T0338513

Computational Psychoanalysis and Formal Bi-Logic Frameworks

Giuseppe Iurato
Independent Researcher, Italy

A volume in the Advances in Human and Social
Aspects of Technology (AHSAT) Book Series

Published in the United States of America by
  IGI Global
  Information Science Reference (an imprint of IGI Global)
  701 E. Chocolate Avenue
  Hershey PA, USA 17033
  Tel: 717-533-8845
  Fax: 717-533-8661
  E-mail: cust@igi-global.com
  Web site: http://www.igi-global.com

                    Library of Congress Cataloging-in-Publication Data

Names: Iurato, Giuseppe, 1972- editor.
Title: Computational psychoanalysis and formal bi-logic frameworks / by
  Giuseppe Iurato.
Description: Hershey, PA : Information Science Reference, [2018]
Identifiers: LCCN 2017028587| ISBN 9781522541288 (hardcover) | ISBN
  9781522541295 (ebook)
Subjects: LCSH: Psychoanalysis. | Logic.
Classification: LCC BF175 .C635 2018 | DDC 150.19/5--dc23 LC record available at https://lccn.loc.gov/2017028587

This book is published in the IGI Global book series Advances in Human and Social Aspects of Technology (AHSAT)
(ISSN: 2328-1316; eISSN: 2328-1324)

British Cataloguing in Publication Data
A Cataloguing in Publication record for this book is available from the British Library.

For electronic access to this publication, please contact: eresources@igi-global.com.

Advances in Human and Social Aspects of Technology (AHSAT) Book Series

Ashish Dwivedi
The University of Hull, UK

ISSN:2328-1316
EISSN:2328-1324

Mission

In recent years, the societal impact of technology has been noted as we become increasingly more connected and are presented with more digital tools and devices. With the popularity of digital devices such as cell phones and tablets, it is crucial to consider the implications of our digital dependence and the presence of technology in our everyday lives.

The **Advances in Human and Social Aspects of Technology (AHSAT) Book Series** seeks to explore the ways in which society and human beings have been affected by technology and how the technological revolution has changed the way we conduct our lives as well as our behavior. The AHSAT book series aims to publish the most cutting-edge research on human behavior and interaction with technology and the ways in which the digital age is changing society.

Coverage

- Technology Dependence
- Cyber Behavior
- ICTs and human empowerment
- Technology and Social Change
- Cultural Influence of ICTs
- Philosophy of technology
- Human-Computer Interaction
- Cyber Bullying
- Technology and Freedom of Speech
- Human Development and Technology

IGI Global is currently accepting manuscripts for publication within this series. To submit a proposal for a volume in this series, please contact our Acquisition Editors at Acquisitions@igi-global.com or visit: http://www.igi-global.com/publish/.

Titles in this Series

For a list of additional titles in this series, please visit: www.igi-global.com/book-series

701 East Chocolate Avenue, Hershey, PA 17033, USA
Tel: 717-533-8845 x100 • Fax: 717-533-8661
E-Mail: cust@igi-global.com • www.igi-global.com

Table of Contents

Preface

Computational psychoanalysis officially is born with the works of the Special Session (A5) kindly hosted by the 13th IEEE ICCI*CC-2014 annual International Conference on Cognitive Informatics & Cognitive Computing, held in London, UK, on August 18-20, 2014. As a truly new discipline, it started, on the basis of the previous primary work made by Ignacio Matte Blanco in working out a formal ground to the Freudian psychoanalysis, with the early basic works and contributions due to Andrei Khrennikov[1], Rosapia Lauro-Grotto and Fionn Murtagh, cited in chronological order. As one of the main purposes, it basically tries to understand what are the primary formal structures and running mechanisms of the unconscious, with the ambitious aim to possibly implement them into the wide computer sciences realm. With respect to the works of the authors just mentioned above, we have anyhow tried to work out, in this book, an independent, alternative framework in which to lay out some of the main concepts and notions of Freudian psychoanalysis, mainly centred on logic.

The central aim of psychoanalysis, as established by Sigmund Freud since the end of 19th century, has been to identify and understand the underlying unconscious mechanisms of consciousness, so trying to clarify what is the role played by unconscious in the mental activity of human being. This has been possible thanks to a particular clinical intervention that sees involved closely patient and analyst in the so-called *analytical setting*, where psychoanalytic therapy is performed according to a certain, well-established *praxis* learned first – to be then professed – within a particular group, that of *community of psychoanalysts*, within which formation and training of the profession of psychoanalyst is possible and obliged to be achieved. Afterwards, the psychoanalyst may exert her or his profession for the psychological well-being of those humans who ask her or his help. From this, it follows a closely personal and individual feature of psychoanalysis and its therapy.

This situation has entailed the "castling" of psychoanalysis in itself, conferring to it a kind of inaccessible self-referentiality that has led this discipline out of scientific ones, even excluding it from those psychological sciences which have a certain methodology thanks to which they may be classified as scientific. All that is mainly due to the lacking of any possible "intersubjective" assessment of psychoanalysis itself. On their part, psychoanalysts counterreply saying that it is not possible to do otherwise, just due to the intimate relationship upon which analytical setting must rely to be as such, but with the consequent effect to make ever more closed their world. This is the main reason why psychoanalysts are so diffident in regard to any other thing that may interfere with their private analytic work, so intimate and personally oriented.

As briefly said above, such a situation is the outcome of the nature itself of psychoanalysis and its therapy, in particular by the subjective feature which distinguishes analytic setting. Nevertheless, this does not prevent a possible, fruitful comparison with other disciplines, in view of a revisiting and a further improvement of psychoanalysis itself. This is just what modestly we have tried to do in this work, that is to say, try to provide a minimal rigorous status to aspects of psychoanalytic framework in the Freudian trend, putting into a fruitful and constructive comparison some main notions, concepts and methods of psychoanalysis with what has been historical offered by other disciplines. Psychoanalysis itself, as having to do with an ever changing and an ever more complex world which is that of human psyche, is an eminently *historic* discipline (as Freud himself more times pointed out), whose theoretical framework is mainly based on what is empirically provided by the clinical experience coming from the analytic setting, as possibly testified by the deontological honesty of every psychoanalyst, who herself or himself puts the handle to modify, if necessary, the theory itself. And, we have based our work just on this precious testimony of many psychoanalysts, who historically have followed Freud, trying to identify a coherently logic pathway for building up a theoretical pattern which has those prerequisites to be classified as rigorous, at least formally.

So, we have started from Freud to French psychoanalytic school, mainly made by Jacques Lacan, Jean Laplanche, Jean-Bertrand Pontalis, Daniel Lagache, André Green and others (but not fully limited to the rich French tradition, which however has been the most opened one towards interdisciplinary perspectives), so identifying a common, persistent "formal theme" which goes from unconscious realm to conscious thought: it is the *phallic logic*, a basic, primordial[2], irreducible logical nucleus, encysted deeply in the unconscious phylogenetically but that manifests itself, along all the epi-ontogenetic route which goes from deepest unconscious to consciousness, in that it is what basically confers that primary, constitutive *binary* and *oppositional* nature (whence, entailing *dichotomization*) to either conscious and unconscious thought. Of course, usual (Aristotelian) binary logic, that basically characterizes conscious thought, is an outcome of this phallic logic along the crucial passage from primary to secondary process, as well as the formal basis of any possible computation. Therefore, phallic logic seems to be the first structural invariant which goes from deep (structural) unconscious to consciousness.

At the basis of phallic logic, there seems to be a primary functional-logical pattern exemplified by the so-called "Fort/Da" reel game. In turn, French school of psychoanalysis, above all with the work of Jacques Lacan, identified the main unconscious mechanisms underlying phallic logic, which were subsequently recollected together, above all by André Green (1993), in a finite set of primary mechanisms which seem to be, in turn, commonly joined around a chief basic psychic operation, that of *negative*. Upon this set of primary psychic unconscious mechanisms, we have delineated a possible theoretical psychoanalytic model for human *symbolic* function, which has been built up on the basis of some considerable contributions due to many psychoanalysts of the French school and others, joined together for giving rise a coherent more comprehending theoretical model whose basic functionality is still a primary *oppositional dialecticity* between certain systems of psychic agencies and subagencies. Also in this case, a primary functional-logical role is played by the *phallic logic*. Therefore, it seems that this irreducible logical nucleus treads the entire route which goes from deepest unconscious to consciousness, so it seems to be a structural invariant of human psyche, already localized – as already said – in the deepest unconscious.

The existence of this phallic logic, which is basically binary and oppositional in its functionality, might be therefore ascribed to a founding *structural unconscious*, universally and ahistorically present as such in every human being, just in the original sense given to it by Claude Lévi-Strauss. Such a phallic logic, therefore, should be meant as a kind of universal, atemporal syntactic structure just based on binary opposition, this being coherent with the meaning that Lévi-Strauss intended to give to his notion of structural unconscious (Dei 2016, Ch. 5, Sect. 4), of which we shall give brief outlines later. It is often said that Lévi-Strauss reached the notion of structural unconscious through Roman Jakobson's work on structural linguistics, but this is not properly correct historically[3]. In fact, according to Lévi-Strauss' testimony (Lévi-Strauss & Eribon, 1988), he worked out this notion during his period in the United States – which was a truly important period for his training – in studying the work of Franz Boas, who had, as early before Jakobson, pointed out, since early 1910s, the fundamental importance of unconscious for language and other social phenomena. Jakobson has then indicated to Lévi-Strauss that structural linguistics could provide to him the right tools to work out formally his related ideas.

The encounter of Lévi-Strauss with structural linguistics marked then the abandon of the classical conception of anthropology as an empirical discipline[4], a favour of an abstract level of reflection, hence identifying those principles (oppositions, structures, formal relations) which are deemed, by Lévi-Strauss, as universals of human soul, and thanks to which it is possible to put into relationship the various elements of empirical research. The passage from the empirical level to the structural one, settled up by Marxism and psychoanalysis, is made explicitly possible just thanks to the tools of structural linguistics. This will lead to the abolishment of the traditional distinction between the so-called logical, rational and civilized thought of modern humans on the one hand, and the prelogical, mystic and wild thought of primitives on the other hand. For Lévi-Strauss, what is really important is the identification and enunciation of those laws and rules of thought (not its content) which are invariant just because as such are the structures by means of human mind organizes the intellection of phenomenological world (Fabietti 2013, p. 32).

Lévi-Strauss introduced his notion of structural unconscious in *Les structures élémentaires de la parenté* of 1949, with which opened the structuralistic trend in anthropology. In this celebrated work, Lévi-Strauss, also with the support of the mathematician André Weil, claimed the importance to shift the attention of anthropological analysis from terms or objects to their relations, which therefore will become central for the whole of anthropology. These relations, then, will be brought back, by Lévi-Strauss, to certain fundamental types, having a main oppositional nature[5]; so, binary oppositions will be the generating transformations[6] of all those possible relations which may be established socially. This is in agreement with the in-depth prevalence of phallic logic as mentioned above, this primordial and irreducible logical nucleus just having a main binary oppositional nature. Lévi-Strauss considered this basic logical nucleus as founding symbolic thought, as early present in the primitives (and therefore called, by Lévi-Strauss, "le pensée sauvage", but not according to a derogatory intention) as such in their mythic formations (Tullio-Altan, 1968, Ch. 1, Sect. 2; 1971, Ch. II, Sect. 9, IV; 1983, Ch. 20).

This phallic logic, as introduced by French school of psychoanalysis, also on the basis of what has been done by Lévi-Strauss (by means of Lacan's work), is moulded, as has been indicated above, by the "Fort/Da" reel game, which, nevertheless, should be meant as introducing only a basic process of opposition between signifiers – i.e., the institution of the trait of difference "/" – without any picking up of signified. This is typical, for instance, of certain mythical thoughts and schizophrenic reasoning, in which there is often an unending chain of multiple oppositions with a mere shifting from a signifier to another, without any meaningful conclusion (Laplanche 2001, p. 307). This – Lacan says – because there is no *anchoring point* with which the net of signifiers may catch at least one signified. But, this does not entail the pinning up of a signified to a signified, but rather the pinning up of a signifier on another, more basic signifier, i.e., the so-called *primal signifier*, or *phallus*[7], which has been chosen symbolically by humanity in its ancestrality, with a mythical act therefore, when the *Name-of-the-Father* was first established, that is to say, when the *Œdipal Law* did its coming into human society. Even according to Lacan, this primal anchoring could take place therefore only when a chain of signifiers stopped or collapsed into a primary signifier, i.e., the *phallus*, already existent even before the existence of unconscious, rather itself founding the (structural) unconscious with a primordial act, whose mechanism Freud says to be the *original* (or *primal*) *repression*.

This last would have given rise to such a primordial signifier that, in turn, would have played its basic function of breaking the continuous and endless shifting of the chain of signifiers, thanks to its basic nature of attractor of this chain, collapsing into it. So, primal repression would have therefore mythically created an attracting *hole* (due to a primordial *absence* coming from "Fort/Da" mechanism) around which to throw down these signifier chains, placed at the deepest meanders of unconscious, the main source of that typical human psyche feature which is the *existential anguish*. In this fashion unconscious arose, and in this sense it should be meant as a maker of meaning by means of its characteristic structure of set of signifiers (Laplanche, 2001). Just the rising of this hole is the first, primordial, mythical, founding act of the phallic logic and its running; this hole, then, arises from an original repression, in that it was primordially a signifier which couldn't remain into consciousness, so it was just originally repressed by fixation.

This primal signifier, however, had to be conscious before it had being repressed, so, mythically, there should have been a primordial stage (of humanity) in which there wasn't a distinction between conscious and preconscious, that is, there had to be a unilinear language made by senseless chains of signifiers, like that of schizophrenics or mythical thought, continuously shifting. Whence, in agreement with Jacques Lacan, Jean Laplanche and Serge Leclaire (Laplanche, 2001), this primal fixation, by anticathexis, inscribed an original signifier (or chain of primal signifiers) which gave rise to the very first, irreducible nucleus of unconscious, i.e., the phallic logic. Just Freud himself, we here note, had an astonishing intuition: he says that this primordial nucleus of unconscious is as if it were sprung out from a hole, from a something which is yet empty, hence, such a phallic logic, binarily oppositional $(+/-)$, is as if it were sprung out from an emptiness, like two opposite electric charges $(+/-)$ sprung out, by splitting, from a nothing[8] (Laplanche 2001, p. 313). Anyway, this original cleavage, according to a re-visitation of original Freudian ideas by Lacan, unconscious producing, should be identified with the existence of certain key-signifiers which will regulate and ordinate all the human language; one of these, is the *phallus* (as paternal metaphor).

Now, following closely Lévi-Strauss' words, we give a simple instance of formalization of the idea of structural unconscious according to Lévi-Strauss which will provide, among other things, an emblematic formal pattern for the further formalization processes carried out later. In this regard, Lévi-Strauss before all says that the notion of structure is unthinkable without making reference to that of transformation which, in turn, was drawn up from history of natural sciences, first of all, from D'Arcy W. Thompson's celebrated work *On the Growth and Form* of 1917, in which he saw the many possible differences between species of the same genus as the outcomes of the action of a transformation of something typical of that genus[9]. Formalizing suitably this idea, Lévi-Strauss reached to consider the category of algebraic systems, i.e., sets equipped with their own relations, so that what he calls *structure* should be nothing but the set of all the possible transformations (like, for instance, the homomorphisms) each of which act from one algebraic system to another. The set of all the possible transformations of this type, then, has naturally the algebraic structure of a group, which therefore acts on the category of these algebraic systems.

Thus, a structure, according to Lévi-Strauss, should be formally given by a certain transformation group acting on a certain set of algebraic systems (like, for instance, a category). Lévi-Strauss then specifies that, in structural anthropology, such transformations have, above all, binary oppositional nature. Anyway, what Lévi-Strauss wishes to point out is the primordial establishment of these transformations, which confer a universal, invariant and ahistorical nature to the basic human behaving. Indeed, Lévi-

Strauss highlights that, for instance, if we wish to account for the diversity of all the marriage rules existing between the subgroups of society, then we may invoke a unique, primary basic syntactic law underlying them, that of *exchange*[10], founded originally by the Œdipal principle, which identifies an original transformation whose possible functional states or realizations are just these possible marriage rules changing, in the time, in their semantic (i.e., the meaning assigned to a marriage) and pragmatic (i.e., the contextual usage and aim of a marriage) features, but however undergoing a universal, atemporal transformation primordially established[11] which intersubjectively rules (together other transformations) human mind, its functioning and the consequent behaviour (Lévi-Strauss & Eribon, 1988, Chs. 11, 13).

In a few words, the group of these transformations, called into question by Lévi-Strauss, should be those deeply enrooted in the deepest meanders of human mind, that is to say, in the unconscious, which therefore assumes a structural nature universally shared. The various historical realizations of the action of these transformations as a group elements, will be what historically make so subjective the life experience of every human being, giving *content* to these *forms* already predetermined or inborn, maybe prehistorically established during homination process. Along this formal line opened by Lévi-Strauss, we have retaken this last formal view claiming a remarkable role played by the action of a certain group of transformations for the development of human consciousness itself, whose elements are defined in the unconscious, and whose realizations are nothing but the product of the historicity of every human being. As such, the action of these transformations is accordingly related unavoidably with the crucial passage from the primary process (regarding unconscious) to the secondary one (regarding consciousness), so that we have followed this line in trying to further formalize this passage.

To this end, we have made appeal first to Ignacio Matte Blanco work, which has reconsidered the Freudian theory from a formal viewpoint, trying to identify its formal aspects, so reaching to a definition of structural unconscious which should be then clarified in its possible relationships with that introduced by Lévi-Strauss. To be precise, the work of Matte Blanco has been mainly turned toward the identification of the formal aspects of the Freudian unconscious as a domain upon which then will functionally act those universal transformations that set up those invariant and ahistorical pre-schemata of human mind. So, we have to distinguish between a *static* structural unconscious as worked out (almost axiomatically) by Matte Blanco, and a *dynamical* structural unconscious as worked out by Lévi-Strauss, or better, Matte Blanco has identified the *static* aspects (like the absence of the space-time dimensions, the occurrence of the internal mechanisms of displacement, condensation and absence of negation, and so on), while Lévi-Strauss has identified the *dynamical* aspects of the structural unconscious (i.e., how functionally it works, for example, by repression[12]), whose next historical realizations will account for the subjective aspects of it, for every human individual experience of life. This, so to say, *Matte Blanco/ Lévi-Strauss structural unconscious*, we hypothesize might be phylogenetically arisen during the common, very long *homination* process which has undergone human evolution before the coming of genus *Homo*, just parallel to the brain formation process[13].

Only supposing phylogenetically pre-existent a model of structural unconscious of this type, then epi-ontogenetically[14] determined subjectively along each individual human life experience, we may look at an objective status to psychoanalysis. Since the latest neuroscience researches applied to psychoanalysis (Kandell, 2005; Kaplan-Solms & Solms, 2000; Mancia, 2006; Oliverio, 1982, 2009, 2011, 2016; Sasso, 2005, 2011; Solms & Turnbull, 2003) point out what fundamental role plays unconscious for the whole psychic life of every human being, whose roots should be identified in the most ancient brain zones (i.e., in the paleoencephalon and mesencephalon), it seems that the primal instincts, whose functions are localized just in these most ancient zones, have been subsequently ruled by the higher functions of the other, most recent (phylogenetically) cerebral zones (from midbrain to forebrain, and above all by this last[15]), so structuring, in a more complex manner, these drives mainly by *attachment* or *anaclisis*, that is, as already stated by Freud himself, through an inseparable coexistence of the sexual drives with the somatic needs, inextricable of each other in the childhood and with the former that only later may become independent gradually from the latter[16].

These last views are quite reasonable for what has been indicated above in regard to embodiment theory of mind. Further, coherently with this viewpoint, Jean Laplanche (2008) has taken into account the possible existence of a *drive subversion* in the sense that, besides the existence of the primary instincts to be satisfied for the life and self-preservation principles ruling *needs*, brain evolution has also entailed a pleasure/displeasure principle ruling (by neopallium) *desire*, which nevertheless often goes against the first needs of instinctual satisfactions (by hindbrain and midbrain), so giving rise to a basic, binary oppositional feature which characterizes human beings, but that implies too the parallel chance to overcome possibly this basic contrast by means of *symbolic* formation and elaboration[17]. These considerations, together the main identification of a basic *phallic logic* by the French school of psychoanalysis (whose work, in turn, is based on Lévi-Strauss' ideas), have led us to give credit to a possible formal pattern for human symbolic function based on embodied mind hypothesis, and whose basic dialecticity is liable to be easily formalized. So, with the phylogenetic rising of neocortex upon subcortical cerebral zones, we have, by means of (psychoanalytic) defence mechanisms ruling (by neopallium, during epi-ontogenesis) basic drives and instincts (coming from paleopallium), the development of consciousness in all its complexity.

But, retaken Lévi-Strauss' ideas as briefly mentioned above in its essential formal sketch, as well as its possible links with Matte Blanco's ideas on structural unconscious, so reaching to identify a more composed construct of structural unconscious (i.e., the Matte Blanco/Lévi-Strauss structural unconscious), we have further worked out other possible formalizations of some Matte Blanco's ideas within this new formal framework, as those of *symmetry* and *asymmetry principles* and their relationships within *bi-logic*, making use of elementary notions of mathematics and theoretical physics, as those of *groupoid* and *symmetry breaking*, to account for the chief feature of human consciousness, that is to say, the *ordering*, from which, for example, arises the temporal dimension and its psychic evaluation. We have then made too other more advanced formalizations on the basis of these first more elementary statements which however are in agreement with the discovery of the above mentioned *phallic logic* in that such an ordering springs out from a basic inversion symmetry breaking. Carrying on along this line, we have then mentioned some further mathematical models of other psychoanalytic notions, based on p-adic analysis, hence we have also briefly recalled the main aspects of the so-called *affect logic*, due to Luc Ciompi, which is a proposal whose pattern seems very close to Matte Blanco's ideas but independently worked out from these latter. We have also mentioned the possible links with physics put forward by Ciompi in regard to his model, to support further what we have done before from the same perspective.

Finally, on the basis of what has been expressed so far, we have put a lot of attention to certain possible computational implementations, applications and developments of unconscious constructs, taking into account the main features of these latter. Indeed, from the previous discussions and arguments achieved, we have indentified some typical features of unconscious, among which are above all the absence of the non-contradiction principle and timelessness. This has been mainly pursued within the framework of logic and its possible trends, identifying and arguing with those which seem to be more able to accomplish the computational realizations of these two chief unconscious features. At the same time, we have also considered those informatic notions, like synchronicity/asynchronicity, parallel/concurrent and sequential circuits, which are liable to be related with these last requests. In particular, we have devoted a part of our treatment to discuss temporal and modal logics and their related applications aimed to achieve possible computational implementations of unconscious constructs as analyzed above.

In conclusion, the main aim of this work has been to identify those possible formal aspects of unconscious processes, above all through the works of French school of humanities. In pursuing this, we have identified a basic, irreducible logical nucleus called *phallic logic*, which characterizes human psyche development and function, from unconscious realm to consciousness, it being the primary ground for the binary oppositional and dichotomical nature featuring human psyche in its wholeness. This early, innate and irreducible logical nucleus is also at the basis of the origin of the usual binary reasoning of Aristotelian logic, hence of elementary Boolean algebra, so that quite evident are the possible implications to informatics. This crucial outcome has been made possible from the overall analysis of formal applications of exact and natural sciences methods and notions to psychoanalytic context, which is licit to be pursued only when we assume that epistemological stance according to which there exist certain universal, inborn pre-schemata of human psyche which therefore, as such, may be objectively grasped hence formally treated.

These have been placed into the so-called structural unconscious, as moulded by Lévi-Strauss and Matte Blanco, and two typical instances of them are just *phallic logic* and *original* (or *primal*) *phantasies*. Afterwards, going on in analysing the formal features of this structural unconscious, it has been possible to identify other aspects which verify this requirement of formality, among which is *timelessness*, which has been then considered further in view of its possible computational usage and implementation. Just in this regard, we stress the fact that what we have mainly considered is the unconscious according to Freud, as revisited by Lévi-Strauss, by Matte Blanco and by French psychoanalysts, not the other constructs of unconscious according to neurosciences[18], of which we have at most taken into account those features that are in common with Freudian unconscious – like timelessness – which is mainly characterized as an entity due to repression mechanism.

ACKNOWLEDGMENT

My thanks go to the Director of IGI Global Publisher, Jan Travers, as well as to my Assistant Development Editor, Jordan Tepper, for what they have done to make possible this new publication.

REFERENCES

Carotenuto, A. (Ed.). (1992). Dizionario Bompiani degli Psicologi Contemporanei. Milano, Italy: Bompiani.

Conrotto, F. (2014). Ripensare l'inconscio. Milano, Italy: FrancoAngeli.

Dei, F. (2016). Antropologia culturale (2nd ed.). Bologna, Italy: Società editrice il Mulino.

Dei, F., & Simonicca, A. (Ed.). (2008). Ragione e forme di vita. Razionalità e relativismo in antropologia (2nd ed.). Milano, Italy: FrancoAngeli.

Deliège, R. (2006). Une historie de l'anthropologie. Écoles, auteurs, théories. Paris: Éditions du Seuil.

Green, A. (1993). Le travail du négatif. Paris: Les Éditions du Minuit.

Fabietti, U. (2013). Moderno, ultramoderno, antimoderno. In Simposio Lévi-Strauss. Uno sguardo dall'oggi. Milano, Italy: il Saggiatore.

Iurato, G. (2013b). Σύμβολου: An attempt toward the early origins, Part 1. *Language & Psychoanalysis*, 2(2), 77–120. doi:10.7565/landp.2013.008

Iurato, G. (2013c). Σύμβολου: An attempt toward the early origins, Part 2. *Language & Psychoanalysis*, 2(2), 121–160. doi:10.7565/landp.2013.009

Iurato, G. (2014c). *Alcune considerazioni critiche sul simbolismo*. Preprint No. hal-00980828 version 1. Available at HAL archives-ouvertes.

Iurato, G. (2015c). A simple phylogenetic remark about certain human blood pressure values. *Journal of Biochemistry International*, 2(4), 162–165.

Iurato, G. (2016d). Some Comments on the Historical Role of *Fetishism* in Economic Anthropology. *Journal of Global Economics, Management and Business Research*, 7(1), 61–82.

Iurato, G. (2016e). *The origins of symbol. An historical-critical study of symbolic function, according to the phylo-ontogenetic perspective, as arising from the comparison of certain patterns of neuro-psychological sciences*. Paper Presented at the Satellite Event "On the edge of disciplines", Florence, Italy.

Kandel, E. R. (2005). Psychiatry, Psychoanalysis, and the New Biology of Mind. Washington, DC: American Psychiatric Association Publishing, Inc.

Kaplan-Solms, K., & Solms, M. (2000). Clinical Studies in Neuro-Psychoanalysis. Introduction to a Depth Neuropsychology. London, UK: Karnac Books, Ltd.

Khrennikov, A. Yu. (2002). *Classical and quantum mental models and Freud's theory of unconscious mind. Series in Mathematical Modelling in Physics, Engineering and Cognitive Sciences* (Vol. 1). Växjö, Sweden: Växjö University Press.

Kim, W. W. (2016). History and Cultural Perspective. In Penile Augmentation. Berlin: Springer-Verlag. doi:10.1007/978-3-662-46753-4_2

Laplanche, J. (2001). *L'inconscio e l'Es*. Bari-Roma, Italy: La Biblioteca.

Laplanche, J. (2008). Sexuale. La sessualità allargata nel senso freudiano. Bari-Roma, Italy: La Biblioteca.

Lévi-Strauss, C., & Eribon, D. (1988). De près et de loin. Paris: Éditions Odile Jacob.

Mancia, M. (Ed.). (2006). Psychoanalysis and Neuroscience. Milan, Italy: Springer-Verlag Italia. doi:10.1007/88-470-0550-7

Matte Blanco, I. (1975). The Unconscious as Infinite Sets. An Essay in Bi-Logic. London, UK: Gerald Duckworth & Company, Ltd.

Matte Blanco, I. (1988). *Thinking, Feeling, and Being. Clinical Reflections of the Fundamental Antinomy on Human Beings and World*. London, UK: Routledge.

Moravia, S. (2004). Ragione strutturale e universi di senso. Saggio su Lévi-Strauss. Firenze, Italy: Casa Editrice Le Lettere.

Oliverio, A. (1982). Biologia e comportamento. Bologna, Italy: Nicola Zanichelli Editore.

Oliverio, A. (2009). La vita nascosta del cervello. Firenze, Italy: Giunti Editore.

Oliverio, A. (2011). Prima lezione di neuroscienze. Roma-Bari, Italy: Laterza Editori.

Oliverio, A. (2016). Il cervello e linconscio. *Psicobiettivo*, *36*(3), 251–259. doi:10.3280/PSOB2016-003015

Piscicelli, U. (1994). Sessuologia. Teoremi psicosomatici e relazionali. Padova, Italy: Piccin Nuova Libraria.

Rosenthal, D. (1971). Genetics of Psychopathology. New York, NY: McGraw-Hill Book Company.

Sasso, G. (2005). Psicoanalisi e Neuroscienze. Roma, Italy: Casa Editrice Astrolabio-Ubaldini Editore.

Sasso, G. (2011). La nascita della coscienza. Roma, Italy: Casa Editrice Astrolabio-Ubaldini Editore.

Silvestri, D. (2013). Linguistica implicita e linguistica esplicita. In Simposio Lévi-Strauss. Uno sguardo dall'oggi. Milano, Italy: il Saggiatore.

Solms, M., & Turnbull, O. (2003). The Brain and the Inner World. An Introduction to the Neuroscience of Subjective Experience. New York, NY: Other Press, LLC.

Tullio-Altan, C. (1968). Antropologia funzionale. Milano, Italy: Casa editrice Valentino Bompiani.

Tullio-Altan, C. (1971). Manuale di antropologia culturale. Storia e metodo. Milano, Italy: Bompiani.

Tullio-Altan, C. (1983). Antropologia. Storia e problemi. Milano, Italy: Giangiacomo Feltrinelli Editore. Tullio

ENDNOTES

[1]   After the pioneering works of Matte Blanco (1975, 1988), which have opened, for the first time, the interdisciplinary intertwinements between psychoanalysis and exact sciences, Khrennikov (2002) has written the first, organic and complete work on a possible mathematical physics treatment of psychological sciences (with a particular attention to psychoanalysis) from an advanced standpoint.

[2]   We believe that this ancestral logical nucleus sprung out during *homination* process – as will be briefly mentioned in the Introduction – according to a psychic pattern based on a set of primary unconscious mechanisms recollected around the *negative*, according to André Green (1993), as exposed in (Iurato 2013b,c, 2014c, 2016e), and supported by the considerations made in (Kim 2016, Part I, Ch. 2).

[3]   Cf. (Moravia 2004, p. 291). Anyhow, the constant reference to the unconscious dimension of linguistic (phonemic, in particular) competence of human language, will become the epistemological foundation of the whole structuralistic anthropology (Carotenuto 1992, p. 173; Silvestri 2013, p. 111).

[4]   See also (Dei & Simonicca, 2008) for some epistemological perspectives in anthropology.

[5]   Cf. (Deliège 2006, Ch. 5).

[6]   According to structural linguistics, in a functional manner similar to the modalities of functioning of genetic code with its finite basis (Fabietti 2013, p. 35).

[7]   Henceforth, when we shall use the term of *phallus*, we refer to its widest psychoanalytic sense, above all to its pregnant symbolic meaning.

[8]   Here, we see a conceptual analogy with Paul Dirac's *hole theory* of electric charges, as well as with the basic elements of the theory of spontaneous symmetry breaking of elementary particle theory (see later).

[9]   Cf. (Lévi-Strauss & Eribon 1988, Ch. 11).

[10]   That Lévi-Strauss puts at the early and basic foundational act of society with its elaborated organization. This act of exchange has concerned firstly exchange of economical assets from which, then, culture arose (Lévi-Strauss & Eribon 1988, Ch. 14); see also (Iurato, 2016d).

[11]   See also (Dei 2014, Ch. 5, Sect. 4).

[12]   A typical instance of this, is just the mechanism of *primal* (or *original*) *repression* giving rise to *original phantasies*, which are just universal features of human psyche, hence to be ascribed to Lévi-Strauss' structural unconscious.

[13]   This is in agreement with latest neuropsychoanalytic trends according to which most of psychic life in humans seems however ruled, in a certain manner (i.e., unconsciously), by those most phylogenetically ancient zones of human brain localized in the paleoencephalon and mesencephalon (Oliverio, 1982, 2009, 2011; Piscicelli, 1994; Rosenthal, 1971; Solms & Turnbull, 2003). Moreover, current presences of phylogenetic remnants in the epi-ontogenetic development of every human being, are retraceable also physiologically; cf. (Iurato, 2015c). In a few words, *phylogenesis* is the chromosomal heredity as results from human species evolution, *ontogenesis* is the extrachromosomal memory which warrants the functional development of all the functional (phylogenetic) acquisitions potentially present into the human species at a given moment of its evolution, while *epigenesis* is the action of the adaptive social and environmental influences (Piscicelli 1994, Cap. I).

[14]   Ontogenesis occurs as an integration point between the individual history of epigenesis and the universal history of phylogenesis (Piscicelli 1994, Cap. I).

[15]   See, above all, (Oliverio 1982, Parte II, Capp. 5, 6; 2011, Cap. II; Piscicelli 1994, Cap. I, pp. 18-26). Three are the main phenomena involved in the phylogenetic evolution of human brain: 1) the augmentation of the cerebral mass, in particular of the neocortex undergoing the so-called *rule of cerebral progression*; 2) the *encephalization*, consisting in a hierarchization of cerebral structures in which the most recent ones dominate on the most ancient ones, in terms of phylogenesis, also with integration and association functions; 3) the cellular reorganization and restructuration of cerebral tissues. In particular, in regard to point 2), a very remarkable factor concurring in the encephalization process is the extensive and capillary *embodiment* of the two-ways neural information going through the whole nervous system, from the peripheral one (as sensory-motor information)

to the central one (as mental content), and vice versa (Oliverio 1982, Cap. 5). This provides solid neurophysiological bases to the embodied theories of mind and related theories of human psyche.

[16]   But never completely disjoined of each other; sublimation, for instance, is due to an independence from the somatic attachment. This is coherent with all those theories of embodied mind, with which we rely, for instance, when we shall describe a possible model of human symbolic function based on fetishism (see next Chapter 2, Sect. 2.8). See also (Piscicelli 1994, Cap. I).

[17]   Cf. (Conrotto 2014, Ch. 3, Sect. 3).

[18]   See (Oliverio, 2009).

Introduction

A possible way to give a formal framework to psychoanalysis (but the argument is also valid for general psychological sciences), is to look at those trends of epistemology of human sciences that claim the existence of innate pre-schemata structurally performing human mind and its psychic manifestations. We argue that these might have been implemented during the long homination process in concomitance with the rising of midbrain and, above all, forebrain, which have played the main role to regulate and control drive pushes coming from hindbrain. In such a manner, it is licit to search for possible formal aspects of these underlying mental structures of human being (like the primal phantasies, in psychoanalytic case), phylogenetically predetermined and epi-ontogenetically re-enacted during the life course of human being. This is the main epistemological stance we have adopted in working out possible formalization attempts of psychoanalysis.

Whatever they (i.e., its detractors) may say about psychoanalysis, a little of intellectual honesty, at least internally evoked[1] and accordingly felt if any, is quite enough to recognize, without any doubt, the great, revolutionary impact exerted by psychoanalysis, by the genius of Sigmund Freud, his foresight, his bravery, his honesty and his perseverance, on the whole of human knowledge, beyond its benefits achieved at the psychological and clinical level. Freud has inexorably inflicted another, harder and deeper "narcissistic wound" to the human beings, reappraising a lot, her or his apparent "omnipotence". Accordingly, the many, violent and continuous attacks that psychoanalysis has undergone, are therefore quite justified, if we may say so, just in the light of what it has really discovered, that is to say, the deep and obscure nature of human psyche. Neglecting fully those criticisms that settle out psychoanalysis as a non-science[2] and wholly devoid of any possible scientific feature, in that they are not reasonable and not deeply discussed or rightly argued as ought, we instead provide herein a brief but complete justification of our intentions and methods pursued in this brief work, mainly aimed to expose some possible formalization attempts of psychoanalysis, according to Freudian trend.

The various criticisms on the alleged non-scientificity of psychoanalysis are "rationally" due to the usual *positivistic* standpoints of the so-called natural and exact sciences, whose models would be the only depository of real objective knowledge, if one admits existing a *unique* reality structured in *only one* level, that of the external world whose empirical phenomenology should be more or less directly determined only with experimental methods. The objectivity of the scientific knowledge would also derive from certain invariance principles which basically establish a certain constant extrasubjective presence of this external reality which warrants its determination in every place and at each instant (*space-time invariance principle*[3]) thanks to a precise methodology scientifically settled according to commonly shared criteria of the so-called *scientific community* of all around the world. The experimental data so gained, are then formally treated, according to a precise statistical methodology, hence laid out within a theoretical framework which will provide a *theory* for those phenomenology so observed.

This latter step, is mainly characterized by the use of mathematical methods, in that mathematics is deemed, after Galileo Galilei, as the "formal language" of nature. Certain trends of philosophy of sciences would want hence to see the notions and structures of mathematics as forming that formal language with which human being is able to know external reality, so having a theoretical framework worked out mathematically, is deemed to be a preliminary condition in order to a theory of knowledge may be considered as rigorous and objective, hence scientifically valid only when there holds a certain methodological correspondence, more or less direct, between what is declared by theory and its empirical counterpart experimentally ascertained in the case of natural science. This last *dialecticity* between theory and experience is an unavoidable requisite for the scientificity of a theory. It is not given once and for all, but it should actuated periodically in the course of time, from which a basic *historic* feature of scientific theories follows too.

Therefore, also scientific knowledge has an intrinsic historical feature in that the knowledge of the external world which it would want to recognize, is not given just as has been already said above, once and for all, but it constantly undergoes to a revision and control under the coming of either new knowledge from other fields and progresses of technology because the close and inseparable relationships between a scientific theory and its experimental verifications, are inevitably *mediated* by technology, which allows us a contact with certain aspects of the external reality, just the object of study of scientific knowledge. This has also allowed us to may suitably *change* and *control* these aspects of external reality, as, for instance, is possible to do in the biological science context. And, just this last capability is that conferring a strong sense of objectivity to the scientific knowledge, as well as an ever more increasing "sense of omnipotence" of human being, together (we hope) to an *ethical* responsibility in handling this capability.

Likewise, if scientific knowledge has a typical historical feature in regard to the examination of an external reality presumed to be objective and spatial-temporally invariant, it follows that historicity is a perspective which has a pregnant epistemological aim[4]. To be precise, it is with the evolution of humanity, meant in its widest sense, that progresses in the knowledge are achievable, even for objects which are supposed to be invariant and independent from humans, like the external reality. For more reason, this discussion is primary for the object of study of humanities, which is often a reality changing with the humanity's evolution itself[5]. This is the case of human psyche, whose changing is mainly due to the inextricable intertwinements between the genotype, phylogenetically[6] established, and its phenotypic expression, occurring along epi-ontogenesis[7] of the human being, depending on the (epigenetic) complexity of the possible environmental influences which it may undergo (Kandel, 2005; Morris, 2015).

In a few words, what is really important for the human epi-ontogenetic evolution is the phenotypic expression of the genotype (as phylogenetically determined[8]), whence the fundamental importance of the environment[9], meant in its widest sense, for the general development of the human being. And this, of course, holds too for the development of human psyche, so that, in the particular case of its theoretical models, a crucial role should be played by the environmental conditions in which human being grows up. For psychoanalysis, this last point is one of its epistemological pillars, in that a primary attention is paid just to the first years of development of the child and to the environment in which he or she grows up, a crucial period of the life of every human being, this, which plays a fundamental *deterministic* role in the next psychic development. The psychoanalytic therapy is just focussed on the events of this period, especially the early part. The analytical setting, then, as a precious intimate moment to be shared only between analyst and patient, is centred on a certain re-actualization of this period, with the aim to solve the conflicts established in the childhood.

And, it is just upon this last scenario that psychoanalysis has received its most violent attacks, declaring as not scientifically pertinent the outcomes of the analytical setting, as well as not liable to be properly assessed, in that the subjectivity there involved is so high to make almost impossible a statistical evaluation of the needed data required by the ordinary scientific methodology. So, for psychoanalysis, the usual psychometric methodology, commonly adopted by other psychological disciplines (deemed, for this, to have a scientific status), is not applicable, just for the impossibility of a statistical treatment of the outcomes of analytical setting. This, independently from any other criticism moved to the theoretical framework of psychoanalysis from an epistemological standpoint, like the celebrated ones due Karl Popper on the lacking of *falsificability* of psychoanalytic theory, in that every its interpretation, of a psychic event or fact, is equally and however valid.

Nevertheless, just for the fundamental importance that *historicity* plays for the general progress of human knowledge, included the scientific one, we should be more inclined to assume another, more comprehensive and reasonable, point of view, besides this last. To be precise, we should be more favourable to undertake the point of view that looks at the founding historical nature owned by the psychoanalytic movement (De Mijolla & De Mijolla Mellor 1998, pp. 5-12), an intrinsic historical feature of psychoanalysis that as early Freud himself claimed. So, it is built up on the multitudinous testimonies, works and practices of who has belonged to the so-called psychoanalytic community, contributing to its theory, therapy, clinic. So, psychoanalysis is being to acquire its own corpus of doctrine meanwhile it gradually assimilates coherently and constructively all these contributions, enlarging and improving its theoretical framework as well as its clinical praxis, and vice versa, in that these latter are inseparable of each other (Freudian *Junktim*[10]).

Now, along this historical process of gradual and progressive enrichment within Freudian *Junktim*, we might adopt a particular method of historical comparison thanks to which *descry* possible, underlying conceptual analogies and constancies leading to the identification of certain almost universal *structures* characterizing human psyche and its functioning, whose *form* is basically predetermined phylogenetically (at the epigenetic level), hence is collective, but whose *content*, being then epi-ontogenetically established, is personal, individual, by means of the so-called *symptom*. This might explain why psychoanalysis has a chief "subjective character" which excludes it from scientific disciplines ordinarily meant as such, a feature, this, that will be put into place, intimately, in the analytical setting. But, the possible testimonies in favour of psychoanalytic technique in regard to its therapeutic efficiency, have been deemed as not valid at an epistemological level[11] (Funari 2007, pp. 156-157).

According to the latest epistemological issues[12], at the early basis of human knowledge there seems to exist pre-existing psychic (or mental) *structures* which resemble Plato's and Kant's related notions, hence we are quite near also to structuralism Lévi-Strauss' ideas as well as to Jerry Fodor's modularity theory of mind[13], and which have been phylogenetically pre-determined (above all, at the epigenetic level[14]) during the very long[15] *homination* process (within *Hominidae*), started about 30 million years ago, and ended with the last remained and not extinguished species of genus *Homo*, that of *Homo sapiens*, appeared about 190,000 years ago. Along this long evolutionary process, it took place an extraordinary regression of the *natural* instincts, gradually replaced by the *culture*, which has been made possible thanks to the rising of *symbolic* function[16] (Cuche, 2004; Tartabini & Giusti, 2006), whence, of the *language*, at around 80,000 years ago[17] when, in a very narrow time interval[18], a small group of African hominids underwent, so to say, a kind of functional "rewiring" of brain structures which established the main functional linguistic operations that only later will be externalized in a sensory-motor way; language, therefore, appeared to accomplish internal functional (hence, mainly qualitative) scopes and aims of thought, and not for communication needs (Berwick & Chomsky, 2016). During this very long course, a parallel evolution of the brain has occurred too, which was characterized above all by the new formations of the neopallium[19], i.e., that region of the brain mainly deputed to the execution and control of higher-order brain functions, such as cognition, sensory-motor perception, language, as well as in presiding over the emotions (above all, thanks to prefrontal cortex, which is interested by most of neural circuits) [20]. Recent neurosciences[21], then, say us that our brain mainly runs according to already preformed functions (or functional pre-schemas or modules[22]), phylogenetically determined (above all, at the epigenetic level) but not closely located or rigidly constrained into certain brain zones, which are then epi-ontogenetically subjectively re-enacted, more or less efficaciously, along the individual life, in dependence on the personal environment and upbringing.

So, we might hypothesize, according to evolutionary biology and psychology[23], that, during this long and crucial period of homination[24], the phylogenetic evolution of the brain[25] together the body (and vice versa), ran parallel to the development of psyche and its (mental) structuration, with the (phylo)genetic implementation (above all, at the epigenetic level) of the actual mental functions mainly by *attachment* (or *anaclisis*, according to the newest psychoanalytic trends[26]), just in agreement with those recent trends of philosophy of mind and neurosciences, which see body and mind as rightly inseparable (*embodied mind*). This should be the early origin of the pre-schemes or modules of psychic functions, so phylo-genetically determined by (epigenetic) implementation occurred along homination, then, from *Homo sapiens* onwards, ready to be ontogenetically re-enacted individually with the phenotypic expression of own genotype. In this view, we might think to psychoanalysis as a particular humanistic discipline which tries to identify and study those (almost) universal (as phylogenetically predetermined) psychic functions understandable according to its explaining model worked out initially by Freud, but afterwards continu-ously, historically underwent, within psychoanalytic community, to changes, improvements and enlarge-ments in dependence on the outcomes of either its therapeutic praxis and its theoretical interpretation.

This, should confer a more objective status to psychoanalysis, being turned towards a collective behaviour rather than an individual one. To be precise, admitted the phylogenetic pre-determination of psychic functions (at the epigenetic level), we may look at the universality feature of these, even when they are studied and approached according to psychoanalytic methods, provided that these are reformu-lated in such a manner to search for the universality feature characterizing them, like for *original* (or *primal*) *phantasies*, as clearly highlighted, for instance, by Jean Laplanche and Jean-Bertrand Pontalis (1967, 1988). It has been the remarkable and wide work of these last two eminent French psychoanalysts (but not strictly limited to them – see later), to have tried to identify that universal feature characterizing concepts and notions of Freudian psychoanalysis, thanks to which it is therefore feasible to looking for a possible "objective" feature of psychoanalytic concepts and notions[27]. This is, besides, coherent with the simple fact that psychoanalysis has mainly to do with *affect*, a primary psychic component not only of human beings but also of all primates and of many other animals (Eibl-Eibesfeldt, 1996; Panksepp & Biven, 2012) which share with us main basic components of it, so, it is presumable that along homi-nation, above all control and execution of affects have been the main evolutionary tasks to be faced[28].

So, psychoanalysis should be viewed from an evolutionary standpoint, in the sense that just in the homination period, most of Freudian concepts, notions and methods find their natural collocation and motivation from a genetic epistemology standpoint. For instance, we might hypothesize that *defence mechanisms* of the Ego (Anna Freud, 1937; Nicasi, 1981), which rule, with their outcomes, consciousness[29], have spring out just along this critical evolutionary course, in which predominated, in a bloody fight, death and life drives (also pushed by hormonal onrushes), and couldn't be otherwise at that state. Therefore, just in this critical period, we should retrace the possible deterministic bases for the human psychic development, for instance searching for possible universal schemas of behaviour, genotypically invariant but liable to be phenotypically developed[30] (as well as changeable at the epigenetic level); among these, we may, for example, lay out just the original (or primal) phantasies, as regard more properly psychoanalytic context. Thus, parallel to an individual biological development and differentiation, we may have a kind of psychic development and differentiation which starts with an undifferentiated mixed between *Id* (or *Es*) and *Ego*, hence with a first phase of differentiation (by phenotype) between these two main agencies by environmental action, to be followed afterwards by a second phase of differentiation by the familial action (*Œdipal triadicity*), with the rising of the third (normative) agency, the *Super-Ego*, so reaching the psychic individuality by each human being (Semi 1988-89, Vol. I, Ch. 7, Sect. 7.3).

In this regard, Freud himself, in *Moses and Monotheism* (of 1934-38), just the last works wrote by him, were extremely foresight in applying psychoanalysis to the historical analysis, stating, among other things, that the crucial passage from "nature" to "culture" took place with the rising of the language[31] and with the shift from *matriarchate*[32] (with the rising of the undifferentiated pair *Es-Ego*) to *patriarchate* (with the rising of *Super-Ego*, mainly by rituality). Maybe, these precious and clear considerations by Freud, should be applied even before the historical period analyzed by him, to be more precise, these should be applied to the homination period, until up the coming of latest species of the genus Homo, above all *Homo sapiens*. Freud also speaks of "mnestic traces of archaic experiences of the human species[33]", as, for instance, the *original phantasies* (Laplanche & Pontalis, 1988). All this, is in part coherent with what recently done, for example, by the work of Giordano Fossi (2003), who has proposed a new trend, just defined as *evolutionary psychoanalysis*, addressed to take into account neuroscience and evolutionary biology discoveries, but not contemplating the existence of any type of unconscious.

Therefore, compared the very brief duration of the period which goes from *Homo sapiens* to our times, with respect to the millions of years of homination, from which follows most of what we are nowadays phylogenetically impressed, even the unconscious, we are inclined to think that the (phylo)genetically preformation functionality and structuration of the brain during the former period surely overbears that of the latter period, mainly governed by culture and symbolism ruled by the former brain structural functionality (phylo)genetically predetermined. So, just this latter, at least in its structural aspects, might be considered as arising during homination process, along which all the possible universal psychic *structures* have crystallized atemporally in their typical *form*, but without *content* (afterwards determined by culture) as claimed, for last, by Lévi-Strauss. The notion of *structure* according to Lévi-Strauss refers to the *logic* (hence, to the internal *order*) of the set of all the possible functional *transformations* to which a given algebraic *system* of *relations* (among the constituent *parts*, or *elements*, of such a system) may undergo (Abbagnano, 1998; Bastide, 1966; Boudon 1970, pp. 30-31; CSFG, 1977; Lévi-Strauss & Eribon 1988, pp. 161-163; Vattimo et al., 1993). Therefore, a structure identifies the *transformational syntax* of a system of relations, which is *invariant* and *ahistorical* (Lévi-Strauss, 1977) in that it refers to the syntactical aspects (i.e., to the mere *forms*) of these transformations, not to their historical valence which will be provided by *semantics* and *pragmatics* (Charles W. Morris), conferring (diachronically) *content* to these "empty" structures; in this regard, see, for instance, (Neubauer, 2004) for a brief survey on the historical semantic and its *semasiologic* method to study diachronic variation of meaning giving pre-eminence to signifier with respect to signified.

According to Lévi-Strauss, any phenomenon of human mind is understandable only identifying (synchronously and) preliminarily its underlying (unconscious) structures from the various systems of ethnographic research. This implies neither a formal dissolution nor a rational stiffening of history, because the search for structures leads to a metahistorical level, implying a rationalization of human nature, as a structure identifies what is intrinsic and invariant of the natural phenomena, that is to say, it should be meant as a mental conceptual schema equipped of its own consistence and autonomy at the unconscious level (*structural unconscious*). The structure is independent of its historical substratum, in that, it is the outcome of the spatial-temporally transversal comparison of many different ethnographic realities and data, so it turns out to be invariant with respect to a certain group of transformations which syntactically characterizes it as such[34]. Then, the various (ethnographic) systems from which such a group arises, are nothing but realizations of it, just in the mathematical sense of this term (Fabietti & Remotti, 1998).

Then, this transformational syntax is nothing but that the *logic* which rules the variations of such systems. Lévi-Strauss, then, gives pre-eminence to the oppositional transformations, hence to a *binary logic*, to be applied to a common (hence, universal), deepest and underlying invariant *ground* (i.e., the structural unconscious) from which springs out the rich and variegated phenomenology of human consciousness. Indeed, starting from an idea due to Franz Boas, according to which under any logical apparatus lies unconscious[35], also consciousness is the outcome of the pre-reflexive and collective unconscious mechanisms. The social-cultural facts may be studied from different levels which, along a continuum, go from full consciousness to unconscious level, or better structural unconscious level, basically meant as opposed to the so-called *événementiel* level. In it, subject and object encounter not phenomenologically but unconsciously and metahistorically, independently of any historical and individual determination, but rather with a universal, formal and ahistorical feature (Fabietti & Remotti, 1998).

Moreover, human mind, according to Lévi-Strauss, is the place of the structures which basically run according to an oppositional logic, as they are at the basis of that universal attitude of human being to *classify*, a function which is typical of every social phenomenon, comprised science. Lévi-Strauss also reaches even to consider as existing a kind of homology (just structural) among mental, social and natural structures, unconsciously mediated (Fabietti & Remotti, 1998). So, Lévi-Strauss, explicitly and peremptory, stresses the fundamental and primary importance of pre-existent, transcendental, innate schemata which hereditarily[36] structurate binarily human being and her or his intellectual activity[37]. At the basis of this view, then, there is the preference for a *binary logic* as it lies at the deepest core of the functioning of any human phenomenology. This precious legacy of Lévi-Strauss[38], was preciously acquired above all by Jacques Lacan, as well as by the French school of psychoanalysis which has always paid a great and deep attention to the possible formal aspects of psychoanalysis, and human sciences in general (Francioni, 1982).

Mario Francioni (1982, Introduction, p. 11), in analysing historically and epistemologically French psychoanalysis along its evolution, has yet identified some general features of the epistemological status of psychoanalysis. Indeed, just from the quite singular historical route followed by French psychoanalysis, which, among other things, has been supported by many other disciplines like arts, literature, philosophy, anthropology, sociology, political sciences, linguistics, exact sciences, Francioni claims that psychoanalysis has to be meant as a "science of support, attachment" (*anaclisis*, to be more precise) rather than a "founding knowledge[39]", as it unavoidably has made reference to (as well as has searched support by) other fields of knowledge, also very far from psychology. In this regard, the scenario of the French culture of 20th century, has been featured by an extremely rich vivacity and pervasive interdisciplinary intertwinements, which have not had equal elsewhere. This, has enriched and enhanced psychoanalysis itself, which is not immune from the contact with other knowledge fields, inasmuch as its conceptual framework is ever evolving and growing for the interdisciplinary relationships it has with other sciences (Francioni 1982, p. 15). Above all in France, a new, foresight and open world has arisen around psychoanalytic knowledge, providing to this latter such a rich amount of new trends and insights, to have made possible the identification and pursuing of new perspective from which to look at psychoanalytic knowledge (Francioni, 1978; Francioni 1982, Ch. 15, Sect. 1).

Now, just within this rich, lively, variegated and exiting cultural community[40] of the France of 20th century, is placed our work. Indeed, reconnecting us with what has been said above, about a part of Lévi-Strauss' oeuvre, there have been important and valuable psychoanalysts and scholars, among whom are Jacques Lacan, Jean Laplanche, Jean-Bertrand Pontalis, Serge Leclaire, André Green, and many others, who have tried, in their interdisciplinary work, to identify those *formal* aspects underlying psychoanalysis and human sciences in general. They are, more or less, tied with Lacan and his teaching that, basically, is centred on a certain *logic of the lack* that structurates the subject of the unconscious, i.e., the logic of the *desire* which, on its turn, springs out from an unbridgeable *écart*, or difference, between the *needs* on the one side and the *demand* of eternal, full and unconditioned love – the perennial *encore* – by *others* (*alterity*) on the other side[41], a gap which may be overcome only by means of *language*. The primeval satisfactions of primary needs, have been inscribed into the *imaginary* register, mainly made by corporal or bodily pleasures received during infancy by mother and transcribed as deep mnestic traces; the infant, mainly moved, by the deadly compulsion to repeat mechanism (which acts according to the *real* register), to relive these lost satisfactions, is able to accomplish this only phantasmatically by *hallucination* (*symptom* at the reality level, or *dream* at the imaginative level) to re-find the lost object, so he or she would like to realize this, but life principle imposes him or her to may pursue this only symbolically, so entering into the *symbolic* register, upon which occurs entire real life. These three registers are inseparable of each other, and their reciprocal intertwinement (*Borromean knot*) rules entire psychic life of every human being (Francioni, 1978; Francioni 1982, Ch. 15, Sect. 1).

But, while, on the one side, the *need* is satisfiable materially by *presence* of real objects (pleasure), and, on the other side, the *demand* of full and unconditioned love[42] by others is almost unrealizable as such (because of its reciprocity function), then only a third way is possible, that of *desire*, which is the desire of something lacking, hence ruled by a *logic of the lack*, which is the logic of the subject of unconscious, i.e., the desire, just arising from the unbridgeable gap between need and demand of primary narcissism. Desire may be accomplished, on the other hand, only symbolically, from which it follows *language*, meant in its widest sense. This explains why Lacan says that unconscious is structured like a language, mediated by symbolic order which should not mean as the field of what stays behind symbol, its content, the symbolized, but rather it refers to the common structure of instinctual (i.e., drive) dynamics of unconscious which follows laws and rules similar to the ones discovered by structural linguistics and anthropology. Thus, Lacan has discovered that, the unconscious support underpinning symbolic register mediating the intersubjective relationships (for example, those of kinship) and the transcendence of the *langue* with respect the single subject (who speaks according to an historical actuation of the *langue*, i.e., the *parole*[43]), are mainly due to the action of the compulsion to repeat mechanism, i.e., the basic structural operation of unconscious (Francioni, 1978; Francioni 1982, Ch. 15, Sect. 1).

Thus, Lacan has above all discovered the basic structurality of unconscious by means of the laws and rules of its subject (i.e., the subject of unconscious, that is to say, the desire), whose logic is a *logic of the lack*, i.e., the lacking of the object (need, love, primary experience of satisfaction, lacking of the penis, etc.), as a necessary outcome to overcome or fill that gap between need and demand. With the realization of this logic, the individual finally enters into the symbolic order – otherwise it falls into the realm of psychosis – leaving primary narcissism (imaginary register) for the secondary narcissism, with the acquisition of language. But, doing so, the individual not only relegates herself or himself, and all the others, into the imaginary register (in that, desire springs out from the impossibility to accomplish really to primary narcissism impellent requests of imaginary register, but however tries to go towards it through a symbolic manoeuvre which is trying to restore however this state of initial and full well-being, that of the fusional state child-mother, which starts since prenatal one), but above all alienates herself or himself under the domain of the *Other*, so becoming a *barrelled subject*, in which there is a kind of inversion of the Kantian relation between a transcendental Ego and a psychological Ego. Thus, human being turns out not only dominated, but above all sequestered by the alterity of symbolic order (the Other), to which he or she accesses leaving, as the main protagonist of the scene, the unconscious in its basic identification with the Other (Francioni, 1978; Francioni 1982, Ch. 15, Sect. 1).

These are the very basic, key elements of Lacan's theory and its revolutionary attainment. Among these, to have discovered the basic structural nature of unconscious by means of its symbolic order, which is structured according to structural linguistics (Ferdinand De Saussure) and anthropology (Claude Lévi-Strauss), whence it follows its universal and atemporal[44] nature, among other things. As has been said above, for Lacan, who besides has been always aimed only to rediscovery Freud[45],

What is crucial for unconscious dynamics is just the compulsion to repeat principle, which rules mainly desire and hallucinatory reproduces childhood perceptions by now became signs or traces of an imaginary satisfaction. Lacan recognized the importance of this unconscious mechanism which is involved in many different types of logics conscious and unconscious. Nevertheless, the real logic of unconscious, according to Lacan, is just the *logic of the lack* (or *logic of the negative*). The lack, on the other hand, takes place according to three main modalities[46], namely *privation*, *frustration* and *castration*, which, in any case, all are functionally characterized by a primary *alternation* of the type presence/absence, which should be however considered always at the symbolic level (or order), in that, in the reality, nothing is lacking; so, the lacking object should not be confused with a lost object of reality (Chemama & Vandermersch, 1998).

Only with the occurrence of a signifier[47] (hence, belonging to the symbolic), it is possible to have a condition of lacking marked by this signifier as a symbol of such an absence, so allowing, to the desiring subject, the access to the language. Lacking therefore is the indispensable condition in order that human being be a *talking* (or *speaking*) *being* depending on a constitutional and indelible *defect* which is so necessary as much as unobservable. Such lacking is then supported and gradually re-found by the *mourning* experience[48] which takes over after a period of full and strong satisfaction of pleasure, like that experienced during fusional state child-mother. So, human being becomes a desiring being when he or she becomes aware that the only condition underpinning his or her being is just this *recurrent lacking*, on its turn supported by the compulsion to repeat mechanism which makes desire as incessant. Now, Lacan identifies, in the so-called *"Fort/Da"* (coming from the Freud's "Fort/Da" reel game described in *Beyond the Pleasure Principle* of 1920), the basic key of functioning of the *logic of the lack*, the founding nucleus of symbolic register in which "the absence is evoked in the presence and, vice versa, the presence in the absence"; whence, the access to the language[49]. This primary logical principle of "Fort/Da" is the one which has given rise to the so-called *phallic logic*, which therefore is the common, primary logical nucleus upon which every other logic relies. Lacan has centred psychoanalytic theory on phallus as main desire signifier; the Œdipus complex itself is seen as a dialectic between the basic alternatives of "to be or not to be the phallus", "to have or not to have the phallus" (Chemama & Vandermersch, 1998; Conrotto, 2014; Laplanche & Pontalis, 1967, 1988; Laplanche, 2000, 2001).

Now, it has been above all the French school of psychoanalysis, mainly along Lacan's tradition, to have tried to identify those unconscious mechanisms underlying "Fort/Da" basic process, hence the phallic logic. As discussed in (Iurato, 2013b,c), initially we had proposed, following an insight due to Jean Laplanche and Jean-Bertrand Pontalis (1967), to consider *disavowal* as one of the main psychic mechanism underlying the formation of symbolic register, in that it relies at the early basis of any other possible logic (just according to what Lacan has said), and regarding general anxiety or anguish states and the defence against them, hence we have applied[50], just in passing, this pattern to a possible phylogenetic origin of the symbolic function (before language), applying it to the human evolution (*homination*), to be precise, after those stages in which early species of the genus *Homo*, having acquired upright position (i.e., *bipedism*[51], that preceded *encephalization* process[52] – with sexual dimorphism already gained – but with which has remained correlated closely until up nowadays), could experience and feel traumatically (hence, with anguish production) primitive early forms of castration anxiety (or *any other* traumatic event, which has however produced a very strong *anxiety*[53]), to be then handled and symbolically elaborated – through a set of unconscious psychic mechanisms recollected around the *negation*, among which is disavowal, according to what stated by André Green (1993) – for reaching, afterwards, certain crucial and deep neural changes, discontinuously occurred, which have entailed the rising of a *symbolic function* preceding language formation and production, in agreement with what very recent neurolinguistics claims[54] (Berwick & Chomsky, 2016). This is therefore coherent with the hypothesis according to which the *phallic logic* lies just at the early and primary basis, as a key founding nucleus (Conrotto 2014, p. 99), of the next developments of all other forms of logics. Further, just the involvement of psychic mechanisms regrouped around the *negative* (according to André Green – see above), is coherent with what is said in (Tartabini & Giusti 2006, Cap. II, Sect. 2.11) about the origin of symbolic function in the genus *Homo*, preceding language, on the basis of some previous hypotheses, put forward by Edgar Morin and Terrence W. Deacon (1997), on the crucial role played by religious and sacred practices, together their unavoidable contrasting meanings whose dialecticism is just overcome by symbolic formation.

So, we might suppose that, along the crucial homination process, during which human brain developed considerably until up to reach almost the same neurophysiological configuration of the present one, certain neural circuits established to give rise almost universal schemata moulding human behaviour, hence phylogenetically implemented and, from time to time, epi-ontogenetically activated during the phenotypic expression of our own genotype. From a psychodynamic point of view, then, these pre-schemata so phylogenetically predisposed, should correspond to those *original* (or *primal*) *phantasies* (or *phantasms*) predicted by psychoanalysis, just epi-ontogenetically re-activated, for instance, by *original* (or *primal*) *repression* (Conrotto 2014, p. 99) which acts as real interpretative schemata, so assigning a semiotic-semantic function just to unconscious, which would arise just in the moment in which these original repression mechanisms run. Likewise, we might consider the Ego defence mechanisms as phylogenetically established and epi-ontogenetically liable to be, more or less, re-activated. Even the unconscious would be established just at the moment of institution of the primordial "Fort/Da" (Conrotto, 2009), just as an early founding act, so restoring epi-ontogenetically those primary, *original* (or *primal*) *phantasies* (in first, castration, as well as others) which therefore *structurate* it, as stable (trans-individual and trans-cultural) associative schemata through different generations and cultures (Moore & Fine, 1990; Petrini et al. 2013, p. 145) or as aprioristic interpretative schemas (i.e., as previously empty *forms* which will receive, then, a *content*[55] – following Lévi-Strauss[56] – accomplishing, thus, to their semiotic-semantic main function), which will give rise then individual *phantasies* (or *phantasms*[57]). The main effort made by Freud as well as by all the psychoanalytic thought, has been that to explain and understanding the stability, the efficacy, and the organized setting of the *phantasmatic* life of every individual, through which desire tries to be fulfilled going through defences and interdictions (Laplanche & Pontalis, 1967, 1988). Anyway, clinical psychoanalysis has verified what role play fantasies which can be qualified as primal, however one regards their historicity, in that they are the basis of every individual fantasy (De Mijolla 2005, p. 552).

The original repression, according to Lacan, is basically due to a primeval hindrance – because of castration – of a primary signifier, namely the *imaginary phallus*[58], to access to consciousness (Chemama & Vandermersch, 1998); instead, according to Freud[59], it is due the action of a primordial counter-cathexis or anticathexis (because, it cannot be otherwise, i.e., neither a cathexis nor a withdrawal of cathexis, in that these require both an already existing unconscious), by the Ego, of certain presentations that cannot enter into consciousness – so undergoing a fixation – and that arose from a crucial yet traumatic event of archaic prehistory, enormously charged because of its traumaticity, which lacerates protective shield; this is the prototypical situation with which first original repressions occurred. Thus, human organism, mobilising a part of the internal energy, created a permanent barrier against traumatic experiences, limiting the flow of external stimuli; and in such a manner, it took place the deepest, impenetrable nucleus of unconscious. So, this phylogenetic process of constitution of the deepest unconscious nucleus by original repression, from then onwards, repeats epi-ontogenetically in every human being[60]. Of course, there should be a close connection between the formation of this shield and the defence mechanisms of the Ego, as well as between original repression and original phantasies (Laplanche & Pontalis, 1967, 1988).

In conclusion, if we wish to looking for a possible scientific status of psychoanalysis, then a reasonable way to be pursued fruitfully to this end, is that turned to look at the *structural* aspects of unconscious, which should be considered as phylogenetically acquired (at the epigenetic level) during the *homination* process[61], along which occurred *encephalization* (whose big increment was mainly due to the enrichment of socialization). This psychic structuration, almost contemporary to encephalization, has probably implemented[62] such mental schemas of pre-interpretations, which nowadays structurally rule our thinking and reasoning; the notions of *original* (or *primal*) *phantasy* and *repression*, are clear instances of these structures and their action, which should be meant (although not in the aim of a mere and full *formal* reductionism[63]) just in the structuralistic sense due to Lévi-Strauss. The unconscious construct is the central pillar of the whole psychoanalytic framework, so that the first step to do in view of a possible formalization attempt of psychoanalysis is just turned towards the possible *structural* aspects of the unconscious, those phylogenetically acquired along homination process, in their basic formal structure, which will be then variously filled epi-ontogenetically (for instance, by repression) by that singular, individual content coming from the life experience of each human being.

On the basis of these latter considerations, we have simply tried to follow a route which could be in agreement with this "neostructuralistic" perspective from which to look "scientifically" at the foundations of psychoanalysis, believing strongly in the phylogenetic constitution of intersubjective deep mental structures (hence, almost universal[64]), epigenetically implemented above all during homination, then epi-ontogenetically re-established individually. So, we have first reconsidered the appreciable work achieved by Ignacio Matte Blanco[65] just on the foundations of psychoanalysis, taking into particular attention his notion of *structural unconscious* and his ideas on the crucial and inseparable intertwinements between primary and secondary processes that he has formalized by means of mathematical logic. This, besides, has led us to may perform a conceptual analysis and a theoretical recognition of the possible psychoanalytic foundations of formal logic, mainly Boolean logic, which, conversely, have also allowed to reconsider and rethink, from these new standpoints, some basic psychoanalytic theoretical concepts and notions, above all that of unconscious and its logic, always in comparison with the related psychic phenomenology. In particular, this route has led us to understand, besides other, the basic *binary* nature of unconscious logic, prelude to the next, basic *discriminating* task and *dialectic*[66] nature of consciousness, and its possible relationships with usual logical binary operators commonly involved in Boolean algebra (hence, Aristotelian logic), so making possible to establish too a very elementary formalization attempt schematizing algebraically the crucial passage from the primary process to the secondary one, within Freudian framework. Furthermore, it seems too that, usually, people reason even making an "unawareness" use of *natural deductions* (Lolli 2000, p. 87), as if these were already present, just in an unconscious fashion, in their deepest soul, without to be neither syntactic nor semantic in their logical nature, but rather, according to H. Paul Grice (1993), conversational (hence, regarding a collective, social and non-conventional metalevel of communication[67]).

So, carrying on along this path, we have reconsidered some theoretical psychoanalytic patterns[68] of human psyche related to symbolic function, whose functioning is mainly centred on those set of psychic unconscious mechanisms revolving around the *negative*, as above all done by André Green (1993), like disavowal, splitting, foreclosure, and so on, which operate not only in pathological cases, but also in the normal psychic life, its course and developments. All that, in particular, has enabled us to take into account, as well as to be coherent and in agreement with, that fundamental binary nature of human structural unconscious as has emerged from Freud's works themselves together the support, the improvements, the progresses made possible thanks to the work of other his successors, among whom are many exponents of French school[69] of psychoanalysis, like André Green, Jacques Lacan, Daniel Lagache, Jean Laplanche, Serge Leclaire, Jean-Bertrand Pontalis, and others, thanks to which we have identified the persistent and pervasive binary logic (to be precise, the *phallic logic*) featuring structural unconscious and its functioning, with obvious repercussions on the consciousness. This has allowed to trace further a special line starting from structural unconscious realm, with its *phallic logic*, towards gradually the usual binary logic of the so-called "rational" thought, mainly featured by the Boolean logic, just thanks to Matte Blanco's work and his *bi-logic*, which has therefore casted the bases for a psychoanalytic foundation of logic, together the works of other as much important and valid psychoanalysts (quoted above).

Then, ever thanks to Matte Blanco's work on structural unconscious and its formal features, in particular from its timelessness, we have understood what primary role plays *ordering* for human consciousness, hence *recursion* processes, which are formally the very early bases of computation. So, taking into loan, some notions and elementary methods of theoretical physics and mathematics, like those of *symmetry breaking* and *groupoid*, we have tried to formalize better some ideas due to Matte Blanco, hence to provide an elementary formal framework within which to lay out the basic notion of ordering and its role for consciousness, showing how is possible to get such a notion by means of a suitable *nuanced* application of the notion of symmetry breaking to the categorial notion of groupoid. From this, further, advanced formal constructions and considerations have followed, ever regarding possible formalizations of some main concepts and processes of psychoanalysis (e.g., ultrametric and p-adic, mathematical physics and topological models of unconscious, possible formal origins of time and its role for consciousness). In particular, from the formal analysis of the temporal aspects and dimensionalities of conscious and unconscious processes, we have outlined, very briefly, the possible role played by unconscious construct in informatics, from a logic stance. On the other hand, also according to André Leroi-Gourhan, the historical domestication of space and time by humans, even much more than the usage and handling of instruments, is the human fact *par excellence*. It is placeable within the most general ability of human being to establish nexuses among things, in that temporal relation may be seen as a kind of triadic relation in which a human interpreting establishes a correlation between two events or durations, in which one is what is measured and the other is what measures. This capability is universal, is at the basis of the scientific thought, and changes only for the reference systems adopted to accomplish this task (Fabietti & Remotti, 1998).

REFERENCES

Abbagnano, N. (1998). Dizionario di Filosofia (3rd ed.). Torino, Italy: UTET Libreria.

Akhtar, S., & O'Neil, M. K. (Eds.). (2011). *On Freud's 'negation'. In The International Psychoanalytic Association – Contemporary Freud. Turning points & critical issues*. London, UK: Karnac Books, Ltd.

Allman, J. M. (2000). *Evolving Brains*. New York, NY: Scientific American Library. A division of HPHLP.

Ammaniti, M., & Gallese, V. (2014). La nascita dell'intersoggettività. Lo sviluppo del Sé fra psicodinamica e neurobiologia. Milano, Italy: Raffaello Cortina Editore.

Andersson, O. (1962). Studies on the Prehistory of Psychoanalysis. Stockholm: Scandinavian University Books.

Arieti, S. (1974). Interpretazione della schizofrenia. Milano, Italy: Giangiacomo Feltrinelli Editore.

Arieti, S. (1976). Creatività. La sintesi magica. Roma, Italy: Il Pensiero Scientifico Editore.

Atkinson, R. L., Atkinson, R. C., Smith, E. E., Bem, D. J., & Nolen-Hoeksema, S. (Eds.). (1996). *Hilgard's Introduction to Psychology* (12th ed.). Orlando, FL: Harcourt Brace.

Badiou, A. (1982). Théorie du sujet. Paris: Éditions du Seuil.

Balsamo, M. (2009). Ripetizione, coazione a ripetere, destino. In *Psiche. Dizionario storico di psicologia, psichiatria, psicoanalisi, neuroscienze* (Vol. 2, pp. 957–962). Torino, Italy: Giulio Einaudi editore.

Balzarotti, R. (Ed.). (1972). Cahiers pour l'Analyse. Scritti scelti di analisi e teoria della scienza, a cura del Centro Ricerche 2. Torino, Italy: Editore Boringhieri.

Barratt, B. B. (2016). *Psychoanalysis and the Postmodern Impulse. Knowing and Being since Freud's Psychology*. New York, NY: Routledge.

Bastide, R. (Ed.). (1966). Usi e significati del termine struttura nelle scienze umane e sociali. Milano, Italy: Giangiacomo Feltrinelli Editore.

Battacchi, M. W. (2006). *La conoscenza psicologia. Il metodo, l'oggetto, la ricerca*. Roma, Itlay: Carocci editore.

Beals, R. L., & Hoijer, H. (1965). An Introduction to Anthropology (2nd ed.). New York, NY: The MacMillan Company.

Berwick, R. C., & Chomsky, N. (2016). Why Only Us. Language and Evolution. Cambridge, MA: The MIT Press. doi:10.7551/mitpress/9780262034241.001.0001

Bianchi, P. (2014). La psicoanalisi e la politica delle singolarità. In L'inconscio è la politica. Milano-Udine, Italy: Mimesis Edizioni.

Boudon, R. (1970). *Strutturalismo e scienze umane*. Torino, Italy: Giulio Einaudi editore.

Bourguignon, A., & Manus, A. (1980). Hallucination nègative, déni de la réalité et scotomisation. *Annales Médico-Psychologiques*, *138*(2), 129–153. PMID:6992686

Bremer, M. (2005). *An Introduction to Paraconsistent Logics*. Frankfurt am Main, Germany: Peter Lang Publishing.

Bria, P. (1981). Introduzione. Pensiero, mondo e problemi di fondazione. In *L'inconscio come insiemi infiniti. Saggio sulla bi-logica* (pp. xix–cxi). Torino, IT: Giulio Einaudi editore.

Bria, P., & Caroppo, E. (2006). Antropologia culturale e psicopatologia. Roma, Italy: Alpes Italia.

Bruner, E. (Ed.). (2015). Human Paleoneurology. Springer International Publishing. doi:10.1007/978-3-319-08500-5

Carotenuto, A. (1982). Discorso sulla metapsicologia. Torino, Italy: Bollati Boringhieri Editore.

Carotenuto, A. (1991). Trattato di psicologia della personalità e delle differenze individuali. Milano, Italy: Raffaello Cortina Editore.

Carotenuto, A. (Ed.). (1992). Dizionario Bompiani degli Psicologi Contemporanei. Milano, Italy: Bompiani.

Castiglioni, M., & Corradini, A. (2011). *Modelli epistemologici in psicologia. Dalla psicoanalisi al costruzionismo*. Roma, Italy: Carocci editore.

Cazeneuve, J. (1971). Sociologie du rite. Paris: PUF-Presses Universitaires de France.

Cellucci, C., & Ippoliti, E. (2016). Logica. Milano, Italy: EGEA Editore.

Chasseguet-Smirgel, J. (1975). L'idéal du moi. Paris: Éditeur Claude Tchou.

Chasseguet-Smirgel, J. (1985). Creativity and perversion. London, UK: Free Association Books, Ltd.

Chemama, R., & Vandermersch, B. (Eds.). (1998). Dictionnaire de la Psychanalyse. Paris: Larousse-Bordas.

Cherubini, P., Giaretta, P., & Mazzocco, A. (Eds.). (2000). Ragionamento: psicologia e logica. Firenze, Italy: Giunti Gruppo Editoriale.

Chianese, D. (2009). Costruzione, Ricostruzione, Interpretazione. In *Psiche. Dizionario storico di psicologia, psichiatria, psicoanalisi, neuroscienze* (Vol. 1, pp. 280–285). Torino, Italy: Giulio Einaudi editore.

Conrotto, F. (2000). Tra il sapere e la cura. Un itinerario freudiano. Milano, Italy: FrancoAngeli.

Conrotto, F. (2009). Negazione. In *Psiche. Dizionario storico di psicologia, psichiatria, psicoanalisi, neuroscienze* (Vol. 2, pp. 728–730). Torino, Italy: Giulio Einaudi editore.

Conrotto, F. (2010). Per una teoria psicoanalitica della conoscenza. Milano, Italy: FrancoAngeli.

Conrotto, F. (2014). Ripensare l'inconscio. Milano, Italy: FrancoAngeli.

Contardi, R. (2010). La prova del labirinto. Processo di simbolizzazione e dinamica rappresentativa in psicoanalisi. Milano, Italy: FrancoAngeli.

Contarello, A., & Mazzara, B. M. (2002). Le dimensioni sociali dei processi psicologici. Roma-Bari, Italy: Laterza Editori.

Conte, M., & Gennaro, A. (Eds.). (1989). Inconscio e processi cognitivi. Bologna, Italy: Società editrice il Mulino.

Conti, L., & Principe, S. (1989). Salute mentale e società. Fondamenti di psichiatria sociale. Padova, Italy: Piccin Nuova Libraria.

Contri, G. (1972). Nozioni fondamentali nella teoria della struttura di Jacques Lacan. In Cahiers pour l'Analyse. Scritti scelti di analisi e teoria della scienza, a cura del Centro Ricerche 2. Torino, Italy: Editore Boringhieri.

Corradi Fiumara, G. (1980). Funzione simbolica e filosofia del linguaggio. Torino, Italy: Editore Boringhieri.

CSFG – Centro di Studi Filosofici di Gallarate. (1977). Dizionario delle idee. Firenze, Italy: G.C. Sansoni Editore.

Cuche, D. (2004). La notion de culture dans les sciences sociales. Paris: Éditions La Découverte.

D'Urso, V., & Trentin, R. (1998). Introduzione alla psicologia delle emozioni. Roma-Bari, Italy: Editori Laterza.

Dalla Chiara Scabia, M. L. (1973). Istanti e individui nelle logiche temporali. *Rivista di Filosofia, 64*(2), 95–122.

Dalla Chiara Scabia, M. L. (1974). Logica. Milano, Italy: ISEDI – Istituto Editoriale Internazionale.

Damasio, A. (1994). Descartes' Error. Emotion, Reason, and the Human Brain. New York, NY: G.P. Putnam's Sons.

De Mijolla, A. (Ed.). (2005). *International Dictionary of Psychoanalysis* (Vols. 1–3). Farmington Hills, MI: Thomson Gale.

De Mijolla, A., & De Mijolla Mellor, S. (Eds.). (1996). Psychanalyse. Paris: PUF-Presses Universitaires de France.

Deacon, T. W. (1997). *The Symbolic Species. The Coevolution of Language and the Brain*. New York, NY: W.W. Norton & Company.

Dei, F., & Meloni, P. (2015). *Antropologia della cultura materiale*. Roma, Italy: Carocci editore.

Devlin, K. (2006). *The Math Instinct: Why You're a Mathematical Genius (Along with Lobsters, Birds, Cats, and Dogs)*. New York, NY: Thunder's Mouth Press.

Dijksterhuis, A., & Nordgren, L. F. (2006). A theory of unconsciouss thought. *Perspectives on Psychological Science*, *1*(2), 95–109. doi:10.1111/j.1745-6916.2006.00007.x PMID:26151465

Donati, P. (2015). L'enigma della relazione. Milano, Italy: Mimesis edizioni.

Durst, M. (1988). Dialettica e bi-logica. L'epistemologia di Ignacio Matte Blanco. Milano, Italy: Marzorati Editore.

Eibl-Eibesfeldt, I. (1996). Amore e odio. Per una storia naturale dei comportamenti elementari. Milano, Italy: Edizioni Adelphi.

Eibl-Eibesfeldt, I. (1997). Le invarianti nell'evoluzione delle specie. Roma, Italy: Di Renzo Editore.

Eibl-Eibesfeldt, I. (2001). Etologia umana. Le basi biologiche e culturali del comportamento. Torino, Italy: Bollati Boringhieri editore.

Eibl-Eibesfeldt, I. (2005). Dall'animale all'uomo. Le invarianti nell'evoluzione delle specie. Roma, Italy: Di Renzo Editore.

Ekstrom, S. R. (2004). The mind beyond our immediate awareness: Freudian, Jungian, and cognitive models of the unconscious. *The Journal of Analytical Psychology*, *49*(5), 657–682. doi:10.1111/j.0021-8774.2004.00494.x PMID:15533197

Fabietti, U., & Remotti, F. (Eds.). (1998). Dizionario di Antropologia. Etnologia, Antropologia Culturale, Antropologia Sociale. Bologna, Italy: Nicola Zanichelli Editore.

Fairlamb, H. L. (1994). *Critical conditions. Postmodernity and the question of foundations*. Cambridge, UK: Cambridge University Press. doi:10.1017/CBO9780511552762

Falzone, A. (2005). Filosofia del linguaggio e psicopatologia evoluzionistica. Soveria Mannelli (CZ), Italy: Rubbettino Editore.

Ferretti, F. (2010). Alle origini del linguaggio umano. Il punto di vista evoluzionistico. Roma-Bari, Italy: Editori Laterza.

Finelli, R. (2010). Perché l'inconscio non è strutturato come un linguaggio. In Compendio di Psicoanalisi e altri scritti. Roma, Italy: Newton Compton editori.

Finelli, R. (2011). Rappresentazione e linguaggio in Freud: a partire dal "Compendio di psicoanalisi". *Consecutio Temporum. Rivista di critica della postmodernità*, *1*, 112-125.

Fodor, N., & Gaynor, F. (1950). Freud: Dictionary of Psychoanalysis. New York, NY: The Philosophical Library.

Fonagy, P., Gergely, G., Jurist, E. L., & Target, M. (2002). Affect Regulation, Mentalization, and the Development of the Self. New York, NY: Other Press.

Fossi, G. (1983). La psicologia dinamica: un'eredità del XX secolo. Roma, Italy: Edizioni Borla.

Fossi, G. (1984). Le teorie psicoanalitiche. Padova, Italy: Piccin Nuova Libraria.

Fossi, G. (1988). Psicoanalisi e psicoterapie dinamiche. Torino, Italy: Bollati Boringhieri editore.

Fossi, G. (2003). Una proposta evoluzionista per la psicoanalisi. Con un manuale per la pratica terapeutica e la ricerca empirica. Milano, Italy: FrancoAngeli.

Francioni, M. (1978). Psicoanalisi linguistica ed epistemologia in Jacques Lacan. Torino, Italy: Editore Boringhieri.

Francioni, M. (1982). Storia della psicoanalisi francese. Teorie e istituzioni freudiane. Torino, Italy: Editore Boringhieri.

Freni, S. (1992). Prefazione all'edizione italiana. In Capire il transfert. Milano, Italy: Raffaello Cortina Editore.

Freud, A. (1937). The Ego and the Mechanisms of Defence. London, UK: The Hogarth Press.

Freud, S. (1938). Abriß der psychoanalyse. Academic Press.

Freud, S. (1957). *The Standard Edition of Complete Psychological Works of Sigmund Freud* (Vols. 1-24; J. Strachey, Trans. & Ed.). London, UK: The Hogarth Press.

Freud, S. (1979). La scissione dell'Io nel processo di difesa (1938). In Opere di Sigmund Freud, 1930-1938. L'uomo Mosè e la religione monoteistica e altri scritti (vol. 11). Torino, Italy: Editore Boringhieri.

Friedman, D. M. (2001). A Mind of Its Own. A Cultural History of the Penis. New York, NY: Simon & Schuster, Inc.

Friedman, M., & Tomšič, S. (Eds.). (2016). Psychoanalysis: Topological Perspectives. New Conceptions of Geometry and Space in Freud and Lacan. Bielefeld, Germany: transcript Verlag. doi:10.14361/9783839434406

Fromm, E. (1951). The Forgotten Language. An Introduction to the Understanding of Dreams, Fairy Tales, and Myths. New York, NY: Holt, Rinehart & Winston Publishing Company, Inc.

Fromm, E. (1976). To have or to be? New York, NY: Harper & Row Publishers, Inc.

Funari, E. (1978). Psicoanalisi: tecnica o Weltanschauung? In *Psicoanalisi e classi sociali* (pp. 147–153). Roma, Italy: Editori Riuniti.

Funari, E. (1988). Contestualità e specificità della psicoanalisi. In Trattato di Psicoanalisi: Vol. 1. Teoria e Tecnica. Milano, Italy: Raffaello Cortina Editore.

Funari, E. (2007). L'irrapresentabile come origine della vita psichica. Milano, Italy: FrancoAngeli.

Fusco, A., & Tomassoni, R. (Eds.). (2013). Creatività nella psicologia letteraria, drammatica e filmica. Milano, Italy: FrancoAngeli.

Galimberti, U. (1979). Psichiatria e fenomenologia. Milano, Italy: Giangiacomo Feltrinelli Editore.

Galimberti, U. (1983). Il corpo. Milano, Italy: Giangiacomo Feltrinelli Editore.

Galimberti, U. (2006). Dizionario di psicologia. Torino, Italy: UTET Libreria.

Gay, P. (2000). Freud. Una vita per i nostri tempi. Milano, Italy: Bompiani.

Giberti, F., & Rossi, R. (Eds.). (1996). Manuale di psichiatria (4th ed.). Padova, Italy: Piccin Nuova Libraria.

Gilliéron, E., & Baldassarre, M. (Eds.). (2012). Perversione e Relazione. Roma, Italy: Alpes Italia.

Giordano, M., Dello Russo, G., Pardi, F., & Patella, G. A. (1984). Tempo e inconscio. Napoli, Italy: Guida editori.

Girotto, V. (Ed.). (2013). Introduzione alla psicologia del pensiero. Bologna, Italy: Società editrice il Mulino.

Goleman, D. (1995). Emotional Intelligence. New York, NY: Bantam Books.

Green, A. (1993). Le travail du négatif. Paris: Les Éditions du Minuit.

Grice, H. P. (1993). Logica e conversazione. Saggi su intenzione, significato e comunicazione. Bologna, Italy: Società editrice il Mulino.

Grinberg, L. (1989). La supervisione psicoanalitica. Teoria e pratica. Milano, Italy: Raffaello Cortina Editore.

Grunberger, B. (1971). *Le narcissisme. Essai de psychanalyse.* Paris: Payot.

Guyton, A. C. (1991). Basic Neuroscience. Anatomy & Physiology (2nd ed.). Philadelphia, PA: W.B. Saunders Company.

Hall, C. S. (1999). *A Primer in Freudian Psychology.* New York, NY: Meridian Books.

Hampe, B., & Grady, J. E. (Eds.). (2005). *From Perception to Meaning. Image Schemas in Cognitive Linguistics.* Berlin: Walter de Gruyter GmbH and Co. doi:10.1515/9783110197532

Hanly, C. (1984). Ego Ideal and Ideal Ego. *The International Journal of Psycho-Analysis, 65*(3), 253–261. PMID:6571602

Hanly, C. (2011). Studi psicoanalitici sul narcisismo. Scritti di Charles Hanly. Roma, Italy: Giovanni Fioriti Editore.

Hickmann, M., & Robert, S. (Eds.). (2006). *Space in Languages – Linguistic Systems and Cognitive Categories.* Amsterdam: John Benjamins Publishing Company. doi:10.1075/tsl.66

Hodges, W. (1977). *Logic. An Introduction to Elementary Logic.* Harmondsworth, UK: Penguin Books, Ltd.

Hodkinson, I., & Reynolds, M. (2007). Temporal Logic. In Handbook of Modal Logic. Amsterdam: Elsevier, B.V.

Holloway, R. L. (1974). The Casts of Fossil Hominid Brains. *Scientific American*, *231*(1), 106–115. doi:10.1038/scientificamerican0774-106 PMID:4858755

Horkheimer, M., & Adorno, T. W. (1947). Dialektik der Aufklärung. Philosophische Fragments. Amsterdam: Querido Verlag N.V.

Imbasciati, A. (2015). Nuove teorie sul funzionamento della mente. L'istituzione psicoanalitica e gli psicoanalisti. Milano, Italy: FrancoAngeli.

Ippoliti, E. (2007). *Il vero e il plausibile*. Morrisville, NC: Lulu Press, Inc.

Iurato, G. (2013a). Mathematical thought in the light of Matte Blanco work. *Philosophy of Mathematics Education Journal*, 27.

Iurato, G. (2013b). Σύμβολου: An attempt toward the early origins, Part 1. *Language & Psychoanalysis*, *2*(2), 77–120. doi:10.7565/landp.2013.008

Iurato, G. (2013c). Σύμβολου: An attempt toward the early origins, Part 2. *Language & Psychoanalysis*, *2*(2), 121–160. doi:10.7565/landp.2013.009

Iurato, G. (2014a). At the grounding of computational psychoanalysis: on the work of Ignacio Matte Blanco. A general history of culture overview of Matte Blanco bilogic in comparison. In *Proceedings of the 2014 IEEE 13th International Conference on Cognitive Informatics and Cognitive Computing*. Los Alamitos, CA: IEEE Computer Society Press.

Iurato, G. (2014b). The dawning of computational psychoanalysis. A proposal for some first elementary formalization attempts. *International Journal of Cognitive Informatics and Natural Intelligence*, *8*(4), 50–82. doi:10.4018/ijcini.2014100104

Iurato, G. (2014c). *Alcune considerazioni critiche sul simbolismo*. Preprint No. hal-00980828 version 1. Available at HAL archives-ouvertes.

Iurato, G. (2015a). A Brief Comparison of the Unconscious as Seen by Jung and Lévi-Strauss. *Anthropology of Consciousness*, *26*(1), 60–107. doi:10.1111/anoc.12032

Iurato, G. (2015b). Fetishism in Marketing. Some First Elementary Psychoanalytic Anthropology Remarks. In Business Management: A Practioners' Guide. Delhi: International Research Publication House.

Iurato, G. (2015c). A simple phylogenetic remark about certain human blood pressure values. *Journal of Biochemistry International*, *2*(4), 162–165.

Iurato, G. (2016a). *A psychoanalytic enquiry on symbolic function*. Preprint No. hal-01361264 version 3. Available at HAL archives-ouvertes.

Iurato, G. (2016b). *A view of LSA/ESA in Computational Psychoanalysis*. Preprint No. hal-01353999 version 1. Available at HAL archives-ouvertes.

Iurato, G. (2016c). On Jacques Lacan Psychosis Theory and ERPs Analysis. *Journal of Biology and Nature*, *5*(4), 234–240.

Iurato, G. (2016d). Some Comments on the Historical Role of *Fetishism* in Economic Anthropology. *Journal of Global Economics, Management and Business Research, 7*(1), 61–82.

Iurato, G. (2016e). *The origins of symbol. An historical-critical study of symbolic function, according to the phylo-ontogenetic perspective, as arising from the comparison of certain patterns of neuro-psychological sciences.* Paper Presented at the Satellite Event "On the edge of disciplines", Florence, Italy.

Iurato, G. (2016f). Two simple questions regarding cultural anthropology. *Journal of Global Research in Education and Social Science, 8*(1), 10–15.

Iurato, G. (2017a). An Essay in Denotational Mathematics. Rigorous Results. In Encyclopedia of Information Science and Technology (4th ed.). Hershey, PA: IGI Global.

Iurato, G. (2017b). Un raffronto critico fra la teoria platonica delle idee ed il paradosso di Kripke-Wittgenstein. In Platone nel pensiero moderno e contemporaneo (vol. 11). Villasanta (MB), Italy: Limina Mentis Edizioni.

Iurato, G. (2017c). *Rigidity of the Generalized Other, narrowness of the Otherness and demodernization, in the framework of symbolic interactionism. Ideology and Political Journal.* (in press)

Iurato, G., & Khrennikov, A. Yu. (2015). Hysteresis model of unconscious-conscious interconnection: Exploring dynamics on m-adic trees. *p-Adic Numbers, Ultrametric Analysis and Applications, 7*(4), 312–321. doi:10.1134/S2070046615040068

Iurato, G., & Khrennikov, A. Yu. (2017). On the topological structure of a mathematical model of human unconscious. *p-Adic Numbers, Ultrametric Analysis and Applications, 9*(1), 78–81. doi:10.1134/S2070046617010071

Iurato, G., Khrennikov, A. Yu., & Murtagh, F. (2016). Formal Foundations for the Origins of Human Consciousness. *p-Adic Numbers, Ultrametric Analysis and Applications, 8*(4), 249–279. doi:10.1134/S2070046616040014

Jablonka, E., & Raz, G. (2009). Transgenerational Epigenetic Inheritance: Prevalence, Mechanisms, and Implications for the Study of Heredity and Evolution. *The Quarterly Review of Biology, 84*(2), 131–176. doi:10.1086/598822 PMID:19606595

Jaffé, R. (2009). Ideale dell'Io, Idealizzazione. In *Psiche. Dizionario storico di psicologia, psichiatria, psicoanalisi, neuroscienze* (Vol. 1, pp. 494–500). Torino, Italy: Giulio Einaudi editore.

Johnson-Laird, P., & Bara, B. (1984). Syllogistic Inference. *Cognition, 16*(1), 1–61. doi:10.1016/0010-0277(84)90035-0 PMID:6540648

Kächele, H. (2001). Are there "Pillars of Therapeutic Wisdom" for Psychoanalytic Therapy? *European Journal of Psychoanalysis. Humanities, Philosophy. Psychothérapies, 12-13*, 151–161.

Kandel, E. R. (2005). Psychiatry, Psychoanalysis, and the New Biology of Mind. Washington, DC: American Psychiatric Association Publishing, Inc.

Kaplan-Solms, K., & Solms, M. (2000). Clinical Studies in Neuro-Psychoanalysis. Introduction to a Depth Neuropsychology. London, UK: Karnac Books, Ltd.

Kemeny, J. G. (1959). A Philosopher Looks at Science. Princeton, NJ: D. Van Nostrand Reinhold Company, Inc.

Kemeny, J. G., Snell, J. L., & Thompson, G. L. (1974). *Introduction to Finite Mathematics* (3rd ed.). Englewood Cliffs, NJ: Prentice-Hall.

Kernberg, O. (2011). Suicide prevention for psychoanalytic institutes and societies. *Journal of the American Psychoanalytic Association, 60*(4), 707–719. doi:10.1177/0003065112449861 PMID:22786850

Khrennikov, A. Yu. (1991). *p*-Adic quantum mechanics with *p*-adic valued functions. *Journal of Mathematical Physics, 32*(4), 932–937. doi:10.1063/1.529353

Khrennikov, A. Yu. (1998). Human subconscious as the *p*-adic dynamical system. *Journal of Theoretical Biology, 193*(2), 179–196. doi:10.1006/jtbi.1997.0604 PMID:9714931

Khrennikov, A. Yu. (2002). *Classical and quantum mental models and Freud's theory of unconscious mind. Series in Mathematical Modelling in Physics, Engineering and Cognitive Sciences* (Vol. 1). Växjö, Sweden: Växjö University Press.

Khrennikov, A. Yu. (2007). Toward an adequate mathematical model of mental space: Conscious/unconscious dynamics on *m*-adic trees. *Bio Systems, 90*(3), 656–675. doi:10.1016/j.biosystems.2007.02.004 PMID:17400367

Kim, W. W. (2016). History and Cultural Perspective. In Penile Augmentation. Berlin: Springer-Verlag. doi:10.1007/978-3-662-46753-4_2

Kissin, B. (1986). *Conscious and Unconscious Programs in the Brain.* New York, NY: Plenum Publishing Corporation. doi:10.1007/978-1-4613-2187-3

Köhler, T. (2007). *Freuds Psychoanalyse. Eine Einführung* (2nd ed.). Stuttgart, Germany: W. Kohlhammer GmbH.

Kultgen, J. (1976). Lévi-Strauss on Unconscious Social Structures. *The Southwestern Journal of Philosophy, 7*(1), 153–159. doi:10.5840/swjphil19767118

Kuper, J. (Ed.). (1988). *A Lexicon of Psychology, Psychiatry and Psychoanalysis.* London, UK: Routledge.

La Forgia, M. (1992). Sincronicità. In Trattato di Psicologia Analitica (Vols. 1-2). Torino, Italy: UTET.

Lacan, J. (2014). *The Seminar of Jacques Lacan. Book X: The Anxiety* (J. A. Miller, Ed.; A. R. Price, Trans.). Malden, MA: Polity Press.

Lacas, M.-L. (2007). La démarche originale de Gisela Pankow. Gisela Pankows original thought processes. *LÉvolution Psychiatrique, 72*(1), 15–24. doi:10.1016/j.evopsy.2006.11.001

Làdavas, E., & Berti, A. (2014). Neuropsicologia (3rd ed.). Bologna, Italy: Società editrice il Mulino.

Lagache, D. (1961). *La psychanalyse et la structure de la personnalité.* Paper Presented au Colloquium International de Royaumont, Paris, France.

Lagache, D. (1965). Le modèle psychanalytique de la personnalité. In *La Folle du Logis. La psychanalyse comme science exacte* (pp. 159–183). Paris: PUF-Presses Universitaires de France.

Lakatos, I. (1978). Philosophical Papers (Vols. 1-2). Cambridge, UK: Cambridge University Press.

Lambert, K., & Brittain, G. G., Jr. (1979). An Introduction to the Philosophy of Science. Reseda, CA: Ridgeview Publishing Company.

Langs, R. (1990). Guida alla psicoterapia. Un'introduzione all'approccio comunicativo. Torino, Italy: Bollati Boringhieri editore.

Laplanche, J. (2000). Problematiche II. Castrazione. Simbolizzazioni. Bari-Roma, Italy: La Biblioteca.

Laplanche, J. (2001). *L'inconscio e l'Es*. Bari-Roma, Italy: La Biblioteca.

Laplanche, J. (2007). *L'après-coup*. Bari-Roma, Italy: La Biblioteca.

Laplanche, J., & Pontalis, J.-B. (1967). Vocabulaire de la psychoanalyse. Paris: Presses Universitaires de France.

Laplanche, J., & Pontalis, J.-B. (1988). Fantasma originario, fantasmi delle origini, origini del fantasma. Bologna, Italy: Società editrice il Mulino.

Lerner, D. (Ed.). (1961). Quality and Quantity. New York, NY: The Free Press of Glencoe.

Lévi-Strauss, C. (1975). *Razza e storia e altri studi di antropologia*. Torino, Italy: Giulio Einaudi editore.

Lévi-Strauss, C. (2008). Sull'Italia. In Claude Lévi-Strauss fotografato da Marion Kalter. Napoli, Italy: Electa Napoli.

Lévi-Strauss, C., & Eribon, D. (1988). De près et de loin. Paris: Éditions Odile Jacob.

Levitz, K., & Levitz, H. (1979). *Logic and Boolean Algebra*. Woodbury, NY: Barron's Educational Series, Inc.

Lis, A., Mazzeschi, C., & Zennaro, A. (2007). *La psicoanalisi. Un percorso concettuale fra tradizione e attualità (2nd ed.)*. Roma, Italy: Carocci editore.

Lis, A., Zennaro, A., Mazzeschi, C., Salcuni, S., & Parolin, L. (2003). *Breve dizionario di psicoanalisi*. Roma, Italy: Carocci editore.

Lolli, G. (1991). Introduzione alla logica formale. Bologna, Italy: Società editrice il Mulino.

Lolli, G. (2000). Un logico esamina i modelli mentali. In Ragionamento: psicologia e logica. Firenze, Italy: Giunti Gruppo Editoriale.

Lolli, G. (2005). QED – Fenomenologia della dimostrazione. Torino, Italy: Bollati Boringhieri editore.

Longhin, L. (1992). Alle origini del pensiero psicoanalitico. Roma, Italy: Edizioni Borla.

Longhin, L. (2016). La mente emotiva. Conoscerla e curarla. Milano, Italy: FrancoAngeli.

Longhin, L., & Mancia, M. (1998). Temi e problemi in psicoanalisi. Torino, Italy: Bollati Boringhieri editore.

Luborsky, L., & Crits-Christoph, P. (1992). Capire il transfert. Milano, Italy: Raffaello Cortina Editore.

Lusetti, V. (2008). Psicopatologia antropologica. Roma, Italy: EUR-Edizioni Universitarie Romane.

Macola, E. (Ed.). (2014). Sublimazione e perversione. Attualità Lacaniana. Rivista della Scuola Lacaniana di Psicoanalisi, 18, 7-108.

Mancia, M. (Ed.). (1990). Super-Io e Ideale dell'Io. Roma, Italy: Casa Editrice Astrolabio-Ubaldini Editore.

Mancia, M. (Ed.). (2006). Psychoanalysis and Neuroscience. Milan, Italy: Springer-Verlag Italia. doi:10.1007/88-470-0550-7

Manzi, G. (2013). Il grande racconto dell'evoluzione umana. Bologna, Italy: Società editrice il Mulino.

Marchi, D. (2016). Il mistero di Homo naledi. Chi era e come viveva il nostro lontano cugino africano: storia di una scoperta rivoluzionaria. Milano, Italy: Mondadori Libri.

Marcuse, H. (1964). One-Dimensional Man. Studies in the Ideology of Advanced Industrial Society. Boston, MA: Beacon Press, Inc.

Matte Blanco, I. (1975). The Unconscious as Infinite Sets. An Essay in Bi-Logic. London, UK: Gerald Duckworth & Company, Ltd.

Matthews, G. C. (1998). Neurobiology. Molecules, Cells, and Systems. Oxford, UK: Blackwell Science, Ltd.

McCulloch, W. S. (1965). *Embodiments of Mind*. Cambridge, MA: The MIT Press.

Mellino, M. (2005). La critica postcoloniale. Decolonizzazione, capitalismo e cosmopolitismo nei postcolonial studies. Roma, Italy: Meltemi editore.

Mendes, E.P.R. (1995). Vicissitudes da clínica psicanalítica contemporânea. *Reverso, Belo Horizonte, 40*.

Miller, P. H. (1983). *Theories of Developmental Psychology*. New York, NY: W.H. Freeman & Co.

Milrod, D. (2002). The superego. Its formation, structure, and functioning. *The Psychoanalytic Study of the Child, 57*, 131–148. PMID:12723129

Mitchell, S. A., & Black, M. J. (1995). *Freud and beyond. A History of Modern Psychoanalysic Thought*. New York, NY: Basic Books. A Division of Harper Collins Publishers.

Moore, B. E., & Fine, B. D. (Eds.). (1990). Psychoanalytic Terms and Concepts. New York, NY: The American Psychoanalytic Association.

Moore, D. S. (2015). *The Developing Genome. An Introduction to Behavioural Epigenetics*. New York, NY: Oxford University Press.

Moravia, S. (2004). Ragione strutturale e universi di senso. Saggio sul pensiero di Claude Lévi-Strauss. Firenze, Italy: Casa Editrice Le Lettere.

Nannini, S. (2007). Naturalismo cognitivo. Per una teoria materialistica della mente. Macerata, Italy: Edizioni Quodlibet.

Nannini, S. (2011). L'anima e il corpo. Un'introduzione storica alla filosofia della mente. Roma-Bari, Italy: Laterza Editori.

Nannini, S. (2015). Time and Consciousness in Cognitive Naturalism. *Rivista Internazionale di Filosofia e Psicologia*, *6*(3), 458–473.

Napolitano, F. (2009). Rappresentazione, 2. In *Psiche. Dizionario storico di psicologia, psichiatria, psicoanalisi, neuroscienze* (Vol. 2, pp. 919–923). Torino, Italy: Giulio Einaudi editore.

Neubauer, K. (2004). Semantica storica. In Dizionario degli studi culturali. Roma, Italy: Meltemi editore.

Nicasi, S. (1981). Meccanismi di difesa. Studio su Freud. Milano, Italy: il Saggiatore.

Øhrstrøm, P., & Hasle, P. F. V. (Eds.). (1995). *Temporal Logic. From Ancient Ideas to Artificial Intelligence. Studies in Linguistics and Philosophy, Volume No. 57*. Dordrecht, The Netherlands: Kluwer Academic Publishers.

Oliverio, A. (1982). Biologia e comportamento. Bologna, Italy: Nicola Zanichelli Editore.

Oliverio, A. (1984). Storia naturale della mente. Torino, Italy: Editore Boringhieri.

Oliverio, A. (2008). Geografia della mente. Territori cerebrali e comportamenti umani. Milano, Italy: Raffaello Cortina Editore.

Oliverio, A. (2009). La vita nascosta del cervello. Firenze, Italy: Giunti Editore.

Oliverio, A. (2011). Prima lezione di neuroscienze. Roma-Bari, Italy: Editori Laterza.

Oliverio, A. (2016). Il cervello e linconscio. *Psicobiettivo*, *36*(3), 251–259. doi:10.3280/PSOB2016-003015

Oliverio, A. (2017). Il cervello che impara. Neuropedagogia dall'infanzia alla vecchiaia. Firenze, Italy: Giunti Editore.

Palombi, F. (2002). Il legame instabile. Attualità del dibattito psicoanalisi-scienza. Milano, Italy: FrancoAngeli.

Pankow, G. (1977). L'uomo e la sua psicosi. Milano, Italy: Giangiacomo Feltrinelli Editore.

Pankow, G. (1979). Struttura familiare e psicosi. Milano, Italy: Giangiacomo Feltrinelli Editore.

Panksepp, J., & Biven, L. (2012). The Archeology of Mind. Neuroevolutionary Origins of Human Emotion. New York, NY: W.W. Norton & Company.

Papagno, C. (2010). Neuropsicologia della memoria. Bologna, Italy: Società editrice il Mulino.

Parsons, T. (1970). *Social Structure and Personality*. New York, NY: The Free Press. A Division of The Macmillan Company.

Peterburs, J., Nitsch, A. M., Miltner, W. H. R., & Straube, T. (2013). Impaired representation of time in schizophrenia is linked to positive symptoms and cognitive demand. *PLoS ONE*, *8*(6), e67615/1–7. doi:10.1371/journal.pone.0067615 PMID:23826328

Petit, C., & Prévost, G. (1971). Genetica ed evoluzione. Milano, Italy: Arnoldo Mondadori Editore.

Petocz, A. (2004). *Freud, psychoanalysis and symbolism*. Cambridge, UK: Cambridge University Press.

Petrilli, S., & Ponzio, A. (2005). *Semiotics Unbounded. Interpretive Routes Through the Open Network of Signs*. Toronto: The University of Toronto Press. doi:10.3138/9781442657113

Petrini, P., Casadei, A., & Chiricozzi, F. (Eds.). (2011). Trasgressione, violazione, perversione. Eziopatogenesi, diagnosi e terapia. Milano, Italy: FrancoAngeli.

Petrini, P., Renzi, A., Casadei, A., & Mandese, A. (2013). Dizionario di psicoanalisi. Con elementi di psichiatria, psicodinamica e psicologia dinamica. Milano, Italy: FrancoAngeli.

Piattelli Palmarini, M. (1987). Scienza come cultura. Protagonisti, luoghi e idee delle scienze contemporanee. Milano, Italy: Arnoldo Mondadori Editore.

Pieri, P. F. (2005). Dizionario junghiano (Edizione ridotta). Torino, Italy: Bollati Boringhieri editore.

Piscicelli, U. (1994). Sessuologia. Teoremi psicosomatici e relazionali. Padova, Italy: Piccin Nuova Libraria.

Pizzi, C. (Ed.). (1974). La logica del tempo. Torino, Italy: Bollati Boringhieri Editore.

Poggi, S. (1977). I sistemi dell'esperienza. Bologna, Italy: Società editrice il Mulino.

Pollo, M. (2016). La nostalgia dell'uroboros. Contributi a una psicologia culturale delle nuove addiction. Milano, Italy: FrancoAngeli.

Possenti, V. (Ed.). (1979). Epistemologia e scienze umane. Milano, Italy: Editore Massimo.

Preziosi, P. (1992). Fondamenti di neuropsicofarmacologia. Padova, Italy: Piccin Nuova Libraria.

Putnam, H. (1956). Mathematics and the Existence of Abstract Entities. *Philosophical Studies*, 7(6), 81–88. doi:10.1007/BF02221758

Putnam, H. (1975). Filosofia della logica. Nominalismo e realismo nella logica contemporanea. Milano, Italy: ISEDI – Istituto Editoriale Internazionale.

Rayner, E. (1995). *Unconscious Logic. An Introduction to Matte Blanco's Bi-Logic and its Uses*. New York, NY: Routledge.

Rayner, E. (1998). Foreword. In *The Unconscious as Infinite Sets. An Essay in Bi-Logic* (pp. xviii–xxiv). London, UK: Karnac Books, Ltd.

Recalcati, M. (2003). Introduzione alla psicoanalisi contemporanea. Milano, Italy: Bruno Mondadori Editore.

Recalcati, M. (2007a). Elogio dell'inconscio. Dodici argomenti in difesa della psicoanalisi. Milano, Italy: Bruno Mondadori.

Recalcati, M. (2007b). Lo psicoanalista e la città. L'inconscio e il discorso del capitalista. Roma, Italy: manifestolibri.

Recalcati, M. (2010). L'uomo senza inconscio. Figure della nuova clinica psicoanalitica. Milano, Italy: Raffaello Cortina Editore.

Recalcati, M. (2016). *Jacques Lacan* (Vols. 1-2). Milano, Italy: Raffaello Cortina Editore.

Riehl, J. P. (2010). *Mirror-Image Asymmetry. An Introduction to the Origin and Consequences of Chirality*. Hoboken, NJ: John Wiley & Sons, Inc. doi:10.1002/9780470588888

Riolo, F. (2009). Trasformazione. In *Psiche. Dizionario storico di psicologia, psichiatria, psicoanalisi, neuroscienze* (Vol. 2, pp. 1112–1116). Torino, Italy: Giulio Einaudi editore.

Rose, J. R. (Ed.). (2011). *Mapping Psychic Reality. Triangulation, Communication, and Insight. Psychoanalytic Ideas*. London, UK: Karnac Books, Ltd.

Rosenzweig, M. R., Bennett, E. L., & Diamond, M. C. (1972). On the Role of Environmental Stimulation on Brain Plasticity. *Scientific American*, *226*(2), 22–29. doi:10.1038/scientificamerican0272-22 PMID:5062027

Rossi, R., De Fazio, F., Gatti, U., & Rocco, G. (2008, Feb.). Perizie e consulenze psichiatriche su Diamante Stefano, Stevanin Gianfranco, Bilancia Donato, Panini Giorgio. *POL.it – The Italian On Line Psychiatric Magazine*.

Roudinesco, E. (1997). Jacques Lacan. Outline of a life, history of a system of thought. Oxford, UK: Polity Press.

Roudinesco, E. (2008). Da vicino e da lontano. Claude Lévi-Strauss e la psicoanalisi. In Lévi-Strauss Fuori di sé. Macerata, Italy: Quodlibet.

Sabbadini, A. (1979). Introduzione. In Il tempo in psicoanalisi. Milano, Italy: Giangiacomo Feltrinelli Editore.

Sannella, D., & Tarlecki, A. (2012). *Foundations of Algebraic Specification and Formal Software Development. Monographs in Theoretical Computer Science. An EATCS Series*. Berlin: Springer-Verlag. doi:10.1007/978-3-642-17336-3

Sasso, G. (1982). Le strutture anagrammatiche della poesia. Milano, Italy: Giangiacomo Feltrinelli Editore.

Sasso, G. (1993). La mente intralinguistica. L'instabilità del segno: anagrammi e parole dentro le parole. Genova, Italy: Marietti Editore.

Sasso, G. (1999). Struttura dell'oggetto e della rappresentazione. Roma, Italy: Casa Editrice Astrolabio-Ubaldini Editore.

Sasso, G. (2005). Psicoanalisi e Neuroscienze. Roma, Italy: Casa Editrice Astrolabio-Ubaldini Editore.

Sasso, G. (2011). La nascita della coscienza. Roma, Italy: Casa Editrice Astrolabio-Ubaldini Editore.

Scabini, E. (1973). Ideazione e psicoanalisi. Milano, Italy: Giangiacomo Feltrinelli Editore.

Segalen, M. (1998). Rites et rituels contemporains. Paris: Les Éditions Nathan.

Semi, A. A. (2003). La coscienza in psicoanalisi. Milano, Italy: Raffaello Cortina Editore.

Semi, A.A. (Ed.). (1989). *Trattato di Psicoanalisi* (Vols. 1-2). Milano, Italy: Raffaello Cortina Editore.

Severino, E. (2008). La strada. La follia e la gioia. Milano, Italy: BUR Saggi.

Siri, G. (Ed.). (1976). Problemi epistemologici della psicologia. Milano, Italy: Vita e Pensiero.

Skelton, R. (1984). Understanding Matte Blanco. *The International Journal of Psycho-Analysis, 65,* 453–460. PMID:6544756

Skelton, R. (1990). Generalizations from Freud to Matte Blanco. *The International Review of Psycho-Analysis, 17,* 471–474.

Skillicorn, D. (1994). *Foundations of Parallel Programming.* Cambridge, UK: Cambridge University Press. doi:10.1017/CBO9780511526626

Sluzki, C. E., & Ransom, D. C. (1979). Il doppio legame: la genesi dell'approccio relazionale allo studio della famiglia. Roma, Italy: Casa Editrice Astrolabio-Ubaldini Editore.

Smirnov, V. N. (1970). *La transaction fétichique. Nouvelle Revue de Psychoanalyse, 2.*

Solomon, P., & Patch, V. D. (1974). Handbook of Psychiatry. Los Altos, CA: Lange Medical Publications.

Somenzi, V. (1998). Prefazione. In Categorie, tempo e linguaggio. Quaderni di Methodologia, N. 5. Roma, Italy: Società Stampa Sportiva.

Spedini, G. (2005). Antropologia evoluzionistica (2nd ed.). Padova, Italy: Piccin Nuova Libraria.

Stirling, C. (2001). *Modal and Temporal Properties of Processes.* New York, NY: Springer-Verlag. doi:10.1007/978-1-4757-3550-5

Tabossi, P. (2009). Rappresentazione, 1. In *Psiche. Dizionario storico di psicologia, psichiatria, psicoanalisi, neuroscienze* (Vol. 2, pp. 914–919). Torino, Italy: Giulio Einaudi editore.

Tallis, R. (2002). Hidden Minds. A History of the Unconscious. New York, NY: Arcade Publishing, Inc.

Tanenbaum, A. S., & Bos, H. (2015). *Modern Operating Systems* (4th ed.). Essex, UK: Pearson Education Limited.

Tartabini, A., & Giusti, F. (2006). Origine ed evoluzione del linguaggio. Scimpanzé, ominidi e uomini moderni. Napoli, Italy: Liguori Editore.

Terminio, N. (2009). Misurare l'inconscio? Coordinate psicoanalitiche nella ricerca in psicoterapia. Milano, Italy: Bruno Mondadori.

Thom, R. (1985). *Modelli matematici della morfogenesi.* Torino, Italy: Giulio Einaudi editore.

Thomä, H., & Kächele, H. (1989). *Psychoanalytic Practice* (Vols. 1-2). Berlin: Springer-Verlag.

Tibaldi, M. (2004). Critica archetipica. In Dizionario degli studi culturali. Roma, Italy: Meltemi editore.

Toraldo di Francia, G. (1976). *L'indagine del mondo fisico.* Torino, Italy: Giulio Einaudi editore.

Uznadze, D. N., Prangisvili, A. S., Bassin, F. V., & Razran, G. (1972). *L'inconscio nella psicologia sovietica.* Roma, Italy: Editori Riuniti.

Vaccarino, G. (2006). Scienza e semantica. Milano, Italy: Edizioni Melquiades.

Vallortigara, G., & Panciera, N. (2014). Cervelli che contano. Milano, Italy: Adelphi Edizioni.

Van Lommel, P. (2016). Coscienza oltre la vita. La scienza delle esperienze di premorte. Torino, Italy: Edizioni Amrita.

Vattimo, G., Ferraris, M., & Marconi, D. (Eds.). (1993). Enciclopedia Garzanti di Filosofia. Milano, Italy: Garzanti Editore.

Venema, Y. (2001). Temporal Logic. In The Blackwell Guide to Philosophical Logic. Oxford, UK: Basil Blackwell Publishers.

Verdiglione, A. (1977). Matematica dell'inconscio. In Feticismo, linguaggio, afasia, matematica dell'inconscio. Venezia, Italy: Marsilio Editori.

Viret, J. (2012). Topological Approach of Jungian Psychology. *Acta Biotheoretica*, *58*(2), 233–245. PMID:20658172

Voevodin, V. V. (1992). Mathematical Foundations of Parallel Computing. Singapore: World Scientific Publishing. doi:10.1142/1533

Von Scheve, C., & Salmela, M. (Eds.). (2014). *Collective Emotions. Perspectives from Psychology, Philosophy, and Sociology*. Oxford, UK: Oxford University Press.

Von Wright, G. H. (1969). *Time, Change and Contradiction*. Cambridge, UK: Cambridge University Press.

Wang, Y., Zadeh, L. A., Widrow, B., Howard, N., Wood, S., Patel, S., & Zhang, D. et al. (2017). Abstract Intelligence: Embodying and Enabling Cognitive Systems by Mathematical Engineering. *International Journal of Cognitive Informatics and Natural Intelligence*, *11*(1), 1–22. doi:10.4018/IJCINI.2017010101

Watzlawick, P., Beavin, J. H., & Jackson, D. D. (1967). Pragmatics of Human Communication. A Study of Interactional Patterns, Pathologies, and Paradoxes. New York, NY: W.W. Norton & Company.

Weinstein, A. (1996). Groupoids: Unifying Internal and External Symmetry. *Notices of the American Mathematical Society*, *43*(7), 744–752.

Westphal, B. (2007). La Géocritique. Réel, fiction, espace. Paris: Les Éditions de Minuit.

White, D. R., & Jorion, P. (1996). Kinship networks and discrete structure theory: Applications and implications. *Social Networks*, *18*(3), 267–314. doi:10.1016/0378-8733(95)00277-4

Whitebook, J. (1995). *Perversion and Utopia. A Study in Psychoanalysis and Critical Theory*. Cambridge, MA: The MIT Press.

Whitrow, G. J. (1988). *Time in History. Views of Time from Prehistory to the Present Day*. Oxford, UK: Oxford University Press.

Zadeh, L. A. (1965). Fuzzy Sets. *Information and Control*, *8*(3), 338–353. doi:10.1016/S0019-9958(65)90241-X

Zadeh, L. A. (1968). Fuzzy Algorithms. *Information and Control*, *12*(2), 94–102. doi:10.1016/S0019-9958(68)90211-8

Zadeh, L. A. (1988). Fuzzy Logic. *Computer*, *21*(4), 83–93. doi:10.1109/2.53

Zanforlin, M. (1971). Prefazione. In Evoluzione e modificazione del comportamento. Torino, Italy: Editore Boringhieri.

Zapparoli, G. C. (1970). La perversione logica. I rapporti tra sessualità e pensiero nella tradizione psicoanalitica. Milano, Italy: Franco Angeli Editore.

Zentall, T. R. (2013). Animals represent the past and the future. *Evolutionary Psychology, 11*(3), 573–590. doi:10.1177/147470491301100307 PMID:24027784

Zepf, S., & Gerlach, A. (2012). Commentary on Kernbergs suicide prevention for psychoanalytic institutes and societies. *Journal of the American Psychoanalytic Association, 61*(4), 771–786. doi:10.1177/0003065113496634 PMID:23918822

ENDNOTES

[1]   In this regard, it is enough that everyone ask to herself or himself: has my life been always conducted in a fully rational and perfect way? Does human life carries on rationally? If not, is it possible to give a rational explanation to all these irrationalities or dissonances never making reference to psychoanalysis? Anyway, recent neurosciences corroborate the main psychoanalytic ideas, concepts and assumptions; cf. (Oliverio, 2009).

[2]   Almost surely, the intellectual oppositions to psychoanalysis are due to those personal *resistances*, just meant in their psychoanalytic sense, which are, in turn, an indirect confirmation that supports psychoanalysis (Francioni 1982, Introduction, p. 11; Laplanche & Pontalis, 1967). Besides this, surely certain "modalities of conduct" internal to the so-called "psychoanalytic community", have discredited and disadvantaged psychoanalysis itself (Francioni 1982, p. 15). On the other hand, it is evident that there exist many psychic phenomena which cannot be otherwise explained enough by means of other psychological trends (Oliverio, 2009).

[3]   Cf. (Toraldo di Francia, 1976).

[4]   Cf. (Francioni 1982, Introduction, 1.).

[5]   Cf. (Petit & Prévost, 1971).

[6]   For the relationships among phylogenesis, ontogenesis and epigenesis, we refer to (Morris, 2015; Piscicelli 1994, Ch. 1; Spedini, 2005). See also (Kandel 2005, Ch. 2) and (Iurato, 2015c). Anyway, independently from genetic data (which, in our case, say that our DNA is similar, up to 98%, to that of other members still living of the subfamily of *Homininae*), we are most interested in phenotype, not in the genotype, in that it is more able to account for the possible diversities of human evolution, so we are more oriented to consider the phenotypic expression as the main reference pattern for studying adaptive and evolutive history of humans (Manzi, 2013; Marchi, 2016). The importance of the role played by environment in changing some physical anthropology parameters, like the cephalic index (which was deemed to be an invariant, used to classify races), has been pointed out since Franz Boas work, which has proved that this last index was instead changeable in dependence on the environment (Lévi-Strauss & Eribon 1988, p. 63).

[7]   Phylogenesis is the chromosomal heredity acquired along historical evolution of human species; ontogenesis is the extra-chromosomal heredity potentially present at the birth of every human being, and that will develop along her or his individual growth inside to a certain genetic pool; and, finally, epigenesis is the integration point between phylogenesis and ontogenesis, where social and environmental factors influence the latter and its development. Ontogenesis and epigenesis are however independent of each other, though closely interrelated (Piscicelli 1994, Cap. I; Zanforlin, 1971).

[8]   Also, at the epigenetic level; cf. (Kandel 2005, Ch. 2; Morris, 2015).

[9]   See also (Rosenthal 1971, Ch. 2).

[10]   Cf. (Funari 2007, pp. 156-159), in which it is discussed this crucial epistemological aspect of psychoanalysis from the perspective offered by so-called *pragmatic phenomenology*, from which to look at psychoanalysis. In this text, there is also an interesting, wider discussion of the general epistemological setting of psychoanalysis, in which it deserves to be signalized, in particular, the attempt to view psychoanalysis as a *research program* in the sense of Imre Lakatos.

[11]   Above all, Adolf Grünbaum has used this argument to settle the question inherent psychoanalysis, reputing it as a non-scientific discipline.

[12]   We follow (Conrotto, 2014).

[13]   But without considering such modules as strictly localized into the brain.

[14]   In this regard, it is enough to simply recall that experience and environment play a very crucial role in structuring brain and its functioning; cf. (Rosenzweig et al., 1972).

[15]   With respect to the temporality related to the history of human evolution from *Homo sapiens* onwards, until up today.

[16]   Denys Cuche (2004, Introduction) has rightly pointed out the fundamental importance of *culture* for human being, who is basically formed, moulded, and just structured, by the culture, even in her or his deepest needs, like feeding, sexuality, and other. The culture has so made possible the adaptation of the environment itself to the needs and desires of human being. Either (Beals & Hoijer 1970, Vol. II, Ch. I) and (Cuche 2004, Introduction) then point out the fundamentally unconscious nature of human culture. Furthermore, it seems that forms of *writing*, meant in its widest sense, preceded language; cf. (Iurato, 2016d) and (Petrilli & Ponzio 2005, Ch. 8, Sect. 8.3).

[17]   In which some other species of the genus *Homo* (not only the *Sapiens*) were present.

[18]   Feature this that, just for its temporal brevity, entails therefore a poor probability for the occurrence of possible genotype changes at molecular level, so leaning instead for an abrupt qualitative change, caused by a very strong, traumatic yet not-well known event, at a phenotype expression level, hence of epigenetic nature.

[19]   With respect to the other species, genus *Homo* has been characterized by a great increasing above all of the frontal and prefrontal areas, besides the other ones (Granit 1977, Ch. 4).

[20]   Cf. (Damasio, 1994; Oliverio, 1982, 2008, 2017; Preziosi 1992, Cap. 1, Sect.1.2). It seems that just prefrontal areas have been the most recent brain regions, in term of phylogenetic evolution. In general, frontal areas has the main task of executive control, so coordinating emotive and sensory-motor systems, with teleological aims (Làdavas & Berti 2014, Ch. IX).

[21]   Cf. (Oliverio, 2017) and references therein.

[22]   Philosophical tradition had already established this principle since its origins; and Lévi-Strauss has further confirmed this from the anthropological perspective, for whom human mind runs according to a finite number of predefined formal schemata (Lévi-Strauss & Eribon 1988, Ch. 14).

23   Cf. (Goleman, 1995, Part I, Ch. 1).

24   Certain scholars, like Ralph Holloway (1974), say us that most of brain evolution is due to social and cultural (above all, by material culture) evolution besides the natural physiological growth, which maybe started even before the usual period (around higher Palaeolithic) in which is deemed first forms of social organizations arose.

25   For the ontogenetic evolution of the brain, see (Matthews 1998, Cap. 2), while, for its phylogenetic evolution, see (Oliverio, 1984, 2008, 2011).

26   Cf. (Conrotto, 2014). In particular, according to Jean Laplanche, the "qualitative jump" achieved by humans in distinguishing from animals, consisted in the rising of an excess of *drives* with respect to the *instincts*, that is to say, for the coming of a surplus of *desire*, ruled by pleasure/displeasure principle, in comparison to natural instincts of survival, a change mainly due to particular transformations of sexual instincts; cf. (Conrotto 2014, Ch. 3, Sect. 3) and references therein.

27   From this perspective, for example, it is possible to use psychoanalytic concepts, notions and methods (at least, the use of an unconscious perspective) to study and interpret sociological or political phenomena, like, for example, done in (Iurato, 2017c); cf. also (Mellino, 2005). This, besides, comes back above all to the tradition of *Frankfurt school* (H. Marcuse, E. Fromm, and so on) as well as to certain trends of cultural anthropology (e.g., *culture and personality* trend, *structuralism*), sociology (e.g., *functionalism*, according to Talcott Parsons), politics (e.g., *Marxism*, according to Louis Althusser), economy (e.g., Jean-Francois Lyotard – cf. (Mellino, 2005)), and so on.

28   And this, even in agreement with evolutionary biology; cf. (Goleman 1995, Part I, Ch. 1).

29   See (Solomon & Patch 1974, Cap. 31). However, a consciousness act always involves simultaneous activation of many cerebral zones, ranging from cortical ones, to thalamus and limbic system, until up trunk-encephalic one (Guyton 1991, Ch. 21). This crucial pathway should be taken into account from a psychoanalytic standpoint for accounting consciousness functions, which, therefore, are closely related with the most ancestral zones of the brain and the related nervous system.

30   In this regard, see (Semi 1988-89, Vol. I, Ch. 7, Sect. 7.3).

31   Or better, with the preliminary rising of the *symbolic* (or *signic*) function, upon which then *language* relies.

32   To be precise, Freud stated that primitive social organization was first patriarchal (primal horde), then matriarchal (with the divinization of woman as mother and the grouping of brothers into totemic clans), and, finally, once again, patriarchal and patrilineal, with a unique God replacing the primal father. Anyway, the notion of the primitive occupied a central place in Freud's thought, where it is often considered as the equivalent, at the collective level, to the infantile at the individual level. This aspect of Freud's work has provided bases for fruitful interactions between anthropology and psychoanalysis (De Mijolla 2005, p. 1319).

33   For instance, among these, we may include the so-called *near-death experiences* (NDE) (Van Lommel, 2016), whose paradisiacal environmental scenes told by patients get out from these, might be, for example, ancestral recalls of living primordial environments of hominids, hence primordial life experiences spent by them in their times.

34   In the Preface, we have already given a very brief formal sketch of these Lévi-Straussian notions.

35   Cf. (Lévi-Strauss & Eribon 1988, p. 161).

36   This statement needs some clarifying remarks. To avoid misunderstandings, here we mean that these structures might have been implemented phylogenetically (above all, at the epigenetic level) during and parallel to homination and the consequent brain evolution (in this regard, *paleoneurol-*

ogy is crucial; cf. (Bruner, 2015) and references therein). So, once human brain reached its almost definitive physiological and anatomical setting, these structural functions have been then acquired and implemented into the human brain, and supported by the related neural circuits. In these terms, we should be meant the phylogenetic origin and constitution (above all at the epigenetic level) of such mental structures (functionally meant), which then may be re-enacted ontogenetically in each individual. Only in this way, we should understand in what sense Lévi-Strauss speaks of inheritance of the structures as meant by him. Amongst these, then, we might include those founding universal structures which psychoanalytic thought has contemplated as such, like primal (or original) phantasies (in the case of Freudian thought), archetypes (in the case of Jungian thought, but considered only in their form, not in their possible content or meaning to which Jung gave universal feature; cf. (Moravia 2004, pp. 302-305), myths (in the case of Lévi-Straussian thought), rites and rituals (and, on the constant actuality of these latter, basically meant as structures equipped with a certain universal ahistorical feature, meaning producing and playing a strong social role of linking, cf. (Cazeneuve, 1971; Segalen, 1998)). These structures should be mainly meant therefore as phylogenetic formations (established, above all, during homination) which should re-enact ontogenetically in each individual on the basis of the general living environment in which he or she grows up, so giving them content (meaning). This is a possible epistemological way to confer an objective status to the objects of study of human sciences, among which is psychoanalysis. What we are trying to do in this work, is just, very modestly, to provide some first elementary formalizations of these structures, meant just in their epistemological sense as pre-existing entities phylogenetically established (as has been said above).

[37] Cf. (Lévi-Strauss 2008, p. 11). This opposition feature is also a distinct, founding trait of information theory, besides to be the central pillar of linguistics according to Roman Jakobson (Fabietti & Remotti, 1998). This support the fact that binary logic is a founding ground of human thought, either conscious and unconscious, as we shall see.

[38] Whose thought has been deeply influenced by that of Freud, and vice versa (Roudinesco, 2008).

[39] Even if, it is undeniable the strong and wide explaining power of psychoanalysis in regard to philosophical questions. For instance, nobody may deny the strong explaining power, for example, of death and life principles, at the general philosophical level; furthermore, certain sociological phenomena, like racism (in this regard, see also what is said in (Beals & Hoijer 1970, Vol. II, Ch. I, Sect. 10, pp. 67-68)), may be better understood within a psychoanalytic framework; and, again in regard to racism, also see for instance (Iurato 2016f).

[40] Surely, together its, as much rich and deep cultural tradition and legacy, which dates back to Enlightenment.

[41] Both *need* and *demand* of love, are instilled into the infant by mother and her body, during the tie child-mother (primary narcissism).

[42] Initially directed to the mother.

[43] It has been Ferdinand De Saussure, for the first time, to have identified two main standpoint of linguistics, the *parole* and the *langue*. The first, is that unique and unrepeatable observable act as due to the individual intelligence, while the second is an act which is invariant with respect to the act of the *parole*, is not observable yet has its own existence in that outcome of the collectivity and made intelligible by the *parole*, i.e., its historical actuation (Fabietti & Remotti, 1998).

[44] Timelessness is, besides, one of the typical features of structural unconscious.

[45] He really has gone farther from what Freud had already done, but always trying to respect his thought and work.

[46] Precisely referred to the agent of the lack, to the object of the lack, and to the lacking in itself.

[47] The chief one being the *phallus*, meant in its widest psychoanalytic sense – cf. (Chemama & Vardermersch, 1998).

[48] Mourning and desire, even etymologically, are closely related of each other and inseparable: indeed, a mourning ever precedes logically a desire, and, inversely, every mourning does revive the traces of a past pleasure, hence its desire.

[49] Just in regard to the context of our discussion, Lacan's ideas are particularly indicated, from the anthropological viewpoint, because what really distinguishes genus *Homo* (at least, its latest species) from other primates, is just the language (Marchi 2016, Ch. XI, p. 153), or better, symbolic function. It seems too that even any other feature, before deemed exclusive prerogative of genus *Homo*, like affects, emotions, expectation capabilities and computing tasks, have been now ascertained to be present also in other primates (Eibl-Eibesfeldt, 1996; Panksepp & Biven, 2012; Marchi 2016, Ch. XI). On the other hand, besides language, which, however, has been a recent acquisition by the species of genus *Homo*, what also distinguishes these from other primates, is the singular modality of regulation, management and development of sexual instinct, so it seems not unreasonable to invoke too, in this regard, sublimation phenomena as meant by psychoanalysis but in an evolutionary context. Furthermore, just to return to the religious practices of above, seen the further fact that also some primates are strangely able to elaborate some rudimental forms of *mourning*, yet quite enough to may suppose that they also experience anguish (in agreement to what has been just said above), we are even more convinced that Lacan's theory is the right way to be pursued according to what is said in this introduction. Anyhow, it seems that anguish, meant in its widest sense, has surely played a crucial role, from the psychic viewpoint, along the process of homination.

[50] Cf. (Iurato, 2014c, 2016e). For a very interesting anthropological history of penis, see (Kim 2016, Part I, Ch. 2), where it is said, among other things, that first hominids started to wear cloths around 170,000 year ago, just the period of *Sapiens*, and it is told which path has been followed by first species of genus *Homo* from conquered bipedal station onwards, in relation to sexuality. A possible, interesting hypothesis put forwards is also that of "runaway selection" underwent by penis due to the fact that, once humans conquered erected station and two-feet walking, with a consequent lost of the general body hairs, this process of "runaway selection" (of penis) consisted in occurrence of some typical mimetic traits, such as prominent plumage and/or body ornamentations, which were much more preferred by women than an erect penis manifestly showed (as before clothing arisen) as selectively strategically advantageous, in such a manner that females preferred to mate much more with males possessing the strongest expression, with the result that, in the subsequent generations, males offspring were more likely to posses that physical trait (Kim 2016, Part I, Ch. 2, pp. 11-13). This "runaway selection" underwent by penis (and, in general, the concealment of the genitalia of both sexes), therefore, is in agreement with our pattern on the origin of symbolic function, just based on disavowal (Iurato, 2013b,c, 2014c,e), in that it involves a fetishism phenomenology whose occurrence is very coherent with this "runaway selection" process. So, we are quite convinced on the reasonable validity of this pattern on the possible (phylogenetic) origin of symbolic function.

[51] Not to be confused with *bipedalism*, which is a wider anatomical term regarding also non-humans. Instead, *bipedism* is an anatomical-functional trait typical of humans, either in phylogenetic and ontogenetic sense.

[52] Cf. (Allman, 2000; Spedini, 2005).

[53] The hypothesis that anguish were an emotion already felt since early hominines (but not only these – see later), is partially supported, besides by the obvious survival instinct, also by the fact that some species of hominines (but not only them – see later) followed religious rituals (Marchi 2016, Ch. XI).

[54] Different studies and researches agree in recognizing a "qualitative jump" occurred at the end of *homination* process, which marked the rising of the latest species of genus *Homo*, i.e., *Homo sapiens*, and whose main feature has been just the activation of some neural circuits mainly around *Broca's area* of the brain (Conrotto 2014, p. 88), just the one mainly involved in the *elaboration* of language; see also (Sasso, 2005, 2011) and references therein.

[55] For instance, by *repression*, as it takes place along individual life pathway, to be distinguished by *original* (or *primal*) *repression*. Freud himself claimed that repression is the central pillar of the whole psychoanalytic edifice (Laplanche & Pontalis, 1967).

[56] For example, the marriage rules basically have the same, almost invariant, ahistorical syntactic nature of *exchange* (Lévi-Strauss & Eribon 1988, Ch. 11; Iurato, 2016d) between two different families, established by the Œdipal principle, but that has an its own historical evolution in dependence on either the meaning (semantics) given to this exchange and the context (pragmatics) in which it takes place. This is only one among the countless instances of social phenomena which may be likewise analyzed. Anyhow, from a logical viewpoint (see above all Kurt Gödel work on completeness theorem), syntax and semantics are inseparable of each other (Lolli 2000, p. 86); if one then wishes to identify a syntactic rule, then, as a general criterion, we may say that it should have a *mechanical* nature (Lolli 2000, p. 88), as if it had a pre-schematic and non-subjective operative modality.

[57] Which, notwithstanding that, seem as well to have a certain trans-cultural feature, which make easier the reciprocal touches and relations, above all at the affective level (Moore & Fine, 1990). Our own *phantasy*, says Freud, always works upon pre-existent schemes (Fodor & Gaynor, 1950). Furthermore, phantasy thought is always and continuously presents, contributing to determine the mental orientation with which we perceive external stimuli and organize them in events of our life, so that what we perceive and lived consciously is the result of the interaction between experience data and unconscious phantasies (Moore & Fine, 1990). In a few words, unconscious phantasies and their derivatives, are the outcome of interaction among desire impulses, cognitive abilities, defence operations and the Super-Ego (Moore & Fine, 1990).

[58] For a general overview of the (non-indifferent) role played by penis in the history of humanity and the widest culture, see (Friedman, 2001).

[59] Anyway, Freud's ideas on the nature of primal repression remained quite obscure (De Mijolla 2005, p. 1309).

[60] The reference to phylogenetic and ontogenetic arguments may be accepted, without great biological reserves, if they (above all, the phylogenetic ones) are carried out, contextually to homination period, at least at the epigenetic level; cf. (Jablonka & Raz, 2009). We take in great consideration the new discipline of *epigenetics*; cf. (Moore, 2015).

61   In that – which is a way in agreement with those programmes which see in close collaboration psychoanalysis and neurosciences; cf. (Kaplan-Solms & Solms, 2000) – we are faithfully close to the last Freud' will which was aimed to search for possible phylogenetic origins and foundations to his psychoanalytic thought, as clearly transpires from his latest works. Furthermore, this standpoint is also coherent with certain ideas of Silvano Arieti (1976) about thinking process; cf. Chapter 7, Sect. 7.3.

62   Just in regard to Jungian archetypes, in that they have in common with Lévi-Straussian notion of structure (as said above, hence in regard to formal aspects of archetypes, not to their semantics), it has been advanced even theses in favour of a their genetic inheritance identified in a possible biological basis (Stevens, 1982) likewise to what takes place in regard to hereditary ethological structures of modern evolutionary biology and human ethology (Eibl-Eibesfeldt, 2001), which is just coherent with our line of thought (Eibl-Eibesfeldt, 1997, 2005).

63   Indeed, maybe a weak point of Lévi-Strauss' view, is the will to completely formalize every human phenomenon, reducing it to the underlying, its composing formal structures, yet neglecting the semantic-pragmatic content they may host, which confers historicity to it.

64   As has been said above, instances of these universal structures may be archetypes (in that they have in common with the notion of structure according to Lévi-Strauss; cf. (Iurato, 2015a)), myths, rites and rituals. We suppose here that all these structures (just mainly meant according to Lévi-Strauss) have to be understood as purely *forms* devoid of any content, which will be then, from time to time, gained in terms of semantics and pragmatics, which confer historicity to such forms which are, per se, ahistorical. Furthermore, just in regard to Jungian archetypes, the recent cultural studies pays attention to them, deeming as motifs that, in a constant and recurrence manner, give *form* to fundamental aspects of human existence, which cannot be explained reductively by neither the biographical standpoint nor the historical-social one, but refer instead to something which stands before all that, i.e., to primordial images, to primal models of form, to original behaviour patterns, to the key rules of human life and sociality, which are all at the basis of visible forms; even in the literary texts, they – i.e., the archetypical constants – refer to those deep connections underlying universal determinants of human existence of all times (Tibaldi, 2004). This view is further supported by the simple clinical datum according to which schizophrenia is a mental disorder which does not entail an impairment of syntactic structures (just the *forms* of above), but rather is mainly characterized by an impairment of the functions of integration between semantics and pragmatics, in the semiotic theory of Charles W. Morris, which provide contextual coherence and meaning; cf. (Falzone, 2005; Ferretti, 2010), as well as (Iurato, 2016c) and references therein. Thus, just in this sense, it should be meant the conception of unconscious as a semiotic producer (Conrotto, 2014).

65   Matte Blanco has been one of the firsts scholars to have pointed out, above all from a formal standpoint, the close and inseparable connections between *affect* and (so-called) *rational thought*; along the same line, we have recalled too the work of Luc Ciompi, who, like Silvano Arieti, has investigated these relationships from an interdisciplinary perspective, making often numerous references to exact and natural sciences, starting from his decennial clinical experience with schizophrenia. All this, much before the advent of cognitive neurosciences applied to study affects (A. Damasio, and so forth).

66   Indeed, we should point out that, however, human reasoning is not so perfectly linear and sequential in the concatenation of its logic inferences (which can be performed no more than three in a unique thought act; cf. (Lolli 2000, p. 87)), so it is not fully rigorous, but rather dialectic, and ever more, *ambiguous* and filled of contradictions.

67   See, in this regard, the surely existent links with the so-called *Kripke-Wittgenstein paradox* (Iurato, 2017b).

68   That, just for this their basic binary nature, are therefore worthy to be taken into serious consideration for possible, further informatics implementations.

69   But not exclusively limited to this.

Chapter 1
An Epistemological Introduction and a General Overview

ABSTRACT

We mention the main foundations and elements of philosophy of sciences to have a rough yet quite complete view of the epistemological framework in which to lay out our discussion on the possible formalizations attempts of psychoanalysis. In particular, we have highlighted the possible relations between exact/ natural sciences and humanities, with a special emphasis on those intertwinements already established between humanities and informatics. We have however chosen to assume a new epistemological stance mainly based on a structuralistic view coming from Claude Lévi-Strauss' pioneering work, which, as reconsidered by the French school of psychoanalysis (above all, Jacques Lacan and Jean Laplanche), has led to identify a universally shared logical structure, irreducible per se, which basically rules human thought; this is the phallic logic (or Ur-logic).

1.1. INTRODUCTION

In this first chapter, we provide, although very briefly, the right epistemological placement of the arguments treated in this book, in such a manner to have a general overview of the philosophical framework within which we shall develop and lay out our work mainly centred on some possible relationships among psychoanalysis and exact/natural sciences, turned toward possible applications to informatics and computer sciences. One of the main aims of this chapter, is to try to justify, from a philosophical standpoint, the work done in the subsequent chapters. Indeed, seen the very little consideration and scant reputation which nowadays unfortunately psychoanalysis has in regard to other psychological sciences, with the few but enough epistemological arguments herein exposed, we hope to make quite clear that, contrarily to these wrong and unjustified prejudices[1], it is possible to start a new treatment of theoretical psychoanalysis with a reformulation of some its main ideas through exact and natural sciences, so conferring a certain scientific status just meant in the terms briefly recalled in this chapter, above all in the last sections. All this, will make also possible to have a first formal elementary basis which will turn out to be useful for possible computational implementations of these psychoanalytic concepts.

DOI: 10.4018/978-1-5225-4128-8.ch001

According to certain pessimistic opinions, the psychoanalysis seems to be destined by now to a net failure (Kernberg, 2011; Zepf & Gerlach, 2012) from either the therapeutic and the theoretical standpoint: in the first case, because it is unable to adequately face the personal requests of individuals belonging to an ever-changing society; in the second case, because it basically lacks suitable scientific criteria of validation (Imbasciati 2015, p. 10). To remedy to this unhappy destiny, new ways have to be found. Antonio Imbasciati (2015) has tried to keep alive psychoanalysis trying to integrate it with other discipline, like experimental psychology, developmental psychology and neurosciences, yet not falling into a sterile and full reductionism (Funari, 2007); likewise, Mauro Mancia (2006), Alberto Oliverio (2016), and so others. All these attempts are essentially linked by the common view to see Freudian theory not as given once and for all, but liable to be modified according to the evolution of general culture.

Along the last century, considerable changes have occurred in the epistemological setting of psychoanalysis. At the same time, philosophy of sciences and epistemology have also undergone notable changes of stance, perspective, point of view. All that, has allowed to cast interesting and unexpected bridges between psychoanalysis and exact/natural sciences. Out of these, we are first interested in the relationships between psychoanalysis and logic, as suggested by the work of Ignacio Matte Blanco. Therefore, our perspective is that turned to look at the possible relationships between psychoanalysis and logic, or else toward the unconscious influences in the rational thought within Freudian framework as seen by Matte Blanco, examined formally by means of algebraic methods; at the same time, the searching for these formal bases underlying such psychoanalytic concepts, will lead naturally to a parallel comparison with natural sciences, physics in particular, but ever looking for to the underlying formal structures.

Our main aim, is to provide a minimal formal framework to some chief concepts and notions of Freudian psychoanalysis, in agreement with certain epistemological stances, like those put forward by Evandro Agazzi (1976, 1979, 1985a,b, 2014) just in reference to humanities, according to which, just on the basis of the models provided by mathematics, one of the main basic requisites to be owned by a *corpus* of knowledge, is its internal coherence and unity, as well as its capability to give a reasonable justification of what is asserted by it. Now, just in relation to psychoanalytic context, from a theoretical viewpoint, a possible formalization through exact and natural sciences (like mathematics and physics), also built up on the basis of an analogical similarity in the meaning, may accomplish to these latter requests of logical coherence and unity, independently of any other question, yet crucial, regarding clinical and therapeutic contexts. So, what we have tried to do, is to give a possible mathematical outlook to some aspects of psychoanalysis and its linguistic structure.

This, because mathematics, according to the certain philosophical stances, mainly due to John G. Kemeny (Lambert & Brittain, 1979, Ch. 5), may be also considered as basically not having a proper object of study but rather as providing only formal arguments to be applied to the contents of other fields of knowledge which therefore provide to mathematics its objects. This, in particular, may be valid also for psychoanalysis, because there is no sufficient reason against that. On the contrary, just the appreciable work of Matte Blanco, which has been unfairly neglected also by psychoanalytic community, has provided the right ground upon which to build up a possible formal framework for psychoanalytic theory, just searching for those formal aspects of the Freudian *oeuvre* which were liable to be identified and treated as such. This Matte Blanco's work has been indispensable to draw up this book.

The applications of mathematics to psychoanalysis is made possible if we consider, in this regard, certain philosophical stances about meaning of mathematics. Indeed, in this work, as already said just above, we choose the ideas of the mathematician and philosopher John George Kemeny (1959), according to whom basically mathematics is the study of the *form* of mathematical argumentations which are meant in a Kantian sense as analytical truths; it is the most general type of knowledge we may have, and, ever according to Kemeny, it is fully devoid of an object of study, so that it may be applied to a very vast range of objects of knowledge – comprised psychoanalytic ones – which will become the *content* of a mathematical knowledge *formally* treated. Nevertheless, we should say mathematics is devoid of any object of study meant in its empirical nature, but also that, instead, such an object may exist but is *abstract*, and may be perceived by a kind of *mathematical intuition*[2] (*d'aprés* Kurt Gödel) as we perceive empirical objects by sensorial intuition (Lambert & Brittan 1979, Ch. 5).

So that, we may apply *formal* mathematical language to psychoanalytic *objects* as its *content*. In pursuing this, we should however put before too the fundamental elements of philosophy of sciences and epistemology, to lay out better, from a philosophical standpoint, psychoanalysis and logic within their own epistemological framework. After having necessarily outlined these preliminary elements of philosophy, to be precise those regarding the latest trends of epistemology and philosophy of sciences, we shall be much more able to see better what possible relationships may be casted between theoretical psychoanalysis and exact/natural sciences, besides the recent, valuable attempts to find an interesting and innovative relationship between psychoanalysis, either theoretic and therapeutic, and neurosciences, very promising, on the wake of the initial attempt pursued by Freud himself in his well-known *Project for a Scientific Psychology* of 1895, yet soon after abandoned for the poorness of the neurological knowledge of the time, but now actual and vivid according to new neurosciences discoveries and progresses (Ekstrom, 2004; Kandel, 2005; Kaplan-Solms & Solms, 2002; Mancia, 2006; Sasso, 2005, 2011).

Nevertheless, instead to look at the objects of exact (mathematics) and natural sciences, as we have briefly discussed above, rather we should look at the *methodology* of study of such disciplines, making use of logical tools the first ones, of experimental practices the second ones. Despite this, there exist higher scientific assertions which are nothing but mathematical assertions in that they are so formal in their own nature, to have by now lost a direct contact with the empirical world; this is the case of most of the modern mathematical and theoretical physics. Anyway, insofar as indirect it may be, a connection between an higher scientific assertion and its experimental bases however should exist, differently from a pure mathematical assertion which may have no link with a some aspect of empirical world. This is coherent with the main fact that mathematics however does not entail any *factual enrichment* to other simplest (or atomic) scientific assertions joined together (Lambert & Brittan 1979, Ch. 5; Putnam, 1956, 1971).

However, mathematics is, without doubt, the language of science, providing the formal tools to express empirical assertions or facts and their reciprocal interrelationships. Furthermore, since the mathematical assertions cannot be refuted by empirical facts, we return to Kemeny's positions for which mathematical assertions are *analytical* (in the Kantian sense) and true in dependence only on their form, while the scientific ones are *synthetic* (in the Kantian sense) in that they may be refuted by a suitable empirical situation and their truth depends on their content and its empirical validation. In any event, we can say that, in general, there is not a net and full distinction between analytical and synthetic assertions or propositions, because, very frequently, many mathematical assertions deemed to be analytical, indeed may yet undergo to a change coming from a mutation in certain contexts of empirical sciences, in dependence on the very close relation between mathematics and natural sciences. Anyhow, as a matter of fact, mathematics is surely the primary formal language of sciences, and very thin as well as factitious often are the distinctions between them (Lambert & Brittan 1979, Ch. 5).

In any case, the main aim of the present work, is not to give a possible scientific status to Freudian psychoanalysis via Matte Blanco's framework, but rather to provide, as much as possible, a formal outlook to certain main concepts of Freudian psychoanalysis in such a manner these may be suitable to be computationally implemented, likewise other neuropsychological patterns which have been right used to the same ends, like in artificial, natural and computational intelligence, cognitive informatics, software sciences, neuroinformatics, human-level machine intelligence, and so on; see for example (Wang et al., 2017) and references therein. In doing so, we have started from the very early bases, relying on the possible relations which link together elementary algebra and logic with founding psychoanalytic concepts. Only after having established such first, elementary bases, it will be possible to carry on toward further, higher computational implementations based on more advanced formal grounds.

1.2. A BRIEF OUTLOOK OF PHILOSOPHY OF SCIENCES AND EPISTEMOLOGY

A knowledge including a certain degree of warranty of its own validity, may be defined a *science*. This warranty may be provided by either: *i) proof* techniques, *ii) explaining* descriptions, or *iii) corrigibility* tools. The lacking of any degree of warranty of validity, gives rise to *opinion*.

The first, classical ideal pattern of science, dating back to Socrates and Aristotle, is that centred on a closed system of statements whose validity is proved by logic proof. It provides a deductive knowledge, historically represented, par excellence, by the Euclid's *Elements*. Mathematics, indeed, became the main ideal of science to be pursued. Fascinated by the perfection reached by geometry, philosophy considered the geometric models for introducing the notion of philosophical system as well as giving, to philosophical knowledge, a basic character of systematicity, unity, coherence and compatibility, as features typical of the scientific knowledge.

Then, in the modern period, a new paradigm of science arose, turned to identify the possible relationships observed, along a phenomenological investigation, among certain objects, from which to infer laws and rules. This is the key aspect of that scientific methodology centred on explaining descriptions. Finally, a recent trend is that recognizing, as unique warranty of validity, the criterion of self-corrigibility, which rejects every claim of absolute warranty (like in the case *i)*) and is based on the assumption of fallibility of human knowledge, in part related with the falsificability of Karl Popper. All that, drops the classical, scientific ideal of *episteme* (of *i)*), characterized by an absolute certainty of knowledge liable of demonstrability, which has turned out to be unrealizable in its full programmatic intent. The self-corrigibility is, instead, the lesser dogmatic and rigid warranty of validity which may be required by a methodology to be classified as scientific.

Until up positivistic period, scientific knowledge was deemed to be the highest form of rational knowledge. Afterwards, post-positivistic epistemology, much more turned to look at the coherence and to be anti-foundationist, has undermined the classical scientific knowledge as meant according to *i)*. The classical patterns of scientific rationality, as in *i)*, are now considered as possible forms of knowledge of the reality among the many others, hence neither the unique nor the highest ones; these forms of knowledge refer to "scientific paradigms" (Thomas Kuhn), "research programmes" (Imre Lakatos), "research traditions" (Larry Laudan), or "styles of reasoning" (Ian Hacking), meant as genetic matrices of scientific knowledge, coherently with the *epistemological anarchism* of Paul Feyerabend.

Attention has been paid to the imposing influence of social-cultural contexts in the rising and development of scientific knowledge, as Kuhn has stressed. This entails the replacement of an objective criterion of truth (as advocated in *i)*) with an historical and social-pragmatic criterion based on common consensus that, according to Kuhn, leads to the creation and the establishment of scientific theories. It follows, according to Richard Rorty, the rejection of a conception of science meant as the result of individual minds operating on a certain objective reality, in favour of a conception of science as a socially built up reality which, contextually (i.e., relatively to a given scientific community), is able to self-validate and self-certificate itself, without making reference to any other meta-scientific, philosophical justification.

Moreover, we remember that current philosophy of science (Boniolo & Vidali, 1999) also allows to consider a certain methodological freedom in regard to inference methods (mainly, induction and abduction) adopted in achieving a scientific knowledge which is impossible to be thought as fully devoid of uncertainty which instead is the main distinctive feature of it. This is a common aspect of either science and historical knowledge, both founded on the central epistemic notion of *possibility*, as Martin Heidegger has clearly pointed out, in turn, based on the *conditional explanation* just of *retrospective possibilities* or *probabilities*, so abandoning any form of strong causal explanation in favour of the *epistemological plausibility*, which is just what science really searches.

Around plausibility, a new philosophy of science trend has grown up. A *theory of epistemological plausibility* has been worked out, with its own inference models for treating beliefs, in searching for a possible *logic of plausibility* following different routes (Abbagnano, 1998; Boniolo & Vidali, 1999; Capozzi & Cellucci, 2014; Cellucci & Ippoliti, 2016; Fairbain, 1994; Ippoliti, 2007; Vattimo et al., 1993). We shall return later on the epistemological foundations of psychoanalysis in the final sections of these chapter, where we shall outline some recent trends which are deemed to be much more close to that line of thought which we wish to pursue.

1.3. ON THE POSSIBLE RELATIONSHIPS BETWEEN EXACT/NATURAL SCIENCES AND HUMANITIES

One possible way to understand the relationships between exact/natural sciences and humanities, is discussing on the philosophical concepts of *explanation* and *understanding*.

The *explanation*, generally speaking, is turned to provide answers to the "why" of the being of an object[3], and its occurrence. To this end, we may identify two main explanation techniques: *a)* the *causal explanation* technique and *b)* the *conditional explanation* technique.

The first one, is related to the notion of *causality*, which, in turn, may be pursued by either logical *deducibility* and *uniformity*. These latter are, then, closely related to the notion of *necessity*, so that, a causal explanation is the proof of the necessity of the object with respect to which it is called into question. So, a causal explanation provides the final necessity for the occurrence of a given object.

The causal explanation based on the deducibility is identified with the classical logical proof of the necessity of the object into question. The causal explanation based on the uniformity is, instead, related to the regular and constant occurrence of certain connections among given phenomena and their reciprocal ratio.

Therefore, causal explanation is however aimed to give an high degree of certainty, contrarily to the conditional explanation whose explicating schema does not claim those features of infallibility and globality typical of the causal explanation mainly invoked by the classical exact and natural sciences. The conditional explanation provides valid reasons for to the possibility of the controlled occurrence of a given object, according to a probabilistic determinism, that is to say, it argues on the possibility for the occurrence of a given object which may be regularly controlled under suitable conditions. This last type of explanation, is usually present in human sciences.

The *understanding*[4] arises just as a specific knowledge activity different from rational knowledge and its explicative techniques. Historically, understanding springs out, in the Romantic period, in relation to the exegesis of biblical texts, to become, then, the key for distinguishing the explicative process of human sciences from that of natural and exact sciences, basically due to the difficulties found in applying the causal techniques of scientific knowledge to humanities (Wilhelm Dilthey). This is due, in turn, to the basic distinction between the objective and invariable external nature and the mutable human reality, always changing. In the latter, human being is either who investigates and who is investigated, the subject of the knowledge is the same object of knowledge.

It is Johann Droysen, around 1860s, to point out the specificity of the historical understanding, distinguishing amongst a philosophical knowledge (*erkennen*), a historical knowledge (*verstehen*) and a scientific knowledge (*erklären*), mainly due to the relative position of the observer with respect to the observed. This distinction will be then reduced, by Droysen, to the basic opposition between the understanding (*verstehen*) and the explaining (*erklären*).

This latter distinction will be then retaken by Dilthey, who at first conceives the *Erlebnis*, i.e., own life experience or personal past, as the main means of the historical understanding and, in general, of the inter-human understanding, not liable of causal explanation. It allows to grasp intrinsically historical reality. But, much before Dilthey, already Friedrich Schleiermacher, around 1820s, points out the need for understanding, theoretically and practically, the reasons and motivations of other persons, in interpreting the text of an author, according to a certain psychological hermeneutics.

Afterwards, with the rising of positivism, still Dilthey, around early 1900s, distinguishes between *Naturwissenschaften* (natural sciences) and *Geisteswissenschaften* (humanities), so delineating the alternative between the naturalistic attitude of the investigator who studies the objects of external reality with a detached behaviour in regard to these, and the degree of empathic disposition with which subject and object are identified in humanistic research, or else, the act of knowledge is not different from the object of knowledge.

For Heinrich Rickert, the understanding allows the reconstruction of the net of relationships of an object, while, for George Simmel, understanding allows to putting into relationship the psychic apparatuses of many people. Hence, Max Weber tries to fill the gap between causal and historical explanation, stating that the latter is also a causal explanation, identifying connections among historical phenomena, but not ruled by a universal law (like in objective reality of natural sciences).

Hence, Droysen and Dilthey point out that, differently from natural phenomena characterized by repeatability and controllability, historic phenomenon is singular in its own nature, so it may be only understood and not explainable according to a universal law. So that, in the understanding process, the awareness of a feeling identifies with the feeling itself. While natural phenomena undergo causal explanations which do not modify their essence, humanities instead use axiological and teleological categories modifying the essence of the phenomenon so observed, in that just the understanding of it necessarily changes its meanings, values, aims.

Finally, radicalizing this last perspective, Martin Heidegger, in his celebrated *Sein und Zeit* (of 1927), tries to unify these two perspectives, showing the basic circularity between understanding and knowledge. He gives pre-eminence to the understanding in regard to the explaining. He also states that explaining has not autonomous function, as it always presupposes a preliminary form of pre-understanding incardinated in the language, because of the basic existential rooting of human being into the world (*Dasein* or *Being-There*).

Such unavoidable pre-understanding, ontologically rooted in the human being, is therefore the transcendental basis for the scientific explanation. With Heidegger, therefore, the understanding springs out from the pre-understanding of the object of knowledge, which takes place from the inclusion of this latter into the own intimate structures of subjectivity, contrarily to the scientific knowledge which presuppose an unavoidable intersubjectivity disposition with respect to this object of knowledge.

This Heideggerian stance has been criticized by neo-positivism which wished to comprehend all field of knowledge under the context of causal explanation. It was instead re-taken by Hans George Gadamer, and put at the foundation of contemporary hermeneutics as an *ontological hermeneutics*, according to which the interpretation, meant as the constitutive dimension of the whole human existence (the human being is "thrown" into the world), is nothing but that an articulation of the understanding which explicitates in existents (in the Heideggerian sense, i.e., *Dasein*) (Cassinari, 2005).

So, this last point of view, provided by Heidegger, seems suitable to be considered a right starting point from which to begin an epistemological discourse about the possible relationships between psychoanalysis and exact/natural sciences. Indeed, in giving precedence to the understanding[5], he presupposes that explanation is based on this, so that they are however closely related of each other, with the latter built up on the former, although functioning according to different logics. So, it is not fully implausible to claim they are two different manifestations of a higher logic, in agreement with Matte Blanco, as we shall see later.

Furthermore, also in agreement with part of the *Port-Royal* program, we might arguing in favour of the thesis according to which what basically gives a *scientificity* feature to a certain discipline, is the existence of a *logic* underlying its methodology, this latter being broadly meant as a set of rules and techniques to achieve, according to a certain procedural order, a valid knowledge, the validity of which being warranted by following just this disciplinary procedure. This is also in agreement with the fact that, in the unconscious realm, a very variegated set of different logics exists, whose effects and manifestations yet regard too conscious thought (Conrotto 2014, Ch. 3, Sect. 3).

Nevertheless, as Paul Feyerabend points out, this founding set of rules and techniques, is not to be meant as given once and for all, from a certain meta-temporal structure of human rationality, but is rather set up from time to time in dependence on the single objectives and specific situations. Just this set will give rise to a logic, if this last is generally meant as the study of valid inferences, or else the study of coherent sets of sentences, to be pursued according to a given operative procedure (syntax). In psychoanalysis, then, what is really important for the psychoanalytic interpretation is just its logical coherence and semantic meaningfulness (Codignola, 1977).

Current philosophy of science has identified three main trends in dependence on the notion of scientific explanation adopted: the *epistemic* trend, the *ontic* trend and the *pragmatic* trend. The first one, is the so-called *nomological* trend of the usual conception of science based on hypothetical-deductive/inductive method providing laws and rules. The second one, is based on the *causal explanation*, so that for a scientific explanation is not sufficient to have an explaining law (as in the epistemic trend) only, but also a causal motivation. Finally, the third trend is intended to answer to questions which basically contain the interrogative adverb "why", hence in dependence on the context in which such question arise and the related knowledge's background in which they are inserted. Just this latter trend is that able to provide reasons and valid answers to a wider range of questions than that of proper scientific disciplines.

So, we have different models of scientific knowledge, hence different conceptions of a scientific explanation in dependence on the different manners to mean science's aims: according to *epistemic* trend, based on a nomological-deductive explanation, science is a process of gradual approach to the regularities of the observable reality by means of formalizations; according to *ontic* approach, based on a statistical inferential-abductive explanation, science tries to understand the latest and deep reasons and motivations underlying natural phenomena; while, the *pragmatic* approach, based on a teleological-functionalistic explanation, sees science in terms of the involved communicative actors aimed to functionally exchange finalized information (Abbagnano, 1998; Boniolo & Vidali, 1999; Vattimo et al., 1993).

1.4. ON CERTAIN INTERTWINEMENTS BETWEEN PSYCHOANALYSIS AND INFORMATICS

Modern epistemology tries to overcome the pernicious gap between *understanding* (typical of humanities) and *explaining* (typical of sciences). This is of interest for the epistemological setting of psychoanalysis in respect to natural sciences, founded on empirical-descriptive bases. In particular, psychoanalysis is turned to understand the theoretical-clinical data from a methodological point of view based on the capacity of intuition and empathic identification of psychoanalyst with respect to the patient, during the dyadic relation of analytical setting, in such a manner to work out a practical operative model warranting a certain objectivity feature and a moderate degree of inference (Freni, 1992). Based on the so-called *historical-clinic method* (M.W. Battacchi[6]), which uses understanding logic, psychoanalytic cure is centred on a double interpretation of what is discussed during setting, the interpretation by analyst and the interpretation by patient; but only observing the *a posteriori* effects produced by analyst interpretation and insights on patient psychic life, psychoanalytic therapy may be considered to have or not a certain degree of scientific objectivity (Castiglioni & Corradini, 2011).

In psychoanalysis, this relation is particularly identifiable in the so-called *Junktim*, that is to say, that inseparable link among research, theory and practice in psychoanalysis. As such, therefore, a particular relevance takes the transference, the main psychic phenomenology established in the analytical setting. In this framework, a particular relevance has the transcription of the talking of the analytical setting, between analyst and patient, as a *narrative unity*, as conducted, for instance, by means of the *CCRT method* due to Lester Luborsky (Luborsky & Crits-Christoph, 1992), which provides an objective formal model for transference and its interpretation, where the principal role of protagonist is played by patient, while analyst undertakes the role of the parents, brothers, sisters, and other meaningful persons. The re-dramatization of precocious and nuclear relations in the analytical current setting, together the insight so acquired by means of therapist's interpretation, are the crucial elements of psychoanalytic cure. Now, these narrative unities may be analyzed with the support of informatics means[7].

Along this line, new computational methods may be placed, like, for example, those achieved by Fionn Murtagh (2012a,b; 2013; 2014a,b; 2017). About narrativization from the psychoanalytic viewpoint, see also (Murtagh, 2017; Murtagh & Iurato, 2017). Murtagh's line of research has been innovative in applying geometrical data analysis on texts (Murtagh, 2017). Furthermore, to be signalled too the wide and multidisciplinary work of Yair Neuman (2014, 2016) on computational cultural psychology and the applications of new technologies in psychology. Other previous formal attempts to identify psychoanalytic aspects in texts, have been made by Giampaolo Sasso (1982, 1993), but without any informatics implementation. Finally, we recall some very early attempts to apply psychoanalytic ideas to cybernetics and artificial intelligence due to Marvin Minsky (1975) describing frame systems as a formalism for representing knowledge, hence focussing on the issue of what the content of knowledge should be in specific domains. Minsky also argues that vision should be viewed symbolically with an emphasis on forming expectations, then he discusses the enormous problem of the volume of background common sense knowledge required to understand even very simple natural language texts and suggests that networks of frames are a reasonable approach for representing such a knowledge. Along the same line is placeable the work of David Bell (2016) on robotics and its developments and outcomes for human beings. To be recalled too the possible applications of semantic differential in psychoanalytic and psychological contexts (Capozza, 1977; Kuper, 1988). Finally, we also recall the work of the psychologist Antonio Fusco and co-workers on the deep psychological meaning underlying literary and artistic works (Fusco & Tomassoni, 2013).

1.5. SOME OUTLINES OF THE CURRENT EPISTEMOLOGICAL SETTING OF PSYCHOANALYSIS

In this section, mainly in the first subsection, we outline the chief philosophical standpoints on the epistemological status of psychoanalysis, that will be the foundational ground upon which our next discourse and formal constructions, will build up.

1.5.1. Introduction: Some First Epistemological Perspectives

As has been already said, in this subsection and the following two, we outline three main stances on the epistemological setting of psychoanalysis, the first is assumed by some psychoanalysts of Brazilian psychoanalytic society, the second is mainly assumed by some psychoanalysts and philosophers of Italian psychoanalytic community, while the third is that proposed by Peter Fonagy; however, other viewpoints, remarks and considerations will follow too. In any event, we can summarily state immediately that, in general, a certain field of knowledge has a scientific status when, equipped with its own methodology, is able to describe (with its own language), predict and suitably *modify*, within a certain approximation, a given "state of things" belonging to its object world. This may be also applied to psychoanalysis which, with its own language (that we are trying to formalize here), is able to describe psychic world of human beings, trying to *modify* it, by means of a certain procedural methodology (analytical setting), in pathological cases mainly[8]. This is the main epistemological stance undertook in this work.

Anyway, we also consider other *constructive* epistemological points of view on psychoanalysis, to which we believe, neglecting those of positivistic and neoempiricistic nature (among which are the arguments of Karl Popper and Adolf Grümbaum) because they do not admit any other scientific status besides that of natural sciences[9], differently from other epistemological trends (one of which is that very briefly delineated in the last subsection of this chapter) which do not deny a possible *scientificity* to psychoanalysis, if suitably defined are the related philosophical notions variably involved. In this regard, we refer (but not exhaustively) to the main literature on the argument (Balzarotti, 1972; Bezoari & Palombi, 2003; Buzzoni, 1989; Conrotto, 2000, 2010, 2014; Funari, 2007; Lauro-Grotto, 2014b; Palombi, 2002; Possenti, 1979; Siri, 1976).

Enzo Funari (1978) has admonished from the attempts to reduce psychoanalysis to other scientific disciplines from which has yet borrowed concepts and notions, by analogy. He instead proposes to look at the objects of study of psychoanalysis, like the unconscious, its language and its relations with consciousness, the position of the (analysed) subject seen from a perspective which overturns the Cartesian cogito, and so on. Psychoanalysis has mainly to do with the *articulation* of the various *phantasies* (from whose universality[10] an intersubjective feature of psychoanalysis may follow) of the subject, along her or his personal history (from which a subjectivity feature of psychoanalysis hence follows), as mainly due to the unconscious' subject, that is, the *desire*. In such terms, it follows that psychoanalysis has its own method (i.e., an operative technique) which may explicate, as a *praxis*, in the cure of the subject. But, anyhow, even this last, always starts from a previous, though minimal, theoretical framework that, just in the case of psychoanalysis, is based and erected on a certain number of hypotheses which are preliminary *interpretations* due to the psychoanalyst, and which will be then verified or not, with a dialectic method, along the course of the analytical setting and her or his overall clinical experience. This is quite similar, at an epistemological level, to what takes place in other so-called scientific disciplines classified as such, even if, in the case of psychoanalysis, we have to do with a new, peculiar world or reality, that of *phantasies*, which constellate all the psychic life of the human being.

But, as Funari notes, following Luis Althusser, this last remark cannot allow us to seeking the possible scientific status of psychoanalysis uniquely in its therapeutic practice, in that any other scientific discipline is *a priori* founded and based on a preliminary theoretical framework which will lead to the next operational setting upon which will rely its so-called scientific status. This consideration was besides well known to Freud himself, who looked at the scientific status of his discipline not by means of its technique or practice but rather looking at its theoretical framework which will suitably change, only *a posteriori*, on the basis of the outcomes of its praxis. The first step is therefore to have a preliminary, minimal theoretical framework from which to start, outlining its objects of study and its field of investigation inside the wider one of psychic phenomenology. Psychoanalysis was born just in those places left empty by other psychological disciplines, where stay objects abandoned by these latter, i.e., the unconscious and its phenomenology in the our case.

Hence, Funari points out that psychoanalysis, only after having defined its minimal theoretical framework of investigation as just described above, may be possibly put in comparison with other scientific disciplines, but only from the perspective for which psychoanalysis has already an its own autonomous disciplinary status as a field of doctrine regarding the study of the unconscious and its language. And this is the point of view undertook in this work, where we are trying only to improve style, language and setting of the theoretical framework of psychoanalysis, from the analogical conceptual comparison with the language and methods of other disciplines, like mathematics and physics, but not extending this also to their respective objects of study and fields of investigation, which are quite different.

On the other hand, following Pietro Bianchi (2014), what is often blamed to psychoanalysis is the lack of some form of objectivity mainly due to the so-called "singularity of the symptom", that is to say, the individuality of the patient's suffering, which precludes any possible intersubjectivity. The subject should be rather the result of an institutionalization, or of an abstract reification, according to certain pre-existent formal rules and laws of the Other, which determines her or his singularity by means of their individual reification. Psychoanalytic cure then should turned to determine this *cut* into the Other, which determines the singularity[11] of the subject of the unconscious (*symptom*). In this regard, Bianchi makes mention to some related ideas of Slavoj Žižek.

But, it might not be otherwise. Indeed, only with this singular actuation of the laws and rules of the symbolic Other, it is possible the manifestation of this last as a singularity in each individual (i.e., the Lacanian *a*), who therefore identifies, determines an "hole" into the Other (i.e., the Lacanian *A*) that, in turn, is recognizable only in this way. The individual, as *singularity a* (i.e., Lacanian *other*), is therefore the hole of the *structure A* (i.e., Lacanian *Other*[12]), thanks to which he or she enters into the field of the *otherness*. Alain Badiou (1982) then points out the importance to look at the *form* of the relation existing between *a* and *A*, between singularity and structure, that is to say, at the form of the relation with which subject *a* (field of the subject) is inscribed into *A* (field of the Other), hence to look at the relation between these two fields, which Badiou says to be universal and rigid, hence liable to be possibly studied scientifically.

Afterwards, the form of such relation should be pre-figured and pre-settled by a kind of metalogic, said to be *Ur-logic*, that, according to Lacanian school, should be the dialectic logic of the signifier, which might be identified with the phallic logic of which we shall talk about in the next Chapter 2, Section 2.8. Such an *Ur-logic*, nevertheless, should not be meant as providing a universal feature to the relationships between structure and singularity, whose rigidity, so, should hinder any singularity feature to the individual subjectivity, who should be therefore fully alienated. To this end, Lacan, in his *Séminaire, Livre XX, Encore* (of 1972-1973), establishes some limits to the range of efficacy of this metalogic, beyond which structure (i.e., *A*) cannot preside and control fully, so making it a weaker logic, a logic of "not-all", which will become then a logic of "female", according to Lacan.

We would like to see a certain similarity between this *Ur-logic* and the one will be discussed in the next Chapter 2, Section 2.8., just the *phallic logic*, which expresses the singularity of every human being moved by her or his own unconscious' desire. It is just the comparison of these individual experiences (of many *a*), arising from the clinical praxis of psychoanalysis, said to be *formalization*, to allow us to descry those common features of this phallic logic.

Finally, just because of the arguments treated in this book, from an epistemological viewpoint we should quote the work of Manuel Sanchez-Cardenas (2011) which starts by observing that, although psychoanalytic pluralism is widespread, there is still a spirit of countraposition among the different theoretical trends of psychological sciences, in particular inside psychoanalysis. Sanchez-Cardenas just says that Matte Blanco's work allows us to think about these questions from a new perspective. Indeed, since direct psychic experience, normally felt to be an indivisible whole, is featured by the symmetrical mode (very close to the unconscious functioning) and projects itself in a multiple and decondensed manner explicating in the asymmetrical mode (consciousness). Thus, psychical facts (as, for example, those that patient says and feels during a clinical session) can be accounted for by multiple possible conscious representations which, however, are not mutually contradictory and coexistent, so giving motif to the existence of different theoretical approaches, hence justifying the epistemological pluralism of psychoanalysis (and psychological sciences, in general). Afterwards, Sanchez-Cardenas (2016) proposes that affective factors may be linked together with the hope of reviving a certain *oceanic feelings* of fusion, considered with respect to a unified and unifying theory of the patient-analyst, so proposing new clinical applications of Matte Blanco's thinking.

1.5.2. The Point of View of Ana Boczar and Co-Workers (Círculo Psicanalítico De Minas Gerais, Brasil)

The[13] paradigmatic theory of modern epistemology tries to confer to psychoanalysis its scientific own statute. Even if there is no systematic epistemological treatment in the Freudian writings, it is yet undeniable that the genesis of psychoanalysis has a rigorous dialectic between theorization and clinical observation. Metapsychology is an organized and consistent system of concepts, capable of explaining and coordinating the analytical experience. On the other hand, it is just through metapsychology that clinical work has the possibility to be laid out within a generalized framework. Clinical experience also confirms the interrelations between psychopathology and culture[14]. For instance, modern times have brought about new versions for psychopathological symptoms, which, in turn, have special effects on the narcissistic personalities and the manifestations of anxiety, giving place to different neurotic configurations. This scenario has shed light in the epistemological framework of psychoanalysis, of which we shall discuss herein.

According to the ancient philosophy, above all with the classical tradition stemming from Plato and Aristotle, *truth* is an equation among a sign, a concept and the reality. Therefore, truth is closely related to reality, as St. Thomas of Aquinas said: "truth is the correspondence between the intellect and the thing" (*adæquatio rei et intellectus*). It is a semantic conception that pertains ontological presumptions about the nature of the notions of "existence", "a priori" and "reality", which prevailed in the past centuries, for which "things" were there, they were immediate data from one's senses, and truth was a linguistic translation of this "something" that had already been previously given. This interpretation reflects the empiricism that dominated the natural consciousness and characterized the pre-critical mode of thought, predominant at the time. Also the logician Alfred Tarski moved from the correspondence theory of truth to build up his semantic theory of truth.

Currently, however, the emphasis has been transferred from specific ontological questions to epistemological themes, where the contemporary epistemological problem consists in establishing a relation between theoretical propositions and observational terms, like to found an empirical basis for a specific theory. The principal objective is to demarcate the field of science, distinguishing it from other fields such as theology, philosophy and humanities. The search for a possible solution to this problem has enlarged the gap between the philosophy of contemporary sciences and the empiricism. The possibility of reducing theoretical propositions to verifiable laboratory propositions has been proven to be impossible. But a total acceptance of this scientific criterion would imply the drastic exclusion of vast areas of knowledge which are already under the domain of science, and entire fields of knowledge might never be legitimated. If it were so, then, for instance, there might never be a verification of history or a direct observation of past happenings.

The epistemological debate on verifiability has brought severe criticisms either to empiricism and inductive logic, as it was expounded in the so-called *principle of verifiability* initially proposed by Moritz Schlick. This principle lost its dogmatic rigidity, having been then reformulated in the more flexible direction of the *principle of falsificability* presented by Karl Raimund Popper. According to Popper, scientific theories cannot be sustained by inductively generalized verifications, because all verifications are precarious when conceived as proof. So, theories are founded on the confrontations of deductively obtained consequences which are reached through hypotheses and conjectures. This modification provided scientific criteria of *deduction-falsification*, instead of *verification-induction*.

This epistemological transformation has assured an intersubjective opening to science, which refers to one of Freud's ways of elaborating knowledge: indeed, many of his metapsychological constructions take place *a posterior*, that is to say, from effect to cause. We know that the universal metapsychological concepts are deduced from clinical work and that, besides this, there is no other empirical verifiability for these concepts, excepts transference context. Therefore, metapsychology is a theoretical framework which deals with the phenomena that appear in clinical psychoanalysis.

Thus, scientific progress is now conceived no longer as an advance in knowledge about objective reality, but it should also be conceived in an historical and sociological sense, in that the acceptance or rejection of hypotheses depends upon certain parameters imposed by paradigmatic theory, which should be considered as a model for all procedures of result validation and evaluation. Paradigmatic theory is instituted by a certain scientific community in a determined historical period, this being what defines "normal science" (T.S. Kuhn). Freud's doctrinarian position was directly influenced by Ernst Mach's *empiriocriticism*, which had been amply diffused in Vienna at the beginning of the century. Empiriocriticism is a philosophical trend that strived to differentiate itself from simple empiricism by using a conventional phenomenism based on phenomenic evidence or a sensible experience, whose data are not necessarily treated according to scientific treatment.

Anyway, there is a fundamental difference between psychoanalysis and other disciplines that recur to the experimental method, like physics, notwithstanding that this last was a model took into consideration by Freud in formulating the theoretical framework of psychoanalysis. However, even if there is no explicit and well-articulated epistemology in the Freudian writings, it is undeniable that the genesis of psychoanalysis upholds a rigorous dialectic between theorization and clinical observation. The concepts were not created arbitrarily but, on the contrary, they were adopted only when they were able to bring about some advances in the comprehension of clinical phenomena, in which they found their very confirmation.

For example, the concept of *repression* (see next chapter) acquired a new theoretical statute with the modification of the concept of trauma, which no longer referred to an external, empirical event – i.e., seduction – but, from then onwards, it referred to the phantasmatical space of representations. Repression's theoretical dislocation did not happen by pure speculation, but was rather determined through clinical observations related to psychoneuroses and, above all, hysteria. Therefore, we can generically declare that if there is any form of confrontation in psychoanalysis, it occurs surely in the clinical domain. On the other hand, we cannot expect to prove the existence of a-historic, extra-linguistic, almost-natural realities such as the "unconscious", "instinct" (drive) or "repression".

This kind of comprehension would be a typically realistic, pre-critical understanding formed by the substantiation of concepts together with the conception of "images" and "representations" of the things that are immediately apprehended through our senses and named in ordinary language. Instead, there is no "reality" that is similar to the "unconscious", but even so when we use it, we are not in the ground of free will and total lack of rational control. This, because metapsychology is an organized, coherent and consistent set of concepts that, since Freud's work, has been able to explain and to coordinate the experience of psychoanalytic clinical work. This experience is then shared by a transcultural community of researchers that has been maintained for almost a century. In this perspective of post-empiricist epistemology, the function of the hard nucleus of psychoanalytic theory (i.e., its fundamental concepts) is to enable understanding and judgment, together consensus and dissension of deeply heterogeneous experiences, in searching of common elements. In other words, with this metapsychological theory, it is possible to go beyond the singularity of clinical knowledge and to establish a certain level of communication which allows to define psychoanalysts and their institutions as a vast research community with its specific tradition that characterizes it at the institutional and social-cultural level (Carotenuto 1992, p. 6).

Thus, despite the possible differences in interpretation and semantic dislocations, psychoanalysts may be identified by their introductory manuals, common language, and the abundant literature that are assimilated and discussed by different groups of people. Above all, they are identified for their ability to uphold the dynamics of differences and complex identities in the same communicational horizon, so that, all the new "discoveries" and "hypotheses" are incorporated or rejected after a long process of discussion and persuasion in the midst of the psychoanalytic community. The Freudian text can and should be restudied and reanalyzed, so it definitely should not be an object of ritualistic repetition that carries the risk of "excommunication" for anyone who repeats it incorrectly. On the contrary, we must acknowledge that psychoanalytic concepts have to be *historically* understood and appraised, which does not mean that we surrender to relativism and irrationalism.

Psychoanalysis has an its own epistemic identity, an identity that does not rely upon an abstract truth, in that it finds its historical weight and recognition in a community that is still able to assure articulation between theory and praxis in justifying or rejecting what has been theoretically worked out. Therefore, it is through metapsychology that we are able to try to universalize clinical work and it is also through continuous clinical work that metapsychology finds the possibility of fulfilment. Anyway, it is the recognition of the basic *historicity* of either the concepts and the psychoanalytic experience that obliges us to ask if psychoanalysis can still be considered a paradigm in the psychic field or if the psychoanalytic community has been irreparably fragmented to the point of not being able to contain the intellectual tradition which was at first inaugurated by Freud, above all after the proliferation of many (non-orthodox) psychoanalytic schools and trends.

Thus, is it possible that the psychoanalytic community no longer relies as a condition enabling communication and confrontation between different hermeneutic options? Or, instead, should we become aware of the existence of not only one, but several clinical matrixes, hence not only one, but several metapsychologies? Does the field that is denominated "psychoanalysis" really conceal a plurality of possible perspectives which may be incommensurable and irreducible to each other? Or, should we recognize that an approximately uniform terminology underlies the several diverse kinds of psychoanalyses which stem from different clinical and cultural contexts, but that instead hide a sort of conceptual invariance?

All these questions are not without consequence. It is obvious that contemporary psychoanalysts no longer have the same clinical experiences as Freud did, due to the deep cultural transformations that have occurred later. As known, psychoanalysis was founded in a society characterized by rigid morals, in which sexual repression and emotional contentions were the social norm. We now meet other types of patients who differ from the hysterical patients those that inspired Freud at the end of the 19th century. Contemporary patients present new versions and symptoms[15]. Clinical work seems to confirm the intimate interrelation between psychopathology and culture (Bria & Caroppo, 2006).

At present, we can observe new psychopathological configurations such as invasive manifestations of anxiety and neo-narcissistic affections. All these manifestations are typical of the exacerbated individualism that exists in post-modern societies, side by side with the helplessness of individuals who belong to a symbolically impoverished culture that is immersed in imaginary fantasies. Modern individuals are cast into specular mazes in which they rotate at such an high velocity that they no longer count on past experiences or future expectations to guide them. The modern-day of this permissive society is featured by abundance, rather than privation, of pervasive communication, invasive media, propaganda, gadgets, technology, sex, etc. This creates a mental pathology (that obeys the laws of high velocity and pleasure principle), while reducing the firmness of cultural values and diluting the points of stable references.

Neurotic repression is gradually being substituted by narcissistic fluctuation. Hence, the emotional emptiness, the impossibility of feeling, and the de-substantiation or the desiccating of the Ego, reveal the really truth of this narcissistic process which is nothing but a strategy for this emptiness. Christopher Lasch, in his book *The Culture of Narcissism* (of 1979), has said that personal relations present high risks of instability, arguing, moreover, that what people really aspire at most, is an emotional detachment because it gives them the feeling of (apparent) invulnerability and emotional independence. Furthermore, Gilles Lipovetsky, in his book *L'ère du vide* (of 1983), affirmed that exaggerated sexual liberation, aggressive feminism and pornography, all tend toward the same finality, namely, to build up barriers against emotions as well as to maintain emotional intensities at a distance. Along the same lines of thought, the work of Zygmunt Bauman is placeable.

Paradoxically, however, men and women desire the intensity of privileged relationships, but the stronger the expectation is, the rarer and briefer becomes the miraculous fusion. The hyper-invested body, lives under the command of perennial "youth and beauty", even though this doesn't mean a complete experience of sexuality. On the contrary, narcissistic fascination rather generally renders a couple's sexual experience more difficult to be pursued. Sexual identity also follows the same rules of "uncommitment" (that is, a mutual and permanently undeveloped relation between two people, usually finalized to get material benefits only), and bisexual identity is, for instance, becoming even more frequent. Through this double identity, people hope to experience all the possible good things that both sexes have to offer, without renouncing to any possible pleasure[16]. Boczar and co-workers rightly suppose, in this regard, that modern sexual identity has been strongly influenced by the decline of the paternal function and the dissolution of the nuclear family.

Concerning anxiety, then, Boczar and co-workers have focused on two main situations. The first is the anxiety signal that appears as a protection to the integrity of the Ego; it is also the element that propels the analytical experience, and we can even say, the very founding human experience. This anxiety signal is yet often quite inefficient, so it frequently gives rise to a second kind of anxiety which is a fluctuating or even annihilating, destructive anxiety. All that remits the individual towards structural helplessness and abandonment, along with other primitive (ancestral) traumatic experiences; this takes place, for example, when one encounters panic disorder configurations.

In the midst of annihilating and fluctuating anxiety, this disorder is however bound to post-modernity due to the crises of values, to the reinvention and refinement of violence in the social space, and also to the increase in the forms of discomfort that surge in civilization. Psychosomatic phenomena can also be included in this last anxiety group. They are basically due to an impossibility of symbolic elaboration and to the Ego's surrender to the real of the body. These are some of the main symptoms which have been found in contemporary psychoanalytic clinical work (Boczar et al., 2001; Recalcati, 2010). The psychoanalysts' task is to bring out the subject of one's Self, where he pretends to be deceased (by the strong death instincts), with psychoanalyst guided by the available universal references provided by metapsychology.

As a conclusion, therefore, from what has been said so far, we may say that, psychoanalysis is modernity's daughter, therefore it suffers from the very era that itself helped to create. So, Boczar and co-workers end advancing some crucial questions, therefore asking, for example, considering the abrupt changes of present times, what has happened to subjectivity? Hence, does Freudian metapsychology remain entirely valid or will it have to be modified in order to attend the new subjectivity of modern individuals? Have the social-cultural transformations merely affected the surface of clinical phenomena or instead have they reached the deepest structures of the psyche? In psychoanalytic psychopathology, how should we deal with phenomenological approaches – that are more sensitive to the singularity of clinical manifestations – and the structural approaches – that try to express the deeper logic of the psyche? Finally, would not a joint effort between psychoanalysis and epistemology be able to re-think the place of this modern subject in crisis and also elaborate the different vicissitudes of different clinical approaches?

All these questions – state, at last, Boczar and co-workers – are extremely complex, but, however, they surely suggest that one of the main study's objects of the epistemology of psychoanalysis should be oriented toward the interrelationship between clinical work, culture and metapsychology, hence in viewing psychoanalysis as laid out within a sociological context, just due to its relevant historical dimension linked with social-cultural context in which it operates. Boczar and co-workers believe that just this kind of discussion is essential if we want to release psychoanalysis from the dogmatic space of "esoteric" doctrines and institutions. Along this line, maybe it is possible to give a scientific status to psychoanalysis if one tries to identify the underlying universal or constant structural aspects of human psyche according to a psychoanalytic pattern suitably laid out within a sociological framework. This because of the above close interrelations between psychoanalytic patterns and social-cultural environment in which human being lives.

So, looking at the sociological applications of psychoanalysis, beyond its strict subjectivity which often it is accused (above all, in relation to unconscious contents by repression) to be lacking in objectivity, for instance as a possible explicative model of sociological phenomena, hence gaining a collective explicative power, perhaps a certain degree of scientific validity may be achieved by psychoanalysis. Historically, possible applications of psychoanalysis to sociological context, have been made by many exponents of Frankfurt school (Theodor W. Adorno, Max Horkheimer, Herbert Marcuse, Erich Fromm, and so on), as well as by other notable sociologists, like Talcott Parsons (1970); alike, on the same level of discussion and in regard to the same directions and ends, it has to be considered the possible, fruitful applications of psychoanalysis to anthropology, as already done, for example, by the so-called *culture and personality* trend.

1.5.3. The Point of View of Objectualistic Epistemology, the Stance of Peter Fonagy, and the Latest Epistemological Positions

Some[17] Italian psychoanalysts, amongst whom are Luigi Longhin (1992, 2016) and Mauro Mancia (Longhin & Mancia, 1998), in regard to the "hot" epistemological debate on the foundations of psychoanalysis, have taken into consideration, as valid just in this context, some epistemological stances put forward[18] by Evandro Agazzi (1976, 1979, 1985a,b, 2014), which, recollected together, have given rise to the so-called *objectualistic* point of view. Agazzi centres his arguments on the so-called *explicative deduction*, which is a logical form of reasoning whose covered range is wider than that of a simple syllogism, and is able to build up a doctrinal corpus internally coherent and unitary, which provides too a rational justification[19] to what is affirmed within it, which is shared and accepted as such by a certain community (*intersubjectivity*), that of psychoanalysts, whose clinical and therapeutic work should be however able, in a certain manner, to give right benefits to patients (psychoanalytic cure[20]). So, from an epistemological standpoint, *explanation* has a major power than a formal syllogism, in agreement with what has been said in previous sections, in that it requires, as minimal requisites of subsistence, the existence of, at least, one logical nexus between the objects (meant in their widest philosophical sense) of this corpus of knowledge[21] (*objectuality*).

Now, the *objectualistic* point of view claims that, besides these latter requirements, a scientific theory should also be able to make *reference* to some extra-linguistic object (that is, not describable with the internal language of the theory into question), that, relatively to the psychoanalytic context, Longhin and Mancia (1998) should identify it into the extra-clinical context, to be precise in the counter-transference suitably redefined and in its supervision by a third person external to the dyadic link of analytical setting; and, just in this last phase, a certain feature of objectivity may be identified, with a methodology quite similar to that of natural sciences, trying to identify the possible invariants involved along the analytical setting. In a few words, what is scientifically relevant in psychoanalysis is the clinical *outcomes* of the analytical setting (Grinberg, 1989; Langs, 1990; Longhin, 2016). However, from a theoretical standpoint, besides this latter as much crucial epistemological request, the remaining ones, as have been mentioned above, are yet central in a philosophical discussion about the foundations of theoretical psychoanalysis, regardless of the next empirical verifiability in the therapeutic setting whose discussion, however, should follow too but only after having previously clarified the theoretical framework.

Finally, we mention too the epistemological stance put forward by Peter Fonagy (1982), whose criticisms to psychoanalytic theory are mainly turned to the weaknesses of its empirical bases and to the logical problems of its metapsychology whose major are anthropomorphism, reification, and the inappropriate use of metaphors. According to Fonagy, as the theoretical structure of psychoanalytic framework is basically erected through yet unavoidable metaphoric tools having a main linguistic nature, it follows that, if one wishes to discover the right theoretical framework in which to lay out psychoanalysis, then it is need to turn towards the implicit mechanisms underlying the formation of such metaphoric expressions of which psychoanalysis is rich. Only in this way, Fonagy says, psychoanalysis may go out of its pre-scientific state in which it stays. And, along this same line of thought is our point of view, for which, tempting to make reference to the formal language of exact and natural sciences, and their theoretical methodology to build up so-called scientific theories, we might maybe descry the underlying formal structures presiding the psychoanalytic phenomenology, and hosting, individually[22], the *personalistic* psychic content stored along each own life experience, so reaching a minimal degree of objectivity with the acknowledgement of certain almost universal, trans-subjective structures and formations[23] presiding general human psyche functioning.

The structural unconscious according to Matte Blanco, is just placeable among these universal and invariant structures, like Lévi-Strauss' unconscious[24], coherently with the outcomes of the latest neurobiological researches and their philosophical conclusions (Panksepp & Biven, 2012) as well as with certain functionalistic standpoints of cognitive sciences, like that of Jerry Fodor on the *theory of modularity* of the mind[25]. On the other hand, the latest epistemological stances (Conrotto, 2014) say us that what really *structurate* human psyche are the *primal phantasies*[26] (Laplanche & Pontalis, 1967, 1988) which are, in turn, basically turned to structurate later *Œdipal complex*. So, there exist innate structures which act as multi-systems of semiotic transduction of corporal experiences, signs producing, which structurate unconscious and rule its functioning. Each of these pre-linguistic semiogenetic systems, on its turn, is mainly ruled internally by a chief, primordial logical nucleus which confers to it, the basic, minimal formal fashion: it is made by the *signifier of castration* ruled by the *pleasure/displeasure principle*, which give rise to a basic binary logic called *phallic logic*[27]. Anyway, we refer to the next Chapter 2, Section 2.8. for a deeper discussion of these last questions.

Furthermore, for an updated and wider recognition on the latest philosophical and epistemological positions related to psychoanalysis, as well as for an overall view of the present epistemological setting of psychoanalysis in regard to other knowledge fields, we refer to the remarkable work of Francesco Conrotto (2014) and references therein, where, among other things, it is stated, rightly, that just psychoanalysis, almost inversely to what required in the above sections, may provide new and unexpected remarks, hints and insights to the epistemology itself, renewing the same concept of human knowledge.

REFERENCES

Abbagnano, N. (1998). *Dizionario di Filosofia. Terza edizione aggiornata e ampliata da Giovanni Fornero*. Torino, Italy: UTET Libreria.

Agazzi, E. (1976). Criteri epistemologici fondamentali delle discipline psicologiche. In *Problemi epistemologici della psicologia*. Milano, Italy: Vita e Pensiero.

Agazzi, E. (1979). Analogicità del concetto di scienza. Il problema del rigore e dell'oggettività nelle scienze umane. In *Epistemologia e scienze umane*. Milano, Italy: Editore Massimo.

Agazzi, E. (1985a). La questione del realismo scientifico. In *Scienza e filosofia. Saggi in onore di Ludovico Geymonat*. Milano, Italy: Garzanti.

Agazzi, E. (1985b). Riflessioni epistemologiche sul tema "Segno, simbolo, sintomo, comunicazione. Implicanze e convergenze fra filosofia, psichiatria e psicoanalisi". In *Segno, simbolo, sintomo, comunicazione. Implicanze e convergenze fra filosofia, psichiatria e psicoanalisi*. Genova, Italy: Edizioni Esagraph.

Agazzi, E. (2014). *Scientific Objectivity and its Contexts*. New York, NY: Springer-Verlag, Inc.; . doi:10.1007/978-3-319-04660-0

Badiou, A. (1982). *Théorie du sujet*. Paris: Éditions du Seuil.

Balzarotti, R. (Ed.). (1972). *Cahiers pour l'Analyse. Scritti scelti di analisi e teoria della scienza, a cura del Centro Ricerche 2*. Torino, Italy: Editore Boringhieri.

Battacchi, M. W. (2006). *La conoscenza psicologia. Il metodo, l'oggetto, la ricerca*. Roma, Italy: Carocci editore.

Bell, D. (2016). *Superintelligence and World-Views*. Surrey, UK: Grosvenor House Publishing, Ltd.

Benvenuto, S. (2005). *Perversioni. Sessualità, etica, psicoanalisi*. Torino, Italy: Bollati Boringhieri editore.

Bezoari, M., & Palombi, F. (Eds.). (2003). *Epistemologia e Psicoanalisi: attualità di un confronto. Quaderni del Centro Milanese di Psicoanalisi*. Milano, Italy: Edizioni del Centro Milanese di Psicoanalisi.

Bianchi, P. (2014). La psicoanalisi e la politica delle singolarità. In *L'inconscio è la politica*. Milano-Udine, Italy: Mimesis Edizioni.

Boczar, A., Teixeira da Costa Salles, A. C., Pimenta, A. C., Drawin, C. R., Eliana Rodrigues Pereira, E., Brandão Lemos Morais, M., & Beaudette Drummond, S. (2001). Psychoanalysis and Epistemology: The Interrelation Between Clinical Work, Culture and Metapsychology. *International Forum of Psychoanalysis*, *10*(2), 145–150.

Boniolo, G., & Vidali, P. (1999). *Filosofia della scienza*. Milano, Italy: Bruno Mondadori.

Bria, P., & Caroppo, E. (2006). *Antropologia culturale e psicopatologia*. Roma, Italy: Alpes Italia.

Buzzoni, M. (1989). Operazionismo ed ermeneutica. Saggio sullo statuto epistemologico della psicoanalisi. Milano, Italy: Franco Angeli Editore.

CA (Collectif d'Auteurs). (1975). *La Psychanalyse*. Paris: Editions Le Livre De Poche.

Capozzi, M., & Cellucci, C. (2014). *Breve storia della logica. Dall'Umanesimo al primo Novecento.* Morrisville, NC: Lulu Press, Inc.

Carotenuto, A. (1982). *Discorso sulla metapsicologia.* Torino, Italy: Bollati Boringhieri Editore.

Carotenuto, A. (1991). *Trattato di psicologia della personalità e delle differenze individuali.* Milano, Italy: Raffaello Cortina Editore.

Carotenuto, A. (Ed.). (1992). *Dizionario Bompiani degli Psicologi Contemporanei.* Milano, Italy: Bompiani.

Castiglioni, M., & Corradini, A. (2011). *Modelli epistemologici in psicologia. Dalla psicoanalisi al costruzionismo.* Roma, Italy: Carocci editore.

Cellucci, C., & Ippoliti, E. (2016). *Logica.* Milano, Italy: EGEA Editore.

Codignola, E. (1977). *Il vero e il falso. Saggio sulla struttura logica dell'interpretazione psicoanalitica.* Torino, Italy: Editore Boringhieri.

Conrotto, F. (2000). *Tra il sapere e la cura. Un itinerario freudiano.* Milano, Italy: FrancoAngeli.

Conrotto, F. (2009). Negazione. In *Psiche. Dizionario storico di psicologia, psichiatria, psicoanalisi, neuroscienze* (Vol. 2, pp. 728–730). Torino, Italy: Giulio Einaudi editore.

Conrotto, F. (2010). *Per una teoria psicoanalitica della conoscenza.* Milano, Italy: FrancoAngeli.

Conrotto, F. (2014). *Ripensare l'inconscio.* Milano, Italy: FrancoAngeli.

Corradi Fiumara, G. (1980). *Funzione simbolica e filosofia del linguaggio* [The symbolic function: Psychoanalysis and the philosophy of language]. Torino, Italy: Editore Boringhieri.

Cuche, D. (2004). *La notion de culture dans les sciences sociales.* Paris: Éditions La Découverte.

D'Urso, V., & Trentin, R. (1998). *Introduzione alla psicologia delle emozioni.* Roma-Bari, Italy: Editori Laterza.

Dalla Chiara Scabia, M. L. (1973). Istanti e individui nelle logiche temporali. *Rivista di Filosofia, 64*(2), 95–122.

Dalla Chiara Scabia, M. L. (1974). *Logica.* Milano, Italy: ISEDI – Istituto Editoriale Internazionale.

Damasio, A. (1994). *Descartes' Error. Emotion, Reason, and the Human Brain.* New York, NY: G.P. Putnam's Sons.

De Glas, M., & Desclés, J.-P. (1996). Du temps linguistique comme idéalisation d'un temps phenomenal. *Intellectica – Le sémiotique/Logiques et sciences cognitives, 23*(2), 159-192.

De Glas, M., & Plane, J.-L. (2005). *Une approche formelle de la typicité. Cahiers du CREA, N. 20.* Paris: Imprimerie de l'École Polytechnique.

De Masi, F. (2016). Which is the relevant superego for clinical analytic work? In F. Borgogno, A. Luchetti, & L. M. Coe (Eds.), *Reading Italian Psychoanalysis* (pp. 279–290). Oxfordshire, UK: Routledge.

De Mijolla, A. (Ed.). (2005). *International Dictionary of Psychoanalysis* (Vol. 1–3). Farmington Hills, MI: Thomson Gale.

De Mijolla, A., & De Mijolla Mellor, S. (Eds.). (1996). *Psychanalyse*. Paris: PUF-Presses Universitaires de France.

De Pasquali, P. (2002). *Figli che uccidono. Da Doretta Graneris a Erika & Omar. Soveria Mannelli (CZ)*. Italy: Rubbettino Editore.

De Waelhens, A., & Ver Eecke, W. (2001). *Phenomenology and Lacan on Schizophrenia, after the Decade of the Brain*. Leuven, Belgium: Leuven University Press.

Dehaene, S., & Brannon, E. (Eds.). (2011). *Space, Time and Number in the Brain. Searching for the Foundations of Mathematical Thought*. Amsterdam: Elsevier, Inc.

Dei, F., & Meloni, P. (2015). *Antropologia della cultura materiale*. Roma, Italy: Carocci editore.

Deng, Y. (2013). *Applied Parallel Computing*. Singapore: World Scientific Publishing.

Derdzinski, A. (1992). *Geometry of the Standard Model of Elementary Particles*. Berlin: Springer-Verlag; . doi:10.1007/978-3-642-50310-8

Desclés, J.-P. (2009). Relations spatiales et mouvements dans l'espace. Communication au le Séminaire GéoTAL, Rennes, France.

Devlin, K. (2006). *The Math Instinct: Why You're a Mathematical Genius (Along with Lobsters, Birds, Cats, and Dogs)*. New York, NY: Thunder's Mouth Press.

Di Gregorio, L. (2003). *Psicopatologia del cellulare. Dipendenza e possesso del telefonino*. Milano, Italy: FrancoAngeli/LeComete.

Dijksterhuis, A., & Nordgren, L. F. (2006). A theory of unconsciouss thought. *Perspectives on Psychological Science*, *1*(2), 95–109. doi:10.1111/j.1745-6916.2006.00007.x

Dolto, F. (1984). *L'image inconsciente du corps*. Paris: Editions du Seuil.

Donati, P. (2015). L'enigma della relazione. Milano, Italy: Mimesis edizioni.

Durst, M. (1988). *Dialettica e bi-logica. L'epistemologia di Ignacio Matte Blanco*. Milano, Italy: Marzorati Editore.

Eco, U. (1981). *Simbolo. Voce dell'Enciclopedia Einaudi* (Vol. 12). Torino, Italy: Giulio Einaudi editore.

Egidi, R. (1979). Il linguaggio delle teorie scientifiche. Esperienza ed ipotesi nell'epistemologia contemporanea. Napoli, Italy: Guida Editori.

Egidi, R. (Ed.). (1992). *La svolta relativistica nell'epistemologia contemporanea*. Milano, Italy: FrancoAngeli.

Ehresmann, A. C., & Vanbremeersch, J. P. (2007). *Memory Evolutive Systems. Hierarchy, Emergence, Cognition*. Amsterdam: Elsevier, B.V.

Eibl-Eibesfeldt, I. (1996). *Amore e odio. Per una storia naturale dei comportamenti elementari.* Milano, Italy: Edizioni Adelphi.

Eibl-Eibesfeldt, I. (1997). *Le invarianti nell'evoluzione delle specie.* Roma, Italy: Di Renzo Editore.

Eibl-Eibesfeldt, I. (2001). Etologia umana. Le basi biologiche e culturali del comportamento. Torino, Italy: Bollati Boringhieri editore.

Eibl-Eibesfeldt, I. (2005). *Dall'animale all'uomo. Le invarianti nell'evoluzione delle specie.* Roma, Italy: Di Renzo Editore.

Ekstrom, S. R. (2004). The mind beyond our immediate awareness: Freudian, Jungian, and cognitive models of the unconscious. *The Journal of Analytical Psychology, 49*(5), 657–682. doi:10.1111/j.0021-8774.2004.00494.x

Ellis, J., Mavromatos, N. E., & Nanopoulos, D. V. (1992). The origin of space-time as W-symmetry breaking in string theory. [Part B]. *Physics Letters, 288*(1-2), 23–30. doi:10.1016/0370-2693(92)91949-A

Endert, E. (2006). Über die emotionale Dimension sozialer Prozesse. *Die Theorie der Affektlogik am Beispiel der Rechtsextremismus und Nationalsozialismusforschung (Theorie und Methode).* Konstanz, Germany: UVK Verlagsgesellschaft mbH.

Enriques, F. (1912). *Scienza e Razionalismo.* Bologna, Italy: Nicola Zanichelli Editore.

Fabietti, U., & Remotti, F. (Eds.). (1998). *Dizionario di Antropologia. Etnologia, Antropologia Culturale, Antropologia Sociale.* Bologna, Italy: Nicola Zanichelli Editore.

Fairlamb, H. L. (1994). *Critical conditions. Postmodernity and the question of foundations.* Cambridge, UK: Cambridge University Press; . doi:10.1017/CBO9780511552762

Falzone, A. (2005). *Filosofia del linguaggio e psicopatologia evoluzionistica.* Soveria Mannelli, Italy: Rubbettino Editore.

Fenichel, O. (1945). *The psychoanalytic theory of neurosis.* New York, NY: W.W. Norton & Company, Inc.

Ferretti, F. (2010). *Alle origini del linguaggio umano. Il punto di vista evoluzionistico.* Roma-Bari, Italy: Editori Laterza.

Ffytche, M. (2012). *The Foundation of the Unconscious. Schelling, Freud and the Birth of the Modern Psyche.* Cambridge, UK: Cambridge University Press.

Figà-Talamanca Dore, L. (1978). *La logica dell'inconscio.* Roma, Italy: Edizioni Studium-Vita Nova.

Finelli, R. (2010). Perché l'inconscio non è strutturato come un linguaggio. In Compendio di Psicoanalisi e altri scritti. Roma, Italy: Newton Compton editori.

Finelli, R. (2011). Rappresentazione e linguaggio in Freud: A partire dal "Compendio di psicoanalisi". *Consecutio Temporum. Rivista di critica della postmodernità, 1,* 112-125.

Fodor, N., & Gaynor, F. (1950). *Freud: Dictionary of Psychoanalysis.* New York, NY: The Philosophical Library.

Fonagy, P. (1982). The Integration of Psychoanalysis and Experimental Science. A Review. *The International Review of Psycho-Analysis*, *9*(2), 125–145.

Fonagy, P., Gergely, G., Jurist, E. L., & Target, M. (2002). *Affect Regulation, Mentalization, and the Development of the Self*. New York, NY: Other Press.

Fornari, F. (2016). Psychic birth. In F. Borgogno, A. Luchetti, & L. M. Coe (Eds.), *Reading Italian Psychoanalysis* (pp. 593–600). Oxfordshire, UK: Routledge.

Fossi, G. (1983). *La psicologia dinamica: un'eredità del XX secolo*. Roma, Italy: Edizioni Borla.

Fossi, G. (1984). *Le teorie psicoanalitiche*. Padova, Italy: Piccin Nuova Libraria.

Fossi, G. (1988). Psicoanalisi e psicoterapie dinamiche. Torino, Italy: Bollati Boringhieri editore.

Fossi, G. (2003). *Una proposta evoluzionista per la psicoanalisi. Con un manuale per la pratica terapeutica e la ricerca empirica*. Milano, Italy: FrancoAngeli.

Francioni, M. (1978). Psicoanalisi linguistica ed epistemologia in Jacques Lacan. Torino, Italy: Editore Boringhieri.

Francioni, M. (1982). *Storia della psicoanalisi francese. Teorie e istituzioni freudiane*. Torino, Italy: Editore Boringhieri.

Freni, S. (1992). Prefazione all'edizione italiana. In *Capire il transfert*. Milano, Italy: Raffaello Cortina Editore.

Freud, S. (1938). Abriß der psychoanalyse [An outline of psychoanalysis]. *The International Journal of Psycho-Analysis*, *21*, 27–84.

Freud, S. (1957). *The Standard Edition of Complete Psychological Works of Sigmund Freud* (Vol. 1-24). (J. Strachey, Trans. & Ed.). London, UK: The Hogarth Press.

Freud, S. (1979). La scissione dell'Io nel processo di difesa (1938). In *Opere di Sigmund Freud, 1930-1938. L'uomo Mosè e la religione monoteistica e altri scritti* (Vol. 11). Torino, Italy: Editore Boringhieri.

Friedman, D. M. (2001). *A Mind of Its Own. A Cultural History of the Penis*. New York, NY: Simon & Schuster, Inc.

Friedman, M., & Tomšič, S. (Eds.). (2016). *Psychoanalysis: Topological Perspectives. New Conceptions of Geometry and Space in Freud and Lacan*. Bielefeld, Germany: Transcript Verlag; . doi:10.14361/9783839434406

Fromm, E. (1951). *The Forgotten Language. An Introduction to the Understanding of Dreams, Fairy Tales, and Myths*. New York, NY: Holt, Rinehart & Winston Publishing Company, Inc.

Fromm, E. (1976). *To have or to be?* New York, NY: Harper & Row Publishers, Inc.

Funari, E. (1978). Psicoanalisi: tecnica o Weltanschauung? In *Psicoanalisi e classi sociali* (pp. 147–153). Roma, Italy: Editori Riuniti.

Funari, E. (1988). Contestualità e specificità della psicoanalisi. In Trattato di Psicoanalisi. Volume I: Teoria e Tecnica. Milano, Italy: Raffaello Cortina Editore.

Funari, E. (2007). *L'irrapresentabile come origine della vita psichica*. Milano, Italy: FrancoAngeli.

Fusco, A., & Tomassoni, R. (Eds.). (2013). *Creatività nella psicologia letteraria, drammatica e filmica*. Milano, Italy: FrancoAngeli.

Galimberti, U. (1979). *Psichiatria e fenomenologia*. Milano, Italy: Giangiacomo Feltrinelli Editore.

Galimberti, U. (1983). *Il corpo*. Milano, Italy: Giangiacomo Feltrinelli Editore.

Galimberti, U. (2006). *Dizionario di psicologia*. Torino, Italy: UTET Libreria.

Gay, P. (2000). *Freud. Una vita per i nostri tempi*. Milano, Italy: Bompiani.

Giberti, F., & Rossi, R. (Eds.). (1996). *Manuale di psichiatria* (4th ed.). Padova, Italy: Piccin Nuova Libraria.

Gilliéron, E., & Baldassarre, M. (Eds.). (2012). *Perversione e Relazione*. Roma, Italy: Alpes Italia.

Giordano, M., Dello Russo, G., Pardi, F., & Patella, G. A. (1984). Tempo e inconscio. Napoli, Italy: Guida editori.

Girotto, V. (Ed.). (2013). Introduzione alla psicologia del pensiero. Bologna, Italy: Società editrice il Mulino.

Glover, E. (1949). *Psychoanalysis*. London, UK: John Bale Medical Publications, Ltd.

Goleman, D. (1995). *Emotional Intelligence*. New York, NY: Bantam Books.

Green, A. (1993). *Le travail du négatif*. Paris: Les Éditions du Minuit.

Greenacre, P. (1971). *Emotional growth. Psychoanalytic studies of the gifted and a great variety of other individuals*. New York, NY: International Universities Press, Inc.

Grice, H. P. (1993). Logica e conversazione. Saggi su intenzione, significato e comunicazione. Bologna, Italy: Società editrice il Mulino.

Grinberg, L. (1989). *La supervisione psicoanalitica. Teoria e pratica*. Milano, Italy: Raffaello Cortina Editore.

Grunberger, B. (1971). *Le narcissisme. Essai de psychanalyse*. Paris: Payot.

Hall, C. S. (1999). *A Primer in Freudian Psychology*. New York, NY: Meridian Books.

Hampe, B., & Grady, J. E. (Eds.). (2005). *From Perception to Meaning. Image Schemas in Cognitive Linguistics*. Berlin: Walter de Gruyter GmbH and Co.; . doi:10.1515/9783110197532

Hanly, C. (1984). Ego Ideal and Ideal Ego. *The International Journal of Psycho-Analysis, 65*(3), 253–261.

Hanly, C. (2011). *Studi psicoanalitici sul narcisismo. Scritti di Charles Hanly*. Roma, Italy: Giovanni Fioriti Editore.

Harary, F., Norman, Z., & Cartwright, D. (Eds.). (1965). *Structural Models*. New York, NY: John Wiley and Sons, Inc.

Hartmann, H., & Loewenstein, R. M. (1962). Notes on the Superego. *The Psychoanalytic Study of the Child*, *17*, 42–81.

Hermann, I. (1989). *Psicoanalisi e logica*. Roma, Italy: Di Renzo Editore.

Hickmann, M., & Robert, S. (Eds.). (2006). *Space in Languages – Linguistic Systems and Cognitive Categories*. Amsterdam: John Benjamins Publishing Company; . doi:10.1075/tsl.66

Hodges, W. (1977). *Logic. An Introduction to Elementary Logic*. Harmondsworth, UK: Penguin Books, Ltd.

Horkheimer, M., & Adorno, T. W. (1947). *Dialektik der Aufklärung. Philosophische Fragments*. Amsterdam: Querido Verlag N.V.

Imbasciati, A. (2015). *Nuove teorie sul funzionamento della mente. L'istituzione psicoanalitica e gli psicoanalisti*. Milano, Italy: FrancoAngeli.

Ippoliti, E. (2007). *Il vero e il plausibile*. Morrisville, NC: Lulu Press, Inc.

Iurato, G. (2013a). Mathematical thought in the light of Matte Blanco work. *Philosophy of Mathematics Education Journal*, 27.

Iurato, G. (2013b). Σύμβολου: An attempt toward the early origins, Part 1. Language & Psychoanalysis, 2(2), 77–120. 10.7565/landp.2013.008

Iurato, G. (2013c). Σύμβολου: An attempt toward the early origins, Part 2. Language & Psychoanalysis, 2(2), 121–160. 10.7565/landp.2013.009

Iurato, G. (2014a). At the grounding of computational psychoanalysis: on the work of Ignacio Matte Blanco. A general history of culture overview of Matte Blanco bilogic in comparison. In *Proceedings of the 2014 IEEE 13th International Conference on Cognitive Informatics and Cognitive Computing*. Los Alamitos, CA: IEEE Computer Society Press.

Iurato, G. (2014b). The dawning of computational psychoanalysis. A proposal for some first elementary formalization attempts. *International Journal of Cognitive Informatics and Natural Intelligence*, *8*(4), 50–82. doi:10.4018/ijcini.2014100104

Iurato, G. (2014c). *Alcune considerazioni critiche sul simbolismo*. Preprint No. hal-00980828 version 1. Available at HAL archives-ouvertes.

Iurato, G. (2015a). A Brief Comparison of the Unconscious as Seen by Jung and Lévi-Strauss. *Anthropology of Consciousness*, *26*(1), 60–107. doi:10.1111/anoc.12032

Iurato, G. (2015b). *Fetishism* in Marketing. Some First Elementary Psychoanalytic Anthropology Remarks. In *Business Management: A Practioners' Guide*. Delhi: International Research Publication House.

Iurato, G. (2015c). A simple phylogenetic remark about certain human blood pressure values. *Journal of Biochemistry International*, *2*(4), 162–165.

Iurato, G. (2016a). *A psychoanalytic enquiry on symbolic function.* Preprint No. hal-01361264 version 3. Available at HAL archives-ouvertes.

Iurato, G. (2016b). *A view of LSA/ESA in Computational Psychoanalysis.* Preprint No. hal-01353999 version 1. Available at HAL archives-ouvertes.

Iurato, G. (2016c). On Jacques Lacan Psychosis Theory and ERPs Analysis. *Journal of Biology and Nature, 5*(4), 234–240.

Iurato, G. (2016d). Some Comments on the Historical Role of *Fetishism* in Economic Anthropology. *Journal of Global Economics. Management and Business Research, 7*(1), 61–82.

Iurato, G. (2016e). *The origins of symbol: An historical-critical study of symbolic function, according to the phylo-ontogenetic perspective, as arising from the comparison of certain patterns of neuro-psychological sciences.* Paper Presented at the Satellite Event "On the edge of disciplines", Florence, Italy.

Iurato, G. (2017a). An Essay in Denotational Mathematics. Rigorous Results. In *Encyclopedia of Information Science and Technology* (4th ed.). Hershey, PA: IGI Global.

Iurato, G. (2017b). Un raffronto critico fra la teoria platonica delle idee ed il paradosso di Kripke-Wittgenstein. In Platone nel pensiero moderno e contemporaneo (vol. 11). Villasanta, Italy: Limina Mentis Edizioni.

Iurato, G. (2017c). (in press). Rigidity of the Generalized Other, narrowness of the Otherness and de-modernization, in the framework of symbolic interactionism. *Ideology and Political Journal.*

Iurato, G., & Khrennikov, A. Yu. (2015). Hysteresis model of unconscious-conscious interconnection: Exploring dynamics on m-adic trees. p-Adic Numbers, Ultrametric. *Analysis and Applications, 7*(4), 312–321. doi:10.1134/S2070046615040068

Iurato, G., & Khrennikov, A. Yu. (2017). On the topological structure of a mathematical model of human unconscious. p-Adic Numbers, Ultrametric. *Analysis and Applications, 9*(1), 78–81. doi:10.1134/S2070046617010071

Iurato, G., Khrennikov, A. Yu., & Murtagh, F. (2016). Formal Foundations for the Origins of Human Consciousness. p-Adic Numbers, Ultrametric. *Analysis and Applications, 8*(4), 249–279. doi:10.1134/S2070046616040014

Jablonka, E., & Raz, G. (2009). Transgenerational Epigenetic Inheritance: Prevalence, Mechanisms, and Implications for the Study of Heredity and Evolution. *The Quarterly Review of Biology, 84*(2), 131–176. doi:10.1086/598822

Jackson, D. D. (1954). Some factors influencing the Œdipus Complex. *The Psychoanalytic Quarterly, 23,* 566–581.

Jaffé, R. (2009). Ideale dell'Io, Idealizzazione. In *Psiche. Dizionario storico di psicologia, psichiatria, psicoanalisi, neuroscienze* (Vol. 1, pp. 494–500). Torino, Italy: Giulio Einaudi editore.

Johnson-Laird, P., & Bara, B. (1984). Syllogistic Inference. *Cognition, 16*(1), 1–61. doi:10.1016/0010-0277(84)90035-0

Kächele, H. (2001). Are there "Pillars of Therapeutic Wisdom" for Psychoanalytic Therapy? *European Journal of Psychoanalysis. Humanities, Philosophy. Psychothérapies, 12-13*, 151–161.

Kandel, E. R. (2005). *Psychiatry, Psychoanalysis, and the New Biology of Mind.* Washington, DC: American Psychiatric Association Publishing, Inc.

Kaplan-Solms, K., & Solms, M. (2000). *Clinical Studies in Neuro-Psychoanalysis. Introduction to a Depth Neuropsychology.* London, UK: Karnac Books, Ltd.

Kemeny, J. G. (1959). *A Philosopher Looks at Science.* Princeton, NJ: D. Van Nostrand Reinhold Company, Inc.

Kemeny, J. G., Snell, J. L., & Thompson, G. L. (1974). *Introduction to Finite Mathematics* (3rd ed.). Englewood Cliffs, NJ: Prentice-Hall.

Kernberg, O. (2011). Suicide prevention for psychoanalytic institutes and societies. *Journal of the American Psychoanalytic Association, 60*(4), 707–719. doi:10.1177/0003065112449861

Khan Masud, R. M. (1970). *Le fétichisme comme négation du soi. Nouvelle Revue de Psychoanalyse, 2, Numéro spécial: Objects du fétichisme. Présentation par J-B. Pontalis.* Paris: Éditions Gallimard.

Khan Masud, R. M. (1979). *Alienation in perversions.* London, UK: The Hogarth Press, Ltd.

Khrennikov, A. Yu. (1991). *p*-Adic quantum mechanics with *p*-adic valued functions. *Journal of Mathematical Physics, 32*(4), 932–937. doi:10.1063/1.529353

Khrennikov, A. Yu. (1998). Human subconscious as the *p*-adic dynamical system. *Journal of Theoretical Biology, 193*(2), 179–196. doi:10.1006/jtbi.1997.0604

Khrennikov, A. Yu. (2002). Classical and quantum mental models and Freud's theory of unconscious mind. In *Series in Mathematical Modelling in Physics, Enginnering and Cognitive Sciences* (Vol. 1). Växjö, Sweden: Växjö University Press.

Khrennikov, A. Yu. (2007). Toward an adequate mathematical model of mental space: Conscious/unconscious dynamics on *m*-adic trees. *Bio Systems, 90*(3), 656–675. doi:10.1016/j.biosystems.2007.02.004

Kissin, B. (1986). *Conscious and Unconscious Programs in the Brain.* New York, NY: Plenum Publishing Corporation; . doi:10.1007/978-1-4613-2187-3

Köhler, T. (2007). *Freuds Psychoanalyse. Eine Einführung* (2nd ed.). Stuttgart, Germany: W. Kohlhammer GmbH.

Kultgen, J. (1976). Lévi-Strauss on Unconscious Social Structures. *The Southwestern Journal of Philosophy, 7*(1), 153–159. doi:10.5840/swjphil19767118

Kuper, J. (Ed.). (1988). *A Lexicon of Psychology, Psychiatry and Psychoanalysis.* London, UK: Routledge.

La Mantia, F. (2017). From Topology to Quasi-Topology. The Complexity of the Notional Domain. In Lecture Notes in Morphogenesis: Vol. 5. Language in Complexity: The Emerging Meaning. Springer International Publishing.

Lacan, J. (2014). *The Seminar of Jacques Lacan. Book X: The Anxiety (J. A. Miller* (A. R. Price Trans. & Ed.). Malden, MA: Polity Press.

Lacas, M.-L. (2007). La démarche originale de Gisela Pankow. Gisela Pankows original thought processes. LÉvolution Psychiatrique, 72(1), 15–24. 10.1016/j.evopsy.2006.11.001

Lagache, D. (1961). La psychanalyse et la structure de la personnalité. In *La psycanalyse. Recherche et enseignement Freudiens de la Société Française de Psychanalyse, N. 6: Perspectives structurales.* Paris: Presses Universitaires de France-PUF.

Lagache, D. (1965). Le modèle psychanalytique de la personnalité. In *La Folle du Logis. La psychanalyse comme science exacte* (pp. 159–183). Paris: PUF-Presses Universitaires de France.

Lakatos, I. (1978). *Philosophical Papers.* Cambridge, UK: Cambridge University Press.

Lambert, K., & Brittain, G. G. Jr. (1979). *An Introduction to the Philosophy of Science.* Reseda, CA: Ridgeview Publishing Company.

Lample-De-Groot, J. (1962). Ego ideal and Superego. *The Psychoanalytic Study of the Child, 17,* 94–106.

Langs, R. (1990). Guida alla psicoterapia. Un'introduzione all'approccio comunicativo. Torino, Italy: Bollati Boringhieri editore.

Laplanche, J. (2000). *Problematiche II. Castrazione. Simbolizzazioni.* Bari-Roma, Italy: La Biblioteca.

Laplanche, J. (2001). *L'inconscio e l'Es.* Bari-Roma, Italy: La Biblioteca.

Laplanche, J. (2007). *L'après-coup.* Bari-Roma, Italy: La Biblioteca.

Laplanche, J., & Pontalis, J.-B. (1967). *Vocabulaire de la psychoanalyse.* Paris: Presses Universitaires de France.

Laplanche, J., & Pontalis, J.-B. (1988). Fantasma originario, fantasmi delle origini, origini del fantasma. Bologna, Italy: Società editrice il Mulino.

Lauro-Grotto, R. (2008). The unconscious as an ultrametric set. *The American Imago, 64*(4), 52–62. doi:10.1353/aim.2008.0009

Lauro-Grotto, R. (2014a). Formal Approaches in the Age of Mirror Neurons. Hints from Psychoanalytic Theories and Practice. In *Proceedings of the 2014 IEEE 13th International Conference on Cognitive Informatics and Cognitive Computing.* Los Alamitos, CA: IEEE Computer Society Press.

Lauro-Grotto, R. (2014b). Paradigmi metapsicologici. Con tre scritti inediti di Freud. Pisa, Italy: ETS-Editrice tecnico-scientifica.

Lenz Dunker, I. (2008). Psychology and Psychoanalysis in Brazil. From Cultural Syncretism to the Collapse of Liberal Individualism. *Theory & Psychology, 18*(2), 223–236. doi:10.1177/0959354307087883

Lerner, D. (Ed.). (1961). *Quality and Quantity.* New York, NY: The Free Press of Glencoe.

Lévi-Strauss, C. (1975). *Razza e storia e altri studi di antropologia.* Torino, Italy: Giulio Einaudi editore.

Lévi-Strauss, C. (2008). Sull'Italia. In *Claude Lévi-Strauss fotografato da Marion Kalter*. Napoli, Italy: Electa Napoli.

Lévi-Strauss, C., & Eribon, D. (1988). *Da vicino e da lontano. Discutendo con Claude Lévi-Strauss.* Milano, Italy: Rizzoli.

Lewin, R. (1996). Communicating with the schizophrenic superego. *The Journal of the American Academy of Psychoanalysis, 24*(4), 709–736.

Lis, A., Mazzeschi, C., & Zennaro, A. (2007). *La psicoanalisi. Un percorso concettuale fra tradizione e attualità* (2nd ed.). Roma, Italy: Carocci editore.

Lis, A., Zennaro, A., Mazzeschi, C., Salcuni, S., & Parolin, L. (2003). *Breve dizionario di psicoanalisi.* Roma, Italy: Carocci editore.

Loewald, H. W. (1962). The Superego and the Ego-Ideal. II. Superego and Time. *The International Journal of Psycho-Analysis, 43*, 264–268.

Loewald, H. W. (1988). *Sublimation. Inquires into Theoretical Psychoanalysis.* New Haven, CT: Yale University Press.

Loewald, H. W. (1989). *Papers on Psychoanalysis.* New Haven, CT: Yale University Press.

Lolli, G. (1991). Introduzione alla logica formale. Bologna, Italy: Società editrice il Mulino.

Lolli, G. (2000). Un logico esamina i modelli mentali. In *Ragionamento: psicologia e logica*. Firenze, Italy: Giunti Gruppo Editoriale.

Lolli, G. (2005). *QED – Fenomenologia della dimostrazione.* Torino, Italy: Bollati Boringhieri editore.

Longhin, L. (1992). *Alle origini del pensiero psicoanalitico.* Roma, Italy: Edizioni Borla.

Longhin, L. (2016). *La mente emotiva. Conoscerla e curarla.* Milano, Italy: FrancoAngeli.

Longhin, L., & Mancia, M. (1998). Temi e problemi in psicoanalisi. Torino, Italy: Bollati Boringhieri editore.

Luborsky, L., & Crits-Christoph, P. (1992). *Capire il transfert.* Milano, Italy: Raffaello Cortina Editore.

Lusetti, V. (2008). *Psicopatologia antropologica.* Roma, Italy: EUR-Edizioni Universitarie Romane.

Macola, E. (Ed.). (2014). Sublimazione e perversione. Attualità Lacaniana. Rivista della Scuola Lacaniana di Psicoanalisi, 18, 7-108.

Maffei, L. (2014). Elogio della lentezza. Bologna, Italy: Società editrice il Mulino.

Maffei, L. (2016). Elogio della ribellione. Bologna, Italy: Società editrice il Mulino.

Mancia, M. (Ed.). (1990). *Super-Io e Ideale dell'Io.* Roma, Italy: Casa Editrice Astrolabio-Ubaldini Editore.

Mancia, M. (Ed.). (2006). *Psychoanalysis and Neuroscience.* Milan, Italy: Springer-Verlag Italia; . doi:10.1007/88-470-0550-7

Manzi, G. (2013). Il grande racconto dell'evoluzione umana. Bologna, Italy: Società editrice il Mulino.

Marchi, D. (2016). *Il mistero di Homo naledi. Chi era e come viveva il nostro lontano cugino africano: storia di una scoperta rivoluzionaria*. Milano, Italy: Mondadori Libri.

Marcuse, H. (1964). *One-Dimensional Man. Studies in the Ideology of Advanced Industrial Society*. Boston, MA: Beacon Press, Inc.

Matte Blanco, I. (1975). *The Unconscious as Infinite Sets. An Essay in Bi-Logic*. London, UK: Gerald Duckworth & Company, Ltd.

McCulloch, W. S. (1965). *Embodiments of Mind*. Cambridge, MA: The MIT Press.

Mendes, E. P. R. (1995). Vicissitudes da clínica psicanalítica contemporânea. *Reverso (Belo Horizonte)*, 40.

Miller, P. H. (1983). *Theories of Developmental Psychology*. New York, NY: W.H. Freeman & Co.

Milrod, D. (2002). The superego. Its formation, structure, and functioning. *The Psychoanalytic Study of the Child*, *57*, 131–148.

Minsky, M. (1975). A Framework for the Representation Knowledge. In *The Psychology of Computer Vision*. New York, NY: McGraw-Hill Book Company.

Mitchell, S. A., & Black, M. J. (1995). *Freud and beyond. A History of Modern Psychoanalysic Thought*. New York, NY: Basic Books. A Division of Harper Collins Publishers.

Moore, B. E., & Fine, B. D. (Eds.). (1990). *Psychoanalytic Terms and Concepts*. New York, NY: The American Psychoanalytic Association.

Moore, D. S. (2015). *The Developing Genome. An Introduction to Behavioural Epigenetics*. New York, NY: Oxford University Press.

Mordant, I. (1990). Using attribute-memories to resolve a contradiction in the work of Matte Blanco. *The International Review of Psycho-Analysis*, *17*, 475–480.

Murtagh, F. (2012a). Ultrametric model of mind, I [Review]. p-Adic Numbers, Ultrametric. *Analysis and Applications*, *4*(3), 193–206. doi:10.1134/S2070046612030041

Murtagh, F. (2012b). Ultrametric model of mind, II. Application to text content analysis. p-Adic Numbers, Ultrametric. *Analysis and Applications*, *4*(3), 207–221. doi:10.1134/S2070046612030053

Murtagh, F. (2013). The new science of complex systems through ultrametric analysis. Application to search and discovery, to narrative and to thinking. p-Adic Numbers, Ultrametric. *Analysis and Applications*, *5*(4), 326–337. doi:10.1134/S2070046613040067

Murtagh, F. (2014a). Pattern recognition of subconscious underpinnings of cognition using ultrametric topological mapping of thinking and memory. *International Journal of Cognitive Informatics and Natural Intelligence*, *8*(4), 1–16. doi:10.4018/ijcini.2014100101

Murtagh, F. (2014b). Mathematical representations of Matte Blancos bi-logic, based on metric space and ultrametric or hierarchical topology: Towards practical application. Language and Psychoanalysis, *3*(2), 40–63. 10.7565/landp.2014.008

Murtagh, F. (2014c). Pattern Recognition in Mental Processes: Determining Vestiges of the Subconscious through Ultrametric Component Analysis. In *Proceedings of the 2014 IEEE 13th International Conference on Cognitive Informatics and Cognitive Computing*. Los Alamitos, CA: IEEE Computer Society Press; . doi:10.1109/ICCI-CC.2014.6921455

Murtagh, F. (2017). *Data Science Foundations. Geometry and Topology of Complex Hierarchic Systems and Big Data Analytics*. Boca Raton, FL: Chapman & Hall/CRC Press.

Murtagh, F., & Iurato, G. (2016). Human Behaviour, Benign or Malevalent: Understanding the Human Psyche, Performing Therapy, based on Affective Mentalization and Matte-Blancos Bi-Logic. *Annals of Translational Medicine*, *4*(24), 486–496. doi:10.21037/atm.2016.12.37

Murtagh, F., & Iurato, G. (2017). (in press). Visualization of Jacques Lacan's Registers of the Psychoanalytic Field, and Discovery of Metaphor and of Metonymy. Analytical Case Study of Edgar Allan Poe's "The Purloined Letter". *Language and Psychoanalysis*.

Nagel, T. (1993). Summary. In *Experimental and Theoretical Studies of Consciousness. Novartis Foundation Symposium No.* 174. New York, NY: John Wiley & Sons, Ltd.

Nannini, S. (2007). *Naturalismo cognitivo. Per una teoria materialistica della mente*. Macerata, Italy: Edizioni Quodlibet.

Nannini, S. (2011). *L'anima e il corpo. Un'introduzione storica alla filosofia della mente*. Roma-Bari, Italy: Laterza Editori.

Nannini, S. (2015). Time and Consciousness in Cognitive Naturalism. *Rivista Internazionale di Filosofia e Psicologia*, *6*(3), 458–473.

Napolitano, F. (2009). Rappresentazione, 2. In *Psiche. Dizionario storico di psicologia, psichiatria, psicoanalisi, neuroscienze* (Vol. 2, pp. 919–923). Torino, IT: Giulio Einaudi editore.

Neubauer, K. (2004). Semantica storica. In Dizionario degli studi culturali. Roma, Italy: Meltemi editore.

Neuman, Y. (2014). *Introduction to Computational Cultural Psychology*. Cambridge, UK: Cambridge University Press.

Neuman, Y. (2016). *Computational Personality Analysis. Introduction, Practical Applications and Novel Directions*. Springer International Publishing.

Nunberg, H. (1932). *Allgemeine Neurosenlehre auf psychoanalytischer Grundlage* [Principles of psychoanalysis: Their application to the neuroses]. Berlin: Verlag Hans Hüber.

Oliverio, A. (1982). *Biologia e comportamento*. Bologna, Italy: Nicola Zanichelli Editore.

Oliverio, A. (2016). Il cervello e linconscio. Psicobiettivo, 36(3), 251–259. 10.3280/PSOB2016-003015

Oliverio, A. (2017). *Il cervello che impara. Neuropedagogia dall'infanzia alla vecchiaia*. Firenze, Italy: Giunti Editore.

Palombi, F. (2002). *Il legame instabile. Attualità del dibattito psicoanalisi-scienza*. Milano, Italy: FrancoAngeli.

Pankow, G. (1977). *L'uomo e la sua psicosi*. Milano, Italy: Giangiacomo Feltrinelli Editore.

Pankow, G. (1979). *Struttura familiare e psicosi*. Milano, Italy: Giangiacomo Feltrinelli Editore.

Panksepp, J., & Biven, L. (2012). *The Archeology of Mind. Neuroevolutionary Origins of Human Emotion*. New York, NY: W.W. Norton & Company.

Papagno, C. (2010). Neuropsicologia della memoria. Bologna, Italy: Società editrice il Mulino.

Parsons, T. (1970). *Social Structure and Personality*. New York, NY: The Free Press. A Division of The Macmillan Company.

Petit, C., & Prévost, G. (1971). Genetica ed evoluzione. Milano, Italy: Arnoldo Mondadori Editore.

Petocz, A. (2004). *Freud, psychoanalysis and symbolism*. Cambridge, UK: Cambridge University Press.

Petrilli, S., & Ponzio, A. (2005). *Semiotics Unbounded. Interpretive Routes Through the Open Network of Signs*. Toronto: The University of Toronto Press; . doi:10.3138/9781442657113

Petrini, P., Casadei, A., & Chiricozzi, F. (Eds.). (2011). *Trasgressione, violazione, perversione. Eziopatogenesi, diagnosi e terapia*. Milano, Italy: FrancoAngeli.

Petrini, P., Renzi, A., Casadei, A., & Mandese, A. (2013). *Dizionario di psicoanalisi. Con elementi di psichiatria, psicodinamica e psicologia dinamica*. Milano, Italy: FrancoAngeli.

Piattelli Palmarini, M. (1987). *Scienza come cultura. Protagonisti, luoghi e idee delle scienze contemporanee*. Milano, Italy: Arnoldo Mondadori Editore.

Pierce, B. C. (2002). *Types and Programming Languages*. Cambridge, MA: The MIT Press.

Pieri, P. F. (2005). *Dizionario junghiano (Edizione ridotta)*. Torino, Italy: Bollati Boringhieri editore.

Piscicelli, U. (1994). *Sessuologia. Teoremi psicosomatici e relazionali*. Padova, Italy: Piccin Nuova Libraria.

Pizzi, C. (Ed.). (1974). *La logica del tempo*. Torino, Italy: Bollati Boringhieri Editore.

Poggi, S. (1977). I sistemi dell'esperienza. Bologna, Italy: Società editrice il Mulino.

Poincaré, H. J. (1958). *The Value of Science*. New York, NY: Dover Publications, Inc.

Pollo, M. (2016). *La nostalgia dell'uroboros. Contributi a una psicologia culturale delle nuove addiction*. Milano, Italy: FrancoAngeli.

Possenti, V. (Ed.). (1979). *Epistemologia e scienze umane*. Milano, Italy: Editore Massimo.

Putnam, H. (1956). Mathematics and the Existence of Abstract Entities. *Philosophical Studies, 7*(6), 81–88. doi:10.1007/BF02221758

Putnam, H. (1975). *Filosofia della logica. Nominalismo e realismo nella logica contemporanea*. Milano, Italy: ISEDI – Istituto Editoriale Internazionale.

Rayner, E. (1995). *Unconscious Logic. An Introduction to Matte Blanco's Bi-Logic and its Uses*. New York, NY: Routledge.

Rayner, E. (1998). Foreword. In *The Unconscious as Infinite Sets. An Essay in Bi-Logic* (pp. xviii–xxiv). London, UK: Karnac Books, Ltd.

Recalcati, M. (2003). *Introduzione alla psicoanalisi contemporanea*. Milano, Italy: Bruno Mondadori Editore.

Recalcati, M. (2007a). *Elogio dell'inconscio. Dodici argomenti in difesa della psicoanalisi*. Milano, Italy: Bruno Mondadori.

Recalcati, M. (2007b). Lo psicoanalista e la città. L'inconscio e il discorso del capitalista. Roma, Italy: manifestolibri.

Recalcati, M. (2010). *L'uomo senza inconscio. Figure della nuova clinica psicoanalitica*. Milano, Italy: Raffaello Cortina Editore.

Recalcati, M. (2016). *Jacques Lacan* (Vol. 1-2). Milano, Italy: Raffaello Cortina Editore.

Redondi, P. (2007). *Storie del tempo*. Roma-Bari, Italy: Editori Laterza.

Reich, A. (1954). Early identifications as archaic elements in the Superego. *Journal of the American Psychoanalytic Association, 2*(2), 218–238. doi:10.1177/000306515400200203

Reverberi, C., Pischedda, D., Burigo, M., & Cherubini, P. (2012). Deduction without awareness. *Acta Psychologica, 139*(1), 244–253. doi:10.1016/j.actpsy.2011.09.011

Riolo, F. (2009). Trasformazione. In *Psiche. Dizionario storico di psicologia, psichiatria, psicoanalisi, neuroscienze* (Vol. 2, pp. 1112–1116). Torino, Italy: Giulio Einaudi editore.

Rose, J. R. (Ed.). (2011). *Mapping Psychic Reality. Triangulation, Communication, and Insight. Psychoanalytic Ideas*. London, UK: Karnac Books, Ltd.

Rossi, R., De Fazio, F., Gatti, U., & Rocco, G. (2008, Feb.). Perizie e consulenze psichiatriche su Diamante Stefano, Stevanin Gianfranco, Bilancia Donato, Panini Giorgio. *POL.it – The Italian On Line Psychiatric Magazine*.

Roudinesco, E. (1997). *Jacques Lacan. Outline of a life, history of a system of thought*. Oxford, UK: Polity Press.

Roudinesco, E. (2008). *Da vicino e da lontano*. Claude Lévi-Strauss e la psicoanalisi. In *Lévi-Strauss Fuori di sé*. Macerata, Italy: Quodlibet.

Russo, J. A. (2007). Psychoanalysis in Brazil – Institutionalization and Dissemination among the Lay Public. *Estudios Interdisciplinarios de America Latina y el Caribe, 18*(1), 63–80.

Rycroft, C. (1968a). *A critical dictionary of psychoanalysis*. London, UK: Thomas Nelson & Sons, Ltd.

Rycroft, C. (1968b). *Imagination and reality. Psychoanalytical essays 1951–1961*. London, UK: The Hogarth Press, Ltd.

Sabbadini, A. (1979). Introduzione. In *Il tempo in psicoanalisi*. Milano, Italy: Giangiacomo Feltrinelli Editore.

Sanchez-Cardenas, M. (2011). Matte Blancos thought and epistemological pluralism in psychoanalysis. *The International Journal of Psycho-Analysis*, *92*(4), 811–831. doi:10.1111/j.1745-8315.2011.00381.x

Sanchez-Cardenas, M. (2016). Clinical applications of Matte Blancos thinking. *The International Journal of Psycho-Analysis*, *97*(6), 1547–1573. doi:10.1111/1745-8315.12515

Sandler, J., Holder, A., & Meers, D. (1963). The Ego Ideal and the Ideal Self. *The Psychoanalytic Study of the Child*, *18*, 139–158.

Sandler, J. J. (Ed.). (1981). La ricerca in psicoanalisi (vols. 1-2). Torino, Italy: Bollati Boringhieri editore.

Sannella, D., & Tarlecki, A. (2012). *Foundations of Algebraic Specification and Formal Software Development. Monographs in Theoretical Computer Science. An EATCS Series*. Berlin: Springer-Verlag; . doi:10.1007/978-3-642-17336-3

Sasso, G. (1982). *Le strutture anagrammatiche della poesia*. Milano, Italy: Giangiacomo Feltrinelli Editore.

Sasso, G. (1993). *La mente intralinguistica. L'instabilità del segno: anagrammi e parole dentro le parole*. Genova, Italy: Marietti Editore.

Sasso, G. (1999). *Struttura dell'oggetto e della rappresentazione*. Roma, Italy: Casa Editrice Astrolabio-Ubaldini Editore.

Sasso, G. (2005). *Psicoanalisi e Neuroscienze* [The development of consciousness]. Roma, Italy: Casa Editrice Astrolabio-Ubaldini Editore.

Sasso, G. (2011). *La nascita della coscienza*. Roma, Italy: Casa Editrice Astrolabio-Ubaldini Editore.

Scabini, E. (1973). *Ideazione e psicoanalisi*. Milano, Italy: Giangiacomo Feltrinelli Editore.

Segalen, M. (1998). *Rites et rituels contemporains*. Paris: Les Éditions Nathan.

Semi, A. A. (Ed.). (1989). *Trattato di Psicoanalisi* (Vol. 1-2). Milano, Italy: Raffaello Cortina Editore.

Semi, A. A. (2003). *La coscienza in psicoanalisi*. Milano, Italy: Raffaello Cortina Editore.

Severino, E. (2008). *La strada. La follia e la gioia*. Milano, Italy: BUR Saggi.

Siri, G. (Ed.). (1976). *Problemi epistemologici della psicologia*. Milano, Italy: Vita e Pensiero.

Skelton, R. (1984). Understanding Matte Blanco. *The International Journal of Psycho-Analysis*, *65*, 453–460.

Skelton, R. (1990). Generalizations from Freud to Matte Blanco. *The International Review of Psycho-Analysis*, *17*, 471–474.

Sluzki, C. E., & Ransom, D. C. (1979). *Il doppio legame: la genesi dell'approccio relazionale allo studio della famiglia*. Roma, Italy: Casa Editrice Astrolabio-Ubaldini Editore.

Smirnov, V. N. (1970). *La transaction fétichique*. Nouvelle Revue de Psychoanalyse, 2.

Somenzi, V. (1998). Prefazione. In *Categorie, tempo e linguaggio. Quaderni di Methodologia, N. 5*. Roma, Italy: Società Stampa Sportiva.

Spedini, G. (2005). *Antropologia evoluzionistica* (2nd ed.). Padova, Italy: Piccin Nuova Libraria.

Spitz, R. A. (1957). *No and yes. On the genesis of human communication*. New York, NY: International University Press, Inc.

Steedman, M. (2000). *Surface Structure and Interpretation*. Boston, MA: The MIT Press.

Tabossi, P. (2009). Rappresentazione, 1. In *Psiche. Dizionario storico di psicologia, psichiatria, psicoanalisi, neuroscienzel* (Vol. 2, pp. 914–919). Torino, Italy: Giulio Einaudi editore.

Tallis, R. (2002). *Hidden Minds. A History of the Unconscious*. New York, NY: Arcade Publishing, Inc.

Target, M., & Fonagy, P. (2002). The role of the father and child development. In *The Importance of Fathers. A Psychoanalytic Re-evaluation*. London, UK: Routledge.

Terminio, N. (2009). Misurare l'inconscio? Coordinate psicoanalitiche nella ricerca in psicoterapia. Milano, IT: Bruno Mondadori.

Thomä, H., & Kächele, H. (1989). *Psychoanalytic Practice* (Vol. 1-2). Berlin: Springer-Verlag.

Tibaldi, M. (2004). Critica archetipica. In Dizionario degli studi culturali. Roma, Italy: Meltemi editore.

Toraldo di Francia, G. (1976). *L'indagine del mondo fisico*. Torino, Italy: Giulio Einaudi editore.

Uznadze, D. N., Prangisvili, A. S., Bassin, F. V., & Razran, G. (1972). *L'inconscio nella psicologia sovietica*. Roma, Italy: Editori Riuniti.

Vaccarino, G. (2006). *Scienza e semantica*. Milano, Italy: Edizioni Melquiades.

Vallortigara, G., & Panciera, N. (2014). *Cervelli che contano*. Milano, Italy: Adelphi Edizioni.

Vattimo, G., Ferraris, M., & Marconi, D. (Eds.). (1993). *Enciclopedia Garzanti di Filosofia*. Milano, Italy: Garzanti Editore.

Vegetti Finzi, S. (Ed.). (1976). *Il bambino nella psicoanalisi*. Bologna, Italy: Nicola Zanichelli Editore.

Verdiglione, A. (1977). Matematica dell'inconscio. In *Feticismo, linguaggio, afasia, matematica dell'inconscio*. Venezia, Italy: Marsilio Editori.

Vicario, G. B. (1997). Il tempo in psicologia. *Le Scienze*, *30*(347), 43–51.

Vicario, G. B. (2005). Il tempo. Saggio di psicologia sperimentale. Bologna, Italy: Società editrice il Mulino.

Viret, J. (2012). Topological Approach of Jungian Psychology. *Acta Biotheoretica*, *58*(2), 233–245.

Von Scheve, C., & Salmela, M. (Eds.). (2014). *Collective Emotions. Perspectives from Psychology, Philosophy, and Sociology*. Oxford, UK: Oxford University Press.

Wang, Y. (2008). On Concept Algebra: A Denotational Mathematical Structure for Knowledge and Software Modeling. *International Journal of Cognitive Informatics and Natural Intelligence*, *2*(2), 1–19. doi:10.4018/jcini.2008040101

Wang, Y. (2010). A Sociopsychological Perspective on Collective Intelligence in Metaheuristic Computing. *International Journal of Applied Metaheuristic Computing, 1*(1), 110–128. doi:10.4018/jamc.2010102606

Wang, Y., Wang, Y., Patel, S., & Patel, D. (2006). A Layered Reference Model of the Brain. *IEEE Transactions on Systems, Man and Cybernetics. Part C, Applications and Reviews, 36*(2), 124–133. doi:10.1109/TSMCC.2006.871126

Wang, Y., Zadeh, L. A., Widrow, B., Howard, N., Wood, S., Patel, S., & Zhang, D. et al. (2017). Abstract Intelligence: Embodying and Enabling Cognitive Systems by Mathematical Engineering. *International Journal of Cognitive Informatics and Natural Intelligence, 11*(1), 1–22. doi:10.4018/IJCINI.2017010101

Wang, Y., Zhang, D., & Kinsner, D. (Eds.). (2011). *Advances in Cognitive Informatics and Cognitive Computing*. Berlin: Springer-Verlag.

Watanabe, S. (1969). *Knowing and Guessing. A Quantitative Study of Inference and Information*. New York, NY: John Wiley & Sons, Inc.

Watzlawick, P., Beavin, J. H., & Jackson, D. D. (1967). *Pragmatics of Human Communication. A Study of Interactional Patterns, Pathologies, and Paradoxes*. New York, NY: W.W. Norton & Company.

Westphal, B. (2007). *La Géocritique. Réel, fiction, espace*. Paris: Les Éditions de Minuit.

White, D. R., & Jorion, P. (1996). Kinship networks and discrete structure theory: Applications and implications. *Social Networks, 18*(3), 267–314. doi:10.1016/0378-8733(95)00277-4

Whitebook, J. (1995). *Perversion and Utopia. A Study in Psychoanalysis and Critical Theory*. Cambridge, MA: The MIT Press.

Whitrow, G. J. (1988). *Time in History. Views of Time from Prehistory to the Present Day*. Oxford, UK: Oxford University Press.

Wimmer, M., & Ciompi, L. (1996). Evolutionary aspects of affective-cognitive interactions in the light of Ciompi's concept of "affect-logic". *Evolution & Cognition, 2*, 37–58.

Yang, J., Kanazawa, S., Yamaguchi, M. K., & Kuriki, I. (2016). Cortical response to categorical colour perception in infants investigated by near-infrared spectroscopy. *Proceedings of the National Academy of Sciences of the United States of America, 113*(9), 2370–2375.

Zadeh, L. A. (1965). Fuzzy Sets. *Information and Control, 8*(3), 338–353. doi:10.1016/S0019-9958(65)90241-X

Zadeh, L. A. (1968). Fuzzy Algorithms. *Information and Control, 12*(2), 94–102. doi:10.1016/S0019-9958(68)90211-8

Zadeh, L. A. (1988). Fuzzy Logic. *Computer, 21*(4), 83–93. doi:10.1109/2.53

Zapparoli, G. C. (1970). *La perversione logica. I rapporti tra sessualità e pensiero nella tradizione psicoanalitica*. Milano, Italy: Franco Angeli Editore.

Zeh, H. D. (2007). *The Physical Basis of the Direction of Time* (5th ed.). Berlin: Springer-Verlag.

Zepf, S., & Gerlach, A. (2012). Commentary on Kernbergs suicide prevention for psychoanalytic institutes and societies. *Journal of the American Psychoanalytic Association*, *61*(4), 771–786. doi:10.1177/0003065113496634

ENDNOTES

[1]   Maybe due to the obvious fact that, seen the arguments treated by psychoanalysis, natural resistances arise just in regard to psychoanalysis itself.

[2]   Which seems nowadays confirmed by recent neuropsychology research on mathematical abilities (Vallortigara & Panciera, 2014).

[3]   Meant in its widest philosophical sense.

[4]   *Comprende* in French, *Verstehen* in German, *comprendere* in Italian.

[5]   Likewise, Umberto Galimberti (1979) has pointed out that psychological sciences cannot use explanation methods typical of natural sciences, because human behaviour must be understood not explained, otherwise we risk to reduce human being to a mere natural phenomenon (as in psychiatry), neglecting all the other complex phenomenology (meant in its widest philosophical sense) that characterizes her or him, which escapes from scientific description and detection.

[6]   See (Battacchi, 2006).

[7]   See also (Iurato, 2016b). On the other hand, Vittorio Somenzi (1998) pointed out that, from certain re-interpretations of Kurt Gödel theorems (as those made by Giuseppe Vaccarino (2006)), it seems impossible to do a rational analysis of the relationships among brain, mind (or thought) and language, with the consequent impossibility to formulate these in terms of the present status of artificial intelligence, so it seems also licit to see toward other directions, like the one falling into the domain of psychoanalysis and its possible relations with exact sciences.

[8]   Just in this regard, see (Terminio, 2009), where a detailed and clear discussion about the existence of unconscious and how it may be empirically detected, is given.

[9]   In this regard, let us say immediately, in what follows we shall make reference to physics and other natural sciences, not for borrowing their scientific patterns in view of their possible application to psychoanalysis, but rather for considering possible conceptual analogies and similarities at a theoretical level (like the linguistic one, hence related to possible formalization attempts on the analogical basis provided by mathematics), not at the procedural or experimental one. This, because psychoanalysis and natural sciences have to do, in general, with different realities, or else, different levels or aspects of the same reality. On the other hand, it seems that *unconscious* is a construct which, just for its peculiar nature, is not liable to undergo measurements in the operative sense of natural sciences; cf. (Terminio, 2009).

[10]   Cf. (Laplanche & Pontalis, 1967, 1988).

[11]   According to a process quite similar, formally, to a *symmetry breaking* (on *A*), as will be discussed later.

[12]   This Other, should be then identified with the *a priori* Kantian forms, or with those universal, pre-existing formal structures of which we shall talk about at the end of this chapter.

[13]   In this section, we closely follow, often almost verbatim, the brief but very meaningful work (Boczar et al., 2001), which explains the main epistemological positions of the *Círculo Psicanalítico de Minas Gerais*, Brazil. See also (Lenz Dunker, 2008) and (Russo, 2007).

[14]   Cf. (Bria & Caroppo, 2006) and (Lusetti, 2008).

[15]   In this regard, see (Mendes, 1995) and (Recalcati, 2010).

[16]   See (Mendes, 1995).

[17]   Here, we follow (Conrotto 2014, Ch. 2).

[18]   See also (Egidi, 1979, 1992) in regard to relativism in contemporary epistemology and other general questions.

[19]   In this regard, Freud himself said that the first, early justification of the psychoanalytic concepts should come from their experimentation or application on herself or himself, deeming they more or less valid in dependence on the result of their comparison with our own life experience and personal past.

[20]   In this regard, see (Freni, 1992). This feature, i.e., the relief from psychic suffering, relying on the outcomes of an analytical setting (and, in general, of every other psychological therapy), which allows to identify epistemological bases conferring scientific status to a psychological discipline, just within the community of operators professing such a clinical treatment, is centrally important and usually accredited as such (Carotenuto 1982, 1991; 1992, Premessa). Nevertheless, just in reference to the psychoanalytic context, it is not the *insights* coming from the analytical setting (no matter the psychoanalytic trend followed) and its related interpretations, to give rise the healing (Benvenuto 2005, Ch. 4, Sect. 4.2.), but rather other intersubjectives factors which, being common to almost all psychoanalytic trends, suggest there are underlying objective reasons to this, which therefore would turn out to be useful just in searching of possible scientific requisites to be conferred to psychoanalytic disciplines (Kächele, 2001).

[21]   *Objectivity* is the typical feature of a scientific knowledge which is reached by means of its own methodology of research related to the objects falling into this field of knowledge; the choice of such objects is what is identified as the *objectuality* of such a knowledge.

[22]   In this, satisfying those personal, singular and subjective requirements that psychoanalysis has always reclaimed as typical and distinctive of its therapeutic praxis (Recalcati, 2007a).

[23]   Instances of these, may be provided by the so-called *primal phantasies*; see (Laplanche & Pontalis, 1967, 1988). On the other hand, recent neurobiological research has identified archaic, ancestral structures, phylogenetically established and very ancient, which preside over emotive-affective phenomenology according to certain mechanisms shared with other animals, hence universal (Panksepp & Biven, 2012).

[24]   See, for example, (Iurato, 2015a) and, above all, (Kultgen, 1976).

[25]   Cf. (Nannini, 2011).

[26]   They basically are innate (i.e., *a priori*, just in the Kantian sense) interpretative schemas, which have arisen from the very long phylogenetic route of human evolution (mainly, during *homination* process), and have a chief *generative* function, in a similar way to that provided by Noam Chomsky's *transformative-generative grammars*.

[27]   Cf. (Conrotto 2014, p. 99).

Chapter 2
Some Basic Elements of Psychoanalysis According to Sigmund Freud

ABSTRACT

After having briefly but exhaustively recalled the main lines of Freudian psychoanalytic thought, we have discussed a possible psychoanalytic theoretical model for human symbolic function mainly centred on the action of a set of primary psychic mechanisms rejoined around the negative, in its widest sense according to the works of André Green. A chief aspect of this pattern has turned out to be an underlying, irreducible dialecticity that reflects on the one hand, the typical feature of human symbolic function, and, on the other hand, the main outcome of the unavoidable presence of a basic dichotomy formalized the so-called phallic logic, that is, that primordial, ancestral and irreducible logical nucleus inevitably present in the deepest meanders of human psyche as an inborn structure phylogenetically preformed and ontogenetically re-established during the psychic evolution of any human being.

2.1. INTRODUCTION

Matte Blanco's psychoanalytic theory starts mainly from orthodox framework of psychoanalysis according to Sigmund Freud. Thus, in this chapter, we recall some basic elements of Freudian theory, which will turn out to be useful in the next chapters. On the basis of these, then, we expose a possible formal model of human symbolic function, mainly centred on splitting processes which confer a binary discreteness as a founding ground which sinks own roots even into the unconscious as we shall see, and however upon which then it will be possible to build up a binary formal logic pattern liable of possible informatics implementations. So, it seems that binary logic is the founding logical nucleus of human psyche, from unconscious to consciousness.

As we have recalled in the previous chapter, many different aspects of human psyche require as much different theories to account for their psychological nature. So, psychology has a typical historical feature inasmuch as the knowledge of human psyche is given by the totality of the various psychological theories

DOI: 10.4018/978-1-5225-4128-8.ch002

as established in a given historical period. This epistemological feature of psychology is mainly due to the intrinsic diachronicity of human psyche.

From this standpoint, psychoanalysis is a theory of human psyche based on the crucial notion of unconscious. It is a corpus of hypotheses related to mental development and functioning of human psyche moulded by dynamical patterns centrally based on the construct of unconscious. Along his whole scientific career, Freud gave different dynamical patterns of human psyche. In what follows, we shall give the strictly indispensable basic notions of psychoanalysis which will be need for working out those formal models underlying computational psychoanalysis simply meant as a reformulation of certain patterns of Freudian psychoanalysis susceptible to be formalized in view of a possible their informatics implementation.

2.2. THE BIRTH OF PSYCHOANALYSIS: A BRIEF HISTORICAL SURVEY AND A GENERAL INTRODUCTORY OVERVIEW

At the turn of the 18th century, from the conjunction between the philosophical thought and the neurological research, Sigmund Freud (1856-1939) started to build up his magnificent, monumental and revolutionary theory of human psyche turned to work out a new theoretical system and to set up an innovative psychotherapeutical method. The psychic apparatus of the human being is indeed theoretically describable on the base of the main assumption by which a fundamental importance for the whole human psychic life, is just played by the unconscious phenomenology, which is approachable only by means of a new, specific technique, the psychoanalytic method.

Freud begins to conceive his psychoanalytic ideas gradually, after a strong preliminary training in neurology. During the studies at the faculty of medicine, he attends the laboratory of physiology of Ernst von Brücke, where he meets Joseph Breuer, and the laboratory of zoology of Carl Friedrich Claus. After the degree in medicine in 1881, he moves to the psychiatric division of the general hospital of Wien, headed by Theodor Meynert.

In 1885, Freud moves to Paris, to attending lessons by Jean-Martin Charcot at the Salpêtrière, where he is fascinated by the new ideas of hysteria, hypnosis, traumatic neuroses introduced by Charcot. Then, he goes to Berlin, for studying paediatrics, hence, in Wien, he works at the institute headed by Max Kassovitz, specialized in neurological paediatrics, until up 1887. In the next decade, it takes place that scientific evolution which will lead Freud to work out his first theoretical and therapeutical system of human psyche.

Just in 1895, Freud publishes, in collaboration with Breuer, the first book on these new ideas, entitled *Studies on Hysteria*. From 1895 to 1899, he is in epistolary correspondence with Wilhelm Fliess, through which his psychoanalytic ideas consolidate even more, also thanks to a personal self-analysis. In 1895, he writes (but not publishes in that left unfinished) the *Project for a Scientific Psychology*, in which he tries to give a neurobiological basis to his new psychoanalytic ideas.

The first organic presentation of Freud's psychoanalytic ideas, is the celebrated book entitled *The Interpretation of Dreams*, published in 1900, which marks the official birth of psychoanalysis as a new theory of mind and as a groundbreaking psychotherapeutical method. In 1901, Freud publishes *The Psychopathology of Everyday Life*, and, in 1905, the *Three Essays on the Theory of Sexuality*, where many clinical cases are also described. Thanks to all these publications, Freud gradually acquires even more international knowledge, and, around him, a group of pupils starts to establish.

In 1908, the *Vienna Psychoanalytic Society* is founded, followed, in 1910, by the foundation of the *International Psychoanalytic Association*. The psychoanalysis starts to become an autonomous psychological discipline, although internal and external contrasts are also present. Some crucial divisions, internal to the new established psychoanalytic movement, give rise new psychological trends, like the *analytical psychology* of Carl Gustav Jung and the *individual psychology* of Alfred Adler. Notwithstanding that, psychoanalysis has gone on thanks to the steadiness of its founding father, until his death.

The route of Freudian thought has had its own gestation, from a twenty-years pre-psychoanalytic period in medicine and physiology until up reaching a metapsychological theory of mind worked out within a multidisciplinary framework including many disciplines, like philosophy, physics, anthropology, sociology, art, etc. From an initial training in anatomy and clinic, Freud reaches to neurophysiology and psychophysics, always with the aim to work out a psychological model of the mind.

The guiding pattern is the dynamical concept of neurosis, as acquired from the previous clinical experience. From this founding nucleus, Freud gradually accrues his dynamical model of human psyche, empirically supported by a new psychotherapeutical technique, which he shall call just *psychoanalysis*. The key theoretical concept of this new psychodynamic theory of mind, is that of *unconscious*, experimentally characterized, with respect to its wider philosophical notion, by the so-called *symptom*.

Many clinical techniques allow to explore unconscious: the *theory of dreams*, inasmuch as they are the fulfilment of an ungratified desire which explicates through manifest and latent contents; the *theory of parapraxes, quips and slips*; the *theory of hysteria*, with the notion of *repression*; the *technique of free association*, replacement of the hypnotic one; the idea of *transference*, around which revolves the whole psychoanalytic praxis. Just from the outcomes of these techniques, Freud builds up his original notion of unconscious, typical of psychoanalysis.

Freud founds his psychoanalytic theory on childhood sexuality, whose period is subdivided into phases of which the chief one is that regarding Œdipus complex. Neuroses are brought back to this crucial period of human life. In the years 1914-15, Freudian theory undergoes a first reorganization, becoming a *metapsychology* in which psychic phenomena are considered from three distinct points of view: the *topographic* standpoint (distinguishing among unconscious, preconscious, conscious – first topography of human psyche), the *dynamical* standpoint (centred on psychic conflicts) and the *economic* standpoint (ruled by pleasure-displeasure principle).

In this first reformulation, Freud prepares the bases for the fundamental notion of narcissism. In 1920, just within this metapsychological framework, Freud gives, on the base of clinical (above all, the compulsion to repeat principle) and epistemological (above all, the second principle of thermodynamics related to the notion of entropy) principles, a first double classification of psychic drives, into *life drive* and *death drive*. The last, remarkable development of the Freudian theoretical framework, is the second topography of human psyche, describing its functioning in terms of three agencies, the *Ego*, the *Super-Ego* and the *Es*.

Anyway, the influence of Freudian work on the whole culture of 20th century is inestimable. Besides the many criticisms moved to psychoanalysis, as conceived by Freud, it has been the great merit to have however vividly stimulated the problematic discussion and the critical reflection in every place of the cultural environment in which it could have some relationship or concern. So, psychoanalysis has surely marked a great and remarkable cultural revolution (Carotenuto, 1992).

2.3. THE MAIN CONCEPTS OF PSYCHOANALYSIS, I: ON THE UNCONSCIOUS

In this section, we give first a brief but complete historical outline of the notion of unconscious before Freud's work on this, which will be briefly outlined later.

2.3.1. The Unconscious Before the Coming of Psychoanalysis

The notion of unconscious has a central position in the dynamical psychology. The early history of the notion of unconscious belongs to the history of philosophical concepts[1], since then human being was aware of the need to admit the existence of a reality which be *other*, which go beyond the own awareness, to enlarge the field of knowledge. From a philosophical standpoint, unconscious may be meant in a three main senses: the psychological, the epistemological and the metaphysical one. The psychological sense refers to a psychic content owned by individual, as, for example, that stored in the memory but actually not thought by the subject. The philosophical sense refers to that content, or form of knowledge, which is deemed not derived from experience yet presents in the subject, coming from the deepest zones of psyche towards perceptive acts and judgments. Finally, the metaphysical one considers unconscious the universal essence of reality transcending every human being, hence the explicative principle of being and becoming (CSFG 1977, pp. 534-535).

First prolegomena to the notion of unconscious, although this term is never used, are retraceable in ancient Greek philosophy, in which unconscious phenomenology is identified in the *daìmon*, to be distinguished from the spirit or soul (*psyché*). Democritus had already understood that human being might be influenced by stimuli of which he or she is not aware. Plato makes then reference to a hidden knowledge into the deepness of soul, trapped by the body, which should be done aware by *anàmnesis*. Plato, in the *Teeteto*, distinguishes between "to posses" and "to have" a knowledge, that is to say, between an unaware (implicit) virtuality and an actual awareness (explicit). Aristotle gives much more weight to Plato's considerations, standing out the importance of those fugacious stimuli which however influence the perceptive experience of everyday life and, in particular, the content of dreams. In particular, unconscious, in its epistemological sense, will be acquired by *innatism*. Plotinus distinguishes between a lower and an upper region of soul, the former as the place of early intuition, the latter as the source of discursive thought.

Obviously, these are simple intuitions which however will appear later in the thought of Galen, St. Augustine, Michael de Montaigne. The unconscious dimension starts to assume a certain role only with Nicholas Malebranche according to whom, into the soul, there is an innate capability to receive an infinity of different changes which soul itself is not able to know as such. This standpoint will be retaken by Gottfried W. Leibniz who will give to it, a much more consistent epistemological basis to Malebranche's intuitions.

Indeed, first hints to a notion of unconscious are due to Leibniz, who speaks of "little perceptions", or "insensible perceptions", continuously operating, but not followed by a further reflection or awareness, that Leibniz calls *apperception*, and that, however, give rise to that "strange state of unknown and uncertainty yet clear in its whole image but confused in its parts"; these perceptions do not reach consciousness unless, integrating among them, they acquire an enough intensity to become apperceivable.

So, with the acknowledgement of little perceptions which escape to consciousness, and that stay at the basis of all the our non-determined actions, a first demarcation line arises between what is unconscious and, at the opposite side, what refers to full awareness or stays at the border of this.

The existence of this dark zone of human psyche, is then reconsidered by Christian Wolff, hence recognized by Immanuel Kant who, in opposition to John Locke's statement for which it is not possible to speak of mental representations which are not conscious because to have just mental representations means that these are conscious, reconsiders the notion of unconscious to state that "we may be *mediately* aware of a representation which is not *immediately* conscious".

With Kant, we shall have an anticipation of a wide range of different thematic trends which will develop later distinct next psychological trends. In particular, the identification of mental activities upon which we cannot have any information through experimentation, is an anticipation of what will be the subsequent cognitive unconscious. In his psychological lectures, Kant distinguishes between "obscure" and "clear" perceptions of objects in dependence on these are conscious or not. Furthermore, what is crucial for Kant, is that rules and laws, underlying the functioning of our psychic functions, are unconscious[2].

Johann F. Herbart retakes some Leibniz's arguments, and establishes a first method of study of psychological phenomena (which he calls *representations*) in relation to a certain threshold (*limen*) discriminating between conscious and unconscious realm, that is, between "strong" representations (of consciousness) and "weak" representations (belonging to unconscious), in dependence on their intensity. In this regard, Herbart speaks of *consciousness threshold*, upon which there are conscious representations, under which instead there are unconscious representations.

From an historical standpoint, Herbart's elaborations will be the starting point of the two main trends of 19th-century psychology: on the one hand, we have an orientation towards quantitative and estimating aspects of psychological phenomena, from which will spring out *psychophysics*, while, on the other hand, we have an orientation towards qualitative and dynamical aspects of these, from which will come *psychoanalysis*.

For instance, Herbart's consciousness threshold will be retaken by Gustav Fechner in the 1860s, according to a strict quantitative approach, to establish a possible relationship between entities of the external world (stimuli) and their psychic reproduction (sensations), introducing two distinct thresholds, namely the *absolute threshold* and the *differential threshold*. In particular, Fechner gives importance to the so-called "negative" sensations, the ones that lie under consciousness level in that related with underthreshold values which set up them into the unconscious realm[3].

But, it is with Friedrich Schelling that the unconscious is explicitly named, so becoming the germ of a first metaphysical conception, considering it as one of the two chief aspects of the *Absolute* which unifies nature and mind (or spirit), that is, unconscious and consciousness, which are closely related of each other. In general, the notion of unconscious is explicit in the romantic period of the philosophy of nature, like, for example, in the thought of Gotthilf V. von Schubert, Ignaz P. Troxler, Carl G. Carus, for which unconscious is the founding principle of the being, the invisible root of the whole universe, in which both nature and mind (or spirit) are joined, and from which then consciousness departs.

Hence, Arthur Schopenhauer considers unconscious as the will to live which forms the *Noumenon* of the world, that is to say, the thing in itself, or else the object of pure knowledge. His conception of unconscious will play a fundamental role in the next formulation of unconscious according to Freud and Jung, inasmuch as Schopenhauer considers it as the irrational and blind will operating in every human being by means of sexual and conservative drives. Finally, from all these conceptions, Eduard von Hartmann assigns to the unconscious the main function of structuration of the whole universal life by strata, of which then matter and mind (or spirit) are nothing but two different manifestations of the same principle, i.e., the unconscious.

Along this wake, the considerations of Henri Bergson are just placeable. Indeed, he strenuously defends the notion of unconscious, declaring that its rejection is simply due to the presupposition that consciousness is the main, essential feature of human psychic life. He notes that consciousness is characterized by the *present* moment of what is currently lived and experienced, that is to say, by what is acting. So, what is not acting may therefore not belong to consciousness, notwithstanding it has an its own existential status (i.e., unconscious). He therefore distinguishes between time and consciousness.

Gradually, from this philosophical conception of the notion of unconscious, also psychology and medicine start to consider it as having a scientific status. Besides the psychophysics contributions, with Carus, finally, the unconscious, in psychopathology, is being deemed the key to understand conscious life; likewise, in medicine, amongst others, Jean-Martin Charcot, Pierre Janet, Theodule Ribot and Théodore Flournoy, refer to the unconscious for understanding better certain notable psychic phenomena, like post-hypnotic suggestion, hysteric symptoms, psychomotor automatisms, sleepwalking.

As has been said above, retaking Herbart's notion of consciousness' threshold, under which all ideas are just unconscious, Fechner gives an image of human psyche as a kind of iceberg of which only the upper peak emerges as a conscious part, just the one usually called sometime into question to heuristically explain human psychic apparatus according to first topography claimed by Freudian psychoanalysis. Then, on the wake of Fechner's work, either Hermann von Helmholtz and Wilhelm Wundt retake some main themes of Leibnitzian-Herbartian tradition, as that of representation, apperception and unconscious inferences, to be treated more quantitatively than predecessors.

Helmholtz distinguishes the receptive sensorial process of external stimulation, i.e., the perception, from the more complex synthesizing process of apperception, which completes the sensorial data, coming from perception, with representations, unconscious inferences and previous experience. The perceptive act therefore explicates through a sequence of representations in which unconscious inferences (as called by Helmholtz) modulates their coordination (like, the spatial one) and warrants its constancy. Thus, the phenomenological horizon of perception is enlarged by representational activity, in that this is turned to involve all the related psychic processes, among which are just the unconscious inferences.

It seems then that unconscious processes are banned by Wundt's psychology, in that this last has, as main methodological principle, that according to which only consciousness phenomena are liable to be considered from a psychological standpoint. Nevertheless, as pointed out in (Poggi, 1977), Wundt himself tacitly sees the unconscious as a presupposition for any conscious psychic activity. Also Filipp V. Bassin[4] points out that, close to a negative view of unconscious by Wundt, there is another viewpoint of unconscious as a latent activity qualitatively specific of the brain, so able to exert its significant influence on behaviour.

From this last standpoint, the unconscious logic processes modulate the activity of consciousness, so it follows that the primary nature of psychic phenomena is basically unconscious, whose activity, suitably modified as a cognizable expression, underlies awareness. In particular, consciousness has the main task "to catch" what comes from intuition in turn closely related to unconscious activity. Therefore, Wundt's psychology admits the existence of a complex net of unconscious connections underlying phenomenological reverberations, which entails a continuum unconscious-conscious.

Also Edward Titchner, in the analysis of experience, admits the existence of a psychic elaboration which escapes from consciousness, like in rapid and automatic behaviours and executions, from which to infer just the existence of an unconscious component. Likewise, Oswald Külpe highlights the existence of a "thought without images", that is to say, the existence of certain mental contents of consciousness without any sensorial counterpart. Finally, also Henry J. Watt, in his studies on the word association, inferred the existence of an unconscious activity able to exert a certain control on the conscious one.

Gradually, from all these stances, unconscious seems to be treated even more theoretical than before, so we have, at the turn of 19th century, first bases for a theoretical construct of unconscious. But, notwithstanding that medicine and psychology of 19th century, given, although unwillingly, a certain scientific acknowledgement to the unconscious realm, only with the coming of Freudian psychoanalysis, this notion will acquire its full and highest importance either from the clinical and the theoretical standpoint, so becoming a theoretical construct which comprehends motivational aspects of human personality either normal and pathological.

Anyway, it is also useful historically to remember that, although unconscious was re-evaluated by psychologists of Würzburg, it was instead quite neglected in the work of Franz Brentano (as well as ambiguously treated by William James), whose studies on psychic phenomena had nevertheless importance for either Edmund Husserl and Freud. Indeed, Brentano's notion of *intentionality* will have a certain role also in the Freudian thought, even if it is considered in relation to the unconscious psychic activity rather than to the consciousness, like in Husserl (Abbagnano, 1998; Conte & Gennaro, 1989; Pieri, 2005; Vattimo et al., 1993).

3.2.2. The Unconscious According to Freud

Only with Freudian psychoanalysis, unconscious loses that indeterminacy and vagueness owned by its previous philosophical and psychological conceptions, for acquiring a more definite content given by the sexual tendencies which are, in some way, hidden into the human psyche. Thus, we can say that, only with Freud, unconscious acquires the specific nature of an autonomous theoretical construct, becoming the main component of a new psychological pattern of human psyche.

Before Freud, as briefly seen in the previous subsection, unconscious is deemed to be the dark and deep place of irrationality, "wild", incognizable and unattainable as such. With Freud, instead, a new definition of unconscious is worked out, with its own logic and rationality, as the place where lies human desire (i.e., the subject of the unconscious) which gives rise to any other consciousness manifestation. Freud, for the first time, tries to overcome that unbridgeable gap between affectivity and rationality which arose during romantic period.

Freud casts intertwinements between rational thought and unconscious realm, not considering any hierarchic structure of human psyche, with the unconscious (to be precise, the "subconscious") put at the early foundations of upper consciousness edifice, topographically separated of each other. Freud has not established a net antithesis between rationality and unconscious, as this latter has in itself its own logic; he rather has stressed on the unavoidable, active presence of unconscious *into* the consciousness, which both are set up in a twice channel of intentionality always in reciprocal interaction of each other. The unconscious is therefore a *ratio* which goes through consciousness. The conscious psychic phenomena are the minor part of the whole psychic life; besides, they are dependent on the unconscious (Recalcati, 2007a).

Nevertheless, these conclusions were accrued by Freud gradually, along the whole pathway of his rich and revolutionary professional life. Indeed, according to his first works, the psychic phenomena themselves are basically unconscious, the conscious ones being only isolated parts of the whole psychic life of humans, which is mainly switched on by sexual tendencies ruling not only individual life but also collective one. Thus, with Freud, it fails Locke's objection according to which a mental state exists only if it is perceived as such, so falling into the consciousness and vice versa, for which an unconscious mental state would be a contradiction in itself.

Instead, in psychoanalysis, a mental state exists when, although not perceived, it may be however put into evidence through well-determined methods and techniques, just those of psychoanalysis. These processes are quite indirect[5], in the sense that unconscious existence may be identified by means of certain circumstantialities or evidences, most of which are said to be *symptoms*, which are systematically observable only through these special psychoanalytic techniques. The symptom is the manifestation of a some psychic phenomenon which cannot be made conscious, or else, the consciousness itself refuses to accept as such, so undergoing to a transformation. So, just the symptom is the warranty of existence of the unconscious. Therefore, in agreement with Kant, Freudian unconscious is not perceivable directly but only indirectly, just *mediately* (Pieri, 2005).

The dreams, for instance, are not those encrypted messages coming from some divinity, but rather the words of the *Other*, that is to say, what has been rejected by ourselves into the unconscious, but that is always present near consciousness; this gives an unavoidable subjectivity's character to the unconscious, which however does not eliminate fully archetypical features. Just the emersion of the content of the unconscious is what will give rise the symptom. Freud has therefore pointed out the unavoidable presence of unconscious' pushes toward consciousness, which in general give rise to a symptomatic scenario (Recalcati, 2007a).

Human mind is always in activity, performing a great number of psychic functions either in vigil and sleep states, but only a little number of these reaches conscious threshold, in a certain temporal range. The affective dispositions closely related to drives, give rise to desires and motivations which aspire to become conscious, but this is hindered by other contrasting psychic forces (later called Ego and Super-Ego), which confer that typical *conflictual* dynamics, featuring human psyche. This dynamical characteristic was, for the first time, proposed by Freud, in a very distantly manner from the psychological tradition of the time. His new *metapsychological* theory is just turned to consider, into a whole, the various *dynamical*, *topographical* and *economical* aspects of psychic phenomena (Chemama & Vandermersch, 1998; Moore & Fine, 1990).

On the other hand, in philosophy, generally speaking, a concept is an idea which is abstract and general, regrouping objects[6] into classes of equivalence with respect to certain relationships. In this regard, the notion of unconscious, as presented by Freud, is further complicated by the fact that the concepts under discussion are just "unconscious", in other words, they are not the result of a process of judgment, to which Freud gives a certain precedence as a mental act[7]. The unconscious concepts, as defined by Freud, come very close to the notion of symbolic equivalence, which is fundamental for the notion of *symptom*. They also highlight the unconscious origins of thought in its connections above all with (anal) sensations and the related fantasy elaboration that arises from these (De Mijolla, 2005).

In Freud, unconscious has been meant in a double modality, namely, in a topographic way and in a descriptive way. These two standpoints have then provided two distinct patterns of human psyche, the former having a *structural* nature, the latter a *systemic* fashion. The *topographic* use of the term unconscious, as a substantive, refers to a certain place (*tòpos*) of human psyche if this latter is metaphorically considered as structured into spatial zones, while the *descriptive* use of the term unconscious, as an adjective, refers to the psychic contents outside current consciousness field; either these uses have however undergone variations, along the many different phases of Freudian thought. In what follows, we sketch the basic elements of both these uses.

The topographic use of unconscious dates back to the *Studies on Hysteria* of 1895, when Freud outlines the first elements of his theory on repression and psychoneuroses of defence, and where the term unconscious is explicitly adopted, for the first time, just as a substantive, for mental contents which are intolerable, forgotten or irreconcilable, hence expelled outside consciousness. Then, Freud considers sexual and pre-sexual childhood psychic traumas and desires, so descrying close and fundamental relations between unconscious contents and infantile sexual experiences, in the celebrated work *The Interpretation of Dreams* of 1900.

Hence, Freud defines psychoanalysis as the science of the unconscious-soul (*unbewusst-seelisch*) or psychology of the unconscious (in short, *Ucs.*). By means of the local aetiology of neurotic symptoms, he discovers that dreams are similarly constructed, so that *Ucs.* becomes a generic psychic system. In particular, from the study of hysteric phenomena, Freud infers that at least two psychic agencies are need to be considered to explain functioning of psychic apparatus, to be precise, a first one (said to be *preconscious*) which subordinates the activity of the other (i.e., the *Ucs.*), to criticize this latter and possibly to hindering, to its content, to go into consciousness. This content mainly consists of wishes – unconscious and indestructible – and repressed psychic contents, cathexed by the libido through free energy and regulated by pleasure-displeasure principle, while certain primary mechanisms (i.e., displacement and condensation) rule the *Ucs.*

The conflict between repressed material and censuring forces – which confers a dynamical feature to human psyche, so that psychoanalysis belongs to *dynamical psychology* – creates dreams and paradigmatic compromise-formations. The existence of *Ucs.* is therefore revealed through certain localized manifestations, such as joking, forgetting words, meaning shifts, image hybridizations, inversions, overlaps, and other symptomatic activities[8], which cannot be explained by means of conscious processes. The abbreviation *Ucs.* refers to unconscious in its substantive sense as a psychic system, while the abbreviation *ucs.* stands for unconscious in its adjective sense in reference to the contents of this system (Petrini et al., 2013; De Mijolla, 2005).

In the topographic use, therefore, unconscious is made by repressed contents whose access to the system preconscious-conscious has been forbidden just by *repression*. These are mainly childhood's desires which undergo a *fixation* into the unconscious[9]. The combination of these contents are ruled by two main mechanisms of primary process, *condensation* and *displacement*. Furthermore, since they are strongly cathexed by drive energy[10], these contents are however aimed always to come back to consciousness. Anyway, they may have access to the system preconscious-conscious only as compromise-formations after these latter having been deformed by censorship placed between the systems preconscious (*Prec.*) and unconscious (*Ucs.*).

By means of a spatial metaphor, Freud conceives unconscious and consciousness as separated by preconscious, which is the only intermediary zone with which either may be put into reciprocal communication; every communication route between unconscious and consciousness necessarily goes through preconscious, so there is not communication route that directly goes from unconscious to consciousness without passing through preconscious. There are then close relationships between consciousness and preconscious. Furthermore, the contents of the latter may be subject to a double censorship, in regard to its double touch with unconscious on the one hand, and with consciousness on the other hand (Fodor & Gaynor, 1950).

The contents of unconscious are the so-called *instinctual representatives* of drive (or *libido*). The *drive*, which is never an object of consciousness, is between the psychic and the somatic, may be only represented, and is placeable beyond conscious and unconscious. In fact, on the one hand, drive never can become conscious, while, on the other hand, it is present into the unconscious only by means of its representatives (i.e., the *instinctual representatives*), on its turn, provided by representations that Freud, in one of his first patterns of human psyche, considers as given by sequences of transcriptions of signs (as mnestic traces). The unconscious representatives are then organized into *phantasies*, that is to say, imaginary stories to which drive is attached or fixed, which may be considered as a real performance of desire.

In the first topography of human psyche, Freud considers unconscious as due to repression, to be precise, to infantile repression. With this occurrence, the separation between unconscious and preconscious-consciousness, takes place. A primary unconscious nucleus is being thus established, which will remain basically unchanged along the entire life course (Sasso, 2011) and that, therefore, might be considered as the basis for a possible deterministic development of human psyche. So, according to Freud, unconscious is being mainly constituted in the childhood, with *primary* (or *original*) *repression*, hence maintained by *secondary* (or *posterior*) *repression* of the so-called *unconscious' derivatives* which mainly are re-invested unconscious contents, coming from primary repression and inclined to become aware, that may reach too preconscious-conscious border.

A *proper repression* then may act on certain contents of the consciousness which are therefore re-sent to preconscious (Moore & Fine, 1990). To be precise, Freud himself distinguished between a *repression* properly said, and a *suppression*, corresponding to the above secondary repression or to this last proper repression, which mainly acts inside conscious-preconscious system, as a second censorship (different from primary censorship acting between the unconscious and the preconscious system, in the first Freudian topography), as well as a conscious mechanism, which does not send material into the unconscious. Dynamically, suppression is due to ethical judgements and proper values of each individual; furthermore, a psychic representation may be repressed (into the unconscious, which therefore should be a set of signifiers if we consider, also according to Lacan, a representation as a signifier), while the related affective charge (corresponding to a signified) may be suppressed or even deleted fully (Laplanche & Pontalis, 1967).

These latter are always active and push toward consciousness: this perennial unconscious activity is the indestructibility of unconscious desire, i.e., the subject of the unconscious, which may be released either somatically or mentally. Moreover, as there is a close relationship in terms of their functionality between primary repression and *primary phantasies*, these latter, to be meant as pre-individual schemes which structurate infantile sexual experiences, confer a certain universal or mythical feature to Freudian unconscious which is, however, basically established subjectively.

In *The Interpretation of Dreams* (of 1900), which, rightly, is still deemed valid by most of psychoanalysts[11], Freud exposes, by means of the explaining of dreaming activity, the main psychic mechanisms that rule unconscious, that is to say, *displacement* and *condensation*, which constitute the so-called *primary process*, presiding over unconscious functioning. The former, is a centring process of unconscious contents (dream thoughts) around an element which apparently seems to have a minor importance; the latter allows to accumulate many different contents upon only one element. Freud discovered such mechanisms by studying various *unconscious' formations* (like slips, parapraxes, and so on), to be considered as equivalent to symptoms, for their common structure of compromise-formation and the equal function of desire (or wish) satisfaction.

The basic nucleus of unconscious is made by instinctual representatives – i.e., by desire impulses featured by cathexis mobility of free energy – which lean to discharge their related cathexed energy by means of displacement and condensation. Thus, an instinctual representative may yield all its cathexed energy content by displacement, or acquire the cathexed energy contents of many other different instinctual representatives by condensation. The psychic processes and representatives of unconscious are atemporal, do not take into account reality, so replacing the internal one (i.e., the psychic reality) with the external reality (with respect to which there is full indifference), undergo to pleasure-displeasure principle, do not know any contradiction neither any reciprocity[12], are finally devoid of doubts and of any gradation of certainty (Laplanche & Pontalis, 1967).

In *Metapsychology* (of 1915), Freud introduces the so-called *economic standpoint* in ruling flow of psychic energy. Here, he discusses deeply preconscious system from a topographic standpoint. Either unconscious (*Ucs.*) and preconscious (*Pcs.*) are out of consciousness (*Cs.*), that is to say, their content is unconscious from a descriptive viewpoint; the content of preconscious may have access to consciousness, being it only temporarily unconscious. The drive psychic energy is freely mobile into the unconscious, while it is constrained into the preconscious. Furthermore, a double censorship system operates into the preconscious: a first part is placed between unconscious and preconscious, while a second part is between preconscious and consciousness.

Cathexis mainly concerns unconscious content from primary repression, and involves free energy. This content, on its turn, tends to go towards consciousness, to which yet preconscious censorship opposes, by secondary repression, detaching (by disinvestment or withdrawal of cathexis) this content of its own energy charge that arose from primary repression. At the same time, the drive energy so available from this disinvestment process, may be re-cathexed by *countercathexis* (or *anticathexis*), to invest another element, which may belong also to the preconscious-conscious system, like for instance a derivative of unconscious. In such a manner, preconscious, with its two censorships, hinders the intrusion of unconscious content, that remains relegated therefore either into the unconscious (by first barrier) or into the preconscious (by second barrier). Anyway, the passage of a given element from one psychic system to the other (i.e., between unconscious and preconscious), is made possible thanks to its disinvestment by one system and the subsequent re-investment by the other (Fodor & Gaynor, 1950; Laplanche & Pontalis, 1967).

Nevertheless, this same process may be repeated into the preconscious-conscious system, by the hindering action of its second censorship barrier, which exerts the defence mechanisms of the Ego. Furthermore, the countercathexed element may be various: a general unconscious representation or a system of representations, as well as a behaviour, a situation, a trait of temperament, and so on. Anyway, the main aim is to stabilize the repression under the incessant pressure of the unconscious desire, which is indestructible, and runs into the rigidity of Ego's defence mechanisms. All this dynamicity requires a constant expenditure of psychic energy employed in defence activities.

The censorship system, as conceived by Freud in his first formulation of human psychic apparatus, has been introduced to explain deformation mechanisms of dreaming. It is a permanent system acting to selectively hindering the passage from unconscious to preconscious-conscious system, so it is at the structural foundation of repression. Freud himself thinks that basically there are not two distinct censorship barriers but rather only one which is quite mobile and may extend its action between the contours of the unconscious and preconscious-conscious regions. Freud furthermore deems that preconscious runs according to the secondary process, stating that a psychic content becomes conscious thanks to a suitable overcathexing of it.

The *countercathexis* (or *anticathexis*) is therefore a defence mechanism of the Ego which hinders, through censorship, dangerous or unacceptable (hence anxiogenic) unconscious representatives to go into consciousness or motility. Countercathexis has the aim to maintain a representative into the psychic system from which derives its cathexis energy. So, to hinder an unconscious representative to go into consciousness, often the countercathexed element is an unconscious derivative, like a replacement formation or a reactive formation. Freud decomposes drive into affective charge and representation, which are closely tied of each other. The various defence mechanisms operate on the representation, deleting, by disinvestment (or de-cathexis), the relative drive energy charge, or affective charge, which therefore is available for further investments of other, more acceptable representations. Hence, according to Freud, the nucleus of the *Ucs.* basically consists of instinctual representatives which seek to discharge their cathexis energy, that is to say, it consists of wishful impulses. Importantly, Freud notes, in 1917, that the *Ucs.* is the missing link between soma and psyche (De Mijolla, 2005).

Either questions related to compulsion to repeat mechanism and various conceptual difficulties linked to unconscious aspects of the Ego, led Freud, around 1920, to leave his first topography of human psyche in favour of a second one, in which unconscious is considered from a descriptive viewpoint, so losing its first substantival meaning for acquiring an adjectival one. In this second topography, mainly characterized by a systemic approach, human psyche is no longer quantitatively structured according to a spatial metaphor, but rather qualitatively, by means of three main psychic agencies, i.e., the *Ego*, the *Super-Ego* and the *Es* (or *Id*), chiefly ruled by two primary instincts, the *life* and *death instincts*. Nevertheless, this second topography is not in conflict with the previous one. Indeed, the *Es* incorporates the *Ucs.* and inherits almost all its features, where the quality to be "unconscious" characterizes, besides the *Id*, also a large extent of the *Ego* (its defence mechanisms, like the resistances to the sense of guilt, as well as its affects, and so on), to most of the *Super-Ego* processes (like ethic norms), and to the various conflicts between agencies. Anyway, in the *Es* hold almost all the traits featuring *Ucs.* as outlined in the first structural topography (Moore & Fine, 1990; De Mijolla, 2005; Pieri, 2005). The *Es* is, furthermore, the primary source of any drive push, of the psychic energy, the origin of any cathexis (Laplanche & Pontalis, 1967).

In the *New Introductory Lectures on Psychoanalysis* (of 1932), Freud says that, into the *Es*, there are nothing but drive investments which require a urgent discharge. The *Es* should be the early, primary origin of human psychic apparatus, a first nucleus which will remain as such for the whole life, just that primary unconscious nucleus recalled above (Sasso, 2011). Upon this initial nucleus, throughout life, a sequence of various and different stratifications of repressed material gradually will shape dynamically around this nucleus (Petrini et al., 2013). From a historical standpoint, in the 1925 work *A Note upon the "Mystic Writing Pad"*, Freud makes an analogy between a writing tool, then said to be "Mystic Writing Pad", and human memory functioning, as it represents a kind of artefact of the system[13] *Ucs./Pcs. – Cs.* According to Freud, the *Ucs.*, i.e., the repository for memory traces, as well as the place of fixations, is even assumed to retain an instinctual foundation analogous to animal knowledge, as well as an inherited place of psychic formations and traces of human history, so conferring to it a kind of collective feature (De Mijolla, 2005).

In any event, Freud has always taken care in separating the basic deep dynamical unconscious from the latent, more superficial part, which is susceptible to becoming then conscious. From the experience with posthypnotic suggestion, the dream, as well as other experiences associated with the first topography, are not deemed, by Freud, as the outcomes of a paradoxical logic of unconscious. In the writings of the late 1930s, Freud himself criticizes aspects of his second topography of human psyche, stating that "What is unsatisfactory in this picture – and I am aware of it as clearly as anyone – is due to our complete ignorance of the dynamic nature of the mental processes. We tell ourselves that what distinguishes a conscious idea from a preconscious one, and the latter from an unconscious one, can only be a modification, or perhaps a different distribution, of psychical energy. We talk of cathexes and hypercathexes, but beyond this we are without any knowledge on the subject or even any starting-point for a serviceable working hypothesis". In this regard, the qualitative dynamic of the first topography permits instead to put forward some working hypotheses which allow to overcome these last issues raised by Freud himself (De Mijolla, 2005).

2.4. THE MAIN CONCEPTS OF PSYCHOANALYSIS, II: ON DEFENCE MECHANISMS

Within Freudian theory, the *defence* refers group of psychic operations aimed at the reduction and elimination of any possible change turned to threaten the integrity and stability of the basic bio-psychological individual. In that the Ego is constituted as a psychic agency which embodies this stability and strives to maintain it, it may be then considered as both the stake and the agent of these operations. Generally speaking, *defence* is directed towards internal excitation (instinct), while, in practice, its action is extended to every *representation* (e.g., memory, phantasy) linked with this excitation as well as directed to any situation which is unpleasurable for the Ego as a result of its incompatibility with individual's equilibrium and, to that extent, liable to spark off the excitation. Unpleasurable affects, which serve as motives or signals for defence, may also become its object.

The defensive process is expressed concretely in mechanisms of defence which are more or less integrated into the Ego. Defence is marked and infiltrated by instincts, against which is directed, and consequently it often takes on a compulsive aspect, and works at least in part in an unconscious way. *Defence mechanisms* are different types of operations through which defence may explain its function. Which of these mechanisms predominate in a given case, depends upon the type of illness under consideration, upon the developmental stage reached, upon the extent to which the defensive conflict has been worked out, and so on. It is generally agreed that the Ego puts the defence mechanisms to use, but the theoretical question of whether their mobilisation always presupposes the existence of an organised Ego capable of sustaining them is an open one. There is no doubt that, from 1926 onwards, the study of the defence mechanisms became a major theme of psycho-analytic research by Freud.

This development was then spearheaded by Anna Freud who, basing herself on concrete examples, attempted to describe the variegation, the complexity and vast action's range of the mechanisms of defence. In particular, she showed how defensive aims may make use of the most varied activities (e.g., phantasy, intellectual activity) and how defence can be directed not only against instinctual claims (as originally conceived by his father) but also against everything which is liable to give rise to the development of *anxiety*: emotions, situations, Super-Ego demands, etc. In what follows (see Chapter 7), we may schematically denote with Θ the set of all the possible defence mechanisms as just recalled above.

It may be noted too that Anna Freud does not claim that her approach is either exhaustive or systematic, a reservation which applies especially to her incidental enumeration of the defence mechanisms, whose list includes: *repression, regression, reaction-formation, isolation, undoing, projection, introjection, turning against the self, reversal into the opposite, sublimation*. Many other defensive procedures have been described. Anna Freud herself further brings under this heading the processes of *denial in phantasy, idealisation, identification with the aggressor*, etc. Melanie Klein further describes what she considers to be very primitive defences: *splitting of the object, projective identification, denial of psychic reality, omnipotent control over objects*, and so forth.

However, a fundamental theoretical distinction ought not to be overlooked, namely, the distinction which marks off *repression* from all other defensive processes. Freud had no qualms about recalling this specificity even after having said that repression was merely a special case of defence. This uniqueness of repression is not due so much to the fact – invoked by Anna Freud – that it may be defined, in essence, as a permanent anticathexis, and that it is at once 'the most efficacious and the most dangerous' of the mechanisms of defence: its special function derives rather from its role in the constitution of the (non-structural) unconscious as such (Laplanche & Pontalis, 1967).

2.5. THE MAIN CONCEPTS OF PSYCHOANALYSIS, III: ON THE TWO FREUDIAN TOPOGRAPHIES OF HUMAN PSYCHE

A *topography* is a theory or point of view which implies a differentiation of the psychical apparatus into a number of subsystems. Each of these has distinct characteristics or functions and a specific position vis-à-vis the others, so that they may be treated, metaphorically speaking, as points in a psychical space which is susceptible of figurative representation. Two topographies are commonly identified in Freud's work: in the first one, the major distinction is that between *Unconscious*, *Preconscious* and *Conscious*, while the second differentiates the three agencies of *Id* (or *Es*), *Ego* and *Super-Ego*. These have been discussed in the previous section 2.3.

The first topographical conceptualisation of the psychical apparatus is proposed in Chapter VII of *The Interpretation of Dreams* (of 1900), but its early elements may be traced already in the *Project for a Scientific Psychology* (of 1895), where it is still embedded in the neurological framework of a neuronal apparatus. This first topography (further developed in the metapsychological papers of 1915) distinguishes between three systems, i.e., *unconscious*, *preconscious* and *conscious*, each of which has its own function, type of process, cathectic energy and specific ideational contents. Between each of these systems, Freud places censorships which inhibit and control transposition from one to another. The term censorship points up the spatial aspect of the theory of the psychical apparatus. The topographical perspective goes beyond this basic differentiation.

But, from 1920 onwards, Freud worked out another conception of the personality, given the concise title of *second topography*. According to the classical account, the principal reason for this was the ever-greater consideration demanded by the unconscious defences, making impossible to go on identifying the poles of the defensive conflict with the systems described with first topography, i.e., respectively the unconscious repressed material and the Ego with the Preconscious-Conscious system, even if, in reality, the motives for the revision in question cannot be fully reduced to this fact, which had in any case long been more or less explicitly present in Freud's work.

In describing briefly this second topography, we follow Daniel Lagache (Bastide 1966, pp. 91-94). Unconscious system is the place of sexual and aggressive instincts, of unconscious desire, of the phantasies charged with free energy which is aimed to discharge immediately and easily shifts; it is an incoherent organization without any regard for identity principle and the non-contradiction one; it is the place of the syncretism. Preconscious, instead, is the place of defensive counter-impulses, charged with bound energy, which are aimed to inhibit as well as to postpone the discharge of impulses; it has a certain autonomy and, in it, first mental processes turned to be conform to identity principle and non-contradiction, start to appear. Consciousness, then, is basically at the dependence of preconscious, and indeed Freud speaks of the system Preconscious-Conscious as opposed to the system of mnestic traces. However, under the functions of attention, consciousness manages free energy available from preconscious, to establish relationships with external world, resisting to the pushes exerted by displeasure affects.

With the second topography, one of the chief discoveries that made it possible was that of the role played by the various identifications in the formation of the personality and of the permanent structures which they leave within it: ideals, critical agencies, self-images, and so on. In its schematic form, this second theory involves three agencies: the *Id* (or *Es*), the instinctual pole of personality; the *Ego*, which puts itself forward as representative of the whole person, and that, as such, is cathexed by narcissistic libido; and the *Super-Ego*, or agency of judgement and criticism, constituted by the internalisation of social and parental demands and prohibitions.

This approach however does not merely set up an interplay between these three agencies: for one thing, other more specific intraformations are isolated within these (e.g., ideal ego, ego-ideal), so that 'intrasystemic' relations are brought into play as well as 'intersystemic' ones; further, special importance comes to be assigned to the 'relations of dependence' obtained between the various systems, particularly in the case of the Ego, where the satisfaction of instinctual demands is found to occur, even within the sphere of the Ego's, and are said to be *adaptative* activities (Laplanche & Pontalis, 1967). Just from this second topography, we may work out, in the final section, a more rigorous model of human psyche which is liable to account for the human symbolic function with a pattern, useful for further possible formalizations to be computationally implemented, and mainly based on a dialectic functioning relying on Freudian psychoanalysis.

In what follows, finally, we quote some excerpts drawn from Freudian work *Die Verdrängung* [The Unconscious] (of 1915), to integrate what has just been said above. The first one, concerns the first topographic sketch of human psyche according to Freud, by which he says that

Proceeding now to an account of the positive findings of psycho-analysis, we may say that in general a psychical act goes through two phases as regards its state, between which is interposed a kind of testing (censorship). In the first phase the psychical act is unconscious and belongs to the system Ucs. If, on testing, it is rejected by the censorship, it is not allowed to pass into the second phase; it is then said to be 'repressed' and must remain unconscious. If, however, it passes this testing, it enters the second phase and thenceforth belongs to the second system, which we will call the system Cs. But the fact that it belongs to that system does not yet unequivocally determine its relation to consciousness.

It is not yet conscious, but it is certainly capable of becoming conscious (to use Breuer's expression) – that is, it can now, given certain conditions, become an object of consciousness without any special resistance. In consideration of this capacity for becoming conscious we also call the system Cs. the 'preconscious'. If it should turn out that a certain censorship also plays a part in determining whether the preconscious becomes conscious, we shall discriminate more sharply between the systems Pcs. and Cs. For the present, let it suffice us to bear in mind that the system Pcs. shares the characteristics of the system Cs. and that the rigorous censorship exercises its office at the point of transition from the Ucs. to the Pcs. (or Cs.). (Freud 1957, Vol. XIV, pp. 172-174)

The second one, is then an excerpt of Freud's discussion on some typical features of this his first topography of human psychic apparatus. He says that

The distinction we have made between the two psychical systems receives fresh significance when we observe that processes in the one system, the Ucs., show characteristics which are not met with again in the system immediately above it. The nucleus of the Ucs. consists of instinctual representatives which seek to discharge their cathexis; that is to say, it consists of wishful impulses. These instinctual impulses are co-ordinate with one another, exist side by side without being influenced by one another, and are exempt from mutual contradiction.

When two wishful impulses whose aims must appear to us incompatible become simultaneously active, the two impulses do not diminish each other or cancel each other out, but combine to form an intermediate aim, a compromise. There are in this system no negation, no doubt, no degrees of certainty: all this is only introduced by the work of the censorship between the Ucs. and the Pcs. Negation is a substitute, at a higher level, for repression. In the Ucs. there are only contents, cathected with greater or lesser strength. The cathectic intensities are much more mobile. By the process of displacement one idea may surrender to another its whole quota of cathexis; by the process of condensation it may appropriate the whole cathexis of several other ideas.

I have proposed to regard these two processes as distinguishing marks of the so-called primary psychical process. In the system Pcs. the secondary process is dominant. When a primary process is allowed to take its course in connection with elements belonging to the system Pcs., it appears 'comic' and excites laughter. The processes of the system Ucs. are timeless; i.e. they are not ordered temporally, are not altered by the passage of time; they have no reference to time at all. Reference to time is bound up, once again, with the work of the system Cs. The Ucs. processes pay just as little regard to reality. They are subject to the pleasure principle; their fate depends only on how strong they are and on whether they fulfil the demands of the pleasure-unpleasure regulation.

To sum up: exemption from mutual contradiction, primary process (mobility of cathexes), timelessness, and replacement of external by psychical reality – these are the characteristics which we may expect to find in processes belonging to the system Ucs. Unconscious processes only become cognizable by us under the conditions of dreaming and of neurosis – that is to say, when processes of the higher, Pcs., system are set back to an earlier stage by being lowered (by regression). In themselves they cannot be recognized, indeed are even incapable of carrying on their existence; for the system Ucs. is at a very early moment overlaid by the Pcs. which has taken over access to consciousness and to motility.

Discharge from the system Ucs. passes into somatic innervation that leads to development of affect; but even this path of discharge is, as we have seen, contested by the Pcs. By itself, the system Ucs. would not in normal conditions be able to bring about any expedient muscular acts, with the exception of those already organized as reflexes. (Freud 1957, Vol. XIV, pp. 185-187)

2.6. THE MAIN CONCEPTS OF PSYCHOANALYSIS, IV: ON THE OBJECT-RELATIONS

The term *object-relation*, in general, refers to the subject's mode of relation to her or his own world, i.e., the modality to relate with this latter; such a relation is the entire complex outcome either of a particular organisation of the personality and of a more or less phantasied apprehension of objects, as well as of certain special types of defence. We may speak of the object-relationships of a specific subject, but also of types of object-relationship making reference either to points in human psychic development (e.g., an oral object-relationship) or else to psychopathology (e.g., a melancholic object-relationship).

Object is to be taken here in the special sense which it has for psycho-analysis in such expressions as 'object-choice' and 'object love'. For instance, a person may be described as an object in so far as the instincts are directed towards her or him; there is nothing pejorative in this, and no particular implication that this person is, in any sense, not a subject. *Relationship* should be understood in the strong sense of the term, i.e., as an interrelationship, in fact, involving not only the way the subject constitutes his objects but also the way these objects shape her or his actions. That we speak of the 'object-relationship' rather than of the relationship to the object, serves to point up this connotation of interaction: to use the second formulation would imply that the object or objects predate the subject's relations with them and, by the same token, that the subject has already been constituted.

The original Freudian theory has been in implicit intertwinement with the current notion of object-relationship. Indeed, in seeking to analyse the concept of instinct, Freud distinguished between the instinctual *source*, *object* and *aim*. The *source* of the instinct is that zone or somatic apparatus which is the seat of the sexual excitation; its importance in Freud's eyes is attested to by the fact that he names each stage of libidinal development after the corresponding predominant erotogenic (somatic) zone. As to the aim and object, Freud preserved the distinction between them throughout his work. Thus, separate sections of the work *Three Essays on the Theory of Sexuality* (of 1905) deal, in turn, with 'deviations in respect of the aim' (e.g., sadism) and 'deviations in respect of the object' (e.g., homosexuality).

Similarly, in the work *Instincts and their Vicissitudes* (of 1915), there is a difference between those transformations of the instinct tied to changes of aim and those where the process essentially concerns the object. The distinction between source, object and aim, which Freud uses as a frame of reference, loses its seeming rigidity when he brings his attention to bear on instinctual life. To say that at a given stage the functioning of a particular somatic apparatus (e.g., the mouth) determines a mode of relationship with the object (e.g., incorporation) is tantamount to treating this functioning as a prototype: all the subject's other activities, somatic or not, may, on this view, be invested with oral meanings. Similarly, numerous connections exist between object and aim.

Modifications of the instinctual aim appear as governed by a dialectic in which the object has its part of play; particularly, in the cases of sadism/masochism and voyeurism/exhibitionism, 'the turning round upon the subject's self (change of object) and the transformation from activity to passivity (change of aim) converge or coincide'. Sublimation is said to supply a further illustration of this correlation between object and aim. Lastly, Freud envisaged character-types and types of relationship to the object in conjunction with each other, and, in his clinical works, he was able to show how the same set of problems may be identified in what are apparently quite distinct activities of a given subject (Laplanche & Pontalis, 1967).

2.7. THE MAIN CONCEPTS OF PSYCHOANALYSIS, V: ON THE CONSCIOUSNESS

In the descriptive sense, consciousness is a transient psychic property which distinguishes between external and internal perceptions from psychical phenomena as a whole. According to Freud's metapsychological theory, consciousness is the main psychic function of a system, the perception-consciousness system (Pct.-C). From the topographical point of view, the perception consciousness system lies on the periphery of the psychical apparatus and receives information both from the outside world and from internal sources: this information is composed of sensations, which impress themselves at some point on the pleasure-unpleasure scale, and of revived memories. Freud often ascribes the function of perception-consciousness to the preconscious system, in which case this is referred to as the preconscious-conscious system (P-C).

From the functional point of view, the perception-consciousness system stands opposed to the unconscious and preconscious as systems of mnestic traces: here no lasting trace of any excitation remains. From the economic point of view, the system is characterised by the fact that it has, at its disposal, a freely mobile energy capable of hypercathecting a given element: this is the mechanism of attention. Consciousness plays an important part in the dynamics of the conflict (conscious avoidance of what is disagreeable; a more selective control over the pleasure principle) and of the treatment (function and limitations of the prise de conscience); yet, it cannot be defined as one of the poles of the defensive conflict. In psychology, then, consciousness is the subjects immediate apprehension of mental activity (Laplanche & Pontalis, 1967).

Although Freud thought that conscious processes are ''the same as the consciousness of the philosophers and of everyday opinion'' and ''a fact without parallel, which defies all explanation or description'', he yet argued that they could not be considered the ''essence'' of mental life. Rather, consciousness has a fugitive quality and does not ''form unbroken sequences which are complete in themselves. [...] The psychical, whatever its nature may be, is in itself unconscious and probably similar in kind to all the other natural processes of which we have obtained knowledge''. Freud stressed, however, that consciousness still plays an important role; indeed, it is ''the one light which illuminates our path and leads us through the darkness of mental life''.

The work of psychoanalysis, as Freud saw it, is ''translating unconscious processes into conscious ones, and thus filling in the gaps in conscious perception''. Consciousness is the qualitative perception of information arising both from the external world and from the internal world: an external world that is unknowable in itself and to which we have access only via subjective elements collected by our sense organs and an internal world that consists of unconscious mental processes and that we are aware of solely through sensations of pleasure/unpleasure and revived memories.

According to Freud, ''A persons own body, and above all its surface, is a place from which both external and internal perceptions may spring''. From the beginning, Freud treated consciousness and perception as indissolubly linked, indeed, so much so that throughout his work he deemed them to constitute a single structure, the perception-consciousness system (Pct.-C). Freud also drew a distinction, within non-conscious phenomena, between latent states susceptible of becoming conscious at any moment, and repressed psychic processes inaccessible to consciousness. This led him to differentiate the unconscious system proper, from a preconscious system, cut off from consciousness by censorship but also controlling access to consciousness.

In this sense, the preconscious and the conscious are very close: both are governed by secondary processes and both draw on a bound form of psychic energy. In *The Interpretation of Dreams* (of 1900), Freud spoke of the preconscious-conscious system, and, in *The Unconscious* (of 1915), he described the preconscious as a ''conscious knowledge'', even if it provides access to unconscious contents and processes, provided that they have been transformed. From his earliest writings on, Freud saw the link between consciousness and the Ego as very close. And although by 1920, Freud viewed the Ego as in large part unconscious in its defensive activities, he continued to attach consciousness to it as both the "nucleus" and the "surface of the mental apparatus". By the early twenty-first century, the problem of perception had become increasingly complex.

Freud's near conflation of perception and consciousness, which required him to postulate that perceptual phenomena and the laying down of memory traces are incompatible, has come in for serious reconsideration. It is worth noting, though, that Freud himself, in his last years, was given pause on this issue by the problem of fetishism, apropos of which it was apparent that perceptions and mnestic traces could be caught up in one and the same conflict. This line of thinking has led to a re-evaluation of all the psychopathologies where disavowal and splitting predominate, such as borderline conditions, and more generally, to a review of all the states involving the relationships between perception and hallucination – cf. also D.W. Winnicott notions of the subjective object and of transitionality (De Mijolla, 2005).

2.8. A POSSIBLE FORMAL PSYCHOANALYTIC MODEL FOR HUMAN SYMBOLIC FUNCTION

Here, we outline a possible formal psychic model worked out within psychoanalytic theory – mainly Freudian theory and its further next extensions due to other psychoanalysts who professed faithful to Freudian orthodoxy – which may provide a rigorous pattern, mainly based on a dialectic interplay, for explaining symbolic function. The outcome of this rigorous attempt of formalization of Freudian psychoanalytic view of symbolic function, in providing a formal psychic scheme, might turn out to be useful too, if suitably formally transcribed further, for a possible computational implementation of this pattern whose importance might be retraceable in the chief fact that the functioning of such a formal model basically relies on the action of splitting, dichotomist[14] psychic phenomena (e.g., disavowal[15], as well as other related defence mechanisms[16]), which are discrete and bivalent, in their essential nature, hence easily implementable in a binary logic, i.e., the primary algebraic basis for an automatic computation.

Indeed, along his life, Freud always paid, more or less explicitly, attention to the mechanism of negation and related psychic operations. However, it is important at least to make mention to what Freud's has done in regard to conceptual and dynamic overlaps between negation and some other defensive operations of the Ego, which have been, afterwards, identified, clarified and classified, to include, besides the *negation*, the following ones: *repudiation, denial, disavowal, isolation of affect*, and *undoing*. We now give a very brief description of each of these, following closely (Akhtar & O'Neil 2011, Introduction).

Repudiation, later called, after Lacan, *foreclosure*, had already been however considered implicitly by Freud in the work *The neuro-psychoses of defence* of 1894, and it is a defence mechanism which refers to the end-point of repression and the elimination of both an idea from consciousness and the fact that this has occurred. According to Freud, "the ego rejects the incompatible idea together with its affect and behaves as if the idea had never occurred to the ego at all". Seen as such, repudiation and negation seem to lie, so to speak, on the opposite ends of the repression spectrum: the former erases repression itself, and the latter creates a partial opening in the repressive barrier of affect. Both repudiation and negation follow repression and alter what it has achieved.

Denial is an unconsciously operative Ego defence which works by obliterating the awareness of a painful external reality, as Freud stated in the 1920s. Hence, Anna Freud, in the 1930s, elaborated further on this concept, but she never departed from her father's view that denial involves the erasure of a piece of perception. In contrast, Melanie Klein, around the same period, used the term denial to denote the obliteration of internal reality, especially the importance of the objects on which one depends. But, a natural question is how does denial is related to negation? The answer depends upon whether one is using the Freudian or Kleinian definition of denial. Freudian denial obliterates perception before it can become a part of psychic reality, whereas negation addresses a repressed content of psychic reality, so the two mechanisms are quite different, while Kleinian denial, comes close instead to negation, since both deal with aspects of psychic reality. The main difference between them is that such denial is violent towards the internal word, whereas negation involves a certain reconciliation with the repressed mental contents.

Disavowal is a term used by Freud for the first time in the late of 1920s, for the little girl's refusal to acknowledge her lack of a penis and, later, to explain fetishist's maintaining of two contradictory attitudes by which he (or she) simultaneously acknowledges and repudiates the absence of a penis in women. Unlike denial, disavowal leads to a splitting of the Ego, this making disavowal distinct from negation, since there is no cleavage of the Ego in the latter. Moreover, while disavowal is characterized by contradictory attitudes in two consciously experienced, though separated, Ego segments (just due to splitting processes), negation, instead, holds one attitude consciously and the other unconsciously. Just for this, we deem disavowal much more indicated, as defence mechanism, to be involved in symbolic formation.

Regarding then *isolation of affect*, in his 1927 paper *On Negation*, Freud stated that "we can see how in this [negation] the intellectual function is separated from the affective process. With the help of negation, only one consequence of the process of repression is undone – the fact, namely, of the ideational content of what is repressed not reaching consciousness. The outcome of this is a kind of intellectual acceptance of the repressed, while at the same time what is essential to the repression persists". Curiously, it is precisely the lack of intellectual acceptance (e.g., "I *never* thought of my mother in this connection") that Freud held to be the hallmark of negation, and put at the origin of the symbol of negation (Conrotto, 2009). How, then, to account for this contradiction?

It is hard to say, but, according to Salman Akhtar, is that Freud, implicitly, wandered around on a new concept here, a concept that would be explicitated, or elucidated better, two decades later by his daughter Anna (in 1936) under the designation of "isolation of affect". In negation, repression is partially undone by allowing the repressed into consciousness in its *negative* form, while, in the isolation of affect, repression is partially undone by allowing the repressed into consciousness in its *positive* form. For example, an individual using negation exclaims, "I *never* thought that my husband should die", as opposed to the one using isolation of affect, who declares, "I *have* thought of my husband dying, but I have no idea why, since I've no feeling of anger or hostility towards him". The two mechanisms are thus quite different. Notwithstanding that, there is some similarity, too, between negation and isolation of affect. This basically resides in the fact that neither permits the emotional counterpart of the de-repressed idea into conscious awareness.

Undoing, finally, is a defence mechanism first described by Freud in 1909, and further elaborated by him in 1926, which involves the Ego's warding off anxiety by committing an act opposite to an instinctual deed that has been actually committed or is imagined to have been committed. In Otto Fenichel's words, in undoing, "something is done which, actually or magically, is the opposite of something which, again actually or in the imagination, was done before". The act often follows a drive intensification as a consequence of external or internal events. For instance, someone stopping over at a friend's apartment, might say "please do not offer me a drink" in a rather transparent effort to instead reverse the morally conflicted and shy desire to ask for a drink; so that, something is becoming conscious here and is reversed by stating its opposite.

And just herein lies the similarity between undoing and negation. In fact, both express the opposite of what is meant, i.e., undoing, in the form of inverse action, and negation, in the form of inverse thought.

But since the boundary between thought and action can get blurred, it is possible to conceive of undoing as "negation via action" and of negation as "undoing via thought". However, and this is quite important, such a parallelism overlooks the fact that undoing diminishes one's contact with internal reality, while negation prepares the ground for increased knowledge of it. Anyway, we may say that, very roughly, all these latter defence operations overall form a set which is however marked, or featured, by negation and the notion of negative, which are funding concepts of psychoanalytic theoretical framework. Indeed, Freud himself, brought back the springing out of the negative to the rise of pushes of primary drives which found the basic, primary dualism upon which relies *pleasure/displeasure principle* (e.g., "I want, this, to eat or to spit"), and Lacan wanted to identify the first step of human psyche functioning, just in the primary contraposition between *Verwerfung* (*foreclosure* – see later) and *Bejahung* (*admission*), hence justifying our position about a predominance of disavowal (see later) in the early deployments of human psyche, above all its symbolic function.

However, according to Freud, the institution of the "negative" (with all the consequent psychic correlates, among which is the set of defence operations of above) should be brought back to the institution (or establishment) of the basic *pleasure/displeasure* duality (borne by pleasure principle), closely related with the qualitative dimension of the economic-dynamical functioning of psyche that André Green defines as *primary symbolization*, having, therefore, a main qualitative nature and connected with the primary rising of *qualia* as primordial nuclei of consciousness (Sasso, 2011). Perhaps, much more precisely, the rising of the "negative" has to be brought back to the mythic moment of the institution of the *difference sign* between the *Fort* ("gone") and the *Da* ("there") in the "*Fort/Da*" reel game described by Freud[17] in *Beyond the Pleasure Principle* of 1920, which, according to Jean Laplanche and Serge Leclaire (Laplanche, 2000, 2001), is the founding moment, the early origin, of the whole human psyche, from which it starts too the formation of unconscious and infantile sexuality, hence the binary logic on the model of the "*Fort/Da*" game (Conrotto, 2009; 2014, Ch. 3, Sect. 3).

Indeed, the "*Fort/Da*" reel game enables first the institution then the encounter with the two values of $(-)$ (i.e., disappearance) and of $(+)$ (i.e., appearance), and establishes the difference between one thing and the other, yet linked together. Indeed, an object is recognizable as such only "in relation" to what is "different from" it: for example, a black mark is identifiable as such only in relation to what is different from, a white page, where the "difference", here, is not a quality "in" the black mark or "in" the white page, and yet this "difference" gives the mark and the page their respective identities. So, "difference itself", difference as such, has no "itself", is not as such, as difference, in the "*Fort-Da*" (or "*Fort/Da*") game, is neither "*Fort*" nor "*Da*" but rather resembles the hyphen – (or /) between them; this therefore entails a meaning of linking, relation. The "*Da*" of every "*Fort/Da*" game, depends on the "*Fort*", and this is given by the "difference" which again, in itself, is never present and never absent (Barratt 2016, Ch. 4).

Thus, from Freud's reel game to death drive (in 1920), hence from a manifest negation (i.e., "this is not my mother!", tells a patient, during a dream) to the latent statement that supports it (i.e., "she is effectively his mother"), Freud reaches (in 1925) to identify the primary role of negation for the thought functions of judgement and the reality examination, which are being to be placed therefore among repression, the lost of the object of primary satisfaction and its re-finding by means of the representative which emancipates the individual from sensory-motor perception of immediate drive discharge ruled by pleasure principle (*perceptive identity*), to thought elaboration (*thought identity*). In working out this crucial passage, Freud identified the foundations underpinning though, i.e., the instinctual substrate underlying it, its basic quality feature (e.g., "good/bad") and its property of absence (e.g., "losing/finding", "disappearance/reappearance") of the object (of thought), so that, basically, thought goes on just to rebuild up this, hence *re-presenting* it, or *re-constructing* an its configuration by *simulation*[18] from its deep mnestic traces, not simply *representing* mentally the image of such an object as it may come from some its perception or past memory (Conrotto 2014, Ch. 3., Set. 3; Semi 1988-89, Vol. I, Sect. 6.1).

As has already been said at the end of Chapter 1, just the latest epistemological stances (Conrotto, 2014) say us that what really *structurate* human psyche are the *primal phantasies*[19] (Laplanche & Pontalis, 1967, 1988) which are, in turn, basically turned to structurate later *Œdipal complex*. So, there exist innate, pre-existent structures which act as multi-systems of semiotic transduction of corporal experiences, signs producing, which structure unconscious and rule its functioning. Each of these pre-linguistic semiogenetic and semantic systems, on its turn, is mainly ruled internally by a chief, primordial logical nucleus which confers to it the basic, minimal formal fashion. Such a key logics is made by the *signifier of castration* ruled by the *pleasure/displeasure principle*, which give rise to a basic binary logic called *phallic logic*[20], just according to the above described mechanism provided by the "*Fort/Da*" reel game, with the institution, among other things, of the *difference sign*, which, as seen, establishes too a basic relation between the two different things, together to the rising of the set of those defence mechanisms linked to negation and the negative (see above). So, "*Fort/Da*" reel game inaugurates the chain of signifiers of primary (or primordial) symbolization (outcome of the compulsion to repeat mechanism, of which "*Fort/Da*" is its early manifestation), hence that *Ur-logic* mentioned in Chapter 1, Section 1.5.1., which develops according to logical nexuses whose capture on what should be signified, takes place by means of metonymy and metaphor. In the words of Lacan, human being spends her or his time entirely in the deployment of the structural alternative in which presence/absence $(+ / -)$ are closely and inseparably linked together, the one calling the other, and vice versa; in this primordial game, the object at stake is fully uninterested for the subject, who instead spends her or his whole life just for the "alternative" $(+ / -)$, not for the "win". Thus, the subject enters into the symbolic order (Contri 1972, pp. 253-255).

The pattern which will be delineated in the next subsections, mainly based on the action of the set of psychic operations related, in some way, to negation (as briefly described at the beginning of this incipit, and many of which are recollected under the name of *primary defences* by André Green[21] to identify certain primary psychic operations which have to do with all the possible "yes and/or no" issues however falling into the domain of action of the Ego), above all disavowal, is closely linked with what has been just said above, because, the "*Fort/Da*" reel game is, on its turn, holds up on compulsion to repeat mechanisms, hence it depends on complex defence mechanisms closely correlated with perversions exerting in the field of action of Ego's Ideal and Ideal Ego agencies whose instances operate under the destructive influences of the primary narcissism (Semi 1988-89, Vol. I, Sect. 6.3.1, p. 419). From this, it follows a close relationship between this pattern (as described herein) and the phallic logic mentioned above.

2.8.1. A Very Brief Sketch on Symbolism in Psychoanalysis

The access to *symbolic universe* provided by *representations* (or better, *presentations*), has marked, along the human evolution, the qualitative distinguishing feature of homination process (Contardi 2010, Introduction, Sect. 2; Tartabini & Giusti 2006, Cap. II). It is not possible to give here than the slightest survey on symbolism, so we will provide a very few outlines on it, just the needful for what follows.

Symbolism is an indirect form of representation. *Symbolization* is a psychic function typical of human beings, through which a mental representation refers to another one according to a not well defined link. Differently from the *sign*, which ties together representations whose meanings are both conscious and related by a conventional but rigid link, the *symbol* is characterized by the fact that the meaning of one representation belongs to unconscious realm (*latent meaning*), the other to consciousness (*manifest meaning*). One of the main hypotheses is that symbolization is prior to any other form of sign function, like language (Bottiroli 2006, p. 176; Moore & Fine, 1990).

In psychoanalysis, the first interest towards symbols dates back to Freud's work *The Interpretation of Dreams* of 1899, considered still valid by most of psychoanalysts (Fossi 1988, p. 41), and remained such throughout his life. Distinguishing, from C.S. Peirce onwards, symbol from sign, in that the link between signifier and signified in latter is arbitrary but rigid, symmetric and mainly belonging to consciousness, while, in the former, is more elusive, weaker, asymmetric, relying between unconscious and consciousness, and endowed of almost universal, ancestral features to be identified in the unconscious realm, maybe the remnants of a primordial and fundamental language forgotten by humanity, as Erich Fromm has pointed out in (Fromm, 1951). From Freud onwards, the symbolism has been a central theme of many other psychoanalysts, like Jung, Melanie Klein, Hanna Segal, Lacan, and so forth (Barale et al., 2009).

Freud conceived symbols as all springing out from unconscious, as a result of primary process whose main aim is to reduce anguish, removing unacceptable ideas and desires. Symbolic formation, in its widest sense, allows the deferment (time delay[22]) of the discharge of psychic tensions or conflicts produced by stimuli, interposing mental mediators (symbols) between stimuli and responses, so postponing the gratification, or else shifting desires from forbidden objects to their licit (often material) substitutes, so allowing an immediate gratification (Moore & Fine, 1990). The main aim of the present paper is just to give a psychoanalytic pattern, worked out within Freudian theory, explaining these latter two aspects.

To be precise, the first result of symbolic formation meant as above, gives rise to sublimation[23], hence to civilization and (non-material) culture just in the Freudian sense[24], while the second result of symbolic formation, reduces to (symbolic) reification at simple and immediate materiality (material culture[25]). Since at the basis of symbolic formation there is, anyway, a compromise between opposite tendencies (in accomplish pleasure and reality principles, as well as life and death principles), we have identified such a basic dialectic in the relationships between two main opposite structural parts of Ego agency arising from a certain crucial division[26] (*Ego's splitting*), namely the subagency Ideal Ego on the one hand, and the subagency system Ego's Ideal–Super-Ego on the other hand[27]. Just from their dialectic opposition, springs out mainly sublimation phenomena (desire) on the one side, and materialistic practices (pleasure) on the other side.

The pattern described herein, is mainly supported, besides the new clinical data (Recalcati, 2010), also by the fact that symbolism, in psychoanalysis, is considered closely related to somatic-sensory components of Self experience (Fossi 1988, p. 101), as well as just by the latest psychoanalytic clinic that has clearly shown the emergence of new pathologies which may be laid out within this framework based on Ego's splitting. Furthermore, a valuable epistemological support to this model is provided too by the recent work of Francesco Conrotto (2010, 2014), even if more or less direct confirmations come from many other different sources and witnesses. For instance, some of these latter are retraceable in (Semi 1988-89, Vol. I, Ch. 6, Sects 6.1 and 6.2), where the negation and related psychic operations (Akhtar & O'Neil 2011, Introduction), are put at the foundation of abstract thought.

Furthermore, another confirmation of the model that will be discussed later, is provided by the work of Pier Mario Masciangelo (Semi 1988-89, Vol. I, p. 418), for which, at the intersystemic level and from the dynamical-structural standpoint, the links existing between castration fear and anguish of fragmentation correspond to a sadomasochistic relation holding between Ego and Super-Ego. Indeed, at the level of Super-Ego, there holds an intrasystemic conflict between a regressive and persecutory Ego's substructure (i.e., the megalomaniac Ideal Ego of primary narcissism, that is, the most primitive part of ideality) and the most mature intrasubjective (i.e., the Ego's Ideal of secondary narcissism) and prohibiting (i.e., the Super-Ego) parts of ideality, as outcomes of the Œdipification. Among these, repression, disavowal and splitting of the Ego, coexist together, associated with the instable sadomasochistic dynamics, among which is just the *fetishism* (Semi 1988-89, Vol. I, p. 418), which we have taken as chief explaining pattern. In the next subsections, however, we shall provide a wider and deeper discussion of this dynamic pattern, here just outlined in its basic features.

2.8.2. On Ego, Ideal Ego, Ego's Ideal and Super-Ego: A First Introductory Overview

According to the last 1938 Freudian thought (Freud, 1938), an Ego's splitting takes place with the formation of two subagencies which will be called *Ego's Ideal* and *Ideal Ego* (Chasseguet-Smirgel, 1975; Hanly, 1984, 2011; Hartmann & Loewenstein, 1962; Lagache, 1961, 1965; Lample-De-Groot, 1962; Laplanche & Pontalis, 1967; Levin, 1996; Loewald, 1962, 1988; Mancia, 1990; Milrod, 2002; Reich, 1954; Sandler et al., 1963; Sandler, 1981). Nevertheless, both these names are due to Hermann Nunberg (1932) and Daniel Lagache (1961, 1965), and not properly to Freud who explicitly introduced and used only the name Ego's Ideal in his 1914 *On Narcissism. An Introduction* to denote an autonomous intrapsychic formation, prior to Super-Ego, to which the Ego refers itself for evaluating its effective realizations or representations (Galimberti, 2006). Nevertheless, Freud himself, in the 1914 *On Narcissism. An Introduction*, as well as in the 1922 *Group Psychology and the Analysis of the Ego* and in the 1923 *The Ego and the Id*, speaks too of an Ideal Ego (*Idealich*) but identifies it with the Ego's Ideal (*Ichideal*) and this, on its turn, with the Super-Ego, even if, in some points of his discussion, a certain distinction between them seems already to be possible.

However, as pointed out in (Hanly, 1984, 2011), Freud starts to use the term Ideal Ego since 1922, to refer to narcissistic phenomena, while Ego's Ideal was being gradually included into the Super-Ego, so Charles Hanly suggests, on the basis of the philosophical tradition as well as of his clinical experience, to use both terms but to be meant in a different manner as referring to different psychic aspects of personality: the former connotes a *state of being*, whereas the latter connotes a *state of becoming*. This is partially justified, for example, by distinguishing these three main cases: an individual may be honest in her or his dealing with others because she or he fears punishment by others (the primary narcissistic motives of self-interest or egoism – Ideal Ego pole), because she or he fears punishment by her or his own guilt (the moral motive or Super-Ego prohibition), or because she or he wishes to be, and to be seen, an honest person (the secondary narcissistic motive – Ego's Ideal pole) (Hanly, 1984, 2011).

The Ideal Ego has in-depth narcissistic origins going back to the primary identification (of primary narcissism) and precedes all further object relations, as well as it is prior to Super-Ego; it was also called the *ein einziger Zug* (i.e., the *unary trait*) by Freud, the unavoidable and unchangeable basis upon which to build up all the next secondary identifications (of the Ego's Ideal and Super-Ego, in secondary narcissism stage). The Ideal Ego springs out from the fusional bodily relation with mother, and is the most archaic agency, which physiologically corresponds to the realization of the primary and secondary circular reactions according to J. Piaget (Petrini et al., 2013). Although the individual should leave such a narcissistic ideal of omnipotence and immediate satisfaction, he or she is however unable to renounce fully to that plain and unconditioned state of pleasure enjoyed in the childhood[28]. Such a first, infant narcissistic state, i.e., the *Idealich*, is afterwards overcome thanks to either parents and society criticisms in regard to the child and the internalization of idealized objects, towards Ego's Ideal (Lis et al., 2003).

To be precise, the next convergence of this primary narcissism with the interiorization of such criticisms and the consequent parental identifications, will give rise to the Ego's Ideal, that, in *On Narcissism. An Introduction* (of 1914), it was introduced, by Freud, to indicate an internal psychic formation that enables Ego to evaluate its own operate constantly comparing it with an already acquired ideal model, i.e., the Ego's Ideal, as outcome of the sunset of Œdipal complex. Therefore, it gives rise to agencies of self-observation as well as of prohibition, together to other secondary identifications[29] of secondary narcissism (as outcomes of the aggressive tendencies, ambivalent relations, introjection of the rival, and internalization of the conflict[30]), which allow the rising of the first psychic components of subjectivity. Then, in *Group Psychology and the Analysis of the Ego* of 1922, Freud puts Ego's Ideal at the basis of the formation of collectivity which may exist only after a common object has been put as an ideal to be shared collectively, in such a way that different individuals may identify among them, for having in common such an ideal in the own Ego; so, it is in the further convergence of the Ego's Ideal owned by many individuals, that Freud saw the early origin of social cohesion. Then, in *The Ego and the Id* of 1923, Freud overlaps Ego's Ideal with the notion of Super-Ego (explicitly mentioned, for the first time, just in this work), hence making a first distinction between them only in the[31] *New Introductory Lectures to Psychoanalysis* of 1932, according to the chain of co-implications[32] "moral consciousness ↔ guilt ↔ Super Ego (feared) ↔ sense of inferiority ↔ ideality function ↔ Ego's Ideal (loved)".

Subsequently, on the basis of these last Freudian conceptions, other authors, as Nunberg in 1932, Lacan in 1936 and Lagache in 1958, retook two such Ego's agencies as distinct from each other[33], even if, as already said, in the last period of his work, Freud himself more or less implicitly started to distinguish between these two Ego's subagencies. Their interplay will play a key role in the following psychic behaviour of every human being. Lagache considers the above Freudian chain of equivalences, explicitly talking of a pair Ego's Ideal–Super Ego in which respectively ideality and prohibition permeates of each other, but always keeping their distinct and oppositional roles but with possible interchange's relations. This is a well-known fact, linked with the basic disaggregated nature of Ego and its components, often in opposition among them; this is also true for Super-Ego, as pointed out by J.A. Arlow (Moore & Fine, 1990; Gay, 2000).

Likewise, Nunberg deems that the obedience to Super-Ego is induced by the fear of punishment (as due to feared persons), while the affection to Ego's Ideal is motivated by the loving sentiment (felt in regard to loved persons), even if he supposes the two agencies of the pair Ego's Ideal–Super Ego, as sharply distinct and opposite of each other. Nevertheless, either Nunberg and Lagache do not exclude at all a relationship of exchange between them, like, for instance, in the relations of the type love-hatred in which possible reference persons there involved, may change their status in respect to the single individual to whom they contribute to form such agencies[34]. Finally, among others, Grunberger (1971) and Chasseguet-Smirgel (1975, 1985) (see also references cited at the beginning of this subsection) have stressed the need to consider distinct the two agencies of Ego's Ideal and Super-Ego, the former pointing out the main internal narcissistic origin of Ego's Ideal on the one hand, and, on the other hand, the dependence of Super-Ego on the external environment, whose origins are retraceable in the Œdipus phase, stating too, that these two agencies follow different pathways which may lead to reciprocal contrasts between them.

Anyway, we may say that all these last authors agree in identifying, just in the Ideal Ego[35], an unconscious narcissistic formation, prior to Super-Ego, characterized by either an omnipotence's ideal bringing back to the early state of indistinctness of Ego from Es (death drive) or a primary identification with mother (child-mother bind) and experienced as omnipotent (narcissistic rigidity). In the Ideal Ego, reigns the symmetry, the indistinctness, so there is no dialectic, for its deep roots in the fusional and symbiotic tie child-mother. Instead, in the pair Ego's Ideal–Super-Ego, there is the fundamental dialectic between the *One* and the *Other*, that is, respectively, what one would like to be (the *One*) with respect to what already exists beyond own individuality (the *Other*). As we shall discuss later, the Ego and its development is closely related just to this dialectic[36] internal to the agency pair Ego's Ideal–Super-Ego.

Indeed, the notion of Ego's Ideal remains however implicit in almost all the Freud's work, until to begin object of his explicit study between 1914 and 1922, in concomitance with the passage from the first to the second topology of human psyche. From the Ego's Ideal, Freud goes to Super-Ego, but, before that, he however points out, as early in *On Narcissism. An Introduction*, the crucial importance played by the former for the development of the Ego itself, which, on its turn, is oriented towards the external reality and the establishment of object relations, so Ego needs to take *enough distance* from primary narcissism (of Ideal Ego) of child-mother tie, but, at the same time, trying to recover it, because of the fact that the immediate satisfaction and the infinite omnipotence of primary narcissism always exert their ascending influence, so they are always present (also due to death drive and mainly acting through compulsion to repeat) just as a sedimentation of the Ego into an area hold by the Ego's Ideal (seen therefore as a kind of precipitate around the initial germ of the Ideal Ego) which runs as a kind of "propeller pole" of the Ego for its evolutive pathway, so first triggering then allowing the channelling of narcissistic libido (at first, polarized all around Ideal Ego) toward objects make available by Super-Ego, and whose related cathexed energy may then come back to the Ego itself and its energy reservoir (Jaffé, 2009).

So, with the breaking of the child-mother bind[37], which takes place along the Œdipal phase, arise Ego's Ideal and Super-Ego agencies, which have wide pieces of their lands in common with Ego where it may interact with them, without excluding possible conflicts between Ego, Super-Ego and Ego's Ideal, which may arise too. In any case, the key of this basic process is the dawning of the Ego's Ideal from the Ideal Ego by means of the intervention of the Œdipal triangulation[38], so transforming primary needs (of Ideal Ego) to desires (of Ego's Ideal) to be accomplished in respect to Super-Ego, and in dependence on related Ego's instructions, even if, as Freud himself pointed out (Fodor & Gaynor, 1950), either Ego and Super-Ego, most of the times, carry on together, being possible to distinguish them only when they enter into conflict of each other, and this mainly occurs in some chief cases.

For instance, out of these, one concerns the case in which a strong push of activation coming from primary narcissism, flattens the Ego on either the object and the Ego's Ideal, these latter being both identified between them in the desperate endeavour to restore the fusional tie child-mother, like in the cases of falling in love, so the Ego will turn out to be emptied of its own resources and at the mercy of the Ego's Ideal, a psychic state, this, that, if is persistent, may lead to maniac-depressive disorders or to melancholia, until up possible Ego's fragments, still remained in the consciousness, may broke this idealized soap inside which the deceived subject lives.

We are interested, in particular, in the formation of Ego's Ideal. It starts from the primary nucleus of the Ideal Ego, acquiring, by internalization, various idealized objects, as bearers of secondary narcissism, from the moment in which the child becomes aware to live as a separate psychic entity detached from the child-mother tie, which takes place when he or she enters into the crucial Œdipal *triangular space* (Britton 2000, Ch. IV). With the breaking of such an embroiling symbiosis child-mother, mainly characterized by the Ideal Ego agency (and upon which a very weak Ego is still flattened), two different psychic agencies begin to stand out, namely the Ego's Ideal and the Super-Ego, which, as has been said above, should be deemed different, yet closely related, of each other. With this bifurcation, the Ego is allowed to issue over them, acquiring a metalevel of control integrating subjectivity (Ego's Ideal) with objectivity (Super-Ego) thanks to the conquer of a *third position* in a *triangular psychic space* springing out from Œdipal phase (Britton 2000, 2003; Jaffé, 2009; Petrini et al., 2013).

So, Ego's Ideal is successive to Ideal Ego, it is its heir, as the outcome of the renunciation by child of her or his primary and predominant narcissistic position, replacing the love for herself or himself with other ideals to be reached, coming from various identifications with parental figures and others in accordance with her or his own previous Ideal Ego. Such identifications will be made possible thanks to the Ego, even if this latter often is not always able to carry forward such a role, as well as to make the right choices; these are taken from family considered in its social-cultural context and environment where child grows up and lives. Hence, Ego's Ideal is the result of a particular series of successive identifications with idealized objects[39], so, according to Freud, the sense of inferiority comes from the comparison between Ego's evaluations and what the model provided by Ego's Ideal is able to furnish to the subject, an ideal model to which he or she always tends to conform herself or himself, but never reaching it, just because of the structural nature of such an agency (Jaffé, 2009; Petrini et al., 2013).

Thus, Ego's Ideal is not only the yearned place of primary narcissism, now re-actualized as a multilayer shell of secondary narcissism built up on the primary narcissism nucleus of Ideal Ego, by means of various identifications with idealized objects drawn up from otherness, but comprehends too consciousness patterns, ethical and cultural conceptions, parental models, educational schemes, present at the junction point with Super-Ego, in that such features are also elements of the latter. So, Ego's Ideal is edified upon that empty space[40] which has come create by the forced abandonment[41] of primary narcissism, with the related consequences due to the losing of that blissful state[42] felt in the symbiosis child-mother in which every primary and secondary need (according to Piaget – see above) was immediately and fully satisfied. The coming of this agency, i.e., the Ego's Ideal, is crucial for the psychological development of the subject, as, in its complexity and peculiarity, it occupies a cardinal junction place between absolute narcissism and objectuality, between pleasure and reality principle (Jaffé, 2009).

Freud himself changed his ideas on Ego's Ideal and Super-Ego: at first, in *The Ego and the Id* (of 1923), he gives pre-eminence to Super-Ego, a part of which is the Ego's Ideal, and with respect to which the Ego compares itself and ever tries to conform; afterwards, in the *New Introductory Lectures on Psycho-Analysis* (of 1932), he instead inverts, in some sense, this perspective, giving major importance to narcissistic aspects of personality, upon which Super-Ego itself builds up. However, this change of perspective was mainly motivated and promoted by the change of topography of human psyche, after which Freud became aware of the impossibility to consider coincident these two agencies, a question inherited by post-Freudian authors who identified, within it, three main problematic themes: the polarity narcissism/Œdipus, the polarity pre-object structure/object relationship, and the polarity ideality/prohibition-guilt-punishment (Jaffé, 2009). Anyway, an essential polarity's feature seems therefore to lie between these two main distinct agencies, that is to say, we may consider to partially hold a basic relationship of the following type: Ego's Ideal $\xleftrightarrow{\text{polarity}}$ Super-Ego.

Therefore, the rising of these two different agencies, is of fundamental importance for the psychic development of every human being, basically because, loosely speaking, the coming of Super-Ego, is associated to reality, to objectual world, to temporality (Loewald, 1962, 1999), to separation, to the father's role, while the Ego's Ideal is related to narcissism, to perfection, to undifferentiation, to the desire to restore the child-mother symbiotic tie (Petrini et al., 2013). These two distinct poles gives rise to a primary dialectic just due to their essentially opposed nature, which lies at the basis of the inter-relationship between respectively *objectivity* (otherness) and *subjectivity*. Upon these, a third agency, the Ego, develops thanks to the intervention of the third position in the Œdipal triangular psychic space, which warrants the possible integration of subjectivity and objectivity. The main function of Ego is to produce *beliefs*, which may become *knowledge* only after a preliminary objective evaluation of them (Britton 2000, 2003).

Freud himself considered the *believing* as a judgement function giving a reality connotation[43], to be ascribed to the Ego (located in the perceptive-conscious system) and explicable only by means of language, so reaching to the basic distinction between *psychic* (or *internal*) *reality* and *material* (or *external*) *reality*. Following Kant, Freud, just at the beginnings of his work, stated that beliefs and doubts belonged to the Ego, not to the unconscious (later, said to be *Es* or *Id*) which does not know the notions of reality, doubt, belief, contradiction, space, time, and all the other typical aspects of perceptive system (from which Ego springs out as a *bodily Ego*). Britton, besides, supposes that beliefs (much more than doubts) are so natural as other features of perceptive system, like feeling, breathing, etc., which are conform to the innate ideas of space and time. For us, events occur inside a three-dimensional space, according to a unidirectional time, in a certain place or in another one, and we cannot do otherwise. Just in such a way, consciousness runs, according to natural, innate (Kantian) forms of human mind, with which imagination[44] discloses (Britton 2000, 2003).

Therefore, the Ego regulates the interaction of the internal psychic experience with what comes from external reality by means of perception; the Ego nominates the experiences, assigns the status of certainty to selected ideas and certain fantasies, hence tests the degree of reality their assigned by means of the reality exam, that assigns them the judgement of truth or falsity. At the same time, it is the nucleus of subjective Self, the one receiving perception and accordingly promotes the action. It is the agency which makes us real. The subjective Self is, then, the observed Self, so Ego is also the place of self-consciousness, the awareness of ourselves. Britton, furthermore, points out that the self-observation and the judgement on themselves are preeminent functions of the Ego, not of the Super-Ego, even if these are often usurped by the latter. So, the reality judgement is competence of the Ego, while the moral judgement regards Super-Ego (Britton, 2003).

What now urges, is to understand how Ego stands out from these other agencies, in particular how Ego emancipates from Super-Ego. On the other hand, Freud, as early in the paper *Remarks on the Theory and Practice of Dream-Interpretation* of 1922, had glimpsed a possible splitting of the Ego in re-analyzing his theory on dreams. He remarked that such a splitting could occur either in vigil and dreaming state, makes reference to Ego's Ideal as a psychic agency separated from Ego, which observes, criticizes and punishes. But, Britton observes that the Ego' functions are quite different from the ones of either Super-Ego and Ego's Ideal: to Ego are due the functions of self-observation and judgement of internal and external reality, while to Super-Ego and Ego's Ideal are respectively due the functions of moral-ethical evaluations and the choice of the models to follow (Britton, 2003).

2.8.3. Further Elementary Considerations on Symbolism

Continuing on the wake of what has already been said in the previous Section 1, according to (Abbagnano, 1998) and (Galimberti, 2006), the word *symbol* derives from the Greek noun σύμβολου (with

Latin transliteration *sȳmbolum*), this from σύμβαλλω, in turn derived from the verb συμβάλλειν (with Latin transliteration *sȳm bállein*) which, in composition, means "throw together". It is characterized, like the *sign*, by an a priori *postponement* which, on the one hand, includes the symbol in the sign's order as a specific case of it (as a conventional symbol), whereas, on the other hand, it is opposed to the sign itself because the latter has a predetermined relationship with what it denotes or connotes (*aliquid stat pro aliquo*[45]), whereas the *symbol*, instead, in evoking its corresponding part, refers to a given reality which is not decided by some form of convection but by the recomposition or assembling of a whole (in respect of its original etymological meaning, as a non-conventional symbol). Roughly speaking, there is no rigid link between a symbol and what it symbolizes.

Nevertheless, the relationships between sign and symbol are never well delineated in a clear manner. The psychoanalytic perspective might yet provide useful clarifications, above all that of the Kleinian trend and that of the British *middle group* headed by Donald W. Winnicott, if one takes into account the early etymological meaning of the term "symbol" (Laplanche & Pontalis, 1967), i.e., the one that refers to the "assembling of a set of things". Following (Petocz 2004, Ch. 1), which quotes a Lévi-Strauss' consideration, the concept of meaning is so difficult to define perhaps because of its intimate reciprocal connection with the notion of symbol. On the other hand, the noun σύμβολου, i.e., a "tally", originally referred to each of the two corresponding pieces of some small object which contracting parties broke between them and kept as proof of identity when rejoined together[46]. That meaning subsequently expanded to include a diversity of meaning such as other kinds of tokens, seal, contract, sign, code, and so forth (Laplanche & Pontalis, 1967).

2.8.4. A Brief Historiographical Outline on Verneinung (Negation), Verleugnung (Disavowal), Verdrängung (Repression) and Verwerfung (Foreclosure)

2.8.4.1. Verneinung, Verleugnung, Verdrängung and Verwerfung: A Brief Introduction

According to (Roudinesco 1995, Part VI, Ch. V) and (Petrini et al., 2013), Freud, for the first time, used the term *negation*[47] (*Verneinung*) in 1917 after a personal re-elaboration of the term *negative hallucination* due to H. Bernheim, following his 1914 reclassification of psychoses, neuroses and perversions, based on castration theory, as made in *On Narcissism. An Introduction*. The term was then explicitly used by Freud in 1925. By *Verneinung*, Freud meant a verbal mechanism through which the repressed material is recognized in a negative logical manner by the subject, but without being accepted. So, negation implies a contestation, that related to the recognition of a repressed thought by the patient. Freud says that every "not" comes from unconscious (Petrini et al., 2013).

Nevertheless, following (Britton 2000, Ch. V), Freud, as early in the *Studies on Hysteria* (of 1892-95), claimed the attention on a particular state of the mind that he described summarily with the motto "the blindness of the eye which does not see", to refer to that mental disposition for which something is known and, at the same time, is not known. Later, he used the term *Verleugnung* to describe this particular form of negation without psychotic features, subsequently translated into *disavowal* by James Strachey, until up to consider it, in 1938, as a "middle measure in which the denegation is followed by an acknowledgement, with the establishment of two concomitant yet opposite settings, independent of each other, which de facto give rise to a splitting of the Ego".

Hence, Britton makes reference to other authors who have fruitfully retaken the last Freudian notion of disavowal, like M. Bash who considers disavowal, differently from psychotic denegation, as a mechanism which nullifies only the sense of things but not their effective perception, that is to say, the external thing is however present in the internal psychic world of the subject. Then, J. Steiner speaks of the action of disavowal mechanism as "turning a blind eye", linking it to the Œdipal complex (Britton 2006, Ch. V, p. 89). This in agreement with Octave Mannoni[48], according to whom Freud began to implicitly use the notion of disavowal after the 1890s in discussing the concept of splitting the Ego, both these notions being closely related to one another.

Likewise, following (Conrotto, 2009), the question of negation compared, in the Freudian work, since its beginnings. The first reflections on it, were done by Freud in relation to psychoses and exposed, in the personal letters to Wilhelm Fliess of the 1890s, in which he discusses of psychotic functioning, in particular of the characteristic elements of paranoid projection[49], for which affects and contents of incompatible representations are however kept in consciousness but projected outside, together the rejection of the related judgements (reproofs, accusations, etc.). So, Freud already held the essence of what will be later called disavowal, since the late of the 1890s. Nevertheless, he subsequently used a great variety of further terms to describe the many aspects of these psychic phenomena.

Indeed, in *On the Sexual Theories of Children* (of 1908) and in *The case of little Hans* (of 1908), Freud explicitly describes the disavowal (*Verleugnung*) as due to the penis' lacking in the woman, hence he comes back to it in 1934, extending this painful perception from the specific case of penis' envy to all the possible perceptions contrasting pleasure principle, denying the reality of the related negative perception so had. Then, Freud specifies that this defence mechanism is quite different from repression, relating it to psychoses rather than neuroses. Afterwards, in *Fetishism* (of 1927), in *An Outline of Psychoanalysis* (of 1938) and in *Splitting of the Ego in the Process of Defence* (of 1938), Freud puts this mechanism in relation with a splitting of the Ego[50] into two independent yet contrasting of each other components giving rise different mental dispositions (Conrotto, 2009).

Nevertheless, this mechanism does not entail the deletion of either a perception or a representation, but rather it entails the rejection of the meaning (signified) that this implies, namely, in the specific case of penis's lacking, the rejection of the castration's phantasm, so that, in general, what is really rejected is the attribution judgement. So, we should say that, while repression (*Verdrängung*) deals with affect, disavowal (*Verleugnung*) deals with representation, in the sense that, as the former does not cancel affect but shifts this to the unconscious, so the latter does not cancel the representation (*signifier*) but deletes its meaning (*signified*). Furthermore, disavowal is always the denegation of a "lack" (widely meant[51]), while negation (*Verneinung*) is the first step towards the preconscious recognition of something however present (Conrotto, 2009).

The relationship between mind and reality has been a controversial theme in Freud's work, debated between two main hypotheses about its functioning: on the one hand, the mind is passively considered to be the result of the reproduction of reality, while, on the other hand, we have a mind that actively creates and transforms reality. In *The Negation* (of 1925), Freud, contrasting a well-established philosophical tradition, considers the *judgement of attribution* prior to the *judgement of existence*, that is to say, we first judge[52], on the basis of pleasure/displeasure principle, then we formulate an existence judgement of the real. Thus, reality would not be reproduced as such by the mind, in its perfect form, but it would be rather a construction resulting from a series of complex operations of assumption and rejection (Chianese, 2009).

By means of negations (by *Verleugnung*) and denials (by *Verleugnung*), precociously included into the language, the child may manipulate and distort reality, so that the language just relies on the power of the primordial (as well as primitive) negations and denials, which therefore should be considered as primitive psychic mechanisms of human being. The Ego develops through language and, in turn, language develops by means of negations and denials so that the latter are constitutive acts of the Ego, which grows up just through these primary acceptances-registrations (by negation) and denials-cancellations (by disavowal). However, a fundamental importance has had the short paper *The Negation* (of 1925), in which Freud discusses the two main aspects of this basic defence mechanism, the second of which will gradually lead to *Verleugnung* (Chianese, 2009).

Indeed, in his short yet fundamental paper *The Negation* (of 1925), Freud discusses the two main aspects of negation: the first one, is that related to the availability to make acceptable, by negation, an unpleasant content so repressed, bringing it at the consciousness level but with a content which is the negation of the repressed one (just by means of the symbol of negation), so that the repressed material is yes recognized but in a negative manner; the second one, instead, concerns the rising of a *judgement* in regard to the external reality in which the psyche of the individual does not find a satisfactory representation, so, in this case, negation deals with foundational bases of reality principle. It is, therefore, the basic ascertainment of an *absence* which leads to the recognition of an external reality independent of the individual, this entailing therefore first forms of separation between intellectual functions and affectivity components, as well as the dawning of judgements. All that is just typical of *Verleugnung* (Conrotto, 2009).

However, the question of the Ego's splitting has always been more or less explicitly considered by Freud throughout his work, since the beginnings. Indeed, in *The Wolf Man* (of 1914), Freud implicitly discusses such a mechanism in a case-study in which no judgement had been expressly given on the existence of castration, but it was only taken into account the non-existence of it, so that, there held, in the patient, two opposite tendencies: on the one hand, he abhorred the eviration, while, on the other hand, he was disposed to accept it, taking comfort by femininity as a compensation. But Freud says too that a third tendency still virtually persisted as well, that is to say, the most ancestral and deepest one, that which restricted to dismiss the eviration, without posing to himself the problem to express any judgement about the reality or not of such a painful perception (Conrotto, 2009).

This last full rejection is terminologically expressed, by Freud, with the verb *Verwerfen*, that is, to dismiss in full, which led to consider a new psychic mechanism, said to be *Verwerfung*, and usually translated in *preclusion*, or *foreclosure* (from Lacan onwards), as the key of psychotic disorder, as discussed by Freud in *The Schreber Case* (of 1910), by which what has been abolished inside us (precluded) will however turn back to us, for example in hallucinatory manner like in psychoses. This early abolishment was named, by Lacan, *foreclosure*, even if such a term has its origins in the definition of the so-called *negative hallucination*, given by Hippolyte Bernheim in[53] 1884, and meant as an absence of the perception of an object anyhow present in the perceptive field. According to Lacan, foreclosure consists in the rejection of a signifier outside the symbolic universe of the individual, or else, in the refusal of the inscription of a signifier in the symbolic chain, so that the *Verwerfung* should be the inverse of the *Bejahung*, i.e., the admission, with which the attributive judgement takes place, as well as the primary process with which something of real is revealed to the being, so opening the way to the symbolic register (Conrotto, 2009; Petrini et al., 2013).

Following (Britton 2000, Ch. V), Freud also used the term *Verleugnung* after 1923, to indicate, in the cases of perversions and obsessive neuroses the refusal, by the subject, to recognizing the reality of a negative or traumatic perception, like the lacking of a female penis; afterwards, in 1938, Freud extended that, to all the possible painful perceptions and experiences which, contrasting with pleasure principle, lead to not recognize reality or to transform it, in a hallucinatory manner, to fulfil desire. The

Verneinung is connected to a mechanism typical of neuroses, whereas the *Verleugnung* is connected to a mechanism typical of perversions[54]. Finally, according to Freud, the *Verdrängung* is a term which indicates a mechanism related to *repression*. Thereafter, in the 1914 *Wolf Man*, Freud also used the term *Verwerfung* to indicate the *rejection* of a reality presented as non-existent, and to be meant as distinct from the previous ones.

So, Freud identified four main defence mechanisms, along his whole route of clinical work and theoretical investigation, processes which should be however more correct to name them *psychic transformations*: *Verdrängung* (repression) and *Verneinung* (negation) in the case of neuroses (and both mainly regarding the relations between Ego and Es), *Verleugnung* (disavowal) and *Verwerfung* (foreclosure) in the case of psychoses (and both mainly regarding Ego). The *Verneinung* allows the partial re-issue of repressed material by means of a linguistic transformation, the *negation*, so making admissible the coming in the consciousness of a content before deemed inacceptable, just considering its negation. The *Verdrängung* eliminates from consciousness field those affects and representations which are, in some way, incompatible either with the pleasure principle (for primary repression) and with the system of self-representations, values and moral-ethical norms which form her or his own conscious identity (for secondary repression); these transformations are mainly somatic as concern affects, while remain as such for the psychic ones (Riolo, 2009).

In the *Verneinung*, there is no repression of neither affect or representation, but the negation of their belonging to the individual, that is to say, the transformation regards the reality judgement and takes place into the Ego field. It is closely related to another form of denial, the *Verleugnung*, in which there is not the negation of a verbal predicate (like in the *Verneinung*) but the negation of a reality object, so a splitting of the Ego occurs, in the sense that, two opposite tendencies – i.e., the denial of the perception of a some reality and, at the same time, its acknowledgement – are both present in the Ego, without any intervention of repression processes. Finally, a fourth psychic transformation, i.e., the *Verwerfung*, takes place when the Ego repudiates, in a stronger and more intense manner, a psychic representation together its affective charge, as if it were never reached to the Ego, so we have an incipit of psychosis. So, differently from *Verleugnung* (in which, as we have said above, the representation however holds in the Ego, although this is split, but not the related affect which is however not treated by this mechanism, as repressed), in the *Verwerfung* there is a preventive expulsion (into the real register, following Lacan) of both affect and representation from the Ego, hence its exclusion, in full, from the symbolic register (again, following Lacan), whence psychosis. Nevertheless, the results of this expulsion will come back to the Ego, from the Real register, just in the form of delirious or hallucination (Riolo, 2009).

These two main forms of negation, i.e., the *Verneinung* and the *Verleugnung*, are however brought back to the primary, irreducible duality pleasure/displeasure principle characterizing the qualitative functioning[55] of the dynamics of human psyche mainly based on the impulsive motion of primary drives, from which, then, all the other opposite pairs spring out, so featuring the intrinsic duality of consciousness (Conrotto, 2009). For these reasons, the *Verneinung* seems to characterize basically the linguistic function of human being (with its symbol of negation), while the *Verleugnung* (which is however in close relation with *Verneinung*) seems rather to be the only psychic transformation, regarding the Ego, to be put in relation with symbolic function, in that the psychic representation[56] (*signifier*) is not repressed, differently from the affect[57] (*signified*), so it remains in the symbolic order, in a de-affectivized state, under the influence of the two opposed subagencies of the Ego as outcomes of the related splitting process undergone by Ego, just entailed by this transformation, so providing that basic opposition feature which is the key element of human symbolic function and its running. Furthermore, as said above, *Verleugnung* is just at the early basis of reality principle as well as of the judgement function. Due to this, we are of the opinion that this primary psychic mechanism if a founding process for the psyche of every human being, as it relies at the early basis of symbolic function. This in agreement with[58] Jean Laplanche and Jean-Bertrand Pontalis (1973), as well as with respect to what Freud himself willed to allude in his last works of the late 1930s, not considering *Verleugnung* as fully and solely related to deep psychosis (in that it takes place for *Verwerfung*), but rather having to do with its incipit or with related limit cases or with its intrusions in the field of consciousness[59].

2.8.4.2. Other Considerations, Hints and Remarks

In France, there were some heated debates (in which Freud himself was involved) about the relations of the term *scotomization*, first proposed by Pichon-Rivière in 1928 to indicate an unconscious mechanism through which a subject makes disappear from the consciousness those facts which are unpleasant, with the previous terms. For instance, R. Laforgue proposed to consider scotomization as comprising either the *Verleugnung* and another repression mechanism typical of psychoses, whilst Freud considered it as distinct from both *Verleugnung* and *Verdrängung*. Laforgue wanted to indicate an annulment of a perception whilst Freud wished to keep the perception within a framework supported by negation, that is to say, not complete closure of a perception in front of a misunderstanding of reality, but rather activation of a perception put between a denegation and a repression. In a nutshell, the real problem consisted in the lack of a specific term to indicate the rejection mechanism typical of psychoses.

And, even Freud had a certain moment of uncertainty between all these terms, *Verleugnung* (disavowal), *Verdrängung* (repression) and *Verneinung* (negation), in relation to the psychosis' mechanisms. Finally, Freud opted for *Verleugnung* (i.e., denegation or disavowal, as it will be called later by James Strachey). *Verleugnung* (i.e., *disavowal*, or *denial*, of the reality), is a term that Freud began to explicitly use, in a specific sense, after the 1925 paper entitled *The Negation*, until it attained a more general sense in the last of his works, namely the 1938 *Abriß der Psychoanalyse*[60] (Freud, 1938), even if such a primary notion did not have a definitive characterization, for which reason it will be retaken by his followers to be studied more deeply.

As stated above, disavowal (*Verleugnung*) is different both from negation (*Verneinung*) and from repression (*Verdrängung*). Following the last Freudian ideas exposed in (Freud 1938, Part III, Chs. 8 and 9), as well as on the basis of the previous considerations, we may suppose disavowal as a fundamental psychic mechanism which relies on the primary basis of any other possible relation with the external reality. Indeed, in this his last works, Freud fully re-examined all his previous ideas about the Ego agency and its functions in the light of the fundamental psychic process of Ego's splitting. In this 1938 work, Freud also states that a certain degree of fetishism is also part of normality, particularly during romantic love[61]. The above-mentioned Freud work *The Negation* has therefore played a primary role in the subsequent studies on consciousness.

In fact, following (De Mijolla, 2005), negation dramatizes a situation of interpretative conflict and is related to a dialogical situation. Negation, unknown at the level of the unconscious, needs to be situated on a secondary level, and we can gain access to it only by way of the symbol (the symbol of negation). The study of the interrelation between oral instinctual motions and the establishment of negative and affirmative behaviour, has been further investigated in the works of René A. Spitz (1957). Then, following (Akhtar & O'Neil, 2011), any elementary content, according to Freud, becomes conscious only in its inverted and negated forms. Subsequent epistemological analyses (Chemama & Vandermersch,

1998) have shown that this 1925 Freudian paper dwells above all on with the disavowal mechanism and not only on with the negation one (as besides already mentioned above), so that his main theses were much more related to the former rather than to the latter.

On the other hand, with his notion of splitting of the Ego, Freud showed his 1938 last thoughts especially concerning fetishism and typical aspects of psychosis. It also enlightens his ideas on the basically non-unified structure of the Ego. He moreover focused on the question of the possible relationships between the Ego agency and the reality, introducing another model different from that of repression and of the re-emersion of the repressed content, just by establishing the notion of disavowal as a specific psychic mechanism regarding Ego agency in its relationships with reality (Bokanowski & Lewkowicz, 2009). However, the initial motivations for the introduction of the disavowal mechanism were mainly due to attempts to give a satisfactory explanation of the main features of psychoses which remained until then out of the psychoanalytic theoretical framework which was mainly turned to explain neuroses.

Broadly speaking, disavowal is therefore a main defence mechanism through which the individual denies the recognition of general painful experiences, impulses, reality data or aspects of herself or himself which generate anguish. Such a notion however might be also understood as a first generalization of a particular initial denial, precisely the one experienced by the individual in recognizing that traumatic perception which consists in the occurred awareness of the lack of a female penis, with consequent supervention of the related castration anxiety due to the interdict of castration threat (Laplanche & Pontalis, 1967). On the other hand, according to the initial 1924 Freudian conception, at the first impressions of this lack of a penis, the baby boy just disavows this absence or lack and *imagines* to see, in an equal manner, a penis which formerly there was but that afterwards has been cut off (castration).

And still according to Freud (1938), this process seems to be quite normal and widespread in children, but that it might become later dangerous in adult age, giving rise either to a psychotic behaviours or a paraphilia, even if, in these last cases, it is yet quite unclear in what specific manner these take place (Petrini et al., 2011, 2013). Girls, instead, reject the acceptance of the *facto datum* of their own castration, persisting in the conviction of having a penis, being therefore forced, later, to behave as if they were males (penis' envy[62]).

Subsequently, as has already been said, this first disavowal conception was then extended to all the painful perceptions which, contrasting with the pleasure principle, lead to not recognizing the reality and to transform it, for example, through hallucinatory modalities, to fulfil desire. Fetishism, besides homosexuality, is the most frequent amongst the paraphilias (Greenacre 1971, Ch. XVII), although it is the most difficult one to be diagnosed due to the fact that it is mainly asymptomatic. In any event, fetish may be determined too by a symbolic unconscious association often depending on the variegated range of multiform sexual experiences had in childhood (Petrini et al. 2011, 2013).

2.8.5. Towards the Ego's Splitting

The 1927 Freudian paradigm of fetishism, which was initially laid down to explain the formation of fetishes by means of castration anxiety due to the observation of the lack of a female penis, has gone beyond the context of sexuality, due to the rigour with which it was formulated by Freud himself. Subsequently, such a paradigm underwent further improvements until a definitive 1938 model centred around the basic notion of Ego's splitting (Freud, 1938). According to the latter, most people overcome such a castration complex through *symbolic elaboration*[63], accepting the gender sexual differences (the basis of the sense of *otherness* or *alterity* (Gilliéron & Baldassarre, 2012), whereas those who do not overcome such a complex will have neurotic developments with possible paraphilic degeneration (Piscicelli 1994, Ch. IX).

In fetishism, the perception that disproves the infant's belief in a female penis is not rejected but is, as some say, displaced upon an object, the *fetish*. It therefore does not imply a hallucination or an alteration of the representation of reality (like in psychoses), but simply it repudiates the reality. After having detected the lack of a female penis, the child has, in a certain sense, modified its initial belief about the female penis, retaining it and, at the same time, abandoning it (*Aufgegeben*). He or she believes that, despite everything, the female has a penis, even if this is no longer that of before, because something has taken its place or replaced it, that is to say, it has been named a "symbolic substitute" for it upon which it will be possible to cathexis the desire to avoid the strong anxiety's pressures due to the castration principle. But, in doing so, the child inevitably goes into a conflict created by the load of the real undesired perception of a penis lack against the force of a counter-desire opposed to this, thereby reaching a basic ambivalence whose resolutive compromise will be possible only thanks to the action of the unconscious thought which dialectically operates through its own primary processes[64].

In short, the fetish is, yes, a symbolic substitute for the phallus, not always an iconic reproduction, but rather a kind of reification of it. Such a fetish reflects, at the same time, the denial and the affirmation of the female castration, this also corresponding to the coexistence of two opposite attitudes in respect of the fetish, which Freud tries to explain by means of a particular psychic mechanism, called *Ego's splitting* (*Ichspaltung*). This splitting takes place when the child undergoes a conflict between the initial instinct's claim (*Anspruch*) and the objection made by reality (*Einsprunch*), but does not choose either one or the other, or else chooses both. In such a manner, the formation of the Ego's synthetic function is perturbed.

Thus, to sum up, a fundamental characteristic of fetishism is that it allows reality to be recognized and, at the same time, disclaimed. It gives rise to the fundamental creation of opposites whose separation, thanks to this splitting mechanism (if correctly operating), is at the basis of first consciousness formation[65]. Such a mechanism, however, is different from the psychotic one because the latter is a mere and simple repudiation of the reality[66] which is never recognized. Nevertheless, the (paraphilic) fetishist cannot avoid a degenerative Ego splitting when this splitting does not give rise to that compensative symbolic elaboration recalled above (Benvenuto, 2005).

2.8.6. On Ego's Splitting, Fetishism and Transitional Phenomena

By means of the disavowal mechanism, Freud glimpses the origins of an intrasystemic Ego's splitting[67] (*Ichspaltung*) through which, within the Ego agency, two distinct and conflictual psychic attitudes take place of which one takes into account the reality denied by the other, and substitutes it with the content of a desire. Or else, following (Laplanche & Pontalis, 1967), through this intrapsychic division, an Ego's splitting takes place both into a part which observes and into a part which is observed.

This last perspective is widely but implicitly used by Freud in his final works, above all to denote a certain dichotomic or separated nature of human psyche. Throughout this paper, when we refer to the notion of Ego's splitting, we mean this last perspective, coherently with the Freudian work in which such a notion starts to be used with the celebrated works *Fetishism* (of 1927), *Splitting of the Ego in the Process of Defence* (of 1938) and in *Abriß der Psychoanalyse* (of 1938). Above all, we will follow the Freudian thought of this last work. According to Freud, disavowal would allow us to explain the typical features of psychoses and fetishism.

Following (Galimberti, 2006), as stated above, the original 1925 Freudian concept of disavowal was extended to all the painful perceptions that, being in contrast with the pleasure principle, lead to not recognizing the reality, transforming it in a hallucinatory manner to satisfy the desire. Hence, disavowal is a very fundamental psychic mechanism which has to do with the external reality, and whose main result is this Ego's splitting. It is the first psychic agency to form for detecting reality. The Ego's splitting is a basic psychic mechanism preliminary to others, like introjective and projective identification, etc.

Following (Greenacre 1971, Ch. XI), in the formation of Ego's agency, a remarkable role is played by pre-Œdipus phases. In the 1930s, there was a considerable need for a deeper knowledge of Ego. In this regard, the author, thanks to her professional psychiatrist activity, had the opportunity to examine many clinical cases of psychosis which turned out to be of great usefulness just to study the Ego's function. After the studies of W. Hoffer, P. Schilder, M. Ribble, M.E. Fries, R.A. Spitz and M.S. Mahler, it had been possible to ascertain that the first formations of this agency (i.e., the Ego) are of a corporal or somatic nature (bodily Ego[68]).

Greenacre herself (and B. Lantos) pointed out a certain primitive predisposition to anxiety, mainly related to the elaboration of primal scenes, which will play a notable role in the Ego's formation, if properly cathexed, together its next splitting. According to Greenacre, the classical 1927 and 1938 Freudian works on fetishism were the best ones on fetishism and perversions. In these works, Freud foregrounds the Ego's splitting which takes place in consequence of the strong castration anxiety when a child has recognized the gender sexual differences. Above all, the kid refuses to recognize the reality of this painful situation. Nevertheless, he assigns a penis to his mother, symbolically represented by the fetish (material[69] or merely symbolic) whose specific form is largely due to the displacement of that energetic amount which has been determined in concomitance with the appearance of castration anguish.

The fetish formation must therefore provide these incongruities in the corporal image formation through suitable surrogates. These may be physical parts of the body (material fetish) or may be abstract formations like more or less complex fantasies (Greenacre 1971, Ch. XVII). The pathological cases mainly take place during the passage from the normal childish fetish of three- to four-year-olds to the latency phase, characterized by the deterioration of the capacity to establish object relations. In (Greenacre 1971, Ch. XII), the author contributed further interesting considerations on fetishism. According to her, the fetish has mainly a phallic meaning, but also a bisexual one.

Fetishism is a disorder which is mainly due to an imperfect development of corporal image and of the bodily Ego, from which derive disorders of reality sense, of identity sense and of object relations. The adult's fetish has something in common with the Winnicott childhood's *transitional object* which, usually, has a certain role in the constitution and development of the reality and of the object relation, and concerns both sexes. The formation of a transitional object takes place within the so-called (Winnicott-Spitz) *transitional space*, which is the space around which the mother-child relationship and related *transitional* phenomenology take place (Vegetti Finzi 1976, Part II).

The persistence in adult age of the fetish reveals a chronic defect of psychosomatic structure, while the transitional object is usually abandoned with the dawning of genitality, at least in normal cases. In most cases, the fetish itself is something of a secret to the fetishist himself (or herself), which is strictly related to the primary meaning of the Œdipus complex, that is to say, the uncovering of the enigma sphinx, to confirm the basic relationships existing between fetish formation and pregenital phases. Following (Greenacre 1971, Ch. XVI), in the phallic phase a consolidation of the recognition of genital organs takes place and, in the case of disorders and failures in the formation of corporal Ego, the fetish formation may cope with this, with a narcissistic reinforcement of Ego itself through it.

Finally, through a rapid analysis of the psychoanalytic literature on fetishism (Khan Masud, 1970, 1979), it will turn out that in the fetish formation process the first forms of condensation and displacement mechanisms take place, which are the two main psychodynamic processes underlying any symbolic formation. Fetish formation and (D.W. Winnicott) transitional object, have pathways which meet frequently, starting from common origins in the childhood until they become different to each other with psychic maturation, distinguishing between two possible choices, namely normality and pathology (perversions[70]). These two entities, i.e., fetish and transitional object, have many common points among them in the first stages of human psychosexual development.

2.8.7. On Ego's Ideal and Ideal Ego

Following (Laplanche & Pontalis, 1967), Freud, as mentioned above, put disavowal as the main psychic mechanism involved in the Ego's splitting. He started from the previous notion of *Spaltung* due to J. Breuer and P. Janet, but gradually reached his original generically oriented conception to indicate an intrapsychic division, above all in the last part of his life, in reference to a splitting of the Ego into an *observing part* (Ego's Ideal) and into an *observed part* (Ideal Ego); the observing part, i.e., the Ego's Ideal, does not evaluate own level of morality and ethics but rather the level of own real psychic efficiency. Later, from his above-mentioned 1927 works on fetishism, gradually Freud posed the disavowal mechanism at the basis of this splitting phenomenon that he wanted, in turn, to put at the basis of psychoses and perversions. Freud however pointed out that in psychoses a full separation from reality never takes place; in every psychosis, even the deepest ones, two antithetic psychic attitudes always exist: the one that takes into account the reality in the normal attitude, and the other that, under the drive influence, detaches the Ego from reality, giving rise to delirious thoughts.

The outcomes of this Ego's splitting are therefore two opposite psychic settings[71], of which each subsists, throughout life, alongside the other and never singly of each other, but with the prevalence, from time to time, of only one of these two, to the detriment of the other. Out of these, there is a normal self-observing component which takes into account the external reality (and is prodromic to the formation of the system *Ego's Ideal–Super-Ego*) mainly through opposition to the contrary subagency (the Ideal Ego), while the other, under the Es' instinct influence, tears out the Ego from the reality (and is prodromic to the unconscious formation of the *Ideal Ego*) assuming a prevalent narcissistic formation on the basis of primary identifications as a result of the mother-child relation from which starts to develop the Super Ego–Ego's Ideal agency pair, which, in its formation stage taking place along the first fusional, symbiotic and incestuous relationship mother-child, has an ambivalent, invasive and archaic maternal feature strongly charged of aggressivity and superpower, viscous tie which, indeed, will be broken by the Father's action (*d'après* Lacan) and that, just through the intervention of the *Father's* (or *Name-of-the-Father*) *law*, gives rise to the Œdipical agency system Ego's Ideal–Super-Ego (Rossi et al., 2008; Iurato 2014a,b).

According to Nunberg and Lagache, the Ideal Ego, genetically prior to the Super-Ego, is the first Ego's component to be formed from the symbiotic mother-child state, upon which the subject will build up her or his further psychic development, and to which he or she comes back in psychotic states (and not only in these). According to Lagache (1961, 1965), Ideal Ego has sadomasochistic implications: in particular, hand in hand with Ideal Ego starting its formation, the negation of the Other, by the basic agency pair Ego's Ideal–Super-Ego, is correlative to the affirmation of Self, thus giving rise to opposite pair formation and to the next separation of their elements (consciousness process – cf. (Iurato, 2015a)).

Thus, following (Laplanche & Pontalis, 1967), we have two basic Ego's psychic components, the one that observes (Ego's Ideal–Super-Ego) and the other that is observed (Ideal Ego[72]).

Human psychic behaviour will be the dialectic result of the concomitant action of these two opposite and inseparable, but independent from each other, Ego's (sub)agencies, hence by the prevalence of one of these two upon the remaining one. However, there is, always, a dialectic interaction[73] between them. Freud put this splitting mechanism at the psychodynamic basis of psychoses and other disorders (including neuroses), justifying the assumption of such a mechanism as one of the main dynamic processes of psychic formation, which basically allows us to relate ourselves to reality. In short, the basic opposition between the (narcissistic) Ideal Ego and the (social) Ego's Ideal is the early source of any further dialectic process of consciousness (Iurato 2015a). Furthermore, within the Lacanian work, disavowal has been the first psychic mechanism involved in a complex epistemological evolution that reached the composite notion of *forclusion* which lies at the basis of the celebrated binomial *O/o* (that is, *discourse of the Other* versus *discourse of the other*) that Lacan derives from the previous binomial Ideal Ego/Ego's Ideal.

As mentioned above, these two Ego's components are not present in the Freudian thought, which introduced only the notion of Ego's Ideal and to which was brought back then the notion of Super-Ego. The history of the agency pair Ideal Ego–Ego's Ideal has undergone quite a hard-working evolutionary history. Following (Laplanche & Pontalis, 1967), Freud introduced the notion of Ego's Ideal in *On Narcissism. An Introduction* (of 1914) to indicate an agency as resulting from the convergence of infantile narcissism and omnipotence (which will form the idealizations of the Ego) and the parental (hence social) agencies and identifications; later, first in *Group Psychology and the Analysis of the Ego* (of 1921), then in *The Id and the Ego* (of 1923), the Ego's Ideal was identified with the Super-Ego agency, whose function is put in the foreground in the formation of critical sense, of prohibition and self-observation agencies and of interpersonal relations. Nevertheless, the psychoanalytic literature identifies a certain difference between the Super-Ego agency and the Ego's Ideal one even if they overlap one another somewhat.

The system Ego's Ideal–Super-Ego is, however, related to social and prohibition agencies as well as to self-observation, moral and critical functions, even if there is no unanimous consensus in the respective attribution of these. As early in *On Narcissism. An Introduction* (of 1914), Freud used the term *Ideal Ego* but substantially as synonymous with Ego's Ideal. These subagencies would be retaken by Nunberg in 1932, of which we will outline some related ideas in the next section, and, in 1958, by Lagache, who indentifies a main opposition between the Ideal Ego and the system Ego's Ideal–Super-Ego. According to Lagache, the Ideal Ego has a narcissistic character of omnipotence which is mainly due to a primary identification with the mother; it is irreducible to the Ego's Ideal agency, and its formation has sadomasochistic implications, including the negation of the Other in correlation to the affirmation of Self, on the basis of the main opposition between the Ideal Ego and the Ego's Ideal–Super-Ego system.

But, following (Roudinesco 1995, Part VI, Ch. V), it was Lacan that, in 1953 – but without quoting Nunberg – considered, in his own way, these two Ego subagencies as distinct from each other, putting them at the foundation of his theoretical framework, highlighting their relevant nature and function. The Ideal Ego is a narcissistic formation belonging to the imaginary register and formed during the *mirror stage* (theorized by Lacan since 1936), whereas the Ego's Ideal refers to a symbolic function that is able to organize the set of the relationships of the subject with others. The institution of the dualism *O/o* is therefore a consequence of the establishment of the dualism Ego's Ideal/Ideal Ego. In this system, Lacan laid out the celebrated Lévi-Straussian splitting from nature to culture operated by universal incest prohibition (Gilliéron & Baldassarre, 2012) because this allowed Lacan to conceive a basic opposition between the *symbolic function* of the *Father* (corresponding to the Ego's Ideal or to the *Other*), representing the culture and incarnation of the law, and the *imaginary position* of the *Mother* (from whom derives the Ideal Ego or the *other*), depending on the order of Nature and destined to merge with the child meant as the phallic object of a missing penis.

It is thanks to the mirror stage that the Œdipus phase starts, in such a manner that, through the paternal metaphor (*Name-of-the-Father*), the child is separated from the mother, giving rise to the Ego's Ideal formation[74]. Therefore, it is just by *naming* the missing mother penis – that is to say, the child – by means of the paternal metaphor (the *phallus*) that the *symbolic register* takes place (Ego's Ideal or *Other O*, or *signifier*), which is related to a secondary process, through disengaging from the *imaginary register* (the Ideal Ego or *other o*, or *signified*), which is strictly related to the primary process.

The consequent *lack of being*, due to this disengaging from the mother womb[75], creates, amongst other things, the unsatisfiable *desire* of the *other* of the imaginary order which will try to be satisfied with other maternal substitutes that she or he will find in the symbolic order of the *Other*. The symbolic register will allow her or himself to be perceived and recognized from the Ideal Ego to the Ego's Ideal, that is to say, through the symbol, whose notion starts from Lévi-Strauss and F. de Saussure's structuralistic theories. However, for Lacan, what is fundamentally important is the signifier structure of the symbolic order and not the link of symbol with the symbolized (or signified), which concerns with the imaginary order, as in Freud.

2.8.8. An Outline of Hermann Nunberg's Ego Psychology

Although little-known, the work of Hermann Nunberg (1932, 1955, 1975) contains a great number of new ideas and insights on psychoanalysis besides being one of the most important treatises[76] on orthodox psychoanalytic theory, as remembered by Freud himself in his preface to this work. For our purposes, we only recall here some points of his work which may have some usefulness for what is expounded here. For instance, in (Nunberg 1975, Ch. 5), a clear and complete discussion of Ego psychology is presented, of which we here outline those main points that are useful for our studies. In it, the primary role of bodily Ego is highlighted, as well as understood as the first central core around which will revolve and build up all the following psychic representations. The perception is the first and basic element for establishing the *reality exam* which develops with great slowness but upon which will depend all the following psychic formation. The Ego will accomplish both internal and external requests, with a suitable right energy distribution.

According to Nunberg, the Ego initially is in an unorganized phase within the Id, whose delimitation identifies a subagency called *Ideal Ego*, which has a full narcissistic and omnipotent character turned only toward the satisfaction of the own needs.[77] It springs out from the fusional relationship child-mother of primary narcissism, in which child has a primary, archaic identification with mother, endowed of omnipotence. During the psychic development, this subagency gradually leaves its role in place of the other rising subagency, with which it will enter in a dialectic relation, called the *Ego's Ideal*, even if, particularly in psychotic states, the individual intends to come back to the Ideal Ego when fantasies of "coming back to the maternal womb" predominate. Children and schizophrenics have great difficulty in disengaging from their strong narcissistic and omnipotent Ideal Ego which has an unconscious nature and is ruled by the principle of pleasure, trying to satisfy every need also in a hallucinatory manner in case of non-immediate satisfaction.

Hence, the main defence mechanisms of Ideal Ego are negation, projection and hallucination to avoid any unpleasantness. Nevertheless, in normality, it is not always possible to disregard the reality, thus giving rise to the formation of the reality principle, which is often mediated by the thought. Between the perception of reality and the action adapted to the perceived reality gradually the thought is inserted, which prepares the action, eventually substituting it. The judgment function of *negation*, according to Freud, is the first transition step from ignorance to recognition. To be precise, recognition takes place thanks to a state of spiritual protection which seeks stimuli from the external world which, in turn, will be apperceived and accepted by the Ego. Therefore, recognition undergoes the influx of impulses which are aimed at establishing a link with the external world and its objects, drawing its energy from life instincts. Ignorance, instead, comes from a state which feels the stimuli of the external world as unpleasant, so perturbing the ever desiderated quite. Thus, the Ego definitively closes the perceptive system against them.

Negation, instead, takes a further step, in the sense that it recognizes what is unpleasant, and, at the same time, eliminates, expels and annihilates (in the unconscious, by repression) all that. Ignorance and negation are energetically supported by death instincts. Therefore, the relationships between the external and internal world are ruled by the interplay between life and death instincts by means of the own bodily image and its borders. The gradual adaptation to reality takes place to inhibit the aggressiveness (Thanatos) through life instincts (Eros) which provide energy for libidinal investments of the first object relationships. In this regard, Nunberg considers the depersonalization states and schizophrenia as patterns to infer as a reality sense starts to form. In pursuing this, as we will see, the last 1938 Freudian thought seems to be re-evoked.

In both cases, there is a retirement of libido from the lost-love object to which are also associated the world's destruction feelings with related aggressiveness tendencies that Nunberg attributes to the anxieties of castration. Furthermore, in these pathological cases, Nunberg detected a certain increase of narcissistic components that he would want to bring back to an identification of the Ego with the phallus due to the retirement of the libidinal cathexis from objects to the Ego, with consequent loss of the reality sense. Therefore, Nunberg deduces two main consequences: first, that the recognition of reality takes place thanks to a certain capacity of the Ego to turn the libido toward external objects; second, that there is a component of the Ego that does not want to recognize the perceived reality, notwithstanding this is just perceived. It seems that this part of the Ego does not want to know of the perceptions, notwithstanding these are rightly perceived. And the remaining perceiving part of the Ego seems as well to be suffering from this denial.

Therefore, there are two subagencies of the Ego, one that perceives and acts, the other that judges the Ego's experiences which need to be approved in order that these may have a sense of reality. This might explain why it is immoral to deny the reality and not instead say the truth. Thus, Nunberg deepens this self-observing and critical agency of Ego which is located in the preconscious system. The first bodily Ego's percepts will be undergone to the critical and observational modalities of the Ego. They will be recognized or denied according to modalities which have no sensorial character and are absent in schizophrenic patients where a deep self-observation prevails, but not over percepts of the external world. In normality, the perceiving and self-observing Ego's subagencies harmonically and constructively co-operate with the critical one; often, these two Ego's subagencies are not easily distinguishable inasmuch as they overlap with one another, becoming quite differentiated or separated only when a conflict arises between them.

These critical and self-observing agencies will form the substrate to the next merely psychic *Super-Ego* agency, which will reach its most complete formation with the end of the Œdipus complex. The Super-Ego will begin to intervene between the Id and the narcissistic Ideal Ego agencies, making itself bearer of the social and reality agencies; it will be the result of successive identifications but, in turn, it is also susceptible to influences from the first ones. Nevertheless, this mediation role is often failed by the Super-Ego because of its extreme difficulty in conciliating the Id and Ideal Ego agencies. Nevertheless, Nunberg highlights that both life and death instincts contribute to determining the structure of the Super-Ego. To be precise, its structure mainly stems from the inhibition of immediate instinctual satisfaction to account for reality needs, and this may take place both from death and life instincts.

The death instincts concur to determine such an inhibition of the rigid, prohibitive and authoritarian structure of the Super-Ego, whereas the life instincts concur to determine another particular structure classified as *Ego's Ideal*, which is carried out as follows. When, for love[78], one gives in to an instinctual satisfaction for fear of losing a loved object, the latter will be taken on into the Ego domain and cathexed by the libido, so becoming a part of Ego which will be called *Ego's Ideal*. It is for love of her or his own ideal that the individual remains emotionally bound to it and undergoes to its requests. So, the Ego obeys both the Super-Ego for fear of a punishment and Ego's Ideal for love. This last love is not sexual because it is the outcome of a transformation of an object libido into an Ego's libido, so that a desexualization takes place, that is to say, a sublimation[79], so that the narcissism of Ego's Ideal has a *secondary* nature, as it is linked to secondary process (secondary narcissism), while that of the Ideal Ego is a narcissism having a primary nature (primary narcissism).

According to Nunberg, the system Ego's Ideal–Super-Ego provides the representation of the external world to the Ego. Therefore, instinctual renunciations may take place either for hate or for fear of a punishment and for love, so that the dual system Ego's Ideal–Super-Ego is characterized by an ambiguous or ambivalent nature moulded on the fundamentally opposite love-hate pair. Nunberg puts in evidences the historical evolution of these notions since the Freudian work: indeed, as stated above, Freud mainly conceived the Ego's Ideal as being synonymous with Super-Ego, hence pointing out its prohibitive agencies and not the loving aspects. Instead, Nunberg retook the system Ego's Ideal–Super-Ego and deepened the distinction between these two agencies, although it is very difficult to descry a net distinction between them.

According to Nunberg, the Ego's Ideal has mainly a maternal libido (as it is an heir of the Ideal Ego), while the Super-Ego has mainly a paternal libido, even if there is a certain merger of both. The Ego's Ideal[80], due to its basically maternal nature, starts to form from pregenital phases, while the Super-Ego[81], due to its mainly paternal nature, starts to form during the genital phase because of the castration fear which puts at risk the whole Ego due to its genital identification. The Super-Ego is responsible for the sense of guilt, while the Ego's Ideal is responsible for the sense of inferiority. The Ego's Ideal springs out from the renunciation, by the child, of her or his omnipotent narcissistic position acquired along Ideal Ego formation, so replacing the love for herself or himself with a relationship with an ideal, a model to be reached and pursued (Other), so opening the way to the subjective existentiality of the child (Petrini et al., 2013).

The Ego's Ideal is an agency of personality coming from the convergence of narcissism given by all the idealizations of Ego (Ideal Ego) with the next identifications coming from others (parents, caregivers, etc.) after the breaking of archaic symbiotic tie child-mother with the action of the Name-of-the-Father law (Iurato, 2014b). So, Ego's Ideal is a model to which child tries to conform. In such a manner, the identification process and its structurating action on personality, takes place from the pre-Œdipal phases to Œdipal complex, till to the emergence of the agency system Ego's Ideal–Super-Ego with the renunciation to the (incestuous) Œdipal desires for the identifications with others (Petrini et al., 2013).

Nunberg stresses the complexity of the system Ego's Ideal–Super-Ego, the first subagency being provided by life instincts and characterized by a prevalence of love while the second subagency is underpinned by death instincts and mainly ruled by severity, austerity and by a general asceticism just to stem these destructive instincts. The internal structure of this system is quite complex and variously subdivided into itself, with continuous oscillations from one component to another: for instance, in certain cases the more severe Super-Ego may prevail, in others the rather milder Ego's Ideal may prevail. The Ego will therefore accomplish control, mediation and synthetic functions in regard to the various requests coming from all these agencies, namely the Id, the system Ego's Ideal–Super-Ego and the Ideal Ego, which are mostly in opposition with each other.

2.8.9. Relationships With Jacques Lacan's Discourse of the Capitalist, and Further Perspectives

From an historical-epistemological standpoint, therefore, Freud reached the conception of an Ego's splitting by studying a particular psychopathological model, that of fetishism, even if his ideas on that, were tacitly thought since the juvenile works[82]. This is mainly meant to be a male perversion in which there is no recognition of the female penile lack since this is a fact that, if it were denied, would turn out to be potentially anxiogenic because of the castration complex which is experienced by most people (due to its universal character, as recalled above). He (or she[83]) therefore recuses his (or her) own sensorial perception[84] which has shown to him (or her) that the female genital apparatus lacks a penis, firmly keeping to the opposite conviction. Nevertheless, this denied perception does not remain without any psychic consequence since he (or she) does not have the courage, or the dishonesty, to affirm seeing a penis, unless he (or she) stays in a psychotic state.

So, to compensate for this, he (or she) either turns towards a further general *symbolic elaboration*[85] (as in most normal cases) or clings to something more material, like a part of the body or an object to which he (or she) ascribes the penis role or considers it to be acting as a material symbolic replacement for this. All this (*fetish creation*) is due to the fact that he (or she) does not admit this lack of a penis, notwithstanding the evidence thereof. However, Freud (1938) himself pointed out that this fetish creation does not provide the exact paradigm of the Ego's splitting mechanism, since the former belongs to the proper psychopathological context whereas the castration complex, with its possible effects (including this Ego splitting), basically concerns normality – that is to say, it concerns every human being, as we shall see later – but without excluding possible pathological degenerations (just like in the fetishism).

Subsequently, Freud was led to consider disavowal (as already seen, essentially based on castration anxiety) as concerning, in pathological cases, the full recusation of external reality by the psychotic, as opposed to the repression carried out by the neurotic. Indeed, the former completely recuses the external reality (due to a structural deficit of the pair Ego's Ideal–Super-Ego), whereas the latter removes the (internal) Es' needs. In the first case, as already said, we have an Ego splitting (with a complete prevalence of the narcissistic Ideal Ego) that is different from other splitting phenomena due to the neurotic repression, because the latter concerns an internal conflict between two distinct agencies, the Ego against the Es, in regard to an internal (and not external) reality. Hence, only the former has some relationship with the external world, and Freud put it at the source of every other form of disavowal of reality that yet may be symbolically reconceived or rebuilt up. Thus, disavowal mainly has to do with primary relationships between these two Ego's subagencies, the Ideal Ego and the Ego's Ideal–Super-Ego, due to the above-mentioned Ego splitting[86].

Anyway, this first Freudian model of fetishism, based on disavowal, was then supposed to be valid for all the possible painful and anxiogenic perceptions and experiences[87], as mainly motivated by separation[88], either for males and females, so generalizing disavowal mechanism and Ego's splitting to all possible painful perceptions (above all, by separation and denial of it): indeed, Freud (1938) himself, already noted that the same castration's anxiety is felt by fetishists as well as by non-fetishists, both reacting to it, in the same manner[89]. In this case, in regard to consciousness as mainly identified in the Ego agency, we still have the formation, by Ego's splitting, of the dual subagency pair *Ideal Ego* vs. the system *Ego's Ideal–Super-Ego*, as characterized, around the end of (Freudian) psychosexual development of every human being, by the fundamental persistence (inheritance of the basic conflictual nature of human psyche) of a primary functional dialectic opposition between them, a feature coming from the handling of desire and its satisfaction with respect to reality, according to Eros and Thanatos basic drives as well as to pleasure and reality principles.

We wish to bring back what is said in (Dolto, 1998), within the above psychoanalytic pattern. To be precise, F. Dolto (1998) says that psychic development of child mainly take place through successive *castrations* (which she calls *symbologenous*, i.e., yielding symbols) each corresponding to one phase of the Freudian psychosexual development, until up Œdipus stage in which there is a kind of bifurcation of drives into sublimation on the one hand, and perversion[90] on the other hand (Dolto 1998, pp. 84-90). Thus, we would like to explain theoretically these Dolto's arguments also in terms of the Ego's splitting as sketchily described above. Precisely, the sublimation branch (*phantasy* creating) roughly corresponds to the prevalence of the action of the double agency system Ego's Ideal–Super-Ego upon the Ideal Ego subagency, while, vice versa, perversion branch (of the *pleasure*) corresponds to the prevalence of the action of the Ideal Ego subagency upon the system Ego's Ideal–Super-Ego, with the occurrence of fetishistic phenomena. This is in coherence with the contemporary notion of unconscious according to which it is the place of a primary knowledge structurally organized in terms of signifiers, in itself devoid of any meaning (signified), which will organize later pleasure and will rule phantasy (Chemama & Vandermersch, 1998).

Nevertheless, both these two opposite tendencies, arising from the above bifurcation process (in turn, springing out from Ego's splitting through disavowal mechanism), are always present in every human being, although in different ratio and in inverse proportion of each other. The prevalence of the sublimation branch with the system Ego's Ideal–Super-Ego, roughly corresponds to the rising of *non-material* culture, while the prevalence of the perversion branch with the subagency Ideal Ego roughly entails the rising of *material* culture[91]. All that seems to find a further confirmation from neurosciences: indeed, in analyzing, cleverly, modern society from the standpoint of philosophy of neurosciences, it has been discussed deeply, in (Maffei, 2014, 2016), the inverse proportion[92] existing between a kind of *"bulimia" of consumptions* (to be put in correspondence with Ideal Ego agency) and a kind of *"anorexia" of ethical-moral, cultural and social values* (to be put in correspondence with the agency pair Ego's Ideal–Super Ego).

Moreover, the above theoretical pattern, mainly worked out within Freudian theory, is also able to comprehensively explain most of the new pathologies identified by the current psychoanalytic clinic as claimed by Recalcati (2010), who, inter alia, put at the centre of his theoretical discussion, the well-known 1969 *Discourse of the Capitalist* by Lacan[93], just very close to what has been said above. Such a discourse cannot be simply reduced to a historical version of capitalism as economic system. It is, rather, a wider theoretical pattern or conceptual figure, worked out by Lacan just to highlight a certain declination of the modern social links featured by the failing of the crucial experience of symbolic castration, so that, the pleasure tasted by the subject, without the symbolic anchorage of castration, is pursued as a satisfaction merely dissipative, without limits, compulsive, dangerously linked with the destructive tendency of death drive.

Indeed, Recalcati (2010) shows the current nihilistic nullification process to which *desire*, i.e., the unconscious' subject, is undergone. Such a process, takes place according to a bifurcation in two main lines: the one, aimed to a narcissistic reinforcement of the Ego (hence, with a derailment towards Ideal Ego), the other turned towards an imperious demand of immediate pleasure (typical of primary process of the *Id*) that crosses every form of the principle of symbolic mediation (typical of secondary process, above all, of sublimation phenomena) which explicates in the basic dialectic of the pair Ego's Ideal–Super Ego whose non-attendance (i.e., the absence of the *Other*), according to Lacan, is said to be *Father's evaporation*. What is required, is the immediate satisfaction of pleasure, and the even more wider global market should meet such a request, this corresponding, as seen above, to a drift towards perversion, meant in its widest sense, that is to say, a pleasure unhooked from desire, eluding any dialectic of repression.

The new clinic highlights the hypermodern tendency of the drive's push to avoid fully symbolic castration and its needful sublimatory canalization within phantasmatic framework, for becoming a sadistic push for a consumption pursued without going through the *Other*. This situation is characterized by the vanishing of the orientating and structurating function of great ideals, by the desacralization, the depoliticization, the demitization, as well as by the predominance of the undisputed power of global market, by the hyperactivity of the own hedonistic individualism, even more dominant, and by the volatilization of own inner time. Hypermodernization is giving a desubstantiation of the subject, making this free of the weight of the ideals of tradition (included in the pair Ego's Ideal–Super Ego) but, at the same time, creating, around her or him, a meaningless empty which paralyzes her or his affective life. So, the compulsory ''machine of pleasure'' replaces the sublimatory ''machine of repression'', that is to say, the falling of either the ideals of tradition and the regulating forms of the drives (whose metapsychological centre is just in the repression activity), has left the place to the unrestrained consumption which, as Lacan said, cyclically will damage nihilistically the consumer herself or himself (death drive).

Lacan has stressed on this dialectic, in which De Sadian deadly pleasure releases perversily from desire, like in the social relations inspired by the *discourse of the capitalist*. The pleasure machine prescinds therefore from the dialectic of repression; the dissipative pleasure of death drive, structurally antagonist and alternative to desire, throws the subject into an autistic derive which separates her or him from the Other. Already Freud had descried such a metapsychological thesis, that is to say, the power of *Todestrieb* (i.e., death drive) breaks the Eros' restraints, dissolving the precious links of the subject with the Other, so nullifying the *élan vital* of desire, destroying the life and disconnecting it from the field of the Other[94]. Thus, Recalcati (2010) points out that current clinic is not a *clinic of desire*, as it was and should be, but rather a *clinic of death drive*; there is no longer the problematic of neurosis and the related vicissitudes of loving with its subjective demands, but rather a *clinic of anti-love*.

Recalcati (2010) once again warns on the fact that, there is no longer the neurotic difficulty to undertake own desire, subjectifying it, freeing from repression; current patients show to have severe difficulties to give a sense to their life, to have deep and true passions and feelings, to animate own existence which appears to be underpinned by an acephalous push towards a damned pleasure, dangerous to the life, devastating, not laid out within a phantasmatic framework, and not articulated according with the subject of the unconscious (i.e., the desire). There is no ethical assumption of the task to bring forward the unconscious programme of own desire, neither its neurotic delegation, but rather there is the pernicious programme to nullify it, cancel it, bypass it, negate it. But, what is the most dramatic one, is the absence of the dimension of the unconscious desire and its phantasmatic elaboration through symbolic articulation (with words and thoughts), together the dissolution of the orientating function of Œdipal ideals which had bound, until last decades, modern society.

This liquefaction of the links with the Other, due to an incandescence of the dimension of the drive pleasure, is due to the absence of the regulatory function given by that symbolic castration acting in the unconscious framework by phantasms, and from which, as Freud said, desire springs out of. What stands out is a clinic of psychoses, narcissism and perversions[95] as, at the centre of setting, there is no the unconscious agency of the desire, as it should be, but rather its negation whose outcomes are or the predominance of a drive action devoid of any symbolic articulation, or the bypassing of symbolic castration with the suspension of the basic gender difference and the related anguish of the encounter with the other, so destroying any creative power of the desire in a deadly compulsion to repeat process. So, the new clinic is aimed to restore, to revitalize, to reanimate the unconscious' subject, i.e., the desire.

Therefore, it seems that there are two distinct and disjoint pathways which may be followed, from the darkness of unconscious realm to the light of consciousness, and either characterized by the elimination of the subject of unconscious, i.e., the desire: or perversely, from the place of the *Id*, where reigns the full disorderliness of drives, which immediately reach consciousness (*acephalous* pleasure) with an unmediated stress-freeing discharge, eluding every form of symbolic mediation, and with a compulsive repetition of the pleasure without any symbolic relationship with the Other; or narcissistically, with a rigid hyperidentification negating every modality of alterity, so creating a narcissistic armour which flattens the individual to the extreme and total social conformism. In both cases, therefore, is fully neglected the original, singular *desiring subjectivity* of every human being, which is the key to open the way to others, i.e., it is the essence of otherness, the actualization of *alterity*, which might be considered as the early, chief root of unconscious experience. This desire is indestructible just because it goes beyond the Ego and its limits, that is to say, it does not depend on the Ego's will, it does not depend by Ego, it is not brought by Ego, and does not depend on it.

In conclusion, all this is quite enough to confirm or support our pattern outlined in the previous sections, based on the main opposition[96] *Ideal Ego* vs. *Ego's Ideal–Super Ego* pair, within which it is possible, roughly, to lay out most of the arguments just discussed above, mainly centred on the far-sighted 1969 Lacanian *Discourse of the Capitalist*, so bringing back psychotic manifestations, narcissisms and perversions to the realm of *Ideal Ego* and its deep, strong links with *Id* (the place of *needs*), while symbolic function, triggered by *desire*, should correspond to the dialectic of the pair *Ego's Ideal–Super Ego*, inside which symbolic castration takes places, and sublimation phenomena arise, so allowing a subjective or personal, singular re-elaboration, of knowledge[97].

This Lacan's *Discourse*, is, on its turn, closely linked with his previous *Seminar VII* in which the remarkable 1960 *Kant with Sade* argument is exposed, a basic dialectic between the imperativeness of Sade for a full pleasure satisfaction, and the opposite imperativeness of Kant which constrains subject to obey moral law; these are two unavoidable and intertwined imperatives inseparable of each other, between which subject is perennially buffeted, to undergoing a miserable destiny: being overcame by a law which nullifies desire and that is impossible to observe always, or falling into the desire which twists law to a net pleasure, annihilating and mortifying, as ruled by compulsion to repeat mechanism[98].

Anyway, all that, is in agreement with what has been said at the end of section 2, in that Ideal Ego, as an unconscious narcissistic formation prior to Super-Ego, is featured by either an omnipotence's ideal bringing back to the early state of indistinctness of the Ego from the Es (death drive) or a primary *specular* identification with mother (child-mother bind) and experienced as omnipotent (narcissistic rigidity[99]); it is the depository of the warranty for an immediate and unlimited pleasure, or else, a return to an incestuous pleasure overcoming any possible form of symbolic Law (by Father's action, introducing the subject to the dimension of *otherness*), or interdict, coming from the Œdipus complex (and leading to the opposite side represented by the dialectic of the pair Ego's Ideal–Super Ego, sublimation producing), a pleasure assured by an immediate object satisfaction, as offered for example by Capitalist (meant in its widest Lacanian sense), without any sublimatory intermediation (of secondary process).

On the other hand, genetically, Ego starts to form bodily from the Es, physiologically thanks to the contact with reality by means of perceptive system (*bodily Ego*); afterwards, still in contact with reality, it undergoes a splitting process, as said above, with the formation of two outcomes due to this bifurcation leading on the one hand to the Ideal Ego agency, place of the antisublimation and immediate pleasure, on the other hand to the pair of subagencies Ego's Ideal–Super Ego, whose internal dialectic gives rise to sublimation. So, Ego agency and its functions have an early corporal origin and a deeply somatic nature[100]; among these functions, there is the *desire*. From an historical viewpoint, this notion played a crucial role since the birth of psychoanalysis.

Indeed, Freud, as early in his celebrated *The Interpretation of Dreams* of 1900, considers desire as springing out from a basic hallucinatory or phantasmatic[101] satisfaction of the tension arising from of a primary need that child didn't able to accomplish directly and immediately, that is to say, bodily, as acquired in the primary child-mother bind upon which builds up Ideal Ego agency. So, desire has a main bodily early origin, as coming from a primary satisfaction experience by hallucination or phantasmatically which takes place, for the first time, just when that need has been really satisfied bodily (e.g., by nutrition), that is to say, with the direct contact or live experience with the related satisfaction's object (e.g., food), provided by caregiver, which will be cathexed by a certain amount of psychic energy.

To this corporal perception, will correspond a mnestic image associated, in turn, with the trace of excitation originated by the need. From this first event onwards, once this latter again occurs, but without the real presence of the satisfaction's object, then the related mnestic image, associated just to the related excitation's trace accordingly left, will be re-enacted by a further cathexing of it, as well as it will be re-evoked, hence reproduced, the related perception, so re-establishing, either in an hallucinatory fashion (through the Ideal Ego agency, according to our pattern) or in a phantasmatic manner (by means of the dialectic of the pair Ego's Ideal–Super-Ego, according to our pattern), the original situation of primary corporal satisfaction when satisfaction's object was just present. This latter psychic manifestation is said to be *desire*, by Freud, and has chiefly an unconscious nature (Petrini et al., 2013).

REFERENCES

Abbagnano, N. (1998). Dizionario di Filosofia. Terza edizione aggiornata e ampliata da Giovanni Fornero. Torino, Italy: UTET Libreria.

Ageno, M. (1962). Le radiazioni e i loro effetti. Torino, Italy: Paolo Boringhieri Editore.

Akhtar, S., & O'Neil, M. K. (Eds.). (2011). *On Freud's 'negation'. In The International Psychoanalytic Association – Contemporary Freud. Turning points & critical issues*. London, UK: Karnac Books, Ltd.

Alexander, F. (1948). Fundamentals of psychoanalysis. New York, NY: W.W. Norton & Company, Inc.

Allman, J. M. (2000). *Evolving Brains*. New York, NY: Scientific American Library. A division of HPHLP.

Ammaniti, M., & Gallese, V. (2014). La nascita dell'intersoggettività. Lo sviluppo del Sé fra psicodinamica e neurobiologia. Milano, Italy: Raffaello Cortina Editore.

Andersson, O. (1962). Studies on the Prehistory of Psychoanalysis. Stockholm, Sweden: Scandinavian University Books.

Arieti, S. (1974). Interpretazione della schizofrenia. Milano, Italy: Giangiacomo Feltrinelli Editore.

Arieti, S. (1976). Creatività. La sintesi magica. Roma, Italy: Il Pensiero Scientifico Editore.

Atkinson, R. L., Atkinson, R. C., Smith, E. E., Bem, D. J., & Nolen-Hoeksema, S. (Eds.). (1996). *Hilgard's Introduction to Psychology* (12th ed.). Orlando, FL: Harcourt Brace.

Baars, B. J. (1993). How does a serial, integrated and very limited stream of consciousness emerge from a nervous system that is mostly unconscious, distributed, parallel and of enormous capacity? In *Experimental and Theoretical Studies of Consciousness, Novartis Foundation Symposium No. 174*. New York, NY: John Wiley & Sons, Ltd.

Badiou, A. (1982). Théorie du sujet. Paris: Éditions du Seuil.

Balsamo, M. (2009). Ripetizione, coazione a ripetere, destino. In *Psiche. Dizionario storico di psicologia, psichiatria, psicoanalisi, neuroscienze* (Vol. 2, pp. 957–962). Torino, Italy: Giulio Einaudi editore.

Balzarotti, R. (Ed.). (1972). Cahiers pour l'Analyse. Scritti scelti di analisi e teoria della scienza, a cura del Centro Ricerche 2. Torino, Italy: Editore Boringhieri.

Bara, B. G. (1990). Scienza Cognitiva. Torino, Italy: Bollati Boringhieri editore.

Barratt, B. B. (2016). *Psychoanalysis and the Postmodern Impulse. Knowing and Being since Freud's Psychology*. New York, NY: Routledge.

Bassin, F. V. (1972). *Il problema dell'inconscio. Sulle forme inconsce dell'attività nervosa superiore*. Roma, Italy: Editori Riuniti.

Bastide, R. (Ed.). (1966). Usi e significati del termine struttura nelle scienze umane e sociali. Milano, Italy: Giangiacomo Feltrinelli Editore.

Bateson, G. (1972). *Steps to an Ecology of Mind. Collected Essays in Anthropology, Psychiatry, Evolution, and Epistemology*. San Francisco, CA: Chandler Publishing Company.

Battacchi, M. W. (2006). *La conoscenza psicologia. Il metodo, l'oggetto, la ricerca*. Roma, Italy: Carocci editore.

Benvenuto, S. (2005). Perversioni. Sessualità, etica, psicoanalisi. Torino, Italy: Bollati Boringhieri editore.

Bernardi, S., Dei, F., & Meloni, P. (Eds.). (2011). La materia del quotidiano. Per un'antropologia degli oggetti ordinari. Pisa, Italy: Pacini Editore.

Berwick, R. C., & Chomsky, N. (2016). Why Only Us. Language and Evolution. Cambridge, MA: The MIT Press. doi:10.7551/mitpress/9780262034241.001.0001

Bezoari, M., & Palombi, F. (Eds.). (2003). Epistemologia e Psicoanalisi: attualità di un confronto. Milano, Italy: Edizioni del Centro Milanese di Psicoanalisi.

Bianchi, P. (2014). La psicoanalisi e la politica delle singolarità. In L'inconscio è la politica. Milano-Udine, Italy: Mimesis Edizioni.

Blumenthal, P., & Tyvaert, J.-E. (Eds.). (2003). *La cognition dans le temps. Etudes cognitives dans le champ historique des langues et des textes.* Tübingen, Germany: Max Niemeyer Verlag. doi:10.1515/9783110949490

Bokanowski, T., & Lewkowicz, S. (Eds.). (2009). *On Freud's 'splitting of the ego in the process of defence'. In The International Psychoanalytic Association – Contemporary Freud: Turning points & critical issues.* London, UK: Karnac Books, Ltd.

Boniolo, G., & Vidali, P. (1999). Filosofia della scienza. Milano, Italy: Bruno Mondadori.

Bonnota, O., de Montalembertb, M., Kermarrecc, S., Botbold, M., Waltere, M., & Coulon, N. (2011). Are impairments of time perception in schizophrenia a neglected phenomenon? *Journal of Physiology, Paris, 105*(4-6), 164–169. doi:10.1016/j.jphysparis.2011.07.006 PMID:21803155

Borgogno, F., Luchetti, A., & Marino Coe, L. (Eds.). (2017). Il pensiero psicoanalitico italiano. Maestri, idee e tendenze dagli anni '20 ad oggi. Milano, Italy: FrancoAngeli.

Bottiroli, G. (2006). *Che cos'è la teoria della letteratura. Fondamenti e problemi.* Torino, Italy: Giulio Einaudi editore.

Boudon, R. (1970). *Strutturalismo e scienze umane.* Torino, Italy: Giulio Einaudi editore.

Bourguignon, A., & Manus, A. (1980). Hallucination nègative, déni de la réalité et scotomisation. *Annales Médico-Psychologiques, 138*(2), 129–153. PMID:6992686

Bria, P. (1981). Introduzione. Pensiero, mondo e problemi di fondazione. In *L'inconscio come insiemi infiniti. Saggio sulla bi-logica* (pp. xix–cxi). Torino, Italy: Giulio Einaudi editore.

Bria, P., & Caroppo, E. (2006). Antropologia culturale e psicopatologia. Roma, Italy: Alpes Italia.

Britton, R. (2000). Belief and Imagination. Explorations in Psychoanalysis. London, UK: Routledge.

Britton, R. (2003). Sex, Death and the Super-Ego. Experiences in Psychoanalysis. London, UK: Karnac Books, Ltd.

Britton, R., Blundell, S., & Youell, B. (2014). Il lato mancante. L'assenza del padre nel mondo interno. Milano, Italy: Mimesis edizioni.

Bucci, W. (1985). Dual coding: A cognitive model for psychoanalytic research. *Journal of the American Psychoanalytic Association, 33*(3), 571–607. doi:10.1177/000306518503300305 PMID:4056301

Bucci, W. (1987). *The dual code model and the interpretation of dreams.* New York, NY: Derner Institute – Adelphi University.

Bucci, W. (1997). *Psychoanalysis and Cognitive Science.* New York, NY: The Guilford Press.

CA (Collectif d'Auteurs). (1975). *La Psychanalyse*. Paris: Editions Le Livre De Poche.

Capa, R. L., Duval, C. Z., Blaison, D., & Giersch, A. (2014). Patients with schizophrenia selectively impaired in temporal order judgments. *Schizophrenia Research*, *156*(1), 51–55. doi:10.1016/j.schres.2014.04.001 PMID:24768441

Capozza, D. (1977). Il differenziale semantico. Problemi teorici e metrici. Bologna, Italy: Casa Editrice Pàtron.

Capozzi, M., & Cellucci, C. (2014). *Breve storia della logica. Dall'Umanesimo al primo Novecento*. Morrisville, NC: Lulu Press, Inc.

Carlson, L. (1999). *Consumption and Depression in Gertrude Stein, Louis Zukofsky, and Ezra Pound*. London, UK: Palgrave-MacMillan Press, Ltd. doi:10.1057/9780230379947

Carotenuto, A. (1982). Discorso sulla metapsicologia. Torino, Italy: Bollati Boringhieri Editore.

Carotenuto, A. (1991). Trattato di psicologia della personalità e delle differenze individuali. Milano, Italy: Raffaello Cortina Editore.

Carotenuto, A. (Ed.). (1992). Dizionario Bompiani degli Psicologi Contemporanei. Milano, Italy: Bompiani.

Carruccio, E. (1971). Mondi della Logica. Bologna, Italy: Nicola Zanichelli Editore.

Cassinari, F. (2005). Tempo e identità. La dinamica di legittimazione nella storia e nel mito. Milano, Italy: FrancoAngeli.

Castiglioni, M., & Corradini, A. (2011). *Modelli epistemologici in psicologia. Dalla psicoanalisi al costruzionismo*. Roma, Italy: Carocci editore.

Cazeneuve, J. (1971). Sociologie du rite. Paris: PUF-Presses Universitaires de France.

Ceylan, E. M., Dönmez, A., Ünsalver, B. A., & Evrensel, A. (2016). Neural synchronization as a hypothetical explanation of the psychoanalytic unconscious. *Consciousness and Cognition*, *40*, 34–44. doi:10.1016/j.concog.2015.12.011 PMID:26744848

Chasseguet-Smirgel, J. (1975). L'idéal du moi. Paris: Éditeur Claude Tchou.

Chasseguet-Smirgel, J. (1985). Creativity and perversion. London, UK: Free Association Books, Ltd.

Chemama, R., & Vandermersch, B. (Eds.). (1998). Dictionnaire de la Psychanalyse. Paris: Larousse-Bordas.

Cherubini, P., Giaretta, P., & Mazzocco, A. (Eds.). (2000). Ragionamento: psicologia e logica. Firenze, Italy: Giunti Gruppo Editoriale.

Chialà, S., & Curi, U. (2016). La brama dell'avere. Trento, Italy: Casa editrice Il Margine.

Chianese, D. (2009). Costruzione, Ricostruzione, Interpretazione. In *Psiche. Dizionario storico di psicologia, psichiatria, psicoanalisi, neuroscienze* (Vol. 1, pp. 280–285). Torino, Italy: Giulio Einaudi editore.

Codignola, E. (1977). Il vero e il falso. Saggio sulla struttura logica dell'interpretazione psicoanalitica. Torino, Italy: Editore Boringhieri.

Cohn, P. M. (1965). Universal Algebra. New York, NY: Harper & Row Publishers.

Conrotto, F. (2000). Tra il sapere e la cura. Un itinerario freudiano. Milano, Italy: FrancoAngeli.

Conrotto, F. (2009). Negazione. In *Psiche. Dizionario storico di psicologia, psichiatria, psicoanalisi, neuroscienze* (Vol. 2, pp. 728–730). Torino, Italy: Giulio Einaudi editore.

Conrotto, F. (2010). Per una teoria psicoanalitica della conoscenza. Milano, Italy: FrancoAngeli.

Conrotto, F. (2014). Ripensare l'inconscio. Milano, Italy: FrancoAngeli.

Contardi, R. (2010). La prova del labirinto. Processo di simbolizzazione e dinamica rappresentativa in psicoanalisi. Milano, Italy: FrancoAngeli.

Contarello, A., & Mazzara, B. M. (2002). Le dimensioni sociali dei processi psicologici. Roma-Bari, Italy: Laterza Editori.

Conte, M., & Gennaro, A. (Eds.). (1989). Inconscio e processi cognitivi. Bologna, Italy: Società editrice il Mulino.

Conti, L., & Principe, S. (1989). Salute mentale e società. Fondamenti di psichiatria sociale. Padova, Italy: Piccin Nuova Libraria.

Contri, G. (1972). Nozioni fondamentali nella teoria della struttura di Jacques Lacan. In Cahiers pour l'Analyse. Scritti scelti di analisi e teoria della scienza, a cura del Centro Ricerche 2. Torino, Italy: Editore Boringhieri, pp. 244-289.

Corradi Fiumara, G. (1980). Funzione simbolica e filosofia del linguaggio. Torino, Italy: Editore Boringhieri.

Cotter, D. (2003). *Joyce and the Perverse Ideal*. London, UK: Routledge.

CSFG – Centro di Studi Filosofici di Gallarate. (1977). Dizionario delle idee. Firenze, Italy: G.C. Sansoni Editore.

Cuche, D. (2004). La notion de culture dans les sciences sociales. Paris: Éditions La Découverte.

D'Urso, V., & Trentin, R. (1998). Introduzione alla psicologia delle emozioni. Roma-Bari, Italy: Editori Laterza.

Dalla Chiara Scabia, M. L. (1973). Istanti e individui nelle logiche temporali. *Rivista di Filosofia*, *64*(2), 95–122.

Dalla Chiara Scabia, M. L. (1974). Logica. Milano, Italy: ISEDI – Istituto Editoriale Internazionale.

De Masi, F. (2016). Which is the relevant superego for clinical analytic work? In F. Borgogno, A. Luchetti, & L. M. Coe (Eds.), *Reading Italian Psychoanalysis* (pp. 279–290). Oxfordshire, UK: Routledge.

De Mijolla, A. (Ed.). (2005). *International Dictionary of Psychoanalysis* (Vols. 1–3). Farmington Hills, MI: Thomson Gale.

De Mijolla, A., & De Mijolla Mellor, S. (Eds.). (1996). Psychanalyse. Paris: PUF-Presses Universitaires de France.

De Pasquali, P. (2002). Figli che uccidono. Da Doretta Graneris a Erika & Omar. Soveria Mannelli (CZ), Italy: Rubbettino Editore.

De Waelhens, A., & Ver Eecke, W. (2001). *Phenomenology and Lacan on Schizophrenia, after the Decade of the Brain*. Leuven, Belgium: Leuven University Press.

Dehaene, S., & Brannon, E. (Eds.). (2011). *Space, Time and Number in the Brain. Searching for the Foundations of Mathematical Thought*. Amsterdam: Elsevier, Inc.

Dei, F. (1998). La discesa agli inferi. James G. Frazer e la cultura del Novecento. Lecce, Italy: Argo Editrice.

Dei, F. (2016). Antropologia culturale (2nd ed.). Bologna, Italy: Società editrice il Mulino.

Dei, F., & Meloni, P. (2015). *Antropologia della cultura materiale*. Roma, Italy: Carocci editore.

Dei, F., & Simonicca, A. (Eds.). (2008). Ragione e forme di vita. Razionalità e relativismo in antropologia (2nd ed.). Milano, Italy: FrancoAngeli.

Deliège, R. (2006). Une historie de l'anthropologie. Écoles, auteurs, théories. Paris: Éditions du Seuil.

Devlin, K. (2006). *The Math Instinct: Why You're a Mathematical Genius (Along with Lobsters, Birds, Cats, and Dogs)*. New York, NY: Thunder's Mouth Press.

Di Gregorio, L. (2003). Psicopatologia del cellulare. Dipendenza e possesso del telefonino. Milano, Italy: FrancoAngeli/LeComete.

Dijksterhuis, A., & Nordgren, L. F. (2006). A theory of unconsciouss thought. *Perspectives on Psychological Science*, *1*(2), 95–109. doi:10.1111/j.1745-6916.2006.00007.x PMID:26151465

Dolto, F. (1984). *L'image inconsciente du corps*. Paris: Editions du Seuil.

Donati, P. (2015). L'enigma della relazione. Milano, Italy: Mimesis edizioni.

Durst, M. (1988). Dialettica e bi-logica. L'epistemologia di Ignacio Matte Blanco. Milano, Italy: Marzorati Editore.

Eco, U. (1981). *Simbolo. Voce dell'Enciclopedia Einaudi* (Vol. 12). Torino, Italy: Giulio Einaudi editore.

Egidi, R. (1979). Il linguaggio delle teorie scientifiche. Esperienza ed ipotesi nell'epistemologia contemporanea. Napoli, Italy: Guida Editori.

Egidi, R. (Ed.). (1992). La svolta relativistica nell'epistemologia contemporanea. Milano, Italy: FrancoAngeli.

Ehresmann, A. C., & Vanbremeersch, J. P. (2007). *Memory Evolutive Systems. Hierarchy, Emergence, Cognition*. Amsterdam: Elsevier, B.V.

Ekstrom, S. R. (2004). The mind beyond our immediate awareness: Freudian, Jungian, and cognitive models of the unconscious. *The Journal of Analytical Psychology*, *49*(5), 657–682. doi:10.1111/j.0021-8774.2004.00494.x PMID:15533197

Endert, E. (2006). Über die emotionale Dimension sozialer Prozesse. Die Theorie der Affektlogik am Beispiel der Rechtsextremismus und Nationalsozialismusforschung (Theorie und Methode). Konstanz, Germany: UVK Verlagsgesellschaft mbH.

Enriques, F. (1912). Scienza e Razionalismo. Bologna, Italy: Nicola Zanichelli Editore.

Even, G., & Medina, M. (2012). *Digital Logic Design. A Rigorous Approach*. Cambridge, UK: Cambridge University Press. doi:10.1017/CBO9781139226455

Fairlamb, H. L. (1994). *Critical conditions. Postmodernity and the question of foundations*. Cambridge, UK: Cambridge University Press. doi:10.1017/CBO9780511552762

Falzone, A. (2005). Filosofia del linguaggio e psicopatologia evoluzionistica. Soveria Mannelli (CZ), Italy: Rubbettino Editore.

Fenichel, O. (1945). The psychoanalytic theory of neurosis. New York, NY: W.W. Norton & Company, Inc.

Ferretti, F. (2010). Alle origini del linguaggio umano. Il punto di vista evoluzionistico. Roma-Bari, Italy: Editori Laterza.

Ffytche, M. (2012). *The Foundation of the Unconscious. Schelling, Freud and the Birth of the Modern Psyche*. Cambridge, UK: Cambridge University Press.

Figà-Talamanca Dore, L. (1978). La logica dell'inconscio. Roma, Italy: Edizioni Studium-Vita Nova.

Finelli, R. (2010). Perché l'inconscio non è strutturato come un linguaggio. In Compendio di Psicoanalisi e altri scritti. Roma, Italy: Newton Compton editori.

Finelli, R. (2011). Rappresentazione e linguaggio in Freud: a partire dal "Compendio di psicoanalisi". *Consecutio Temporum. Rivista di critica della postmodernità*, *1*, 112-125.

Fink, K. (1993). The Bi-Logic Perception of Time. *The International Journal of Psycho-Analysis*, *74*, 303–312. PMID:8491534

Fodor, N., & Gaynor, F. (1950). Freud: Dictionary of Psychoanalysis. New York, NY: The Philosophical Library.

Fonagy, P., Gergely, G., Jurist, E. L., & Target, M. (2002). Affect Regulation, Mentalization, and the Development of the Self. New York, NY: Other Press.

Fornari, F. (2016). Psychic birth. In F. Borgogno, A. Luchetti, & L. M. Coe (Eds.), *Reading Italian Psychoanalysis* (pp. 593–600). Oxfordshire, UK: Routledge.

Fossi, G. (1983). La psicologia dinamica: un'eredità del XX secolo. Roma, Italy: Edizioni Borla.

Fossi, G. (1984). Le teorie psicoanalitiche. Padova, Italy: Piccin Nuova Libraria.

Fossi, G. (1988). Psicoanalisi e psicoterapie dinamiche. Torino, Italy: Bollati Boringhieri editore.

Fossi, G. (2003). Una proposta evoluzionista per la psicoanalisi. Con un manuale per la pratica terapeutica e la ricerca empirica. Milano, Italy: FrancoAngeli.

Francioni, M. (1978). Psicoanalisi linguistica ed epistemologia in Jacques Lacan. Torino, Italy: Editore Boringhieri.

Freud, S. (1938). Abriß der psychoanalyse. Academic Press.

Freud, S. (1957). *The Standard Edition of Complete Psychological Works of Sigmund Freud* (Vols. 1-24; J. Strachey, Trans. & Ed.). London, UK: The Hogarth Press.

Freud, S. (1979). La scissione dell'Io nel processo di difesa (1938). In Opere di Sigmund Freud, 1930-1938. L'uomo Mosè e la religione monoteistica e altri scritti (vol. 11). Torino, Italy: Editore Boringhieri.

Friedman, D. M. (2001). A Mind of Its Own. A Cultural History of the Penis. New York, NY: Simon & Schuster, Inc.

Friedman, M., & Tomšič, S. (Eds.). (2016). Psychoanalysis: Topological Perspectives. New Conceptions of Geometry and Space in Freud and Lacan. Bielefeld, Germany: transcript Verlag. doi:10.14361/9783839434406

Fromm, E. (1951). The Forgotten Language. An Introduction to the Understanding of Dreams, Fairy Tales, and Myths. New York, NY: Holt, Rinehart & Winston Publishing Company, Inc.

Fromm, E. (1976). To have or to be? New York, NY: Harper & Row Publishers, Inc.

Funari, E. (1978). Psicoanalisi: tecnica o Weltanschauung? In *Psicoanalisi e classi sociali* (pp. 147–153). Roma, Italy: Editori Riuniti.

Funari, E. (1988). Contestualità e specificità della psicoanalisi. In Trattato di Psicoanalisi: Vol. 1. Teoria e Tecnica. Milano, Italy: Raffaello Cortina Editore.

Funari, E. (2007). L'irrapresentabile come origine della vita psichica. Milano, Italy: FrancoAngeli.

Fusco, A., & Tomassoni, R. (Eds.). (2013). Creatività nella psicologia letteraria, drammatica e filmica. Milano, Italy: FrancoAngeli.

Gabbay, D. M., Hodkinson, I., & Reynolds, M. A. (1994). *Temporal Logic. Mathematical Foundations and Computational Aspects* (Vol. 1). Oxford, UK: Clarendon Press.

Gabbay, D. M., Reynolds, M. A., & Finger, M. (2000). *Temporal Logic. Mathematical Foundations and Computational Aspects* (Vol. 2). Oxford, UK: Oxford University Press.

Galimberti, U. (1979). Psichiatria e fenomenologia. Milano, Italy: Giangiacomo Feltrinelli Editore.

Galimberti, U. (1983). Il corpo. Milano, Italy: Giangiacomo Feltrinelli Editore.

Galimberti, U. (2006). Dizionario di psicologia. Torino, Italy: UTET Libreria.

Galton, A. (Ed.). (1987). *Temporal Logic and its Applications*. New York, NY: Academic Press, Inc.

Gay, P. (2000). Freud. Una vita per i nostri tempi. Milano, Italy: Bompiani.

Giberti, F., & Rossi, R. (Eds.). (1996). Manuale di psichiatria (4th ed.). Padova, Italy: Piccin Nuova Libraria.

Giersch, A., Lalanne, L., van Assche, M., & Elliott, M.A. (2013). On disturbed time continuity in schizophrenia: an elementary impairment in visual perception? *Frontiers in Psychology, 4,* 281-290.

Gilliéron, E., & Baldassarre, M. (Eds.). (2012). Perversione e Relazione. Roma, Italy: Alpes Italia.

Giordano, M., Dello Russo, G., Pardi, F., & Patella, G. A. (1984). Tempo e inconscio. Napoli, Italy: Guida editori.

Girotto, V. (Ed.). (2013). Introduzione alla psicologia del pensiero. Bologna, Italy: Società editrice il Mulino.

Glover, E. (1949). Psychoanalysis. London, UK: John Bale Medical Publications, Ltd.

Goleman, D. (1995). Emotional Intelligence. New York, NY: Bantam Books.

Green, A. (1993). Le travail du négatif. Paris: Les Éditions du Minuit.

Greenacre, P. (1971). Emotional growth. Psychoanalytic studies of the gifted and a great variety of other individuals. New York, NY: International Universities Press, Inc.

Grice, H. P. (1993). Logica e conversazione. Saggi su intenzione, significato e comunicazione. Bologna, Italy: Società editrice il Mulino.

Grinberg, L. (1989). La supervisione psicoanalitica. Teoria e pratica. Milano, Italy: Raffaello Cortina Editore.

Grunberger, B. (1971). *Le narcissisme. Essai de psychanalyse.* Paris: Payot.

Hall, C. S. (1999). *A Primer in Freudian Psychology.* New York, NY: Meridian Books.

Hampe, B., & Grady, J. E. (Eds.). (2005). *From Perception to Meaning. Image Schemas in Cognitive Linguistics.* Berlin: Walter de Gruyter GmbH and Co. doi:10.1515/9783110197532

Hanly, C. (1984). Ego Ideal and Ideal Ego. *The International Journal of Psycho-Analysis, 65*(3), 253–261. PMID:6571602

Hanly, C. (2011). Studi psicoanalitici sul narcisismo. Scritti di Charles Hanly. Roma, Italy: Giovanni Fioriti Editore.

Harary, F., Norman, Z., & Cartwright, D. (Eds.). (1965). *Structural Models.* New York, NY: John Wiley and Sons, Inc.

Hartmann, H., & Loewenstein, R. M. (1962). Notes on the Superego. *The Psychoanalytic Study of the Child, 17,* 42–81.

Hermann, I. (1989). Psicoanalisi e logica. Roma, Italy: Di Renzo Editore.

Hermann, R. (1968). *Lie Groups for Physicists.* New York, NY: W.A. Benjamin, Inc.

Hickmann, M., & Robert, S. (Eds.). (2006). *Space in Languages – Linguistic Systems and Cognitive Categories.* Amsterdam: John Benjamins Publishing Company. doi:10.1075/tsl.66

Hodkinson, I., & Reynolds, M. (2007). Temporal Logic. In Handbook of Modal Logic. Amsterdam: Elsevier.

Horkheimer, M., & Adorno, T. W. (1947). Dialektik der Aufklärung. Philosophische Fragments. Amsterdam: Querido Verlag N.V.

Imbasciati, A. (2015). Nuove teorie sul funzionamento della mente. L'istituzione psicoanalitica e gli psicoanalisti. Milano, Italy: FrancoAngeli.

Ippoliti, E. (2007). *Il vero e il plausibile*. Morrisville, NC: Lulu Press, Inc.

Iurato, G. (2013a). Mathematical thought in the light of Matte Blanco work. *Philosophy of Mathematics Education Journal*, 27.

Iurato, G. (2013b). Σύμβολου: An attempt toward the early origins, Part 1. *Language & Psychoanalysis*, 2(2), 77–120. doi:10.7565/landp.2013.008

Iurato, G. (2013c). Σύμβολου: An attempt toward the early origins, Part 2. *Language & Psychoanalysis*, 2(2), 121–160. doi:10.7565/landp.2013.009

Iurato, G. (2014a). At the grounding of computational psychoanalysis: on the work of Ignacio Matte Blanco. A general history of culture overview of Matte Blanco bilogic in comparison. In *Proceedings of the 2014 IEEE 13th International Conference on Cognitive Informatics and Cognitive Computing.* Los Alamitos, CA: IEEE Computer Society Press.

Iurato, G. (2014b). The dawning of computational psychoanalysis. A proposal for some first elementary formalization attempts. *International Journal of Cognitive Informatics and Natural Intelligence*, 8(4), 50–82. doi:10.4018/ijcini.2014100104

Iurato, G. (2014c). *Alcune considerazioni critiche sul simbolismo.* Preprint No. hal-00980828 version 1. Available at HAL archives-ouvertes.

Iurato, G. (2015a). A Brief Comparison of the Unconscious as Seen by Jung and Lévi-Strauss. *Anthropology of Consciousness*, 26(1), 60–107. doi:10.1111/anoc.12032

Iurato, G. (2015b). Fetishism in Marketing. Some First Elementary Psychoanalytic Anthropology Remarks. In Business Management: A Practioners' Guide. Delhi: International Research Publication House.

Iurato, G. (2015c). A simple phylogenetic remark about certain human blood pressure values. *Journal of Biochemistry International*, 2(4), 162–165.

Iurato, G. (2016a). *A psychoanalytic enquiry on symbolic function.* Preprint No. hal-01361264 version 3. Available at HAL archives-ouvertes.

Iurato, G. (2016b). *A view of LSA/ESA in Computational Psychoanalysis.* Preprint No. hal-01353999 version 1. Available at HAL archives-ouvertes.

Iurato, G. (2016c). On Jacques Lacan Psychosis Theory and ERPs Analysis. *Journal of Biology and Nature*, 5(4), 234–240.

Iurato, G. (2016d). Some Comments on the Historical Role of *Fetishism* in Economic Anthropology. *Journal of Global Economics, Management and Business Research, 7*(1), 61–82.

Iurato, G. (2016e). *The origins of symbol. An historical-critical study of symbolic function, according to the phylo-ontogenetic perspective, as arising from the comparison of certain patterns of neuro-psychological sciences.* Paper Presented at the Satellite Event "On the edge of disciplines", Florence, Italy.

Iurato, G. (2016f). Two simple questions regarding cultural anthropology. *Journal of Global Research in Education and Social Science, 8*(1), 10–15.

Iurato, G. (2017a). An Essay in Denotational Mathematics. Rigorous Results. In Encyclopedia of Information Science and Technology (4th ed.). Hershey, PA: IGI Global.

Iurato, G. (2017b). Un raffronto critico fra la teoria platonica delle idee ed il paradosso di Kripke-Wittgenstein. In Platone nel pensiero moderno e contemporaneo (vol. 11). Villasanta (MB), Italy: Limina Mentis Edizioni.

Iurato, G. (2017c). *Rigidity of the Generalized Other, narrowness of the Otherness and demodernization, in the framework of symbolic interactionism. Ideology and Political Journal.* (in press)

Iurato, G., & Khrennikov, A. Yu. (2015). Hysteresis model of unconscious-conscious interconnection: Exploring dynamics on *m*-adic trees. *p-Adic Numbers, Ultrametric Analysis and Applications, 7*(4), 312–321. doi:10.1134/S2070046615040068

Iurato, G., & Khrennikov, A. Yu. (2017). On the topological structure of a mathematical model of human unconscious. *p-Adic Numbers, Ultrametric Analysis and Applications, 9*(1), 78–81. doi:10.1134/S2070046617010071

Iurato, G., Khrennikov, A. Yu., & Murtagh, F. (2016). Formal Foundations for the Origins of Human Consciousness. *p-Adic Numbers, Ultrametric Analysis and Applications, 8*(4), 249–279. doi:10.1134/S2070046616040014

Jablonka, E., & Raz, G. (2009). Transgenerational Epigenetic Inheritance: Prevalence, Mechanisms, and Implications for the Study of Heredity and Evolution. *The Quarterly Review of Biology, 84*(2), 131–176. doi:10.1086/598822 PMID:19606595

Jackson, D. D. (1954). Some factors influencing the Œdipus Complex. *The Psychoanalytic Quarterly, 23*, 566–581. PMID:13215675

Jaffé, R. (2009). Ideale dell'Io, Idealizzazione. In *Psiche. Dizionario storico di psicologia, psichiatria, psicoanalisi, neuroscienze* (Vol. 1, pp. 494–500). Torino, Italy: Giulio Einaudi editore.

Johnson-Laird, P., & Bara, B. (1984). Syllogistic Inference. *Cognition, 16*(1), 1–61. doi:10.1016/0010-0277(84)90035-0 PMID:6540648

Juhás, G. (1999). On Semantics of Petri Nets over Partial Algebra. In *SOFSEM'99: Theory and Practice of Informatics. Proceedings of the 26th Conference on Current Trends in Theory and Practice of Informatics.* Berlin: Springer-Verlag. doi:10.1007/3-540-47849-3_29

Kandel, E. R. (2005). Psychiatry, Psychoanalysis, and the New Biology of Mind. Washington, DC: American Psychiatric Association Publishing, Inc.

Kaplan-Solms, K., & Solms, M. (2000). Clinical Studies in Neuro-Psychoanalysis. Introduction to a Depth Neuropsychology. London, UK: Karnac Books, Ltd.

Kemeny, J. G. (1959). A Philosopher Looks at Science. Princeton, NJ: D. Van Nostrand Reinhold Company, Inc.

Kemeny, J. G., Snell, J. L., & Thompson, G. L. (1974). *Introduction to Finite Mathematics* (3rd ed.). Englewood Cliffs, NJ: Prentice-Hall.

Kernberg, O. (2011). Suicide prevention for psychoanalytic institutes and societies. *Journal of the American Psychoanalytic Association, 60*(4), 707–719. doi:10.1177/0003065112449861 PMID:22786850

Khan Masud, R. M. (1970). *Le fétichisme comme négation du soi. Nouvelle Revue de Psychoanalyse, 2*.

Khan Masud, R. M. (1979). Alienation in perversions. London, UK: The Hogarth Press, Ltd.

Khrennikov, A. Yu. (2002). *Classical and quantum mental models and Freud's theory of unconscious mind. Series in Mathematical Modelling in Physics, Enginnering and Cognitive Sciences* (Vol. 1). Växjö, Sweden: Växjö University Press.

Kim, W. W. (2016). History and Cultural Perspective. In Penile Augmentation. Berlin: Springer-Verlag. doi:10.1007/978-3-662-46753-4_2

Kissin, B. (1986). *Conscious and Unconscious Programs in the Brain*. New York, NY: Plenum Publishing Corporation. doi:10.1007/978-1-4613-2187-3

Köhler, T. (2007). *Freuds Psychoanalyse. Eine Einführung* (2nd ed.). Stuttgart, Germany: W. Kohlhammer GmbH.

Kultgen, J. (1976). Lévi-Strauss on Unconscious Social Structures. *The Southwestern Journal of Philosophy, 7*(1), 153–159. doi:10.5840/swjphil19767118

Kuper, J. (Ed.). (1988). *A Lexicon of Psychology, Psychiatry and Psychoanalysis*. London, UK: Routledge.

La Forgia, M. (1992). Sincronicità. In Trattato di Psicologia Analitica (vol. 2). Torino, Italy: UTET.

Lacan, J. (2014). *The Seminar of Jacques Lacan. Book X: The Anxiety* (J. A. Miller, Ed.; A. R. Price, Trans.). Malden, MA: Polity Press.

Lacas, M.-L. (2007). La démarche originale de Gisela Pankow. Gisela Pankows original thought processes. *LÉvolution Psychiatrique, 72*(1), 15–24. doi:10.1016/j.evopsy.2006.11.001

Làdavas, E., & Berti, A. (2014). Neuropsicologia (3rd ed.). Bologna, Italy: Società editrice il Mulino.

Lagache, D. (1961). *La psychanalyse et la structure de la personnalité*. Paper Presented au Colloquium International de Royaumont, Paris, France.

Lagache, D. (1965). Le modèle psychanalytique de la personnalité. In *La Folle du Logis. La psychanalyse comme science exacte* (pp. 159–183). Paris: PUF-Presses Universitaires de France.

Lample-De-Groot, J. (1962). Ego ideal and Superego. *The Psychoanalytic Study of the Child*, *17*, 94–106.

Langs, R. (1990). Guida alla psicoterapia. Un'introduzione all'approccio comunicativo. Torino, Italy: Bollati Boringhieri editore.

Laplanche, J. (2000). Problematiche II. Castrazione. Simbolizzazioni. Bari-Roma, Italy: La Biblioteca.

Laplanche, J. (2001). *L'inconscio e l'Es*. Bari-Roma, Italy: La Biblioteca.

Laplanche, J. (2007). *L'après-coup*. Bari-Roma, Italy: La Biblioteca.

Laplanche, J. (2008). Sexuale. La sessualità allargata nel senso freudiano. Bari-Roma, Italy: La Biblioteca.

Laplanche, J., & Pontalis, J.-B. (1967). Vocabulaire de la psychoanalyse. Paris: Presses Universitaires de France.

Laplanche, J., & Pontalis, J.-B. (1988). Fantasma originario, fantasmi delle origini, origini del fantasma. Bologna, Italy: Società editrice il Mulino.

Lauro-Grotto, R. (2008). The unconscious as an ultrametric set. *The American Imago*, *64*(4), 52–62. doi:10.1353/aim.2008.0009

Lauro-Grotto, R. (2014a). Formal Approaches in the Age of Mirror Neurons. Hints from Psychoanalytic Theories and Practice. In *Proceedings of the 2014 IEEE 13th International Conference on Cognitive Informatics and Cognitive Computing*. Los Alamitos, CA: IEEE Computer Society Press.

Lauro-Grotto, R. (2014b). Paradigmi metapsicologici. Con tre scritti inediti di Freud. Pisa, Italy: ETS-Editrice tecnico-scientifica.

Lawson, M. K. (2005). Constructing ordered groupoids. *Cahiers de Topologie et Géométrie Différentielle Catégoriques*, *46*(2), 123–138.

Lenz Dunker, I. (2008). Psychology and Psychoanalysis in Brazil. From Cultural Syncretism to the Collapse of Liberal Individualism. *Theory & Psychology*, *18*(2), 223–236. doi:10.1177/0959354307087883

Lerner, D. (Ed.). (1961). Quality and Quantity. New York, NY: The Free Press of Glencoe.

Lévi-Strauss, C. (1975). *Razza e storia e altri studi di antropologia*. Torino, Italy: Giulio Einaudi editore.

Lévi-Strauss, C. (2008). Sull'Italia. In Claude Lévi-Strauss fotografato da Marion Kalter. Napoli, Italy: Electa Napoli.

Lévi-Strauss, C., & Eribon, D. (1988). De près et de loin. Paris: Éditions Odile Jacob.

Lewin, R. (1996). Communicating with the schizophrenic superego. *The Journal of the American Academy of Psychoanalysis*, *24*(4), 709–736. PMID:9220382

Lis, A., Mazzeschi, C., & Zennaro, A. (2007). *La psicoanalisi. Un percorso concettuale fra tradizione e attualità (2nd ed.)*. Roma, Italy: Carocci editore.

Lis, A., Zennaro, A., Mazzeschi, C., Salcuni, S., & Parolin, L. (2003). *Breve dizionario di psicoanalisi*. Roma, Italy: Carocci editore.

Loewald, H. W. (1962). The Superego and the Ego-Ideal. II. Superego and Time. *The International Journal of Psycho-Analysis*, *43*, 264–268. PMID:13931287

Loewald, H. W. (1988). Sublimation. Inquires into Theoretical Psychoanalysis. New Haven, CT: Yale University Press.

Loewald, H. W. (1989). Papers on Psychoanalysis. New Haven, CT: Yale University Press.

Lolli, G. (1991). Introduzione alla logica formale. Bologna, Italy: Società editrice il Mulino.

Longhin, L. (1992). Alle origini del pensiero psicoanalitico. Roma, Italy: Edizioni Borla.

Longhin, L. (2016). La mente emotiva. Conoscerla e curarla. Milano, Italy: FrancoAngeli.

Longhin, L., & Mancia, M. (1998). Temi e problemi in psicoanalisi. Torino, Italy: Bollati Boringhieri editore.

Luborsky, L., & Crits-Christoph, P. (1992). Capire il transfert. Milano, Italy: Raffaello Cortina Editore.

Lusetti, V. (2008). Psicopatologia antropologica. Roma, Italy: EUR-Edizioni Universitarie Romane.

Macola, E. (Ed.). (2014). Sublimazione e perversione. Attualità Lacaniana. Rivista della Scuola Lacaniana di Psicoanalisi, 18, 7-108.

Maffei, L. (2014). Elogio della lentezza. Bologna, Italy: Società editrice il Mulino.

Maffei, L. (2016). Elogio della ribellione. Bologna, Italy: Società editrice il Mulino.

Main, R. (2014). The cultural significance of synchronicity for Jung and Pauli. *The Journal of Analytical Psychology*, *59*(2), 174–180. doi:10.1111/1468-5922.12067 PMID:24673272

Mancia, M. (Ed.). (1990). Super-Io e Ideale dell'Io. Roma, Italy: Casa Editrice Astrolabio-Ubaldini Editore.

Mancia, M. (Ed.). (2006). Psychoanalysis and Neuroscience. Milan, Italy: Springer-Verlag Italia. doi:10.1007/88-470-0550-7

Marcuse, H. (1964). One-Dimensional Man. Studies in the Ideology of Advanced Industrial Society. Boston, MA: Beacon Press, Inc.

Matte Blanco, I. (1975). The Unconscious as Infinite Sets. An Essay in Bi-Logic. London, UK: Gerald Duckworth & Company, Ltd.

Matte Blanco, I. (1988). *Thinking, Feeling, and Being. Clinical Reflections of the Fundamental Antinomy on Human Beings and World.* London, UK: Routledge.

Matthews, P. T. (1974). *Introduction to Quantum Mechanics.* Maidenhead, UK: McGraw-Hill Publishing Company Limited.

Maurin, K. (1997). *The Riemann Legacy. Riemann Ideas in Mathematics and Physics.* Dordrecht, The Netherlands: Kluwer Academic Publishers. doi:10.1007/978-94-015-8939-0

McCulloch, W. S. (1965). *Embodiments of Mind.* Cambridge, MA: The MIT Press.

Mellino, M. (2005). La critica postcoloniale. Decolonizzazione, capitalismo e cosmopolitismo nei post-colonial studies. Roma, Italy: Meltemi editore.

Miller, P. H. (1983). *Theories of Developmental Psychology*. New York, NY: W.H. Freeman & Co.

Milrod, D. (2002). The superego. Its formation, structure, and functioning. *The Psychoanalytic Study of the Child*, *57*, 131–148. PMID:12723129

Minsky, M. (1975). A Framework for the Representation Knowledge. In The Psychology of Computer Vision. New York, NY: McGraw-Hill Book Company.

Mitchell, S. A., & Black, M. J. (1995). *Freud and beyond. A History of Modern Psychoanalysic Thought*. New York, NY: Basic Books. A Division of Harper Collins Publishers.

Moore, B. E., & Fine, B. D. (Eds.). (1990). Psychoanalytic Terms and Concepts. New York, NY: The American Psychoanalytic Association.

Moore, D. S. (2015). *The Developing Genome. An Introduction to Behavioural Epigenetics*. New York, NY: Oxford University Press.

Moravia, S. (2004). Ragione strutturale e universi di senso. Saggio su Lévi-Strauss. Firenze, Italy: Casa Editrice Le Lettere.

Mordant, I. (1990). Using attribute-memories to resolve a contradiction in the work of Matte Blanco. *The International Review of Psycho-Analysis*, *17*, 475–480.

Murtagh, F. (2012a). Ultrametric model of mind, I [Review]. *p-Adic Numbers, Ultrametric Analysis and Applications*, *4*(3), 193–206. doi:10.1134/S2070046612030041

Murtagh, F. (2012b). Ultrametric model of mind, II. Application to text content analysis. *p-Adic Numbers, Ultrametric Analysis and Applications*, *4*(3), 207–221. doi:10.1134/S2070046612030053

Murtagh, F. (2013). The new science of complex systems through ultrametric analysis. Application to search and discovery, to narrative and to thinking. *p-Adic Numbers, Ultrametric Analysis and Applications*, *5*(4), 326–337. doi:10.1134/S2070046613040067

Murtagh, F. (2014a). Pattern recognition of subconscious underpinnings of cognition using ultrametric topological mapping of thinking and memory. *International Journal of Cognitive Informatics and Natural Intelligence*, *8*(4), 1–16. doi:10.4018/ijcini.2014100101

Murtagh, F. (2014b). Mathematical representations of Matte Blancos bi-logic, based on metric space and ultrametric or hierarchical topology: Towards practical application. *Language and Psychoanalysis*, *3*(2), 40–63. doi:10.7565/landp.2014.008

Murtagh, F. (2014c). Pattern Recognition in Mental Processes: Determining Vestiges of the Subconscious through Ultrametric Component Analysis. In *Proceedings of the 2014 IEEE 13th International Conference on Cognitive Informatics and Cognitive Computing*. Los Alamitos, CA: IEEE Computer Society Press. doi:10.1109/ICCI-CC.2014.6921455

Murtagh, F., & Iurato, G. (2016). Human Behaviour, Benign or Malevalent: Understanding the Human Psyche, Performing Therapy, based on Affective Mentalization and Matte-Blancos Bi-Logic. *Annals of Translational Medicine, 4*(24), 486–496. doi:10.21037/atm.2016.12.37 PMID:28149848

Murtagh, F., & Iurato, G. (2017). Visualization of Jacques Lacan's Registers of the Psychoanalytic Field, and Discovery of Metaphor and of Metonymy. Analytical Case Study of Edgar Allan Poe's "The Purloined Letter". *Language and Psychoanalysis.* (in press)

Nagel, T. (1993). Summary. In *Experimental and Theoretical Studies of Consciousness. Novartis Foundation Symposium No. 174.* New York, NY: John Wiley & Sons, Ltd.

Nannini, S. (2007). Naturalismo cognitivo. Per una teoria materialistica della mente. Macerata, Italy: Edizioni Quodlibet.

Nannini, S. (2011). L'anima e il corpo. Un'introduzione storica alla filosofia della mente. Roma-Bari, Italy: Laterza Editori.

Nannini, S. (2015). Time and Consciousness in Cognitive Naturalism. *Rivista Internazionale di Filosofia e Psicologia, 6*(3), 458–473.

Napolitano, F. (2009). Rappresentazione, 2. In *Psiche. Dizionario storico di psicologia, psichiatria, psicoanalisi, neuroscienze* (Vol. 2, pp. 919–923). Torino, Italy: Giulio Einaudi editore.

Neubauer, K. (2004). Semantica storica. In Dizionario degli studi culturali. Roma, Italy: Meltemi editore.

Neuman, Y. (2014). *Introduction to Computational Cultural Psychology.* Cambridge, UK: Cambridge University Press.

Neuman, Y. (2016). Computational Personality Analysis. Introduction, Practical Applications and Novel Directions. Springer International Publishing.

Nunberg, H. (1932). Allgemeine Neurosenlehre auf psychoanalytischer Grundlage. Berlin: Verlag Hans Hüber.

Øhrstrøm, P., & Hasle, P. F. V. (Eds.). (1995). *Temporal Logic. From Ancient Ideas to Artificial Intelligence. Studies in Linguistics and Philosophy, Volume No. 57.* Dordrecht, The Netherlands: Kluwer Academic Publishers.

Oliverio, A. (1982). Biologia e comportamento. Bologna, Italy: Nicola Zanichelli Editore.

Oliverio, A. (2016). Il cervello e l'inconscio. *Psicobiettivo, 36*(3), 251–259. doi:10.3280/PSOB2016-003015

Oliverio, A. (2017). Il cervello che impara. Neuropedagogia dall'infanzia alla vecchiaia. Firenze, Italy: Giunti Editore.

Pankow, G. (1977). L'uomo e la sua psicosi. Milano, Italy: Giangiacomo Feltrinelli Editore.

Pankow, G. (1979). Struttura familiare e psicosi. Milano, Italy: Giangiacomo Feltrinelli Editore.

Panksepp, J., & Biven, L. (2012). The Archeology of Mind. Neuroevolutionary Origins of Human Emotion. New York, NY: W.W. Norton & Company.

Papagno, C. (2010). Neuropsicologia della memoria. Bologna, Italy: Società editrice il Mulino.

Parsons, T. (1970). *Social Structure and Personality*. New York, NY: The Free Press. A Division of The Macmillan Company.

Peterburs, J., Nitsch, A. M., Miltner, W. H. R., & Straube, T. (2013). Impaired representation of time in schizophrenia is linked to positive symptoms and cognitive demand. *PLoS ONE, 8*(6), e67615/1–7. doi:10.1371/journal.pone.0067615 PMID:23826328

Petocz, A. (2004). *Freud, psychoanalysis and symbolism*. Cambridge, UK: Cambridge University Press.

Petrilli, S., & Ponzio, A. (2005). *Semiotics Unbounded. Interpretive Routes Through the Open Network of Signs*. Toronto: The University of Toronto Press. doi:10.3138/9781442657113

Petrini, P., Casadei, A., & Chiricozzi, F. (Eds.). (2011). Trasgressione, violazione, perversione. Eziopatogenesi, diagnosi e terapia. Milano, Italy: FrancoAngeli.

Petrini, P., Renzi, A., Casadei, A., & Mandese, A. (2013). Dizionario di psicoanalisi. Con elementi di psichiatria, psicodinamica e psicologia dinamica. Milano, Italy: FrancoAngeli.

Piattelli Palmarini, M. (1987). Scienza come cultura. Protagonisti, luoghi e idee delle scienze contemporanee. Milano, Italy: Arnoldo Mondadori Editore.

Pierce, B. C. (2002). *Types and Programming Languages*. Cambridge, MA: The MIT Press.

Pieri, P. F. (2005). Dizionario junghiano (Edizione ridotta). Torino, Italy: Bollati Boringhieri editore.

Piras, F., Piras, F., Ciullo, V., Danese, E., Caltagirone, C. & Spalletta, G. (2013). Time dysperception perspective for acquired brain injury. *Frontiers in Neurology, 4*, 217-226.

Piscicelli, U. (1994). Sessuologia. Teoremi psicosomatici e relazionali. Padova, Italy: Piccin Nuova Libraria.

Pizzi, C. (Ed.). (1974). La logica del tempo. Torino, Italy: Bollati Boringhieri Editore.

Poggi, S. (1977). I sistemi dell'esperienza. Bologna, Italy: Società editrice il Mulino.

Poincaré, H. J. (1958). The Value of Science. New York, NY: Dover Publications, Inc.

Pollo, M. (2016). La nostalgia dell'uroboros. Contributi a una psicologia culturale delle nuove addiction. Milano, Italy: FrancoAngeli.

Putnam, H. (1956). Mathematics and the Existence of Abstract Entities. *Philosophical Studies, 7*(6), 81–88. doi:10.1007/BF02221758

Putnam, H. (1975). Filosofia della logica. Nominalismo e realismo nella logica contemporanea. Milano, Italy: ISEDI – Istituto Editoriale Internazionale.

Quan, P. M. (1969). *Introduction a la géométrie des variétés différentiables*. Paris: Éditions Dunod.

Rayner, E. (1995). *Unconscious Logic. An Introduction to Matte Blanco's Bi-Logic and its Uses*. New York, NY: Routledge.

Rayner, E. (1998). Foreword. In *The Unconscious as Infinite Sets. An Essay in Bi-Logic* (pp. xviii–xxiv). London, UK: Karnac Books, Ltd.

Recalcati, M. (2003). Introduzione alla psicoanalisi contemporanea. Milano, Italy: Bruno Mondadori Editore.

Recalcati, M. (2007a). Elogio dell'inconscio. Dodici argomenti in difesa della psicoanalisi. Milano, Italy: Bruno Mondadori.

Recalcati, M. (2007b). Lo psicoanalista e la città. L'inconscio e il discorso del capitalista. Roma, Italy: manifestolibri.

Recalcati, M. (2010). L'uomo senza inconscio. Figure della nuova clinica psicoanalitica. Milano, Italy: Raffaello Cortina Editore.

Recalcati, M. (2016). *Jacques Lacan* (vols. 1-2). Milano, Italy: Raffaello Cortina Editore.

Redondi, P. (2007). Storie del tempo. Roma-Bari, Italy: Editori Laterza.

Reich, A. (1954). Early identifications as archaic elements in the Superego. *Journal of the American Psychoanalytic Association*, *2*(2), 218–238. doi:10.1177/000306515400200203 PMID:13151996

Reverberi, C., Pischedda, D., Burigo, M., & Cherubini, P. (2012). Deduction without awareness. *Acta Psychologica*, *139*(1), 244–253. doi:10.1016/j.actpsy.2011.09.011 PMID:22019058

Riehl, J. P. (2010). *Mirror-Image Asymmetry. An Introduction to the Origin and Consequences of Chirality*. Hoboken, NJ: John Wiley & Sons, Inc. doi:10.1002/9780470588888

Riolo, F. (2009). Trasformazione. In *Psiche. Dizionario storico di psicologia, psichiatria, psicoanalisi, neuroscienze* (Vol. 2, pp. 1112–1116). Torino, Italy: Giulio Einaudi editore.

Rose, J. R. (Ed.). (2011). *Mapping Psychic Reality. Triangulation, Communication, and Insight. Psychoanalytic Ideas*. London, UK: Karnac Books, Ltd.

Rossi, R., De Fazio, F., Gatti, U., & Rocco, G. (2008, Feb.). Perizie e consulenze psichiatriche su Diamante Stefano, Stevanin Gianfranco, Bilancia Donato, Panini Giorgio. *POL.it – The Italian On Line Psychiatric Magazine*.

Roudinesco, E. (1997). Jacques Lacan. Outline of a life, history of a system of thought. Oxford, UK: Polity Press.

Roudinesco, E. (2008). Da vicino e da lontano. Claude Lévi-Strauss e la psicoanalisi. In Lévi-Strauss Fuori di sé. Macerata, Italy: Quodlibet.

Rycroft, C. (1968a). A critical dictionary of psychoanalysis. London, UK: Thomas Nelson & Sons, Ltd.

Rycroft, C. (1968b). Imagination and reality. Psychoanalytical essays 1951–1961. London, UK: The Hogarth Press, Ltd.

Sabbadini, A. (1979). Introduzione. In Il tempo in psicoanalisi. Milano, Italy: Giangiacomo Feltrinelli Editore.

Sandler, J., Holder, A., & Meers, D. (1963). The Ego Ideal and the Ideal Self. *The Psychoanalytic Study of the Child*, *18*, 139–158. PMID:14147277

Sandler, J. J. (Ed.). (1981). La ricerca in psicoanalisi (vols. 1-2). Torino, Italy: Bollati Boringhieri editore.

Sannella, D., & Tarlecki, A. (2012). *Foundations of Algebraic Specification and Formal Software Development. Monographs in Theoretical Computer Science. An EATCS Series*. Berlin: Springer-Verlag. doi:10.1007/978-3-642-17336-3

Sasso, G. (1982). Le strutture anagrammatiche della poesia. Milano, Italy: Giangiacomo Feltrinelli Editore.

Sasso, G. (1993). La mente intralinguistica. L'instabilità del segno: anagrammi e parole dentro le parole. Genova, Italy: Marietti Editore.

Sasso, G. (1999). Struttura dell'oggetto e della rappresentazione. Roma, Italy: Casa Editrice Astrolabio-Ubaldini Editore.

Sasso, G. (2005). Psicoanalisi e Neuroscienze. Roma, Italy: Casa Editrice Astrolabio-Ubaldini Editore.

Sasso, G. (2011). La nascita della coscienza. Roma, Italy: Casa Editrice Astrolabio-Ubaldini Editore.

Scabini, E. (1973). Ideazione e psicoanalisi. Milano, Italy: Giangiacomo Feltrinelli Editore.

Schmitt, A., Hasan, A., Gruber, O., & Falkai, P. (2011). Schizophrenia as a disorder of disconnectivity. *European Archives of Psychiatry and Clinical Neuroscience*, *261*(2), S150–S154. doi:10.1007/s00406-011-0242-2 PMID:21866371

Segalen, M. (1998). Rites et rituels contemporains. Paris: Les Éditions Nathan.

Semi, A. A. (2003). La coscienza in psicoanalisi. Milano, Italy: Raffaello Cortina Editore.

Semi, A.A. (Ed.). (1989). *Trattato di Psicoanalisi* (Vols. 1-2). Milano, Italy: Raffaello Cortina Editore.

Severino, E. (2008). La strada. La follia e la gioia. Milano, Italy: BUR Saggi.

Silvestri, D. (2013). Linguistica implicita e linguistica esplicita. In Simposio Lévi-Strauss. Uno sguardo dall'oggi. Milano, Italy: il Saggiatore.

Skelton, R. (1984). Understanding Matte Blanco. *The International Journal of Psycho-Analysis*, *65*, 453–460. PMID:6544756

Skelton, R. (1990). Generalizations from Freud to Matte Blanco. *The International Review of Psycho-Analysis*, *17*, 471–474.

Skillicorn, D. (1994). *Foundations of Parallel Programming*. Cambridge, UK: Cambridge University Press. doi:10.1017/CBO9780511526626

Sluzki, C. E., & Ransom, D. C. (1979). Il doppio legame: la genesi dell'approccio relazionale allo studio della famiglia. Roma, Italy: Casa Editrice Astrolabio-Ubaldini Editore.

Smirnov, V. N. (1970). *La transaction fétichique. Nouvelle Revue de Psychoanalyse, 2*.

Solms, M., & Turnbull, O. (2003). The Brain and the Inner World. An Introduction to the Neuroscience of Subjective Experience. New York, NY: Other Press, LLC.

Somenzi, V. (1998). Prefazione. In Categorie, tempo e linguaggio. Roma, Italy: Società Stampa Sportiva.

Sossinsky, A. (2000). Nodi. Genesi di una teoria matematica. Torino, Italy: Bollati Boringhieri editore.

Sparsø, J., & Furber, S. (Eds.). (2001). Principles of Asynchronous Circuit Design. A Systems Perspective. Dordrecht, The Netherlands: Springer-Science + Business Media, B.V. doi:10.1007/978-1-4757-3385-3

Spedini, G. (2005). Antropologia evoluzionistica (2nd ed.). Padova, Italy: Piccin Nuova Libraria.

Spitz, R. A. (1957). No and yes. On the genesis of human communication. New York, NY: International University Press, Inc.

Stanghellini, G., Ballerini, M., Presenza, S., Mancini, M., Raballo, A., Blasi, S., & Cutting, J. (2016). Psychopathology of lived time: Abnormal time experience in persons with schizophrenia. *Schizophrenia Bulletin. The Journal of Psychoses and Related Disorders*, *42*(1), 45–55.

Steedman, M. (2000). *Surface Structure and Interpretation*. Boston, MA: The MIT Press.

Stirling, C. (2001). *Modal and Temporal Properties of Processes*. New York, NY: Springer-Verlag. doi:10.1007/978-1-4757-3550-5

Tabossi, P. (2009). Rappresentazione, 1. In *Psiche. Dizionario storico di psicologia, psichiatria, psicoanalisi, neuroscienze* (Vol. 2, pp. 914–919). Torino, Italy: Giulio Einaudi editore.

Tallis, R. (2002). Hidden Minds. A History of the Unconscious. New York, NY: Arcade Publishing, Inc.

Tanenbaum, A. S., & Bos, H. (2015). *Modern Operating Systems* (4th ed.). Essex, UK: Pearson Education Limited.

Target, M., & Fonagy, P. (2002). The role of the father and child development. In The Importance of Fathers. A Psychoanalytic Re-evaluation. London, UK: Routledge.

Tartabini, A., & Giusti, F. (2006). Origine ed evoluzione del linguaggio. Scimpanzé, Ominidi e uomini moderni. Napoli, Italy: Liguori Editore.

Terminio, N. (2009). Misurare l'inconscio? Coordinate psicoanalitiche nella ricerca in psicoterapia. Milano, Italy: Bruno Mondadori.

Thom, R. (1972). Symmetries Gained and Lost. In *Broken Symmetries. Proceedings of the 3rd GIFT International Seminar in Theoretical Physics organized by the Spanish-Inter-University Group in Theoretical Physics*. Saragoza, Spain: Scientific Information Service, Ltd.

Thom, R. (1980). *Stabilità strutturale e morfogenesi. Saggio di una teoria generale dei modelli*. Torino, Italy: Giulio Einaudi editore.

Thom, R. (1985). *Modelli matematici della morfogenesi*. Torino, Italy: Giulio Einaudi editore.

Thomä, H., & Kächele, H. (1989). *Psychoanalytic Practice* (vols. 1-2). Berlin: Springer-Verlag.

Tibaldi, M. (2004). Critica archetipica. In Dizionario degli studi culturali. Roma, Italy: Meltemi editore, pp. 115-121.

Tokhi, M. O., Hossain, M. A., & Shaheed, M. H. (2003). *Parallel Computing for Real-time Signal Processing and Control*. London, UK: Springer-Verlag London. doi:10.1007/978-1-4471-0087-4

Toraldo di Francia, G. (1976). *L'indagine del mondo fisico*. Torino, Italy: Giulio Einaudi editore.

Uznadze, D. N., Prangisvili, A. S., Bassin, F. V., & Razran, G. (1972). *L'inconscio nella psicologia sovietica*. Roma, Italy: Editori Riuniti.

Vaccarino, G. (2006). Scienza e semantica. Milano, Italy: Edizioni Melquiades.

Vallortigara, G., & Panciera, N. (2014). Cervelli che contano. Milano, Italy: Adelphi Edizioni.

Vattimo, G., Ferraris, M., & Marconi, D. (Eds.). (1993). Enciclopedia Garzanti di Filosofia. Milano, Italy: Garzanti Editore.

Vegetti Finzi, S. (Ed.). (1976). Il bambino nella psicoanalisi. Testi di S. Freud, Jung, Reich, Klein, A. Freud, Spitz, Winnicott, Musatti, Fornari, Erikson, Laing, Lacan, Mannoni. Bologna, Italy: Nicola Zanichelli Editore.

Venema, Y. (2001). Temporal Logic. In The Blackwell Guide to Philosophical Logic. Oxford, UK: Basil Blackwell Publishers.

Verdiglione, A. (1977). Matematica dell'inconscio. In Feticismo, linguaggio, afasia, matematica dell'inconscio. Fa parte di VEL – Collana-rivista di psicoanalisi diretta da Armando Verdiglione. Venezia, Italy: Marsilio Editori.

Vicario, G. B. (1997). Il tempo in psicologia. *Le Scienze, 30*(347), 43–51.

Vicario, G. B. (2005). Il tempo. Saggio di psicologia sperimentale. Bologna, Italy: Società editrice il Mulino.

Viret, J. (2012). Topological Approach of Jungian Psychology. *Acta Biotheoretica, 58*(2), 233–245. PMID:20658172

Voevodin, V. V. (1992). Mathematical Foundations of Parallel Computing. Singapore: World Scientific Publishing. doi:10.1142/1533

von Karger, B. (1995). An algebraic approach to temporal logic. In *Lecture Notes in Computer Science: Vol. 915. Proceedings of the Sixth International Joint Conference on Theory and Practice of Software Development (TAPSOFT '95)*. Berlin: Springer-Verlag. doi:10.1007/3-540-59293-8_198

von Karger, B. (2002). Temporal Algebra. In Lecture Notes in Computer Science: Vol. 2297. Algebraic and Coalgebraic Methods in the Mathematics of Program Construction. Berlin: Springer-Verlag. doi:10.1007/3-540-47797-7_9

Von Scheve, C., & Salmela, M. (Eds.). (2014). *Collective Emotions. Perspectives from Psychology, Philosophy, and Sociology*. Oxford, UK: Oxford University Press.

Von Wright, G. H. (1969). *Time, Change and Contradiction*. Cambridge, UK: Cambridge University Press.

Wang, Y. (2008). On Concept Algebra: A Denotational Mathematical Structure for Knowledge and Software Modeling. *International Journal of Cognitive Informatics and Natural Intelligence, 2*(2), 1–19. doi:10.4018/jcini.2008040101

Wang, Y. (2010). A Sociopsychological Perspective on Collective Intelligence in Metaheuristic Computing. *International Journal of Applied Metaheuristic Computing, 1*(1), 110–128. doi:10.4018/jamc.2010102606

Wang, Y., Wang, Y., Patel, S., & Patel, D. (2006). A Layered Reference Model of the Brain. *IEEE Transactions on Systems, Man and Cybernetics. Part C, Applications and Reviews, 36*(2), 124–133. doi:10.1109/TSMCC.2006.871126

Wang, Y., Zadeh, L. A., Widrow, B., Howard, N., Wood, S., Patel, S., & Zhang, D. et al. (2017). Abstract Intelligence: Embodying and Enabling Cognitive Systems by Mathematical Engineering. *International Journal of Cognitive Informatics and Natural Intelligence, 11*(1), 1–22. doi:10.4018/IJCINI.2017010101

Wang, Y., Zhang, D., & Kinsner, D. (Eds.). (2011). *Advances in Cognitive Informatics and Cognitive Computing*. Berlin: Springer-Verlag.

Watanabe, S. (1969). *Knowing and Guessing. A Quantitative Study of Inference and Information*. New York, NY: John Wiley & Sons, Inc.

Watzlawick, P., Beavin, J. H., & Jackson, D. D. (1967). Pragmatics of Human Communication. A Study of Interactional Patterns, Pathologies, and Paradoxes. New York, NY: W.W. Norton & Company.

Weinstein, A. (1996). Groupoids: Unifying Internal and External Symmetry. *Notices of the American Mathematical Society, 43*(7), 744–752.

Westphal, B. (2007). La Géocritique. Réel, fiction, espace. Paris: Les Éditions de Minuit.

White, D. R., & Jorion, P. (1996). Kinship networks and discrete structure theory: Applications and implications. *Social Networks, 18*(3), 267–314. doi:10.1016/0378-8733(95)00277-4

Whitebook, J. (1995). *Perversion and Utopia. A Study in Psychoanalysis and Critical Theory*. Cambridge, MA: The MIT Press.

Whitrow, G. J. (1988). *Time in History. Views of Time from Prehistory to the Present Day*. Oxford, UK: Oxford University Press.

Wimmer, M., & Ciompi, L. (1996). Evolutionary aspects of affective-cognitive interactions in the light of Ciompi's concept of "affect-logic". *Evolution & Cognition, 2*, 37–58.

Yang, J., Kanazawa, S., Yamaguchi, M. K., & Kuriki, I. (2016). Cortical response to categorical colour perception in infants investigated by near-infrared spectroscopy. *Proceedings of the National Academy of Sciences of the United States of America, 113*(9), 2370-2375.

Zapparoli, G. C. (1970). La perversione logica. I rapporti tra sessualità e pensiero nella tradizione psicoanalitica. Milano, Italy: Franco Angeli Editore.

Zeh, H. D. (2007). *The Physical Basis of the Direction of Time* (5th ed.). Berlin: Springer-Verlag.

Zentall, T. R. (2013). Animals represent the past and the future. *Evolutionary Psychology*, *11*(3), 573–590. doi:10.1177/147470491301100307 PMID:24027784

Zepf, S., & Gerlach, A. (2012). Commentary on Kernbergs suicide prevention for psychoanalytic institutes and societies. *Journal of the American Psychoanalytic Association*, *61*(4), 771–786. doi:10.1177/0003065113496634 PMID:23918822

ENDNOTES

[1] In what follows, we refer to (Dei, 1998; Ffytche, 2012; Funari, 2007; Galimberti, 1983; Recalcati, 2007a; Semi 1988-89, Vol. I; Tallis, 2003) for a historical deepening of the arguments considered in this section.

[2] This might be put into a certain relationship with Ludwig Wittgenstein arguments on rules and private language and the related *Kripke-Wittgenstein paradox* (see also (Iurato, 2017b)).

[3] See (Funari, 1988).

[4] See (Bassin, 1972; Uznadze et al., 1972).

[5] Similarly to methodological processes of quantum physics.

[6] Here, we mean *object* in its widest philosophical sense (Abbagnano, 1998).

[7] See (Iurato, 2016a) and references therein.

[8] Which are, overall, said to be *unconscious' formations*.

[9] Nevertheless, not all childhood's experiences fall into unconscious: for example, some of them may refall into unreflective consciousness (for example, according to Russian psychological school).

[10] Nevertheless, these last remarks about processing of drive psychic energy and its flow, are established by Freud at the early beginnings of his second theory of human psyche, after 1915, when he introduces the so-called *economic standpoint*.

[11] See (Fossi 1988, p. 41).

[12] That is to say, they may stay altogether without reciprocal contraposition nor to be influenced of each other.

[13] This same system is used by Freud to explain too the rising of temporal dimension, as an outcome of discontinuities occurring between preconscious and conscious, and just characterizing consciousness; in this regard, see also (Iurato et al., 2016), where the rising of temporal dimension is just formally related with a certain discontinuity feature presents in the human psychic functioning according to Freudian first topography. We however shall return later on this last argument linked to temporality.

[14] See also (Conrotto 2014, p. 33).

[15] This choice, besides to its own theoretical motivations (Iurato, 2013b,c), is also motivated by some epistemological considerations due to Jacques Lacan, according to whom science is nothing but a psychosis in which operate mainly *Verwerfung* (i.e., foreclosure) mechanisms (Balzarotti 1972, p. 16). Disavowal alone yet is, in itself, unable to produce symbolization since the emptiness left by it, for the denying of a painful external perception, excludes per se conflicts as well as is devoid of any structuring function; this empty may be, at most, filled by mere illusion, which is asymbolic and demetaphorizating (Semi 1988-89, Volume I, App. 6.1, p. 451). Instead, its symbolic action may arise from the splitting of the Ego that it may imply (Iurato, 2013b,c).

[16] See just below. Anyway, we refer to (Akhtar & O'Neil, 2011) for a deepening of these arguments.

[17] Cf. (Iurato, 2013b,c) and references therein. See also (Friedman & Tomšič 2016, p. 181).

[18] Often, metaphorically conducted at an unconscious level.

[19] They basically are innate (i.e., *a priori*, just in the Kantian sense) interpretative schemas, which have arisen from the very long phylogenetic route of human evolution (mainly, during *homination* process), and have a chief *generative* function, in a similar way to that provided by Noam Chomsky's *transformative-generative grammars*.

[20] Cf. (Conrotto 2014, p. 99).

[21] See (Green, 1993). See also what is said in (De Mijolla & De Mijolla Mellor 1998, Ch. II, Sect. VII, No. 4, *f*). The work of André Green is very important, because, among other things, he states that the *negative* recollects, around it, all the other defence mechanisms which play a fundamental importance for the psychic functioning not only pathological but even normal. Green states that they are linked together just to form a unitary set of operations which identify the real structure of the subject, being its reference points.

[22] André Green speaks of "temporal dyscrhony and spatial distance", occurring with the secondary process and that separate desiring subject, desired object and the possibility of satisfaction, in reference to the relation between primary and secondary process (Semi 1988-89, Vol. I, p. 414).

[23] Cf. (Loewald, 1988).

[24] On the other hand, it is well-known that cultural work, according to Freud, comes from repression and conversion of pervert sexual elements (Petrini et al., 2013; Vattimo et al., 1993).

[25] Understood in its widest sense, beyond the anthropological meaning; cf. (Bernardi et al., 2011; Dei & Meloni, 2015). A further, in-depth discussion of what is said in this sentence, will be given in the last subsections.

[26] For the fundamental importance of splitting psychic phenomena in the rising of bivalent logic, see (Conrotto, 2010) and, above all, (Conrotto 2014, p. 33), as well as what has been already said above, just in the incipit of this section 2.8.

[27] These agencies, however, warrant the existence of the needful links with unconscious realm.

[28] Ant that it starts since prenatal phase, in the maternal womb, to which every human being unconsciously tends to return back, as pointed out by Franco Fornari (2016).

[29] Belonging to the Ego's Ideal and Super-Ego agencies, understood as distinct between them according to the next work of other post-Freudian scholars (e.g., Nunberg, Lagache, Lacan, Grunberger, Chasseguet-Smirgel, Hanly, and others more). See the references quoted at the beginning of this subsection, as well as (Iurato, 2013b,c) for further bibliographical references.

[30] See (Semi 1988-89, Vol. I, p. 411).

[31] Cf. (Gay, 2000).

[32] Cf. (Gay, 2000).

[33] See also (Chasseguet-Smirgel, 1975, 1985).

[34] See also (Gay, 2000).

[35] See (Vattimo et al., 1993).

[36] In passing, we recall as well that this dialectics of the agency pair Ego's Ideal–Super-Ego explicates symbolically and represents that basic generational difference with which every individual may grow up. On the other hand, in his last work, Freud (1938) considers Super-Ego as a particular agency which forms into the Ego, above all under parental influences and by public institutions (schools, clubs, educational and recreational centres, and so forth) which, in turn, are moulded by traditions,

uses, customs, and the general culture of the society in which they live. Furthermore, Es, Ego and Super-Ego are the bearers of, respectively, the deepest inherited ancestral past, the individual past (i.e., the own lived experiences) and the institutional past (i.e., that made by others).

[37] Which explicates along the imaginary relation axis a-a' of the well-known *Schema L* due to Lacan. For this breaking, see also (Iurato, 2014a,b).

[38] See also (Murtagh & Iurato, 2016) and references therein.

[39] Here, the term "object" is used in its widest sense.

[40] Giving rise something near to the Lacanian *lack of being* ("*manque*"), desire producing.

[41] Occurring during Œdipal phase, and needful to enter into the real life, with the acquisition of her or his own autonomy and personality.

[42] Similar to the so-called *béance* of Lacan.

[43] Which, in general, takes place by means of either an external perception or an internal correlation with some other already acquired objective datum, known fact or established belief (Britton 2004, Ch. 6, p. 93).

[44] In this regard, Britton refers cleverly to a right and well-fitting example drew from quantum mechanics. Indeed, he recalls that the typical case in which a particle may stay in two different places at the same time, in quantum mechanics may be described only formally, but cannot be imagined according to our usual thinking ways (Britton 2003, Ch. 6).

[45] In other words, "something stands for something else".

[46] So that its meaning refers to something, like an object, and, through its fragmentation, to the idea of a link or bond. This will be coherent with what is pursued in this paper about bodily image formation in fetishism, Ego's splitting and their relations with symbolism.

[47] Or *denegation*, as called by Jean Hyppolite in the 1950s. However, for a precise historical clarification about linguistic usage, meaning and related translation of the original Freudian terms of *Verneinung*, *Verleugnung*, *Verdrängung* and *Verwerfung*, we refer to (Laplanche & Pontalis, 1967).

[48] See the Introduction to the Italian translation of (Freud, 1938), that is to say, (Freud 1999, Foreword, pp. 7-12).

[49] Chianese (2009) points out the recurrence of the themes treated in these letters to Fliess (of the period 1887-1904) in the last Freudian work of the 1930s.

[50] As Cesare L. Musatti points out in the foreword to the Italian translation of *Splitting of the Ego in the Process of Defence* (Freud 1979, p. 556), the Freudian notion of splitting of the Ego has a relevance wider than that given by Freud himself in the course of his work, which started from a particular yet crucial anguish experience felt by child in recognizing penis' lacking in woman. Nevertheless, Freud himself, in the beginning of this last paper, talks about an Ego's splitting arising from a general anguish experience not particularly due to a specific cause (Freud 1979, p. 557). Furthermore, in the beginning of this work, Freud states too that what he is talking about is something new with respect to his previous work (De Mijolla & De Mijolla Mellor 1998, p. 213; Semi 1988-89, Vol. I).

[51] From his clinical experience, Freud noted that "trauma" (just due to lacking) precedes always the "word" (Chianese, 2009).

[52] So, we may say that aesthetic moment precedes almost every other form of mental activity, basically due to the primary action of pleasure-displeasure principle. This besides had already been preached by ancient philosophy which gives precedence to the *aistheta* (the act of early perception) with respect to the *noemata* (the act of pure thinking), and in the middle of which there is located,

as an intermediate moment between them, the *phainestai*, that is to say, the apparition, the appearance, hence the *phantasia*, the *phantasma*, the *phantaston*, and so on, to be meant, therefore, as precursors of mental representations (Napolitano, 2009). Besides, also recent neuropsychology confirms the precedence of an aestethic sense (of beauty) with respect to certain rational functions, like language, in that, for example, it has been discovered, in the children, an innate sense of colours before any linguistic abilities (Yang et al., 2016). Also Susanne Langer has then pointed out that, after her long research route, started with the investigation of different forms of symbolism and ended over twenty years later, beauty is experienced whenever deep feelings are truthfully expressed (Rayner 1995, p. 16). Also Antonio Alberto Semi (2003) points out that one of the main features of conscious system according to Freudian theory, is the qualifying and judgement function. Finally, to further support this, we may call into question the so-called *ugly duckling theorem* due to Satosi Watanabe, according to which every classification process (typical of consciousness, according to Ignacio Matte Blanco) is impossible without a previous, already established system of biases and prejudges (Watanabe, 1969).

[53] Historically, Bernheim coined the expression of *negative hallucination* in 1884, and Freud used such a term from 1895 until 1917, when he discarded it. In the meanwhile, Freud put forward the concept of *disavowal* (as *Verleugnung*) in 1914, even if, in its wider meaning, it is basically equivalent to negative hallucination, but, in its more specific meaning, it designates the simultaneous acknowledgement and non-acknowledgement of a traumatic perception. *Scotomization*, instead, was introduced by Enrique Pichon-Rivière and René Laforgue, but it is basically identical to negative hallucination. Freud and Laforgue had a long and polemical discussion just about it. However, from a psychological, a metapsychological and a psychopathological standpoint, only the concepts of negative hallucination and disavowal, in their more specific meaning, ought to be considered. In their first three phases of action, both these processes run identically: the first phase is a "preliminary position", a conception of the things just related to the wishes and the pleasure principle (attribution judgement), while the second phase is marked by a stimulus which is unconsciously perceived as "unbearable"; during the third phase, then, perception is suspended by various processes, whereas, it is only with the fourth phase that these two mechanisms basically differ: in the negative hallucination, the Ego keeps the perception unconsciously, whereas, in the disavowal (in its specific meaning), it is split (Ego's splitting), one part acknowledges the perception, while the other disavows it (Bourguignon & Manus, 1980).

[54] The *Verleugnung* has to do with external reality, but in an opposite manner with respect to repression. It is the first step towards psychosis. If neurotic is aimed to repress instinctual drives of *Id* (or *Es*), the psychotic refuses reality. After 1927, Freud started to consider *Verleugnung* as a psychic mechanism specifically related to fetishism, and perversions in general, until up 1938, when Freud settled up a theory of Ego's splitting just based on this mechanism.

[55] That André Green defines as *primary symbolization*. Lacan, instead, brings back the negation to the primary act of contraposition between *Bejahung* (admission) and *Verwerfung* (denial), so giving precedence to the latter, also with respect to the language, therefore, if this last is considered to be based just on negation.

[56] On the other hand, representations have many featuring aspects in common with symbolism. Indeed, a *representation* (from a general standpoint) is something which stands for something else, real or imaginary, reproducing this in an approximate fashion and not in a bijective manner, within a

certain universe (*representational universe*) inside which there exist those relations involving all the objects to be represented (Tabossi, 2009).

57   It is just the emotive-affective component to giving rise the meaning (*signified*) of a psychic representation (*signifier*) (Riolo, 2009; Conrotto, 2009).

58   See the final part of their item on *Disavowal*.

59   Seen too the vague and often sharply undefined bounds between normal and pathological psychic behaviour, this also in agreement with the relationships prescribed between the so-called *symmetric* and *asymmetric* thought according to Matte Blanco.

60   This last (partially unfinished) work may be considered as the Freud's spiritual testament of his doctrine, in which he almost axiomatically tried to delineate the main lines of his theory as it historically evolved from its first ideas to the final form, together with some of its unsolved questions to which the author was not able to give a relevant answer.

61   This psychic phenomenon is almost ubiquitous in childhood if it is laid out in the Winnicott framework of transitional objects and their relations with fetish.

62   On this, Lacan will speak of the child as a prolongation of the mother penis.

63   The degree of this is directly correlated with (and proportional to) the emotive content associated with it.

64   See (Benvenuto 2005, Sect. 4.2; Khan Masud, 1970, 1979; Smirnov, 1970).

65   The constitution and separation of opposite pairs, as already said, is a fundamental and characterizing task for consciousness (Laplanche & Pontalis, 1967). Here, we have discussed such psychodynamic processes from the Freudian perspective, but they also play a fundamental role in the Jungian theory of consciousness (Iurato, 2015a).

66   Which has mainly external sources.

67   Which should be kept distinct from the analogous notion related to schizophrenia in which it is preferable to use the term *dissociation*.

68   In this regard, the work of Gisela Pankow has been very remarkable. Indeed, she has provided, among other, new insightful therapeutic views of psychosis and other psychical disorganisation forms (Pankow, 1977, 1979). The E. Kretschmer legacy – whom she has been either a disciple and a collaborator at Tubingen – as well as phenomenology, have been unavoidable sources to understand her new concept of *bodily image* and the related process of symbolisation considered to be prior to any sign process as well as to language. This notion of bodily image is much more a dynamic organisation than a mirror picture which is nothing but its projection into space. The access to language and the genesis of the sign have precursors into an already-lived and an already-felt body, which will allow the access to the other, hence providing a possibility of symbolisation (Lacas, 2007).

69   In this case, the (material) fetish may be considered as a materialized effect of screen memory (related to implicit memory – cf. (Mancia, 2006)) or cover memory.

70   In this regard, it is useful to remember the incisive Freudian expression according to which "perversions are, in a certain sense, the 'negative' of neuroses". Herein, we refer to the widest meaning of the term "perversion" (Moore & Fine, 1990).

71   Which might be considered as forming the first precursor of an opposite pair (or else the source of any other possible philosophical pair), which will play a fundamental role in the dialectic reasoning, as already stated above.

72   In passing, we recall that these two Ego's agencies, as the result of an intrasystemic agency separation (i.e., the Ego's splitting), play a fundamental role in Lacan's theoretical framework.

73   Which is not present in psychoses.

74   A support to our discussion, is also (Target & Fonagy, 2002).

75   Just at this point occurs the *foreclosure*, a specific Lacanian splitting mechanism based on reality's *rejection* (*Verwerfung*) and derived both from the Freudian *spaltung* and from Laforgue and Pichon-Rivière's *scotomization*. This mechanism roughly consists in the primordial rejection of a fundamental signifier (the name-of-the-father, hence the symbolic phallus) out of the symbolic register of the subject, so giving rise to a psychotic state. Therefore, the (symbolic) phallus is a cornerstone of Lacanian theory basically because it is the primordial symbol to enter into the symbolic order. Hence, also in the Lacan theory of the symbolic, the phallus, with related castration phenomena, plays a fundamental role (Recalcati 2003, Sect. 2.7; Macola, 2014).

76   Together the well-known treatise of Otto Fenichel (1945).

77   Subsequently, Lagache (1961) will bring back this subagency to the maternal predominance or to the phallic mother. He brings back to it possible deviant behaviours.

78   Here, when one speaks of love, we refer to the wider general sense of this term, not only to the sensual one.

79   Subsequently, Chasseguet-Smirgel (1985) identified various possible outcomes for the Ego's Ideal, perverse as well as creative.

80   It is linked to narcissism, to perfection, to undifferentiation, and to the desire in restoring symbiotic union with mother (Petrini et al., 2013).

81   It is linked to reality, to object world, to temporality, to separation, to the father (Petrini et al., 2013).

82   Indeed, as early in *The Interpretation of Dreams*, Freud speaks of a splitting of the Ego (Britton 2004, p. 95).

83   We have intentionally given precedence to males over females because these phenomena mainly concern the former, although not exclusively. Only for this reason have we put the female third person individual pronoun "she" within brackets. In any other case, when we have used (or shall use) personal pronouns, as a unique criterion we have chosen the one arranging them in alphabetical order.

84   Which still turns out to be not compromised.

85   Considering this in the general framework describing the crucial passage from nature to culture, that is to say, we regard the symbolic function as the main landmark of this. Sublimation therefore has to be meant as a consequence of it.

86   Which is a mechanism in some respects quite similar to the *scotomization* process of E. Pichon-Rivière and R. Laforgue (Rycroft, 1968a).

87   Anguish is an affect felt by every human being who does not belong to pathological disorder spectrum. Indeed, only in dementia and other sever psychotic illnesses, anguish disappears completely (Durst 1988, p. 222).

88   As has been said at the beginning of this section, this defence mechanism is considered to be an archaic psychic process which took place from the tendency to not tolerate any form of contradiction (as anxiety producing) which may appear in the affective-emotive reality of human being, which is aimed to the search for good and rewarding relationships to avoiding any form of frustration. Furthermore, in the last period of his work, Freud himself put the anguish at the centre of his reflections on the psychic functioning either normal and pathological, assigning to the Ego

the main function to contain, cope and facing it. Indeed, Freud, since his first works on dreaming, describes how child tries to control her or his instinctual fears and internal anguishes projecting them externally by means of playing, then analogically linking this usage of the playing to the role of dreaming in neurotics. As is well-known, this standpoint was then retaken, deepen and extended, in an original manner, by Melanie Klein (Britton 2004, p. 88).

[89]   Cf. (Di Lorenzo 2003, Ch. 3, Sect. 2) where an interesting and clever psychological analysis of the pathological use of mobile communications and related technologies has been pursued. His study dates back to 2002, but surely it is of current interest and validity, even more nowadays, seen that wide and capillary proliferation of online networks, against which there exist outstanding criticisms (Maffei, 2014, 2016).

[90]   To be meant in its widest sense (Moore & Fine, 1990).

[91]   Applications of this pattern to economic anthropology, are briefly outlined in (Iurato, 2015b, 2016d), also on the basis of what has been suggested in (Horkheimer & Adorno 1947, 1966, 2002) and in (Carson 1999, Introduction), about possible relationships between consumption and fetishism. On the other hand, as early the *Frankfurt School* had stressed these problematic centred just on the severe risk of derive of every capitalist society towards a full and flat consumption's tendency, total-izing human being as, for instance, has clearly claimed Herbert Marcuse (1964, 1967). However, as early Fromm (1976, 1977) as well as theological and philosophical reflection (cf. (Chialà & Curi, 2016)), from time, have admonished humans to put attention to this risk of the derive toward careless materialism, stigmatizing the current tendency towards the *having* rather than towards the *being*, the latter – i.e., *to have* and *to be* – being the two main categories within which oscillates every human existence since birth of society, a dichotomy already pointed out by Gabriel Marcel and by Jean-Paul Sartre but autonomously developed and masterly re-contextualized by Fromm. Furthermore, Umberto Curi, in (Chialà & Curi, 2016), points out that already in the St. Paul's letter to Colossians, the insatiable avarice (*pleonexia* or *pleonexy*) must be condemned as an idolatry. Thus, also the Sacred Scriptures (with St. Paul but also in the Gospel of Luke) reveal what deep connections there exist between *pleonexia* (i.e, the having) and idolatry, so referring to fetishist phenomena.

[92]   Cf. (Maffei, 2016, p. 33).

[93]   See, above all, (Recalcati, 2007b).

[94]   This clinic of the new and multi-variegated dependences or addictions, all intended to bringing back humans to their original status (death drive), is also exposed, in a clear, clever and lucid manner, in (Pollo, 2016).

[95]   Coherently with our pattern of above, in which a central role is played by fetishism just invoked by Freud to try to explain psychoses and perversions.

[96]   A corroboration of this opposition, may come from the theoretical underpinnings to the analytic treatment of certain serious psychopathologies in which mental structures originate from early traumatic areas and develop in isolation and lack of enough relationships, in particular, with the agency pair Ego's Ideal–Super-Ego, due to the pre-existence of a destructive organization, turning out to be structured in the absence of internal parents, so expressing a narcissistic hatred of need and dependence, hence with psychic structure collapsing to Ideal Ego agency. Such unelaborated areas become psychic structures – say, virtual ''neo-creations'' – in which aggression, seduction, terror and fascination hold sway. Structures of this kind may be said to have developed instead of the Super-Ego and Ego's Ideal, so that they are unable to grow into more mature forms as in the

case of primitive formations. However, Freud's theory turned out be unable to fill the gap between the formation of the normal Super-Ego and that of its pathological counterpart, identified in melancholic disturbs. To be precise, in *Mourning and Melancholia* (of 1915), he refers to a consciousness imbued with powerful sadism that gives rise to an intrapsychic vicious circle, but then, in *The Ego and the Id* (of 1922), he instead describes a Super-Ego which now springs out from the introjection of parental images and becomes the representative of all the value and moral judgements. Such a polarity in the conception of Super-Ego seems to remain implicitly present throughout Freud's framework: on the one hand, it is seen as the expression of sociality and of positive identifications with the father figure and other social-cultural models, while, on the other hand, it is the heir to the cannibalistic and aggressive destructiveness of melancholia. At the same time, the importance of the aggressive instinct is implicit in Freud's conception of Super-Ego pathology: he indeed writes that in melancholia the Super-Ego is "as it were, a pure culture of the death instinct", while later, in *The Economic Problem of Masochism* (of 1924), he notes that, due to the defusion (meant in the psychological sense) of the death instinct, the Super-Ego becomes too cruel and inexorable against the Ego; hence, in *Civilization and its Discontents* (of 1929), the aggression of the Super-Ego is said to be turned against the Ego itself and transformed into the sense of guilt, in anguish. Considering all that, Freud notes that the severity of the Super-Ego no longer coincides with that of the real parents, but rather depends instead on a combination of environmental and innate constitutional factors (De Masi, 2016). So, we should be inclined to invoke just the main opposition *Ideal Ego* vs. *Ego's Ideal–Super-Ego* in trying to dissolve such a contradiction regarding these opposite functions owned by Super-Ego, just relegating these aggressive aspects of Super-Ego to the Ideal Ego agency, rather than to the pair Ego's Ideal–Super-Ego to which, instead, is attributed only the task of representing the parental interdictions and the social-cultural laws as initially worked out by Freud.

[97] Cf. also (Cotter 2003, pp. 92-95), where Ideal Ego is called *narcissistic Ego*, while Ego's Ideal is called *Ideal Ego*. Furthermore, according to (Petrini et al., 2011), perversions are seen as the outcome of an opposition to Law. Indeed, Petrini and co-workers, observe that psychoanalysis may be also seen as a theory built up on the relationship between human beings and Law, this latter understood in its widest sense as ruling the desire, the pleasure and the power in the individuals. A pervert is simply seen as one who needs just of Law to get her or his pleasure in transgressing it (cf. Ideal Ego), putting herself or himself in opposition to Law (cf. Ego's Ideal–Super Ego), above all moral law, just to get her or his full, unconditioned and immediate pleasure (a merely narcissistic aim, therefore, belonging to Ideal Ego agency) to detriment of the others (just represented by the agency pair Ego's Ideal–Super Ego).

[98] Which, maybe, is pushed by the fascinating remembrance of the great omnipotence and infinite pleasure felt by child in her or his infancy, during the strong child-mother tie (Ideal Ego) established since pre-natal stage, and that operates, according to Thanatos, always contrasting the as much present and unavoidable *élan vital* due to Eros. In any case, the compulsion to repeat mechanism is one of the fundamental mechanisms with which unconscious runs; it overcomes the pleasure principle, and seems to concern almost every psychic drive in respect to their relationships with Thanatos. It may be correlated with Ideal Ego meant as the main agency coming from archaic child-mother tie, which is, in its deep nature, an incestuous bind drenched by ambivalence, invasiveness and viscosity which may lead to a tragic end like that of the Orestes' myth in the version provided either

by Aeschylus or by Euripides (De Pasquali, 2002). From all that, a possible motivation underlying the close link among Ideal Ego, Thanatos and compulsion to repeat mechanism, may follow.

[99] See also (Whitebook 1995, pp. 63-68, p. 278).

[100] Cf. (Iurato, 2013b,c) for more information.

[101] Which is the prodromic germ of the next symbolic function and sublimation phenomena; cf. (Loewald, 1992) as well as (Zapparoli, 1970).

Chapter 3
A Brief Account of Ignacio Matte Blanco Theory and Other Related Psychoanalytic Themes

ABSTRACT

Besides the crucial work achieved by Claude Lévi-Strauss on the structural aspects of human mind, among which is the so-called structural unconscious (according to Lévi-Strauss) as a main psychic component of human being, also Ignacio Matte Blanco has greatly contributed to determine those structural features of human psyche which could be suitably formalized, reaching to an his own notion of structural unconscious (according to Matte Blanco), which he wants to lay out within Freudian framework. He has also identified other interesting formal aspects of Freudian theory, above all those regarding the central passage from primary process to secondary one. In doing so, he has introduced the notion of symmetry and asymmetry, then rejoined into the most general notion of bi-logic, as the overlying logic system presiding the overall functioning of human psyche. So, in this chapter, we have briefly recalled the main notions of Matte Blanco's psychoanalytic theory.

3.1. INTRODUCTION

Ignacio Matte Blanco has given a solid and valid contribution to the theoretical and epistemological systematization of the foundations of Freudian psychoanalysis. He has masterfully joined together feeling and thinking. In this chapter, we outline his work, also contextualized in relation to the general and wider psychoanalytic scenario. Main references for this chapter are (Matte Blanco, 1975) and, above all, (Rayner, 1995), this last almost verbatim.

Until short time ago, thinking and feeling have been mainly compared and contrasted of each other. Matte Blanco has been one of the firsts to have brought them together by looking at feeling in order to introspect about it for a few moments and consider it as a crucial phenomenon in our live.

Among others, however, also John Bowlby, inspired by Susanne Langer work on symbolization (which distinguishes between a *discursive symbolization*, mainly taking place at the social linguistic level as a

DOI: 10.4018/978-1-5225-4128-8.ch003

sign, and a non-discursive or *presentational* one, in which the symbol has an immediate idiosyncratic sensory reference and there is a direct isomorphism between the thing symbolized and the symbol) has noted that, in animals and humans, *emotion* is an instantaneous appraisal and evaluation of the state of the external environment *simultaneously* at the internal physiological and psychological condition of the organism.

Therefore, emotion contains, in a whole and *at the same time*, data about both exteroception and interoception systems, bodily functions (both visceral and skeletal), memories, anticipations of the future, and the state of the own *Self* with others. To be noted here that, in human beings at least, the sense of the Self is central to any developed emotion. So, a feeling is basically an overall evaluation of the internal and external worlds together in one experience, with a two-way views integrated of each other.

Although rough and ready, as well as often incomplete and mistaken compared with the step-by-step analytic thinking, a feeling can have a quickness and efficiency which logical thought lacks. It is a somatopsychic event, a *gestalt*, a holistic experience of multiplicity. Moreover, if one considers its elements singly, apart from the others (hence, *analytically* identified), then the feeling magically disappears, while if them come together again (*synthetically* recollected), then the emotion returns.

Thus, if affect is an undivided whole event of quick appraisal, then the classical view that emotion is simply a disruptive force of reason must be discarded. Rather, it appears that feeling can be both a preliminary and an end stage of any thinking process. Therefore, an overall (emotive) appraisal of fear, curiosity or dissatisfaction, say, may give the incipit to thinking. From this standpoint, thinking contains a motive or drive element within it, an emotive charge which is not simple a mere psychic drive, in that there are other aspects, above all the ones related to body, mainly exteroceptive and interoceptive-physiological.

Therefore, emotion, synthetically perceived, can be viewed as an analysable structure with its own recognizable constituents and relations. Moreover, since an emotion has basic motivational aspects (intentionality), it is a complex structure controlled by feedback arcs, so that emotions are dynamic systems rather than mere static states.

It has been said above that an emotion (or feeling[1]) is both a preliminary and an end stage of any thinking process. With regard to the end of a thinking sequence, marked by an emotion, there is so an affect appraisal that ends such a sequence, for example by satisfaction, triumph, ecstasy, delight, orgasm or gloomy failure.

Between the beginning and the end, other emotions will be evaluating in the meanwhile thought sequence goes on. Note also that interpersonal atonements and empathy give rise to intersubjective experiences, which are usually central to the development of emotions and hence of deeply engaged thinking processes.

To sum up, an emotion, or feeling is, by its nature, an undivided whole, which runs to appraise overall the internal and external situation together. Detailed thinking, on the other hand, in its problem-solving aspects, is analytic. It deals with discriminating the significant constituents of a whole circumstance and their relationships in the situation. Analytic thought of any sort starts with awareness of a whole (synthetic) question, but is not holistic in its own nature.

Seen from this stance, feeling and thinking should not be put against of each other. They are stages or aspects of an adaptive, maladaptive or creative process. Nevertheless, Matte Blanco's framework about this view is not like Bowlby's one, as it is not rooted in an evolutionary or biological systems theory, but rather is phenomenological and based on a precise definition of mental processes by introspection.

Nevertheless, their views of emotions are remarkably similar in many respects, but Matte Blanco has always considered feeling and thought together from a more structural standpoint. More than any other analyst, his frame comprehends both the logical and thoughtful aspects of emotions, linked together in an original manner. He illuminates the emotions which lie in thinking, and this is surely his great achievement.

For a moment, we image, at a general level of ideas, the emotion and thought states of any human being living in and moving through any kind of environment. In order to survive, every animal, including human beings, must, in each waking moment and whatever their emotion, be aware of the objects, surfaces and spaces, as well as locate and recognize them. Recognition system of some kind and sort is basic to all livings; it involves systems of memory.

However, the location of objects and of the own self in their midst, also involves registration of the possible relationships between things, and, in this regard, the discrimination of differences is of paramount importance: these latter might, for instance, concern the different geometrical distances between the things in the space before the eyes, or about differences in sound sequences as another person speaks.

Importantly, such discriminations must involve the primary *intuitions* that lie behind the formation of the concepts that make up formal logic and mathematics. For instance, there are, although brief and approximate, ideas of temporal and spatial sequence, quantity, counting, distance and interval. This is the realm of the action of the own self dealing with real objects. We now know that exercise in these discriminations starts since within hours of birth; among them, there are the *preconcepts* of mathematics, almost placed at a physiological level; cf. (Vallortigara & Panciera, 2014). In any case, also in these last activities and processes, emotions are involved.

These discriminating relationships can also be recognized when the same conditions and situations in which they have been perceived for the first time, have to repeat again ("same again" activity). This obviously saves (in memory) a great deal of learning anew by trial and error method, and such recognition using memory is at the core of any meaningfulness and learning. It is such a capacity for discrimination and recognition, or "same again" activity, about complex and subtle events, to put higher vertebrates, and humans more than any other, among the widely adaptive species.

Significantly, just thanks to this "same again" activity, it is possible to identify and register what *quality* is in common among different things, that requires the mind to be crucially a classificatory organ. This is based on matching or one-to-one correspondence, already acquired, which lies at the heart of all thinking process and is, basically, a comparison procedure estimation providing. The mathematical consideration of such a primary classification process leads to *set theory*. Set and class are defined slightly differently, even if, for our purposes, we need not distinguish them.

One of Matte Blanco's starting points was just set theory. Notice here that the idea of something belonging to a certain set or class, involves recognition that it has at least some *quality* that matches (i.e., has a one-to-one correspondence with) other things in this set. There is here, however dimly, an awareness of belonging to a collection or plurality. There must here be, however vaguely, a certain sense of quantity and 'counting', hence the precursor of number must be present, or else, is an innate sense, as confirmed by recent neuropsychology; cf. also (Vallortigara & Panciera, 2014).

The interplay between difference discrimination and sameness registration is at the core of Matte Blanco's thinking. At a first sight, these primary functions may seem to be of such generality and abstractness to be considered of little practical interest. Furthermore, they have not previously been dwelt upon at length in psychoanalysis. However, derivatives of sameness registration such as "identification of", "identifying with", "similarity with", "equation" and "equivalence" are common enough.

Perhaps the most, basic conceptual constituent in the theoretical tradition of psychoanalysis is the dynamical one, intention, drive and motive being so central. Matte Blanco's main focus, however, is about thinking and the related ways of knowing, i.e. cognition. So, his great contribution is really epistemological. Psychodynamics, therefore, with Matte Blanco, gives also emphasis to cognitive structures; his model of the mind does not pretend to be complete in itself, as well as has differences from much of traditional psychoanalysis; anyway, he suggests that emotion and thinking need each other.

Thus, Matte Blanco suggests to put particular attention to the discrimination of difference relations and recognition of "samenesses", as well as to the dialectic interplay, mainly as an argument (in that such a recognition is most appropriately performed with a verbal-level thinking), between them. Instantaneous awareness and integration of vast networks of such perceptible relations are vital since they enable the location and evaluation of the significance of internal and external objects and conditions. Basically, this is the main functional mechanism of the emotionality.

3.2. IGNACIO MATTE BLANCO AND HIS WORK: A BRIEF BIO-BIBLIOGRAPHICAL SKETCH

Ignacio Matte Blanco was born in 1908 in Santiago, Chile. In 1928, he graduated in medicine at the University of Chile in Santiago and became an associate professor of physiology in 1933. In the meanwhile, he was interested in psychiatry, and psychoanalysis in particular. His father persuaded him that then England was the only place to study, so that, in the mid-1930s, he went to London and trained at the Institute of Psychiatry and at the Institute of Psycho-Analysis. His personal analyst was Walter Schmideberg, while, among his teachers, there were the main exponents of the British group, like Ernest Jones, Melanie Klein, John Bowlby.

As a member of the British Psycho-Analytical Society, he considered himself as an independent. Anyway, most significant for him was surely Melanie Klein, who he ranked second only to Freud in his theoretical estimation. Matte Blanco's admiration for the theories of these two together comes from their clear-eyed view of the dark side of human mind. He however deemed their common pessimism was essential for their discoveries but, at the same time, he didn't lay out himself along this cool point of view. In the 1930s, Matte Blanco began to study mathematical logic intensively, particularly the celebrated Russell and Whitehead's *Principia Mathematica* (of 1910-13). In 1940, he went to United States of America where he spent the next four years and where he devoted himself to psychoanalysis and psychiatry, first at Johns Hopkins Hospital in Baltimore, then at Duke University, North Carolina, and finally at the Medical Centre in New York. He continued his formal logical studies, attending Richard Courant's famous weekly seminar in the Mathematical Department at Columbia University.

After the mid-1940s, Matte Blanco returned to Chile and accepted the chair of psychiatry at the University of Chile. As professor of psychiatry, he was administrative head of the department and an inexhaustible reformer. His modern clinical treatment for psychotic patients became a model for much of South America. However, he wished to continue his own particular creative activity, and in 1966 moved to Italy with his family and became a training analyst of the Italian Psychoanalytical Society. He was also invited by the chairman of psychiatry at the Catholic University of Rome to teach at the postgraduate school, where he could continue his studies and psychoanalytic work without administrative encumbers.

Matte Blanco's attention to logic was similar to that towards psychoanalysis. He devoted himself passionately to both, developing his original ideas between two great conceptual poles: on the one side, we have Freudian theory, while, on the other, we have Russell and Whitehead work on the foundations of mathematics. But, also Wilfred Bion used formal logic in his psychoanalytic studies, referring to

Model Theory according to Alfred Tarski; likewise, Imre Hermann made deep studies on the possible correlations between logic and psychoanalysis. A severe accident occurred to Matte Blanco in 1990, leaving his brain severely damaged, so that his memory was irremediably impaired. This was dramatic for him and for his family. He died, in Rome, in 1995.

Since 1950s, Ignacio Matte Blanco has worked on the relationships between mathematical logic and psychoanalysis to investigate unconscious and emotional processes. The celebrated *Unconscious as Infinite Sets*, of 1975, for the first time recollects systematically the outcomes of these studies and researches, marking a milestone in the epistemology of psychoanalysis. This interrelation between mathematical logic and psychoanalysis, led Matte Blanco to conclude that human mind can usefully be conceived as functioning by the combination of two distinct modalities which are polarized. This is said to be the *bi-logical* point of view.

Freud's greatest contribution has been to show the importance of unconscious processes in mental life and how they could be revealed and understood. Matte Blanco's fundamental contribution is placed along this line. Freud discovered particular characteristics of the unconscious, even if their remained quite uncoordinated. Matte Blanco has successfully remedied to this lack proposing a new theoretical framework in which to lay out these unconscious features to be understood basically in terms of the interaction of a few fundamental processes which, however, can give rise to highly complex dynamic mental structures. These basic structure are said to be *bi-logical* structures.

Matte Blanco reached his new ideas starting from formal logic, with the aim to investigate the *process of thinking*, emphasizing the essential centrality of the *classificatory* activity at all levels of thought, even in the unconscious. The underlying viewpoint of Matte Blanco's theory is that actual sequences of thinking are at the very core of the psychoanalytic trade, as thinking and disturbances in it are however present in every clinical minute of a psychoanalytic therapist's day. It is likely that every psychopathological disorder entails at least some disturbance in thinking, this being quite obvious in the psychoses, but also neurotic pathology involves at least some thought disturbance. Either neurotic symptoms and disabling character imply manifest distortions of thinking processes. This is clear when we recognize that any defensive act concerns with thought, otherwise it could not have a defence feature.

Historically, western culture has always considered holding a definite and net distinction between feeling and thinking, with Greeks dividing study of communication into rhetoric and logic, which reflects such a distinction. They were aimed to giving them an equal status, but intellectuals of the modern era (from Descartes onwards) have often set one against the other, giving pride of place to reasoning and logical thought. Emotion was often seen as a mere disruption or immature form of logical reasoning, which was viewed as the supreme achievement of the human mind.

Even early psychoanalysis theorized emotionality as a form of breakdown of, or regression from, clear logical thought. However, it was just Freud, more than anyone, to begin to see the general interpersonal dyadic link in a systematic way involving emotional issues, giving to the feeling states a proper status of subject of study, seen as mainly aimed to emotional change. Freud therefore gave equal attention to either feeling and thinking. Although sceptical from a philosophical standpoint, Freud, faithful to positivistic view, always taken into account carefully logical analysis. It was just his point-by-point comparison of dream with classical logic that enabled him to identify the specific characteristics of the unconscious processes, as done in the book *The Interpretation of Dreams* (of 1900) and in the work *The Unconscious* (of 1915), that do not undergo the rules of ordinary logic. This has been the core of the psychoanalytic contribution to human thought. It is just at this point of Freudian work that Matte Blanco starts his work concerning the process of thinking.

The next thing to be seen is that out of this emotional interaction Freud begins to think about the patient's logicality. He notes an underlying equivalence for the patient between florin notes and the girls' genitalia. In one way they both belong to the same class – that of being handleable; this is crucial to Matte Blanco's thinking. Freud then spots a logical inconsistency (at least from the point of view of everyday assumptions) between the patient's unnecessary care about the handling of florin notes and his careless unscrupulousness about sexually abusive handling of the girls. What is more, Freud appeals to our natural sense of logical consistency to get readers to agree with his assumptions about cleanliness and abuse rather than those of the patient, and of course most of us would feel that he is quite right in this. We can then go on to understand the explanatory model he provides about a displacement occurring, and this displacement model, too, aims to be logically consistent.

Analyzing theoretically the clinical case exposed in the work *Notes Upon a Case of Obsessional Neurosis* (of 1909), just prior to the work *Rat Man* (of 1909), Freud first identifies an underlying equivalence, regarding patient, between florin notes and the girls' genitalia, as they both rely in the same level (or belong to the same *class*, as Matte Blanco should say), i.e., that of being handleable. Then, Freud recognizes to hold a logical inconsistency (at least, from the standpoint of everyday assumptions) between the patient's unnecessary care about handling of florin notes and his careless unscrupulousness about sexually abusive handling of the girl's masturbation. But, Freud appeals to our own natural sense of logical consistency to support his assumptions about cleanliness and sexual abuse rather than those of the patient, making reference to a rough explanatory model, aimed to be logically consistent, based on a displacement process occurring just between cleanliness and sexual abuse.

3.3. THE PRINCIPLES OF SYMMETRY AND ASYMMETRY, ACCORDING TO MATTE BLANCO

As has been said in section 1, the dichotomous model of "samenesses" registration and difference discrimination, i.e., the two main forms of human mental activity, *similarity* and *difference*, whose interaction, dialectic or argument seems to underlie not only peculiarities of unconscious processes but also of emotional experiences generally, has been due to Matte Blanco's studies on affectivity and his crucial focus upon Freud's works of the early 1900s, in particular on a work dealing with the illogicality of the mind of a government official in passing from the airy unscrupulousness about a sexual abuse to the hyper-scrupulosity about dirty banknotes, and that Freud defines as a typical instance of *displacement*, which he sees as one of the characteristics of the unconscious.

These latter are *condensation, displacement, timelessness, absence of mutual contradiction* and *replacement of external by internal reality*. They probably represent the Freud's most fundamental achievement as they form the path to understand the coding of both dreams and symptoms. Matte Blanco claims that this is that vital area which has been much neglected by psychoanalysis, which suffers in clarity just because of that.

From this, Matte Blanco detects the two main principles of mental functioning whose combination gives rise to an economical understanding of unconscious working generally. They inherit the deep, basic and primary activities of mental life in health and also illness. Here, the use of the concept of "principle" is not optimal as such a term usually refers to a law which is always true; Matte Blanco uses such a term because he feels that his two above principles are fundamental to normal life.

Matte Blanco starts by saying that unconscious processes work with *classificatory* activity; they seek out the similarities between things, so that unconscious leaps to generalization. From this, Matte Blanco works out the so-called *principle of generalization*, by which the system unconscious treats an individual thing (e.g., person, object, concept) as if it were a member or element of a set or class which contains other members; in turn, it treats this class as a subclass of a more general class, and this more general class as a subclass of a still more general class, and so on.

In other words, unconscious process jumps to seeing a particular thing in terms of belonging to wider and wider class membership; so, it sets up class hierarchies. Later, Matte Blanco refers to the principle of *abstraction* and *generalization*. This has been an important addition because, it has become clear to us that a certain form of abstraction is basic and endemic in unconscious processes.

Matte Blanco's second basic discovery takes the form of a complex proposition, the *principle of symmetry*, which is crucial. It is best approached in terms of two fundamental proposals. The first is about *logical asymmetry*, and is as follows: many relationships that are discriminated in the physical world are asymmetrical; an asymmetrical relationship is one whose converse is not identical to it. The second proposal instead is about *logic symmetry* and is as follows: some perceived relationships are, however, symmetrical; a symmetrical relation is one whose converse is identical to it. Many other relations are however ambiguous.

Furthermore, we note that many symmetrical relations do not seem, at first sight, to be as common as asymmetrical ones when we are perceiving the external world with its geometry and geography of things, which are replete with difference relations between places, points, lines, surfaces, spaces and solid things. However, at the same time, we must continuously use sameness relations when dealing with the world.

Perhaps *asymmetry* stands out first because a prime use of consciousness is to locate the own Self within a world of objects. This is a central function of the focus of attention. Notice also that we are concerned with logically asymmetrical and symmetrical relations, which are respectively defined by the identity or not of their converses; they apply to much more than spatial relations.

The word *symmetry* simply refers to sameness between at least two things and thus to match and set up a one-to-one correspondence. We often think only of visual, lefthand, righthand or bilateral symmetry, but there are symmetries of rotation, displacement, as well as those of colour, weight, time, electric charge and many others. In all logical symmetries, a transformation from one state to another brings about, when repeated, a coming back to the initial state. This is precisely what identical converse means, as well as the key aspect of a group structure.

Using the concepts of symmetry and asymmetry, Matte Blanco comes to the heart of his discovery and makes two fundamental hypotheses whose their linkage is most unusual yet simple. The first one is that ordinary conscious logical reasoning, which includes scientific and everyday thought about the physical world, consistently entertains propositions about asymmetrical relations. Hence, the mind is conceived as made of relations whose converses are not identical to them.

This naturally involves the discrimination of difference relations. At the same time, symmetrical relations will not be entertained, but, if thought is ordinarily logical, then they will however remain consistently interwoven with, yet do not obliterate, the asymmetrical ones; and, the functioning of such a thought is similar to Freud's secondary process. Here is the realm of two-valued or bivalent Archimedean logic. It is this that must rule at the conscious and preconscious levels of thought if mental coherence of the Self and world has to hold.

The system unconscious selectively treats the converse of any relation as identical to it. It treats logically asymmetrical relations as if they were symmetrical. These very simple proposals are the keystones of Matte Blanco's work. It is these that he calls the *principle of symmetry*. Functioning in the mode of this principle, is more or less synonymous with Freud's primary process.

As the unconscious selectively treats asymmetrical relations as symmetrical, it follows that some aspects of unconscious process can still behave asymmetrically also according to two-valued logic, while, in other unconscious aspects, symmetry and sameness of converses may prevail. Thus, certain asymmetrical elements, in dreams for instance, can still retain clear logical discrimination, like, for example, spatial representations and sequences.

The primary process of selectively ignoring certain asymmetrical or difference relations, is said to be *symmetrisation* by Matte Blanco; sometimes, this process is also called "identicalization", but this is less evocative than the more precise term symmetrisation. At this point, it should be noted also that symmetrisation suggests a move into greater simplicity, as a slippage or regression into an evasive or avoidant activity, that is to say, symmetrisation very often works as a defence, but this is not its primary function, which is just to experience sameness. It has been also suggested that symmetrisation basically functions in the service of recognition, as we shall see later.

The conscious level appears to be the one that is most sensitive in discriminating asymmetries and differences of converses. Likewise, at a less conscious level, the mind seems much more interested in similarities and samenesses. Because it is a coordinator for dealing with the world, consciousness cannot manage too many samenesses. The unconscious, on the other hand, can manage this, and, in fact, it seems marvellously equipped to do just this, even if it is not so estranged from differences.

The psychoanalyst Kenneth Wright says that registration of sameness and symmetry is primary and certainly necessary for survival. However, symmetric and asymmetric thought, leaning on each other, give rise, from a refined combination of them, logical thinking, and this is undoubtedly what Matte Blanco intended, who saw too symmetrisation as vital to life. Note also that neither symmetry nor asymmetry is, in itself, abnormal, but they can both serve for defensive and avoidant purposes. Remember, too, that symmetrised logic is endemic not only in unconscious processes but also in emotional states generally.

Visible, above all in early infancy, are then certain physiological processes which evoke crude and instantaneous reactions. These are primitive, largely physiological, body-dominated emotions. They basically have an all-or-nothing, *either-or* polarized quality. These reactions are also instantaneous, physiological classificatory actions. However, it would not be right to equate primitiveness with the system unconscious, but, primitive or not, unconscious seems also to deal often with things and events in just these polarized classificatory ways. It appears then to be the work of conscious levels to articulate, integrate or bring together, and hence to recognize as likenesses and differences, the multitude of disparate things and events that unconscious knows.

Furthermore, according to Matte Blanco, unconscious, besides symmetrisation, is responsible of a main *splitting* process that dichotomizes, that is, unconscious both symmetrises and dichotomizes. Moreover, Elisabeth Bott Spillius points out that splitting process involves greater, more crude or exaggerated differences than what the full awareness of consciousness does. Splitting thus involves a "gross" process of asymmetrisation, so that, the unconscious appears, then, as seen by logical and conscious thought, as accentuating both symmetrisation and asymmetrisation, so it is not only symmetry that the unconscious slips into, as Matte Blanco tends to consider, at least in his earlier works.

Now, we mention some chief modalities in which symmetrisation can ordinarily occur.

3.3.1. Time

In considering the basic conception of a *time* relation, ordinarily we discriminate saying for instance that 'event B follows event A', then, recognizing an asymmetrical relation, we easily conclude that 'A is followed by B'. Now, if a symmetrisation taken place, then we would have that 'B follows A' and 'A follows B', so a succession would not be possible, hence there would not be awareness of time sequence, and our knowing of time would disappear. This happens most obviously in dreams, and through these cases Freud made his historic leap to understanding the timelessness of the unconscious. From another point of view, there is also a timelessness about well-established long-term memories at levels where 'time labels' are not attached, as manifestly happens in dreams.

3.3.2. Space

The as much basic conception of *space*, like that of time, involves relations which are basically asymmetrical. For instance, having preliminarily chosen an orientation, then, taking two points in a line, they must stand to the viewer in an asymmetrical relation to each other: thus, if B is to the left of A, then A must be (in the opposite direction) to the right of B. But, if there is too an insertion of symmetry, then we would say that, 'B is to the left of A' and 'A is to the left of B', so that, the points of this line would become interchangeable of each other, hence might not be distinguishable. Therefore, there would not be awareness of *extension*, and the conception of space would disappear.

This occurrence certainly happens, without any difficult, at the unconscious level, like, for example, in the condensation of ideas into the dream imagery.

Although Freud described the unconscious as being timeless, he omitted to refer explicitly to the spacelessness of unconscious, even if this is surely implicit in the displacement and condensation processes which characterize unconscious. The omission of spacelessness as a characteristic of the unconscious by Freud, may have given the impression that the use of the notion of "psychic space" is licit. Matte Blanco insists that mental space may be a useful concept but it is necessary to be clear about its use, as psychic spacelessness is omnipresent in unconscious phenomena and confusions may easily arise. Finally it is important to note that the phenomenon of *merging of selves* rests upon a spatial symmetrisation.

3.3.3. The Equation Between a Whole and Its Parts ("Part = Whole" Equation)

Thinking about a whole object, say 'B', and a part of it, say 'b', involves a space or time relation between them such that B *includes* b, while b *is included* in B. Such statements or propositions naturally use asymmetrical logic, but, when symmetrised, they entail that 'B includes b' and 'b includes B', that is, space within the object 'B' will disappear. Thus, where symmetry rules, whole objects are experienced as identical to their constitutive parts.

At a first sight, this should seem a dotty and pointless exercise, but our everyday emotional thought has almost always to do with such 'part = whole' equations. This is very important from a psychological standpoint. Indeed, this type of equations is most obvious in psychosis when, say, someone may feel, for instance, that the whole spirit of evil is emerging through a boil on the nose. Another, very emblematic case of the occurrence of such an equation, is when usually a man is able to recognize, in a vigil state, that his penis is part of his body in a certain location, but in normal dreams, as well as consciously in psychosis, it is commonplace for penis, whole body and Self to be undifferentiated, identical or inter-changeable.

In a more muffled fashion, it probably occurs too in those neuroses where feeling the impotence refers equally to the experience of a particular dysfunction of the penis, to weakness of the whole body and to the incompetence of the overall Self. In normal circumstances, the 'part = whole' equation is easily seen, for instance, with the failing of an examination: an ordinary person might simply say 'I have failed this time', a neurotically depressive person might say 'I am an utter failure', while a psychotic person may say 'I am failure'. To be noted here the different degrees of conscious and preconscious level of symmetrisation. Another example would be when a parent, quite emotively, says 'You are a bad boy' when an otherwise nice child has done some small thing wrong.

3.4. THE NOTIONS OF BI-LOGICALITY AND BI-MODALITY ACCORDING TO MATTE BLANCO

Rough polarized, *all-or-nothing* states occur very frequently. Only later, when other experiences have been related with asymmetricity, one can say to oneself, 'I was weak, bad or a failure on that occasion but it has not always been so with me'. It is an important phenomenon in any emotionality, both healthy and pathological.

A *class*, or a *set*, is a collection of any kind of things which have at least one characteristic, quality or attribute, in common. First, being a collection, thus having an extensive, quantitative, numerable, 'counting' or 'population' aspect, it deals not only with attributes, that is, with a *qualitative* feature, but also in 'more than oneness', that is to say, it deals also with a *quantitative* feature. This however does not necessarily involve a precise counting, but rather an estimating process. Second, members having a defining attribute or quality in common means that a set has also a *qualitative* aspect.

One of the functions of symmetrisation is to rely *only* upon the common quality, the defining at-tribute, of the members or things in a set. This ignores the individuality of its members and entails the *obliteration of the quantitative aspects* of the class or set. Matte Blanco (1975) had already discussed this, but it has been Mordant (1990) who has clearly shown that when a class attribute is separated from its members, then it becomes an *abstract* notion, and Skelton (1990) has addressed the same question equally cogently using the conception of predicate thinking.

Let us look further into this question. The specific idea of a class usually refers to a set whose mem-bers need bear no consistent relation to each other except that they have some attribute in common. An individual becomes a member of the (social) class if he, she or it is seen to bear the common attribute. Thus members of the class 'English' can be scattered anywhere over the globe

but they still remain English as long as they carry the attributes of Englishness. Dwelling only upon the attribute of a class, say Englishness, is an act of abstraction, so the characteristic *quality* of a class without its members can be seen as an abstracted attribute, conception or notion.

Now, to be fully a member of, or to be in the relationship of belonging to, a class, necessitates asym-metrical thinking on at least two counts. First, members must be *located* in space or time to be individuals; second, the relationship of 'belonging to a collection' is obviously also asymmetrical.

However, if a symmetrisation runs *within the whole class*, then the locatable individuality of the members has been obliterated or ignored; further, the belongingness of its members to the class disap-pears. The class and its members are then only known or experienced as the same. The whole class and its parts become identical. Note that this is also exactly what can happen to a *whole object* and its parts under the effect of symmetrisation. This is the *principle of symmetry* according to Matte Blanco.

This again may seem an absurd exercise but every day we engross ourselves in such logic both pathologically and in normal emotionality. De Gaulle, for instance, did this in his well-known phrase, 'La France c'est moi'. This may not be good logic but it is definitely not meaningless it

even carried an important truth at the time of the Second World War which probably could not have been conveyed by means of a chain of logically consistent phrases. The whole realm of emotional communication, useful or not, is imbued with symmetrisation or identicalizations. This could be, for example, in intimate love, anger or pain, in gossip, politics, poetry or literature, in any rhetorical expressions, and so on.

Such emotional activity uses both ordinary logic, which scrupulously adheres to asymmetrical relations, together with symmetrical logic *at the same time*. Matte Blanco calls this a *bi-logical mode,* be it in unconscious or emotional thought. Following Spillius' observation mentioned earlier, a biological mode can perhaps best be viewed as thought where there is an *accentuation* of either symmetrical or asymmetrical inferences, or both, as compared to fully logical consciousness.

Patterns of feeling-thought, where symmetrisations occur enmeshed with asymmetrical relations, are called *bi-logical structures* by Matte Blanco. Pathological thought with its tricky, avoidant defensive systems involves exaggeration, or slippage in certain regions away from consistent use of both asymmetrical discriminations and symmetrical recognitions. When symmetrisations, as well as *accentuated* asymmetrisations, serve to obliterate painful affects, then we can say that they serve defences; they are then 'economical with the truth'. For more usefully creative purposes, bi-logic and symmetrisations can function by consciously controlled intentional 'dipping' into symmetries; this will not be in the service of avoidance, but for rich and meaningful emotional communication.

Matte Blanco naturally defines separately the operation of symmetry and asymmetry but shows that their *interaction*, or *dialectic* (Durst, 1988), is psychologically very important. Incidentally, Matte Blanco at one time put forward the terms *homogeneity* and *heterogeneity* in interplay but finally settled for *symmetry* and *asymmetry* since they describe very well the logical functions involved. However, we recall that registration of sameness or symmetry is a necessary function in even the most logical and rational of thought. But it must function together consistently with asymmetry.

For instance, any class or set, including a mathematically rigorous one, is defined by its members being the same in some way, i.e., symmetry. However, if it is ordinarily logical and not a bi-logical structure, its standing with regard to its frame of asymmetrical relations is still strictly definable and consistent, so gross symmetrisation will not have to occur. Neither symmetry nor asymmetry operate singularly, but rather they run always coupled.

Therefore, a symmetrisation is seen to emerge, or 'insert' itself, only when a difference relation, an asymmetrical converse, *detectable to the consciously logical mind*, is *ignored* in favour of a simple registration of sameness which is a symmetrical relation. The same situation can occur where symmetries are ignored and some asymmetries are exaggerated. In other words, it can be said that *bi-logic*, as a discipline, concerns itself with the systematic investigation of complex combinations between identical and non-identical relationships.

Of course, the purely logical thought is also never devoid of *both* asymmetrical and symmetrical relations. Further, there can be no thought without recognition and this entails classification with its symmetry or sameness registration. But when thought is ordinarily logical, symmetries are bound or contained by definite asymmetrical relations, so that consistency of inference is maintained. Matte Blanco calls the structure of such consistent thought *bi-modal*, as opposed to bi-logical.

As an instance, by its nature, any external *physical object* can, on the one hand, be perceived as a whole which is distinct from (in that, asymmetrically related to) other things. On the other hand, all the parts of the object must also have at least one symmetry or sameness in common. i.e., that they are all together members of that one whole object. Thus, for instance, it is vital for survival to perceive that one's motor car is distinct from, and asymmetrically related in a multitude of ways, to other cars. But the parts of the car – wheels, engine, seats, etc. – must also have a symmetry in common: they all belong together as members of that unique car.

Wholeness and uniqueness of an object depend upon both asymmetrical and symmetrical relations, which, for survival in the physical world, these must be consistently related to each other. The concept of the car is then bi-modally structured. However, *at the same time*, cars can have all sorts of other more *emotional meanings*; for instance, they can be symbols of potency or of maternal care. Where this happens, the notion of the car has become a bi-logical structure. So, *bi-modality* and *bi-logicality* are the two main components of thought always and at the same time present together, as well as closely and inextricably intertwined of each other: bi-logicality gives rise to syntactic dimensions, while bi-modality gives rise to semantic-pragmatic dimensions of thought. This is besides in agreement with Charles W. Morris[2] ideas on the structure of human language and its main tri-partition in syntax, semantics and pragmatics.

To illustrate bi-logicality in action, we expose an everyday life case of hierarchical classification using both bivalent and symmetrised logics; it is also an example of Matte Blanco's *principle of generalization*. We discriminate, say, a baby. In doing this, we can readily leap to a *hierarchy*: "this is a baby in some ways the same as and in some ways different from all other babies, who are in some ways the same as all human beings, who are in some ways the same as all living things, who are in some ways the same as all touchable things".

Although it seems that we are using symmetry, the logic is yet consistently bivalent, and no symmetrisation is clearly evident. For instance, we can recognize that babies and stones are the same in that they are both touchable, but both symmetry and asymmetrical relations are consistently used, in that we still know that babies and stones are also different, and they are simply *equivalent* with regard to the class attribute of touchability.

However, if *one or more asymmetrical relations are ignored or obliterated*, then symmetrisation emerges. Then, when it comes to the most general level of this hierarchy, symmetry could rule. When that happens, a baby is known *only as the same* as anything touchable, and so too is a stone. So, in this case, a baby, all babies, all human beings, all living things and all stones are only known as *identical*. All that is known about them is their common attribute, i.e., something like *'there is touchability'* or *'touching is'*.

For Matte Blanco, this happens at the deepest levels of the system unconscious, like in psychotic thinking. This can seem a pedantic intellectual exercise but instead it can highlight serious matters. For instance, some mothers, even in moments of apparent intimacy, refer to their babies as nothing but 'it' and this can send a shudder down the listener's spine. Such a mother seems to be revealing a level where ordinary feeling has disappeared and she is automatically equating her baby with a 'thing', anything alive or dead.

Likewise a psychotic person may experience no incompatibility between being alive and dead at the same time. Here live and inanimate or dead things are all touchable, so it appears that a symmetrisation of psychotic proportions has obliterated all discrimination of the manifold differences that can occur between the members of the class of touchable things. At this level of thought all touchable things are nothing but the same. Again, feeling will have disappeared when symmetrisation is very gross.

Even so, the two logics can normally operate together in ordinary rich and emotionally evocative imagination. For instance, a child may lie on the beach lapped by the waves and declaim 'I am a stone'. If he or she is playing, he or she will know very well that he or she *is not* really a stone but the point of the game is that he or she *is* a stone. This is a *paradox* inherent in any make-believe play. Without symmetry, there is no metaphor and with no metaphor there is no make-believe play. But without the Self having a containing framework of awareness of asymmetrical relations, play breaks down into delusion, and the child *believes* he or she is just a stone.

This occurs in psychosis of course and also normally in dreams. It is muted in affective states and in neurotic anxiety when a person may *feel* he or she has turned to stone but knows very well consciously that he or she has not. What is more, the simple dramatic play of 'I am a stone' can perhaps be the beginning of a poetic drama. For instance: "A stone I was, washed by the waves of life, battered by storms, rubbing against my fellow men, my Self remained the same".

Returning back to metaphor, it reminds us Susanne Langer's presentational symbolism which is naturally evocative and used for quick communication of emotional states. Symmetrisation plays a vital part in the *simplification* necessary for this form of communication. Freud was aware of the similarity or isomorphism between symbol and symbolized involved in dream imagery, realizing that it was quite crucial. For instance, he recalls that Aristotle remarked, in this regard, that the best interpreter of dreams was who could best grasp similarities.

Ernest Jones was also quite explicit about the central importance of similarity as a characteristic of psychoanalytic symbolism. Ella Freeman Sharpe likewise described both metaphor and dream imagery as being alike in both having a crucial similarity between the form of the symbol and the symbolized. Other authors have done the same; they usually refer loosely to 'similarity', and this concept combines sameness with a certain lot of difference. It has been Matte Blanco's inspiration and task to link systematically a host of apparently disparate mental functions by seeing that they have the fundamental function of symmetry with its pure sameness registration in common, to which varying degrees of asymmetry may be necessarily added.

The bi-logical viewpoint provides one disciplined way of investigating the symbolization which is a keystone of psychoanalysis. Here, it is possible to see that psychotic symbolic equations involve gross symmetrisations which *distort the extent of the Self* in relation to external and internal reality. Quite different is metaphor which, though still symmetrising, is a valuable means of communication and can enhance Self. Conventional symbols (like signs), though involving symmetries, need use no unbounded symmetrisation and would thus not be based on bi-logical structures.

Symmetrised and bi-logical structures also predominate in *pre-object* states. Perhaps, in order to avoid unwarranted developmental assumptions, it would be better to call these *non-object states*. These would be found most commonly in mood states but also in oceanic feelings, self-object fusions and symbiosis, not to mention more sophisticated mystic experiences. Symmetrisation is then crucial for intersubjectivity.

Indeed, there is now much evidence of sensitivity to other people from the earliest days of life and even the first hours after birth. Infants and mothers are seen to resonate, mimic, tune-in or *attune*, taking turns with each other in their movements and gestures at feeding and in other times. Intersubjectivity is fundamental for the humans and starts very early. This becomes most apparent where emotional expressions are concerned. Such early infant resonant matching appears to be at the heart of sympathy, empathy and mutuality, which act as the very keystones of psychoanalytic therapy, not to mention ordinary friendship and affection generally.

Matte Blanco was aware that such mutuality does in fact involve *interpersonal symmetrisation*, but he did not make it a central aspect of his theory. This was a pity as there is now a great body of research and thought (see Daniel Stern, Joseph Sandler, Peter Fonagy, and so on) that is seeing how important interpersonal mutual experiences are in the development of even the most intellectual of activities.

One has only to glance at the infant research and attachment literature to see how strong is this line of thought. Matte Blanco's apparent lack of central interest in developmental matters has tended to leave his ideas isolated and unheeded in this region. It quickly becomes obvious that experiences of such symmetrical awareness is an essence not only in intersubjective mutuality, attunement and empathy but also in the structuring of any consistent adaptive identification. In this regard, see (Murtagh & Iurato, 2016) where the authors argue that the key concept of Matte Blanco's bi-logic is the unavoidable but variable presence of primary process (symmetric thought) in the secondary one (asymmetric thought) ruling consciousness, for every human being. This variable and dynamic presence allows us, by therapeutic intervention, to convert suitably the symmetric thought into the asymmetric one. The former erupts into the latter by means of affectivity which, accordingly, should be suitably treated to be rightly modulated, regulated and symbolically represented to accomplish the aims of secondary process. This transition has been termed affective mentalization by Peter Fonagy and co-workers (2002). Accordingly, any therapeutic intervention should take into account these facts, aiming to treat the impetuous affective charge to accomplish this, through analytical means or the psychotherapeutic setting.

3.5. THE UNCONSCIOUS, ITS STRUCTURE AND PROPERTIES, ACCORDING TO MATTE BLANCO

The first theme of *The Unconscious as Infinite Sets* (Matte Blanco, 1975) follows closely Freud's works on unconscious and argues how the main characteristics of unconscious functioning can be seen as arising out of symmetrised thought taking over where full consciousness would see asymmetrical relations as well. In this regard, Freud basically distinguishes five characteristics of unconscious, namely timelessness, displacement, condensation, replacement of external by internal reality and absence of mutual contradiction.

At this point we note first that when one is arguing and reading theoretically, our own minds' basic frame of reference must be that of *conscious* level ordinary logical thought which consistently uses asymmetrically structured relations. Seen from this level, it is appropriate to speak (to another person also thinking at a conscious level) of the symmetrisation of thought at an unconscious level; for that is how the unconscious will appear to two consciously structured minds. However, at the unconscious level, in our dreaming selves for instance, we would be in no position to discriminate that such a process was occurring.

Matte Blanco's work has mainly consisted in highlighting those implicit features of unconscious already described by Freud, but never explicitly stated by him. Matte Blanco has instead stood out these features, so he has been able to identify an underlying formal logic structure of unconscious, as a trans-individual entity (in this, resembling Jung's and Levi-Strauss' ideas on unconscious), in which to lay out personal or individual (unconscious) contents by means of repression, which qualifies unconscious as such.

We now discuss briefly these five main features of *structural* unconscious according to Freud, as revised by Matte Blanco.

1. **Timelessness:** This has already been mentioned above, where we have noted that when the converse of a time relation is experienced as identical to it, as happens when a symmetrisation emerges, then sequentiality cannot be known and time, as is well-know, is not discriminated as existing. In this case, therefore, 'after' is felt as no different from 'before' or 'at the same moment'.

    A selective emergence or insertion of timelessness occurred, for instance, with a child who believes for a time that cats were cats, adults were adults, and all children would always remain children. He had not, of course, lost all sense of time, but only that children did not transform with time into grown-ups; it is a selective symmetrisation. Timelessness is also obvious in sleep, as well as, we often wake up in the night and have no idea how long we have slept. However, this time symmetrisation is *only partial*, as many unconscious biological clocks still operate. For instance, the timing of REM and non-REM periods of brain activity proceed consistently throughout sleep.

    On the other hand, a prime example of timelessness occurs in the way dreams readily manifest events; the distant past and the previous day may come together as if at the same time. Such sleep examples are quite normal, but we often have waking instances where serious blocking of thought is associated with a sudden loss in the time sense. What makes the dividing line between a *normal* and *pathological* symmetrisation?

    It seems have to do with whether a symmetry is 'held', i.e., contained or integrated by the central organizing Self or Ego at its appropriate level, so that it does not invade the conscious use of logical inference in the service of an adaptive judgement. Exactly the same applies to the holding of relevant asymmetries in consciousness, and keeping these too in bounds in such a manner that maladaptive splitting and disintegration do not occur.

    We have also noted earlier how awareness of *space* disappears with symmetry. Freud however did not mention spacelessness, but the next three of Freudian unconscious characteristics imply it. Furthermore, Matte Blanco points out that already the timelessness entails the spacelessness, so structural unconscious is devoid of any possible space-time idea, which nonetheless is basic for any consciousness development. So, space-time organization and non-contradiction principle are the founding nuclei of human consciousness, hence their lacking is the distinguishing feature of human unconscious.

2. **Replacement of External by Internal Reality:** The idea of *external* reality necessitates the asymmetrical conception of *space*, of 'inside' and 'outside' or 'psychic' and 'material' reality. With a symmetrisation of it, space ceases to be known there. Thus to the experiencer, *inside and outside become the same* in that region. However, to an outside observer the difference may still be evident, so, to that person, the experiencer appears to be replacing external by internal reality. Perhaps, it would be better to say that external and internal are replaced by non-discrimination. Such non-differentiation is apparent in any person when self-absorbed; it is also most obvious and well documented furthermore in the appearance of any projection or projective identification.

3. **Condensation:** Here, ideas derived from different times and object relations, differently placed in space, are experienced as belonging to a singly located object in time and space. The separation of places in space and time have disappeared; individualities have gone. This can occur naturally with a symmetrisation in one or more spatial or temporal aspect or dimension. Remember that a pure state of symmetry or total sameness is unknowable to consciousness. The condensed images we remember from dreams are mixtures of symmetrical and asymmetrical and are bi-logical structures.

Examples of condensation come every day in analytic practice. Freud's *Interpretation of Dreams* (of 1900) and early case studies, are full of them. Here is two present-day dreams, drawn from Eric Rayner experience of analyst.

First dream. ''Before an holiday, a patient dreamt that she was going down a ski slope with her instructor. Part of the way down, he stopped but she continued the rest of the way easily by herself. The session then showed how she had experienced parting from 'givers of instruction' at different times of her life''. The ski instructor could be recognized as a condensed timeless image of her mother, father, elder brother and her analyst, as well as the knowledgeable side of herself.

Second dream. A patient's parents came to stay in her flat for the weekend and she gave them her bedroom. She then had the following dream. ''Mice were in the bedroom, her mother was phobic of mice, so she had to kill them for her, but they then turned into rabbits, so she would have to kill them too, but they had long ears, which turned into fierce long teeth''. We can see that the mice and fierce rabbits condensed several contradictory or conflicting aspects not only of herself but also of her mother, father, brother, analyst, men in general. The dream images condensed not only many parts of the Self and objects but also various forms of sexual or aggressive impulse and emotional state. The dream then contains many quiet and hidden equations through symmetrisation.

4. **Displacement:** This is perhaps the most crucial characteristic of the unconscious since it lies at the basis of *symbolization, transference, projection, introjection* and *sublimation*. Matte Blanco points out that in displacement a person is seen, by an *outside* observer, to be shifting feelings and ideas from one primary object-relation to another. But, from the point of view of the unconscious of the person, both objects are only known as identical. To the conscious-level self, objects may well be registered as having a *similarity*, as belonging to the same class, which is having a quality in common but also with differences.

Then, with symmetrisation endemic in the unconscious, the objects are conceived as identical, as being nothing but the same. When this occurs, one object can be felt as having any of the qualities of the other. Like for the fear objects of the second dream of above, a defence process of *denial* may then come into play so that the idea or feeling (of fear) is *not consciously* recognized as belonging to the primary object, but (symbolically) only to the secondary one.

5. **Absence of Mutual Contradiction:** Here, Freud refers to wishes which, for to the ordinary logic of consciousness, are contradictory and would thus be expected to nullify each other; this does not occur in the unconscious. Matte Blanco says that Freud is saying that conflict is *not* experienced at this level in the unconscious, while for others, like Melanie Klein, such a conflict would persist even until the very heart of the system unconscious.

Nevertheless, Matte Blanco sees the deepest unconscious level as conflict free, whereas levels nearer consciousness (as the preconscious) are likely to be full of conflict. If we consider the simple case of two wishes, then the functioning of a symmetrisation may be seen in the following way. To be experienced as contradictory, the two wishes must be felt to *oppose* each other. This is the same as each wish being the non-identical *converse* of the other, which is essentially asymmetrical. When a symmetrisation occurs within this idea, only that which is the same between the wishes will be known, and this largely unconsciously; they will be experienced as identical and not as different and contradictory.

That completes this consideration of Freud's characteristics of the unconscious in the light of the working of logical symmetry and asymmetry in a combinatorial dialectical way. It is this that is the primary key in Matte Blanco's work. We now reconsider some of these concepts by looking at them from a few alternative perspectives, among which very important is the consideration of negation.

3.5.1. Negation

Absence of mutual contradiction of impulses is probably a particular case of absence of negation. This, too, can be seen as a function of a logic that has symmetrised elements in it. The very act of a negation is to assert that there is a difference in a relationship, a 'this is *not* that'. This is an essential awareness in asymmetricality, which is that noting that a converse is *not* the same as the original relation. Myriads of instantaneous acts of negation seem to permeate every moment of the waking mental life; they occur in every asymmetrical discrimination. Maybe these experiences are the outcome of some patterning of the 'on-off', or the 'yes-no' of neural functioning.

The same phenomenon of negation can be seen at more complex levels as follows. According to Freud, without negation, there is no sense of external reality as the well-known Freud's 1925 paper on negation points out the importance of negative judgements in the development of the sense of external reality. Matte Blanco comes to a similar conclusion but starting from different premises. For him, the sense of external reality depends on the already present ideas of space and time.

The location of external real objects is obviously important for any animal. All these, i.e., space, time and their offspring location, have been seen to be depending on a logical functioning of the mind which includes asymmetrical relations. These, in turn, depend on negation functions where a conceived relationship and its converse are *not* the same. In particular, when these are symmetrised, awareness of the 'externalness' of reality can disappear. Negation and its absence are both at the very core of any bi-logical thought.

But, a serious difficulty appears to arise here. It is obvious that valid inference depends upon the logical consistency inherent in ordinary conscious level, traditional two-valued logic. It has already been said that the essence of two-valuedness is that things which 'are so' are not 'not so' *at the same time*. Here, the non-contradiction 'If A, then not not-A' is crucial. However, if Matte Blanco is proposing a system where this principle of contradiction can be absent, then surely everything and nothing can be explained by it and the theory is useless (Skelton, 1984; Iurato, 2013).

Matte Blanco argued back that he was sorry; he did not invent the way the unconscious levels of the mind work, nor he is proposing a mind that *never* knows negation or contradiction anywhere. His view is rather that *selective,* localized symmetrisations occur in the unconscious, and thence in emotionally charged thinking of any kind. Furthermore, though minds at unconscious levels may grossly symmetrise, it is the job of the theorist to remain firmly on a level where two-valued logic still consistently applies. The theorist's task is to specify when, where and how the symmetrisation occurs within the object of study.

A similar challenge faces the analytic therapist who must symmetrise between personal self and the patient's self. This arises in the very early act of empathetic instantaneous identification with a patient. The first step in psychotherapeutic understanding is by the therapist symmetrically matching or *attuning* his or her mind with the patient's *mood,* which will lie behind or between the overt words spoken. This is vital to the necessary emotionality of the analytic dialogue.

However, a psychoanalytic therapist must not rest there, but always, at the same time, maintain a combination with asymmetrical two-valued logical functioning, which is necessary for objectivity. It has been argued that the facility for free, *unbiased movement* (using asymmetricality) of often highly emotional identifications (using symmetrisation), seems to define analytic *neutrality*, as defined by Eric Rayner.

3.5.2. Unconscious, Abstraction, Prepositional Functions, and Predicate Thinking

Symmetry plays a part in classification. Indeed, when a classification process works with two-valued logicality, different members of a class remain distinct individuals but are seen as similar though different to belong to the same class, as they have some class-defining quality or attribute in common. But the result of a symmetrisation *within a class* can be that not only do the differences between the members themselves disappear but also between them and the idea of the whole class. When this happens all that is known about the class will be that which is in *common* between the members. This will be the *defining attribute* of the class itself.

In taking, for instance, the idea of several whole collections of different objects (like prey's birds, books, and so on), hence symmetrising all the differences between the members of each of these classes, then what happens are the essential attributes which distinguishes all the objects of each set from those of the other sets (like rapacity, knowledge, and so on). Following Ian Mordant, these attributes are really *abstracted* conceptions or attributes.

If they are abstractions of sort, then we are driven to a remarkable conclusion: if the unconscious is mainly characterized by symmetrisation, and if the outcome of much symmetrisation are abstracted attributes, then *the unconscious deals in something close to abstraction*. However, it should be recognized here that the abstracted ideas *within* themselves, contain asymmetrical relations. For instance, the notion of 'drain', say, involves spatial and distinct part – whole relations – of liquid into a conduit, distinct movements in one direction, and so on. But the whole gestalt, or form, of the abstract idea of 'drainness' itself, floats free of other relations; it can be anywhere at any time. Thus, abstractions, so to speak, 'float in a sea of symmetrisation'.

Mordant thinks that the phrase 'unconscious notion' is useful for such imprecisely abstracted ideas, but the terms 'conception' or 'intuition' will do as well. So, the unconscious notion appears to be the most abstract one. This seems to go against the model produced by our ordinary thinking, for which abstraction is the preserve and fruit of the highest conscious thought processes. Therefore, argument would be: it is the unconscious that is full of primitive urges and their particular symbols, and surely primitive urges cannot be abstractions?

An answer might be as follows. Abstract thinking usually refers to consistent combinatorial activity using logically definable abstract concepts. The instances of such usable concepts, like 'the square root of two' or 'justice', *cannot be directly presented to the senses*. In other words, they cannot be seen, heard, touched or smelled. It is well known from such researchers, as Jean Piaget, that such thinking with abstract concepts is not normally possible until later in childhood, while no one would say that the unconscious only starts functioning then.

However, Piaget, Daniel Stern and many others, directly studying mental functions in the early infancy, have noted that there is considerable evidence for a more simple level of abstraction occurring. This can be called *sensory abstraction*, which is a form of *selection*. For instance, the very understanding of the *general meaning of a word*, such as a noun or a verb, depends upon distinguishing a class attribute. This is usually observed by about a year old onwards, as long as actual instances of the objects of the words are easily visible and tangible.

Incidentally, Piaget used the term 'abstraction' for an aspect of this naming function which can be involved in any early classificatory activity. What is more, it has already been noted that very early abstraction has recently been discovered in another aspect of development. Indeed, infants of only a few days old can pick up a *pattern* in *one sense modality* (touch, say) and use their knowledge of this to *generalize* to something of the same pattern in *another modality* (sight, say). Or again, a rhythmic pattern, picked up first by sound, will be recognized as the same pattern if presented later visually. This is called *cross-sensory* or *amodal* perception, and the scientific evidence for its early importance is by now very well established. It is abstraction of a primitive kind.

There are therefore little doubts that simple abstractions must easily form part of early life. It does not necessarily mean that they then must join the great array of the unconscious realm, but it makes it possible. Others, like Horacio Etchegoyen, Jorge L. Ahumada, Robert M. Emde, Stern and so on, observe that patterns of emotional activity are, in health, automatically selected or abstracted from their context and reacted to, from the earliest infancy onwards. Ahumada, for instance, notes that Gregory Bateson saw that imitation of *emotional* patterns was the basis of animal communication. Bateson called this *analogic* communication.

When such an emotional pattern is selected out from its context, it must at least partially be 'floating freely' of the context; it is then acting as one of above Mordant's abstracted attributes. Also Robert J. Langs seems to have thought along similar lines when he speaks of the abstracting and particularizing aspects of mental activity. Less specifically than Mordant, but much before him in time, Matte Blanco too indicated that many of the prime inhabitants of unconscious imagination are sensory abstractions.

Following Klein, he says, for instance, that we do not talk of a particular locatable 'left or right breast', it is '*the* breast', '*the* good breast', '*the* bad breast', '*the* nipple', '*the* penis', 'faeces'. These are notions, conceptions or imaginary objects, that is to say, they are *generalized ideas*; they are not representations of particular locatable objects of actually perceived reality. These ideas must have qualities which are imaginative but not fantastic, as they however refer to aspects of real things but in a generalized or abstracted way.

Thus, when described by Freud, Klein or any other analyst, unconscious objects are certainly abstractions of a sort. They appear to be simple abstractions both in the infant's mind, and also in anyone else's at unconscious levels. However, 'the good breast' or 'the penis' are now traditionally called *part objects* by psychoanalysts. So *part objects are primitive abstractions* and they are also based on symmetrisations. They are not simple fragments, three-dimensional things, but are of an abstract nature and the product of symmetrisation. Such notions can be 'pure' and dissociated, that is, split off at the unconscious levels. Perhaps splitting must play an essential part in their formation. When this invades conscious structuring then, of course, mental disturbance is manifest.

We shall emphasize too that symmetrisation mixed with asymmetrical discrimination is not only a characteristic of unconscious activity but also of emotionality, even at more conscious levels. Such an emotional activity is crude and liable to prejudice. It may have been initiated by splitting for pathological reasons, but it can also enable *quick evaluations* to be made, communicated and carried out.

Matte Blanco didn't consider the question of the *primitiveness* of the abstraction. He was neither particularly interested in developmental dating, nor did he have recent infant research findings available, as Stern himself noted. He simply approached the question with great imagination from the introspective and the logical-deductive points of view. Based on the well-known 1910 *Principia Mathematica* of Bertrand Russell and Alfred North Whitehead, he pointed to what they called a *propositional function*.

This is a thought which is only very general indeed because it contains as yet neither a *defined subject* nor a *specified object*. It is thus *so general* that it is not yet a definite proposition about anything. Thus a statement such as '*x* is hurt' is a propositional function. In this case *x*, called a *variable* in logic, is so general that the statement is saying nothing specific as yet. It is pointing nowhere in particular, *x* could be a mouse, a cat, a human or any being, even an imaginary one. It only becomes a definite proposition when *x* is specified, for example, to 'my friend John Jones is hurt'.

This specification of a particular person or thing involves clear asymmetrical discriminations. On the other hand, phrases like 'hurtness is happening', 'rage is occurring', 'adoration is' and 'there is threat' are all more or less propositional functions. These refer to endogenous *moods,* and it appears that something close to them populate the unconscious. In summary, Matte Blanco considers that, through symmetrisation, the *unconscious deals largely with propositional functions* and not with fully specific logical propositions.

Similarly, as just mentioned, the unconscious does not deal with fully defined classes, which are definite collections of different members. Rather, it deals with abstract class attributes, notions or conceptions (like hatefulness, loneliness, lovingness, mousiness, cattiness or humanness, and so on) which are the equivalent of the prepositional functions of the given class. The same phenomenon repeatedly impresses itself.

The unconscious largely deals not with particular logically asymmetrically locatable subjects and objects, but with abstract attributes, qualities or notions. Put in another way, these prepositional functions are adjectival and adverbial; they lie behind verbal nouns: lovingness, frighteningness, and so on. So prepositional functions or abstract attributes are fundamental constituents of the unconscious. This is perhaps the most revolutionary contribution of bi-logic.

Freud, in *The Unconscious* (of 1915), wrote that a characterisation of the schizophrenic's mode of thought is that it treats concrete things as though they were abstract, a feature that, albeit not quoted directly about the unconscious as such, may be referred to it since, for Freud, both schizophrenic thought and unconscious operate largely with primary process.

Ross Skelton refers to this sort of 'promiscuous' unconscious use of abstractions as *predicate thinking*. Here, the specificity of the subject and object of a proposition are of such little interest that they are interchangeable; all that matters, is the predicate of the thought. Skelton also drew attention to the fact that this was first noted as a characteristic of schizophrenic thinking by Eilhard Von Domarus in the 1940s, and then used by Calvin Hall and Silvano Arieti in the 1950s, before Matte Blanco's ideas arose. Hanna Segal, in the late of 1950s, also began thinking along these lines many years ago, when she differentiated *symbolic equations* from truly differentiated symbols.

However, it is Matte Blanco who has systematically developed this question. It is of interest that logicians appear to have focused on a similar area of functioning when discussing *equivalence relations* of Algebra, where they note that, "every equivalence is expressed by some sameness predicate" (Hodges, 1977). What is more important, when such predicates are drawn together, the result is called the 'abstraction' of the predicates, similarly to what has been said above. This is not surprising since we are finding out that the unconscious is remarkably suitable at handling great numbers of equations, samenesses, equivalences, *at the same time*. But it makes this by selectively ignoring many asymmetries and difference relations which would be recognizable to consciousness. So, metaphorically speaking with Eric Rayner, "what is gained on the roundabouts is lost on the swings".

Concluding, the remarkable unconscious facility for the *intuitive* detection of similarities, is of constant use in *rapid* evaluations; it is also a central characteristic of emotional thought. But there are drawbacks: its very quickness is prone to promote *prejudices* which readily remain untamed, and become antisocial. When such instantaneous evaluations abound and then go out of the central ego's control, mental breakdown is likely.

Kenneth Wright, in a personal note to Eric Rayner, said that the notion of 'rapid evaluation' links symmetrisation clearly to the processes of actually living and responding in immediate ways in the world, rather than to the relative 'luxury' of thinking and reflecting in a time rightly enough. In the primitive world, for instance, what is important initially is to know what sort of thing is looming up, not the kind of thing that it is not. In the wild, life would depend upon this, and, so to say, it would be better ''to kill an innocent intruder than to miss a dangerous one'', so it seems that life in the raw has to be built on paranoid premises; it seems too that the 'fight/flight' response of the organism fits well with symmetrical thinking.

REFERENCES

Bria, P. (1981). Introduzione. Pensiero, mondo e problemi di fondazione. In *L'inconscio come insiemi infiniti. Saggio sulla bi-logica* (pp. xix–cxi). Torino, Italy: Giulio Einaudi editore.

D'Urso, V., & Trentin, R. (1998). Introduzione alla psicologia delle emozioni. Roma-Bari, Italy: Editori Laterza.

Durst, M. (1988). Dialettica e bi-logica. L'epistemologia di Ignacio Matte Blanco. Milano, Italy: Marzorati Editore.

Figà-Talamanca Dore, L. (1978). La logica dell'inconscio. Roma, Italy: Edizioni Studium-Vita Nova.

Fonagy, P., Gergely, G., Jurist, E. L., & Target, M. (2002). Affect Regulation, Mentalization, and the Development of the Self. New York, NY: Other Press.

Hodges, W. (1977). *Logic. An Introduction to Elementary Logic*. Harmondsworth, UK: Penguin Books, Ltd.

Iurato, G. (2013). Mathematical thought in the light of Matte Blanco work. *Philosophy of Mathematics Education Journal*, 27.

Matte Blanco, I. (1975). The Unconscious as Infinite Sets. An Essay in Bi-Logic. London, UK: Gerald Duckworth & Company, Ltd.

Matte Blanco, I. (1988). *Thinking, Feeling, and Being. Clinical Reflections of the Fundamental Antinomy on Human Beings and World*. London, UK: Routledge.

Mordant, I. (1990). Using attribute-memories to resolve a contradiction in the work of Matte Blanco. *The International Review of Psycho-Analysis*, *17*, 475–480.

Murtagh, F., & Iurato, G. (2016). Human Behaviour, Benign or Malevalent: Understanding the Human Psyche, Performing Therapy, based on Affective Mentalization and Matte-Blancos Bi-Logic. *Annals of Translational Medicine, 4*(24), 486–496. doi:10.21037/atm.2016.12.37 PMID:28149848

Rayner, E. (1995). *Unconscious Logic. An Introduction to Matte Blanco's Bi-Logic and its Uses.* New York, NY: Routledge.

Rayner, E. (1998). Foreword. In *The Unconscious as Infinite Sets. An Essay in Bi-Logic* (pp. xviii–xxiv). London, UK: Karnac Books, Ltd.

Skelton, R. (1984). Understanding Matte Blanco. *The International Journal of Psycho-Analysis, 65*, 453–460. PMID:6544756

Skelton, R. (1990). Generalizations from Freud to Matte Blanco. *The International Review of Psycho-Analysis, 17*, 471–474.

Vallortigara, G., & Panciera, N. (2014). Cervelli che contano. Milano, Italy: Adelphi Edizioni.

Vattimo, G., Ferraris, M., & Marconi, D. (Eds.). (1993). Enciclopedia Garzanti di Filosofia. Milano, Italy: Garzanti Editore.

Vegetti Finzi, S. (1990). Storia della psicoanalisi. Autori, opere, teorie (1895-1990). Milano, Italy: Arnoldo Mondadori Editore.

ENDNOTES

[1] Generally speaking, *emotions* are biological and universal, while *feelings* are individual and particular, social-culturally determined. Then, *affects* include both emotions and feelings (D'Urso & Trentin, 1998; Fonagy et al., 2002).

[2] Cf. (Vattimo et al., 1993).

Chapter 4

First Attempts to Formalize Some Main Aspects of Psychoanalysis:
Towards a Computational Psychoanalysis

ABSTRACT

In this chapter, we have tried to join Lévi-Strauss' ideas with Matte Blanco's ones, in that they have in common from the structuralistic standpoint and psychoanalytically aimed. To this end, we have mainly made use of some notions and methods drawn from elementary mathematics and theoretical physics, in particular the notions of groupoid and symmetry breaking, which are suitable, from a conceptual-analogical viewpoint, to formalize together Lévi-Strauss' and Matte Blanco's ideas. Besides to have mentioned as well other formalizations attempts turned towards psychoanalytic domain, what we have originally reached is that, the typical feature of human consciousness, is that of oppositional dichotomy, a basic distinguishing binary task typical of humans, formalized in the notion of ordering, in which besides falls the temporal dimension, another distinguishing feature of human psyche with its possible different senses. This basic oppositional feature is then in agreement with the unavoidable presence of phallic logic.

4.0 BACKGROUND

Matte Blanco's ideas have been recently formalized variously. One of the first attempts made along this direction is that achieved in (Lauro-Grotto, 2008), a resume of its results being recalled briefly in the following section. Then, we outline other attempts to formalize psychoanalytic concepts on the wake of Matte Blanco's work, making use of category theory[1], to be precise groupoids theory, in relation with some main concepts of theoretical physics; just by means of category theory, we may retrace useful link with computing theory. Hence, even along this pathway, we proceed with further formalizations of certain psychoanalytic patterns (among which is the Giampaolo Sasso's model) involving further

DOI: 10.4018/978-1-5225-4128-8.ch004

advanced notions of category theory, dynamical systems and differential geometry, thanks to which it will be possible to delineate some new ways leading to logic domain, with the perspective to may think to further, possible applications to informatics.

Afterwards, we shall give a brief overview of a possible formal model of unconscious based on hysteresis, within solid state physics and condensed matter physics frameworks, whence we shall mention, along this route, possible applications to the origins of consciousness just in relation to the rising of the temporal dimensions. Then, we make a brief summary of the main psychoanalytic reflections on time, standing out those aspects of the variegated temporal dimensionality which are liable to be formalized suitably for computational aims. Anyway, the framework of a possible formalization of psychoanalysis as will result from what will be said in this Chapter, especially in the Section 4., together to what will be said in the next Chapters 6 and 7, will be the central portrait of our attempt to formalize psychoanalysis, mainly from the logic standpoint.

However, from an historical standpoint, the first attempts to formalize mathematically unconscious processes and concepts, date back to Andrei Khrennikov who, in 1990s (Khrennikov, 1998), used, for first, ultrametric and p-adic analysis methods to work out a formal framework in which to lay out main Freudian ideas. He proposes a mathematical model of the process of thinking based on p-adic dynamical systems over a configuration space of ideas. These dynamical systems are assumed to be placed into the human unconscious and are mainly controlled by human conscious (defence mechanisms of the *Ego*) which fixes parameters of the dynamical systems in the unconscious and transmits to the subconscious generating ideas which initiate iterations of the dynamical systems in the subconscious itself. Thus, Khrennikov presents a mathematical model which is not based on the rule of reasoning, which has opened a new way in modelizing psychological processes.

Mathematically, the configuration space of ideas is described by p-adic numbers, as a p-adic metric on the space of ideas corresponds to the following nearness between ideas: two ideas, say x and y, are close if and only if they have sufficiently long common root (in the sense of p-adic number system). Along this line of thought, Khrennikov and co-workers (Albeverio et al., 1998) proposed as well a mathematical model of the human memory-retrieval process based on dynamical systems over a metric space of p-adic numbers, where the elements of this space represent ideas which are close if and only if they have a sufficiently long initial segment in common. They also assumed that this dynamical system is located into the unconscious and is controlled by the conscious, which specifies the system parameters and provides the ideas that initiate the related typical iteration of the dynamical system. Hence, they also show that even simple p-adic dynamical systems are able to describe essential features of the human memory-retrieval process.

Afterwards, Rosapia Lauro-Grotto (2008) discovered an underlying ultrametric structure owned by Matte-Blanco's formal notion of structural unconscious and its relationship with his related bi-logic conception (see next section). She basically elaborates a suitable recontextualization of the formal theory due to Ignacio Matte Blanco, from either the point of view of neurocognitive science and psychoanalysis. Starting from an approach mainly based on information theory, she has provided a formal description of mental space in terms of a peculiar topographical structure laid out within ultrametric analysis framework. This formal structure is showed to fit as well the constraints of primary process thinking, as presented by Matte Blanco in his essays on bi-logic, so that Lauro-Grotto's model is able to give an exact formal style to some main aspects of Matte Blanco's theory.

4.1. THE LAURO-GROTTO'S FORMALIZATION OF MATTE BLANCO'S IDEAS

In this section, we closely follow (Lauro-Grotto, 2008). This paper starts with a kind of homology regarding two ways of thinking on the deep structure of the mind, falling into the field of cognitive neuroscience of memory in pathological situations[2]. Lauro-Grotto's discussion is based on a quantitative method relying on the well-known Claude Shannon information theory of the 1940s, applied in decoding single cell recordings. When an animal is turned to identify a set of visual stimuli, then the activity's traces of the cells involved in the related recognition process can be interpreted in terms of the degree of similarity between the pairs of recordings so established. Lauro-Grotto, then, describes the results of a psychological experiment, settled up and conducted together other her co-workers, hence they discuss the related implications and conclusions.

The stimuli presented to the subjects involved in this text, are pictures of some famous people from several decades, which must be classified into a grid of semantic dimensions, such as nationality and profession. When the subject possibly fails to recognize the picture, to her or him is nevertheless required to provide the most plausible classification. Then, by analyzing the so-called *confusion matrix*, that is to say, the matrix presenting both correct and incorrect classifications, then it is possible to get a quantitative index providing an estimate of the extent of the relationships of similarity that the subject is able to perceive into the set of stimuli. This is an indirect yet useful estimation parameter of the degree of richness of the conceptual structure underlying the classification process, in dependence on the experimental data. The index they have derived is called the *metric content* of the mental representations.

Their results[3] were however based mainly on a previous work related with patients suffering from neurodegenerative diseases such as Alzheimer's dementia, but the same method was then applied to pick up the evolution of semantic representations through different phases of life, from youth to senescence. Along the entire life course, *semantic memory*, i.e., roughly the mental lexicon with which our knowledge of the world is stored and organized, is slowly enriched by new incoming information, while the network of links and associations among concepts is quite hindered. Nonetheless, Lauro-Grotto and co-workers identified, strangely enough, a simultaneous increasing of information and of the metric content. Furthermore, it has been seen too that, in dementia, when neural resources progressively and inexorably undergo a general pauperization, a loss of information content is parallel to a marked increasing in the metric content of the representations.

Importantly, it seems that the semantic network tends to become even more dominated by similarities and less sensitive to differences. So, Lauro-Grotto and co-workers propose that the mind, so to speak, having less space at its disposal in order to record knowledge, to economize keeps, for instance, a same, common image for two different concepts (that is, related to different classes, for example, those of cats and dogs), expelling all the distinctive features that would keep these two concepts as distinct of each other. So, a new "dog-cat" super-class is thus created, and into this class all the individual attributes are either shared or lost.

The tendency to generate *clusters* of concepts that, in turn, become more and more homogeneous in their inner structure, can be described mathematically as a transition from a metric space to an *ultrametric* one. Both metricity and ultrametricity are topological properties, in the general sense that they define "who is close to whom" in a spatial representation of a given set. In a semantic space metrically equipped, a concept as that of "cat" would be closer to the concept of "dog" than to either that of "butterfly" or of "car". If a semantic space has an ultrametric structure, on the contrary, all the items are organized in a hierarchical sequence of clusters of increasing generality, while inside each cluster all the concepts are equidistant from each other, as is the case for the vertices of an equilateral triangle.

In an ultrametric set, if two concepts belong to the same cluster, they become *ipso facto* indistinguishable; to some extent, they are interchangeable with each other, as well as with the whole cluster. All that has the remarkable consequence that the proper parts of a set and the whole of the set itself, are to be considered as equivalent to each other. Now, according to Matte Blanco, two opposite and apparently irreducible and contradictory ways of being coexist in mental life: the *asymmetric* (or heterogeneous) mode, following the rules of classical reasoning, and the *symmetric* (or homogeneous) mode, which can be described as a system of logic operating on the basis of two fundamental principles.

The first principle, known as *generalization principle*, states that the unconscious treats an individual thing (person, object, concept) as if it were a member or element of a set or class which contains other members; it treats this class as a subclass of a more general class, and, on its turn, this more general class as a subclass or subset of a more general class, etc. The second principle, known as *symmetry principle*, states that the unconscious treats the converse of any relationship as identical to this. In other words, it treats asymmetrical relations as if they were symmetrical. Matte Blanco shows furthermore how to derive from these two principles alone the whole set of unconscious features that, according to the first Freudian topography, characterize unconscious mental activity, i.e., the absence of mutual exclusion and negation, displacement, condensation, atemporality, and the replacement of the inner reality with the external one.

Every mental phenomenon, from abstract thinking to emotion, seems to be marked by the co-presence in various proportions of the symmetric and the asymmetric modes, i.e., the mind is bi-logical in its structure. Now, here comes Lauro-Grotto's observation: the structural unconscious, in the way it is reformulated by Matte Blanco, i.e., the symmetric mode, is homologous to an ultrametric structure. The generalization principle then reflects the hierarchical arrangement in which all the stimuli (or concepts) are perceived as belonging to classes, and the classes are clustered into super-classes of increasing generality.

The symmetry principle reflects the property of the ultrametric organization according to which all the elements of a given class are equidistant from each other, and all of them are placed at the same distance from any other element of any different class. This formulation is appropriately provided by a corollary of the second principle, stating that "when the principle of symmetry is applied there can be no relations of contiguity between the parts of a whole" (Matte Blanco, 1975). As said above in regard to Lauro-Grotto and co-workers' experiment, distance in a semantic space can be considered as an estimate of the difference among concepts.

In an ultrametric set, all the concepts are at the same distance from each other, all the possible "positions" are to be considered as equivalent, and there is no way to distinguish one position from the other. To be clearer, we may consider, for example, a single ultrametric class comprising three concepts: so, in an ordinary Euclidean space, we can imagine them as placed at the vertices of an equilateral triangle. An ultrametric structure might be then considered as isomorphic to an ordinary metric structure of two-dimensional space (i.e., the equilateral triangle) only if we assumed that every vertex of this triangle were at exactly the same distance from every other point of the ordinary space, a situation, this, quite difficult to be imagined by our usual intuition.

However, something similar to this, might be experienced in a finite space when we look at a very distant three-dimensional structure, that will be perceived as it were a single point. Symmetrization of relationships can therefore be described as a transition from a metric to an ultrametric conceptual arrangement. Conversely, instead, that is to say, by *deployment*, as Matte Blanco calls the inverse phenomenon consisting in the opposite shift, i.e., from an ultrametric to a metric structure, there is an apparent increase of the available information and oppositional-contradictory aspects arise as well, as typical, primary features of consciousness. So, bi-logic might be reformulated in terms of a unitary super-logic which unfolds in symmetric and asymmetric modes of being. Finally, Lauro-Grotto notes that a *Hopfield neural network* in fact shows a spontaneous transition from a metric to an ultrametric regime when the storage capacity limit of the system is exceeded, so it provides a neural pattern based on a bi-logic process.

4.2. FIRST ATTEMPTS TO FORMALIZE SOME MAIN CONCEPTS OF PSYCHOANALYSIS VIA MATTE BLANCO'S WORK, THEORETICAL PHYSICS AND CATEGORY THEORY

In this section, we outlines other attempts turned to give a formal framework to some main concepts of psychoanalysis, by means of main Matte Blanco's ideas. We shall introduce some elementary theoretical physics and mathematical notions which will be able to give first formalizations to the main concepts of psychoanalysis, among which are those due to Matte Blanco. The first formal framework which will come out in this section, will be the first portrait of a possible computational psychoanalysis, as developed and applied in the follows. So, the present section will play a very fundamental role in our conception of computational psychoanalysis, in that we shall expose some main case-studies in which certain notions, methods and operations of theoretical physics and mathematics, are analogically used to conceptually formalize, where possible, some chief elements and aspects of psychoanalysis according to Freudian thought.

4.2.1. Introduction

Ignacio Matte Blanco, as already said, was an outstanding psychiatrist and psychoanalyst who gave, among other things, notable contributions to the epistemological status of psychoanalysis starting from the Freudian theoretical framework. At the basis of his rigorous formulation of psychoanalytic foundations based on *bi-logic*, he put two main principles, namely the *generalization principle* and the *symmetry principle*. We refer to (Matte Blanco, 1975) for any further deepening of his thought. One of the central points of Matte Blanco thought is then the crucial transition from *symmetric* to *asymmetric* thinking. In this article, we want to make some formal remarks on the symmetry-asymmetry duality of Matte Blanco bi-logic, within the context of theoretical computational psychoanalysis.

We think that Matte Blanco bi-logic is the most suitable one to be used for trying to employ a creative dimension from a computational standpoint, if one considers the unconscious as the main source of insight. Indeed, the basic inseparability between the *symmetric logic* and the *asymmetric logic* within the bi-logic context, might turn out to be useful just to this end. In this brief article, in particular, we would like to put into evidence some elementary formalizations which are offered as possible formal tools that may shed light upon the above mentioned link between symmetric and asymmetric logic. This is the chief point upon which we want to focus in the present section. Within the general cultural context, we shall try to clarify Matte Blanco's intertwining of symmetric and asymmetric logic by means of certain very elementary mathematical tools and notions drawn from theoretical physics and algebra.

4.2.2. The Bases for a Formalization Attempt via Matte Blanco's Bi-Logic

The central point of Matte Blanco's bi-logic is the inextricable intertwining of *symmetric logic*, which reigns in the unconscious realm and is mainly regulated by the generalization and symmetry principles, and the *asymmetric logic*, which rules conscious thought. We are mainly interested in the passage from the former to the latter, this being that process which, if appropriately formalized, may turn out to be of some usefulness from a computational viewpoint[4]. In pursuing this, we follow a line of contextualization which includes some outstanding figures of the history of culture, amongst whom are Gregory Bateson, Claude Lévi-Strauss, André Weil and Robert R. Bush, as well as some elementary but basic formal tools and notions drawn from theoretical physics and algebra. Herein, we outline some main points of Matte Blanco's thought, following (Figà-Talamanca Dore, 1978).

Matte Blanco's work has been centred around the new and ambitious intention of analysing unconscious logic through rational thought. To do this, he put two main principles at the basis of his framework, the generalization and symmetry principles, which are able to explain the main characteristics of the Freudian unconscious, namely displacement, condensation, absence of time, replacement of the external reality with the internal one, and absence of contradiction. Matte Blanco's work allows us to clarify the concept of consciousness. Starting from the paradigm of visual perception, based on the dual relationships between macular (or central) and peripheral vision, the focus on one object is perceivable only through a series of continuous eye pupil oscillations around it and not with a direct, fixed and central focusing on the object itself that will lead to an evanescence of the field of view.

Analogously, consciousness, like eye movements, builds up asymmetric relationships around the object which is perceivable only through the latter, allowing to distinguish a thing from another. An object of consciousness is the result of a kind of bridling net of asymmetric relations[5] built up around an emotional nucleus of symmetric relations. Consciousness, therefore, acts in an analytical manner, whereas general emotion, running symmetrically, acts in a global or synthetic manner. Nevertheless, both dimensions, or modes of being, are always inseparable and continuously interacting amongst each other. Psychoanalysis has pointed out the fundamental importance of emotion for the psychic life of every human being.

The characters of consciousness may be detected only through introspection, which is an asymmetric phenomenon that concerns the time immediately prior to the introspection act itself. Hence, we may only have a retrospective introspection, because it is not possible to think something and, at the same time, to be aware of thinking. This is mainly due to the basic fact that, into the consciousness, not more than one asymmetric relation per time is presentable. Thus, the typical feature of rational thinking seems to be that of reflecting itself upon consciousness. In this sense, questions on psychological and physical time arise, reaching to touch philosophical issues concerning existentialism and phenomenology.

A pure sensation is something having an elusive and fleeting character, which can be caught by consciousness in an extremely brief time before it is inextricably harnessed into some implicit or explicit proposition (asymmetric relation). At a given instant of time, in the consciousness field there may be present only one phenomenon, the other ones going out from the field. Matte Blanco points out the primary fact according to which any human psychic act is roughly an inseparable pair made both by an emotional nucleus and by a surrounding rational thought component, with a variable ratio of reciprocal combination. The emotional component is made by symmetric relations, whereas the rational thought component is made by asymmetric relations. These two components are inseparable from each other, and in continuous reciprocal interaction.

Analysing some types of emotions, like falling in love, fear and discouragement, it emerges that the main aspect of the symmetric relations characterizing emotion, is that each emotion refers not only to the intentional concrete object but to the wider and whole class to which such an object belongs, that is to say, to the equivalence class of which such an object is one of its representative elements. Indeed, when one, for instance, loves a person, this latter is seen as someone who goes on beyond herself or himself, personifying the attraction and representing all the attractive persons (maximization – see below). Therefore, three main features of the symmetric relations involved in a (strong) emotional status, are identifiable, namely: *i)* the generalization of all the properties of the intentioned object; *ii)* the maximization of the properties of this object; *iii)* the transposition of this object to every other one who may be represented by it.

All this recalls in mind the basic features of an algebraic equivalence relation. Then, the rational thought will build up a covering net made by asymmetric relations around such an emotional nucleus, made by symmetric relations, which constitutes the first and unavoidable apperceptive capture moment of the intentional cathexis object. The main consciousness activity is essentially analytic because it basically subdivides such a globally intentioned object (by emotion) into its constitutive parts, to give rise then to those asymmetric relations which will characterize the consciousness grasp of such an object[6]. Symmetric and asymmetric modes of being are inseparable from each other because an utterly symmetric mode is a typical feature of psychotic or loss of consciousness states, whereas a complete asymmetric mode is also impossible since it would entail a total absence of any cathexis object, which is impossible because of the intentional nature of human desire.

As we will see later, we shall try to formalize in an elementary way this last basic process of consciousness putting it into analogy with a formal process consisting of a kind of truly elementary (inversion) symmetry breaking of equivalence relations (of symmetry thought) into asymmetric ones (asymmetry thought). These very simple considerations may also be laid out within a wider and ambitious research program of a sort of *psychoanalytic physics* centred around the general relationships between primary and secondary psychic process, and whose early origins may be retraced in the Freudian *Project for a Scientific Psychology*[7] (of 1895). On the other hand, as early André Green has noted that a distinguishing feature of the functioning of the primary and secondary process, is just in the realization of an *inversion symmetry* (with negation) in passing from one to the other, so putting negation as the main psychic operation ruling functioning of human psyche (Semi 1988-89, Vol. I, Ch. 6, Sect. 6.1.1, p. 398).

4.2.2.1. From Theoretical Physics: On Symmetry Breaking

Symmetry arguments are very important in natural sciences. These have also played a certain role in linguistics, starting from Noam Chomsky's formalization attempts up until recent linguistic invariant theory (Guay & Hepburn, 2009). Following almost verbatim (Brading & Castellani, 2013), the symmetry of the initial state of a given situation implies the complete equivalence between the existing possible alternatives (for example, the left bundle of hay with respect to the right one of Buridan's ass argument).

If the alternatives are completely equivalent, then there is not a sufficient reason for choosing between them, the initial situation remaining unchanged if also the Leibnizean *principle of sufficient reason* (in short, PSR) cannot be applied to settle the question. Arguments of this kind – that is, arguments leading to definite conclusions on the basis of an initial symmetry of the situation plus PSR – have been used in science since antiquity. The form they most frequently take is the following: a situation with a certain symmetry evolves in such a way that, in the absence of an asymmetric cause, the initial symmetry is preserved. In other words, a breaking of the initial symmetry cannot happen without a reason, or an asymmetry cannot originate spontaneously. So, the notion of symmetry breaking in physics makes its appearance, which historically dates back to some works made in 19th-century solid state physics.

To be precise, the study of symmetry breaking goes back to Pierre Curie, who formulated three principles about crystal symmetry on the basis of some of his notable crystallographic research made in the 1890s. Following (Radicati, 1985), he was primarily concerned, not with the symmetry of the dynamical equations, but rather with that of their solutions, i.e., with the symmetry of the physical states. This phenomenological approach led him naturally to emphasize the role of *asymmetry* rather than that of *symmetry*. A symmetry can be classified as *exact*, *approximate* or *broken*. *Exact* means unconditionally valid; *approximate* means valid under certain conditions; and *broken* can mean different things, depending on the object considered and its context.

According to Curie, *symmetry breaking* has the following role: for the occurrence of a phenomenon in a medium, the original symmetry group of the medium must be lowered (broken, in today's terminology) to the symmetry group of the phenomenon (or to a subgroup of the phenomenon's symmetry group) by the *action* of some cause. In this sense symmetry breaking, or asymmetry, is what creates a phenomenon. Following (Radicati, 1985), Curie was in a better position to appreciate the role of symmetry breaking as a necessary condition for the existence of phenomena. Generally, the breaking of a certain symmetry does not imply that no symmetry is present, but rather that the situation where this symmetry is broken is characterized by a lower symmetry than the original one. In group-theoretic terms, this means that the initial symmetry group is broken into one of its non-trivial subgroups.

It is therefore possible to describe symmetry breaking also in terms of relations between transformation groups, in particular between a group (the unbroken symmetry group) and its non-trivial subgroups. As has been clearly illustrated by Stewart and Golubitsky (2006), starting from this point of view, a general theory of symmetry breaking can be developed by tackling such questions as which non-trivial subgroups can occur?; and, when does a given subgroup occur? – In this regard, see also (Stewart & Golubitsky, 2006), and the next subsection. However, the notion of symmetry breaking is emblematic to explain the paradigmatic dialectic contraposition between symmetry and asymmetry.

Symmetry breaking was first explicitly studied in classical physics with respect to physical objects and phenomena. This is not surprising, since the theory of symmetry originated with the visible symmetry properties of familiar spatial figures and everyday objects. As has been said above, it was Curie's works on crystal symmetry that opened this new perspective. However, it is with respect to the laws that symmetry breaking has acquired special significance in physics. There are two different types of symmetry breaking of the laws, *explicit* and *spontaneous*, the case of spontaneous symmetry breaking being the more interesting from a physical as well as philosophical point of view.

Explicit symmetry breaking (ESB) refers to a situation where the related dynamical equations are not manifestly invariant under a certain symmetry group. This means, in the Lagrangian or Hamiltonian formulation, that the Lagrangian or Hamiltonian operator of the system contains one or more terms (like *anomalies*) which are explicitly breaking the symmetry. *Spontaneous symmetry breaking* (SSB) instead occurs in a situation where, given a symmetry of the equations of motion, solutions exist but are not invariant under the action of this symmetry often without any explicit asymmetric input[8] (hence the attribute 'spontaneous').

A situation of symmetry breaking can be first illustrated by means of simple cases taken from classical physics: an emblematic and meaningful example is given by the phenomenology of the well-known *Euler's elastic bar*. In this case, the actual breaking of the symmetry may then easily occur by effect of a (however small) external cause, and the stick bends until it reaches one of the infinite possible stable asymmetric equilibrium configurations. In substance, what happens in the above kind of situation is the following: when some parameter reaches a critical value, the lowest energy solution respecting the symmetry of the theory ceases to be stable under small perturbations and new asymmetric (but stable) lowest energy solutions appear.

The new lowest energy solutions are asymmetric but are all related through the action of the symmetry transformations (which are asymmetric relations in the Matte Blanco sense). Therefore, it seems that for reaching equilibrium solutions of a given dynamically unstable problem, it is needed to break the initial symmetry of unstable and unrelated states, so obtaining solutions with less symmetry (asymmetry) but more stability; furthermore these latter equilibrium states, meant as asymmetric solutions of the given dynamical problem, are related among each other by (asymmetric) relations given by the action of a transformation group. In quantum physics, instead, SSB is applicable only to infinitely extended systems (like unconscious, according to Matte Blanco). These last considerations might also turn out to be useful in regard to further formal considerations about an object's relationship.

Historically, the concept of spontaneous symmetry breaking first emerged in condensed matter physics of the first half of 20th century, and was later transferred to quantum field theory (QFT) in the 1960s, above all in relation to weak interactions. The notion of symmetry breaking still waits to be laid out within a unified formal treatment because of its variegated nature and the different contexts in which such a notable mechanism is involved. Herein, we shall consider only the quantum context in which it is better known and studied from a formal viewpoint. The spontaneous breakdown of a global continuous internal symmetry gives rise to massless bosons (known as *Goldstone bosons*) according to a general QFT theorem, known as *Goldstone theorem*, stated by J. Goldstone in the early 1960s and valid only in the case of global continuous symmetries; moreover, other important elements are *locality* and infinite dimensionality (Strocchi, 2012).

Subsequently, starting from the previous notion of *dynamical symmetry breaking* (DSB) related to the creation, via Higgs mechanisms, of massive gauge vector bosons from symmetry-violating vacuum expectation values of Higgs scalar fields, a more general mechanism was proposed, today also known as the *Englert-Brout-Higgs-Guralnik-Hagen-Kibble mechanism* (hereafter briefly called *Higgs phenomenon*), according to which, when a *global* internal gauge symmetry is promoted to a *local* gauge symmetry, then Goldstone bosons disappear and gauge bosons acquire mass, this taking place often without explicitly breaking the gauge invariance of the theory.

Following (Strocchi, 2012), in the Haag-Kastler algebraic approach to quantum field theory, the essence of a spontaneous symmetry breaking for an infinitely extended system, with a *locality* condition related to the algebra of local fields (i.e., local operators) F which, in turn, contains, as subalgebra, the C^*-algebra of observable fields F_{obs} associated with the given system, is as follows. From the pioneering works by E.P. Wigner, the physical observables of such an algebra can be obtained only through a suitable Hilbert space representation π of F_{obs}.

There is a symmetry group G acting on a ray Hilbert space H to give a group of unitary operators $U(g)$ of the latter. This gives rise to a group of algebraic automorphisms of F_{obs} through the algebraic map $g \rightarrow \alpha_g$ given by $\alpha_g(A) = U(g)A\,U(g)^{-1}$ for each $A \in F_{obs}$, which induces an action of the group G on F_{obs} via the assigned Hilbert space representation π, in turn induced by the group of unitary operators $\left\{ U(g); g \in G \right\}$ via the Wigner's theorem. Nevertheless, in the case of an infinitely extended system, there may be automorphisms α_g which are not described by unitary operators provided by a representation π of F_{obs}, that is to say, g exists as a symmetry at the algebraic level, but it is not a symmetry of the realization of the system provided by the representation π in H_π, that is, it is not implemented by unitary operators in H_π. In this case, we say that the symmetry g is *broken* in H_π. Therefore, there is a substantial level detachment between the algebraic and the functional stance of a symmetry when this is broken.

This fact, that is to say disjoint realizations of the physical system induced by inequivalent representations of F_{obs}, is the main essence of the mechanism of symmetry breaking. It is just this inequivalence of, at least, two distinct representations to give rise asymmetry, for infinitely extended systems: in this case, the breaking of color symmetry mentioned in (Strocchi, 2000) and made possible thanks to the comparison with the environment or background, is very meaningful to clarify the idea. From quantum cromodynamics case studies, it is also known that highest symmetry levels imply a flattening of reality, so that asymmetry – arising from symmetry breaking – is a fundamental element to detect this, as well as to account for diversity.

As has already been said above, symmetry breaking raises a number of deep philosophical questions, such as the one asking about the evidence for the (hidden) symmetry underlying the directly observable asymmetry. SSB allows symmetric theories (like those concerning unconscious) to describe asymmetric reality (of consciousness), assuming the salient fact that an observed asymmetry requires the *action* of a cause which can be an explicit breaking of the symmetry of the laws or asymmetrical initial conditions or SSB. This last consideration is very similar to the aim of the Curie principle that, when extended to include the case of SSB, is substantially equivalent to the methodological principle according to which an asymmetry of the phenomena must come from the explicit or spontaneous breaking of symmetry of fundamental laws. This might be called an *extended Curie principle*.

Following (Strocchi, 2000), roughly we might say that the general mechanism of spontaneous symmetry breaking related to a physical system is characterized by symmetric interactions between its parts, but the environment in which the system stays is not symmetric (like the vacuum), this implying an asymmetric behaviour of the above interactions. In general, the lowest energy states lie at the bases of this asymmetry. However, in agreement with (Strocchi, 2000), it is just the comparison between, at least, two different realizations that highlights the paradigmatic duality symmetry-asymmetry through the symmetry breaking mechanism, this being just one of the possible philosophical aspects inherent the general symmetry breaking phenomena, to which we shall refer later.

4.2.2.2 From Mathematics: On Groupoids

The groupoid structures have a wide range of applications, ranging from pure and applied mathematics to physics and computer science, until to logic[9]. We refer to (Brown, 1987), (Weinstein, 1996), (Buneci, 2003) and (Harary et al., 1965) for more information. In what follows, we are interested in a particular groupoid structure which is the most suitable one to formalize in an elementary way what is our object of discussion. Roughly speaking, a *groupoid* is simply an algebraic system with a partial binary relation. A more precise but succinct definition is that a groupoid G is a small category in which every morphism is an isomorphism. Thus G has a set of morphisms, which we shall call just *elements* of G, a set $Ob(G)$ of *objects* or *vertices*, together with two functions, say $s, t : G \rightarrow Ob(G)$, $i : Ob(G) \rightarrow G$ such that

$si = ti = 1$. The functions s, t are sometimes called the *source* and *target* maps respectively. If $a, b \in G$ and $ta = sb$, then a *product* or *composite* ab exists such that $s(ab) = as$, $t(ab) = tb$. Further, this product is associative; the elements $ix, x \in Ob(J)$, act as identities; and each element a has an inverse a^{-1} with $s(a^{-1}) = ta$, $t(a^{-1}) = sa$, $aa^{-1} = isa$, $aa^{-1}a^{-1}a = ita$

An equivalence relation R on X becomes a groupoid with $s, t : R \to X$ the two natural projections, and product $(x, y)(y, z) = (x, z)$ whenever $(x, y), (y, z) \in R$. There is an identity, namely $(x, x) \in \Delta(R)$, for each $x \in R$. A special case of this groupoid is the *coarse* or *natural groupoid* $X \times X$, which is obtained by taking $R = X \times X$. This apparently banal and foolish example is found to play instead a key role in the theory and applications. At the opposite extreme to the coarse groupoid $X \times X$, is the *fine groupoid* on X that can be considered as the diagonal equivalence relation on X, or alternatively as the groupoid X consisting only of identities, namely the elements of X. This consideration of an equivalence relation as a groupoid also suggests the utility of groupoids for studying quotienting constructions, particularly in cases where the quotient set X / R cannot carry the appropriate structure. We are just interested in these last types of groupoid structures. Following the preprint of F. Latremoliere, given any set X endowed with an equivalence relation $\approx$, we define a groupoid structure over X by letting $G_{\approx} \doteq \left\{ (x, y) \in X^2, x \approx y \right\}$ together with the following multiplication

$$\circ : \left\{ (x, y), (y, z) \in G_{\approx}, (x, y, z) \in X^3 \right\} \to G_{\approx}$$

$$\left((x, y), (y, z) \right) \overset{\circ}{\longrightarrow} (x, z) .$$

This operation is well-defined by the transitivity of the equivalence relation, which also gives the associativity property. Now, the symmetry of $\approx$ ensures that for all $(x, y) \in G_{\approx}$, (y, x) is also in $G_{\approx}$, the latter being clearly the inverse of the former. Finally, the reflexivity is not required to define the structure; the set of units of this groupoid is the set of elements x of X such that $x \approx x$, so when $\approx$ is reflexive, then $G^0 \doteq \left\{ (x, x); x \in X \right\} \cong X$. Note that, for any $(x, y) \in G_{\approx}$, $s((x, y)) = x$ and $r((x, y)) = y$, whilst $(x, y)^{-1} = (y, x)$. We shall name this groupoid the *groupoid graph* of the relation $\approx$. Also (Weinstein, 1996) considers groupoids as generalized equivalence relations.

4.2.3. Some Elementary Formalization Attempts Within Category Theory

4.2.3.1. Again on Groupoids

The above mentioned groupoid structures will make possible certain formalization attempts of some main aspects of Matte Blanco's bi-logic. The groupoid structure has been proved to be at the early bases of almost all the most basic commutative and non-commutative algebraic structures, so that they lie at the deeper roots of the general algebraic formalization. In particular, groupoid structures are also at the basis of graph and combinatorial structures (see (Živaljević, 2006) and references therein) as well as having applications in type theory (see (Barthe et al., 2003)); likewise, ordered groupoids are at the foundations of other algebraic structures, like groups and inverse semigroups (Gilbert & Miller, 2011). Finally, groupoids have recently received remarkable attention also in non-linear dynamics of networks:

in this regard, see (Golubitsky & Stewart, 2006), where a very interesting discussion of network synchrony, asynchrony and related symmetry breaking phenomena, in the context of groupoid formalism, is made[10]. The main feature and potentiality of a groupoid structure is just the partiality of its binary operation, that makes this structure quite versatile.

On the other hand, following (Guay & Hepburn, 2009), for some time mathematicians have argued for the more general groupoids as more suitable structures for treating symmetries. At the crossroads between groups and groupoids, lies a distinction between local and global symmetries. For physicists, the local-global symmetry distinction is aligned with the distinction between local and global transformations. For mathematicians, the distinction is based on whether part or the entire structure is conserved (the former requiring a groupoid and not a group representation). Therefore, groupoids are offering more flexible mathematical structures embracing a wider formal tool box to treat symmetry and related phenomena. Groupoids can be understood not only as generalized groups but we can also see them as generalized equivalence relations: to be precise, it is possible to prove the existence of a certain two-way correspondence between groupoids and equivalence relations: see (Guay & Hepburn, 2009) and (Weinstein, 1996) for more details.

Meant as a generalization of equivalence relations between parts of an object, groupoids open the door to local symmetries. The group, instead, can only represent global symmetries, that is to say it is unable to put into relation parts of those (whole) objects which are involved in the group transformations. Groupoids will be those unifying formal structures which will comprise either local and global symmetries, both from physical and mathematical standpoint (Weinstein, 1996). Thus, since we stress the fact that equivalence relations, according to Matte Blanco, characterize the structural unconscious, it is immediately realized that groupoids are the most suitable elementary formal structures to try to give a minimal theoretical framework of this psychoanalytic construct.

Finally, we consider ordered groupoids, that is to say groupoids equipped with a compatible partial order relation. Following for example (Lawson, 2005), it is possible to prove formally that every ordered groupoid is isomorphic to one constructed from a certain category acting in a suitable fashion upon a groupoid arising from an equivalence relation. To this end, Lawson considers the possible simplest groupoids, that is to say, those arising from equivalence relations and specifically named *combinatorial groupoids*. Then, going on, he formally constructs ordered groupoids from combinatorial ones plus some further data, namely a partial order in turn inferred from a partial preorder relation that, by quotienting, gives rise to a partial order. In turn, such a preorder relation may be induced by a suitable category action on the given combinatorial groupoid. Thus, to sum up, the essential steps of this formal construction, are as follows:

- A category C acts on a combinatorial groupoid H.
- It induces a preorder[11] $\prec$ on H whose associated equivalence relation is $\equiv$.
- The quotient structure $H/\equiv$ is a groupoid $J(C, H)$ on which the preorder induces an order.
- The groupoid $H/\equiv$ is ordered and every ordered groupoid is isomorphic to one constructed in this way.

This is the clear formal treatment given by Lawson, in which a final universality property is proved, namely, that every ordered groupoid is isomorphic to one of the form $J(C, H)$ for some action of a category C on a combinatorial groupoid H. Roughly, if the above action of C on H is of the general type[12] $(a, x) \to a \cdot x$ (e.g., it may provide some interpersonal relation), then we put $x \prec y$ in H if and only if there exists $a \in C$ such that $x = a \cdot y$, being then easy to prove that $\prec$ is a preorder; then, $x \equiv y$ if and only if $x \prec y$ and $y \prec x$, is an equivalence relation on H. Hence, an order on $H/\equiv$ is given by setting $[x] \leq [y]$ if and only if $x \prec y$, that is to say, if and only if there exists $a \in C$ such that $x = a \cdot y$, this last definition turning out to be well-posed. Finally, given $O(x) \doteq \{a \cdot x; a \in C\}$ the orbit of x under the given action of C on H, then it is easy to prove that $[x] < [y]$ if and only if $y \notin O(x)$, that is to say $O(x) \cap O(y) = \varnothing$, with a consequent violation, with respect to the given action, of the inversion symmetry $(x, y) \to (y, x)$, which is the simplest instance of a permutation symmetry breaking with respect to the diagonal.

Therefore, a strict order arises from a simple inversion symmetry breaking, which basically expresses an asymmetry condition as a simple outcome of the inequivalence of at least two different representations. Furthermore, following (Hermann 1968, Ch. 2), every transitive action of a group/groupoid structure G on a set M induces on it a *homogeneous space* structure. It is possible to prove that the study of homogeneous spaces can, in principle, be reduced to the study of coset spaces G/H when H is a sub-group of G, hence to the study of pairs (G, H) of the type group/groupoid-subgroup/subgroupoid, just the typical formal pair of algebraic structures involved in the above formulation of symmetry breaking phenomena. On the other hand, a strict ordering is, in a certain sense, a formal condition characterizing the asymmetry involved in every possible hierarchical structure which is a strictly ordered structure too. In conclusion, we can say that, in a certain sense, inversion symmetry breaking is a compatible mechanism that, for instance, via combinatorial groupoid or groupoid graph structure, is able to formalize the passage from (Matte Blanco) symmetry (essentially represented by an equivalence relation) to (Matte Blanco) asymmetry (essentially represented by a strict order relation[13]).

As has been said above, a groupoid structure is naturally associated with every equivalence relation, where reflexivity is not necessarily required. Now, the properties of an equivalence relation approximately correspond, by means of a kind of cryptomorphism theorem, to Matte Blanco's generalization[14] and symmetry principles, whereas a preorder is simply a reflexive and transitive binary relation. An order [strict order] is an antisymmetric preorder that differs from an equivalence relation simply replacing the symmetry condition with an antisymmetric [asymmetric] one. Thus, with a breaking of inversion symmetry, we obtain an asymmetric relation. Therefore, via groupoid graph or combinatorial groupoids, it is possible to go from an equivalence relation to an order one, basically through a suitable inversion symmetry breaking.

4.2.3.2. On the Formal Structure of Kinship, on Gregory Bateson Double Bind, and All That

Following (White & Jorion, 1996), it was André Weil and Robert R. Bush to give, starting from *Murngin* system, a first attempt to formalize kinship by means of permutation group structures, exposed in a very interesting appendix to chapter XIV of the celebrated Claude Lévi-Stauss 1949 work *Les Structures Élémentaires de la Parenté*; see also (Kemeny et al., 1974). While the empirical cultural content remains to be filled in, the problem of formal representation of kinship is concerned with the relations or orderings between culturally given unions such as reproductive or other types of matings, not the cultural characteristics of the unions themselves. In graph theoretic terms, vertices and their labels, even while associated, are distinct. Therefore, ordered structures are at the early bases of every further attempt to formalize kinship.

After this work of Weil and Bush, other formalizing attempts were attained by other scholars, mainly using graphs and other ordered structures. But, having seen that groupoids are at the basis of all these just mentioned structures and having seen too that not all binary relationships are allowed in any possible kinship structure theory, it seems quite natural to think groupoids (like combinatorial groupoids or groupoid graphs) as the most suitable structures to formalize kinship and, in general, interpersonal relationships, just due to partiality of its binary operation. In any case, every possible formal structure used so far to formalize kinship, is an a priori given ordered structure which may be thought as a formal framework of a social structure as it really appears, without giving any hint on the possible early origins of it, that is to say, how and whence it came about.

On the other hand, according to (Lerner 1961, Model 2), thanks to the Weil and Bush work, the matrimonial rules of primitive societies are aimed to hinder the marriage between close kin even in the case in which the involved individuals weren't aware of being in a kin relationship; this was possible because there exist primitive[15] societies where familiar links are liable to be quickly forgotten. This means that implicitly (or unconsciously) they follow just these group rules, so that it is allowed to consider group/groupoid structures as tools suitable to formalize such questions, in a very precise manner. Not all marriage types are allowed, the marriages between brother and sister turning out to be automatically hindered, so that it is as if Oedipal rules unconsciously acted to shape kinship[16].

This is a notable fact because it is very amazing to see how a primitive society, through trial and error, has been able to perform formal structures of a certain complexity, like the group ones. Then, since psychology (see (Atkinson et al., 1996)) and social anthropology (see (Lévi-Strauss, 1975)) are nowadays even more oriented to consider a familial nucleus as the primary structural key of society as well as the natural environment that much more influences the psychological growth of an individual, in agreement with this, we would want to put forward the hypothesis that the familial triadic structure is the key component which lies at the early basis of any possible further social formal structure in agreement with what Lévi-Strauss himself states in (Lévi-Strauss, 1975). Therefore, we want to focus on the family structure, believing that it is just its deep triadic structure that mostly contributes to the individual's basic psychological formation.

Now, according to Matte Blanco, the main feature of consciousness is just the passage from the symmetric logic to the asymmetric one, so that it is of extreme importance to shed light on this crucial step. The minimal cardinality of a non-trivial ordered groupoid is three for two chief reasons: first, to warrant a non-trivial transitive property, second because of the fashion with which an ordered groupoid is obtainable, that is to say by means of non-trivial action of a non-trivial category with at least two elements, on a non-trivial combinatorial groupoid with at least two elements. Now, in the 1950s, Gregory Bateson, Don D. Jackson, John Weakland and Jay Haley gave a possible (interpersonal) interpretation of schizophrenia based on the so-called *double bind* (see (Bateson 1972, Part III)), in which the familiar nucleus plays a fundamental role. Let us briefly discuss it.

Bateson, likewise Matte Blanco, knew Bertand Russell and Alfred Norton Whitehead *type theory*, the first one that enabled to identify different levels of abstraction, pointing out the criticalities and potentialities of two crucial axioms of formal set theory, the *axiom of specification* and the *axiom of extensionality*, which allow to clearly distinguish between element, set and class, starting from the well-known Cantor *naïve set theory*. So, the way towards metamathematics had been opened. Taking into account this theory, as well as previous notable studies made by Rudolf Carnap, Ludwig Wittgenstein,

Frieda Fromm-Reichmann and Benjamin Lee Whorf, first Bateson considered the possibility of the existence of many abstraction levels in human communication, with the logical distinction between different *types*[17]. For instance, in schizophrenia, there is often a confusion between literal and metaphoric levels of either her or his own and other messages (inability to metacommunicate).

He also argues on the lack of the main formal properties characterizing an equivalence relation, that is to say reflexivity, symmetry and transitivity, which are almost totally disregarded by primary process[18]. There, indistinguishable are everyone from someone and no-one, as well as the whole from the part, which are features of conscious processes. Then, Bateson and his collaborators point out the chief fact that a schizophrenic is mainly unable to contextualize (to realize *metacommunicative frameworks*, according to Bateson), that is to say, he or she has serious problems in semantics and pragmatics tasks[19], as well as in discriminating the various logical types. Bateson and co-workers[20] bring this back to the presence of a double bind. The double bind will be retaken by the *Palo Alto school* of Paul Watzlawick on pragmatic communication (see (Watzlawick et al., 1967)).

The notion of *double bind* is quite original, and refers to the presence of a double and logically ambiguous link between mother and daughter/son which moulds two-way interpersonal relations centred around an emotively ambiguous and, at the same time, logically contradictory communication between mother and daughter/son, and that will engrave, in a negative manner, upon the next emotive states and logical abilities of the girl or boy, hindering the capacity to distinguish the logical status of the thoughts, if the paternal figure does not act as an intermediary[21], a kind of "breaker" coherently with what will be said later. Indeed, it is as if such a paternal figure acted by breaking the inversion symmetry between mother and daughter/son, re-establishing the right hierarchical position within the familial nucleus. The paternal figure (or paternal caregiver) acts to make inequivalent at least those two primary representations given by maternal and paternal figures, as a kind of symmetry breaking, according to what has been said above.

The double bind plays a fundamental role in structuring the family[22]. Indeed, following (Jackson, 1954), from the clinical analysis of the triadic familial structure of six female patients, it turns out that in all these cases but a psychotic patient, the mother permitted a third person – like father – to be present between the double bind given by mother-daughter, acting as a sort of "role inverter": in fact, Jackson reports, for instance, that the father's closeness and overt interest in his daughter, was the reverse of the mother's in that it tended to decrease as the child grew older and, in some instance, was abruptly terminated at the menarche. These patients have been trained symbiotically to feed on triadic involvement. This is most apparent when they are interacting with only one person and must in fantasy involve a third as though they feel no "ego wholeness" without a collection of "part egos".

One price paid for this need to interact in two directions at the same time is a multifaceted inferiority feeling. For example, these women equate head and penis, hence intellect and maleness. The parental interaction constituted a *nidus* for the development of the girl's hysterical and phobic symptoms and acting out. Therefore, the paternal figure could be seen as *acting*[23] on the double bind to break the often dangerous inversion symmetry mother-daughter/son[24], distinguishing between, at least, two different realizations, so giving rise to an order relation; as regard symmetry of double bind, see (Watzlawick, 1967). On the other hand, psychoanalytic history (from Œdipal phase till to Lacan's theory[25]) has always stressed the primary and unavoidable role played by a paternal figure in breaking the dangerous symbiotic and aphasic reciprocity of child-mother. In agreement with Matte Blanco's bi-logic, *triadicity*, therefore, is a primary and essential structural element to have the primary presuppositions for a normal psychic development.

There exists literature on the relationships between Matte Blanco and Bateson. The above supposition concerning symmetry breaking made by the paternal figure is supported by the interesting work of Klaus Fink (1993) about the bi-logic perception of time. Fink reports a clinical case of a young man (John) who had not a really present paternal figure but a dominant, incorporating and prevaricating maternal figure who caused a spread of symmetrical thought which entailed, amongst other things, a distortion of time perception, with an impairment of time ordering. Only through the transference intervention of the psychoanalyst, it was possible to try to restore a stronger paternal role, so recovering the right time perception, hence stemming maternal symmetric thought drives. John gradually re-acquired his own sense of individuality and awareness, a right time perception, a normal balanced relationship between physical and psychological time[26], all elements, these, which gave rise to a right phenomenological psychology relationship between *here-and-now* and *there-and-then*, roughly between psychic (or internal) and external reality.

On the other hand, also Bateson and co-workers had already pointed out about the possibility to implicitly change rules only under transference setting[27]. Therefore, according to Fink, a correct reality-testing just consists in putting (also by means of transference intervention) the right relationships between symmetrical and asymmetrical thinking. Again according to Fink, the resolution of psychic conflicts has been considered as a sort of *catastrophic point* (also in the René Thom sense) by W. Bion, as well as an *uncanny point* by Freud himself, to highlight the criticality of the turning-point element marking the equally crucial transition point from symmetrical to asymmetrical thought. Fink's considerations also justify our view of this passage as a kind of symmetry breaking development. On the other hand, Freud too considered time as one of the main features of the passage from primary to secondary process, related to delaying of desire's satisfiability.

Taking into account what has been said above, if one considers the passage from symmetric to asymmetric thought as due to a kind of inversion symmetry breaking, besides that as an overcoming of Bateson and co-workers double bind mother-daughter/son through father action, then it is possible to account for the rising of ordering, hence hierarchical structures. In particular, taking into account what has been said about Higgs mechanism, the SSB allows the transition from a *global* to a *local* symmetry with a generation of massive bosons (asymmetry), which might be interpreted as an unavoidable presence of symmetry interstices into the asymmetry, a thing quite analogous to the bi-modal presence of symmetric and asymmetric thought. Therefore, although a global symmetry has broken into local symmetries, these latter never utterly disappear (because symmetry breaking in any case involves non-trivial groups), consistent with Matte Blanco according to whom conscious thought may include only few asymmetrised pieces of symmetry.

On the other hand – see for instance (Wetterich, 2005) and (Ellis et al., 1992) – at the early origins of space and time and their difference, there could be basically symmetry breaking phenomena. The unavoidable presence of symmetry interstices into the asymmetry might also be put into comparison with the so-called *paraconsistent logics* in which not all contradictions (due to symmetric thought) of a formal system have serious implications or relevance for the whole system; these contradictions may be relegated into neighbourhoods, or circumscribed regions, in such a way that they cannot influence the coherence of the system, without having trivializations of it. Thus, also in logic, with this last type of confinement operations, it is possible, as the saying goes, to conceive a kind of contemporaneous presence of symmetric and asymmetric thought elements, coherently with Matte Blanco bi-logic. Finally, what has been said so far is also coherent with many points of the rich thought of Jean Piaget on the genesis of consciousness in children.

4.2.3.3. Other Formal Remarks

Following the work of Klaus Fink (1993), we have pointed out the primary role played by transference intervention in setting up the right *ratio* between symmetric and asymmetric thinking. Also Bateson and co-workers pointed out the great force exerted by transference to implicitly change interpersonal rules which are the symbolic transposition of the familiar ones. The two main dimensions which characterize the transference, where the essence of childish Oedipus complex is re-evoked, are the actualization of past experience and the displacement towards the paternal figure. The paternal imago, in general, is the one that has major load in the transference intervention; other imago, like the maternal one, may also be involved in transference setting. Therefore, following Bateson and co-workers, we agree with the assumption that the paternal figure plays a very fundamental role in establishing the right interpersonal relationships (according to Freud, symbolically moulded on the familial ones) and in overcoming the pernicious double bind.

In the previous subsections, we have tried to formalize, in an elementary fashion, the crucial passage from symmetric to asymmetric thinking, taking into account some elementary notions drawn from theoretical physics, and certain basic structures drawn from algebra. In particular, we have considered some groupoid structures which are offered to formalize certain notable aspects of Matte Blanco's bi-logic. Now, recent research on computational psychoanalysis made by Lauro-Grotto (2008) and Murtagh (2012) about structure of the semantic field, have realized that the main aspects of the unconscious realm, via Matte Blanco bi-logic, can be formalized by means of ultrametric structure and that the passage from symmetric to asymmetric thinking might be put into analogical comparison with the formal passage from ultrametric to metric. But as early Khrennikov (1998, 2002, 2007), even before, had extended p-adic dynamical systems and analysis to mathematical modelling of mental space and psychoanalysis. To be precise, an ultrametric is a metric which satisfies a stronger triangular inequality, namely the following

$$d(x,y) \leq \max\left\{d(x,z), d(z,y)\right\}, \forall x, y, z .$$

Now, Lauro-Grotto (2008) claims that if one considers, following Matte Blanco, an ultrametric space model of unconscious, due to the intrinsic properties of such a type of formal space, there follows a notable restriction of semantic field because of the great number of clusters of concepts that become indistinguishable due to a loss of homogeneity in their inner structure, with a consequent loss of hierarchical ordering. Therefore, the Matte Blanco symmetric-asymmetric thinking duality could also be stigmatized by the formal duality ultrametric-metric. On the other hand, the inseparability of these last two notions, essentially given by the various isometric embedding theorems of ultrametric spaces into a Euclidean space (see (Murtagh, 2012) and references therein) could refer to the inseparability between symmetric and asymmetric thinking within the Matte Blanco framework. Finally, from this standpoint, Lauro-Grotto also claims the possible usefulness of the consideration of the *replica symmetry breaking* concept of spin glass theory, coherently with what has been said above about symmetry breaking phenomena. Moreover, the above considered groupoid structures might also be usefully and suitably implemented by these last metric structures to reach a most complete and general formal framework of computational psychoanalysis modelling the unconscious construct.

We conclude with a final but important remark. It could seem quite contradictory to use an order relation, like $\leq$, in defining a property that holds in the unconscious realm, such as the one expressed by the above ultrametric triangular inequality. Indeed, just in the unconscious realm, due to symmetry principle, it is unconceivable to think any order relation. But, again following Klaus Fink's work (see (Fink, 1993) and references therein), such an apparent contradiction may be easily clarified. In fact, as said above, in transference, it is possible to re-establish the right relationship between external and internal reality through the institution of the right correspondence between external and internal time perception.

This was possible just thanks to transference action that allowed the patient to make him aware how something *conceived* symmetrically[28] (unconscious disorder) must be *judged* asymmetrically[29] (usage of an order relation $\leq$ in the ultrametricity condition); there are no other ways to do this[30] because, having seen the nature itself of the unconscious, it couldn't be otherwise; according to Fink, this is ultimately what a reality-testing should consist of. On the other hand, the Matte Blanco epistemological program consists just in searching to explain unconscious phenomenology by means of rational thought. Therefore, in this only apparently contradictory sense, the Lauro-Grotto formal view must be understood, based on ultrametric spaces[31]. In any case, this last type of question would deserve further attention[32]. *En passant*, just for what has been said above about rule changing in transference, we would also want to put forward the hypothesis according to which the celebrated Kripke-Wittgenstein paradox, inasmuch as it is strictly involved in the critical question around the origins of rules, could receive a useful clarification from the psychoanalytic epistemology standpoint.

4.2.4. Further Remarks

In this first part of the section, we have mainly discussed, within the general context of the history of culture, the crucial passage from symmetric to asymmetric thinking within the Matte Blanco framework, trying to formalize it through some elementary formal algebraic structures, the groupoids, with respect to which critical comparisons between equivalence and order binary relations have been made possible. Some simple formal considerations have been then put forward, also taking into account some elementary basic notions drawn from theoretical physics. But the landmark point which we wish to highlight in this section is how order (asymmetry) springs out of that utterly disordered and chaotic realm that is the unconscious. This has been summarized masterfully by the following beautiful Greek maxim due to Anaxagoras of Clazomenæ[33]

«*In the beginning, all the things were together;*

then, it came the mind (ὁ νοῦζ), and set them in order».

Hence, once again, is a great appreciation for the foresight of classical wisdom. Now, in the following subsections, we carry on with other psychoanalytic considerations and further formal attempts which also confirm what has been said above or are linked with them.

4.2.5. Brief Outlines of the Giampaolo Sasso's Model

The recent work achieved by Giampaolo Sasso, and exposed in (Sasso, 1999; 2005; 2011), has been centred on the critical relationships between neurosciences and psychoanalytic theories, taking into account the outcomes of the latest *Infant Research*. From it, as well as following what has already been very briefly outlined above (and published in (Iurato, 2014)), some further brief discussions and suggestions concerning possible formalization attempts of certain main aspects of the Freudian psychoanalytic framework may be usefully worked out. In the meanwhile, throughout the subsection, clear and continuous recalls of Husserlian phenomenology and its historical roots are easily identifiable, until we reach a sort of phenomenological psychoanalysis[34].

4.2.5.1. A Brief Sketch of the Model: First Elements and Basic Notions

From his experience as psychoanalyst and psychotherapist, Sasso has cast the first bases for a new unitary framework of the object relationships in (Sasso, 1999), trying to take into the right account the recent developments achieved by neurosciences. Following (Sasso 1999, Introduction), the functionality of the brain is mainly due to the dynamical action of a set of certain non-localized *mobile functions*, variously dislocated around all the general network of the nervous system which enact different perceptive-sensorial zones of it through *cerebral maps*, whose globally unitary dynamicity is the chief characteristic of the mind that, thanks to the running of distinct cerebral zones, allows to analyse different properties of an intentioned *object*.

These functions basically represent flows of information, along neural lines, given by the known psychic *introjective* and *projective* mechanisms. These latter neural pathways are called *s-o lines* (or *s-o pairs*) and locally connect two elements, namely an element s, representing a mind element approximately located in the frontal, motor and premotor areas, and an element o, codifying a somatic-sensorial or a perceptive property of the object. Thus, neurophysiologically, a *s-o* line is a motor-perceptive path which connects a motor element s, aimed to reach the subject functions, with a perceptive element o, devoted to attain object functions. Along the human ontophylogenetic evolution, a very great amount of *s-o* lines arises, also with the support of the *neural redundancy* which neurobiologically characterizes the ontogenetic evolution of the human brain.

The s elements (where s stands for subject), at first, explicate simple control and motor functions upon the perceptive o elements (where o stands for object), hence they locally couple for giving rise to a *s-o* pair, that is to say to an *object relationship*, which will move along *s-o* lines. This simple dynamics is the essence of the mobility feature of the mind, roughly carried out by the dislocation ensuing from the double mobility given by both s and o elements that locally reconnect to produce *s-o* pairs which accomplish the basic role to locally represent, according to a general *vicariance principle*, a distal or global process just by means of multiple and structural integration process of various primary *s-o* lines. This last principle, which allows a flexible functional dislocation or mobility, formalizes the well-known Freudian processes of displacement and condensation (see (Sasso 1999, Ch. 2, Sect. 2.4)).

Therefore, an object representation, within this model, is mainly based on a structural assemblage of primary *s-o* lines, each of which establishes an inseparable constraint between the representational structure of the o elements and the subject function of the s elements. The system of the *s-o* relations is already present since the prenatal phase and its potential strength to structurally organize is meaningful in regard to the *intentionality* of the child to early establish object relationships. The structuring of this rich system of relations through suitable reorganization and reconnection of its elements, is not an easy task that will be at the basis of the general psychic development. In doing this, the mother will play a truly fundamental role, since she is the first and closest human figure who the child approaches, hence the first object. Such an interaction takes place, by resonance[35], between an autonomous projective-introjective (*P-I*) endogenous dynamics, connate with the child and continuously turned on by the reticular formation, and the action of the mother who alternatively stimulates the functional properties of the s element and of the elements o, contributing to their reconnection into the s-o lines.

The neural information so stimulated, goes through the s-o lines in either directions $s{\rightarrow}o$ (roughly comparable with a *bottom-up* process) and $s{\leftarrow}o$ (roughly comparable with a *top-down* process) forming a net with capacity of rapid reconnection. Therefore, a s-o line should be more properly written as follows[36] $s \rightleftarrows o$ since it is the superposition of two unidirectional flows, namely $s{\rightarrow}o$ and $s{\leftarrow}o$, each of which provides a *proto-object relationship*. The flow $s{\leftarrow}o$ integrates, into the perceptive element o, the information coming from environment, and its codification as internal information is the basis of the introjective processes. The flow $s{\rightarrow}o$, instead, sprung out of the internal information already codified into the motor element s, and is aimed at anticipating and completing the external information, underlying a projective process.

The continuous construction of the s-o line network, which constitutes the basis of the P-I endogenous dynamics[37], at first starts from the stimulation of the own reticular formation of the cerebral trunk through the combinatorial action of basic elementary functions ψ (d'après Freud) which provide ancestral innate abilities of reconnection of the elements s and o, so giving rise to the first nuclei of the *Self* that will relate with objects. The mother is at first support for the set of elements o of the child's net, then she contributes to the various identificatory meanings to be assigned to the information conveyed by the s-o lines through the directions $s{\rightarrow}o$ and $s{\leftarrow}o$, through an integrative modulation and coordination by maternal introjective information (Im).

From a functional viewpoint, a link of the type $s{\leftarrow}o$ assigns an object property o to the subjective element s, so giving rise to an identificatory constraint of *introjective* type (I); instead, a link of the type $s{\rightarrow}o$ entails that a subjective function s is assigned to an object property o, so giving rise to an identificatory constraint of *projective* type (P). When these latter pathways undertake a preferential role, they provide stable introjective and projective properties. If the information given by maternal object (Im) is massively present, then introjective proto-object influences of the type $s{\leftarrow}o$ prevail, whereas, if Im lacks, then projective proto-object developments of the type $s{\rightarrow}o$ prevail.

The maternal introjective information Im greatly influences, above all through the procedural memory structures, the growing up of the representational network given by the articulating bundle of the s-o lines, through a continuous re-organization of the endogenous and exogenous flows involved in the first autonomous P-I endogenous dynamics, and that constitute the proto-object relationships from which derives the Freudian drive structure and that will take object nature just by means of the action of Im, so giving rise to the Freudian object relationship structure. The crucial point is the right interplay between the constructive endogenous P-I dynamics and the exogenous object maternal influence Im, the former having to projectively regulate, at the primary proto-object level, the introjective modulation by the latter, to give rise to advanced object relationships. The above mentioned basic interaction $(P$-$I) - Im$, will be re-enacted and restored, in the right terms, during the crucial transferral-countertransferral relation involved in a psychoanalytic setting, which operates through linguistic nets.

4.2.5.2. A Brief Sketch of the Model: Further Developments

In (Sasso, 2011), the author retakes what was covered in his previous works (Sasso, 1999; 2005) to try to clarify a possible origin of consciousness[38]. Sasso again stresses the primary role played by the child's personal P-I endogenous oscillatory dynamics $s \rightleftarrows o$ which will drive the fundamental psychoanalytic identificatory development by means of the building of the representational system of the child which, in turn, will be greatly ruled and moulded, again through a periodic oscillatory dynamical mechanism, by the available introjective *Im* influences of the mother whose unconscious representations, already quite well-rooted in her, will converge into the incoming consciousness of the child just thanks to this endogenous dynamics with which the child naturally interacts and to whom is phylogenetically predisposed.

So, the psychic development of the child begins at once with the institution of the identificatory relations from her or his early stages, the mother greatly influencing this frail process with her own consciousness states[39]. The primary psychic development is centred upon procedural (or implicit, hence unconscious) memories, which remain inaccessible to the next accrual of the declarative (or explicit) memories, hence with denied access to the psychoanalytic exploration that just makes use of declarative memory functions only. This implies a basic distinction between two chief types of repression mechanisms, namely a deeper *non-removed primary repression* (correlated with a *dynamical unconscious*) and a *removed repression* (correlated with a *removed unconscious*), a distinction, this, already sketched but left incomplete by Freud himself, which, instead, can now be quite well clarified and formalized within the Sasso's model.

Into the s-o line network, one should distinguish a particular subset of it, namely the one formed by those lines of the type s_i-o_i characterizing the internal psychic states related to the *representational* (or *perceptive*) *internal objects* o_i. The formation of the latter is needed for giving a wider and even more articulated reticular formation by means of a continuous going inwards and onwards along the initial line s-o, due to the intermediary presence of an internal object, say o_1, inside it, that is s-o_1-o, with the formation of another level line, s-o_1, but in a higher level than that of s-o, which, in turn, will require another element s, say s_1, to settle the new higher level line s_1-o_1, and so forth. This is the typical iterative process with which the s-o line system grows up and develops, the appearance of the various intermediary internal elements o_i depending on the sensorial stimulation or excitation, whilst the consequent production of the elements s_i, needs to maintain the related stability of the system, and greatly depends on the *Im* action.

In such a fashion, the basic reticular formation evolves, with even more complexification of its structure, from its lowest bases, placed into the most ancient cerebral structures, through the sub-cortical and limbic structures toward the high cortical ones. The various elements o will concentrate into the posterior perceptive-sensorial cerebral zones to give rise to the *object function*, whilst the consequent control elements s will converge into the anterior control cerebral zones to give rise to the *subject function*, and to control the former ones.

Initially, the various internal representational elements o_i are distributed amongst many different cerebral zones, just this variegation standing at the basis of the human capability to identify and to represent the various distinct properties of an external object o whose phenomenological individuation is therefore characterized by the series of such representational objects $o_1, o_2, ..., o_i, ...$ which are the codified perceptive information originated (or is the trace left) by o, hence from the external environment. But the control of these internal objects must be ruled by the representational system given by the (frontal) elements s, so that, for instance, when an external object o, which had already given rise to a perceptive internal object, say o_i, tries to recover the initial line s-o to be re-evoked, now it first meets o_i along this pathway, but the new intermediary line $o_i \leftarrow o$ is a non-phenomenological elaboration since it does not provide any phenomenological consciousness content due to the absence of any s element.

To this end, therefore, a new element s is needed to restore a consciousness constraint of the type s-o, so giving rise to a phenomenological consciousness content or intentional act through the following new elaboration $s_i \leftarrow (o_i \leftarrow o)$. Often, the external information is firstly worked out by those many cerebral zones devoted to the codification of the various possible perceptive elements o_i, amongst which, nevertheless, homologous bonds of the type o-o are possible, which however remain unconscious because their elaboration takes place mainly into procedural memories. But little by little such homologous links arise, they stimulate the representational system of the elements s (which, in any case, starts from albeit minimal innate equipment of unitary representational patterns), choosing one of its elements, say s_i, that will control and regulate the sensory-motor-perceptive element[40] o_i through a one-way re-entering projective line $s_i \rightarrow o_i$ (providing a *representational access*[41], with which the sensorial-perceptive flows enter into the brain) codifying the information of o_i by means of the internal restoring of the one-way introjective line $s_i \leftarrow o_i$ (providing a *representational restoring*, with which the frontal zones of the brain drive and control the sensorial-perceptive information), just promoted by $s_i \rightarrow o_i$, which reproduces, although in a less sensitive fashion with respect to the original or initial way[42] $s \leftarrow o$, the environmental information and that is needed for a sufficiently normal psychic development to prevent a projective excess of investment not adequately counterbalanced by introjective responses; hence, once such an introjective re-entries $s_i \leftarrow o_i$ assumes a stable asset, then o_i institutes a constraint on the frontal zone that therefore acquires a property of the object o, codified by the set of internal objects o_i, so determining an introjective effect. The mother action always operates through introjective lines of the type $s_i \leftarrow o_i$, so that her influence superposes with the other introjections.

In any way, the elements involved in any line $s \rightleftarrows o$ are inseparable from each other, and this serves to highlight the indissoluble intertwining between the object's properties o and the subject's intentions s, this unitary coupling giving rise to an irreducible and primitive elementary nucleus of consciousness, i.e. a *qualia*. The indivisibility of the constraint $s \rightleftarrows o$, allows to introduce the fundamental property of *binding* of the phenomenological constraint s-o, which comprises different functionalities, like the *conjunction binding* of projection's signals coming from distinct cerebral zones and the *dynamical binding* of synchronous signals activated in the same zone or in the bordering one; furthermore, a distinction between *spatial* and *temporal binding* is considered as well.

A chief theoretical problem of the binding is the possible synchronization of oscillatory responses with regard to spatially separated regions of the cerebral cortex, issue which requires the presupposition of a stimulating intrinsic cerebral dynamical switchboard to build up the oscillatory fibre of the $s \rightleftarrows o$ lines, and upon which the bending relies. From what has been just said above, we may state a general principle[43] of the *joined elaboration* concerning the two main elements s and o of any primary phenomenological constraining line $s \rightleftarrows o$, according to which any phenomenological consciousness content exclusively springs out from the joined elaboration of an element o with an element s. Nevertheless, as we have seen above, there may exist as well links between homologous elements, for instance of the type o-o or s-s, but without giving a consciousness phenomenological content.

Therefore, together the formation of the representational internal objects o_i, a related set of representational elements s_i is also available little by little that representational accesses $s_i \leftarrow o_i$ arise, where each element s_i is into correspondence with the original (frontal) representational element s through a non-phenomenological homologous (frontal) bond of the type s-s, that is to say $s_i \rightarrow s$, recalling that s_i and o_i are memory stored elements[44]. Thereafter, once that a frontal element s_i is primed, an attempt at restoring the original frontal representation s takes place, this being possible, due to the above principle of the joined elaboration, only re-evoking the corresponding perceptive object o, hence one of its partial internal objects o_i, so restoring a phenomenological constraint of the type s-o, to be precise s_i-o_i, until up the completion of this process with the frontal non-phenomenological elaboration $s_i \leftarrow s$ in such a manner as to have a phenomenological perceptive elaboration of the type $(s_i \leftarrow s) \leftarrow (o_i \leftarrow o)$; and all this, of course, requires a non-zero temporal interval to be realized, in this case being a fundamental prerequisite to ascertain what type of time notion we are using (see, besides to what has been said above, (Iurato et al., 2016) for further brief mentions about physical and psychic time distinction[45]). Thus, to summarize, the original perceptive object o will be re-evoked by means of a series of partial internal objects o_i each of which, in turn, pushing on the original representation s of the original perceptive object o, gives rise to a series of (frontal) representational elements s_i such that a relation of the type $s_i \leftarrow s$ holds, each of these last homologous bonds not having any phenomenological content if it is considered without to the homologous bond $o_i \leftarrow o$.

Notwithstanding that they are void of any consciousness content, both the above mentioned frontal homologous elaborations $s_i \rightarrow s$ and $s_i \leftarrow s$ play a very fundamental role for the human psychic development. Indeed, as a main characteristic, they may run either with partial consciousness states or even with absence of phenomenological consciousness, that is to say, in an unconsciously manner. Therefore, it is clear too what fundamental role they may play for understanding the possible mechanisms with which unconscious does work. Thus, the elaboration of elements of the type s, notwithstanding takes place for a main object-environmental control purpose, may be phenomenological present either in a partial manner or even wholly absent. Furthermore, ideal, intuitive, attentive, self-reflexive and early states of consciousness may be brought back to the action of the homologous bonds of the type s-s with respect to the set of representational objects o, the former undergoing certain basic *hierarchical ordering* operations producing meaning[46], coming from the personal live experience and from the related live environment[47], which will allow to structurally build up the representational system of the s-o constraints, having the primary property to identify unitary patterns. This latter ordering processes will play a very fundamental role for human consciousness, because them are also related with the possible orders coming from the dynamics and topology of the cerebral maps.

4.2.5.3. A Brief Sketch of the Model: Advanced Notions

The above mentioned system of double representations s-s and o-o, is able to explain as well what the main distinction between a primary non-removed unconscious and a secondary removed unconscious consist of. The former mainly concerns deregulations of the representational system of the frontal lines s-s, with damages, in general due to a basic lacking of an adequately and enough maternal interaction child-mother in forming homologous bonds between elements s_i and s, hence with a basic impossibility to have phenomenological contents provided by relations of the type $(s_i \leftarrow s) \leftarrow (o_i \leftarrow o)$, in this case, generally writing $s \xrightarrow{\ not\ }$ to denote the simple fact that there exist persistent and consistent inhibitory representational frontal elements s hindering hierarchical orderings into the s-s system with gaps in the abstract representational *mental states* s_i-s. The latter, instead, mainly relies on the inability to establish stable s-o phenomenological relationships due to the fact that frontal elements s, with the occurrence of suitable re-entering mental processes s-s, hinder the reaching of sensor-perceptive occipital-parietal objects o_i, so not allowing the formation of a consciousness content; in this case, we simply write $s \xrightarrow{\ not\ } \hat{o}$ to mean the general fact that the representational frontal element s hinders the approaching of consciousness by the perceptive element $\hat{o}$.

Now, after having outlined the fundamental role played by the endogenous dynamics s-o (with its functional correlate in the *P-I* dynamics) in resonant periodic interaction with the mother, we can consider the next two main stages of the psychic development of the child, that is to say, the basic *identificatory system* and the next *mentalization*[48] process. The latter has mainly due to the structuration of the *s-s* line system, whereas the former requires something more. Indeed, along the primary psychodynamic development of the child, roughly codified by the well-known oral-anal-genital sequence, we observe here a convergence of identificatory traits due to both familial figures (i.e., mother and father), at first that of the mother then the one of the father, so giving rise to all that complex series of *identificatory constellations* but which, in general, turns out to be quite unstable.

According to E.Z. Tronick, the first consciousness states are the outcome of the running of an *asymmetric*[49] *dyadic system* centred on the early interrelation between the child and the mother, from which starts a *dyadic expansion* of consciousness states which spring out from a projective-introjective (*P-I*) oscillatory dynamics, having a basic periodic recursive character[50], through which a remarkable transfer of consciousness states may take place, from mother to child, just thanks to an innate *intentional need* by the child due to the childhood attachment models. Therefore, the child intentionality is inherent with the *P-I* endogenous dynamics, directly oriented to maintain and to control the object relation, gradually engaging either the primary and secondary associative nets involving the elements *s*. With different action and running in dependence on the involved cerebral lobe, the introjective *I* and projective *P* oscillatory flows revolve around the elements o_i upon which engrave with a dynamics of the general type $P \rightarrow o_i \leftarrow I$, where the introjective flows *I*, in normality conditions, excite bodily or somatic zones[51] in such a manner that is locally regulated and counterbalanced (as a kind of a restraining 'protective shield') by the re-entering projective flows *P*, so giving rise to a Freudian energetic cathexis which 'engrave' the stimulation (or excitement) into a certain element of the psychic apparatus, so giving rise, in turn, to that rich and variegated frontal representational grid of human mind given by the elements *s*. Steady imbalances of such a two-flow dynamics give rise to pathological psychic illnesses. On the other hand, the above mentioned asymmetric aspect of the basic intentional function involved in the crucial dyadic system mother-child discussed above, gives rise to a kind of implicit hierarchical structure into the consciousness dyadic state. Furthermore, all the discussions above, should be made for both the right and left cerebral lobes, for instance making use of a double sign ± to appoint one of these to the *s* and *o* elements, with related homologous and heterogeneous combination lines, for distinguishing these two zones.

A very important issue concerns the *topology* of an object relationship. The repression should not be understood as a kind of *area transfer* from one psychic place to another one but rather as a non-topological *local dynamical change* of the cathexis itself in such a manner it may be under the action of different psychic agencies. According to the Sasso's model, this may be explained as the *access* of an element *s* upon an element *o* through a *s-o* lines that modify its *local elaboration*. Therefore, the Freudian unconscious should not be meant as a set of topic agencies but rather as dynamically characterized by a continuous distribution of the various accesses *s-o*. Just in this regard, we may say that dynamical system theory might provide useful insights about this last dynamics. Indeed, if one takes into consideration the main fact that compulsion to repeat mechanism is a typical feature of unconscious, which goes beyond pleasure principle and is closely linked to death drive (Laplanche & Pontalis, 1967; Petrini et al., 2013); this is an automatic, incoercible mechanism independent from typical conflictual-dynamical processes of human psyche between pleasure and reality principle, but rather this mechanism of automatic repetition seems to be the place of the perennial conflict between life and death; it is the result of a primary, basic lacking of symbolization of traumatic experiences (hence, not elaborated enough) which therefore push to re-emerge as such. From the analysis of transference outcomes, Freud understands that repetition is an attempt to counterbalance the infantile amnesia, that is, the impossibility to reach, by means of memory (hence, individually), the deepest unconscious zones, i.e., what is ever unreachable, of non-symbolized pre-subjective experiences, mnestic traces not suitably represented or symbolized, stored definitively at a unchangeable pre-representational status (Balsamo, 2009). In this sense, it should be meant the deepest unconscious nucleus as a strong attractor, placed into the unconscious realm.

Now, we may hypothesize that, for instance, the breaking of these periodical cycles, linked to this process of compulsion to repeat, may give rise to a series of conscious phenomena, like the rising of temporal phenomena[52] as well as the binding of psychic energy along the passage from primary to secondary process. This last is in agreement with the fact that, reality principle instances occur when there are threatens to survival of the individual, so compulsions to repeat appear in defence of self-preservation of the individual, bounding or holding pleasure principle (turned to an immediate and unconditioned satisfaction, which often undermine life), so taming impulsive drives with the coming of reality principle. In a few words, bound psychic energy, typical of secondary process, may arise from the holding action due to compulsion to repeat mechanism operating on the free psychic energy available in the unconscious and ruled by pleasure principle[53].

On the other hand, already Freud himself, in his work *The Unconscious* (of 1915), had to do with similar issues, just in considering the question whether the repression is characterized by *topical* displacement and condensation mechanisms (*topical hypothesis*) or rather it is characterized by a kind of *local state* or *phase transition* which takes place in the same locality, regarding the same material (*functional hypothesis*). Initially, Freud chose the first hypothesis, but next he decided upon the second one, considering as a basic repression mechanism, the one consisting in a sort of *cathexis subtraction* of either the unconscious mnestic *vestiges* or conscious mnestic traces, hence as a local state change of the cathexis: in other words, a certain subtraction of energy weakens the cathexis itself, with a consequent changing or transformation of it. Nevertheless, thought within Sasso *s-o* model, these two Freudian hypotheses are not in contradiction with each other, because both should be seen as mainly due to changes of networks, in which either the object cathexis and countercathexis differently acts, distributing itself amongst the primary and the secondary nets; in turn, a different situation takes place in dependence on the cerebral lobe under consideration. Therefore, this multiplicity of phase (or state) changes, differently distributed amongst many distinct cerebral levels, basically characterizes the crucial link unconscious-conscious within the *s-o* model.

The very early interactions of the child with the mother and the related environment, essentially take place for innate physiological reasons, whilst the fundamental *identificatory development* takes place only later, thanks to a disaggregative condition of the previous stages of the child psychic development (mainly ruled by the mother action) which entails an *instability of identity* that will promote and will drive all the next psychic development comprising four main sequential steps: the first one given by the primary child-mother tuning in; the second one given by the identificatory development (studied by psychoanalysis); the third one converging into the various attachment models, and fourth and last one given by the mentalization process, which takes place when the primary cerebral net starts to differentiate into other higher levels. This last process provides distinct secondary networks, from the primary one which was mainly ruled by the primary relation maternal object, departing from this with the acceptance of new object relationships extending the initial introjective-projective dynamics of the *dual* type to the more complex one having of *group* type, with the occurrence of a paternal figure.

This incoming group development, even due to the above mentioned dynamical instability, naturally characterizes that multiple dynamics of the cerebral mind, ever undergoing to continuous transformations and re-organization procedures all featured by hierarchy-producing associative-dissociative coordination processes, providing a differentiated set of various object relationships. The associative character regards the convergence integration of the primary cerebral net, moulded by the mother one and having a fundamental sensory-motor nature, during the initial basic child-mother interaction, whereas the dissociation feature has to do with the divergence proliferation of the secondary cerebral nets, which underlies any psychic splitting (like the *disavowal* mechanism) process[54], and that, therefore, has need of a re-organization for a basic psychic unity, although an essentially dissociated nature characterizes the psyche of every human being. In this latter step, the (mind-producing) mentalization will operate to coordinate the introjective-projective flows within the secondary cerebral net framework, in such a manner as to regulate the identitary nuclei which spring out from the primary net (having sensory-motor source) of the *dual* relation child-mother to the secondary nets due to the action of the *group* function upon the first dual nucleus.

Thus, as a crucial point of the mature psychic development, the so-called *Œdipus situation* arises, forcing the child to come out from the initial *dual* relationship with the mother, pushing the child to find her or his own identity. All this is quite similar to the symmetry breaking like phenomena, outlined in the first part of this section and mainly due to a paternal figure action, regarding the famous child-mother *double bind*, which includes many aspects and notions similar to either the optimal and pathogen mother influences provided by the primary child-mother *P-I* dynamical relation. Also belonging to this class of relations, characterized by symmetry breakdown like phenomena, might be considered the so-called Otto Rank's *double* (of 1914) and the related transformational function which gives rise to the *identificatory* function by means of the main passages from primary to secondary nets, with consequent intentionality diversifications.

In the Sasso *s-o* model, the psychoanalytic identificatory process, which implies a consciousness growing up, might be formalized as a *bundle of identificatory traits* each of which is the coordination of a finite sequence of elements[55] of the type $<s_i\text{-}s\text{-}o>_1, ..., <s_i\text{-}s\text{-}o>_n$, whose every element is formed by an *intentional nucleus* $s_i\text{-}s$ that acts upon an object o to give rise to a consciousness content $s_i\text{-}s\text{-}o$ on the basis of the reciprocal and perpetual child's comparative interrogation between what the mother has firstly implemented into her or him by primary interaction child-mother with the related environments, the above mentioned instability of this dual link leading to be opened to new identifications (corresponding to the passage from the primary to secondary cerebral nets). The various non-phenomenological identitary nuclei $<s_i\text{-}s>_j$ will be organized, by the mind, into the secondary cerebral nets according to a certain hierarchical order of them which starts from the original founding nucleus of the primary cerebral net to develop into the secondary ones.

Therefore, the mind is not the identity in itself but rather is the hierarchical ordering of the various intentional nuclei $<s_i\text{-}s>_i$ distributed amongst the primary and secondary cerebral nets; the consciousness, in turn, is not the mind but rather is the phenomenological representational contents $<s\text{-}o>$ from time to time available to the non-phenomenological nuclei $<s_i\text{-}s>_j$ which form the mind coordination. The main feature of this process is the fact that we really do not perceive the *pattern* but its unitary (Gestalt) *hierarchical categorical configuration* that emerges from the action of a non-decreasing *temporal function* (to account for the basic and unavoidable consciousness temporal dimension) that regulates and controls the integrative processes of the ever evolving multilevel cerebral networks mainly according to a combinatorial dynamics. Therefore, we again highlight the fact that the temporal dimension plays a very fundamental role for consciousness and its integration, as already pointed out in the first part of this section, giving a unitary and cohesive character to consciousness due to the primary founding nuclei of the *Self* (primary consciousness).

We once again stress the truly unavoidable fundamental hypothesis on the consciousness origin and structure, according to which it is centred on the constraints *s-o* meant as a founding *ontological unity* of the consciousness itself, through which a sensorial elaboration *o* is liable to be linked with a motor elaboration *s* (in this, a preeminent role being played by mirror neuron systems – see also (Lauro Grotto, 2014)) to give rise to an elementary consciousness content *s-o* (a *qualia*) whose dynamics is promoted and ruled through the primary interaction child-mother given by the *P-I* oscillatory dynamics $s \rightleftarrows o$ which is needed for the development and integration of the composite cerebral network. The consciousness then evolves trying to integrate and coordinate the manifold of the various constraints *s-o* along the parallel evolution of the manifold of the various cerebral networks whose instability is mainly due to the phylogenetic *neural redundancy* that pushes to produce high level cerebral networks (amongst which the one related to the language).

4.2.6. Toward Some First Formalization Attempts of the Sasso's Model via Category Theory, Differential Geometry, and Dynamical System

In the previous subsections, we have seen what fundamental role may play the sensory-motor *bundle* B_{s-o} of all the possible phenomenological constraints $s \rightleftarrows o$, each of which may be considered as a kind of algebraic maps[56] of the type $s \rightarrow o$ and $s \leftarrow o$, together its main properties, amongst which are the *locality* one and the *vicariance principle*. All that plays a crucial role in the dawning and in the development of the human psyche, through the interplay between the child *P-I* endogenous dynamics and the introjective maternal influence *Im*. Thus, we may surely state that the bundle B_{s-o} in the child is, above all, the outcome of the decisive two-way dynamical interaction of periodic oscillatory type $P - I \rightleftarrows \text{Im}$, respectively between the *P-I* endogenous dynamics – ruling the primary identificatory processes of the child – and the so-called *mother-child tuning in*, so that the following pair $P_c \doteq \left\{ B_{s-o}, P - I \rightleftarrows \text{Im} \right\}$, made by the bundle of functions B_{s-o} and by the oscillatory dynamical system $P - I \rightleftarrows \text{Im}$ structuring B_{s-o}, gives rise to a formal basis, say P_c, for the psychic development of the child. These latter simple claims, may imply, from a general history of science standpoint, some possible brief elementary formal remarks such as the following ones.

4.2.6.1. On Bundles, Logic, and Dynamical Systems

In mathematics and theoretical physics, a very notable role is played by the wide class of the so-called *fibred structures*, amongst which there are *bundles*, *fibre bundles* and *fibre spaces* (see (Husemoller, 1975) and (Souriau, 1964)), whose notions first arose out of questions posed in the 1930s about issues on the topology and geometry of manifolds, and whose first rigorous formulations date back to the 1950s. We shall refer to a very simpler basic notion, that of bundle of functions, from which some of the other ones may be built up. Following (Bruhat 1961, Sect. 1.1) (see also (Godement 1959, Sect. 3.1), (Quan 1969, Ch. I, Sect. II.3) and (Cabras et al., 1991)), given two abstract sets[57] X and Y, a *bundle* $B(X, Y)$ *of functions* from X to Y, is a class of sets of functions, say $F(U, Y)$, of the type $f : U \subseteq X \rightarrow Y$ for each $U \subseteq X$, such that, for every covering $\left\{ U_i \right\}_{i \in J}$ of U, we have $f \mid_{U_i} \in F(U_i, Y) \ \forall i \in J$, this last property expressing a *locality condition*. Moreover, following (Borceux, 1989), the basic idea underlying the notion of bundle is just that of *locality*, that is, the existence of elements locally defined and having enough properties of gluing and restriction.

But, what is important is the fact that a bundle defined between topological spaces, besides having local elements, has too a *local logic* through which one may establish the truth values of every local property by means of the construction of an appropriate *Heyting algebra* on it, recalling that every Boole algebra is a Heyting algebra as well. Therefore, if properly contextualized, it would not be fully out of place to consider what has just been said above referred to $\mathfrak{F}_{s-o}$, the fact that the consciousness is mainly the result of the integration, into unitary and temporal-hierarchically ordered patterns called *qualia* (or primitive *psychic qualities*), of the various emerging phenomenological outcomes at most unconsciously coming out from a multiple system of centres placed into different cerebral networks, together with the various *binding* and *hierarchical ordering* operations basically ruled by a primary temporal dimension, which might be suitably formalized within this context or framework.

Following (Thom 1980, Ch. VII, Sect. 7.3.A-C), within the general dynamical system framework (above all, catastrophe theory), between two dynamical systems presenting recurrence (like metabolic ones), resonances will always appear, the stability of the corresponding dynamical system resulting from the topological product of the two given systems depending on the ratio of the corresponding resonances. In particular, between two metabolic systems in a free interaction promoted by a weak perturbation with stochastic direction, an exchange of information always takes place. In general, the topological product of two dynamical systems put into free interaction between them (like two oscillators that enter into resonance), is structurally unstable and has a wide and variable range of possible resonances in competition amongst them, the related stability depending on the nature of the initial perturbation. In the topological product-system, each factor-system loses its individuality, converging into a new unstable and mixed dynamical system (*resonance system*) whose initial instability gradually goes towards a more stable regime through the reaching of a resonance state chose amongst the possible ones. By the way, we note that the mathematical framework suitable for the treatment of this last issue involves a fibration of the product topological space; finally, we also note that René Thom, in (Thom 1980, Ch. XIII, App. 1), provides a very interesting formal model of the a memory from a dynamical system point of view, which might have as many interesting applications from a computational psychoanalysis standpoint[58].

In (Thom 1985, Ch. X, Sect. 10.2), a lucky formal geometrical model, centred around the dynamical notion of resonance, is proposed to try to formalize the notion of *signification*. The *resonance* is one of the key notions of modern dynamical system theory and, from what has already been said above, it may be put at the basis of the first most elementary attempts to formalize communication transmission phenomena. On the other hand, already E.C. Zeeman, in his celebrated 1965 paper *Topology of the Brain*, considered the totality of our own cerebral activities as forming a topological dynamical system, amongst other things predicting and foreshadowed many results which would be later confirmed by the subsequent mirror neuron research. Later works of Zeeman[59] confirmed the usefulness of general topological dynamics in modelling the brain, whose chief dynamical feature seems just be that oscillatory nature of its phenomena (see (Zeeman, 1976a,b) and references therein). The above mentioned basic interaction between the *P-I* endogenous dynamics and the maternal introjective influence *Im*, might be laid out within the above sketchily described framework of the theory of dynamical systems, for instance formally identifying, in the activation promoted by the cerebral reticular formation of the cerebral trunk, the dynamical action of an *attractor*.

Obviously, the dynamical system approach to cognitive systems is by now well-stated but, following the brief lines outlined in this note, it might deserve interesting further perspectives on the computational psychoanalytic side. Furthermore, also in the early history of neural computation, after the pioneering works by J.J. Hopfield, several formal architectures were set up between the 1970s and the 1980s, considering some dynamical system notions and concepts, like that of resonance and self-organization: to be precise, the *adaptive resonance theory*, mainly developed by S. Grossberg and G. Carmeking, considers the hypothesis that the brain autonomously runs in such a manner as to organize it according to certain recognition codes, whilst T. Kohonen developed the idea according to which neurons self-organize themselves for variable adaptive purposes through the institution of *self-organizing maps*.

4.2.6.2. On Symmetry Breakdown, Generative Structures, and Other

On the other hand, modern differential geometry techniques have allowed to work out symmetry breaking formalism in the most general fashion through fibre bundle tools within gauge theory framework: in this regard, see (Bleecker 1981, Ch. 10, Sect. 10.3), (Percacci 1986, Ch. 4, Sect. 4.4) and (Derdzinski 1992, Ch. 11). Moreover, the real essence of symmetry breaking relies on functional analysis of operator spaces, like Hilbert spaces. Indeed, following (Strocchi, 1981, 1999) and references therein, roughly we may say that, from a formal viewpoint, the spontaneous symmetry breaking mechanism for infinite dimensional classical systems involves maps between Hilbert space sectors in relation to actions of certain related symmetry groups (e.g., the group of internal symmetries of a certain mathematical entity – like an equation – and the related stability group). All these formal considerations might be suitably reworked in relation to B_{s-o}, where a crucial point is the comparison between different representations of non-phenomenological intentional nuclei $<s_i\text{-}s>_i$ to give rise to phenomenological contents when we approach an object o.

On the other hand, in (Thom 1980, Ch.10, Sect. 10.3, Remark 10.3.11), the author stresses which formal analogies, similarities and common points may exist between symmetry breaking phenomena – via the Higgs mechanism – and catastrophe theory of dynamical systems, this last theory being the most suitably formal framework in which possibly to put P_c. Furthermore, in (Thom 1972, Sect. II.1), the author provides a very interesting discussion of the possible formal relationships existing between (macroscopic) broken symmetry phenomena and the resonance ones, bearing, as a main example, the case of two periodic linear oscillators in interaction between them whose structural instability may be overcome by means of a (macroscopic) symmetry breaking phenomenon with the consequent appearance of a resonance[60]. In conclusion, from these very simple remarks, we would want to put forward possible and plausible useful comparisons and transpositions between the symmetry breaking phenomena theory, as taking place within the general framework of dynamical systems (d'après the pioneering works of R. Thom, I. Prigogine, L. Von Bertalanffy, M.A. Brazier, and others), and the formal system P_c where some main features have been identified, amongst which are the fibre structure of its elements, the basically resonant oscillatory nature of its dynamics, some main topological aspects (amongst which the locality and the functional hypothesis of the object relationships) and the hierarchical ordering character provided by an innate temporal dimension.

The latter should be meant as a primitive psychic function rooted into the primary and most ancient structures of the *Self*, which regulates and controls all the running of P_c. The temporal dimension belongs to the set of *generative structures* which are considered, from a more properly structuralistic viewpoint, as those early, primitive (structural) archetypical bases of the human psyche upon which to build up the next psychic development of every human being. In fact, following Yuri I. Manin, as early as the human individual has taken consciousness of the own Ego in front of a world that changes, the notion of time has gradually undertaken even a more prominent role along the course of the history of culture. Since the primitive epoch, the human being has always had some method to measure time, usually by means of recurrent phenomena. The time originally makes its phenomenological appearance as a consciousness' flow characterized by the awareness both of the transiency of the present and of the content of the various thought entities. Furthermore, following too (Miller 1983, Ch. 1), since the known pioneering Piaget works on child psychic development, the psychological bases of mathematical thinking have been studied from a structuralistic point of view.

Precisely, certain primary biological mechanisms have been ascertained to be at the basis of certain elementary formal structures, called *generative structures* (so named after N. Bourbaki), from which all the other ones constructively follow according to a well-defined *architecture des mathématiques*. These generative structures are classified into three main classes, respectively containing the *algebraic*, the *topological* and the *ordered* structures. According to this view, the psychological bases for the ordered generative structures is the primitive idea of *time*, both discrete and continuous, while the topological generative structures have their psychological bases in the idea of *closeness* which, in turn, find their roots in the biological mechanisms of the organization of the perceptive space around a privileged centre, namely the human body. In concluding this brief note, we would want to further stress the following fact that, according to us, plays a very fundamental role in the psychic development of human psyche, namely, the truly founding and primary role played by the triadic familial structure in structuring and developing the human psyche of the child.

4.2.7. Final Remarks and Further Hints

Computational psychoanalysis officially is born with the works of the Special Session (A5) kindly hosted by the 13th IEEE ICCI*CC-2014 *International Conference on Cognitive Informatics & Cognitive Computing* held in London, UK, on August 18-20, 2014 (see the related Proceedings quoted in (Iurato, 2014)). As a truly new discipline, it started, on the basis of the previous primary work made by Ignacio Matte Blanco in working out a formal ground to the Freudian psychoanalysis, with the early basic works and contributions due to Andrei Khrennikov[61], Rosapia Lauro Grotto and Fionn Murtagh (in chronological order). As one of the main purposes, it basically tries to understand what are the primary formal structures and running mechanisms of the unconscious, with the ambitious aim to possibly implement them into the wide computer science framework. With respect to the work of the authors just mentioned above, we have however worked out, in this section, an independent, alternative framework in which to lay out some main concepts and notions of psychoanalysis. On the other hand, recent progress in cognitive informatics has also pointed out what primary role may be played by unconscious phenomena[62].

On the other hand, in this subsection (above all, in the first part), we have very briefly outlined, in passing, the possible use of certain elementary algebraic structures (like the groupoid ones) to formalize some basic notions and concepts of psychoanalysis. In pursuing this, we have spoken about some special binary relations, amongst which are order relations and partially defined binary relations involved in groupoid structures. Now, the latest results in cognitive informatics (see (Wang, 2008)) make use of new algebraic structures in which binary relations are involved, amongst which are the so-called *concept algebra* which puts into relation generic elements called *concepts*. Roughly, a *concept*, defined on an arbitrary set O, is an algebraic system of the type (O, A, R^c, R^i, R^o) where $O \subseteq P(O)$ (= power set of O), A is a non-empty set of attributes, R^c is a set of internal relations, R^i is a set of input relations, and R^o is a set of output relations. Concept algebras, furthermore, are closely related to lattice structures. Therefore, it is evident[63] what possible generalizations might be achieved when one implements, into a concept, partially defined binary relations as well as orderings. Concept algebra provides a rigorous mathematical model as well as a formal semantics for object-oriented class modelling and analyses.

Moreover, concept algebra provides a *denotational mathematical*[64] means for algebraic manipulations of abstract concepts. Concept algebra is an abstract mathematical structure for the formal treatment of concepts and their algebraic relations, operations, and associative rules for composing complex concepts, and they can be used to model, specify, and manipulate generic "to be" type problems, particularly system architectures, knowledge bases, and detail-level system designs in computing, software engineering, system engineering, and cognitive informatics. On the other hand, cognitive informatics has also turned its attention to sociological context (see (Wang, 2010), coherently with one of the lines of thought followed in this subsection. Therefore, the various formal aspects treated in (Wang, 2010) might be usefully contextualized with what has been said in this subsection about social-anthropological features. In conclusion, computational psychoanalysis and cognitive informatics have promising and interesting relationships which deserve further analysis and deepening.

4.3. THE ROLE OF TIME FOR HUMAN CONSCIOUSNESS FROM THE PSYCHOANALYTIC STANDPOINT

Time is a central and founding dimension of consciousness, as philosophy has pointed out from centuries, but it has been quite neglected from the psychoanalytic viewpoint. As briefly suggested in the previous section, compulsion to reapet mechanisms are features of unconscious realm and its functioning, which entail non-progressive processes mainly characterized by a cyclic temporality, coherently with conservative feature of drives; instead, consciousness acts in such a manner that a sort of symmetry breaking of this cyclic time, might give rise to a linear time, just as a typical feature of consciousness. This, coherently with what has been just said in the previous section. In the present section, therefore, we first argue just on this crucial aspect of time both for unconscious and, above all, for consciousness, following closely (Iurato et al., 2016), then we shall give a wider discussion on time from either a psychoanalytic and a philosophical standpoint.

4.3.1. The Rising of Time Dimension According to a Possible *P*-Adic Formal Model of Consciousness

In (Iurato & Khrennikov, 2015), attention has been paid to a possible implementation of a basic hysteresis pattern[65] (the Preisach one), suitably generalized, into a formal model of unconscious-conscious interconnection and based on the representation of mental entities by m-adic numbers, where $m = 2, 3,$

4, ... Algebraically, the systems of m-adic numbers are particular algebraic rings, while geometrically these are homogeneous trees with m branches leaving each vertex). One of the central points of the theoretical framework which lays out the basic concepts and notions of psychology and psychoanalysis concerning the unconscious-conscious relationships, is the use of m-adic dynamical systems (Khrennikov, 1997). Mathematically, it is fruitful to proceed with the fields of p-adic numbers, where $p > 1$ is a prime number. However, in cognitive and psychological applications, there would not be a priori reasons to restrict models to prime number bases, being more natural to work with the rings of m-adic numbers, where $m > 1$ is an arbitrary natural number.

Nevertheless, from the conclusions of (Iurato & Khrennikov, 2015), it has turned out to be more relevant to consider fields of p-adic numbers, with p a prime number, instead of arbitrary m-adic numbers. As has been seen in (Iurato & Khrennikov, 2015), in the unconscious domain, say U, there works a gigantic dynamical system, and one of the interesting consequences of the presented model in (Iurato & Khrennikov, 2015), is just that information processed unconsciously and consciously has different geometric structures, different mental trees have to be in the use. Pure mathematics tells us that hysteresis type memory effects are possible only if they are accommodated with transition from one type of mental tree to another. It is just this latter type of formal process which might underlie the crucial phenomenology involving conscious-unconscious pair.

Nonetheless, in (Iurato & Khrennikov, 2015), we have not given enough attention either to the exact domains in which certain formal operators run and to the various temporal aspects involved in the formal model therein considered, because the main intention was only to stress the relevance of hysteresis effects in modelling conscious-unconscious relationships. So, it has turned to be necessary to deepen and clarify the question related above all to the role played by time in such a model, referring to (Iurato et al., 2016) for a wider treatment. The psychophysical (hydraulic) model of Freud in combination with the p-adic mathematical representation gives us a possibility to apply (for a moment just formally) the theory of spontaneous symmetry breaking which was developed for physical processes to mental processes and, in particular, to make the first step towards modelling of interrelation between the physical time (at the level of emotional order) and psychic time at the levels of the thing and word representations.

4.3.1.1. The Three Levels (or Orders) of a Psychic Representation[66], According to Freud

From a psychoanalytic viewpoint, Freud stated first patterns of human psyche taking into account models of physics, mainly adopting an energetic pattern drawn from hydrodynamics, and in particular choosing a diffusion scheme for the energy flow. This framework is clearly identifiable in the initial Freudian neurophysiological theories on human psychic mechanisms as exposed in the known *Project for a Scientific Psychology* of 1895. Following (Chemana & Vandermersch, 2005; de Mijolla, 2005; Finelli, 2011; Fossi 1983, 1984; Laplanche & Pontalis, 1967), since the first works till to the final ones, as for example the celebrated yet unfinished compendium *An Outline of Psychoanalysis* of 1938, Freud never left out his initial hydraulic model of psychic energy, ever trying to implement it with the other formulations worked out along the maturation and the evolution of his thought. Indeed, in this latest compendium, Freud gave a configuration of human psychic system based on the reciprocal and contemporary presence of three orders, namely the *emotional order*, the *thing representation order* and the *word representation order*. In the Freudian oeuvre, these three orders, which provide the most elementary psychic act (*cathexis*) through object relationships[67], keep unchanged their presence although with at most role changing.

They respectively rely on the *Triebrepräsentant* (or *Triebrepräsentanz*), that is, the drive or instinctual representation, on the *Sachvorstellung* (or *Objektvorstellung*), that is, the thing representation, and on the *Wortvorstellung,* that is, the word representation.

In any case, from a historical stance, Freud started from considering the notion of representation as meant by philosophy, that is, as the operation, or the act, with which consciousness reproduces an objective content. This is broadly speaking meant as follows, i.e., made by external objets or by internal psychic states, or else one of these objects themselves. Then, Freud considered a more specific psychological sense of this concept, to be precise, he intended to refer to the renewal of a perceptive experience in absence of the sensorial stimulus, which should be meant as a knowledge act comprised by the mere sensation and the next abstracting intellection (Galimberti, 2006). From this point onwards, Freud started to gradually consider three possible levels, or orders, of a representation understood in the latter terms.

Following (De Mijolla, 2005), the *representation of affect* can be defined as a medium for the affective expression, in a sense serving as its vehicle in mental dynamics. In the metapsychological texts of 1915, Freud clearly established that instinct, situated, so to speak, at the "frontier" between body and mind, is expressed in mental dynamics by means of two main components: on the one hand, the *ideational representative,* and on the other, an energy charge, the *quota of affect (Affektbetrag)*, whose fate can be distinct. This energy change, when it is temporarily without a representational support, can be qualitatively transformed into various emotions (e.g., fear, pleasure, anxiety, and so on) and, under certain conditions, cathexis ideational representations can await the arrival of such a charge that will embody and validate them. This is the case, for example, when anxiety "without an object" (that is, without a conscious object) becomes focused around a clearly identifiable phobogenic object. This process was clearly demonstrated in the work *Analysis of a Phobia in a Five-year-old Boy* (of 1909), in which the castration anxiety of the "little Hans" was found to be embodied in horses.

Thus, if we wish to make the idea of what representation of affect is, then we may metaphorically consider a travelling salesman 'representing' a product, who has been delegated by his or her employer to pursue this function for the clients, in this analogy, the instinct being the employer, and consciousness being the client. This last metaphor is coherent with the use of the term *Repräsentanz* by Freud to which he intended to give the meaning of "delegate", "deputy", or "representative" just in the commercial sense. Following (Chemana & Vandermersch, 1998), Freud used the term *Repräsentanz* just to mean this function, that is to say, the representing or delegating function, and introduced it to explain that instinctual work imposed on the psyche because of its unavoidable and inseparable link with body. The drive or instinct coming from body is considered, in *Three Essays on the Theory of Sexuality* (of 1905), as the *psychische Repräsentanz*, while, in *Instincts and Their Vicissitudes* (of 1915), this is considered as the *psychische Repräsentant.*

The *psychische Repräsentanz* should be meant as psychic representative, while the *psychische Repräsentant* should be meant as a psychic representation. Subsequently, from 1915 onward, Freud used only the latter, leaving out the former, but ever keeping a certain semantic ambiguity. In two metapsychological essays of 1915, namely *Die Verdrängung* [The Repression] (of 1915) and *Das Unbewusste* [The Unconscious] (of 1915), Freud first claims a clean distinction between an ideational element (representation) and an affective element (*Affektbetrag*). As claimed in (Iurato & Khrennikov, 2015), there is a control centre *CC*, containing second censorship agencies, which has functions of control, formulates problems and sends them to the preconscious *Pr.* domain; first censorships instead act between the preconscious and the (repressed) unconscious domain *U*.

Now, following (Laplanche & Pontalis, 1967), among the many first censorship functions played by *Pr.*, there is above all that of *primary repression*[68] which gives rise to the very early repressed material, the one lying into the deepest meanders of unconscious, the first hard core, say *UCC* (see later), of the unconscious which is unexplorable in the psychoanalytic setting (Sasso, 2011); it is roughly placeable into the implicit memories and is inaccessible to the next explicit memories (Mancia, 2006). This first core will run as an attractor of the other next repressed contents, coming from censorship functions which mainly work as repulsion centres, and mainly operating by means of *fixation* processes through which *Affektbetrag* attaches to ideational element (representation). Therefore, the concept of representation, in Freud, has undergone a complex evolution in which he paid attention first to the initial triad *Triebrepräsentant-Sachvorstellung-Wortvorstellung*, then to the pair *Sachvorstellung-Wortvorstellung*, until to the last notion of *purposive idea* (or *finalized representation*), although all them are present more or less explicitly in the Freudian thought since its early steps.

The *Triebrepräsentant* is meant, by Freud, as the primary instinctual representative with which drives and endosomatic excitations find their psychic expressions. Sometimes, in the Freudian view, such a term refers to the ideational element, while, other times, it is wider and comprehends also affective elements. On the other hand, as recalled in (Laplanche & Pontalis, 1967), instinctual representative (*Triebrepräsentant*), ideational representative and psychical representative should be meant as synonymous of each other, to roughly mean some representative of the somatic with the psychic. In any case, Freud then pointed out the clean distinction between *Affektbetrag* and representation because both undergo a different fate, hence he carried on with a deeper discussion on representation, distinguishing between things-representation and words-representation on the basis of his juvenile study on aphasia of 1891 which has tacitly played a fundamental role in the next development of the Freudian thought (Fossi, 1984).

Nevertheless, also in this case, Freud seems not to depart much from the above semantic field identified by instinctual representative (*Triebrepräsentant*), ideational representative and psychical representative. Furthermore, as again pointed out in (Laplanche & Pontalis, 1967), even things-representation and words-representation might be considered as belonging to the same semantic field, so that it is allowed, eventually, to focus only on this last pair thing representation-word representation, if nothing else because Freud himself will give later a major load to it in the dawning of consciousness. However, along the main path comprehending the three representation orders *Triebrepräsentant*, *Sachvorstellung* and *Wortvorstellung*, which herein we wish to suppose to be distinct, it is possible to consider the main link between corporal affect, phantasmagoric and/or hallucinatory things-representation of the scene of satisfaction and/or dissatisfaction through which the affect's charge fulfils, hence their symbolic representation by means of language[69] and through which secondary process mainly performs, as one of the keystones of psychic functioning according to Freud.

But two crucial points of Freudian thought are that the instinctual charge, meant as an affective element, is independent of the representation, meant as an ideation element, and that things-representation and words-representation are tied together to give rise to a conscious representation (Sasso 2011, Sect. 13.3) belonging to the secondary process (say this, assumption *AC*). The third representation order therefore bears in itself – approximately, like in a (non-isolated) closed thermodynamical system – that received bodily energy amount (*Affektbetrag*) brought by the pair – approximately, like in a (non-isolated) open thermodynamic system[70] – made by the first two representation orders tied together into the third one, that is to say, the secondary process, in the third representation order, makes bound[71] (*bound energy*), through systems of symbols (among which are the linguistic ones) which replace or "stand for" things and affects, the open energy (*free energy*) freely arising from the primary process composed by the first two representation orders[72]. This takes place similarly to a Hegelian *Aufheben,* that is to say, sticking at the thing representation affectively charged (around the cathexis object or thing) – that is, a signified – a chain of words as signifiers[73] (see also *associative chains*), which is possible thanks to verbalization system which mainly associates a mental image with a word (Rycroft, 1968a,b).

The concept of affect had a great importance in the Freudian framework since the first works of J. Breuer and Freud on hysteria whose symptoms are retraceable in a traumatic event without a suitable energy discharge (locked affect). These studies showed that affect may be not linked with representation. The problem was then treated deeply in the metapsychological studies *Die Verdrängung* [The Repression] (of 1915) and *Das Unbewusste* [The Unconscious] (of 1915)[74].

This first representation refers therefore to the basic *Affektbetrag,* that is to say, the primary emotional charge which is tied all around the object of cathexis. According to Freud, the affectivity concerns the bodily context, and is defined as the subjective transposition of the quantity of instinctual energy. The body is broadly meant as the resonant place of emotions whose early roots are basically embodied; it is the early source of every human action and thought, as well as the primary means between internal and external world. The body enables the fundamental transformation of the quantitative kinesthetic, sense-perceptive and somatic energy to other qualitative and quantitative forms of energy, including the qualitative one related to the emotional and rational thought (Iurato, 2013a,b,c). Freud considered an hydrodynamic model of corporal energy flow based on free diffusion processes of energy mainly regulated from pleasure and displeasure principles. Therefore, we must search out the early and primary origins of every human mental state in the corporal encompassing of bodily energy[75] providing the *Triebrepräsentant.*

Broadly speaking, following Freud's original ideas, this bodily energy seems to be a physiological one meant in its truly quantitative nature and springing out from natural biochemical-physic processes which occur in our own body since prenatal stage[76]. It will be just the *Triebrepräsentant* to convert part of this energetic amount into other qualitative forms of energy like the affective ones and those related to hysteretic and conversion phenomena. As indicated above, Freud adopted (also with J. Breuer) an hydraulic (physics) model for the energy flow questions variously involved in his framework, mainly based on the psychophysical and thermodynamical works of H. von Helmholtz, E.W. von Brücke, W.J. Rankine and Sir W. Thompson. Furthermore, it seems that Freud was also inspired by the psychological theory of mechanical representations (*Vorstellungmechanik*) according to J.F. Herbart, in drawing up his theory of the three order psychic representations (Andersson, 1962)[77].

Therefore, the second representation order, namely the *Sachvorstellung*, gives rise to the eidetic-perceptive representations of external objects, to *gestalt* effects, spatial-temporally coordinated amongst them in a varied manner, while the third representation order, namely the *Wortvorstellung*, provides the linguistic-symbolic representation. In the first order prevails, so to say, a quantitative-diffusive logic due to bodily energy encompassment, in the second order a qualitative-associative (or combinatory) logic due to the cooperative action of different sensory inputs and imagines, and in the third order a set of formal logics related with the previous ones. The intertwinement among these three orders for giving rise explicitly (as a consciousness act) to the third one, in which the first two are implicitly present and tied together, is the basis of the Freudian non-pathological running of consciousness. This basic interlacement is also placeable into the above framework considering the relationships conscious-unconscious *C-U*, because the first two representation orders mainly are in the unconscious domain and arrange the primary process, while the third one is in the (preconscious-)conscious domain but is closely related with the first two.

4.3.1.2. The Rising of Temporal Dimension

The main aims of the works (Iurato & Khrennikov, 2015; Iurato et al., 2016), achieved in the framework of elementary *p*-adic analysis (the simplest version of analysis on trees in which hierarchic structures are presented through ultrametric distance) applied to formalize psychic phenomena, have been to propose some possible first hypotheses about the origins of human consciousness centred on the basic notion of time symmetry breaking as meant according to quantum field theory of infinite systems and condensed matter physics[78]. To be precise, starting from Freud's psychophysical (hydraulic) model of unconscious and conscious flows of psychic energy based on the three-orders mental representation, namely the emotional order, the thing representation order, and the word representation order, the authors have used the *p*-adic (treelike) mental spaces to model transition from unconsciousness to pre-consciousness and, then, to consciousness.

In this formal framework, it has been explored the theory of hysteresis dynamics, where conscious states are generated as the outcome of the integration of unconscious memories. One of the main mathematical consequences of this *p*-adic formal model is that trees representing unconscious and conscious mental states have to have different structures of branching and distinct procedures of clustering. The first psychophysical model of Freud in combination with the *p*-adic mathematical representation, has given the fruitful possibility to apply (for a moment just formally) the theory of spontaneous symmetry breaking of infinite dimensional field theory, to mental processes and, in particular, to make the first step towards modelling of interrelation between the physical time (at the level of the emotional order) and psychic time at the levels of the thing and word representations. Within this model, a discussion on the distinction and rising of different dimensions of time, has been achieved.

As has been said above, time is a fundamental aspect of human consciousness and its dawning, even to be its characterizing feature[79] (Reale, 1982). According to Freud, time is a distinctive trait of the secondary process with respect to the primary one which has not cognition of it, differently from the former. This is due, following Freud, to the fact that the sense of time arises from the delay or postponement experience between desire and its immediate satisfaction, so that primary process pushes to dilate and deny time, whilst life instincts and adaptation inclinations, as typical features of secondary process, going beyond pleasure principle, necessarily lead to the institution of a temporal dimension; and this in agreement with the action of compulsion to repeat mechanism, as discussed above. Again according to Freud, time is also a constitutive trait of human memory whereby past experiences are able to exert effects on the present with neurotic consequences when futurity does not entail any pleasant novelty because the subject is harnessed to pursue a behaviour acquired in the past which he or she does not want to give up (Galimberti, 2006). This last remark is coherent with the previously mentioned formal model based on hysteresis effects (Iurato & Khrennikov, 2015; Iurato et al., 2016), as hysteresis phenomenology is closely related to temporality. According to this formal model, just in the region of human psyche (according to Freudian first topography) corresponding to preconscious-conscious, temporal dimension arises, coherently with Freud's remark, expressed just at the end of *A Note upon the "Mystic Writing Pad"* (of 1925), for which consciousness basically runs discontinuously (due to its connections with preconscious) which, on its turn, is at the early origin of temporal dimension (De Mijolla & De Mijolla Mellor 1998, Ch. VI, Sect. II, pp. 281-282).

There exist at least two different types of time, say a *psychological* or *mental* time and a *physical* time which are distinct[80] (Khrennikov 2002, Ch. 5). Recently, physics has turned its attention towards early origins of time, speculating just on certain symmetry breaking phenomena as possible physical mechanisms producing physical time. Amongst them, there are some arguments (Kastner, 2011) which, starting from the Wheeler-Feynman absorber theory of electrodynamics, put forward the hypothesis that physical time might spring out from symmetry breaking due to the occurrence of relevant and contingent boundary conditions in macroscopic phenomena involving energy transfer. To be precise, taking into account that energy operator is canonically conjugated – as quantum observable – to time operator in the framework of field theory, it is the broken symmetry of the physical laws governing energy propagation that establishes the directionality of time (anisotropy of time). So, with suitable analogical extensions, it is possible to suppose that a certain sense of the arrow of time might spring out from the unavoidable imposition of relevant boundary conditions, as those given by human body, to the bulk of physiological energy involved in the *Triebrepräsentant*, and whose propagation, by diffusion, will prepare the basis for the occurrence of the next further representation orders of either *Sachvorstellung* and *Wortvorstellung*.

4.3.2. The Temporality From the Psychoanalytic Standpoint: Further Remarks

We refer to (Iurato et al., 2016) for a deep discussion of a possible theory on the rising of temporal dimension according to a *p*-adic framework of human psyche worked out on the basis of Freudian psychoanalysis, as briefly mention above. Here, instead, we set up a further although brief analysis of temporality and its human acquisition, from the psychoanalytic viewpoints[81], highlighting the possible formal aspects rising from these disquisitions. Anyway, the main formal feature of time, as well as of any other consciousness activity and function, is the ordering property, so that the coming of an order relation is a preeminent one from a computational psychoanalysis standpoint. This is also in agreement with the fact that, one of the main common features of conscious processes (and even the biological ones) is *recursion* (Conrotto 2014, p. 104), which might not exist without some ordering; hence, another confirmation of the primary importance of ordering for human life. On the other hand, also in (Zapparoli 1970, p. 49), it is stated that time is the crucial ingredient of logic, hence of the so-called rational thought: to be precise, he states that the main object of logic is just the retardation of pleasure, while the main aim of logic is the regulation of human behaving through this retardation. From that, we deduce the crucial, primary importance of temporal dimension for human being behaviour, as many times already pointed out by philosophical tradition.

From[82] an evolutionary point of view, the *Es* (or *Id*) and the formation of the *Super-Ego* precede the rising of the *Ego*. The latter and, in general, the whole conscious system, which has control and adaptive to reality functions, are embedded into the temporality, so that the relationships of human psyche with temporality, are to be retraced in the activity of conscious system and regard reality principle, not the pleasure one. The unconscious, instead, is *atemporal*, as has already been said widely, while temporal dimension seems to spring out from perceptive-conscious system, and self-perceptively acquired (Reale, 1982). To give an empirical evidence to Freudian assumption on the timelessness of unconscious, in the late 1950s, some long-period tests have been made, which seem to corroborate it (Sabbadini 1979, pp. 21-22). The manifest content of dreams seems furthermore to show that often effect precedes cause and that simultaneity replaces logical connection between these; so, from this, it turns out the relevance of time in the explanation of logical connections. Often, says Freud, dreaming activity transposes temporal events into spatial ones: for instance, the appearance of small and far persons in a dream, with respect to other ones present in the dream scene, would want to mean that the formers are, with respect to other people of greater dimensions, temporally farther (Sabbadini 1979, pp. 22-23).

From this, it follows that the awareness of a temporal dimension is the main discrimination point between unconscious and conscious zones (in the topographical model of human psyche) as well as between primary and secondary processes (in the dynamical model of human psyche). In the primary process, the psychic energy flows freely from a presentation (o representation) to another, according to the primitive mechanisms of condensation and displacement, which have none respect in regard to temporality which rules our conscious life. Instead, the control of psychic energy stably cathexed upon an object or presentation (bound energy), is instead the typical feature of secondary process. Such an energy control (a function gradually played by *Ego*), requires a capacity to hold, to keep pushes due to impulse (ruled by pleasure principle) to satisfying desires, hence tolerating consequent frustration that such a delay[83] entails, as due to the principle of reality which rules secondary process, differently from the case of primary process in which an immediate satisfaction if required, in either hallucinatory or real manner (Sabbadini 1979, pp. 24-15).

At first, instinct (or drive) and its satisfaction are in an inseparable and timelessness unity, in an eternal present that does not know any displeasure due to remembrance or expectation. In this phase, the Self is charged or invested by a narcissistic omnipotence (primary narcissism), is not still differentiated from the external world, and subject and object are an inseparable whole in a fusional state with mother. In this phase, maternal body and what mother may give in satisfying any child's desire, is seen as an integral thing of the child, with a consequent disclaimer of any interpersonal relation. Instead, with the dilation and retardation of desire's satisfaction, it takes place a first separation between Self and non-Self, a differentiation between internal and external world, and, with the absence of mother, the original narcissistic omnipotence, magically atemporal, is now reduced to a present time in which prevails either the discomfort of the need still unsatisfied and the phantasmatic expectation of a next satisfaction. So, it seems that just in the crucial passage from a fusional, intimate state with mother to a relatively separated and autonomous state from mother, a first, basic awareness of a psychological time takes place (Sabbatini 1979, pp. 24-25; Giordano et al., 1984).

On the other hand, we recall that the integrative function of the symbolic system and its dialectic process of knowledge, has its main feature in the diachronic integration process of the past, that is to say, the capability to make meaningful connections with previous vicissitudes, from the darkest and deepest ones (of unconscious) to those near to the awareness (of preconscious). Only with the emergence of a diachronic perspective, the subject can make reference to past, hence to insert affective-cognitive experiences into more evolved structures of the relational organization. The diachronic dimension of cognitive life, coming just in the moment in which one has access to the consciousness, is not thinkable as the result of something coming from external world. Indeed, according to Freud and Marie Bonaparte, time is closely related to consciousness work which, when it arises, then we perceives an internal flow (i.e., the time flow) which will be later projected into the external world (Corradi Fiumara, 1980).

Just in relation with what has been said in the previous subsection, the early problems of lost of the rewarding object cannot exist in a spatial dimensionality only, since the tolerance of frustration entails not only the awareness of the presence or absence of the desiring object which is placed, in a given situation, into a certain space by drive expectation. The tolerance of frustration indeed implies an incipit of temporal stretching which is a prelude to the constitution of a time in which events may be itemized sequentially, hence it is possible to establish a non-spatial prospective dimension on which previous and future things in such a manner to open the possibility to make projects and with which thought may arise. But only symbolically it is possible to reconnect – with regret, so one tries to retrieve – with something which has went lost, which is missing, and that therefore is being to constitute our previous history. Such an historicization, as symbolically mediated, is always present, in a parallel manner, to every other projectual aim (Corradi Fiumara, 1980).

REFERENCES

Abbagnano, N. (1998). Dizionario di Filosofia (3rd ed.). Torino, Italy: UTET Libreria.

Akhtar, S., & O'Neil, M. K. (Eds.). (2011). *On Freud's 'negation'. In The International Psychoanalytic Association – Contemporary Freud. Turning points & critical issues.* London, UK: Karnac Books, Ltd.

Albertson, M. O., & Collins, K. L. (1996). Symmetry Breaking in Graphs. *The Electronic Journal of Combinatorics, 3*(1), R18.

Albeverio, S., Kloeden, P. E., & Khrennikov, A. Yu. (1998). Human Memory as a p-Adic Dynamic System. *Theoretical and Mathematical Physics, 117*(3), 1414–1422. doi:10.1007/BF02557180

Alexander, F. (1948). Fundamentals of psychoanalysis. New York, NY: W.W. Norton & Company, Inc.

Alling, N. G. (1987). *Foundations of analysis over surreal number fields.* Amsterdam: North-Holland Publishing Company.

Allman, J. M. (2000). *Evolving Brains.* New York, NY: Scientific American Library. A division of HPHLP.

Ammaniti, M., & Gallese, V. (2014). La nascita dell'intersoggettività. Lo sviluppo del Sé fra psicodinamica e neurobiologia. Milano, Italy: Raffaello Cortina Editore.

Andersson, O. (1962). Studies on the Prehistory of Psychoanalysis. Stockholm: Scandinavian University Books.

Arieti, S. (1974). Interpretazione della schizofrenia. Milano, Italy: Giangiacomo Feltrinelli Editore.

Arieti, S. (1976). Creatività. La sintesi magica. Roma, Italy: Il Pensiero Scientifico Editore.

Atiyah, M. F., & Macdonald, I. G. (1969). Introduction to Commutative Algebra. Reading, MA: Addison-Wesley Publishing Company, Inc.

Atkinson, R. L., Atkinson, R. C., Smith, E. E., Bem, D. J., & Nolen-Hoeksema, S. (Eds.). (1996). *Hilgard's Introduction to Psychology* (12th ed.). Orlando, FL: Harcourt Brace.

Baars, B. J. (1993). How does a serial, integrated and very limited stream of consciousness emerge from a nervous system that is mostly unconscious, distributed, parallel and of enormous capacity? In *Experimental and Theoretical Studies of Consciousness, Novartis Foundation Symposium No. 174*. New York, NY: John Wiley & Sons, Ltd.

Badiou, A. (1982). Théorie du sujet. Paris: Éditions du Seuil.

Bajnok, B. (2013). *An Invitation to Abstract Mathematics*. New York, NY: Springer-Verlag, Inc. doi:10.1007/978-1-4614-6636-9

Balsamo, M. (2009). Ripetizione, coazione a ripetere, destino. In *Psiche. Dizionario storico di psicologia, psichiatria, psicoanalisi, neuroscienze* (Vol. 2, pp. 957–962). Torino, Italy: Giulio Einaudi editore.

Balzarotti, R. (Ed.). (1972). Cahiers pour l'Analyse. Scritti scelti di analisi e teoria della scienza, a cura del Centro Ricerche 2. Torino, Italy: Editore Boringhieri.

Bandyopadhyay, P. (2003). *Geometry, Topology and Quantum Field Theory*. Dordrecht, The Netherlands: Springer Science & Business Media, B.V. doi:10.1007/978-94-017-1697-0

Bara, B. G. (1990). Scienza Cognitiva. Torino, Italy: Bollati Boringhieri editore.

Barone, F. (1965). Logica Formale e Logica Trascendentale (Vols. 1-2). Torino, Italy: Edizioni di «Filosofia».

Barratt, B. B. (2016). *Psychoanalysis and the Postmodern Impulse. Knowing and Being since Freud's Psychology*. New York, NY: Routledge.

Barthe, G., Capretta, V., & Pons, O. (2003). Setoids in type theory. *Journal of Functional Programming, 13*(2), 261–293. doi:10.1017/S0956796802004501

Bateson, G. (1972). *Steps to an Ecology of Mind. Collected Essays in Anthropology, Psychiatry, Evolution, and Epistemology*. San Francisco, CA: Chandler Publishing Company.

Battacchi, M. W. (2006). *La conoscenza psicologia. Il metodo, l'oggetto, la ricerca*. Roma, Italy: Carocci editore.

Ben-Ari, M. (1993). Mathematical Logic for Computer Science. Hemel Hempstead, UK: Prentice Hall International, Ltd.

Benvenuto, S. (2005). Perversioni. Sessualità, etica, psicoanalisi. Torino, Italy: Bollati Boringhieri editore.

Bernardi, S., Dei, F., & Meloni, P. (Eds.). (2011). La materia del quotidiano. Per un'antropologia degli oggetti ordinari. Pisa, Italy: Pacini Editore.

Berwick, R. C., & Chomsky, N. (2016). Why Only Us. Language and Evolution. Cambridge, MA: The MIT Press. doi:10.7551/mitpress/9780262034241.001.0001

Bleecker, D. (1981). *Gauge Theory and Variational Principles*. Reading, MA: Addison-Wesley Publishing Company, Inc.

Blumenthal, P., & Tyvaert, J.-E. (Eds.). (2003). *La cognition dans le temps. Etudes cognitives dans le champ historique des langues et des textes*. Tübingen, Germany: Max Niemeyer Verlag. doi:10.1515/9783110949490

Bokanowski, T., & Lewkowicz, S. (Eds.). (2009). *On Freud's 'splitting of the ego in the process of defence'. In The International Psychoanalytic Association – Contemporary Freud: Turning points & critical issues*. London, UK: Karnac Books, Ltd.

Boniolo, G., & Vidali, P. (1999). Filosofia della scienza. Milano, Italy: Bruno Mondadori.

Bonnota, O., de Montalembertb, M., Kermarrecc, S., Botbold, M., Waltere, M., & Coulon, N. (2011). Are impairments of time perception in schizophrenia a neglected phenomenon? *Journal of Physiology, Paris*, *105*(4-6), 164–169. doi:10.1016/j.jphysparis.2011.07.006 PMID:21803155

Borceux, F. (1989). Fasci, logica e topoi. Quaderni dell'Unione Matematica Italiana, N. 34. Bologna, Italy: Pitagora Editrice.

Borgogno, F., Luchetti, A., & Marino Coe, L. (Eds.). (2017). Il pensiero psicoanalitico italiano. Maestri, idee e tendenze dagli anni '20 ad oggi. Milano, Italy: FrancoAngeli.

Borisyuk, R., Borisyuk, G., & Kazanovich, Y. (1998). Synchronization of neural activity and information processing. *Behavioral and Brain Sciences*, *21*(6), 833. doi:10.1017/S0140525X98241768

Bottiroli, G. (2006). *Che cos'è la teoria della letteratura. Fondamenti e problemi*. Torino, Italy: Giulio Einaudi editore.

Boudon, R. (1970). *Strutturalismo e scienze umane*. Torino, Italy: Giulio Einaudi editore.

Bourguignon, A., & Manus, A. (1980). Hallucination nègative, déni de la réalité et scotomisation. *Annales Médico-Psychologiques*, *138*(2), 129–153. PMID:6992686

Brading, K., & Castellani, E. (2013). Symmetry and Symmetry Breaking. In The Stanford Encyclopedia of Philosophy. Stanford University Press.

Bremer, M. (2005). *An Introduction to Paraconsistent Logics*. Frankfurt am Main, Germany: Peter Lang Publishing.

Bria, P. (1981). Introduzione. Pensiero, mondo e problemi di fondazione. In *L'inconscio come insiemi infiniti. Saggio sulla bi-logica* (pp. xix–cxi). Torino, Italy: Giulio Einaudi editore.

Bria, P., & Caroppo, E. (2006). Antropologia culturale e psicopatologia. Roma, Italy: Alpes Italia.

Britton, R. (2000). Belief and Imagination. Explorations in Psychoanalysis. London, UK: Routledge.

Britton, R. (2003). Sex, Death and the Super-Ego. Experiences in Psychoanalysis. London, UK: Karnac Books, Ltd.

Britton, R., Blundell, S., & Youell, B. (2014). Il lato mancante. L'assenza del padre nel mondo interno. Milano, Italy: Mimesis edizioni.

Brown, R. (1987). From Groups to Groupoids: A Brief Survey. *Bulletin of the London Mathematical Society*, *19*(2), 113–134. doi:10.1112/blms/19.2.113

Bruhat, F. (1961). Algèbres de Lie et groupes de Lie (2nd ed.). Recife, Brazil: Instituto de Física e Matemática, Universidade do Recife.

Bucci, W. (1985). Dual coding: A cognitive model for psychoanalytic research. *Journal of the American Psychoanalytic Association, 33*(3), 571–607. doi:10.1177/000306518503300305 PMID:4056301

Bucci, W. (1987). *The dual code model and the interpretation of dreams.* New York, NY: Derner Institute – Adelphi University.

Bucci, W. (1997). *Psychoanalysis and Cognitive Science.* New York, NY: The Guilford Press.

Buneci, M. R. (2003). Topologies on the graph of the equivalence relation associated to a groupoid. *Proceedings of the International Conference on Theory and Applications of Mathematics and Informatics*, 23-32.

CA (Collectif d'Auteurs). (1975). *La Psychanalyse.* Paris: Editions Le Livre De Poche.

Cabras, A., Canarutto, D., Kolář, I., & Modugno, M. (1991). Structured Bundles. Bologna, Italy: Pitagora Editrice.

Capa, R. L., Duval, C. Z., Blaison, D., & Giersch, A. (2014). Patients with schizophrenia selectively impaired in temporal order judgments. *Schizophrenia Research, 156*(1), 51–55. doi:10.1016/j.schres.2014.04.001 PMID:24768441

Capozza, D. (1977). Il differenziale semantico. Problemi teorici e metrici. Bologna, Italy: Casa Editrice Pàtron.

Capozzi, M., & Cellucci, C. (2014). *Breve storia della logica. Dall'Umanesimo al primo Novecento.* Morrisville, NC: Lulu Press, Inc.

Carlson, L. (1999). *Consumption and Depression in Gertrude Stein, Louis Zukofsky, and Ezra Pound.* London, UK: Palgrave-MacMillan Press, Ltd. doi:10.1057/9780230379947

Carotenuto, A. (1982). Discorso sulla metapsicologia. Torino, Italy: Bollati Boringhieri Editore.

Carotenuto, A. (1991). Trattato di psicologia della personalità e delle differenze individuali. Milano, Italy: Raffaello Cortina Editore.

Carotenuto, A. (Ed.). (1992). Dizionario Bompiani degli Psicologi Contemporanei. Milano, Italy: Bompiani.

Carruccio, E. (1971). Mondi della Logica. Bologna, Italy: Nicola Zanichelli Editore.

Casari, E. (1972). Questioni di Filosofia della Matematica. Milano, Italy: Giangiacomo Feltrinelli Editore.

Cassinari, F. (2005). Tempo e identità. La dinamica di legittimazione nella storia e nel mito. Milano, Italy: FrancoAngeli.

Cellucci, C., & Ippoliti, E. (2016). Logica. Milano, Italy: EGEA Editore.

Chang, C.-C., & Keisler, H. J. (1973). Model Theory. Amsterdam: North-Holland Publishing Company, Inc.

Chasseguet-Smirgel, J. (1975). L'idéal du moi. Paris: Éditeur Claude Tchou.

Chasseguet-Smirgel, J. (1985). Creativity and perversion. London, UK: Free Association Books, Ltd.

Chemama, R., & Vandermersch, B. (Eds.). (1998). Dictionnaire de la Psychanalyse. Paris: Larousse-Bordas.

Cherubini, P., Giaretta, P., & Mazzocco, A. (Eds.). (2000). Ragionamento: psicologia e logica. Firenze, Italy: Giunti Gruppo Editoriale.

Chialà, S., & Curi, U. (2016). La brama dell'avere. Trento, Italy: Casa editrice Il Margine.

Chianese, D. (2009). Costruzione, Ricostruzione, Interpretazione. In *Psiche. Dizionario storico di psicologia, psichiatria, psicoanalisi, neuroscienze* (Vol. 1, pp. 280–285). Torino, Italy: Giulio Einaudi editore.

Choquet-Bruhat, Y., De Witt-Morette, C., & Dillard-Bleick, M. (1982). *Analysis, Manifolds and Physics* (Revised Edition). Amsterdam: North-Holland Publishing Company.

Codignola, E. (1977). Il vero e il falso. Saggio sulla struttura logica dell'interpretazione psicoanalitica. Torino, Italy: Editore Boringhieri.

Cohn, P. M. (1965). Universal Algebra. New York, NY: Harper & Row Publishers.

Conrotto, F. (2000). Tra il sapere e la cura. Un itinerario freudiano. Milano, Italy: FrancoAngeli.

Conrotto, F. (2009). Negazione. In *Psiche. Dizionario storico di psicologia, psichiatria, psicoanalisi, neuroscienze* (Vol. 2, pp. 728–730). Torino, Italy: Giulio Einaudi editore.

Conrotto, F. (2010). Per una teoria psicoanalitica della conoscenza. Milano, Italy: FrancoAngeli.

Conrotto, F. (2014). Ripensare l'inconscio. Milano, Italy: FrancoAngeli.

Contardi, R. (2010). La prova del labirinto. Processo di simbolizzazione e dinamica rappresentativa in psicoanalisi. Milano, Italy: FrancoAngeli.

Contarello, A., & Mazzara, B. M. (2002). Le dimensioni sociali dei processi psicologici. Roma-Bari, Italy: Laterza Editori.

Conte, M., & Gennaro, A. (Eds.). (1989). Inconscio e processi cognitivi. Bologna, Italy: Società editrice il Mulino.

Conti, L., & Principe, S. (1989). Salute mentale e società. Fondamenti di psichiatria sociale. Padova, Italy: Piccin Nuova Libraria.

Contri, G. (1972). Nozioni fondamentali nella teoria della struttura di Jacques Lacan. In Cahiers pour l'Analyse. Scritti scelti di analisi e teoria della scienza, a cura del Centro Ricerche 2. Torino, Italy: Editore Boringhieri.

Corradi Fiumara, G. (1980). Funzione simbolica e filosofia del linguaggio. Torino, Italy: Editore Boringhieri.

Cotter, D. (2003). *Joyce and the Perverse Ideal*. London, UK: Routledge.

CSFG – Centro di Studi Filosofici di Gallarate. (1977). Dizionario delle idee. Firenze, Italy: G.C. Sansoni Editore.

Cuche, D. (2004). La notion de culture dans les sciences sociales. Paris: Éditions La Découverte.

Culioli, A. (2014). L'arco e la freccia. Scritti scelti. Bologna, Italy: Società editrice il Mulino.

D'Urso, V., & Trentin, R. (1998). Introduzione alla psicologia delle emozioni. Roma-Bari, Italy: Editori Laterza.

Dalla Chiara Scabia, M. L. (1973). Istanti e individui nelle logiche temporali. *Rivista di Filosofia, 64*(2), 95–122.

Dalla Chiara Scabia, M. L. (1974). Logica. Milano, Italy: ISEDI – Istituto Editoriale Internazionale.

De Masi, F. (2016). Which is the relevant superego for clinical analytic work? In F. Borgogno, A. Luchetti, & L. M. Coe (Eds.), *Reading Italian Psychoanalysis* (pp. 279–290). Oxfordshire, UK: Routledge.

De Mijolla, A. (Ed.). (2005). *International Dictionary of Psychoanalysis* (Vols. 1–3). Farmington Hills, MI: Thomson Gale.

De Mijolla, A., & De Mijolla Mellor, S. (Eds.). (1996). Psychanalyse. Paris: PUF-Presses Universitaires de France.

De Pasquali, P. (2002). Figli che uccidono. Da Doretta Graneris a Erika & Omar. Soveria Mannelli (CZ), Italy: Rubbettino Editore.

De Waelhens, A., & Ver Eecke, W. (2001). *Phenomenology and Lacan on Schizophrenia, after the Decade of the Brain.* Leuven, Belgium: Leuven University Press.

Dehaene, S., & Brannon, E. (Eds.). (2011). *Space, Time and Number in the Brain. Searching for the Foundations of Mathematical Thought.* Amsterdam: Elsevier, Inc.

Dei, F. (2016). Antropologia culturale (2nd ed.). Bologna, Italy: Società editrice il Mulino.

Dei, F., & Meloni, P. (2015). *Antropologia della cultura materiale.* Roma, Italy: Carocci editore.

Dei, F., & Simonicca, A. (Eds.). (2008). Ragione e forme di vita. Razionalità e relativismo in antropologia (2nd ed.). Milano, Italy: FrancoAngeli.

Deng, Y. (2013). Applied Parallel Computing. Singapore: World Scientific Publishing.

Derdzinski, A. (1992). *Geometry of the Standard Model of Elementary Particles.* Berlin: Springer-Verlag. doi:10.1007/978-3-642-50310-8

Di Gregorio, L. (2003). Psicopatologia del cellulare. Dipendenza e possesso del telefonino. Milano, Italy: FrancoAngeli/LeComete.

Dijksterhuis, A., & Nordgren, L. F. (2006). A theory of unconsciouss thought. *Perspectives on Psychological Science, 1*(2), 95–109. doi:10.1111/j.1745-6916.2006.00007.x PMID:26151465

Dolto, F. (1984). *L'image inconsciente du corps.* Paris: Editions du Seuil.

Donati, P. (2015). L'enigma della relazione. Milano, Italy: Mimesis edizioni.

Durst, M. (1988). Dialettica e bi-logica. L'epistemologia di Ignacio Matte Blanco. Milano, Italy: Marzorati Editore.

Eco, U. (1981). *Simbolo. Voce dell'Enciclopedia Einaudi* (Vol. 12). Torino, Italy: Giulio Einaudi editore.

Ehresmann, A. C., & Vanbremeersch, J. P. (2007). *Memory Evolutive Systems. Hierarchy, Emergence, Cognition.* Amsterdam: Elsevier, B.V.

Ellis, J., Mavromatos, N. E., & Nanopoulos, D. V. (1992). The origin of space-time as W-symmetry breaking in string theory. *Physics Letters. [Part B], 288*(1-2), 23–30. doi:10.1016/0370-2693(92)91949-A

Endert, E. (2006). Über die emotionale Dimension sozialer Prozesse. Die Theorie der Affektlogik am Beispiel der Rechtsextremismus und Nationalsozialismusforschung (Theorie und Methode). Konstanz, Germany: UVK Verlagsgesellschaft mbH.

Enriques, F. (1912). Scienza e Razionalismo. Bologna, Italy: Nicola Zanichelli Editore.

Even, G., & Medina, M. (2012). *Digital Logic Design. A Rigorous Approach.* Cambridge, UK: Cambridge University Press. doi:10.1017/CBO9781139226455

Fairlamb, H. L. (1994). *Critical conditions. Postmodernity and the question of foundations.* Cambridge, UK: Cambridge University Press. doi:10.1017/CBO9780511552762

Falzone, A. (2005). Filosofia del linguaggio e psicopatologia evoluzionistica. Soveria Mannelli (CZ), Italy: Rubbettino Editore.

Feng, E. H., & Crooks, G. E. (2008). Lenghts of time arrow. *Physical Review Letters, 101*(9), 090602/1–4. doi:10.1103/PhysRevLett.101.090602

Fenichel, O. (1945). The psychoanalytic theory of neurosis. New York, NY: W.W. Norton & Company, Inc.

Field, M. (1996). *Symmetry Breaking for Compact Lie Groups. Memoir of the AMS No. 574.* Providence, RI: American Mathematical Society Publications.

Figà-Talamanca Dore, L. (1978). La logica dell'inconscio. Roma, Italy: Edizioni Studium-Vita Nova.

Finelli, R. (2010). Perché l'inconscio non è strutturato come un linguaggio. In Compendio di Psicoanalisi e altri scritti. Roma, Italy: Newton Compton editori.

Finelli, R. (2011). Rappresentazione e linguaggio in Freud: a partire dal "Compendio di psicoanalisi". *Consecutio Temporum. Rivista di critica della postmodernità, 1,* 112-125.

Fink, K. (1993). The Bi-Logic Perception of Time. *The International Journal of Psycho-Analysis, 74,* 303–312. PMID:8491534

Fodor, N., & Gaynor, F. (1950). Freud: Dictionary of Psychoanalysis. New York, NY: The Philosophical Library.

Fonagy, P., Gergely, G., Jurist, E. L., & Target, M. (2002). Affect Regulation, Mentalization, and the Development of the Self. New York, NY: Other Press.

Fornari, F. (2016). Psychic birth. In F. Borgogno, A. Luchetti, & L. M. Coe (Eds.), *Reading Italian Psychoanalysis* (pp. 593–600). Oxfordshire, UK: Routledge.

Fossi, G. (1983). La psicologia dinamica: un'eredità del XX secolo. Roma, Italy: Edizioni Borla.

Fossi, G. (1984). Le teorie psicoanalitiche. Padova, Italy: Piccin Nuova Libraria.

Fossi, G. (1988). Psicoanalisi e psicoterapie dinamiche. Torino, Italy: Bollati Boringhieri editore.

Fossi, G. (2003). Una proposta evoluzionista per la psicoanalisi. Con un manuale per la pratica terapeutica e la ricerca empirica. Milano, Italy: FrancoAngeli.

Francioni, M. (1978). Psicoanalisi linguistica ed epistemologia in Jacques Lacan. Torino, Italy: Editore Boringhieri.

Freud, S. (1938). Abriß der psychoanalyse. Academic Press.

Freud, S. (1957). *The Standard Edition of Complete Psychological Works of Sigmund Freud* (Vols. 1-24; J. Strachey, Trans. & Ed.). London, UK: The Hogarth Press.

Freud, S. (1979). La scissione dell'Io nel processo di difesa (1938). In Opere di Sigmund Freud, 1930-1938. L'uomo Mosè e la religione monoteistica e altri scritti (vol. 11). Torino, Italy: Editore Boringhieri.

Friedman, D. M. (2001). A Mind of Its Own. A Cultural History of the Penis. New York, NY: Simon & Schuster, Inc.

Friedman, M., & Tomšič, S. (Eds.). (2016). Psychoanalysis: Topological Perspectives. New Conceptions of Geometry and Space in Freud and Lacan. Bielefeld, Germany: transcript Verlag. doi:10.14361/9783839434406

Fromm, E. (1951). The Forgotten Language. An Introduction to the Understanding of Dreams, Fairy Tales, and Myths. New York, NY: Holt, Rinehart & Winston Publishing Company, Inc.

Fromm, E. (1976). To have or to be? New York, NY: Harper & Row Publishers, Inc.

Funari, E. (1978). Psicoanalisi: tecnica o Weltanschauung? In *Psicoanalisi e classi sociali* (pp. 147–153). Roma, Italy: Editori Riuniti.

Funari, E. (1988). Contestualità e specificità della psicoanalisi. In Trattato di Psicoanalisi: Vol. 1. Teoria e Tecnica. Milano, Italy: Raffaello Cortina Editore.

Funari, E. (2007). L'irrapresentabile come origine della vita psichica. Milano, Italy: FrancoAngeli.

Fusco, A., & Tomassoni, R. (Eds.). (2013). Creatività nella psicologia letteraria, drammatica e filmica. Milano, Italy: FrancoAngeli.

Gabbay, D. M., Hodkinson, I., & Reynolds, M. A. (1994). *Temporal Logic. Mathematical Foundations and Computational Aspects* (Vol. 1). Oxford, UK: Clarendon Press.

Gabbay, D. M., Reynolds, M. A., & Finger, M. (2000). *Temporal Logic. Mathematical Foundations and Computational Aspects* (Vol. 2). Oxford, UK: Oxford University Press.

Galimberti, U. (1979). Psichiatria e fenomenologia. Milano, Italy: Giangiacomo Feltrinelli Editore.

Galimberti, U. (1983). Il corpo. Milano, Italy: Giangiacomo Feltrinelli Editore.

Galimberti, U. (2006). Dizionario di psicologia. Torino, Italy: UTET Libreria.

Galton, A. (Ed.). (1987). *Temporal Logic and its Applications*. New York, NY: Academic Press, Inc.

Gay, P. (2000). Freud. Una vita per i nostri tempi. Milano, Italy: Bompiani.

Giberti, F., & Rossi, R. (Eds.). (1996). Manuale di psichiatria (4th ed.). Padova, Italy: Piccin Nuova Libraria.

Giersch, A., Lalanne, L., van Assche, M., & Elliott, M.A. (2013). On disturbed time continuity in schizophrenia: an elementary impairment in visual perception? *Frontiers in Psychology*, *4*, 281-290.

Gilbert, N. D., & Miller, E. C. (2011). The graph expansion of an ordered groupoid. *Algebra Colloquium*, *18*(1), 827-842.

Gilliéron, E., & Baldassarre, M. (Eds.). (2012). Perversione e Relazione. Roma, Italy: Alpes Italia.

Giordano, M., Dello Russo, G., Pardi, F., & Patella, G. A. (1984). Tempo e inconscio. Napoli, Italy: Guida editori.

Girotto, V. (Ed.). (2013). Introduzione alla psicologia del pensiero. Bologna, Italy: Società editrice il Mulino.

Givant, S., & Halmos, P. (2009). Introduction to Boolean Algebras. New York, NY: Springer Science + Business Media, LLC.

Glover, E. (1949). Psychoanalysis. London, UK: John Bale Medical Publications, Ltd.

Godement, R. (1959). Variétés Différentiables. Résumé des leçons, Textos de Matemática No. 2. Recife, Brazil: Instituto de Física e Matemática – Universidade do Recife.

Goleman, D. (1995). Emotional Intelligence. New York, NY: Bantam Books.

Golubitsky, M., & Stewart, I. (2006). Nonlinear dynamics of networks: The groupoid formalism. *Bulletin of the American Mathematical Society*, *43*(3), 305–364. doi:10.1090/S0273-0979-06-01108-6

Green, A. (1993). Le travail du négatif. Paris: Les Éditions du Minuit.

Greenacre, P. (1971). Emotional growth. Psychoanalytic studies of the gifted and a great variety of other individuals. New York, NY: International Universities Press, Inc.

Grice, H. P. (1993). Logica e conversazione. Saggi su intenzione, significato e comunicazione. Bologna, Italy: Società editrice il Mulino.

Grinberg, L. (1989). La supervisione psicoanalitica. Teoria e pratica. Milano, Italy: Raffaello Cortina Editore.

Grunberger, B. (1971). *Le narcissisme. Essai de psychanalyse*. Paris: Payot.

Guay, A., & Hepburn, B. (2009). Symmetry and its Formalisms: Mathematical Aspects. *Philosophy of Science*, *76*(2), 160–178. doi:10.1086/600154

Hall, C. S. (1999). *A Primer in Freudian Psychology*. New York, NY: Meridian Books.

Hampe, B., & Grady, J. E. (Eds.). (2005). *From Perception to Meaning. Image Schemas in Cognitive Linguistics*. Berlin: Walter de Gruyter GmbH and Co. doi:10.1515/9783110197532

Hanly, C. (1984). Ego Ideal and Ideal Ego. *The International Journal of Psycho-Analysis*, *65*(3), 253–261. PMID:6571602

Hanly, C. (2011). Studi psicoanalitici sul narcisismo. Scritti di Charles Hanly. Roma, Italy: Giovanni Fioriti Editore.

Harary, F., Norman, Z., & Cartwright, D. (Eds.). (1965). *Structural Models*. New York, NY: John Wiley and Sons, Inc.

Hartmann, H., & Loewenstein, R. M. (1962). Notes on the Superego. *The Psychoanalytic Study of the Child*, *17*, 42–81.

Hermann, I. (1989). Psicoanalisi e logica. Roma, Italy: Di Renzo Editore.

Hermann, R. (1968). *Lie Groups for Physicists*. New York, NY: W.A. Benjamin, Inc.

Hickmann, M., & Robert, S. (Eds.). (2006). *Space in Languages – Linguistic Systems and Cognitive Categories*. Amsterdam: John Benjamins Publishing Company. doi:10.1075/tsl.66

Hildebrand, S., & Tromba, A. (1996). *The Parsimonious Universe. Shape and Form in the Natural World*. New York, NY: Springer-Verlag, Inc. doi:10.1007/978-1-4612-2424-2

Hirsch, M. W. (1976). *Differential Topology*. New York, NY: Springer-Verlag, Inc. doi:10.1007/978-1-4684-9449-5

Hodges, W. (1977). *Logic. An Introduction to Elementary Logic*. Harmondsworth, UK: Penguin Books, Ltd.

Hodkinson, I., & Reynolds, M. (2007). Temporal Logic. In Handbook of Modal Logic. Amsterdam: Elsevier, B.V.

Horkheimer, M., & Adorno, T. W. (1947). Dialektik der Aufklärung. Philosophische Fragments. Amsterdam: Querido Verlag N.V.

Hsu, P.-J., Mauerer, T., Vogt, M., Yang, J. J., Seok Oh, Y., Cheong, S.-W., & Wu, W. et al. (2013). Hysteretic melting transition of a soliton lattice in a commensurate charge modulation. *Physical Review Letters*, *111*(26), 266401–266406. doi:10.1103/PhysRevLett.111.266401 PMID:24483807

Husemoller, D. (1975). *Fibre Bundles* (2nd ed.). New York, NY: Springer-Verlag, Inc.

Imbasciati, A. (2015). Nuove teorie sul funzionamento della mente. L'istituzione psicoanalitica e gli psicoanalisti. Milano, Italy: FrancoAngeli.

Ippoliti, E. (2007). *Il vero e il plausibile*. Morrisville, NC: Lulu Press, Inc.

Iurato, G. (2013a). Mathematical thought in the light of Matte Blanco work. *Philosophy of Mathematics Education Journal*, 27.

Iurato, G. (2013b). Σύμβολου: An attempt toward the early origins, Part 1. *Language & Psychoanalysis*, 2(2), 77–120. doi:10.7565/landp.2013.008

Iurato, G. (2013c). Σύμβολου: An attempt toward the early origins, Part 2. *Language & Psychoanalysis*, 2(2), 121–160. doi:10.7565/landp.2013.009

Iurato, G. (2014a). At the grounding of computational psychoanalysis: on the work of Ignacio Matte Blanco. A general history of culture overview of Matte Blanco bilogic in comparison. In *Proceedings of the 2014 IEEE 13th International Conference on Cognitive Informatics and Cognitive Computing*. Los Alamitos, CA: IEEE Computer Society Press.

Iurato, G. (2014b). The dawning of computational psychoanalysis. A proposal for some first elementary formalization attempts. *International Journal of Cognitive Informatics and Natural Intelligence*, 8(4), 50–82. doi:10.4018/ijcini.2014100104

Iurato, G. (2014c). *Alcune considerazioni critiche sul simbolismo*. Preprint No. hal-00980828 version 1. Available at HAL archives-ouvertes.

Iurato, G. (2015a). A Brief Comparison of the Unconscious as Seen by Jung and Lévi-Strauss. *Anthropology of Consciousness*, 26(1), 60–107. doi:10.1111/anoc.12032

Iurato, G. (2015b). Fetishism in Marketing. Some First Elementary Psychoanalytic Anthropology Remarks. In Business Management: A Practioners' Guide. Delhi: International Research Publication House.

Iurato, G. (2015c). A simple phylogenetic remark about certain human blood pressure values. *Journal of Biochemistry International*, 2(4), 162–165.

Iurato, G. (2016a). *A psychoanalytic enquiry on symbolic function*. Preprint No. hal-01361264 version 3. Available at HAL archives-ouvertes.

Iurato, G. (2016b). *A view of LSA/ESA in Computational Psychoanalysis*. Preprint No. hal-01353999 version 1. Available at HAL archives-ouvertes.

Iurato, G. (2016c). On Jacques Lacan Psychosis Theory and ERPs Analysis. *Journal of Biology and Nature*, 5(4), 234–240.

Iurato, G. (2016d). Some Comments on the Historical Role of *Fetishism* in Economic Anthropology. *Journal of Global Economics, Management and Business Research*, 7(1), 61–82.

Iurato, G. (2016e). The origins of symbol. *An historical-critical study of symbolic function, according to the phylo-ontogenetic perspective, as arising from the comparison of certain patterns of neuro-psychological sciences*. Paper Presented at the Satellite Event "On the edge of disciplines", Florence, Italy.

Iurato, G. (2016f). Two simple questions regarding cultural anthropology. *Journal of Global Research in Education and Social Science*, 8(1), 10–15.

Iurato, G. (2017a). An Essay in Denotational Mathematics. Rigorous Results. In Encyclopedia of Information Science and Technology (4th ed.). Hershey, PA: IGI Global.

Iurato, G. (2017b). Un raffronto critico fra la teoria platonica delle idee ed il paradosso di Kripke-Wittgenstein. In Platone nel pensiero moderno e contemporaneo (vol. 11). Villasanta (MB), Italy: Limina Mentis Edizioni.

Iurato, G. (2017c). *Rigidity of the Generalized Other, narrowness of the Otherness and demodernization, in the framework of symbolic interactionism. Ideology and Political Journal.* (in press)

Iurato, G., & Khrennikov, A. Yu. (2015). Hysteresis model of unconscious-conscious interconnection: Exploring dynamics on *m*-adic trees. *p-Adic Numbers, Ultrametric Analysis and Applications, 7*(4), 312–321. doi:10.1134/S2070046615040068

Iurato, G., & Khrennikov, A. Yu. (2017). On the topological structure of a mathematical model of human unconscious. *p-Adic Numbers, Ultrametric Analysis and Applications, 9*(1), 78–81. doi:10.1134/S2070046617010071

Iurato, G., Khrennikov, A. Yu., & Murtagh, F. (2016). Formal Foundations for the Origins of Human Consciousness. *p-Adic Numbers, Ultrametric Analysis and Applications, 8*(4), 249–279. doi:10.1134/S2070046616040014

Jackson, D. D. (1954). Some factors influencing the Œdipus Complex. *The Psychoanalytic Quarterly, 23*, 566–581. PMID:13215675

Jaffé, R. (2009). Ideale dell'Io, Idealizzazione. In *Psiche. Dizionario storico di psicologia, psichiatria, psicoanalisi, neuroscienze* (Vol. 1, pp. 494–500). Torino, Italy: Giulio Einaudi editore.

Johnson-Laird, P., & Bara, B. (1984). Syllogistic Inference. *Cognition, 16*(1), 1–61. doi:10.1016/0010-0277(84)90035-0 PMID:6540648

Juhás, G. (1999). On Semantics of Petri Nets over Partial Algebra. In *SOFSEM'99: Theory and Practice of Informatics. Proceedings of the 26th Conference on Current Trends in Theory and Practice of Informatics.* Berlin: Springer-Verlag. doi:10.1007/3-540-47849-3_29

Kafri, R., Markovitch, O., & Lancet, D. (2010). Spontaneous chiral symmetry breaking in early molecular networks. *Biology Direct, 5*(38), 1–13. PMID:20507625

Kandel, E. R. (2005). Psychiatry, Psychoanalysis, and the New Biology of Mind. Washington, DC: American Psychiatric Association Publishing, Inc.

Kaplan-Solms, K., & Solms, M. (2000). Clinical Studies in Neuro-Psychoanalysis. Introduction to a Depth Neuropsychology. London, UK: Karnac Books, Ltd.

Kastner, R. E. (2011). The broken symmetry of time. In Quantum Retrocausation: Theory and Experiment. Melville, NY: AIP Publications. doi:10.1063/1.3663714

Kemeny, J. G. (1959). A Philosopher Looks at Science. Princeton, NJ: D. Van Nostrand Reinhold Company, Inc.

Kemeny, J. G., Snell, J. L., & Thompson, G. L. (1974). *Introduction to Finite Mathematics* (3rd ed.). Englewood Cliffs, NJ: Prentice-Hall.

Kernberg, O. (2011). Suicide prevention for psychoanalytic institutes and societies. *Journal of the American Psychoanalytic Association, 60*(4), 707–719. doi:10.1177/0003065112449861 PMID:22786850

Khan Masud, R. M. (1970). *Le fétichisme comme négation du soi. Nouvelle Revue de Psychoanalyse, 2*.

Khan Masud, R. M. (1979). Alienation in perversions. London, UK: The Hogarth Press, Ltd.

Khrennikov, A. Yu. (1991). *p*-Adic quantum mechanics with *p*-adic valued functions. *Journal of Mathematical Physics, 32*(4), 932–937. doi:10.1063/1.529353

Khrennikov, A. Yu. (1998). Human subconscious as the *p*-adic dynamical system. *Journal of Theoretical Biology, 193*(2), 179–196. doi:10.1006/jtbi.1997.0604 PMID:9714931

Khrennikov, A. Yu. (2002). *Classical and quantum mental models and Freud's theory of unconscious mind. Series in Mathematical Modelling in Physics, Enginnering and Cognitive Sciences* (Vol. 1). Växjö, Sweden: Växjö University Press.

Khrennikov, A. Yu. (2007). Toward an adequate mathematical model of mental space: Conscious/unconscious dynamics on *m*-adic trees. *Bio Systems, 90*(3), 656–675. doi:10.1016/j.biosystems.2007.02.004 PMID:17400367

Kissin, B. (1986). *Conscious and Unconscious Programs in the Brain*. New York, NY: Plenum Publishing Corporation. doi:10.1007/978-1-4613-2187-3

Köhler, T. (2007). *Freuds Psychoanalyse. Eine Einführung* (2nd ed.). Stuttgart, Germany: W. Kohlhammer GmbH.

Kovacs, A. L. (1989). Degeneracy and asymmetry in Biology. In *Nonlinear Structures in Physical Systems. Pattern Formation, Chaos, and Waves. Proceedings of the 2nd Woodward Conference*. New York, NY: Springer-Verlag, Inc.

Kultgen, J. (1976). Lévi-Strauss on Unconscious Social Structures. *The Southwestern Journal of Philosophy, 7*(1), 153–159. doi:10.5840/swjphil19767118

Kuper, J. (Ed.). (1988). *A Lexicon of Psychology, Psychiatry and Psychoanalysis*. London, UK: Routledge.

Lacan, J. (2014). *The Seminar of Jacques Lacan. Book X: The Anxiety* (J. A. Miller, Ed.; A. R. Price, Trans.). Malden, MA: Polity Press.

Lacas, M.-L. (2007). La démarche originale de Gisela Pankow. Gisela Pankows original thought processes. *LÉvolution Psychiatrique, 72*(1), 15–24. doi:10.1016/j.evopsy.2006.11.001

Làdavas, E., & Berti, A. (2014). Neuropsicologia (3rd ed.). Bologna, Italy: Società editrice il Mulino.

Lagache, D. (1961). *La psychanalyse et la structure de la personnalité*. Paper Presented au Colloquium International de Royaumont, Paris, France.

Lagache, D. (1965). Le modèle psychanalytique de la personnalité. In *La Folle du Logis. La psychanalyse comme science exacte* (pp. 159–183). Paris: PUF-Presses Universitaires de France.

Lample-De-Groot, J. (1962). Ego ideal and Superego. *The Psychoanalytic Study of the Child, 17*, 94–106.

Langs, R. (1990). Guida alla psicoterapia. Un'introduzione all'approccio comunicativo. Torino, Italy: Bollati Boringhieri editore.

Laplanche, J. (2000). Problematiche II. Castrazione. Simbolizzazioni. Bari-Roma, Italy: La Biblioteca.

Laplanche, J. (2001). *L'inconscio e l'Es*. Bari-Roma, Italy: La Biblioteca.

Laplanche, J. (2007). *L'après-coup. Bari-Roma, Italy: La Biblioteca*. Preprint available at www.math. berkeley.edu

Laplanche, J., & Pontalis, J.-B. (1967). Vocabulaire de la psychoanalyse. Paris: Presses Universitaires de France.

Laplanche, J., & Pontalis, J.-B. (1988). Fantasma originario, fantasmi delle origini, origini del fantasma. Bologna, Italy: Società editrice il Mulino.

Lauro-Grotto, R. (2008). The unconscious as an ultrametric set. *The American Imago, 64*(4), 52–62. doi:10.1353/aim.2008.0009

Lauro-Grotto, R. (2014a). Formal Approaches in the Age of Mirror Neurons. Hints from Psychoanalytic Theories and Practice. In *Proceedings of the 2014 IEEE 13th International Conference on Cognitive Informatics and Cognitive Computing*. Los Alamitos, CA: IEEE Computer Society Press.

Lawson, M. K. (2005). Constructing ordered groupoids. *Cahiers de Topologie et Géométrie Différentielle Catégoriques, 46*(2), 123–138.

Lenz Dunker, I. (2008). Psychology and Psychoanalysis in Brazil. From Cultural Syncretism to the Collapse of Liberal Individualism. *Theory & Psychology, 18*(2), 223–236. doi:10.1177/0959354307087883

Lerner, D. (Ed.). (1961). Quality and Quantity. New York, NY: The Free Press of Glencoe.

Levitz, K., & Levitz, H. (1979). *Logic and Boolean Algebra*. Woodbury, NY: Barron's Educational Series, Inc.

Lewin, R. (1996). Communicating with the schizophrenic superego. *The Journal of the American Academy of Psychoanalysis, 24*(4), 709–736. PMID:9220382

Lewis, C. I. (1912). Implication and the Algebra of Logic. *Mind, 21*(84), 522–531. doi:10.1093/mind/XXI.84.522

Lis, A., Mazzeschi, C., & Zennaro, A. (2007). *La psicoanalisi. Un percorso concettuale fra tradizione e attualità (2nd ed.)*. Roma, Italy: Carocci editore.

Lis, A., Zennaro, A., Mazzeschi, C., Salcuni, S., & Parolin, L. (2003). *Breve dizionario di psicoanalisi*. Roma, Italy: Carocci editore.

Loewald, H. W. (1962). The Superego and the Ego-Ideal. II. Superego and Time. *The International Journal of Psycho-Analysis, 43*, 264–268. PMID:13931287

Loewald, H. W. (1988). Sublimation. Inquires into Theoretical Psychoanalysis. New Haven, CT: Yale University Press.

Loewald, H. W. (1989). Papers on Psychoanalysis. New Haven, CT: Yale University Press.

Lolli, G. (1991). Introduzione alla logica formale. Bologna, Italy: Società editrice il Mulino.

Lolli, G. (2000). Un logico esamina i modelli mentali. In Ragionamento: psicologia e logica. Firenze, Italy: Giunti Gruppo Editoriale.

Lolli, G. (2005). QED – Fenomenologia della dimostrazione. Torino, Italy: Bollati Boringhieri editore.

Macola, E. (Ed.). (2014). Sublimazione e perversione. Attualità Lacaniana. Rivista della Scuola Lacaniana di Psicoanalisi, 18, 7-108.

Maffei, L. (2014). Elogio della lentezza. Bologna, Italy: Società editrice il Mulino.

Maffei, L. (2016). Elogio della ribellione. Bologna, Italy: Società editrice il Mulino.

Mancia, M. (Ed.). (1990). Super-Io e Ideale dell'Io. Roma, Italy: Casa Editrice Astrolabio-Ubaldini Editore.

Mancia, M. (Ed.). (2006). Psychoanalysis and Neuroscience. Milan, Italy: Springer-Verlag Italia. doi:10.1007/88-470-0550-7

Marcuse, H. (1964). One-Dimensional Man. Studies in the Ideology of Advanced Industrial Society. Boston, MA: Beacon Press, Inc.

Matte Blanco, I. (1975). The Unconscious as Infinite Sets. An Essay in Bi-Logic. London, UK: Gerald Duckworth & Company, Ltd.

Matte Blanco, I. (1988). *Thinking, Feeling, and Being. Clinical Reflections of the Fundamental Antinomy on Human Beings and World*. London, UK: Routledge.

Matthews, P. T. (1974). *Introduction to Quantum Mechanics*. Maidenhead, UK: McGraw-Hill Publishing Company Limited.

Maurin, K. (1997). *The Riemann Legacy. Riemann Ideas in Mathematics and Physics*. Dordrecht, The Netherlands: Kluwer Academic Publishers. doi:10.1007/978-94-015-8939-0

McCulloch, W. S. (1965). *Embodiments of Mind*. Cambridge, MA: The MIT Press.

Miller, P. H. (1983). *Theories of Developmental Psychology*. New York, NY: W.H. Freeman & Co.

Milrod, D. (2002). The superego. Its formation, structure, and functioning. *The Psychoanalytic Study of the Child, 57*, 131–148. PMID:12723129

Minsky, M. (1975). A Framework for the Representation Knowledge. In The Psychology of Computer Vision. New York, NY: McGraw-Hill Book Company.

Mitchell, S. A., & Black, M. J. (1995). *Freud and beyond. A History of Modern Psychoanalysic Thought*. New York, NY: Basic Books. A Division of Harper Collins Publishers.

Moore, B. E., & Fine, B. D. (Eds.). (1990). Psychoanalytic Terms and Concepts. New York, NY: The American Psychoanalytic Association.

Moore, D. S. (2015). *The Developing Genome. An Introduction to Behavioural Epigenetics*. New York, NY: Oxford University Press.

Mordant, I. (1990). Using attribute-memories to resolve a contradiction in the work of Matte Blanco. *The International Review of Psycho-Analysis*, *17*, 475–480.

Morgan, J., & Tian, G. (2007). *Ricci Flow and the Poincaré Conjecture. Clay Mathematics Monographs, Volume No. 3*. Providence, RI: American Mathematical Society Publications.

Murtagh, F. (2012a). Ultrametric model of mind, I [Review]. *p-Adic Numbers, Ultrametric Analysis and Applications*, *4*(3), 193–206. doi:10.1134/S2070046612030041

Murtagh, F. (2012b). Ultrametric model of mind, II. Application to text content analysis. *p-Adic Numbers, Ultrametric Analysis and Applications*, *4*(3), 207–221. doi:10.1134/S2070046612030053

Murtagh, F. (2013). The new science of complex systems through ultrametric analysis. Application to search and discovery, to narrative and to thinking. *p-Adic Numbers, Ultrametric Analysis and Applications*, *5*(4), 326–337. doi:10.1134/S2070046613040067

Murtagh, F. (2014a). Pattern recognition of subconscious underpinnings of cognition using ultrametric topological mapping of thinking and memory. *International Journal of Cognitive Informatics and Natural Intelligence*, *8*(4), 1–16. doi:10.4018/ijcini.2014100101

Murtagh, F. (2014b). Mathematical representations of Matte Blancos bi-logic, based on metric space and ultrametric or hierarchical topology: Towards practical application. *Language and Psychoanalysis*, *3*(2), 40–63. doi:10.7565/landp.2014.008

Murtagh, F. (2014c). Pattern Recognition in Mental Processes: Determining Vestiges of the Subconscious through Ultrametric Component Analysis. In *Proceedings of the 2014 IEEE 13th International Conference on Cognitive Informatics and Cognitive Computing*. Los Alamitos, CA: IEEE Computer Society Press. doi:10.1109/ICCI-CC.2014.6921455

Murtagh, F. (2017). *Data Science Foundations. Geometry and Topology of Complex Hierarchic Systems and Big Data Analytics*. Boca Raton, FL: Chapman & Hall/CRC Press.

Murtagh, F., & Iurato, G. (2016). Human Behaviour, Benign or Malevalent: Understanding the Human Psyche, Performing Therapy, based on Affective Mentalization and Matte-Blancos Bi-Logic. *Annals of Translational Medicine*, *4*(24), 486–496. doi:10.21037/atm.2016.12.37 PMID:28149848

Murtagh, F., & Iurato, G. (2017). Visualization of Jacques Lacan's Registers of the Psychoanalytic Field, and Discovery of Metaphor and of Metonymy. Analytical Case Study of Edgar Allan Poe's "The Purloined Letter". *Language and Psychoanalysis*. (in press)

Nagel, T. (1993). Summary. In *Experimental and Theoretical Studies of Consciousness. Novartis Foundation Symposium No. 174*. New York, NY: John Wiley & Sons, Ltd.

Nannini, S. (2007). Naturalismo cognitivo. Per una teoria materialistica della mente. Macerata, Italy: Edizioni Quodlibet.

Nannini, S. (2011). L'anima e il corpo. Un'introduzione storica alla filosofia della mente. Roma-Bari, Italy: Laterza Editori.

Nannini, S. (2015). Time and Consciousness in Cognitive Naturalism. *Rivista Internazionale di Filosofia e Psicologia*, *6*(3), 458–473.

Napolitano, F. (2009). Rappresentazione, 2. In *Psiche. Dizionario storico di psicologia, psichiatria, psicoanalisi, neuroscienze* (Vol. 2, pp. 919–923). Torino, Italy: Giulio Einaudi editore.

Neubauer, K. (2004). Semantica storica. In Dizionario degli studi culturali. Roma, Italy: Meltemi editore.

Nunberg, H. (1932). Allgemeine Neurosenlehre auf psychoanalytischer Grundlage. Berlin: Verlag Hans Hüber.

Øhrstrøm, P., & Hasle, P. F. V. (Eds.). (1995). *Temporal Logic. From Ancient Ideas to Artificial Intelligence. Studies in Linguistics and Philosophy, Volume No. 57.* Dordrecht, The Netherlands: Kluwer Academic Publishers.

Oliverio, A. (1982). Biologia e comportamento. Bologna, Italy: Nicola Zanichelli Editore.

Oliverio, A. (2016). Il cervello e linconscio. *Psicobiettivo*, *36*(3), 251–259. doi:10.3280/PSOB2016-003015

Oliverio, A. (2017). Il cervello che impara. Neuropedagogia dall'infanzia alla vecchiaia. Firenze, Italy: Giunti Editore.

Pankow, G. (1977). L'uomo e la sua psicosi. Milano, Italy: Giangiacomo Feltrinelli Editore.

Pankow, G. (1979). Struttura familiare e psicosi. Milano, Italy: Giangiacomo Feltrinelli Editore.

Panksepp, J., & Biven, L. (2012). The Archeology of Mind. Neuroevolutionary Origins of Human Emotion. New York, NY: W.W. Norton & Company.

Papagno, C. (2010). Neuropsicologia della memoria. Bologna, Italy: Società editrice il Mulino.

Parsons, T. (1970). *Social Structure and Personality*. New York, NY: The Free Press. A Division of The Macmillan Company.

Percacci, R. (1986). Geometry of Nonlinear Field Theories. Singapore: World Scientific Publishing. doi:10.1142/0251

Peterburs, J., Nitsch, A. M., Miltner, W. H. R., & Straube, T. (2013). Impaired representation of time in schizophrenia is linked to positive symptoms and cognitive demand. *PLoS ONE*, *8*(6), e67615/1–7. doi:10.1371/journal.pone.0067615 PMID:23826328

Petersen, W. P., & Arbenz, P. (2004). *Introduction to Parallel Computing*. New York, NY: Oxford University Press, Inc.

Petit, C., & Prévost, G. (1971). Genetica ed evoluzione. Milano, Italy: Arnoldo Mondadori Editore.

Petocz, A. (2004). *Freud, psychoanalysis and symbolism*. Cambridge, UK: Cambridge University Press.

Petrilli, S., & Ponzio, A. (2005). *Semiotics Unbounded. Interpretive Routes Through the Open Network of Signs*. Toronto: The University of Toronto Press. doi:10.3138/9781442657113

Petrini, P., Casadei, A., & Chiricozzi, F. (Eds.). (2011). Trasgressione, violazione, perversione. Eziopatogenesi, diagnosi e terapia. Milano, Italy: FrancoAngeli.

Petrini, P., Renzi, A., Casadei, A., & Mandese, A. (2013). Dizionario di psicoanalisi. Con elementi di psichiatria, psicodinamica e psicologia dinamica. Milano, Italy: FrancoAngeli.

Piattelli Palmarini, M. (1987). Scienza come cultura. Protagonisti, luoghi e idee delle scienze contemporanee. Milano, Italy: Arnoldo Mondadori Editore.

Pierce, B. C. (2002). *Types and Programming Languages*. Cambridge, MA: The MIT Press.

Pieri, P. F. (2005). Dizionario junghiano (Edizione ridotta). Torino, Italy: Bollati Boringhieri editore.

Pini, B. (1967). Primo Corso di Algebra. Bologna, Italy: CLUEB Editrice.

Piras, F., Piras, F., Ciullo, V., Danese, E., Caltagirone, C. & Spalletta, G. (2013). Time dysperception perspective for acquired brain injury. *Frontiers in Neurology*, *4*, 217-226.

Piscicelli, U. (1994). Sessuologia. Teoremi psicosomatici e relazionali. Padova, Italy: Piccin Nuova Libraria.

Pizzi, C. (Ed.). (1974). La logica del tempo. Torino, Italy: Bollati Boringhieri Editore.

Poggi, S. (1977). I sistemi dell'esperienza. Bologna, Italy: Società editrice il Mulino.

Pollo, M. (2016). La nostalgia dell'uroboros. Contributi a una psicologia culturale delle nuove addiction. Milano, Italy: FrancoAngeli.

Putnam, H. (1956). Mathematics and the Existence of Abstract Entities. *Philosophical Studies*, *7*(6), 81–88. doi:10.1007/BF02221758

Putnam, H. (1975). Filosofia della logica. Nominalismo e realismo nella logica contemporanea. Milano, Italy: ISEDI – Istituto Editoriale Internazionale.

Quan, P. M. (1969). *Introduction a la géométrie des variétés différentiables*. Paris: Éditions Dunod.

Radicati, L. A. (1985). Remarks on the early developments of the notion of symmetry breaking. In *Symmetries in Physics (1600-1980). Proceedings of the 1st International Meeting on the History of Scientific Ideas*. Barcelona: Servei de Publicacions, Bellaterra.

Rayner, E. (1995). *Unconscious Logic. An Introduction to Matte Blanco's Bi-Logic and its Uses*. New York, NY: Routledge.

Rayner, E. (1998). Foreword. In *The Unconscious as Infinite Sets. An Essay in Bi-Logic* (pp. xviii–xxiv). London, UK: Karnac Books, Ltd.

Recalcati, M. (2003). Introduzione alla psicoanalisi contemporanea. Milano, Italy: Bruno Mondadori Editore.

Recalcati, M. (2007a). Elogio dell'inconscio. Dodici argomenti in difesa della psicoanalisi. Milano, Italy: Bruno Mondadori.

Recalcati, M. (2007b). Lo psicoanalista e la città. L'inconscio e il discorso del capitalista. Roma, Italy: manifestolibri.

Recalcati, M. (2010). L'uomo senza inconscio. Figure della nuova clinica psicoanalitica. Milano, Italy: Raffaello Cortina Editore.

Recalcati, M. (2016). *Jacques Lacan* (Vols. 1-2). Milano, Italy: Raffaello Cortina Editore.

Redondi, P. (2007). Storie del tempo. Roma-Bari, Italy: Editori Laterza.

Reich, A. (1954). Early identifications as archaic elements in the Superego. *Journal of the American Psychoanalytic Association*, *2*(2), 218–238. doi:10.1177/000306515400200203 PMID:13151996

Reisig, W. (1988). Temporal Logic and Causality in Concurrent Systems. In R. H. Voght (Ed.), Lecture Notes in Computer Science: Vol. 335. *CONCURRENCY 1988* (pp. 121–139). Berlin: Springer-Verlag. doi:10.1007/3-540-50403-6_37

Rentz, J. (Ed.). (2002). Lecture Notes in Computer Science: Vol. 2293. Qualitative spatial reasoning with topological information. Berlin: Springer-Verlag. doi:10.1007/3-540-70736-0

Rescher, N., & Urquhart, A. (1971). Temporal Logic. Wien, Austria: Springer-Verlag GmbH. doi:10.1007/978-3-7091-7664-1

Reverberi, C., Pischedda, D., Burigo, M., & Cherubini, P. (2012). Deduction without awareness. *Acta Psychologica*, *139*(1), 244–253. doi:10.1016/j.actpsy.2011.09.011 PMID:22019058

Riehl, J. P. (2010). *Mirror-Image Asymmetry. An Introduction to the Origin and Consequences of Chirality*. Hoboken, NJ: John Wiley & Sons, Inc. doi:10.1002/9780470588888

Riolo, F. (2009). Trasformazione. In *Psiche. Dizionario storico di psicologia, psichiatria, psicoanalisi, neuroscienze* (Vol. 2, pp. 1112–1116). Torino, Italy: Giulio Einaudi editore.

Rose, J. R. (Ed.). (2011). *Mapping Psychic Reality. Triangulation, Communication, and Insight. Psychoanalytic Ideas*. London, UK: Karnac Books, Ltd.

Rossi, R., De Fazio, F., Gatti, U., & Rocco, G. (2008, Feb.). Perizie e consulenze psichiatriche su Diamante Stefano, Stevanin Gianfranco, Bilancia Donato, Panini Giorgio. *POL.it – The Italian On Line Psychiatric Magazine*.

Roudinesco, E. (1997). Jacques Lacan. Outline of a life, history of a system of thought. Oxford, UK: Polity Press.

Rycroft, C. (1968a). A critical dictionary of psychoanalysis. London, UK: Thomas Nelson & Sons, Ltd.

Rycroft, C. (1968b). Imagination and reality. Psychoanalytical essays 1951–1961. London, UK: The Hogarth Press, Ltd.

Sabbadini, A. (1979). Introduzione. In Il tempo in psicoanalisi. Milano, Italy: Giangiacomo Feltrinelli Editore.

Sandler, J., Holder, A., & Meers, D. (1963). The Ego Ideal and the Ideal Self. *The Psychoanalytic Study of the Child*, *18*, 139–158. PMID:14147277

Sandler, J. J. (Ed.). (1981). La ricerca in psicoanalisi (Vols. 1-2). Torino, Italy: Bollati Boringhieri editore.

Sannella, D., & Tarlecki, A. (2012). *Foundations of Algebraic Specification and Formal Software Development. Monographs in Theoretical Computer Science. An EATCS Series.* Berlin: Springer-Verlag. doi:10.1007/978-3-642-17336-3

Sasso, G. (1982). Le strutture anagrammatiche della poesia. Milano, Italy: Giangiacomo Feltrinelli Editore.

Sasso, G. (1993). La mente intralinguistica. L'instabilità del segno: anagrammi e parole dentro le parole. Genova, Italy: Marietti Editore.

Sasso, G. (1999). Struttura dell'oggetto e della rappresentazione. Roma, Italy: Casa Editrice Astrolabio-Ubaldini Editore.

Sasso, G. (2005). Psicoanalisi e Neuroscienze. Roma, Italy: Casa Editrice Astrolabio-Ubaldini Editore.

Sasso, G. (2011). La nascita della coscienza. Roma, Italy: Casa Editrice Astrolabio-Ubaldini Editore.

Scabini, E. (1973). Ideazione e psicoanalisi. Milano, Italy: Giangiacomo Feltrinelli Editore.

Schmitt, A., Hasan, A., Gruber, O., & Falkai, P. (2011). Schizophrenia as a disorder of disconnectivity. *European Archives of Psychiatry and Clinical Neuroscience, 261*(2), S150–S154. doi:10.1007/s00406-011-0242-2 PMID:21866371

Segalen, M. (1998). Rites et rituels contemporains. Paris: Les Éditions Nathan.

Semi, A. A. (2003). La coscienza in psicoanalisi. Milano, Italy: Raffaello Cortina Editore.

Semi, A.A. (Ed.). (1989). *Trattato di Psicoanalisi* (Vols. 1-2). Milano, Italy: Raffaello Cortina Editore.

Severino, E. (2008). La strada. La follia e la gioia. Milano, Italy: BUR Saggi.

Silvestri, D. (2013). Linguistica implicita e linguistica esplicita. In Simposio Lévi-Strauss. Uno sguardo dall'oggi. Milano, Italy: il Saggiatore.

Skelton, R. (1984). Understanding Matte Blanco. *The International Journal of Psycho-Analysis, 65*, 453–460. PMID:6544756

Skelton, R. (1990). Generalizations from Freud to Matte Blanco. *The International Review of Psycho-Analysis, 17*, 471–474.

Skillicorn, D. (1994). *Foundations of Parallel Programming.* Cambridge, UK: Cambridge University Press. doi:10.1017/CBO9780511526626

Sluzki, C. E., & Ransom, D. C. (1979). Il doppio legame: la genesi dell'approccio relazionale allo studio della famiglia. Roma, Italy: Casa Editrice Astrolabio-Ubaldini Editore.

Smirnov, V. N. (1970). *La transaction fétichique. Nouvelle Revue de Psychoanalyse, 2.*

Solms, M., & Turnbull, O. (2003). The Brain and the Inner World. An Introduction to the Neuroscience of Subjective Experience. New York, NY: Other Press, LLC.

Somenzi, V. (1998). Prefazione. In Categorie, tempo e linguaggio. Quaderni di Methodologia, N. 5. Roma, Italy: Società Stampa Sportiva.

Sossinsky, A. (2000). Nodi. Genesi di una teoria matematica. Torino, Italy: Bollati Boringhieri editore.

Souriau, J. M. (1964). *Géométrie et relativité*. Paris: Éditions Hermann.

Sparsø, J., & Furber, S. (Eds.). (2001). Principles of Asynchronous Circuit Design. A Systems Perspective. Dordrecht, The Netherlands: Springer-Science + Business Media, B.V. doi:10.1007/978-1-4757-3385-3

Spedini, G. (2005). Antropologia evoluzionistica (2nd ed.). Padova, Italy: Piccin Nuova Libraria.

Spitz, R. A. (1957). No and yes. On the genesis of human communication. New York, NY: International University Press, Inc.

Stanghellini, G., Ballerini, M., Presenza, S., Mancini, M., Raballo, A., Blasi, S., & Cutting, J. (2016). Psychopathology of lived time: Abnormal time experience in persons with schizophrenia. *Schizophrenia Bulletin. The Journal of Psychoses and Related Disorders*, *42*(1), 45–55.

Steedman, M. (2000). *Surface Structure and Interpretation*. Boston, MA: The MIT Press.

Stich, M., Blanco, C., & Hochberg, D. (2013). Chiral and chemical oscillations in a simple dimerization model. *Physical Chemistry Chemical Physics*, *15*(1), 255–261. doi:10.1039/C2CP42620J PMID:23064600

Stirling, C. (2001). *Modal and Temporal Properties of Processes*. New York, NY: Springer-Verlag. doi:10.1007/978-1-4757-3550-5

Strocchi, F. (1981). Classification of Solutions of Non-Linear Hyperbolic Equations and Non-Linear Elliptic Problems. In Topics in Functional Analysis 1980-81. Pisa, Italy: Pubblicazioni della Scuola Normale Superiore.

Strocchi, F. (1999). Symmetry Breaking in Classical Systems and Nonlinear Functional Analysis. Pisa, Italy: Pubblicazioni della Scuola Normale Superiore.

Strocchi, F. (2000). Simmetrie e rotture di simmetrie in fisica. Corso di orientamento preuniversitario, Cortona, Italy.

Strocchi, F. (2008). *Symmetry Breaking* (2nd ed.). Berlin: Springer-Verlag. doi:10.1007/978-3-540-73593-9

Strocchi, F. (2012). *Spontaneous Symmetry Breaking in Quantum Systems. A review for Scholarpedia*. Preprint arXiv:1201.5459v1

Tabossi, P. (2009). Rappresentazione, 1. In *Psiche. Dizionario storico di psicologia, psichiatria, psicoanalisi, neuroscienze* (Vol. 2, pp. 914–919). Torino, Italy: Giulio Einaudi editore.

Tallis, R. (2002). Hidden Minds. A History of the Unconscious. New York, NY: Arcade Publishing, Inc.

Tanenbaum, A. S., & Bos, H. (2015). *Modern Operating Systems* (4th ed.). Essex, UK: Pearson Education Limited.

Target, M., & Fonagy, P. (2002). The role of the father and child development. In The Importance of Fathers. A Psychoanalytic Re-Evaluation. London, UK: Routledge.

Terminio, N. (2009). Misurare l'inconscio? Coordinate psicoanalitiche nella ricerca in psicoterapia. Milano, Italy: Bruno Mondadori.

Thom, R. (1972). Symmetries Gained and Lost. In *Broken Symmetries. Proceedings of the 3rd GIFT International Seminar in Theoretical Physics organized by the Spanish-Inter-University Group in Theoretical Physics*. Saragoza, Spain: Scientific Information Service, Ltd.

Thom, R. (1980). *Stabilità strutturale e morfogenesi. Saggio di una teoria generale dei modelli*. Torino, Italy: Giulio Einaudi editore.

Thom, R. (1985). *Modelli matematici della morfogenesi*. Torino, Italy: Giulio Einaudi editore.

Thomä, H., & Kächele, H. (1989). *Psychoanalytic Practice* (Vols. 1-2). Berlin: Springer-Verlag.

Tibaldi, M. (2004). Critica archetipica. In Dizionario degli studi culturali. Roma, Italy: Meltemi editore.

Tokhi, M. O., Hossain, M. A., & Shaheed, M. H. (2003). *Parallel Computing for Real-time Signal Processing and Control*. London, UK: Springer-Verlag London. doi:10.1007/978-1-4471-0087-4

Toraldo di Francia, G. (1976). *L'indagine del mondo fisico*. Torino, Italy: Giulio Einaudi editore.

Uznadze, D. N., Prangisvili, A. S., Bassin, F. V., & Razran, G. (1972). *L'inconscio nella psicologia sovietica*. Roma, Italy: Editori Riuniti.

Vaccarino, G. (2006). Scienza e semantica. Milano, Italy: Edizioni Melquiades.

Vallortigara, G., & Panciera, N. (2014). Cervelli che contano. Milano, Italy: Adelphi Edizioni.

Van Wezel, J., & Littlewood, P. (2010). Chiral symmetry breaking and charge order. *Physics*, *3*, 87. doi:10.1103/Physics.3.87

Vattimo, G., Ferraris, M., & Marconi, D. (Eds.). (1993). Enciclopedia Garzanti di Filosofia. Milano, Italy: Garzanti Editore.

Vegetti Finzi, S. (Ed.). (1976). Il bambino nella psicoanalisi. Testi di S. Freud, Jung, Reich, Klein, A. Freud, Spitz, Winnicott, Musatti, Fornari, Erikson, Laing, Lacan, Mannoni. Bologna, Italy: Nicola Zanichelli Editore.

Venema, Y. (2001). Temporal Logic. In The Blackwell Guide to Philosophical Logic. Oxford, UK: Basil Blackwell Publishers.

Verdiglione, A. (1977). Matematica dell'inconscio. In Feticismo, linguaggio, afasia, matematica dell'inconscio. Venezia, Italy: Marsilio Editori.

Vicario, G. B. (1997). Il tempo in psicologia. *Le Scienze*, *30*(347), 43–51.

Vicario, G. B. (2005). Il tempo. Saggio di psicologia sperimentale. Bologna, Italy: Società editrice il Mulino.

Viret, J. (2012). Topological Approach of Jungian Psychology. *Acta Biotheoretica*, *58*(2), 233–245. PMID:20658172

Voevodin, V. V. (1992). Mathematical Foundations of Parallel Computing. Singapore: World Scientific Publishing. doi:10.1142/1533

von Karger, B. (1995). An algebraic approach to temporal logic. In *Lecture Notes on Computer Science: Vol. 915. Proceedings of the Sixth International Joint Conference on Theory and Practice of Software Development (TAPSOFT '95)*. Berlin: Springer-Verlag. doi:10.1007/3-540-59293-8_198

von Karger, B. (2002). Temporal Algebra. In Lecture Notes in Computer Science: Vol. 2297. Algebraic and Coalgebraic Methods in the Mathematics of Program Construction. Berlin: Springer-Verlag. doi:10.1007/3-540-47797-7_9

Von Scheve, C., & Salmela, M. (Eds.). (2014). *Collective Emotions. Perspectives from Psychology, Philosophy, and Sociology*. Oxford, UK: Oxford University Press.

Von Wright, G. H. (1969). *Time, Change and Contradiction*. Cambridge, UK: Cambridge University Press.

Wang, Y. (2008). On Concept Algebra: A Denotational Mathematical Structure for Knowledge and Software Modeling. *International Journal of Cognitive Informatics and Natural Intelligence, 2*(2), 1–19. doi:10.4018/jcini.2008040101

Wang, Y. (2010). A Sociopsychological Perspective on Collective Intelligence in Metaheuristic Computing. *International Journal of Applied Metaheuristic Computing, 1*(1), 110–128. doi:10.4018/jamc.2010102606

Wang, Y., Wang, Y., Patel, S., & Patel, D. (2006). A Layered Reference Model of the Brain. *IEEE Transactions on Systems, Man and Cybernetics. Part C, Applications and Reviews, 36*(2), 124–133. doi:10.1109/TSMCC.2006.871126

Wang, Y., Zadeh, L. A., Widrow, B., Howard, N., Wood, S., Patel, S., & Zhang, D. et al. (2017). Abstract Intelligence: Embodying and Enabling Cognitive Systems by Mathematical Engineering. *International Journal of Cognitive Informatics and Natural Intelligence, 11*(1), 1–22. doi:10.4018/IJCINI.2017010101

Wang, Y., Zhang, D., & Kinsner, D. (Eds.). (2011). *Advances in Cognitive Informatics and Cognitive Computing*. Berlin: Springer-Verlag.

Watanabe, S. (1969). *Knowing and Guessing. A Quantitative Study of Inference and Information*. New York, NY: John Wiley & Sons, Inc.

Watzlawick, P., Beavin, J. H., & Jackson, D. D. (1967). Pragmatics of Human Communication. A Study of Interactional Patterns, Pathologies, and Paradoxes. New York, NY: W.W. Norton & Company.

Weinstein, A. (1996). Groupoids: Unifying Internal and External Symmetry. *Notices of the American Mathematical Society, 43*(7), 744–752.

Westphal, B. (2007). La Géocritique. Réel, fiction, espace. Paris: Les Éditions de Minuit.

Wetterich, C. (2005). Spontaneous Symmetry Breaking Origins for the Difference Between Time and Space. *Physical Review Letters, 94*(1), 011692–011696. doi:10.1103/PhysRevLett.94.011602 PMID:15698063

White, D. R., & Jorion, P. (1996). Kinship networks and discrete structure theory: Applications and implications. *Social Networks, 18*(3), 267–314. doi:10.1016/0378-8733(95)00277-4

Whitebook, J. (1995). *Perversion and Utopia. A Study in Psychoanalysis and Critical Theory*. Cambridge, MA: The MIT Press.

Whitrow, G. J. (1988). *Time in History. Views of Time from Prehistory to the Present Day*. Oxford, UK: Oxford University Press.

Wimmer, M., & Ciompi, L. (1996). Evolutionary aspects of affective-cognitive interactions in the light of Ciompi's concept of "affect-logic". *Evolution & Cognition, 2*, 37–58.

Yang, J., Kanazawa, S., Yamaguchi, M. K., & Kuriki, I. (2016). Cortical response to categorical colour perception in infants investigated by near-infrared spectroscopy. *Proceedings of the National Academy of Sciences of the United States of America, 113*(9), 2370-2375.

Zadeh, L. A. (1965). Fuzzy Sets. *Information and Control, 8*(3), 338–353. doi:10.1016/S0019-9958(65)90241-X

Zadeh, L. A. (1968). Fuzzy Algorithms. *Information and Control, 12*(2), 94–102. doi:10.1016/S0019-9958(68)90211-8

Zadeh, L. A. (1988). Fuzzy Logic. *Computer, 21*(4), 83–93. doi:10.1109/2.53

Zapparoli, G. C. (1970). La perversione logica. I rapporti tra sessualità e pensiero nella tradizione psicoanalitica. Milano, Italy: Franco Angeli Editore.

Zeeman, E. C. (1961). The topology of the brain and the visual perception. *Topology of 3-manifolds and related topics. Proceedings of the University of Georgia Institute*.

Zeeman, E. C. (1976a). Brain Modelling. In *Lecture Notes in Mathematics: Vol. 525. Structural Stability. The Theory of Catastrophes, and Applications in the Sciences. Proceedings of the Conference*. Berlin: Springer-Verlag.

Zeeman, E. C. (1976b). Catastrophe Theory. *Scientific American, 234*(April), 65–83. doi:10.1038/scientificamerican0476-65

Zeh, H. D. (2007). *The Physical Basis of the Direction of Time* (5th ed.). Berlin: Springer-Verlag.

Zentall, T. R. (2013). Animals represent the past and the future. *Evolutionary Psychology, 11*(3), 573–590. doi:10.1177/147470491301100307 PMID:24027784

Zepf, S., & Gerlach, A. (2012). Commentary on Kernbergs suicide prevention for psychoanalytic institutes and societies. *Journal of the American Psychoanalytic Association, 61*(4), 771–786. doi:10.1177/0003065113496634 PMID:23918822

Živaljević, R. T. (2006). *Groupoids in combinatorics – applications of a theory of local symmetries*. Preprint arXiv: math/0605508v1 [math.CO]

ENDNOTES

[1]   An important monograph regarding applications of advanced mathematical methods – mainly category theory – to psychological sciences and neurophysiology, is (Ehresmann & Vanbremeersch, 2007).

[2]   Cf. (Papagno, 2010).

[3]   See (Lauro-Grotto, 2008) and references therein.

[4]   In this section, we mainly stress the passage from symmetric to asymmetric thought. Nevertheless, if one considers the symmetry-asymmetry duality as, in a certain sense, analogous to the Freudian primary-secondary process duality, then it will be very interesting, above all from a computational psychoanalysis standpoint, to look at the general relationships between the elements of these dual pairs. In this regard, for instance, the reverse passage from the asymmetric logic to the symmetric one, presumably is domain of the repression, trauma and dream.

[5]   A mental image, which often is prior to a definition, is also a set of relationships, hence an asymmetric thought outcome.

[6]   This situation is paradigmatically similar to the essence of the so-called *inverse scattering* according to which a given non-directly observable physical object is indirectly detectable only through the set of asymmetric relations emerging from it (like those forming the scattered field emerging from the scattered object). This resembles a metaphoric explanation of what scattering is, due to Paul T. Matthews (1974, Ch. 10), according to which the essence of the scattering methods is like to determine the form of an invisible statue (i.e., the mathematical form of the scattering potential) from the angular distribution and intensity of the emerging rays due to a watering of it.

[7]   For instance, Freud's notions of *contact-barriers* and *protective shield*, may be identified, according to a certain conceptual analogy, with the notion of *potential well* of elementary quantum mechanics. From an historical viewpoint, the positivistic thought (above all, physics) of the 19th-century greatly influenced Freud; in this regard, see (Hall, 1999).

[8]   In this regard, Strocchi (2012) states that in the development of theoretical physics, the standard way of describing a broken symmetry has been that of introducing an explicit non-symmetric term in the equations of motion. A real revolution occurred with the realization of a much more economical and powerful mechanism, called *spontaneous symmetry breaking*, by which symmetry breaking may be realized even if the equations of motion are symmetric. Furthermore, Strocchi (2012) points out that there also exist cases in which asymmetric inputs are needed.

[9]   For interesting applications of basic groupoids to temporal logic (see also next Chapter 6), cf. (von Karger 2002, pp. 235-236).

[10] As regard possible links between Matte Blanco thought and synchronous/asynchronous logic, see Chapter 6.

[11] This preorder has to be meant as weak, hence it should be more appropriated to denote it as $\precsim$. Anyway, we should continue to use the symbol $\prec$ but meant in a weak sense.

[12] The expression $a \cdot x$ does not stand for a "product" of a by x in the usual (arithmetical) sense of this operation, but denotes simply the action of a on x.

[13] Furthermore, the strict set inclusion is a (partial) strict order which allows to distinguish, for instance, between set and (proper) subset, hence to introduce a minimal hierarchical setting.

[14] Matte Blanco generalization principle shouldn't be literally meant as it is commonly stated, because its usual definitions could lead to the wrong possibility to clearly distinguish between set and subset

in a hierarchical way, a thing which is impossible to do in the unconscious realm. Instead, such a generalization principle should be rather understood as expressing the ability to make equivalence classes and partitions. Only overcoming symmetry and generalization principles, it will be possible to reach communicative metalevels, the simplest of which having been those concerned with the various distinctions among element, subset, set and class arose, with the rising of type theory.

[15] The primitiveness condition is a primary working hypothesis which puts us closest to unconscious behaviour.

[16] This is coherent with what Lévi-Strauss claims about the origin of culture and society (hence consciousness), because he puts the Oedipus complex at the basis of the crucial passage from nature to culture. Moreover, from this standpoint, we might also identify a kind of anthropomorphic origin of group structures.

[17] A very useful and interesting application of Russell-Whitehead type theory in informatics has been given by B.C. Pierce in (Pierce, 2002), with his *type system*.

[18] For instance, in (McCulloch 1965, pp. 40-44), it is reported the case of the intransitivity of psychological preferences, a kind of psychological basis for the well-known Kenneth Arrow theorem on social choices. See also (Harary et al., 1965) and references therein, about other interesting remarks on transitivity or not, concerning many examples of interpersonal relationships.

[19] Modern neurophysiologic research confirms this last fact, that is, schizophrenics have mainly impaired the basic semantic-pragmatic integration functions (see (Iurato, 2016c) for a very brief review).

[20] The main components of this research group (*Palo Alto school*) were Gregory Bateson, Donald D. Jackson, John Weakland, Bill Fry, Paul Watzlawick, Janet Helmick Beavin and Jay Haley.

[21] In this, recalling the famous Lacanian *name-of-the-father*; see (Iurato, 2016c).

[22] The Bateson and co-workers theory is based on a set of controlled studies as well as on a wide series of observations, even if related only to schizophrenic disorders. First extensions to the general social context of this theory, going beyond the schizophrenic domain, have been proposed by Carlos E. Sluzki and Eliseo Veron. Nevertheless, the Bateson hypothesis on double bind has found experimental validation only within the familial group (see (Sluzki & Ransom, 1979)). All this would require further attention.

[23] For a technical treatment of the theory of symmetry breaking via group action, see, for example, (Albertson & Collins, 1996) as regard graph theory, and (Field, 1996) as regard bifurcation symmetry breaking theory.

[24] On the symmetry or reciprocity character of double bind, as well as on other interesting remarks and considerations, see (Watzlawick et al., 1967, 6.43) and references therein. In this work, the general presence and relevance of double bind, as well as the need for overcoming it, in regard to all those systems having a certain intelligence autonomy (including animals), is highlighted.

[25] Indeed, the (symbolic) father mediation between mother and child is needed for making a separation between the imaginary register and the symbolic one.

[26] In this regard, it would also be possible to suppose that the crucial passage from symmetric to asymmetric thought might be related to the equally crucial relationships between physical time (*chrónos*) and psychological time (*kairós*), amongst which there is no a priori two-way correspondence. The latter, as subjective time, flows separately from the former, as real time, which is used to realize a strange and estranging mental state of suspension in which immobility and movement are paradoxically in dialectic relation (Semi 1988-89, Vol. I. Sect. 6.3.1, p. 420). Psychology of

time, as well, from Paul Fraisse onwards (Vicario, 1997), says that these last two times are independent amongst them. Perhaps, the acquisition of physical time perception, considered having an ontological dimension, might exert, according to Klaus Fink, a structuring action on psychological time, making easier or even inducing the passage from symmetric to asymmetric thinking. Fink's work has been confirmed by further studies on time distortion in the transference (Rose, 2011), supporting the idea that psychic reality is strictly influenced by physical time, as experienced in psychoanalytic transference that, as known, above all reproduces the childish Oedipus conflicts, re-evoking the various familiar images. *En passant*, we remember that also the mathematician L. Brouwer claimed the primary importance of a sort of (Kantian) *temporal a-priori* in the mathematical reasoning, that is to say, he gave much attention to the basic role played by the temporal dimension. Likewise, some remarkable phenomenological-existentialistic trends of philosophy pay much attention to the role played by temporal dimension from a psychic standpoint. Finally, we recall that time perception seems to be impaired in schizophrenic patients (Bonnota et al., 2011).

[27] And this could reflect also on Krikpe-Wittgenstein paradox and on a clarifying psychoanalytic revisitation of it. Following (Piattelli Palmarini 1987, I), Kripke provides a kind of collective solution to this paradox, that is to say, the reason (even if the usage of this term is paradoxical just in this context, unless we distinguish between implicit and explicit reasons – in this case, it would be better to speak of an *implicit* reason which will become *explicit* at the consciousness level) why we follow a rule should be a collective fact, not an individual one, as if it belonged to a sort of collective unconscious (like, for instance, the one described by C.G. Jung and C. Lévi-Strauss – cf. (Iurato, 2015a) and (Kultgen, 1976)); on Kripke-Wittgenstein paradox, viewed from these last perspectives, see (Iurato, 2017b).

[28] Like in apprehension.

[29] Like in the expressed thought.

[30] Following (Mitchell & Black, 1995), maybe only Lacan was able to give an original and expressive description of mode of manifestation of the unconscious. Indeed, the elusive-allusive-illusive modality, the incrustations of rhetorical figures, the kaleidoscopic erudition, the intentional ambiguity, the grandiose expression, the perverse echoes of past authors, the oblique irony, the disdain of logical sequence, the humour and sarcasm, are all forms of an affected and precious modality with which Lacan wanted to deliberately show, with his celebrated verbal eloquence, what perverse manners are used by the unconscious to manifest itself.

[31] In this regard, see also what is said in section 5. of the preface, by Remo Bodei, to (Matte Blanco, 2000).

[32] In any case, it seems that all these last types of considerations are part of a more general and wider epistemological discussion inherent in the origin, meaning and validity of the contradiction principle, its possible levels, types and interpretations, in the light of the critical relationships between mythological and rational thought.

[33] See the well-known Diogenes Lærtius, *Lives of Eminent Philosophers*, Volume II, Chapter III.

[34] This is, besides, not fully unfounded historically because, throughout the Freudian work, close parallels, meaningful comparisons and immediate analogies jump to the eye if one points out what primary role the *object* has played, and related notions (like object relationship or object cathexis, intentionality, and so on), in both contexts.

[35] The author, in (Sasso 2005, Introduction), considers the brain very similarly, although in a simplistic manner, to a composite musical instrument which runs through a complex resonance which is made active from reciprocal interactions.

[36] As early Jean Piaget used a similar notation to mean the indissoluble active and dialectic relation between subject S and object O, from which the knowledge springs out of.

[37] This P-I endogenous dynamics should be meant as a sort of 'internal breath' of the cerebral system, almost analogous to a physiological one.

[38] In what follows, if not otherwise specified, we shall always refer to (Sasso, 2011), which is the main reference for this second part of the present subsection.

[39] On the fundamental, primary importance of the early dyadic relation child-mother, there exists by now a very vast literature confirming that; in this regard, see also (Murtagh & Iurato, 2016) and references therein.

[40] Which takes place in the perceptive-sensorial cerebral zones.

[41] Which takes place in the frontal, motor and premotor cerebral zones and allows to access to the representational information content given by o_i. These lines $s \rightarrow o$ are always running in the brain, also without perceptive inputs, otherwise the cerebral activity would turn out, this also explaining why the child has normally needed this for a right counterbalanced supply of introjective feedback. A kind of limbic switchboard is assumed to be mainly responsible for the continuous activation of the various peripheral cortex zones to catch information. This might be considered as the neurophysiological counterpart of *human intentionality*. The restoring of a constraint of the type s-o implies the different (topological) *localization* given both by a frontal element s and a parietal-occipital element o: the former approaches the latter, revealing a consciousness element which is not localized in the element s but *elsewhere* (this recalling the Lacanian *Other*), that is, in the element o, which is needed for its phenomenological occurrence. According to the original Freudian thought, the various *object relationships* arose by relationships amongst different mental s_i-s representations of the objects o, that otherwise might not have phenomenological content.

[42] Because every internal object o_i codifies, in general, only partial properties with respect to the ones codified by the original perceptive elaboration $s \leftarrow o$. It is very difficult to succeed to reach the first original perceptive element o, because the various perceptive internal objects o_i are 'encapsulated' amongst them according to J. Fodor. The psychic mechanism that tries to pursue this, is findable, for instance, in the hallucinatory and dreaming phenomena, in the vivid imagination of the child, and in the artistic skills (in which the so-called 'eidetic' memory plays a very fundamental role).

[43] Which has deep roots into the Husserlian phenomenology.

[44] Both elements s and o have representational nature in the human brain, so we might speak of a *double representational* nature of the system of basic constraints s-o.

[45] In turn, just this issue might be puts at the basis of a clarifying inquiring examination or of a deepening study, about one of the crucial problem of psychology, just that concerning nature and properties of the *physical* and *psychic* time, which might turn out to be of some usefulness also from a computational cognitive science standpoint.

[46] That is to say, having semantic functions.

[47] In this basic interaction, a truly fundamental role being played by *mirror neuron* systems, which allow the mother-child primary resonance interaction to come about, hence it is the primary basis for human intentionality.

48   That is to say, the comprehension of the mental states of other people's, which ensues from the suitable regularization between the two main systems of the maternal introjective flows $s \leftarrow o$ (*maternal intention*) and of the projective re-entries $s \rightarrow o$ controlling the representational grid (*child intentionality*) of the elements o. This intentionality comparison is of primary interest because, otherwise, the child would not be able to distinguish between the own intentionality and any other one if, at least, the intentionality of the mother did not make its appearance. Also this last fact refers to Husserl's phenomenology. The child intentionality increases as the interactions coming from mother and environment enhance, but the first founding nucleus is given by the recursive oscillatory-dynamical interactions with the mother. See also (Fonagy et al., 2002).

49   This asymmetry implicitly implies the presence of a first form of a hierarchical structure into the dyadic consciousness states.

50   And the mirror neuron systems as a primary neurophysiological support.

51   That is to say, the *source* of an object cathexis of the general type $source \xrightarrow{\;object\;} drive\ destination$.

52   In this regard, cyclic time, characterizing internal psychic reflection and psychic time, and linked to these cycles of compulsions to repeat, contrasts with physical time, which is linear and progressive and thinkable as springing out from a kind of symmetry breaking of the former. Furthermore, Freud himself said that the modality of functionality of temporal dimension, springing out from perceptive-conscious system, consists in the periodical alternation between excitability phases and non-excitability phases in facing external stimuli by perceptive-conscious system. It is just this last discontinuity of the perceptive-conscious system, that relies at the early basis of temporal representation; cf. (Sabbadini 1979, pp. 23-24).

53   In this regard, therefore, *dynamical system theory* may come in help, in providing a suitable formal setting, if one considers unconscious as a dynamical system. For other applications of dynamical system theory, see also next Chapter 7, Section 7.3.3.

54   The recent *theories of the multiple structure of the Self* claim attention on the dissociated states of the human psyche, on a basic inhomogeneity of the processes which concur to form consciousness. Freud himself always pointed out the fundamental *disunity of the Ego*, in either normal and pathological cases. All that confirms many points exposed in (Iurato, 2013b,c).

55   This sequence may also give an explanation to the *psychic group* nature of the psychoanalytic setting studied by René Kaës, who has also stressed, starting from the previous work made by Kurt Lewin, Émile Durkheim and Freud himself (about the mass psychology), on the unavoidable role played by the psychic group feature for the human inter-subjectivity which has an irreducible basic group structure meant in a precise manner.

56   Just in passing, we recall the Wilfred Bion's formalistic point of view of psychic mechanisms and functions, which makes use of mathematical function theory in modelizing these; cf. (Conrotto 2014, Ch. 2, Sect.1, *E)*).

57   In general, X is, at least, a topological space.

58   Just in this regard, we quote the work of Jacques Viret (2012) on an interesting correlation, above all at a qualitative and conceptual level, between some notable René Thom's morphologies (like *swallowtail*) of catastrophe theory and the Jungian unconscious structure comprehending either collective and personal one.

59   See also (Zeeman, 1976a,b).

[60] With the change of the two periods in such a way to get a rational ratio, the choosing of the phase of the periodic composite process obtained in this way being a further symmetry breaking phenomenon.

[61] The first one to have considered interesting and valuable theoretical models of human psyche and its functioning, worked out from the dynamical systems standpoint within the framework of *p*-adic analysis, has been Andrei Khrennikov (1991, 1998, 2002, 2007).

[62] In fact, textually following (Wang et al., 2006), we have that: *According to the Layer Reference Model of the Brain…the cognitive processes of the brain can be categorized into six layers and then two subsystems. The subconscious subsystem of the brain is inherited and fixed; while the conscious subsystem is acquired and highly plastic. It is noteworthy that the subconscious life functions determine the majority of human behaviours and cognitive processes and this might be overlooked in psychology and cognitive science…. Although Sigmund Freud focused on the psychological effects of sex-related desires of human beings, he probably over simplified a whole set of other subconscious life functions…. Therefore, a study on the subconscious behaviours of the brain and their mechanisms may be the key to understand how the brain works.*

[63] And perhaps this might be, for example, pursued in another place.

[64] See (Iurato, 2017a).

[65] Hysteresis is the time-based dependence of a system's output on current and past inputs. The dependence arises because the history affects the value of an internal state. To predict its future outputs, either its internal state or its history must be known.

[66] As rightly suggested and argued in (Conrotto 2014, Ch. 3, Sect. 3), the term *representation* is incorrect, so that it should be used more properly the right term *presentation*. Indeed, knowledge is not the result of a representation of what is experienced externally as an external object, but rather it the re-presentation of what is lacking, to fill an empty hole, something which there was but actually is just lacking. All this will be just replaced by re-presentation by the use of *signifiers*, in that, it is just the signifier function to accomplish to this task of re-presentation, just producing a symbol which will be signifier for the lacking object, to the main aim to restore the initial satisfaction that that object had produced (*perceptual identity*) and that left its mnestic trace (not memory or recall), from which perceptual identity will spring out; cf. (Contri 1972, p. 249). Nevertheless, even if unconscious' desire pushes for the rising of such a re-presentation (like a dream), almost always it does not make see really the object which is lacking but rather refers to something other that is, however, in a certain (although not directly explainable in terms of conscious logic) relations with it (and forming the so-called *manifest meaning* of dream). It will be the right interpretation of the analyst, so finding the so-called *latent meaning* of dream, to re-find the lost object, so reconstructing, with asymmetric logic, the *sequential* reasoning path which will led to it, to its finding (*thought identity*). For Lacan, unconscious is satisfied only when it finds the lost object.

[67] Here, we briefly recall that a *cathexis* is a neologism introduced by English translators of Freud's works related to the German term *Besetzung*. It is a Freudian concept which would roughly refer to that charge of (psychic) energy associated with a thing, this last being meant in its widest sense (abstract or concrete thing, person, etc.), that is, cathexis is defined as the general process of investment or adhesion of mental or emotional energy to a person, object, representation, or idea. Such a term, like many other ones, has undergone a complex evolution along the whole Freudian thought in a way that makes impossible to have a precise and unique meaning. In any case, its deepest roots should be retraced in the unconscious itself, where Freud even speaks of *unconscious cathexis*

for the unrestrainable tendency of unconscious to produce representation orders (like the ones we shall analyze below), that is to say, to refer to that intrinsic dynamicity of unconscious which will give rise to every human intentional act (also in the sense of phenomenology – cf. (Laplanche & Pontalis, 1967).

68 The secondary censorships acting between *CC* and *Pr.*, concern *secondary repression* of psychic content from the former to the latter.

69 Nevertheless, there are other manners or ways of satisfaction not related with pure symbolic processes due to sublimation (and certain substitutive) phenomena, but linked to other degenerate phenomena like fetishism (Iurato, 2013b, 2013c; 2016a).

70 Thanks to the openness of this thermodynamical system, that is to say, thanks to the unavoidable great sensible perception of the human body to put itself in touch with the external world, it is possible to have the triggering of those irreversible processes (among which is the diffusion process of *Triebrepräsentant*) which will give rise to the human life pathway and its temporal evolution, and mainly due to those instability conditions of non-equilibrium (Conti & Principe, 1989; Prigogine & Kondepudi, 2002) given by the basic contrast life instincts – death instincts, ruling unconscious dynamics by *UCC*.

71 Cf. with what has been said in the previous section.

72 Cf. with what has been said in the previous section.

73 We are very close to Lacan's theory.

74 To be precise, in the first work, Freud states that: *We have dealt with the repression of an instinctual representative, and by the latter we have understood an idea or group of ideas which is cathexed with a definite quota of psychical energy (libido or interest) coming from an instinct. Clinical observation now obliges us to divide up what we have hitherto regarded as a single entity; for it shows us that besides the idea, some other element representing the instinct has to be taken into account, and that this other element undergoes vicissitudes of repression which may be quite different from those undergone by the idea. For this other element of the psychical representative the term quota of affect* [Affektbetrag] *has been generally adopted. It corresponds to the instinct in so far as the latter has become detached from the idea and finds expression, proportionate to its quantity, in processes which are sensed as affects. From this point on, in describing a case of repression, we shall have to follow up separately what, as the result of repression, becomes of the idea, and what becomes of the instinctual energy linked to it.* (Freud, 1957, Vol. 14, p. 152)

75 This, also because cathexis almost always explicates by *anaclisis*, that is, sexual instincts find their support on life and self-preservation instincts, closely and directly correlated with body (Chemama & Vandermersch, 1998; Laplanche & Pontalis, 1967).

76 Nevertheless, following the patterns of natural sciences, Freud didn't make hypotheses on the possible nature of the energy involved in the many issues raised along his studies and researches. He considered energy in the same manner natural sciences treat energy questions (Laplanche & Pontalis, 1967).

77 As regard, then, the other two representation orders, that is to say, the *Sachvorstellung* (i.e., the presentation of the thing or thing-presentation) and the *Wortvorstellung* (i.e., the presentation of the word or word-presentation), we first quote what Freud himself says in *Das Unbewusste* [The Unconscious], that is to say: *In schizophrenia words are subjected to the same process as that which makes the dream images out of latent dream-thoughts – to what we have called the primary psychical process. They undergo condensation, and by means of displacement transfer their cathexes to one*

another in their entirety. The process may go so far that a single word, if it is specially suitable on account of its numerous connections, takes over the representation of a whole train of thought.... If we ask ourselves what it is that gives the character of strangeness to the substitutive formation and the symptom in schizophrenia, we eventually come to realize that it is the predominance of what has to do with words over what has to do with things.... What has dictated the substitution is not the resemblance between the things denoted but the sameness of the words used to express them. Where the two – word and thing – do not coincide, the formation of substitutes in schizophrenia deviates from that in the transference neuroses. If now we put this finding alongside the hypothesis that in schizophrenia object-cathexes are given up, we shall be obliged to modify the hypothesis by adding that the cathexis of the word-presentations of objects is retained. What we have permissibly called the conscious presentation of the object can now be split up into the presentation of the word and the presentation of the thing; the latter consists in the cathexis, if not of the direct memory-images of the thing, at least of remoter memory-traces derived from these. We now seem to know all at once what the difference is between a conscious and an unconscious presentation. The two are not, as we supposed, different registrations of the same content in different psychical localities, nor yet different functional states of cathexis in the same locality; but the conscious presentation comprises the presentation of the thing plus the presentation of the word belonging to it, while the unconscious presentation is the presentation of the thing alone. The system Ucs. contains the thing cathexes of the objects, the first and true object-cathexes; the system Pcs. Comes about by this thing-presentation being hypercathexed through being linked with the word presentations corresponding to it. It is these hypercathexes, we may suppose, that bring about a higher psychical organization and make it possible for the primary process to be succeeded by the secondary process which is dominant in the Pcs. Now, too, we are in a position to state precisely what it is that repression denies to the rejected presentation in the transference neuroses: what it denies to the presentation is translation into words which shall remain attached to the object. A presentation which is not put into words, or a psychical act which is not hypercathexed, remains thereafter in the Ucs. in a state of repression. (Freud, 1957, Vol. 14, pp. 200-201)

[78] For another, very interesting analysis of the relationships between time and consciousness from the neuroscience standpoint, mediated by a new philosophical position called *cognitive naturalism* (Nannini, 2007) and aimed to solve the crucial problem mind-brain, as well as supported by a competent physics discussion on classical and relativistic mechanics, see (Nannini, 2015).

[79] For relationships between time sense, its impairments and psychopathology, see, for instance (Bonnota et al., 2011; Peterburs et al., 2013; Piras et al., 2013; Schmitt et al., 2011; Stanghellini et al., 2016).

[80] See also (Semi 1988-89, Vol. I, Sect. 6.3.1, p. 420).

[81] For an almost overall view of the various conceptions of time in their historical evolution, see (Redondi, 2007; Whitrow, 1988; Zeh, 2007).

[82] Here, we discuss temporality only from the Freudian standpoint, referring to (Reale, 1982) for other standpoints.

[83] Just at this point, we mention the role of the so-called *après-coup* as temporal dimension typical of human psyche (Laplanche, 2007). Furthermore, also in (Zapparoli 1970, p. 49), it is clearly stated that the main object of logic is the retardation of pleasure, while the main aim of logic is the regulation of human behaving just through this retardation. From this, the importance of time as psychic dimension ruling pleasure principle in dependence on reality principle.

Chapter 5
Foundations of Classical Logic and Its Applications to Informatics

ABSTRACT

This is a brief chapter recalling the essential elements of classical Boolean logic, its foundations and the first possible relationships with certain basic notions of psychoanalysis, in view of the wider discussions of the next chapters. We have also basically recalled, in a very sketchily fashion, the usual applications of Boolean logic in informatics, which are well-known. This, because the truly important aim of this chapter is simply to prepare the logic ground for a possible psychoanalytic interpretation of the basic elements of Aristotelian logics, to be identified in the unconscious realm, as we shall see better in the next chapters.

5.1. INTRODUCTION

In this chapter, we outline the main elements of classical logic with a view towards its applications to informatics. We focus on the simplest and unavoidable fundamental logical bases of computing, those provided by the so-called *Boolean logic*. From this, we shall try to cast, in the next chapters, a bridge with the main ideas of Matte Blanco's *bi-logic*, with the main aim to may establish further possible links with other aspects of logic.

The first relationships between logic and informatics come back to the early origins of the so-called *artificial intelligence*, turned towards the project and realization of artificial systems able to perform intelligence functions and tasks analogous to the human ones. It is an area of research in which converge logic, psychology and linguistics, to be treated from an *information science* standpoint. As a part of cognitive science, artificial intelligence tries to either simulate and emulate human mental functions. It is born around 1950s, in relation to the elaborative capabilities of the new machines invented by Alan M. Turing and John von Neumann, which were not limited to numerical tasks only but also to other data suitably codified. For example, the first programming language called LISP, due to John McCarthy in 1960, was based on Alonzo Church λ-calculus and was able to treat any symbolic data.

DOI: 10.4018/978-1-5225-4128-8.ch005

5.2. A BRIEF HISTORICAL ACCOUNT OF LOGIC AND ITS APPLICATIONS

Since the beginnings, logic is inseparable from philosophy, and vice versa. Aristotle is however unanimously recognized as the founder of logic as an autonomous discipline, giving it a systematic framework and a formal outlook. Around the first century BC, he exposes the doctrine of logic in the *Organon*, the canonical text of Aristotelian corpus just devoted to logic. Differently from the Euclid's *Elements*, it seems that Aristotle's work on logic does not have antecedents. He is therefore the founder of classical logic, also said to be *Aristotelian logic*, to be meant as a symbolic way to conduct formal reasoning.

Aristotelian logical theories analyse the discourse, that is to say, they spring out from the formal analysis of language, distinguishing, into a sentence or proposition, terms or concepts (i.e., noun and verb) in dependence on subject and predicate, and their relative internal position. Furthermore, in dependence on their quality and quantity, the propositions are classified according to their possible logical interrelationships, so giving rise to the known *Aristotelian square of opposition*, and identifying certain *conversion laws* ruling the derivation of propositions from others.

Aristotle's main contribution is on the theory of proof, in which he discusses inferences. In particular, it is in the *Prior Analytics* that Aristotle discusses the theory of inferences, giving pre-eminence to the *syllogistic inference*, deemed to be the logical mechanism par excellence. Then, he discusses the logical argumentations, distinguishing between *dialectic* and *proof* argumentations in dependence on the degree of certainty of the premises; both these two types of argumentation are however carried on according to a common logical mechanism, that of syllogistic inference.

The Megarian-Stoical school then privileges the analysis of the persuasive discourse from a logical standpoint, distinguishing between *rhetoric* and *dialectics*, and giving pre-eminence to sentences rather than to argumentations, so developing a refined analysis of *logical connectives*. This school privileges the study of the possible relationships amongst sentences related to each other through logical connectives, makes a distinction between *validity* and *truth*, as well as between *argument* and *sentence*, and points out the existence of many logical paradoxes.

With the rising of Latin tradition from the Greek and Arabic one, the formal disciplines, like sciences and mathematics, are quite disregarded, at the expense of an interest towards rhetoric and theology. However, from around the end of ancient period onwards, the above two main trends of Greek logic mix of each other, inasmuch as rhetoric and theology required anyway a strengthening in logic for their argumentations. In this regard, Boethius tries to unify the Megarian-Stoical tradition with the Peripatetic one. In the medieval period, logic undergoes a great development, with a rich textbook tradition. The syntactic and semantic analysis of propositions starts to have a systematic treatment. Scholastic logic, in particular, develops the logic of sentences and their meaning in dependence on the constitutive terms, as well as the logic of valid consequences.

First systematic elements of a theory of reference, a general theory of logical implication, a systematization of the theory of syllogisms, detailed modal logic investigations, and a further analysis of logical paradoxes, are the chief currents of medieval logic, which sees, among the main protagonists, Peter Abelard, Robert Grosseteste, Thomas Aquinas, Albertus Magnus, William of Sherwood, Petrus Ferrandi Hispanus, William of Ockham, Walter Burleigh, John Buridan. Moreover, to be highlighted are also numerous attempts to apply formal thought to almost all other liberal arts, like architecture, music, play, as well as at the service of technique[1].

With the opposition of Humanism and Renaissance against Scholastic thought, from 15th to 16th century, the logic is little considered. Instead, it is re-evaluated as a rhetorical logic of Cicero's tradition, founded on the persuasion by means of discourse and dialogue. Only the 16th century Padua school retakes and develops Aristotelian tradition, renewing the methodology of logic with the rediscovery of the proof rigour models by analyzing the formal techniques of new editions of Euclid's *Elements*, with a preference towards syllogism.

Besides the contributions of Francis Bacon, René Descartes and Thomas Hobbes, only with the rising of François Viète algebra, first connections between logical and algebraic operations begin to be outlined. As a consequence of that, from this moment onwards, there will be a thickening of the intertwinement net between logic and mathematics: in fact, on the one hand, mathematical proof benefits from logical tools and techniques to achieve the highest degree of rigour, while, on the other hand, logic takes algebra as a main formal pattern of logical calculus.

Afterwards, in the 17th century, Gottfried Leibniz conceives a more articulated project centred on a mathematization of logic: it is the birth of the *mathematical logic*. He explicitly makes use of alphabetic letters as symbols, so casting the bases of literal calculus through a suitable axiomatic foundation. He furthermore distinguishes the logical calculus as such from all its possible interpretations, guarantying to it the more general setting in order to be interpretable with respect to the widest range of object domains (universes of the discourse). Nevertheless, Leibniz's work will be really known and appreciated only thanks to the next work of 20th century Giuseppe Peano's school. Moreover, also to be mentioned is the *Port-Royal* programme.

Around the mid-18th century, Christian Wolff is turned to give a rigorous logical reformulation of many geometrical and mathematical proofs, so reaching new results in logic. At the same time, other authors, such as Johann Bernoulli, Johann E. Lambert, Gottfried Ploucquet, Johann A. von Segner, in the wake of Leibniz's program, follow too an attempt of mathematization of the logic, by means of algebraic methods, although in a not quite developed fashion.

Against Wolff's dogmatic metaphysics, Immanuel Kant then argues on the need to consider a *transcendental logic* besides the formal one. Indeed, he deems that the formal deduction of a reasoning is a necessary but not always a sufficient condition for its truth, which, to be revealed, above all in reference to empirical contents, a transcendental investigation has to be performed.

But, it is only with George Boole and August De Morgan, around the mid-1800s, that the major part of Leibnizian program starts to develop. He establishes new algebraic structures which are liable of a logical interpretation. So, with their pioneering works, a new mathematical discipline, called the *algebra of logic*, springs out. Other mathematicians, like William S. Jevons, Charles S. Peirce, Ernst Schröder, Hugh McColl, will give fundamental contributions to it, until the 1930s.

Besides this first algebraic trend of logic, around the same period, an analytical trend of logic starts to develop from the works of Georg Cantor, Richard Dedekind, Karl Weierstrass, Gottlob Frege on the arithmetization of mathematical analysis and the foundations of mathematics. In particular, Frege is aimed to bringing back the concepts and principles of arithmetic to logic, so giving rise to the so-called *logicist program*, based on an extremely rigorous and abstract symbolic language. This program didn't have yet success. With Frege, a first complete formulation of both the calculus of first order predicates and the calculus of sentences, is achieved.

The modern mathematical logic was mainly built up, around 19th and 20th century, thanks to the works, among others, of Giuseppe Peano, Bertrand Russell, Alfred N. Whitehead, David Hilbert, Kurt Gödel, Alfred Tarski, Luitzen Brouwer, Arend Heyting. The celebrated works *Principia Mathematica* (3 vols., 1910-13) of Russell and Whitehead, still based on Frege's logicist program, and *The Foundations of Geometry* (1900) of Hilbert, essentially mark the birth of modern mathematical logic in its *formalistic* trend, alongside the *intuitionistic* one due to Brouwer, and both arising from the failure of logicist program.

The former trend gives a precise and rigorous formulation of a pure syntactic theory of formal systems, centred on the founding principles of non-contradiction and formal coherence (*Hilbert's formal programme*). Hilbert also establishes a *theory of proof* from the logical analysis of the formal structure of finitistic arithmetic, from which also derive *recursive function theory* and *combinatorial logic*. Hilbert's programme is the central pillar of metamathematics which is aimed to prove the formal coherence and non-contradictoriety of a mathematical theory based on a given numerical system.

But, in the 1930s, Gödel proves the inconsistency of Hilbert's program, so decreeing its failure. Gödel himself suggests how to overcome this impasse, making appeal to the notion of true formula, but only with Tarski this problematic, opened with the failing of Hilbert's program, will have a full solution by means of his *semantic metatheory* of languages, which will give rise to the so-called *model theory*. Tarski's work allows to give a meaning (or an interpretation) to the abstract symbolic language of a formal system, as well as it allows to treat the notion of truth of sentences. However, Hilbert's program was retaken by Gerhard Gentzen in his important works on theory of proof and natural deductions.

From about 1918 to 1931, Gödel provides a series of fundamental metatheorems: among these, the consistency of the calculus of sentences, the validity, the completeness and the non-decidability of the calculus of first order predicates, from which he leans Platonistic view of mathematics, giving their own ontological status to mathematical entities, and arguing on the irreducibility of truth to proof. But, at the same time, besides formalistic trends, the intuitionistic one should be as much highlighted. Model theory, the theory of sets, the theory of recursion, and the theory of proof, are deemed to be the main four chapters of modern logic.

From the second half of 20th century onward, a pluralistic tendency in logic gradually establishes. So, a rich variety of new trends of logic takes place, this comprehending modal logic, temporal logic, paraconsistent logic, many-value logic, free logic, deontic logic, quantum logic, dialogical logic, relevance logic, fuzzy logic, and so on (Abbagnano, 1998; Ben-Ari, 1993; Vattimo et al., 1993). Anyway, we shall return on some of these latter, in the next Chapter 6.

5.3. THE FOUNDATIONS OF CLASSICAL LOGIC AND THEIR ALGEBRAIC FORMULATION

Roughly, logic deals with reasoning, and its central concern is to distinguish good arguments from poor ones. As indicated above, the first scholar who set down systematically and organically the rules of reasoning was Aristotle. After more than two thousand years, logic remained basically as Aristotle had left it. At the end of the eighteenth century Kant, one of the great philosophers of modern times, expressed the opinion that logic was by now completed subject-matter.

About fifty years later, however, new insights and results on logic started to come forth as a result of the investigations of George Boole and others. In his work, Boole employed algebraic symbolism in a new and suggestive manner that, since then, logic and mathematics interacted to the point that it no longer seems possible to draw a boundary line between them. In particular, Boole's work casts the unavoidable bases for the next development of any formal programming language. We briefly delineate it, closely following (Levitz & Levitz, 1979).

Roughly, compound sentences are obtained from simpler sentences by means of five basic *logical operations* (or *connectives*). These latter, and their symbols, are: *conjunction* $\wedge$, *disjunction* $\vee$, *negation* $\neg$, *implication* $\rightarrow$, *bi-implication* $\leftrightarrow$. In classical logic, a fundamental property of each declarative sentence is that it is *true* or *false*, but not both. If a sentence is true, it has truth value *t*, while, if it is false, it has truth value *f*. It is possible to compute the truth value of a compound sentence built up from composing simpler sentences through logical operations and *logical forms* – i.e., symbolic composition of sentences with parentheses and logical operations – if known are the truth values of these composing simpler sentences. This can be done by means of the well-known truth tables of logical operations.

For every sentence A, the basic tautology $A \vee \neg A$ is denoted by T (which stands for "true"), while the basic contradiction $A \wedge \neg A$ is denoted by F (which stands for "false"). Furthermore, the algebra of logic, after George Boole and Augustus de Morgan, is built up on the set of all elementary sentences ruled by a finite number of the following fundamental properties:

1. $A = \neg \neg A$ (law of double negation);
2. $A \vee B = B \vee A, A \wedge B = B \wedge A$ (commutative law);
3. $\left(A \wedge B\right) \wedge C = A \wedge \left(B \wedge C\right), \left(A \vee B\right) \vee C = A \vee \left(B \vee C\right)$ (associative law);
4. $A \wedge \left(B \vee C\right) = \left(A \wedge B\right) \vee \left(A \wedge C\right), A \vee \left(B \wedge C\right) = \left(A \vee B\right) \wedge \left(A \vee C\right)$ (distributive law);
5. $\neg \left(A \vee B\right) = \left(\neg A\right) \wedge \left(\neg B\right), \neg \left(A \wedge B\right) = \left(\neg A\right) \vee \left(\neg B\right)$ (de Morgan's law);
6. $A \wedge A = A \vee A = A$ (idempotent law);
7. $A \wedge \left(A \vee B\right) = A \vee \left(A \wedge B\right) = A$ (absorption law);
8. $A \vee F = A \wedge T = A$ (identity law);
9. $A \wedge F = F, A \vee T = T$ (domination law).

These properties lead to the so-called *Boolean algebra*, a formal algebraic structure that formalizes propositional calculus, or else, Aristotelian logic, if defined on the set of all sentences, say Ξ. Indeed, John Concoran (2003) proved that Boole's logic fully formalizes the Aristotelian one. If we denote such a structure – i.e., Boolean algebra – by $\wp$, then it is basically identified by the five logical operations $\wedge, \vee, \neg, \rightarrow, \leftrightarrow$. In this work, then, we consider only *modus ponens*, not *modus tollens*, at most as inference rule linked to $\rightarrow$ and supposed to be already present in human mind (see next Chapter 6).

Anyway, as Charles S. Peirce (Barone 1965, Ch. V) pointed out, there hold interdependence relations among the five logical operations $\wedge, \vee, \neg, \rightarrow, \leftrightarrow$, in such a way that only two are the real independent ones, i.e., negation and conjunction or, equivalently, negation and disjunction. In fact, taking into account the above properties 1. – 9., we have the following interdependence relations:

1. $A \leftrightarrow B = \left(A \rightarrow B\right) \wedge \left(B \rightarrow A\right)$;
2. $A \rightarrow B = \left(\neg A\right) \vee B$;
3. $A \wedge B = \neg \left(\left(\neg A\right) \vee \left(\neg B\right)\right)$.

So, we may consider only negation $\neg$ and disjunction $\vee$ as the two basic logical operations needed to identify $\wp$ (Akhtar & O'Neil, 2011); and, as we shall see later, just this latter remark may lead to possible connections with psychoanalytic context (see next Chapter 7). Moreover, from a logical viewpoint, all *logical truths* may be obtained by four fundamental ones: the negation $\neg$, the (*vel*) disjunction $\vee$, the quantifier "all" ($\forall$), and the relation of belonging ($\in$) "it is an element of" (Lambert & Brittain 1979, Ch. 5, Sect. 2); even better, the fundamental pair, negation $\neg$ and disjunction $\vee$, is logically equivalent to the basic expression "neither ... nor" (Lambert & Brittain 1979, Notes to the Chapter 5, Note 4), which will lead us directly to the domain of psychoanalysis and its defence mechanisms (above all, those related to negation[2]). Furthermore, above all in regard to *ii)*, we should distinguish the two main cases provided by the inclusive (*vel*) or exclusive (*aut*) use of the disjunction $\vee$ (Lewis, 1912); in general (but not always), it is considered the exclusive use of the disjunction (Pizzi 1974, N. 4, p. 259) in that, traditionally, formal logic has mainly had to do with *static* situations of a temporally invariant world, not dynamic, so *dialectic* questions have been put out of its domain.

In the algebra of logic, the operator "p implies q" is defined to mean "either p is false or q is true", that is, $p \rightarrow q$ is logically equivalent to $\neg p \vee q$. But this last expression may turn out to be quite equivocal. Indeed, implication is defined in terms of disjunction, but "either-or" ($\vee$) propositions may have at least three different meanings. One of these is ruled out when we understand that "p or q", i.e., either p is true or q is true, must not be taken to exclude the possibility that both p and q may be true. Disjunctions in the algebra do not signify mutual exclusion: so, if p is true, this does not imply that q is false. A convenient statement of this takes the form, "*at least one* of the propositions p and q" is true. Two meanings of disjunction still remain. The implication of the algebra of logic bears the same relation to the one of these that the Aristotelian "implies" bears to the other. Hence the need of distinguishing carefully between these two sorts of disjunction.

For instance, comparing the following two propositions made by disjunctions: *i)* "either Caesar died or the moon is made of green gruyere", and *ii)* "either Matilda does not love me or I am beloved", it follows that, in both cases, at least one of the disjoined propositions *is* true. The difference between these two may be expressed in a variety of ways. The second disjunction is such that at least one of the disjoined propositions is "necessarily" true: i.e., reject one of the two possibilities and thereby embrace the other. Suppose one of its propositions is false and you are in consistency, or accordingly, bound to suppose the other true. If either lemma *were* false, the other would, by the same token, be true. But, none of these statements will hold for the first disjunction. Indeed, at least one of its propositions is, as a fact, true. But, even to suppose it is false that Caesar died, this would not bind one to suppose the moon made of green cheese. If "Caesar died" *were* false, the moon would not necessarily be made of green cheese, if conditions contrary to fact have any meaning at all. It is this last which the algebra is, according to its meaning of disjunction and implication, bound to deny.

The most significant distinction, however, remains to be noted. More accurately, the truth of a composite proposition should be (syntactically) known *a priori*, while it is still problematic *which* of its lemmas is the true one. It (syntactically) has a truth which is *prior to* the determination of the *facts in question*. For instance, the truth of "Caesar died or the moon is made of green cheese" has not this purely logical or formal character. It lacks this independence of facts (semantically-pragmatically). It requires careful analysis to separate these two meanings of "either-or" propositions, though their main features may seem sufficiently distinct. We may call disjunctions like *i)*, whose truth cannot be known apart from the facts, *extensional disjunctions*; those of the type of *ii)*, whose truth can be known *a priori* while it is still problematic which member is true, or whether both are true, we may call *intensional*.

These two, in turn, may be further distinguished by considering their negatives. The truth of extensional disjunction is secured by the truth of either member, regardless of "logical connexions", and the negation of extensional disjunction accordingly negates both the disjoined propositions. That the meaning of disjunction in the algebra of logic should consistently be confined to the extensional, follows from the fact that, in the algebra, the negative of a disjunction is the negation of both its members, while the negative of a conjunction is the disjunction of the negatives of its members. Every intensional disjunction is also extensional, or, more accurately, the intensional disjunction of p and q implies their extensional disjunction also. But the reverse does not hold. Of every intensional disjunction, at least one member is true, but not every "either-or" proposition with at least one true member is an intensional disjunction (Lewis, 1912).

5.4. THE BASIC ELEMENTS OF BOOLEAN LOGIC AND ITS FIRST ELEMENTARY APPLICATIONS TO INFORMATICS: A VERY BRIEF SKETCH

Boolean logic is the simplest one. It lies at the basis of every programming language, providing the minimal, unavoidable syntactic foundation. It also plays a fundamental role in the formalization of digital electronics, as well as in computation theory.

Roughly speaking, Boolean algebra is an algebraic structure whose operations are the conjunction $\land$, the disjunction $\lor$, and the negation $\neg$. It provides formal bases for describing logical relations.

Boolean algebra has been introduced by George Boole in *The Mathematical Analysis of Logic* of 1847, and in *An Investigation of the Laws of Thought* of 1854. But, Edward V. Huntington says that the term "Boolean algebra" was explicitly used, for the first time, by Henry M. Sheffer in 1913. In the 1930s, Claude Shannon, taking Boolean algebra as a pattern, introduced a new formal structure, said to be *switching algebra*, to analyze and formally design switching circuits. Boolean algebras are also used in the design of combinational logic circuits.

Then, logic sentences of classical propositional calculus, have an equivalent expression in Boolean algebra, so that, *Boolean logic* just refers to propositional calculus performed in this algebraic way. Nevertheless, Boolean algebra is not able to formalize predicative calculus. The many and various relationships between algebra and logic have given rise to a new discipline, said to be *algebraic logic*, which is not limited to classical logic only. Anyway, Boolean algebra has been at the foundation of theoretical computer science, being the basic algebraic structure presents in almost every other higher formal structure employed in theoretical informatics and computing sciences (Givant & Halmos, 2009).

REFERENCES

Abbagnano, N. (1998). Dizionario di Filosofia (3rd ed.). Torino, Italy: UTET Libreria.

Akhtar, S., & O'Neil, M. K. (Eds.). (2011). *On Freud's 'negation'. In The International Psychoanalytic Association – Contemporary Freud. Turning points & critical issues.* London, UK: Karnac Books, Ltd.

Bajnok, B. (2013). *An Invitation to Abstract Mathematics.* New York, NY: Springer-Verlag, Inc. doi:10.1007/978-1-4614-6636-9

Balsamo, M. (2009). Ripetizione, coazione a ripetere, destino. In *Psiche. Dizionario storico di psicologia, psichiatria, psicoanalisi, neuroscienze* (Vol. 2, pp. 957–962). Torino, Italy: Giulio Einaudi editore.

Balzarotti, R. (Ed.). (1972). Cahiers pour l'Analyse. Scritti scelti di analisi e teoria della scienza, a cura del Centro Ricerche 2. Torino, Italy: Editore Boringhieri.

Bara, B. G. (1990). Scienza Cognitiva. Torino, Italy: Bollati Boringhieri editore.

Barone, F. (1965). Logica Formale e Logica Trascendentale (2nd ed.; Vols. 1-2). Torino, Italy: Edizioni di «Filosofia».

Ben-Ari, M. (1993). Mathematical Logic for Computer Science. Hemel Hempstead, UK: Prentice Hall International, Ltd.

Borceux, F. (1989). Fasci, logica e topoi. Quaderni dell'Unione Matematica Italiana, N. 34. Bologna, Italy: Pitagora Editrice.

Brading, K., & Castellani, E. (2013). Symmetry and Symmetry Breaking. In The Stanford Encyclopedia of Philosophy. Stanford University Press.

Bremer, M. (2005). *An Introduction to Paraconsistent Logics*. Frankfurt am Main, Germany: Peter Lang Publishing.

Bria, P. (1981). Introduzione. Pensiero, mondo e problemi di fondazione. In *L'inconscio come insiemi infiniti. Saggio sulla bi-logica* (pp. xix–cxi). Torino, Italy: Giulio Einaudi editore.

Bucci, W. (1985). Dual coding: A cognitive model for psychoanalytic research. *Journal of the American Psychoanalytic Association*, *33*(3), 571–607. doi:10.1177/000306518503300305 PMID:4056301

Bucci, W. (1987). *The dual code model and the interpretation of dreams*. New York, NY: Derner Institute – Adelphi University.

Bucci, W. (1997). *Psychoanalysis and Cognitive Science*. New York, NY: The Guilford Press.

Capozzi, M., & Cellucci, C. (2014). *Breve storia della logica. Dall'Umanesimo al primo Novecento*. Morrisville, NC: Lulu Press, Inc.

Carruccio, E. (1971). Mondi della Logica. Bologna, Italy: Nicola Zanichelli Editore.

Casari, E. (1972). Questioni di Filosofia della Matematica. Milano, Italy: Giangiacomo Feltrinelli Editore.

Cellucci, C., & Ippoliti, E. (2016). Logica. Milano, Italy: EGEA Editore.

Chang, C.-C., & Keisler, H. J. (1973). Model Theory. Amsterdam: North-Holland Publishing Company, Inc.

Chemama, R., & Vandermersch, B. (Eds.). (1998). Dictionnaire de la Psychanalyse. Paris: Larousse-Bordas.

Cherubini, P., Giaretta, P., & Mazzocco, A. (Eds.). (2000). Ragionamento: psicologia e logica. Firenze, Italy: Giunti Gruppo Editoriale.

Chianese, D. (2009). Costruzione, Ricostruzione, Interpretazione. In *Psiche. Dizionario storico di psicologia, psichiatria, psicoanalisi, neuroscienze* (Vol. 1, pp. 280–285). Torino, Italy: Giulio Einaudi editore.

Codignola, E. (1977). Il vero e il falso. Saggio sulla struttura logica dell'interpretazione psicoanalitica. Torino, Italy: Editore Boringhieri.

Cohn, P. M. (1965). Universal Algebra. New York, NY: Harper & Row Publishers.

Conrotto, F. (2000). Tra il sapere e la cura. Un itinerario freudiano. Milano, Italy: FrancoAngeli.

Conrotto, F. (2009). Negazione. In *Psiche. Dizionario storico di psicologia, psichiatria, psicoanalisi, neuroscienze* (Vol. 2, pp. 728–730). Torino, Italy: Giulio Einaudi editore.

Conrotto, F. (2010). Per una teoria psicoanalitica della conoscenza. Milano, Italy: FrancoAngeli.

Conrotto, F. (2014). Ripensare l'inconscio. Milano, Italy: FrancoAngeli.

Contardi, R. (2010). La prova del labirinto. Processo di simbolizzazione e dinamica rappresentativa in psicoanalisi. Milano, Italy: FrancoAngeli.

Conte, M., & Gennaro, A. (Eds.). (1989). Inconscio e processi cognitivi. Bologna, Italy: Società editrice il Mulino.

Contri, G. (1972). Nozioni fondamentali nella teoria della struttura di Jacques Lacan. In Cahiers pour l'Analyse. Scritti scelti di analisi e teoria della scienza, a cura del Centro Ricerche 2. Torino, Italy: Editore Boringhieri.

Corradi Fiumara, G. (1980). Funzione simbolica e filosofia del linguaggio. Torino, Italy: Editore Boringhieri.

CSFG – Centro di Studi Filosofici di Gallarate. (1977). Dizionario delle idee. Firenze, Italy: G.C. Sansoni Editore.

Dalla Chiara Scabia, M. L. (1973). Istanti e individui nelle logiche temporali. *Rivista di Filosofia, 64*(2), 95–122.

Dalla Chiara Scabia, M. L. (1974). Logica. Milano, Italy: ISEDI – Istituto Editoriale Internazionale.

De Mijolla, A. (Ed.). (2005). *International Dictionary of Psychoanalysis* (Vols. 1–3). Farmington Hills, MI: Thomson Gale.

De Mijolla, A., & De Mijolla Mellor, S. (Eds.). (1996). Psychanalyse. Paris: PUF-Presses Universitaires de France.

Durst, M. (1988). Dialettica e bi-logica. L'epistemologia di Ignacio Matte Blanco. Milano, Italy: Marzorati Editore.

Enriques, F. (1912). Scienza e Razionalismo. Bologna, Italy: Nicola Zanichelli Editore.

Even, G., & Medina, M. (2012). *Digital Logic Design. A Rigorous Approach*. Cambridge, UK: Cambridge University Press. doi:10.1017/CBO9781139226455

Figà-Talamanca Dore, L. (1978). La logica dell'inconscio. Roma, Italy: Edizioni Studium-Vita Nova.

Finelli, R. (2010). Perché l'inconscio non è strutturato come un linguaggio. In Compendio di Psicoanalisi e altri scritti. Roma, Italy: Newton Compton editori.

Finelli, R. (2011). Rappresentazione e linguaggio in Freud: a partire dal "Compendio di psicoanalisi". *Consecutio Temporum. Rivista di critica della postmodernità*, *1*, 112-125.

Fink, K. (1993). The Bi-Logic Perception of Time. *The International Journal of Psycho-Analysis*, *74*, 303–312. PMID:8491534

Fodor, N., & Gaynor, F. (1950). Freud: Dictionary of Psychoanalysis. New York, NY: The Philosophical Library.

Freud, S. (1938). Abriß der psychoanalyse. Academic Press.

Freud, S. (1957). *The Standard Edition of Complete Psychological Works of Sigmund Freud* (Vols. 1-24; J. Strachey, Trans. & Ed.). London, UK: The Hogarth Press.

Freud, S. (1979). La scissione dell'Io nel processo di difesa (1938). In Opere di Sigmund Freud, 1930-1938. L'uomo Mosè e la religione monoteistica e altri scritti (vol. 11). Torino, Italy: Editore Boringhieri.

Gabbay, D. M., Hodkinson, I., & Reynolds, M. A. (1994). *Temporal Logic. Mathematical Foundations and Computational Aspects* (Vol. 1). Oxford, UK: Clarendon Press.

Gabbay, D. M., Reynolds, M. A., & Finger, M. (2000). *Temporal Logic. Mathematical Foundations and Computational Aspects* (Vol. 2). Oxford, UK: Oxford University Press.

Galimberti, U. (2006). Dizionario di psicologia. Torino, Italy: UTET Libreria.

Galton, A. (Ed.). (1987). *Temporal Logic and its Applications*. New York, NY: Academic Press, Inc.

Giordano, M., Dello Russo, G., Pardi, F., & Patella, G. A. (1984). Tempo e inconscio. Napoli, Italy: Guida editori.

Girotto, V. (Eds.). (2013). Introduzione alla psicologia del pensiero. Bologna, Italy: Società editrice il Mulino.

Givant, S., & Halmos, P. (2009). Introduction to Boolean Algebras. New York, NY: Springer Science + Business Media, LLC.

Green, A. (1993). Le travail du négatif. Paris: Les Éditions du Minuit.

Hermann, I. (1989). Psicoanalisi e logica. Roma, Italy: Di Renzo Editore.

Hickmann, M., & Robert, S. (Eds.). (2006). *Space in Languages – Linguistic Systems and Cognitive Categories*. Amsterdam: John Benjamins Publishing Company. doi:10.1075/tsl.66

Hodges, W. (1977). *Logic. An Introduction to Elementary Logic*. Harmondsworth, UK: Penguin Books, Ltd.

Hodkinson, I., & Reynolds, M. (2007). Temporal Logic. In Handbook of Modal Logic. Amsterdam: Elsevier, B.V.

Ippoliti, E. (2007). *Il vero e il plausibile*. Morrisville, NC: Lulu Press, Inc.

Iurato, G. (2013a). Mathematical thought in the light of Matte Blanco work. *Philosophy of Mathematics Education Journal*, *27*.

Iurato, G. (2013b). Σύμβολου: An attempt toward the early origins, Part 1. *Language & Psychoanalysis*, *2*(2), 77–120. doi:10.7565/landp.2013.008

Iurato, G. (2013c). Σύμβολου: An attempt toward the early origins, Part 2. *Language & Psychoanalysis*, *2*(2), 121–160. doi:10.7565/landp.2013.009

Iurato, G. (2014a). At the grounding of computational psychoanalysis: on the work of Ignacio Matte Blanco. A general history of culture overview of Matte Blanco bilogic in comparison. In *Proceedings of the 2014 IEEE 13th International Conference on Cognitive Informatics and Cognitive Computing*. Los Alamitos, CA: IEEE Computer Society Press.

Iurato, G. (2014b). The dawning of computational psychoanalysis. A proposal for some first elementary formalization attempts. *International Journal of Cognitive Informatics and Natural Intelligence*, *8*(4), 50–82. doi:10.4018/ijcini.2014100104

Iurato, G. (2014c). *Alcune considerazioni critiche sul simbolismo*. Preprint No. hal-00980828 version 1. Available at HAL archives-ouvertes.

Iurato, G. (2015a). A Brief Comparison of the Unconscious as Seen by Jung and Lévi-Strauss. *Anthropology of Consciousness*, *26*(1), 60–107. doi:10.1111/anoc.12032

Iurato, G. (2015b). Fetishism in Marketing. Some First Elementary Psychoanalytic Anthropology Remarks. In Business Management: A Practitioners' Guide. Delhi: International Research Publication House.

Iurato, G. (2015c). A simple phylogenetic remark about certain human blood pressure values. *Journal of Biochemistry International*, *2*(4), 162–165.

Iurato, G. (2016a). *A psychoanalytic enquiry on symbolic function*. Preprint No. hal-01361264 version 3. Available at HAL archives-ouvertes.

Iurato, G. (2016b). *A view of LSA/ESA in Computational Psychoanalysis*. Preprint No. hal-01353999 version 1. Available at HAL archives-ouvertes.

Iurato, G. (2016c). On Jacques Lacan Psychosis Theory and ERPs Analysis. *Journal of Biology and Nature*, *5*(4), 234–240.

Iurato, G. (2016d). Some Comments on the Historical Role of *Fetishism* in Economic Anthropology. *Journal of Global Economics. Management and Business Research*, *7*(1), 61–82.

Iurato, G. (2016e). *The origins of symbol. An historical-critical study of symbolic function, according to the phylo-ontogenetic perspective, as arising from the comparison of certain patterns of neuro-psychological sciences*. Paper Presented at the Satellite Event "On the edge of disciplines", Florence, Italy.

Iurato, G. (2016f). Two simple questions regarding cultural anthropology. *Journal of Global Research in Education and Social Science*, *8*(1), 10–15.

Iurato, G. (2017a). An Essay in Denotational Mathematics. Rigorous Results. In Encyclopedia of Information Science and Technology (4th ed.). Hershey, PA: IGI Global.

Iurato, G. (2017b). Un raffronto critico fra la teoria platonica delle idee ed il paradosso di Kripke-Wittgenstein. In Platone nel pensiero moderno e contemporaneo (vol. 11). Villasanta (MB), Italy: Limina Mentis Edizioni.

Iurato, G. (2017c). *Rigidity of the Generalized Other, narrowness of the Otherness and demodernization, in the framework of symbolic interactionism. Ideology and Political Journal.* (in press)

Iurato, G., & Khrennikov, A. Yu. (2015). Hysteresis model of unconscious-conscious interconnection: Exploring dynamics on *m*-adic trees. *p-Adic Numbers, Ultrametric Analysis and Applications*, *7*(4), 312–321. doi:10.1134/S2070046615040068

Iurato, G., & Khrennikov, A. Yu. (2017). On the topological structure of a mathematical model of human unconscious. *p-Adic Numbers, Ultrametric Analysis and Applications*, *9*(1), 78–81. doi:10.1134/S2070046617010071

Iurato, G., Khrennikov, A. Yu., & Murtagh, F. (2016). Formal Foundations for the Origins of Human Consciousness. *p-Adic Numbers, Ultrametric Analysis and Applications*, *8*(4), 249–279. doi:10.1134/S2070046616040014

Johnson-Laird, P., & Bara, B. (1984). Syllogistic Inference. *Cognition*, *16*(1), 1–61. doi:10.1016/0010-0277(84)90035-0 PMID:6540648

Juhás, G. (1999). On Semantics of Petri Nets over Partial Algebra. In *SOFSEM'99: Theory and Practice of Informatics. Proceedings of the 26th Conference on Current Trends in Theory and Practice of Informatics*. Berlin: Springer-Verlag. doi:10.1007/3-540-47849-3_29

Kastner, R. E. (2011). The broken symmetry of time. In Quantum Retrocausation: Theory and Experiment. Melville, NY: AIP Publications. doi:10.1063/1.3663714

Kemeny, J. G. (1959). A Philosopher Looks at Science. Princeton, NJ: D. Van Nostrand Reinhold Company, Inc.

Kemeny, J. G., Snell, J. L., & Thompson, G. L. (1974). *Introduction to Finite Mathematics* (3rd ed.). Englewood Cliffs, NJ: Prentice-Hall.

Kissin, B. (1986). *Conscious and Unconscious Programs in the Brain.* New York, NY: Plenum Publishing Corporation. doi:10.1007/978-1-4613-2187-3

Lacan, J. (2014). *The Seminar of Jacques Lacan. Book X: The Anxiety* (J. A. Miller, Ed.; A. R. Price, Trans.). Malden, MA: Polity Press.

Lagache, D. (1961). *La psychanalyse et la structure de la personnalité*. Paper Presented au Colloquium International de Royaumont, Paris, France.

Lagache, D. (1965). Le modèle psychanalytique de la personnalité. In *La Folle du Logis. La psychanalyse comme science exacte* (pp. 159–183). Paris: PUF-Presses Universitaires de France.

Laplanche, J. (2000). Problematiche II. Castrazione. Simbolizzazioni. Bari-Roma, Italy: La Biblioteca.

Laplanche, J. (2001). *L'inconscio e l'Es*. Bari-Roma, Italy: La Biblioteca.

Laplanche, J. (2007). *L'après-coup*. Bari-Roma, Italy: La Biblioteca.

Laplanche, J. (2008). Sexuale. La sessualità allargata nel senso freudiano. Bari-Roma, Italy: La Biblioteca.

Laplanche, J., & Pontalis, J.-B. (1967). Vocabulaire de la psychoanalyse. Paris: Presses Universitaires de France.

Laplanche, J., & Pontalis, J.-B. (1988). Fantasma originario, fantasmi delle origini, origini del fantasma. Bologna, Italy: Società editrice il Mulino.

Lawson, M. K. (2005). Constructing ordered groupoids. *Cahiers de Topologie et Géométrie Différentielle Catégoriques, 46*(2), 123–138.

Levitz, K., & Levitz, H. (1979). *Logic and Boolean Algebra*. Woodbury, NY: Barron's Educational Series, Inc.

Lewis, C. I. (1912). Implication and the Algebra of Logic. *Mind, 21*(84), 522–531. doi:10.1093/mind/XXI.84.522

Lis, A., Mazzeschi, C., & Zennaro, A. (2007). *La psicoanalisi. Un percorso concettuale fra tradizione e attualità (2nd ed.)*. Roma, Italy: Carocci editore.

Lis, A., Zennaro, A., Mazzeschi, C., Salcuni, S., & Parolin, L. (2003). *Breve dizionario di psicoanalisi*. Roma, Italy: Carocci editore.

Lolli, G. (1991). Introduzione alla logica formale. Bologna, Italy: Società editrice il Mulino.

Lolli, G. (2000). Un logico esamina i modelli mentali. In Ragionamento: psicologia e logica. Firenze, Italy: Giunti Gruppo Editoriale.

Lolli, G. (2005). QED – Fenomenologia della dimostrazione. Torino, Italy: Bollati Boringhieri editore.

Matte Blanco, I. (1975). The Unconscious as Infinite Sets. An Essay in Bi-Logic. London, UK: Gerald Duckworth & Company, Ltd.

Matte Blanco, I. (1988). *Thinking, Feeling, and Being. Clinical Reflections of the Fundamental Antinomy on Human Beings and World*. London, UK: Routledge.

Moore, B. E., & Fine, B. D. (Eds.). (1990). Psychoanalytic Terms and Concepts. New York, NY: The American Psychoanalytic Association.

Mordant, I. (1990). Using attribute-memories to resolve a contradiction in the work of Matte Blanco. *The International Review of Psycho-Analysis, 17*, 475–480.

Nagel, T. (1993). Summary. In *Experimental and Theoretical Studies of Consciousness. Novartis Foundation Symposium No*. 174. New York, NY: John Wiley & Sons, Ltd.

Øhrstrøm, P., & Hasle, P. F. V. (Eds.). (1995). *Temporal Logic. From Ancient Ideas to Artificial Intelligence. Studies in Linguistics and Philosophy, Volume No. 57*. Dordrecht, The Netherlands: Kluwer Academic Publishers.

Papagno, C. (2010). Neuropsicologia della memoria. Bologna, Italy: Società editrice il Mulino.

Petersen, W. P., & Arbenz, P. (2004). *Introduction to Parallel Computing*. New York, NY: Oxford University Press, Inc.

Petrilli, S., & Ponzio, A. (2005). *Semiotics Unbounded. Interpretive Routes Through the Open Network of Signs*. Toronto: The University of Toronto Press. doi:10.3138/9781442657113

Petrini, P., Renzi, A., Casadei, A., & Mandese, A. (2013). Dizionario di psicoanalisi. Con elementi di psichiatria, psicodinamica e psicologia dinamica. Milano, Italy: FrancoAngeli.

Piattelli Palmarini, M. (1987). Scienza come cultura. Protagonisti, luoghi e idee delle scienze contemporanee. Milano, Italy: Arnoldo Mondadori Editore.

Pierce, B. C. (2002). *Types and Programming Languages*. Cambridge, MA: The MIT Press.

Pini, B. (1967). Primo Corso di Algebra. Bologna, Italy: CLUEB Editrice.

Pizzi, C. (Ed.). (1974). La logica del tempo. Torino, Italy: Bollati Boringhieri Editore.

Poggi, S. (1977). I sistemi dell'esperienza. Bologna, Italy: Società editrice il Mulino.

Putnam, H. (1956). Mathematics and the Existence of Abstract Entities. *Philosophical Studies*, *7*(6), 81–88. doi:10.1007/BF02221758

Putnam, H. (1975). Filosofia della logica. Nominalismo e realismo nella logica contemporanea. Milano, Italy: ISEDI – Istituto Editoriale Internazionale.

Rayner, E. (1995). *Unconscious Logic. An Introduction to Matte Blanco's Bi-Logic and its Uses*. New York, NY: Routledge.

Rayner, E. (1998). Foreword. In *The Unconscious as Infinite Sets. An Essay in Bi-Logic* (pp. xviii–xxiv). London, UK: Karnac Books, Ltd.

Reisig, W. (1988). Temporal Logic and Causality in Concurrent Systems. In R. H. Voght (Ed.), Lecture Notes in Computer Science: Vol. 335. *CONCURRENCY 1988* (pp. 121–139). Berlin: Springer-Verlag. doi:10.1007/3-540-50403-6_37

Rentz, J. (Ed.). (2002). Lecture Notes in Computer Science: Vol. 2293. Qualitative spatial reasoning with topological information. Berlin: Springer-Verlag. doi:10.1007/3-540-70736-0

Rescher, N., & Urquhart, A. (1971). Temporal Logic. Wien, Austria: Springer-Verlag GmbH. doi:10.1007/978-3-7091-7664-1

Reverberi, C., Pischedda, D., Burigo, M., & Cherubini, P. (2012). Deduction without awareness. *Acta Psychologica*, *139*(1), 244–253. doi:10.1016/j.actpsy.2011.09.011 PMID:22019058

Riehl, J. P. (2010). *Mirror-Image Asymmetry. An Introduction to the Origin and Consequences of Chirality*. Hoboken, NJ: John Wiley & Sons, Inc. doi:10.1002/9780470588888

Rose, J. R. (Ed.). (2011). *Mapping Psychic Reality. Triangulation, Communication, and Insight. Psychoanalytic Ideas*. London, UK: Karnac Books, Ltd.

Rycroft, C. (1968a). A critical dictionary of psychoanalysis. London, UK: Thomas Nelson & Sons, Ltd.

Rycroft, C. (1968b). Imagination and reality. Psychoanalytical essays 1951–1961. London, UK: The Hogarth Press, Ltd.

Sabbadini, A. (1979). Introduzione. In Il tempo in psicoanalisi. Milano, Italy: Giangiacomo Feltrinelli Editore.

Sannella, D., & Tarlecki, A. (2012). *Foundations of Algebraic Specification and Formal Software Development. Monographs in Theoretical Computer Science. An EATCS Series*. Berlin: Springer-Verlag. doi:10.1007/978-3-642-17336-3

Semi, A.A. (Ed.). (1989). *Trattato di Psicoanalisi* (Vols. 1-2). Milano, Italy: Raffaello Cortina Editore.

Skillicorn, D. (1994). *Foundations of Parallel Programming*. Cambridge, UK: Cambridge University Press. doi:10.1017/CBO9780511526626

Somenzi, V. (1998). Prefazione. In Categorie, tempo e linguaggio. Quaderni di Methodologia, N. 5. Roma, Italy: Società Stampa Sportiva.

Sossinsky, A. (2000). Nodi. Genesi di una teoria matematica. Torino, Italy: Bollati Boringhieri editore.

Souriau, J. M. (1964). *Géométrie et relativité*. Paris: Éditions Hermann.

Sparsø, J., & Furber, S. (Eds.). (2001). Principles of Asynchronous Circuit Design. A Systems Perspective. Dordrecht, The Netherlands: Springer-Science + Business Media, B.V. doi:10.1007/978-1-4757-3385-3

Steedman, M. (2000). *Surface Structure and Interpretation*. Boston, MA: The MIT Press.

Stich, M., Blanco, C., & Hochberg, D. (2013). Chiral and chemical oscillations in a simple dimerization model. *Physical Chemistry Chemical Physics*, *15*(1), 255–261. doi:10.1039/C2CP42620J PMID:23064600

Stirling, C. (2001). *Modal and Temporal Properties of Processes*. New York, NY: Springer-Verlag. doi:10.1007/978-1-4757-3550-5

Tanenbaum, A. S., & Bos, H. (2015). *Modern Operating Systems* (4th ed.). Essex, UK: Pearson Education Limited.

Terminio, N. (2009). Misurare l'inconscio? Coordinate psicoanalitiche nella ricerca in psicoterapia. Milano, Italy: Bruno Mondadori.

Tokhi, M. O., Hossain, M. A., & Shaheed, M. H. (2003). *Parallel Computing for Real-time Signal Processing and Control*. London, UK: Springer-Verlag London. doi:10.1007/978-1-4471-0087-4

Toraldo di Francia, G. (1976). *L'indagine del mondo fisico*. Torino, Italy: Giulio Einaudi editore.

Vaccarino, G. (2006). Scienza e semantica. Milano, Italy: Edizioni Melquiades.

Vallortigara, G., & Panciera, N. (2014). Cervelli che contano. Milano, Italy: Adelphi Edizioni.

Vattimo, G., Ferraris, M., & Marconi, D. (Eds.). (1993). Enciclopedia Garzanti di Filosofia. Milano, Italy: Garzanti Editore.

Venema, Y. (2001). Temporal Logic. In The Blackwell Guide to Philosophical Logic. Oxford, UK: Basil Blackwell Publishers.

Verdiglione, A. (1977). Matematica dell'inconscio. In Feticismo, linguaggio, afasia, matematica dell'inconscio. Venezia, Italy: Marsilio Editori.

Vicario, G. B. (1997). Il tempo in psicologia. *Le Scienze*, *30*(347), 43–51.

Vicario, G. B. (2005). Il tempo. Saggio di psicologia sperimentale. Bologna, Italy: Società editrice il Mulino.

Voevodin, V. V. (1992). Mathematical Foundations of Parallel Computing. Singapore: World Scientific Publishing. doi:10.1142/1533

von Karger, B. (1995). An algebraic approach to temporal logic. In *Lecture Notes on Computer Science: Vol. 915. Proceedings of the Sixth International Joint Conference on Theory and Practice of Software Development (TAPSOFT '95)*. Berlin: Springer-Verlag. doi:10.1007/3-540-59293-8_198

von Karger, B. (2002). Temporal Algebra. In Lecture Notes in Computer Science: Vol. 2297. Algebraic and Coalgebraic Methods in the Mathematics of Program Construction. Berlin: Springer-Verlag. doi:10.1007/3-540-47797-7_9

Von Scheve, C., & Salmela, M. (Eds.). (2014). *Collective Emotions. Perspectives from Psychology, Philosophy, and Sociology*. Oxford, UK: Oxford University Press.

Von Wright, G. H. (1969). *Time, Change and Contradiction*. Cambridge, UK: Cambridge University Press.

ENDNOTES

[1]   See, for example, the construction of the so-called *rotating circles* of Raymond Lull, for the syllogistic calculus.

[2]   Cf. (Akhtar & O'Neil, 2011).

Chapter 6
The Role of Unconscious Constructs in Logic and Their Applications to Informatics

ABSTRACT

Since phallic logic is the ancestral, irreducible and primordial logical nucleus of human psyche, phylogenetically implemented in its deepest unconscious meanders (we hypothesize that structural unconscious, according to Lévi-Strauss and Matte Blanco, springs out during homination process in concomitance with human brain formation and evolution) and afterwards ontogenetically re-enacted individually as a binary logic in the human consciousness, we may consider structural unconscious features as useful from a computational standpoint, so that we have compared this psychoanalytic construct with certain notions of computer sciences, like those of concurrent/parallel processes, synchronous/asynchronous circuits, temporal/modal logics, with the main purpose to formalize the main features of structural unconscious, like timelessness and the presence of logical contradictions. This has been mainly pursued from the standpoint of logic and its various trends.

6.1 INTRODUCTION

In this chapter, we discuss the role played by certain constructs of unconscious – as briefly outlined previously, above all according to Matte Blanco – mainly in logic, hence suggesting some related, possible applications to theoretical informatics and computing sciences, with the aim of trying to mould functioning of human psyche. Nevertheless, the notion of unconscious to which we wish to refer in this work, is that structural according to Freud and as revisited by Matte Blanco. We do not refer to cognitive unconscious of neurocognitive psychology, which seems to be much more close to preconscious than the Freudian one; we refer instead to the deep unconscious structures, just formalized by the work of Matte Blanco, hoping to may use it for computational aims. From more than a century, since Freud described the basic motivations and Ivan Pavlov the basic mechanisms of human behaviour, we have now a reasonable framework of the forces that drive us. But, a crucial yet unresolved issue concerns the

DOI: 10.4018/978-1-5225-4128-8.ch006

primary relations between conscious and unconscious mental states. Most of people seem comfortable with the concept of an unconscious mental state, even if only for things like beliefs which we are not currently thinking about.

But there seems to be a division between those who think that the only legitimate conception of this sort is one that can be analysed in terms of a disposition to have the corresponding conscious experiences under certain conditions, and those who instead think, as Freud did, that it is legitimate to speak of unconscious mental phenomena, provided they operate in causing action and other mental events in ways sufficiently similar to those of the states of which we can become introspectively aware. Such states could be mental even though permanently unconscious. Freud himself thought they were all physical states of the central nervous system, but that we could in the present state of knowledge describe them only by means of a mentalistic theory. However, it seems that the scientific study of consciousness should include more discussion, to which philosophers may be able to contribute, of the place of consciousness in the larger domain of the mental, and of the extent of that domain and the relations, logical and otherwise, between its conscious and unconscious aspects (Kissin, 1986; Nagel, 1993).

After the decline of *behaviourism* and the consequent coming of *cognitivism*, basic concepts as those of attention, consciousness and unconscious, gradually came back as themes of psychology. This has enabled a possible empirical appraisal of the unconscious mental processes. Beyond previous either methodological and ideological prejudices, cognitivists themselves have became even more aware of the need for putting attention also to the interface between conscious and unconscious, until to speak of a *cognitive unconscious* (Conte & Gennaro, 1989; Kissin, 1986).

The first attempts to relate perception (P), consciousness (C) and unconscious (U) date back to the early neurophysiological studies made by Freud in the 1890s, which led to the drawing up of the fundamental work *The Interpretation of Dreams* (of 1899), where the basic distinction between perception (P) and consciousness (C) is laid out in a theoretical framework in which predominates the *desiring* dimension of a predominant underflow of *unconscious phantasies* which inescapably exist between subject and object, just at an unconscious level, and dynamically animated by an *instinctual* reservoir, yet ruled by a psychic agency said to be *Ego* (Conte & Gennaro, 1989; Kissin, 1986).

So, with Freud, the problem of *unconscious*, meant as the main construct of a possible model of human psyche, reached its highest levels of attention and interest. Afterwards, other psychological next trends tried to undervalue the role of unconscious, while other retook it but through other ways. Anyway, after pioneering Freudian work, the unconscious phenomenology yet undertook a not negligible role in the psychological research, even differently from the psychoanalytic standpoint. A particular relevance assumed the notion of unconscious in the post-Pavlovian Russian school, which tried to give experimental bases to this notion by means of scientific knowledge like neurology, cybernetics, linguistics, so giving, at the same time, a materialistic criticism to Freudian ideology (Bassin, 1972; Uznadze et al., 1972; Kissin, 1986).

Also Piagetian theory of intellective development, together to other approaches like the *gestaltic*, the *perceptogenetic*, and the *microgenetic*, more or less made reference to unconscious aspects of mental life in studying perception, put at the foundation of their study and research work. Hence, the *behaviourism* marked a breaking in the psychological research, banishing any possible reference to the psychological notions of unconscious, consciousness, memory, attention, and so forth. This course, dominated therefore by behaviourism and by the functionalistic culture promoted by the so-called *New Look* trend (Conte & Gennaro, 1989), gradually prepared the ground for the next *cognitive* trend, which even more became leader in the psychological sciences domain. It arose from the behavioural model based on the stimulus-response (S-R) cyclic pattern, to which every psychic conscious phenomenon was reducible, putting out any unconscious phenomenon which was however relegated to an inaccessible *black-box* (Conte & Gennaro, 1989; Kissin, 1986).

However, in the meanwhile this development took place, yet the previously banished concepts of consciousness, memory, attention, and others, accordingly re-emerged, so also the new cognitive trend could not doing without these. The notion of memory, above all, taken a central role. Indeed, it was used to build up the so-called *multi-layers memory pattern*, upon which relies the so-called *human information processing* (HIP) *model* of consciousness information elaboration, according to which that coming from experience is, at first, recorded in the sensorial registers, hence, after to have been elaborated in neural information, and considered as relevant by attention, is then treated first by *short-term memory* (STM), in which it takes place most of consciousness acts (problem solving, evaluations, inferences, etc.), then "automatically" compared with contents of *long-term memory* (LTM), along a process of conscious and complex repeated *rehearsals* which may lead, by reinforcements, to storing new information just in LTM (Conte & Gennaro, 1989; Kissin, 1986).

This was the chief *sequential model* of consciousness of the early cognitive science of 1960s and 1970s. It was based on the attention, as a key component of consciousness, ruling perceptions, remembrances, actions under the control of attention, so that unconscious should refer to either those elements of perceptive system (as incipit of consciousness) which have escaped to the control of the system STM-LTM, which have not undergone to repetitive processes, or to those elements of LTM which have had not access to STM. So, both disregarded stimuli and LTM mnestic traces not activated by STM, are classified as unconscious, which yet operates *simultaneously* to the above conscious acts (Conte & Gennaro, 1989; Kissin, 1986).

Thus, from 1970s onwards, new more complex models taking into account these latter aspects occurring *in parallel* to the conscious ones (*sequentially* performed), were worked out, in which more advanced levels of information elaboration have been considered, like the so-called *parallel distributed processing* (PDP) model or the *parallel distributed elaboration* (PDE) model. In this regard, new models of memory have been outlined, which take into account above all procedural automatic mechanisms. The new cognitive sciences see therefore human being as a multi-channels processor of information, who unconsciously uses inference rules as well as often reasons with non-probabilistic models. At the same time, numerous empirical new techniques have been established to identify unconscious phenomenology as seen from different stances and standpoints (Conte & Gennaro, 1989; Kissin, 1986).

6.2 THE RELATIONSHIPS BETWEEN PSYCHOLOGICAL SCIENCE AND LOGIC

It seems that reflexivity and transitivity are the two main, basilar formal properties of relationships undergoing stably organized groups of living beings (animals, humans), the two minimal properties to have a hierarchy (Girotto, 2013), hence a pre-order, as this last is just a relation which satisfies these two basic properties. But, as we have seen in Chapter 4, a pre-order may spring out from symmetry breaking phenomena applied to groupoids structures, to be precise, we have considered this for combinatorial groupoids, that is to say, for groupoids coming from equivalence relations which will break down, for breaking of inversion symmetry, to give rise just to pre-order relations, hence to order relations.

The typical feature of human mind is that to build up and evaluate *arguments*, which are at least partially explicit, with the main aim to persuade other persons. They regard rational propositions or enunciates that are related of each other by *reasoning* which, in turn, entails the main fact that, if one accepts the premises of a reasoning, then it is quite unavoidable does not accept the related, inherent conclusions. Reasoning may be conducted by means of either *inductive* and *deductive inferences*. Nevertheless, recent psychological sciences does not give pre-eminence to logic, in that human beings often fail in doing correct and valid inferences, it has to be considered invalid the so-called *mental logic*, which deems formal Aristotelian logic followed by human mind, that is, as implemented into the latter, or else, the logic is viewed as a formal expression of mental laws. Indeed, many fallacious inferences are very frequently achieved by most of the people, as if the main logical inference rules were lacking in the human mind, that instead seems to work according to the functional framework provided by the theory of *mental models* (Girotto, 2013).

So, human mind evolved in pursuing *argumentative* theory. Although argumentation has a main individualistic ends, nevertheless it has also collective features inasmuch as it is aimed to confirm own personal beliefs, hypotheses or expectations in convincing who is turned our argumentation. Nevertheless that, very often people does not correctly evaluate the right probabilities of related uncertain events, not always they take optimal decisions, not always they planning appropriately their own future activities, and not always they simulate alternatives which are functional to the past ones. This implies that mental logic is quite inadequate as a paradigm of human mental reasoning, while mental model theory is more appropriate to this end, in that it explains, for instance, why human mind often performs invalid inferences. Indeed, according to this theory, human being, prior to pursue a reasoning, very often sets up erroneous or inappropriate premises to the reasoning to be pursued, in dependence on the social-cultural context in which they are worked out and set up. They often make a mistake because of the erroneous or incomplete previous mental framework built up around premises, and this agrees more with the theory of mental models (Girotto, 2013).

Recent psychology has shown that basic logic rules and laws are present in human being as is present language; among these, there is the valuable *modus ponens*, the usual logic inference for which if p and if $p \rightarrow q$, then q, but not always the *modus tollens* for which if $p \rightarrow q$ and if $\neg q$, then $\neg p$. So, it seems that one of the main deductive inference rules, that is, the modus ponens, is naturally acquainted by human being, even unconsciously, as proved in (Reverberi et al., 2012) where it is shown that modus ponens inference, in contrast to other deductive inferences (like modus tollens), can be carried out automatically and unconsciously; furthermore, other their findings suggest that critical deductive inference schemata can be included in the range of high-level cognitive activities which are carried out unconsciously. This explains why, in the previous chapter, we have pointed out that our main interest is in the modus ponens when we deal with deductive inferences; this also justifies our attempts to search for possible unconscious routes of classical logic, at least of those basic (syntactic) logic operators which fall into the so-called *mental logic* (Girotto, 2013).

In fact, higher logic operators do not fall into mental logic simply because certain inferences, like modus tollens, are not executed equally by many people, but rather they depend on the personal view of the related premises and of the content they assigned. So, basic deductive inferences (like modus ponens and material implication) are carried out *syntactically* independently of the content of the premises, differently from the case of other deductive inferences, like modus tollens, whose outcomes depend on the *pragmatic-semantic* context in which the related premises are embedded, as well as the interpretations given to them; therefore, the semantic-pragmatic context plays a very fundamental role in the psychology of reasoning[1]. Instead, it seems that the *theory of mental models* is a good theory explaining most of the phenomenology of reasoning, supposing first that every human being, before applies an inference, builds up a preliminary mental framework of all the premises involved by inference, comprises their content. This takes place for every inference, but for the simplest ones, like material implication and modus ponens, the validity is however warranted even this preliminary mental representation is partial and not complete, while for the other, it is need to have the most complete framework of the full range of possibilities assumed by premises; this also explains why human being often makes fallacious inferences, due to an incomplete or erroneous reconstruction of the mental framework of premises (Cherubini et al., 2000; Girotto, 2013).

6.3 THE VARIETY OF THE POSSIBLE CONSTRUCTS OF UNCONSCIOUS IN PSYCHOLOGY, SCIENCES AND HUMANITIES

In psychological context, the attempts of identification of unconscious phenomenology necessarily are experimentally settled up with an *indirect* methodology, in so far as we have clearly to do with a *non-manifest* psychological processes. So, a possible way to follow, is that for which we constantly should refer to constructs and notions related to certain psychological entities which are *directly* identifiable empirically but which are, at the same time, closely related with unconscious, through basic conceptual oppositions, based on the chief opposite pair conscious-unconscious (Conte & Gennaro, 1989). This is quite obvious seen the fundamental and basic oppositional nature of symbolic function of human being, upon which relies and explicates most of consciousness activity (Iurato, 2015).

Following Howard Shevrin, we may have numerous possible definitions of unconscious from a *descriptive* standpoint, in dependence on we assume a psychoanalytic or a cognitive stance. For example, we have the following (but not all the possible) descriptive views of unconscious:

- The unconscious processes may be considered as innate or acquired schemes which, once activated, manifest according to more or less predetermined sequences (like driving a bike, playing a guitar, and so on);
- The unconscious processes may be seen as a kind of programmes able to organize behaviour, or else consider them as a series of "files" belonging to certain programmes, at the moment, not recalled or retrieved;
- The unconscious processes may be seen as forms of elaboration of information which precede the rising of phenomenal experience of psychic life;
- The unconscious processes may be considered as preceding any form of awareness of either a conscious representation or content, and inaccessible to consciousness;
- The unconscious processes are structurally and functionally different from the conscious ones;
- The unconscious processes are structurally and functionally similar to conscious ones, yet qualitatively different.

At the same time, as recalled above, the pervasive presence of unconscious activity into the human neuropsychic life, in some cases even assessed empirically by the finding of modifications in neural circuits (Ekstrom, 2004; Kandel, 2005), allows to take into account, just for this unconscious omnipresence, certain contexts of psychic life as suitable to be seen as places in which to try to search out manifestations of unconscious phenomenology. So, empirical methods in searching of unconscious activity have concerned with those possible processes underlying conscious activity, some of which have been accordingly related to the field of study and research regarding attention, memory, altered states of consciousness, as well as to neuropsychophysiological context (Conte & Gennaro, 1989; Maffei 2014, Ch. V; Oliverio, 2016). Nevertheless, we should remark that most of experimental methods which have been used so far to identify such unconscious phenomenology, have mainly concerned with a notion of unconscious much more near to the cognitive one (on its turn, close to the Freudian notion of pre-conscious), rather than the Freudian one, so the following our discussion is not a repetition of what has been already done, but rather is turned to try to apply, as far as possible, Freudian notion of structural unconscious (deeper than preconscious and cognitive unconscious, which are quite superficial), as found by Freud and formally revised by Matte Blanco, computationally by means of a possible implementation of this notion previously laid out within a suitable logic framework.

6.4 THE POSSIBLE APPLICATIONS OF THE UNCONSCIOUS' CONSTRUCTS IN INFORMATICS: THE CASE OF CONCURRENT, PARALLEL AND SEQUENTIAL COMPUTING

In a *concurrent computing* process or thread, a certain number of different computations are performed along many time ranges which overlap among them, that is to say, such computations occur according to a *concurrency modality*, instead that *sequentially* (see later), so that, in a concurrent computing system, a constituent computation process can go on without waiting for the completion of all the other constituent computations. So, from a programming theory standpoint, concurrent computing is a modular programming, in that it decomposes an overall computation into a certain number of constituent computations (or *sub-computations*) which may be executed concurrently, in general according to a previously scheduled timing (Deng, 2013; Even & Medina, 2012; Petersen & Arbenz, 2004; Tanenbaum & Bos, 2015; Tokhi et al. 2003).

In theoretical computer science, *concurrency* has to be meant as that decomposability property of a computing process or thread into more elementary constituent components or sub-units (*sub-compo-nents*), which may be partially ordered or not, as well as may reciprocally interact or not; furthermore, independently these concurrent sub-units of the process are executed out-of-order or in partial order, the final outcome will not change. This allows a parallel execution of the concurrent sub-units, which may significantly improve overall speed of the execution in multi-processor and multi-core systems (Deng, 2013; Even & Medina, 2012; Petersen & Arbenz, 2004; Tanenbaum & Bos, 2015; Tokhi et al. 2003). Temporal logic may be also fruitfully applied to concurrent systems (Stirling, 2001).

The notion of concurrent computing has close connections with the related yet distinct notion of *parallel computing*, in that both may be generally considered as multi-component processes whose units or sub-components may be executed during the same time interval. In a parallel computing, nevertheless, the execution of the sub-computations occurs exactly at the same physical instant, and only one sub-computation per time can occur at every instant, during each single clock cycle, while, in a concurrent computing, though process' time ranges overlap, execution need not run at exactly the same instant. Thus, concurrent computations might be executed in parallel, but not vice versa, in general; furthermore, many distributed algorithms are both concurrent and parallel (Deng, 2013; Even & Medina, 2012; Petersen & Arbenz, 2004; Tanenbaum & Bos, 2015; Tokhi et al. 2003).

The term "sequential" is, then, used in an antinomical sense with respect to that of both terms "concurrent" and "parallel", so concurrent/sequential and parallel/serial have to be meant as opposed pairs. Sequential programming involves a consecutive and ordered execution of processes or threads one after the other, that is to say, in a sequential programming, processes or threads run one after another in a chronological succession, while in a parallel computing, multiple processes or threads execute at the same time. In such cases, the program will execute only one process or thread per time, without communicating with the remaining ones, while, in a parallel programming, in the meantime processes or threads might execute concurrently, yet its sub-units may communicate during execution (Deng, 2013; Even & Medina, 2012; Petersen & Arbenz, 2004; Tanenbaum & Bos, 2015; Tokhi et al. 2003).

A sequential programming often needs schedules; a schedule, then, in which related tasks are executed one at each time (i.e., serially, not in parallel), without interleaving (i.e., sequentially, not concurrently, that is to say, no task begins until the prior ends), is called a *serial schedule*. Finally, a set of tasks which can be scheduled serially, is said to be *serializable*. Most of standard computer programs or threads are sequential, so that sequentiality is often an implicit assumption. In general, given same input data, a sequential program will always execute the same sequence of instructions, and it will always produce, as outputs, the same results. Furthermore, sequential program execution is deterministic (Deng, 2013; Even & Medina, 2012; Petersen & Arbenz, 2004; Tanenbaum & Bos, 2015; Tokhi et al., 2003).

Then, from the computational psychoanalysis standpoint, seen too the main fact according to which unconscious is basically a-temporal, while consciousness is instead temporally featured, it follows immediately that a suitable coupling of concurrent or, even better, parallel processes[2] with sequential ones, notwithstanding their oppositional status due to their principles of functioning, may give rise to a certain composite process whose running might mould human psyche functioning. In this regard, see also what will be said at the end of the next section, in that, as we have mentioned above, temporal logic may be suitably applied to concurrent computation; on its turn, temporal logic may be usefully linked to unconscious processes via groupoids theory, as we shall see in the next section 6.6.

On the other hand, graph theory, whose structures are basically ordered structures, is one of the main formal tool of parallel computing (Voevodin, 1992); see also (Skillicorn, 1994) for other algebraic methods of parallel computing. Finally, from what has been said in Chapter 4, Section 4.1.5.3., all these computer science notions should be suitably taken into account for giving rise a complex computing framework to be worked out also taking into account the inherent notions of dynamical system theory which, as seen, are indispensable to formalize the main unconscious phenomenology related to the crucial interplay between primary and secondary process and the involved bounding energetic processes. Of course, the comparison, then, with neural network theory, should require another deeper discussion which is not possible to do in this place, at least for this moment. Anyway, it seems historically interesting, and perhaps also from a computational standpoint, to reconsider original Freudian works on possible neurobiological substrates to human psyche functioning according to his psychodynamic ideas, as mainly made in his *Project for a Scientific Psychology* (of 1895), as well as to consider, just in this place, what possible analogies may hold between parallel/concurrent processes, as well as synchronous/asynchronous ones, and those basic discontinuities of the excitations inherent preconscious-conscious system taking place in its touches with external reality, of which Freud in passing mentions in his brief work of 1925 entitled *A Note upon the ''Mystic Writing Pad''*, in turn, linked with the rising of consciousness and its temporal dimension.

6.5 THE POSSIBLE APPLICATIONS OF THE UNCONSCIOUS' CONSTRUCTS IN INFORMATICS: THE CASE OF SYNCHRONOUS AND ASYNCHRONOUS LOGIC SYSTEMS

By means of binary numerical system, the principles of arithmetic and classical logic have could be combined together. Hence, Charles Sanders Peirce, for first described, in the 1880s, how logical operations could be carried out through *electrical switching circuits* with suitable *logic gates*. In particular, in the 1930s, it was showed that operations of switching circuits and their functioning, may be represented by two-valued Boolean algebra. Later, Claude E. Shannon extensively used Boolean algebra in the analysis and design of switching circuits. This property of electrical switches to implement logic is the fundamental concept that underlies all the electronic digital computers. So, switching circuit theory became the foundation of *digital logic circuit* design, from around 1940s onward (Even & Medina, 2012; Sparsø & Furber, 2001).

In turn, digital logic circuits can be divided into *combinational logic circuits*, in which the output signals depend only on the current input signals, and *sequential logic circuits*, in which the output depends both on current input and the past history of inputs by means of a memory system. In other words, we may say that sequential logic circuits are combinational logic circuits with memory that goes through a sequence of states. Virtually all practical digital devices are built up on sequential logic circuits. Sequential logic circuits can be divided then into two further types, *synchronous logic* circuits, defined from the knowledge of its signals at discrete instants of time, and *asynchronous logic* circuits, depending on the input signals at any instant of time and their change order (Even & Medina, 2012; Sparsø & Furber, 2001).

In synchronous logic circuits, the distinguishing feature is that the circuit only changes in response to a system clock made by an electronic oscillator which generates a repetitive or periodic series of equally spaced clock pulses, each of which is called a *clock signal*, simultaneously applied to every storage element of the memory. In synchronous circuits settled in the *canonical form*, the clock signal is applied to all the edge-triggered memory elements of the circuit, data storing, called *flip-flops* or *latches*. A feature of these circuits is that changes to the logic signals throughout the circuit all begin at the same time, at regular intervals synchronized by the clock. The outputs of all the memory elements in a synchronous circuit is called the *state of the circuit*, which changes only on the clock pulse. Nevertheless, the changes in logic signal require a certain amount of time to propagate through the combinational logic gates of the circuit, and this is called *propagation delay* (Even & Medina, 2012; Sparsø & Furber, 2001).

The period of the clock signal is expressly regulated long enough in such a manner that the output of all the logic gates have time to reach stable values before the next clock pulse starts. As long as this condition is established, synchronous circuits will operate stably. A possible disadvantage of synchronous circuits is however that they can be slow. Instead, since in asynchronous circuits, there is no clock, so the state of the circuit changes as soon as the input changes, it follows that they don't have to wait for a clock pulse to begin processing inputs, so that asynchronous circuits can be faster than synchronous circuits, and their speed is theoretically limited only by the propagation delays of the logic gates (Even & Medina, 2012; Sparsø & Furber, 2001).

However, asynchronous circuits are more difficult to design and subjected to certain problems not found in synchronous circuits. This is because the resulting state of an asynchronous circuit can be sensitive to the relative arrival times of inputs at gates. If transitions on two inputs arrive then at almost the same time, then the circuit can go into the wrong state depending on slight differences in the propagation delays of the gates. This situation is called a *race condition*. In synchronous circuits this problem is instead less severe because race conditions can occur only for certain inputs – said to be *asynchronous inputs* – coming from outside the synchronous system (Even & Medina, 2012; Sparsø & Furber, 2001).

Asynchronous logic is thus the logic required for designing asynchronous digital systems. Their functioning does not use a clock signal, so their individual logic elements cannot assume discrete values for true/false states, at any given time. Accordingly, Boolean logic is inadequate for this, so that other algebraic structures are required, like, for example, those based on a set of discrete values more than two (Even & Medina, 2012; Sparsø & Furber, 2001); on the other hand, just for asynchronous computing, simplicial complexes have been called into question (Herlihy & Shavit, 1999). In this regard, then, maybe groupoids structures, as briefly exposed in Chapter 4, and that we have seen to be susceptible to formalize the main aspects of structural unconscious and its functioning in relation to consciousness, might be used to accomplish this requirement.

We have seen that such formal algebraic structures – i.e., groupoids – are also suitable to take into account temporal dimensionality, the main feature of consciousness (see again Chapter 4), which, from the Freudian standpoint, comes from a basic discontinuity between exciting and de-exciting processes of psychic energy, and their control by the *Ego* (see Chapter 4, Section 4.2.2), so that, just to this end, asynchronous and synchronous circuits, suitably coupled, may provide the electronic counterpart simulating this psychic function time producing. Moreover, these arguments may have useful links with *proof theory* and its informatics implementations, in that theoretical computer sciences is also interested in attempts which try to build a logic for reasoning executed in parallel. Indeed, most of the formal reasoning proceed in a sequential way, that is, they are describable by means of a basic linear sequence of distinct steps, while unconscious mechanisms usually proceed in parallel (in this regard, see also what will be said in the last section of next chapter). So, a central question of proof theory (and its automatic applications) is whether it is possible to implement to formal (conscious) thought certain typical functional mechanisms of unconscious by means of suitable electronic circuits. We think that asynchronous and synchronous circuits, suitably coupled, might satisfy these last requests.

On the other hand, since 1990s, new research areas have emerged along this direction. Indeed, much of the nervous system can be viewed as a massively parallel, distributed system of highly specialized but unconscious processors. Humans conscious experience, on the other hand, is traditionally viewed as a serial *stream* that integrates different sources of information but is limited to only one internally consistent content at any given moment. Now, the so-called *global workspace theory* had already suggested that the conscious experience emerges from a nervous system in which multiple input processors parallel compete for access to a broadcasting capability; and the winning processor can disseminate its information *globally* throughout the brain. Furthermore, global workspace architectures have been widely employed in computer systems to integrate separate modules when they must work together to solve a novel problem or to control a coherent new response.

This global workspace theory has articulated a series of increasingly complex models, able to account for more and more evidence about conscious functioning, from perceptual consciousness to conscious problem-solving, voluntary control of action, and directed attention. Nonetheless, global workspace theory has turned out to be consistent with, but not reducible to, other theories of limited-capacity mechanisms. Moreover, global workspace architectures has shown competition for input to a neural global workspace and global distribution of its output. Brain structures that are demonstrably required for normal conscious experience can carry out these two functions, and the theory has shown testable predictions, especially for newly emerging, high-speed brain imaging technology (Baars, 1993).

From what has been said above, namely just at the end of the previous section, here we say again that, just in regard to possible applications of synchronous/asynchronous logics to trying to simulate unconscious functioning, we refer either to the end of the next section as well as to the next Chapter 7, Section 7.3. On the other hand, we should say that the notion of synchronization has already been used widely in neurosciences, above all in the neural network theory, from 1980s onwards, until recent times. Indeed, cognitive scientists have tried to identify and explain the possible neural mechanisms underlying cognitive unconscious mental states, such as coma, epileptic seizures, and anaesthesia-induced unconsciousness, from which cognitive unconscious states may be seen as different from the psychoanalytic unconscious ones (Ceylan et al. 2016).

Indeed, Mehmet E. Ceylan and co-workers (Ceylan et al., 2016) have yet recently reconsidered hypothesis about the neural correlates underlying psychoanalytic unconscious, firstly reviewing the previous explanations about the neural correlates of conscious and unconscious mental states, such as brain oscillations, synchronicity of neural networks[3], cognitive binding, hence casting a neuroscientific ground for their hypothesis about neural correlates of psychoanalytic unconscious, as well as parallel but unsynchronized neural networks between different layers of consciousness and unconsciousness. Likewise, they have also proposed a neuroscientific mechanism about how the repressed mental events may reach the conscious awareness, and the lock of neural synchronization between two mental layers of conscious and unconscious. They have also discussed the data about schizophrenia as a clinical example of their proposed hypothesis.

However, what we would like to specify just in this regard, is that our approach has started from a logical stance, as that proposed by Matte Blanco (see above all next Chapter 7, Section 7.3.), for reaching to a set of conclusions which may open different perspectives of further discussion on the formal nature of the structural unconscious according to Matte Blanco, among which is just that regarding synchronous/asynchronous circuits and their underlying logics. This latter, as we have wished to underscore right above, is a point of view quite reasonable, insofar as it has been already treated following other routes, like that of networks as neural correlates of unconscious processes, which therefore justify our aim, that of synchronous/asynchronous processes, reached starting from Matte Blanco's ideas. Finally, in regard to the notion of synchronicity as discussed within Jungian framework in comparison with physical sciences, see (La Forgia, 1992) and references therein. Just in regard to Jungian thought, Richard Carvalho (2014) has used Matte Blanco's ideas to provide a formal basis, of which Jung himself complained of lacking, with which to validate the notion of synchronicity and to demonstrate that it is one of the inevitable properties of an unconscious which is unrepressed, such as Jung's collective unconscious, and that such an unconscious will also be affective and interpersonal (hence, equipped with objective features) as well as intrapersonal, which also have important clinical implications. After an exposition of Matte Blanco's thinking, Carvalho exposes some clinical material regarding mainly psychosomatic symptoms, hence making some possible correlations between Matte Blanco's ideas and Jung's ones. Also on the basis of this work, then, H. Atmanspacher (2014a,b), analyzing further Jung's synchronicity and its psychophysical correlations, has proposed further epistemological remarks about formalizations of structural unconscious. Finally, for the vast implications of the Jungian notion of synchronicity, see (Main, 2014).

6.6 THE POSSIBLE APPLICATIONS OF THE UNCONSCIOUS' CONSTRUCTS IN INFORMATICS: THE CASE OF TEMPORAL AND MODAL LOGICS

Loosely speaking, *temporal logic* may be defined as the study of those aspects of temporality which are logically relevant. Among others, Aristotle and Diodorus Chrono, in ancient philosophy, as well as Avicenna and Occam, in medieval philosophy, dealt with temporalized arguments. Instead, temporal dimension seems to have been quite neglected in modern logic, as this arose mainly from the questions inherent foundations of mathematics, differently from ancient and mediaeval logic in which were centred on structural logic of language, where temporality is a predominant aspect. Even in recent informatics and artificial intelligence, very scant attention has been paid to tenses, where the idea that the property of an object or the holding of a relation among more objects, should be conceived atemporally (Gabbay et al., 1994, 2000; Hodkinson & Reynolds, 2007; Øhrstrøm & Hasle, 1995; Pizzi, 1974; Venema, 2001).

Willard V.O. Quine introduced variables and constants *ad hoc* in account for time in logical enunciates, so including temporal logic into classical logic, while Arthur N. Prior, the founder of temporal logic, studied temporalized enunciates as such. Temporal logic then comprises the design and study of specific systems for representing and reasoning about time. These tasks may have both an applied and a theoretical development, the former consisting in designing a system (chiefly, making choices in the fields of ontology, syntax and semantic), formalizing temporal phenomena in it, and then putting it to work (perhaps through implementing it), while, on the theoretical side, one aims is to proving formal properties, such as completeness and decidability. Temporal logic furthermore has had important applications in computer sciences (Gabbay et al., 1994, 2000; Galton, 1987; Hodkinson & Reynolds, 2007; Øhrstrøm & Hasle, 1995; Pizzi, 1974; Venema, 2001).

Temporal logic provides a recognized technique to specify programming systems, particularly concurrent systems, and to formulate and prove properties of them. The main task of temporal logic is to define the right and reasonable semantic conditions for temporal operators, hence to establish the right syntactic rules to handle these last, as well as to make temporal inferences which depend on the temporal nature[4] of hypotheses. Temporal logic is particularly adequate for properties to hold continuously during functioning. As said above, concurrent systems consist of components which partly operate mutually independent, so that the occurrence of an event affects, and on its turn is affected, by a limited subarea of a system, called the *event's scope*. Occurrences of events with disjoint scopes are not related to global system states; nevertheless, such states may be enforced from outside the system, but its essential properties should be independent thereof. Conventional temporal logic is interpreted over transition systems and their runs, and global states are essential in this context (Gabbay et al., 1994, 2000; Øhrstrøm & Hasle, 1995; Pizzi, 1974; Reising, 1988).

Temporal logic is often considered as a branch of *modal logic* which is a logic system, of the 1960s, turned to extend classical propositional and predicate logic to a new formal theory which deals with *modality*. A *modal proposition* expresses the way, the manner, the fashion (i.e., the *modus*) in which the composition (i.e., the *dictum*) between subject and predicate takes place, often given by inserting an adverbial locution changing verb. The modus, in turn, may be: necessary, possible, impossible, contingent. These are said to be *alethic* modalities. Other modalities which have been formalized in modal logic include *temporal* modalities (from which it follows temporal logic), *deontic* modalities, including obligations or orders, *epistemic* modalities, concerning the knowledge, *doxastic* modalities, related to beliefs, *causal* modalities, *existential* modalities (basically given by quantifiers), *bulomaich* modalities, regarding conation and desire, and so on (Dalla Chiara, 1974).

Modal logic dates back to Aristotle. Jacques Lacan considered it as an unconscious logic, with an original re-interpretation of modality as meant by Aristotle in his treatise *De Interpretatione*, in which he introduced, for the first time, the notion of modality. Lacan gives a psychoanalytic reading of Aristotelian modalities: for instance, the necessary is what never ceases to be written, the possible is what ceases to be written, the contingent is what ceases to be not written, while the impossible is what never ceases to be not writable; here, the reference to be written is meant in term of the symbolic of unconscious, which is structured like a language (Chemama & Vandermersch, 1998).

In his XXI Seminary, entitled *Les non-dupes errent* (of 1974), Lacan underscores the relevance of writing in the relationship between subject and language, just by means of the logic of modalities. Lacan identifies the impossible with the Real, that is, the deepest, unspeakable, ineffable dimension of unconscious, where, for each logical statement p, both p and $\neg p$ persist at the same time, and are logically unverifiable. The Real escapes to every form of knowledge, in that it does not belong to any symbolic register. The symptom, arising from the Real and the only empirical manifestation of it, with its impossible content, may become contingent, that is it ceases to be not writable, only by means of the cure and its analytical interpretation; the symptom expresses the need for the subject to be put, in some way, into relationship with Law and Desire, whose content, nevertheless, is at first unknowledgeable as it escapes from any form of symbolization, mainly writing (Chemama & Vandermersch, 1998).

Following (von Karger 1995, 2002), it is possible to work out an algebraic framework to temporal logic introducing new temporal operators like "next" $(\bigcirc)$, "previous" $(\odot)$ and "eventually" $(\square)$. Sequential calculus is basically an algebraic calculus meant for reasoning about phenomena with a duration and their sequencing. It can be further specialized to various domains used for reasoning about programs and systems, including Tarski's calculus of binary relations, Kleene's regular expressions, Hoare's CSP and Dijkstra's regularity calculus. Burghard von Karger (1995) uses sequential calculus as a tool for algebraizing temporal logics, showing that temporal operators are definable in terms of sequencing and showing how a specific logic may be selected by introducing additional axioms. All axioms of the complete proof system for discrete linear temporal logic are then obtained as theorems of *sequential algebra*, as developed in (von Karger, 2002) and references therein.

So, von Karger has embedded temporal logic into an algebra naturally equipped with sequencing constructs, where recursion is also definable. This might be a first step towards a design calculus for transforming temporal specifications by stepwise refinement into executable programs. The basic idea underlying von Karger's method is to join a precise semigroup structure to the usual Boolean algebra. Semigroups and Boolean algebras with operators, have been thoroughly investigated subject-matters of algebra, and suitable connections to temporal logic might enable valuable cross fertilization, and indeed von Karger's work consists in embedding temporal logic into an algebra which is naturally equipped with certain programming constructs, like sequential composition, non-deterministic choice and conditionals, and in which recursion is definable (von Karger, 1995).

Sequential algebra provides a new alternative way to arriving at the set of operators of temporal logic, equipping a space of observations, which may already have an underlying Boolean algebra structure, with a suitable groupoid structure to be suitably implemented, which takes into account the sequentiality feature of temporality by means of certain evolution operators having a semigroup structure (von Karger, 1995; 2002). Hence, it seems that temporality may be formalized too through a certain groupoid structure, which has a wider categorial nature embracing other more particular structures. Thus, the central, basic algebraic structure around which revolve all the other structures mentioned above, seems to be the groupoid one, that has been discussed in the previous Chapter 4, Section 4.1.5. As just discussed above, therefore, a basic groupoid structure[5], suitably formalizing temporality, may be implemented in a pre-assigned Boolean algebra structure, to give a formal algebraic framework to temporal logic, according to sequential algebra as for example stated by von Karger (1995, 2002).

Finally, in regard to the important remark, made in the previous sections, about the possibility to mould chief unconscious features, mainly a-temporality, we may clarify the risen question within temporal logic in the following manner. To be precise, we have above claimed how operatively synchronicity or parallel processes could simulate at best unconscious functioning, above all its typical feature, the a-temporality. We have also highlighted that surely synchronicity and parallel running do not are equivalent to the a-temporality but rather they may approximate it. Anyway, within temporal logic, we are able to lay out better such a question for making it clearer, succeeding also to justifying why synchronicity or parallel processes, may roughly simulate unconscious functioning.

Indeed, we recall that temporal logic has been the result of the introduction in logic of the temporal dimension, since then, indeed, a characteristic of formal logic was the abstraction from time, this explaining why it was unable to take into account dialectic viewpoint, that is to say, the becoming of the real. But, with the works of either Arthur Prior and Nino B. Cocchiarella, of the 1950s, time has coming in logic. In our case, however, Saul Kripke's semantic may provide the right framework to lay out our question. In fact, we may image a changing situation (hence, temporally variable) as formally describable through a Kripkian realization[6] $\{M_i\}_{i \in I}$ (said to be a *Kripkian history*) where each M_i represents the state of a certain world M at the instant i, while I is a time interval (i.e., a set of instants) in which the evolutionary situation takes place (Dalla Chiara 1974, Ch. 3, Sect. 3.3.).

But, another fundamental and central problem of temporal logic, is the definition of the concept of time *instant*. This has been initially borrowed from physics, hence considering a physical time as a kind of "atom of time", namely, time as the points of an oriented number line (*time arrow*), that is, the classical notion of linear time, experimentally liable to be detected with suitable instruments (clocks). In every time instant, any change cannot take place. This last hypothesis will be assumed by Kripkian point of view of modal logics, considering, for each M_i, a set of transformations, say $\left\{f_j^{M_i}(t)\right\}_{j \in J_i}$ (with J_i a set of indices depending on M_i), of the truth values of the propositions – built up in the language of M_i – which change with the variation of the possible states of the world M_i where both non-contradiction principle and the law of excluded middle hold in each instant of time t (Dalla Chiara 1974, Ch. 3, Sect. 3.3.).

Now, is it possible to leave out the hypothesis of instant of time? Maria Luisa Dalla Chiara Scabia (1973) analyses just this question on the basis of the previous works made by Arthur N. Prior and George von Wright on the punctual structure of time in instants, hence on the topology of time[7], asking whether is it possible to consider not an instant of time (or an "atom of time", homogeneous and indivisible) but rather an infinitesimal time, say Δt, as small as desired but not reduced only to the instant t, during which a variation or change takes place; it is also a threshold under which the truth value of the propositions considered with respect to a certain context that turns out possible in Δt, is undetermined. In this case, the instant t loses its punctual character to opening towards a minimal extent in which a proposition undertakes meaning (Dalla Chiara 1974, Ch. 3, Sect. 3.3.; Westphal 2007, Ch. I). This is coherent with the leaving out of physical (instant) time in favour of (range) psychological time, needed for the human consciousness for understanding (Iurato et al., 2016).

In this new framework, mainly outlined by Dalla Chiara (1973), we may have too the possibility that, for a proposition α, in a given infinitesimal interval Δt, both α and $\neg\alpha$ are true, so it is possible that, just in this little range of time Δt, negligible (but not zero) with respect to the usual whole ranges of time variously and globally involved, the non-contradiction principle is not valid; likewise for the principle of excluded middle. Thus, in Δt, we may have that both α and $\neg\alpha$ are true, that is to say, the non-validity of non-contradiction principle which is, among other things, one of the main features of unconscious logic, as is well-know; this infinitesimal interval Δt, moreover, cannot be further divided into non-void partial intervals in which separately holds definitively α or $\neg\alpha$ (so restoring the non-contradiction principle). In other words, a changing Δt may implies a contradiction, which nevertheless should hold "briefly enough" (lesser, in duration, than Δt itself).

On the other hand, just in regard Δt, hyperreal number system, which comprehends as well real numbers, is suitable to explain the close intertwinements between conscious logic and unconscious one (in the hyperreal numbers Δt), in that, in pure hyperreal numbers, as Δt, the non-contradiction principle is not valid (like in the unconscious), while, in the real number counterpart of this system, such a basic principle is valid (as a typical feature of consciousness). So, just hyperreal number system, which comprises also real numbers, seems to be a promising formal system for describing human psyche functioning, according to Matte Blanco's main framework based on bi-logic. So, interestingly, it should turn out to be further studies on the possible relationships between hyperreal number system (and, even better, surreal number system) with bi-logic as conceived according to Matte-Blanco.

Therefore, instead of having a Kripkian history of the type $\{M_i\}_{i \in I}$, based on the notion of "atom of time", and indicized by the set of time instants I, we may now consider a more general history of the type $\{M_{\Delta t}\}_{\Delta t \in I}$, where each world M is now indicized by the infinitesimal time interval Δt, with, on its turn, $\Delta t \in I$ where I is a set of (infinitesimal) temporal intervals, non-void subset of the (pure) hyperreal numbers system. Thus, in each $M_{\Delta t}$, a logic contradiction may take place, so that, in such a world, we may suppose to hold a multi-values logic (like, for example, the *fuzzy logic*, just in the context of our discussion about computational psychoanalysis – see next Chapter 7, Section 7.5.1.), provided that Δt be "briefly enough". Therefore, if we consider a Kripkian history of the general type $\{M_{\Delta t}\}_{\Delta t \in I}$, with I a non-empty subset of the hyperreal numbers system, then we have the alternation of worlds $M_{\Delta t}$ in which it holds either (Aristotelian) bivalent logic, when Δt is a pure real number (i.e., an instant, an "atom of time") or a polyvalent logic, when Δt is a pure hyperreal number.

Concluding, just these last arguments on the possible subsistence of temporally localized (in an infinitesimal time interval Δt) contradictions[8], hence in violation of the (Aristotelian) principle of non-contradiction, one of the main features of unconscious functioning, suggest how is it possible that synchronicity or parallel/concurrent processes (physically realizable and actuated just with this very small Δt), may suitably simulate unconscious functioning in its main feature, that is to say, the principle of non-contradiction. This, basically in obligation of what has been said above, just in the previous sections, in regard to the legitimacy to operationally use either synchronous circuits and parallel/concurrent processes in trying to simulate some chief functions of structural unconscious. Alike, we have also see that hyperreal numbers system is able to provide a possible, simple formal system describing the crucial interconnection unconscious-conscious called into question by the well-known Matte Blanco's bi-logic system. Anyway, standard references for the computational applications of temporal logic, are (Gabbay et al., 1994, 2000).

REFERENCES

Akhtar, S., & O'Neil, M. K. (Eds.). (2011). *On Freud's 'negation'. In The International Psychoanalytic Association – Contemporary Freud. Turning points & critical issues*. London, UK: Karnac Books, Ltd.

Albertson, M. O., & Collins, K. L. (1996). Symmetry Breaking in Graphs. *The Electronic Journal of Combinatorics, 3*(1), R18.

Alexander, F. (1948). Fundamentals of psychoanalysis. New York, NY: W.W. Norton & Company, Inc.

Allman, J. M. (2000). *Evolving Brains*. New York, NY: Scientific American Library. A division of HPHLP.

Ammaniti, M., & Gallese, V. (2014). La nascita dell'intersoggettività. Lo sviluppo del Sé fra psicodinamica e neurobiologia. Milano, Italy: Raffaello Cortina Editore.

Andersson, O. (1962). Studies on the Prehistory of Psychoanalysis. Stockholm: Scandinavian University Books.

Arieti, S. (1974). Interpretazione della schizofrenia. Milano, Italy: Giangiacomo Feltrinelli Editore.

Arieti, S. (1976). Creatività. La sintesi magica. Roma, Italy: Il Pensiero Scientifico Editore.

Atkinson, R. L., Atkinson, R. C., Smith, E. E., Bem, D. J., & Nolen-Hoeksema, S. (Eds.). (1996). *Hilgard's Introduction to Psychology* (12th ed.). Orlando, FL: Harcourt Brace.

Atmanspacher, H. (2014a). Psychophysical correlations, synchronicity and meaning. *The Journal of Analytical Psychology, 59*(2), 181–188. doi:10.1111/1468-5922.12068 PMID:24673273

Atmanspacher, H. (2014b). Levels of unconsciousness and their formal structures. *The Journal of Analytical Psychology, 59*(3), 385–390. doi:10.1111/1468-5922.12087 PMID:24919630

Baars, B. J. (1993). How does a serial, integrated and very limited stream of consciousness emerge from a nervous system that is mostly unconscious, distributed, parallel and of enormous capacity? In *Experimental and Theoretical Studies of Consciousness, Novartis Foundation Symposium No.* 174. New York, NY: John Wiley & Sons, Ltd.

Badiou, A. (1982). Théorie du sujet. Paris: Éditions du Seuil.

Balsamo, M. (2009). Ripetizione, coazione a ripetere, destino. In *Psiche. Dizionario storico di psicologia, psichiatria, psicoanalisi, neuroscienze* (Vol. 2, pp. 957–962). Torino, Italy: Giulio Einaudi editore.

Balzarotti, R. (Ed.). (1972). Cahiers pour l'Analyse. Scritti scelti di analisi e teoria della scienza, a cura del Centro Ricerche 2. Torino, Italy: Editore Boringhieri.

Bara, B. G. (1990). Scienza Cognitiva. Torino, Italy: Bollati Boringhieri editore.

Barratt, B. B. (2016). *Psychoanalysis and the Postmodern Impulse. Knowing and Being since Freud's Psychology*. New York, NY: Routledge.

Battacchi, M. W. (2006). *La conoscenza psicologia. Il metodo, l'oggetto, la ricerca*. Roma, Italy: Carocci editore.

Ben-Ari, M. (1993). Mathematical Logic for Computer Science. Hemel Hempstead, UK: Prentice Hall International, Ltd.

Benvenuto, S. (2005). Perversioni. Sessualità, etica, psicoanalisi. Torino, Italy: Bollati Boringhieri editore.

Berwick, R. C., & Chomsky, N. (2016). Why Only Us. Language and Evolution. Cambridge, MA: The MIT Press. doi:10.7551/mitpress/9780262034241.001.0001

Blumenthal, P., & Tyvaert, J.-E. (Eds.). (2003). *La cognition dans le temps. Etudes cognitives dans le champ historique des langues et des textes*. Tübingen, Germany: Max Niemeyer Verlag. doi:10.1515/9783110949490

Bokanowski, T., & Lewkowicz, S. (Eds.). (2009). *On Freud's 'splitting of the ego in the process of defence'. In The International Psychoanalytic Association – Contemporary Freud: Turning points & critical issues*. London, UK: Karnac Books, Ltd.

Bonnota, O., de Montalembertb, M., Kermarrecc, S., Botbold, M., Waltere, M., & Coulon, N. (2011). Are impairments of time perception in schizophrenia a neglected phenomenon? *Journal of Physiology, Paris, 105*(4-6), 164–169. doi:10.1016/j.jphysparis.2011.07.006 PMID:21803155

Borgogno, F., Luchetti, A., & Marino Coe, L. (Eds.). (2017). Il pensiero psicoanalitico italiano. Maestri, idee e tendenze dagli anni '20 ad oggi. Milano, Italy: FrancoAngeli.

Borisyuk, R., Borisyuk, G., & Kazanovich, Y. (1998). Synchronization of neural activity and information processing. *Behavioral and Brain Sciences, 21*(6), 833. doi:10.1017/S0140525X98241768

Bottiroli, G. (2006). *Che cos'è la teoria della letteratura. Fondamenti e problemi*. Torino, Italy: Giulio Einaudi editore.

Boudon, R. (1970). *Strutturalismo e scienze umane*. Torino, Italy: Giulio Einaudi editore.

Bourguignon, A., & Manus, A. (1980). Hallucination nègative, déni de la réalité et scotomisation. *Annales Médico-Psychologiques, 138*(2), 129–153. PMID:6992686

Bremer, M. (2005). *An Introduction to Paraconsistent Logics*. Frankfurt am Main, Germany: Peter Lang Publishing.

Bria, P. (1981). Introduzione. Pensiero, mondo e problemi di fondazione. In *L'inconscio come insiemi infiniti. Saggio sulla bi-logica* (pp. xix–cxi). Torino, Italy: Giulio Einaudi editore.

Bria, P., & Caroppo, E. (2006). Antropologia culturale e psicopatologia. Roma, Italy: Alpes Italia.

Britton, R. (2000). Belief and Imagination. Explorations in Psychoanalysis. London, UK: Routledge.

Britton, R. (2003). Sex, Death and the Super-Ego. Experiences in Psychoanalysis. London, UK: Karnac Books, Ltd.

Bruner, E. (Ed.). (2015). Human Paleoneurology. Springer International Publishing. doi:10.1007/978-3-319-08500-5

Bucci, W. (1985). Dual coding: A cognitive model for psychoanalytic research. *Journal of the American Psychoanalytic Association, 33*(3), 571–607. doi:10.1177/000306518503300305 PMID:4056301

Bucci, W. (1987). *The dual code model and the interpretation of dreams*. New York, NY: Derner Institute – Adelphi University.

Bucci, W. (1997). *Psychoanalysis and Cognitive Science*. New York, NY: The Guilford Press.

CA (Collectif d'Auteurs). (1975). *La Psychanalyse*. Paris: Editions Le Livre De Poche.

Capa, R. L., Duval, C. Z., Blaison, D., & Giersch, A. (2014). Patients with schizophrenia selectively impaired in temporal order judgments. *Schizophrenia Research, 156*(1), 51–55. doi:10.1016/j.schres.2014.04.001 PMID:24768441

Capozza, D. (1977). Il differenziale semantico. Problemi teorici e metrici. Bologna, Italy: Casa Editrice Pàtron.

Capozzi, M., & Cellucci, C. (2014). *Breve storia della logica. Dall'Umanesimo al primo Novecento*. Morrisville, NC: Lulu Press, Inc.

Carlson, L. (1999). *Consumption and Depression in Gertrude Stein, Louis Zukofsky, and Ezra Pound*. London, UK: Palgrave-MacMillan Press, Ltd. doi:10.1057/9780230379947

Carotenuto, A. (1982). Discorso sulla metapsicologia. Torino, Italy: Bollati Boringhieri Editore.

Carotenuto, A. (1991). Trattato di psicologia della personalità e delle differenze individuali. Milano, Italy: Raffaello Cortina Editore.

Carotenuto, A. (Ed.). (1992). Dizionario Bompiani degli Psicologi Contemporanei. Milano, Italy: Bompiani.

Carruccio, E. (1971). Mondi della Logica. Bologna, Italy: Nicola Zanichelli Editore.

Carvalho, R. (2014). Synchronicity, the infinite unrepressed, dissociation and the interpersonal. *The Journal of Analytical Psychology, 59*(3), 366–384. doi:10.1111/1468-5922.12085 PMID:24919629

Casari, E. (1972). Questioni di Filosofia della Matematica. Milano, Italy: Giangiacomo Feltrinelli Editore.

Cassinari, F. (2005). Tempo e identità. La dinamica di legittimazione nella storia e nel mito. Milano, Italy: FrancoAngeli.

Cellucci, C., & Ippoliti, E. (2016). Logica. Milano, Italy: EGEA Editore.

Ceylan, E. M., Dönmez, A., Ünsalver, B. A., & Evrensel, A. (2016). Neural synchronization as a hypothetical explanation of the psychoanalytic unconscious. *Consciousness and Cognition, 40*, 34–44. doi:10.1016/j.concog.2015.12.011 PMID:26744848

Chang, C.-C., & Keisler, H. J. (1973). Model Theory. Amsterdam: North-Holland Publishing Company, Inc.

Chemama, R., & Vandermersch, B. (Eds.). (1998). Dictionnaire de la Psychanalyse. Paris: Larousse-Bordas.

Cherubini, P., Giaretta, P., & Mazzocco, A. (Eds.). (2000). Ragionamento: psicologia e logica. Firenze, Italy: Giunti Gruppo Editoriale.

Chianese, D. (2009). Costruzione, Ricostruzione, Interpretazione. In *Psiche. Dizionario storico di psicologia, psichiatria, psicoanalisi, neuroscienze* (Vol. 1, pp. 280–285). Torino, Italy: Giulio Einaudi editore.

Codignola, E. (1977). Il vero e il falso. Saggio sulla struttura logica dell'interpretazione psicoanalitica. Torino, Italy: Editore Boringhieri.

Cohn, P. M. (1965). Universal Algebra. New York, NY: Harper & Row Publishers.

Conrotto, F. (2000). Tra il sapere e la cura. Un itinerario freudiano. Milano, Italy: FrancoAngeli.

Conrotto, F. (2009). Negazione. In *Psiche. Dizionario storico di psicologia, psichiatria, psicoanalisi, neuroscienze* (Vol. 2, pp. 728–730). Torino, Italy: Giulio Einaudi editore.

Conrotto, F. (2010). Per una teoria psicoanalitica della conoscenza. Milano, Italy: FrancoAngeli.

Conrotto, F. (2014). Ripensare l'inconscio. Milano, Italy: FrancoAngeli.

Contardi, R. (2010). La prova del labirinto. Processo di simbolizzazione e dinamica rappresentativa in psicoanalisi. Milano, Italy: FrancoAngeli.

Contarello, A., & Mazzara, B. M. (2002). Le dimensioni sociali dei processi psicologici. Roma-Bari, Italy: Laterza Editori.

Conte, M., & Gennaro, A. (Eds.). (1989). Inconscio e processi cognitivi. Bologna, Italy: Società editrice il Mulino.

Conti, L., & Principe, S. (1989). Salute mentale e società. Fondamenti di psichiatria sociale. Padova, Italy: Piccin Nuova Libraria.

Contri, G. (1972). Nozioni fondamentali nella teoria della struttura di Jacques Lacan. In Cahiers pour l'Analyse. Scritti scelti di analisi e teoria della scienza, a cura del Centro Ricerche 2. Torino, Italy: Editore Boringhieri.

Corradi Fiumara, G. (1980). Funzione simbolica e filosofia del linguaggio. Torino, Italy: Editore Boringhieri.

Cotter, D. (2003). *Joyce and the Perverse Ideal*. London, UK: Routledge.

CSFG – Centro di Studi Filosofici di Gallarate. (1977). Dizionario delle idee. Firenze, Italy: G.C. Sansoni Editore.

Cuche, D. (2004). La notion de culture dans les sciences sociales. Paris: Éditions La Découverte.

Culioli, A. (2014). L'arco e la freccia. Scritti scelti. Bologna, Italy: Società editrice il Mulino.

D'Urso, V., & Trentin, R. (1998). Introduzione alla psicologia delle emozioni. Roma-Bari, Italy: Editori Laterza.

Dalla Chiara Scabia, M. L. (1973). Istanti e individui nelle logiche temporali. *Rivista di Filosofia, 64*(2), 95–122.

Dalla Chiara Scabia, M. L. (1974). Logica. Milano, Italy: ISEDI – Istituto Editoriale Internazionale.

De Masi, F. (2016). Which is the relevant superego for clinical analytic work? In F. Borgogno, A. Luchetti, & L. M. Coe (Eds.), *Reading Italian Psychoanalysis* (pp. 279–290). Oxfordshire, UK: Routledge.

De Mijolla, A. (Ed.). (2005). *International Dictionary of Psychoanalysis* (Vols. 1–3). Farmington Hills, MI: Thomson Gale.

De Mijolla, A., & De Mijolla Mellor, S. (Eds.). (1996). Psychanalyse. Paris: PUF-Presses Universitaires de France.

De Waelhens, A., & Ver Eecke, W. (2001). *Phenomenology and Lacan on Schizophrenia, after the Decade of the Brain*. Leuven, Belgium: Leuven University Press.

Deng, Y. (2013). Applied Parallel Computing. Singapore: World Scientific Publishing.

Dijksterhuis, A., & Nordgren, L. F. (2006). A theory of unconsciouss thought. *Perspectives on Psychological Science*, *1*(2), 95–109. doi:10.1111/j.1745-6916.2006.00007.x PMID:26151465

Dolto, F. (1984). *L'image inconsciente du corps*. Paris: Editions du Seuil.

Donati, P. (2015). L'enigma della relazione. Milano, Italy: Mimesis edizioni.

Durst, M. (1988). Dialettica e bi-logica. L'epistemologia di Ignacio Matte Blanco. Milano, Italy: Marzorati Editore.

Eco, U. (1981). *Simbolo. Voce dell'Enciclopedia Einaudi* (Vol. 12). Torino, Italy: Giulio Einaudi editore.

Ehresmann, A. C., & Vanbremeersch, J. P. (2007). *Memory Evolutive Systems. Hierarchy, Emergence, Cognition*. Amsterdam: Elsevier, B.V.

Ekstrom, S. R. (2004). The mind beyond our immediate awareness: Freudian, Jungian, and cognitive models of the unconscious. *The Journal of Analytical Psychology*, *49*(5), 657–682. doi:10.1111/j.0021-8774.2004.00494.x PMID:15533197

Ellis, J., Mavromatos, N. E., & Nanopoulos, D. V. (1992). The origin of space-time as W-symmetry breaking in string theory. *Physics Letters. [Part B]*, *288*(1-2), 23–30. doi:10.1016/0370-2693(92)91949-A

Endert, E. (2006). Über die emotionale Dimension sozialer Prozesse. Die Theorie der Affektlogik am Beispiel der Rechtsextremismus und Nationalsozialismusforschung (Theorie und Methode). Konstanz, Germany: UVK Verlagsgesellschaft mbH.

Even, G., & Medina, M. (2012). *Digital Logic Design. A Rigorous Approach*. Cambridge, UK: Cambridge University Press. doi:10.1017/CBO9781139226455

Fairlamb, H. L. (1994). *Critical conditions. Postmodernity and the question of foundations*. Cambridge, UK: Cambridge University Press. doi:10.1017/CBO9780511552762

Falzone, A. (2005). Filosofia del linguaggio e psicopatologia evoluzionistica. Soveria Mannelli (CZ), Italy: Rubbettino Editore.

Feng, E. H., & Crooks, G. E. (2008). Lenghts of time arrow. *Physical Review Letters*, *101*(9), 090602/1–4. doi:10.1103/PhysRevLett.101.090602

Fenichel, O. (1945). The psychoanalytic theory of neurosis. New York, NY: W.W. Norton & Company, Inc.

Figà-Talamanca Dore, L. (1978). La logica dell'inconscio. Roma, Italy: Edizioni Studium-Vita Nova.

Finelli, R. (2010). Perché l'inconscio non è strutturato come un linguaggio. In Compendio di Psicoanalisi e altri scritti. Roma, Italy: Newton Compton editori.

Finelli, R. (2011). Rappresentazione e linguaggio in Freud: a partire dal "Compendio di psicoanalisi". *Consecutio Temporum. Rivista di critica della postmodernità, 1*, 112-125.

Fink, K. (1993). The Bi-Logic Perception of Time. *The International Journal of Psycho-Analysis, 74*, 303–312. PMID:8491534

Fodor, N., & Gaynor, F. (1950). Freud: Dictionary of Psychoanalysis. New York, NY: The Philosophical Library.

Fonagy, P., Gergely, G., Jurist, E. L., & Target, M. (2002). Affect Regulation, Mentalization, and the Development of the Self. New York, NY: Other Press.

Fornari, F. (2016). Psychic birth. In F. Borgogno, A. Luchetti, & L. M. Coe (Eds.), *Reading Italian Psychoanalysis* (pp. 593–600). Oxfordshire, UK: Routledge.

Fossi, G. (1983). La psicologia dinamica: un'eredità del XX secolo. Roma, Italy: Edizioni Borla.

Fossi, G. (1984). Le teorie psicoanalitiche. Padova, Italy: Piccin Nuova Libraria.

Fossi, G. (1988). Psicoanalisi e psicoterapie dinamiche. Torino, Italy: Bollati Boringhieri editore.

Fossi, G. (2003). Una proposta evoluzionista per la psicoanalisi. Con un manuale per la pratica terapeutica e la ricerca empirica. Milano, Italy: FrancoAngeli.

Freud, S. (1938). Abriß der psychoanalyse. Academic Press.

Freud, S. (1957). *The Standard Edition of Complete Psychological Works of Sigmund Freud* (Vols. 1-24; J. Strachey, Trans. & Ed.). London, UK: The Hogarth Press.

Freud, S. (1979). La scissione dell'Io nel processo di difesa (1938). In Opere di Sigmund Freud, 1930-1938. L'uomo Mosè e la religione monoteistica e altri scritti (vol. 11). Torino, Italy: Editore Boringhieri.

Friedman, M., & Tomšič, S. (Eds.). (2016). Psychoanalysis: Topological Perspectives. New Conceptions of Geometry and Space in Freud and Lacan. Bielefeld, Germany: transcript Verlag. doi:10.14361/9783839434406

Fromm, E. (1951). The Forgotten Language. An Introduction to the Understanding of Dreams, Fairy Tales, and Myths. New York, NY: Holt, Rinehart & Winston Publishing Company, Inc.

Fromm, E. (1976). To have or to be? New York, NY: Harper & Row Publishers, Inc.

Funari, E. (1978). Psicoanalisi: tecnica o Weltanschauung? In *Psicoanalisi e classi sociali* (pp. 147–153). Roma, Italy: Editori Riuniti.

Funari, E. (1988). Contestualità e specificità della psicoanalisi. In Trattato di Psicoanalisi: Vol. 1. Teoria e Tecnica. Milano, Italy: Raffaello Cortina Editore.

Funari, E. (2007). L'irrapresentabile come origine della vita psichica. Milano, Italy: FrancoAngeli.

Fusco, A., & Tomassoni, R. (Eds.). (2013). Creatività nella psicologia letteraria, drammatica e filmica. Milano, Italy: FrancoAngeli.

Gabbay, D. M., Hodkinson, I., & Reynolds, M. A. (1994). *Temporal Logic. Mathematical Foundations and Computational Aspects* (Vol. 1). Oxford, UK: Clarendon Press.

Gabbay, D. M., Reynolds, M. A., & Finger, M. (2000). *Temporal Logic. Mathematical Foundations and Computational Aspects* (Vol. 2). Oxford, UK: Oxford University Press.

Galimberti, U. (1979). Psichiatria e fenomenologia. Milano, Italy: Giangiacomo Feltrinelli Editore.

Galimberti, U. (1983). Il corpo. Milano, Italy: Giangiacomo Feltrinelli Editore.

Galimberti, U. (2006). Dizionario di psicologia. Torino, Italy: UTET Libreria.

Galton, A. (Ed.). (1987). *Temporal Logic and its Applications*. New York, NY: Academic Press, Inc.

Gay, P. (2000). Freud. Una vita per i nostri tempi. Milano, Italy: Bompiani.

Giberti, F., & Rossi, R. (Eds.). (1996). Manuale di psichiatria (4th ed.). Padova, Italy: Piccin Nuova Libraria.

Giersch, A., Lalanne, L., van Assche, M., & Elliott, M.A. (2013). On disturbed time continuity in schizophrenia: an elementary impairment in visual perception? *Frontiers in Psychology*, *4*, 281-290.

Gilliéron, E., & Baldassarre, M. (Ed.). (2012). Perversione e Relazione. Roma, Italy: Alpes Italia.

Giordano, M., Dello Russo, G., Pardi, F., & Patella, G. A. (1984). Tempo e inconscio. Napoli, Italy: Guida editori.

Girotto, V. (Ed.). (2013). Introduzione alla psicologia del pensiero. Bologna, Italy: Società editrice il Mulino.

Glover, E. (1949). Psychoanalysis. London, UK: John Bale Medical Publications, Ltd.

Goleman, D. (1995). Emotional Intelligence. New York, NY: Bantam Books.

Green, A. (1993). Le travail du négatif. Paris: Les Éditions du Minuit.

Greenacre, P. (1971). Emotional growth. Psychoanalytic studies of the gifted and a great variety of other individuals. New York, NY: International Universities Press, Inc.

Grice, H. P. (1993). Logica e conversazione. Saggi su intenzione, significato e comunicazione. Bologna, Italy: Società editrice il Mulino.

Grinberg, L. (1989). La supervisione psicoanalitica. Teoria e pratica. Milano, Italy: Raffaello Cortina Editore.

Grunberger, B. (1971). *Le narcissisme. Essai de psychanalyse.* Paris: Payot.

Hall, C. S. (1999). *A Primer in Freudian Psychology.* New York, NY: Meridian Books.

Hampe, B., & Grady, J. E. (Eds.). (2005). *From Perception to Meaning. Image Schemas in Cognitive Linguistics.* Berlin: Walter de Gruyter GmbH and Co. doi:10.1515/9783110197532

Harary, F., Norman, Z., & Cartwright, D. (Eds.). (1965). *Structural Models*. New York, NY: John Wiley and Sons, Inc.

Herlihy, M., & Shavit, H. (1999). The Topological Structure of Asynchronous Computability. *Journal of the Association for Computing Machinery, 46*(6), 858–923. doi:10.1145/331524.331529

Hermann, I. (1989). Psicoanalisi e logica. Roma, Italy: Di Renzo Editore.

Hickmann, M., & Robert, S. (Eds.). (2006). *Space in Languages – Linguistic Systems and Cognitive Categories*. Amsterdam: John Benjamins Publishing Company. doi:10.1075/tsl.66

Hirsch, M. W. (1976). *Differential Topology*. New York, NY: Springer-Verlag, Inc. doi:10.1007/978-1-4684-9449-5

Hodges, W. (1977). *Logic. An Introduction to Elementary Logic*. Harmondsworth, UK: Penguin Books, Ltd.

Hodkinson, I., & Reynolds, M. (2007). Temporal Logic. In Handbook of Modal Logic. Amsterdam: Elsevier, B.V.

Husemoller, D. (1975). *Fibre Bundles* (2nd ed.). New York, NY: Springer-Verlag, Inc.

Imbasciati, A. (2015). Nuove teorie sul funzionamento della mente. L'istituzione psicoanalitica e gli psicoanalisti. Milano, Italy: FrancoAngeli.

Ippoliti, E. (2007). *Il vero e il plausibile*. Morrisville, NC: Lulu Press, Inc.

Iurato, G. (2013a). Mathematical thought in the light of Matte Blanco work. *Philosophy of Mathematics Education Journal, 27*.

Iurato, G. (2013b). Σύμβολου: An attempt toward the early origins, Part 1. *Language & Psychoanalysis, 2*(2), 77–120. doi:10.7565/landp.2013.008

Iurato, G. (2013c). Σύμβολου: An attempt toward the early origins, Part 2. *Language & Psychoanalysis, 2*(2), 121–160. doi:10.7565/landp.2013.009

Iurato, G. (2014a). At the grounding of computational psychoanalysis: on the work of Ignacio Matte Blanco. A general history of culture overview of Matte Blanco bilogic in comparison. In *Proceedings of the 2014 IEEE 13th International Conference on Cognitive Informatics and Cognitive Computing*. Los Alamitos, CA: IEEE Computer Society Press.

Iurato, G. (2014b). The dawning of computational psychoanalysis. A proposal for some first elementary formalization attempts. *International Journal of Cognitive Informatics and Natural Intelligence, 8*(4), 50–82. doi:10.4018/ijcini.2014100104

Iurato, G. (2014c). *Alcune considerazioni critiche sul simbolismo*. Preprint No. hal-00980828 version 1. Available at HAL archives-ouvertes.

Iurato, G. (2015a). A Brief Comparison of the Unconscious as Seen by Jung and Lévi-Strauss. *Anthropology of Consciousness, 26*(1), 60–107. doi:10.1111/anoc.12032

Iurato, G. (2015b). Fetishism in Marketing. Some First Elementary Psychoanalytic Anthropology Remarks. In Business Management: A Practioners' Guide. Delhi: International Research Publication House.

Iurato, G. (2015c). A simple phylogenetic remark about certain human blood pressure values. *Journal of Biochemistry International*, 2(4), 162–165.

Iurato, G. (2016a). *A psychoanalytic enquiry on symbolic function*. Preprint No. hal-01361264 version 3. Available at HAL archives-ouvertes.

Iurato, G. (2016b). *A view of LSA/ESA in Computational Psychoanalysis*. Preprint No. hal-01353999 version 1. Available at HAL archives-ouvertes.

Iurato, G. (2016c). On Jacques Lacan Psychosis Theory and ERPs Analysis. *Journal of Biology and Nature*, 5(4), 234–240.

Iurato, G. (2016d). Some Comments on the Historical Role of *Fetishism* in Economic Anthropology. *Journal of Global Economics, Management and Business Research*, 7(1), 61–82.

Iurato, G. (2016e). *The origins of symbol. An historical-critical study of symbolic function, according to the phylo-ontogenetic perspective, as arising from the comparison of certain patterns of neuro-psychological sciences*. Paper Presented at the Satellite Event "On the edge of disciplines", Florence, Italy.

Iurato, G. (2016f). Two simple questions regarding cultural anthropology. *Journal of Global Research in Education and Social Science*, 8(1), 10–15.

Iurato, G. (2017a). An Essay in Denotational Mathematics. Rigorous Results. In Encyclopedia of Information Science and Technology (4th ed.). Hershey, PA: IGI Global.

Iurato, G. (2017b). Un raffronto critico fra la teoria platonica delle idee ed il paradosso di Kripke-Wittgenstein. In Platone nel pensiero moderno e contemporaneo (vol. 11). Villasanta (MB), Italy: Limina Mentis Edizioni.

Iurato, G. (2017c). *Rigidity of the Generalized Other, narrowness of the Otherness and demodernization, in the framework of symbolic interactionism. Ideology and Political Journal*. (in press)

Iurato, G., & Khrennikov, A. Yu. (2015). Hysteresis model of unconscious-conscious interconnection: Exploring dynamics on *m*-adic trees. *p-Adic Numbers, Ultrametric Analysis and Applications*, 7(4), 312–321. doi:10.1134/S2070046615040068

Iurato, G., & Khrennikov, A. Yu. (2017). On the topological structure of a mathematical model of human unconscious. *p-Adic Numbers, Ultrametric Analysis and Applications*, 9(1), 78–81. doi:10.1134/S2070046617010071

Iurato, G., Khrennikov, A. Yu., & Murtagh, F. (2016). Formal Foundations for the Origins of Human Consciousness. *p-Adic Numbers, Ultrametric Analysis and Applications*, 8(4), 249–279. doi:10.1134/S2070046616040014

Jackson, D. D. (1954). Some factors influencing the Œdipus Complex. *The Psychoanalytic Quarterly*, 23, 566–581. PMID:13215675

Jaffé, R. (2009). Ideale dell'Io, Idealizzazione. In *Psiche. Dizionario storico di psicologia, psichiatria, psicoanalisi, neuroscienze* (Vol. 1, pp. 494–500). Torino, Italy: Giulio Einaudi editore.

Johnson-Laird, P., & Bara, B. (1984). Syllogistic Inference. *Cognition*, *16*(1), 1–61. doi:10.1016/0010-0277(84)90035-0 PMID:6540648

Juhás, G. (1999). On Semantics of Petri Nets over Partial Algebra. In *SOFSEM'99: Theory and Practice of Informatics. Proceedings of the 26th Conference on Current Trends in Theory and Practice of Informatics*. Berlin: Springer-Verlag. doi:10.1007/3-540-47849-3_29

Kaplan-Solms, K., & Solms, M. (2000). Clinical Studies in Neuro-Psychoanalysis. Introduction to a Depth Neuropsychology. London, UK: Karnac Books, Ltd.

Kastner, R. E. (2011). The broken symmetry of time. In Quantum Retrocausation: Theory and Experiment. Melville, NY: AIP Publications. doi:10.1063/1.3663714

Khrennikov, A. Yu. (1991). *p*-Adic quantum mechanics with *p*-adic valued functions. *Journal of Mathematical Physics*, *32*(4), 932–937. doi:10.1063/1.529353

Khrennikov, A. Yu. (1998). Human subconscious as the *p*-adic dynamical system. *Journal of Theoretical Biology*, *193*(2), 179–196. doi:10.1006/jtbi.1997.0604 PMID:9714931

Khrennikov, A. Yu. (2002). *Classical and quantum mental models and Freud's theory of unconscious mind. Series in Mathematical Modelling in Physics, Enginnering and Cognitive Sciences* (Vol. 1). Växjö, Sweden: Växjö University Press.

Khrennikov, A. Yu. (2007). Toward an adequate mathematical model of mental space: Conscious/unconscious dynamics on *m*-adic trees. *Bio Systems*, *90*(3), 656–675. doi:10.1016/j.biosystems.2007.02.004 PMID:17400367

Kissin, B. (1986). *Conscious and Unconscious Programs in the Brain*. New York, NY: Plenum Publishing Corporation. doi:10.1007/978-1-4613-2187-3

Köhler, T. (2007). *Freuds Psychoanalyse. Eine Einführung* (2nd ed.). Stuttgart, Germany: W. Kohlhammer GmbH.

Kultgen, J. (1976). Lévi-Strauss on Unconscious Social Structures. *The Southwestern Journal of Philosophy*, *7*(1), 153–159. doi:10.5840/swjphil19767118

Kuper, J. (Ed.). (1988). *A Lexicon of Psychology, Psychiatry and Psychoanalysis*. London, UK: Routledge.

La Forgia, M. (1992). Sincronicità. In Trattato di Psicologia Analitica (Vols. 1-2). Torino, Italy: UTET.

La Mantia, F. (2017). From Topology to Quasi-Topology. The Complexity of the Notional Domain. In Lecture Notes in Morphogenesis: Vol. 5. Language in Complexity. The Emerging Meaning. Springer International Publishing.

Lacan, J. (2014). *The Seminar of Jacques Lacan. Book X: The Anxiety* (J. A. Miller, Ed.; A. R. Price, Trans.). Malden, MA: Polity Press.

Lacas, M.-L. (2007). La démarche originale de Gisela Pankow. Gisela Pankows original thought processes. *LÉvolution Psychiatrique, 72*(1), 15–24. doi:10.1016/j.evopsy.2006.11.001

Làdavas, E., & Berti, A. (2014). Neuropsicologia (3rd ed.). Bologna, Italy: Società editrice il Mulino.

Lagache, D. (1961). *La psychanalyse et la structure de la personnalité.* Paper Presented au Colloquium International de Royaumont, Paris, France.

Lagache, D. (1965). Le modèle psychanalytique de la personnalité. In *La Folle du Logis. La psychanalyse comme science exacte* (pp. 159–183). Paris: PUF-Presses Universitaires de France.

Langs, R. (1990). Guida alla psicoterapia. Un'introduzione all'approccio comunicativo. Torino, Italy: Bollati Boringhieri editore.

Laplanche, J. (2000). Problematiche II. Castrazione. Simbolizzazioni. Bari-Roma, Italy: La Biblioteca.

Laplanche, J. (2001). *L'inconscio e l'Es.* Bari-Roma, Italy: La Biblioteca.

Laplanche, J. (2007). *L'après-coup.* Bari-Roma, Italy: La Biblioteca.

Laplanche, J. (2008). Sexuale. La sessualità allargata nel senso freudiano. Bari-Roma, Italy: La Biblioteca.

Laplanche, J., & Pontalis, J.-B. (1967). Vocabulaire de la psychoanalyse. Paris: Presses Universitaires de France.

Laplanche, J., & Pontalis, J.-B. (1988). Fantasma originario, fantasmi delle origini, origini del fantasma. Bologna, Italy: Società editrice il Mulino.

Lawson, M. K. (2005). Constructing ordered groupoids. *Cahiers de Topologie et Géométrie Différentielle Catégoriques, 46*(2), 123–138.

Lerner, D. (Ed.). (1961). Quality and Quantity. New York, NY: The Free Press of Glencoe.

Lévi-Strauss, C. (1975). *Razza e storia e altri studi di antropologia.* Torino, Italy: Giulio Einaudi editore.

Lévi-Strauss, C. (2008). Sull'Italia. In Claude Lévi-Strauss fotografato da Marion Kalter. Napoli, Italy: Electa Napoli.

Lévi-Strauss, C., & Eribon, D. (1988). De près et de loin. Paris: Éditions Odile Jacob.

Levitz, K., & Levitz, H. (1979). *Logic and Boolean Algebra.* Woodbury, NY: Barron's Educational Series, Inc.

Lewin, R. (1996). Communicating with the schizophrenic superego. *The Journal of the American Academy of Psychoanalysis, 24*(4), 709–736. PMID:9220382

Lewis, C. I. (1912). Implication and the Algebra of Logic. *Mind, 21*(84), 522–531. doi:10.1093/mind/XXI.84.522

Lis, A., Mazzeschi, C., & Zennaro, A. (2007). *La psicoanalisi. Un percorso concettuale fra tradizione e attualità (2nd ed.).* Roma, Italy: Carocci editore.

Lis, A., Zennaro, A., Mazzeschi, C., Salcuni, S., & Parolin, L. (2003). *Breve dizionario di psicoanalisi*. Roma, Italy: Carocci editore.

Lolli, G. (1991). Introduzione alla logica formale. Bologna, Italy: Società editrice il Mulino.

Lolli, G. (2000). Un logico esamina i modelli mentali. In Ragionamento: psicologia e logica. Firenze, Italy: Giunti Gruppo Editoriale.

Lolli, G. (2005). QED – Fenomenologia della dimostrazione. Torino, Italy: Bollati Boringhieri editore.

Macola, E. (Ed.). (2014). Sublimazione e perversione. Attualità Lacaniana. Rivista della Scuola Lacaniana di Psicoanalisi, 18, 7-108.

Main, R. (2014). The cultural significance of synchronicity for Jung and Pauli. *The Journal of Analytical Psychology*, 59(2), 174–180. doi:10.1111/1468-5922.12067 PMID:24673272

Mancia, M. (Ed.). (1990). Super-Io e Ideale dell'Io. Roma, Italy: Casa Editrice Astrolabio-Ubaldini Editore.

Mancia, M. (Ed.). (2006). Psychoanalysis and Neuroscience. Milan, Italy: Springer-Verlag Italia. doi:10.1007/88-470-0550-7

Matte Blanco, I. (1975). The Unconscious as Infinite Sets. An Essay in Bi-Logic. London, UK: Gerald Duckworth & Company, Ltd.

Matte Blanco, I. (1988). *Thinking, Feeling, and Being. Clinical Reflections of the Fundamental Antinomy on Human Beings and World*. London, UK: Routledge.

McCulloch, W. S. (1965). *Embodiments of Mind*. Cambridge, MA: The MIT Press.

Miller, P. H. (1983). *Theories of Developmental Psychology*. New York, NY: W.H. Freeman & Co.

Milrod, D. (2002). The superego. Its formation, structure, and functioning. *The Psychoanalytic Study of the Child*, 57, 131–148. PMID:12723129

Mitchell, S. A., & Black, M. J. (1995). *Freud and beyond. A History of Modern Psychoanalysic Thought*. New York, NY: Basic Books. A Division of Harper Collins Publishers.

Moore, B. E., & Fine, B. D. (Eds.). (1990). Psychoanalytic Terms and Concepts. New York, NY: The American Psychoanalytic Association.

Moravia, S. (2004). Ragione strutturale e universi di senso. Saggio su Lévi-Strauss. Firenze, Italy: Casa Editrice Le Lettere.

Mordant, I. (1990). Using attribute-memories to resolve a contradiction in the work of Matte Blanco. *The International Review of Psycho-Analysis*, 17, 475–480.

Murtagh, F., & Iurato, G. (2016). Human Behaviour, Benign or Malevalent: Understanding the Human Psyche, Performing Therapy, based on Affective Mentalization and Matte-Blancos Bi-Logic. *Annals of Translational Medicine*, 4(24), 486–496. doi:10.21037/atm.2016.12.37 PMID:28149848

Murtagh, F., & Iurato, G. (2017). Visualization of Jacques Lacan's Registers of the Psychoanalytic Field, and Discovery of Metaphor and of Metonymy. Analytical Case Study of Edgar Allan Poe's "The Purloined Letter". *Language and Psychoanalysis*. (in press)

Nagel, T. (1993). Summary. In *Experimental and Theoretical Studies of Consciousness. Novartis Foundation Symposium No. 174*. New York, NY: John Wiley & Sons, Ltd.

Nannini, S. (2007). Naturalismo cognitivo. Per una teoria materialistica della mente. Macerata, Italy: Edizioni Quodlibet.

Nannini, S. (2011). L'anima e il corpo. Un'introduzione storica alla filosofia della mente. Roma-Bari, Italy: Laterza Editori.

Nannini, S. (2015). Time and Consciousness in Cognitive Naturalism. *Rivista Internazionale di Filosofia e Psicologia*, *6*(3), 458–473.

Napolitano, F. (2009). Rappresentazione, 2. In *Psiche. Dizionario storico di psicologia, psichiatria, psicoanalisi, neuroscienze* (Vol. 2, pp. 919–923). Torino, Italy: Giulio Einaudi editore.

Neubauer, K. (2004). Semantica storica. In Dizionario degli studi culturali. Roma, Italy: Meltemi editore.

Nunberg, H. (1932). Allgemeine Neurosenlehre auf psychoanalytischer Grundlage. Berlin: Verlag Hans Hüber.

Øhrstrøm, P., & Hasle, P. F. V. (Eds.). (1995). *Temporal Logic. From Ancient Ideas to Artificial Intelligence. Studies in Linguistics and Philosophy, Volume No. 57*. Dordrecht, The Netherlands: Kluwer Academic Publishers.

Oliverio, A. (1982). Biologia e comportamento. Bologna, Italy: Nicola Zanichelli Editore.

Oliverio, A. (2016). Il cervello e linconscio. *Psicobiettivo*, *36*(3), 251–259. doi:10.3280/PSOB2016-003015

Oliverio, A. (2017). Il cervello che impara. Neuropedagogia dall'infanzia alla vecchiaia. Firenze, Italy: Giunti Editore.

Pankow, G. (1977). L'uomo e la sua psicosi. Milano, Italy: Giangiacomo Feltrinelli Editore.

Pankow, G. (1979). Struttura familiare e psicosi. Milano, Italy: Giangiacomo Feltrinelli Editore.

Panksepp, J., & Biven, L. (2012). The Archeology of Mind. Neuroevolutionary Origins of Human Emotion. New York, NY: W.W. Norton & Company.

Papagno, C. (2010). Neuropsicologia della memoria. Bologna, Italy: Società editrice il Mulino.

Peterburs, J., Nitsch, A. M., Miltner, W. H. R., & Straube, T. (2013). Impaired representation of time in schizophrenia is linked to positive symptoms and cognitive demand. *PLoS ONE*, *8*(6), e67615/1–7. doi:10.1371/journal.pone.0067615 PMID:23826328

Petersen, W. P., & Arbenz, P. (2004). *Introduction to Parallel Computing*. New York, NY: Oxford University Press, Inc.

Petocz, A. (2004). *Freud, psychoanalysis and symbolism*. Cambridge, UK: Cambridge University Press.

Petrilli, S., & Ponzio, A. (2005). *Semiotics Unbounded. Interpretive Routes Through the Open Network of Signs*. Toronto, CA: The University of Toronto Press. doi:10.3138/9781442657113

Petrini, P., Renzi, A., Casadei, A., & Mandese, A. (2013). Dizionario di psicoanalisi. Con elementi di psichiatria, psicodinamica e psicologia dinamica. Milano, Italy: FrancoAngeli.

Piattelli Palmarini, M. (1987). Scienza come cultura. Protagonisti, luoghi e idee delle scienze contemporanee. Milano, Italy: Arnoldo Mondadori Editore.

Pierce, B. C. (2002). *Types and Programming Languages*. Cambridge, MA: The MIT Press.

Piras, F., Piras, F., Ciullo, V., Danese, E., Caltagirone, C. & Spalletta, G. (2013). Time dysperception perspective for acquired brain injury. *Frontiers in Neurology, 4*, 217-226.

Piscicelli, U. (1994). Sessuologia. Teoremi psicosomatici e relazionali. Padova, Italy: Piccin Nuova Libraria.

Pizzi, C. (Ed.). (1974). La logica del tempo. Torino, Italy: Bollati Boringhieri Editore.

Poggi, S. (1977). I sistemi dell'esperienza. Bologna, Italy: Società editrice il Mulino.

Rayner, E. (1995). *Unconscious Logic. An Introduction to Matte Blanco's Bi-Logic and its Uses*. New York, NY: Routledge.

Rayner, E. (1998). Foreword. In *The Unconscious as Infinite Sets. An Essay in Bi-Logic* (pp. xviii–xxiv). London, UK: Karnac Books, Ltd.

Redondi, P. (2007). Storie del tempo. Roma-Bari, Italy: Editori Laterza.

Reich, A. (1954). Early identifications as archaic elements in the Superego. *Journal of the American Psychoanalytic Association, 2*(2), 218–238. doi:10.1177/000306515400200203 PMID:13151996

Reisig, W. (1988). Temporal Logic and Causality in Concurrent Systems. In R. H. Voght (Ed.), Lecture Notes in Computer Science: Vol. 335. *CONCURRENCY 1988* (pp. 121–139). Berlin: Springer-Verlag. doi:10.1007/3-540-50403-6_37

Rentz, J. (Ed.). (2002). Lecture Notes in Computer Science: Vol. 2293. Qualitative spatial reasoning with topological information. Berlin: Springer-Verlag. doi:10.1007/3-540-70736-0

Rescher, N., & Urquhart, A. (1971). Temporal Logic. Wien, Austria: Springer-Verlag GmbH. doi:10.1007/978-3-7091-7664-1

Reverberi, C., Pischedda, D., Burigo, M., & Cherubini, P. (2012). Deduction without awareness. *Acta Psychologica, 139*(1), 244–253. doi:10.1016/j.actpsy.2011.09.011 PMID:22019058

Riehl, J. P. (2010). *Mirror-Image Asymmetry. An Introduction to the Origin and Consequences of Chirality*. Hoboken, NJ: John Wiley & Sons, Inc. doi:10.1002/9780470588888

Riolo, F. (2009). Trasformazione. In *Psiche. Dizionario storico di psicologia, psichiatria, psicoanalisi, neuroscienze* (Vol. 2, pp. 1112–1116). Torino, Italy: Giulio Einaudi editore.

Rose, J. R. (Ed.). (2011). *Mapping Psychic Reality. Triangulation, Communication, and Insight. Psychoanalytic Ideas*. London, UK: Karnac Books, Ltd.

Rossi, R., De Fazio, F., Gatti, U., & Rocco, G. (2008, Feb.). Perizie e consulenze psichiatriche su Diamante Stefano, Stevanin Gianfranco, Bilancia Donato, Panini Giorgio. *POL.it – The Italian On Line Psychiatric Magazine*.

Rycroft, C. (1968a). A critical dictionary of psychoanalysis. London, UK: Thomas Nelson & Sons, Ltd.

Rycroft, C. (1968b). Imagination and reality. Psychoanalytical essays 1951–1961. London, UK: The Hogarth Press, Ltd.

Sabbadini, A. (1979). Introduzione. In Il tempo in psicoanalisi. Milano, Italy: Giangiacomo Feltrinelli Editore.

Sannella, D., & Tarlecki, A. (2012). *Foundations of Algebraic Specification and Formal Software Development. Monographs in Theoretical Computer Science. An EATCS Series*. Berlin: Springer-Verlag. doi:10.1007/978-3-642-17336-3

Sasso, G. (1982). Le strutture anagrammatiche della poesia. Milano, Italy: Giangiacomo Feltrinelli Editore.

Sasso, G. (1993). La mente intralinguistica. L'instabilità del segno: anagrammi e parole dentro le parole. Genova, Italy: Marietti Editore.

Sasso, G. (1999). Struttura dell'oggetto e della rappresentazione. Roma, Italy: Casa Editrice Astrolabio-Ubaldini Editore.

Sasso, G. (2005). Psicoanalisi e Neuroscienze. Roma, Italy: Casa Editrice Astrolabio-Ubaldini Editore.

Sasso, G. (2011). La nascita della coscienza. Roma, Italy: Casa Editrice Astrolabio-Ubaldini Editore.

Scabini, E. (1973). Ideazione e psicoanalisi. Milano, Italy: Giangiacomo Feltrinelli Editore.

Schmitt, A., Hasan, A., Gruber, O., & Falkai, P. (2011). Schizophrenia as a disorder of disconnectivity. *European Archives of Psychiatry and Clinical Neuroscience*, *261*(2), S150–S154. doi:10.1007/s00406-011-0242-2 PMID:21866371

Segalen, M. (1998). Rites et rituels contemporains. Paris: Les Éditions Nathan.

Semi, A. A. (2003). La coscienza in psicoanalisi. Milano, Italy: Raffaello Cortina Editore.

Semi, A.A. (Ed.). (1989). *Trattato di Psicoanalisi* (Vols. 1-2). Milano, Italy: Raffaello Cortina Editore.

Skelton, R. (1984). Understanding Matte Blanco. *The International Journal of Psycho-Analysis*, *65*, 453–460. PMID:6544756

Skelton, R. (1990). Generalizations from Freud to Matte Blanco. *The International Review of Psycho-Analysis*, *17*, 471–474.

Skillicorn, D. (1994). *Foundations of Parallel Programming*. Cambridge, UK: Cambridge University Press. doi:10.1017/CBO9780511526626

Sluzki, C. E., & Ransom, D. C. (1979). Il doppio legame: la genesi dell'approccio relazionale allo studio della famiglia. Roma, Italy: Casa Editrice Astrolabio-Ubaldini Editore.

Smirnov, V. N. (1970). *La transaction fétichique. Nouvelle Revue de Psychoanalyse, 2.*

Solms, M., & Turnbull, O. (2003). The Brain and the Inner World. An Introduction to the Neuroscience of Subjective Experience. New York, NY: Other Press, LLC.

Somenzi, V. (1998). Prefazione. In Categorie, tempo e linguaggio. Quaderni di Methodologia, N. 5. Roma, Italy: Società Stampa Sportiva.

Sparsø, J., & Furber, S. (Eds.). (2001). Principles of Asynchronous Circuit Design. A Systems Perspective. Dordrecht, The Netherlands: Springer-Science + Business Media, B.V. doi:10.1007/978-1-4757-3385-3

Spitz, R. A. (1957). No and yes. On the genesis of human communication. New York, NY: International University Press, Inc.

Stanghellini, G., Ballerini, M., Presenza, S., Mancini, M., Raballo, A., Blasi, S., & Cutting, J. (2016). Psychopathology of lived time: Abnormal time experience in persons with schizophrenia. *Schizophrenia Bulletin. The Journal of Psychoses and Related Disorders*, *42*(1), 45–55.

Steedman, M. (2000). *Surface Structure and Interpretation*. Boston, MA: The MIT Press.

Stirling, C. (2001). *Modal and Temporal Properties of Processes*. New York, NY: Springer-Verlag. doi:10.1007/978-1-4757-3550-5

Tabossi, P. (2009). Rappresentazione, 1. In *Psiche. Dizionario storico di psicologia, psichiatria, psicoanalisi, neuroscienze* (Vol. 2, pp. 914–919). Torino, Italy: Giulio Einaudi editore.

Tanenbaum, A. S., & Bos, H. (2015). *Modern Operating Systems* (4th ed.). Essex, UK: Pearson Education Limited.

Target, M., & Fonagy, P. (2002). The role of the father and child development. In The Importance of Fathers. A Psychoanalytic Re-evaluation. London, UK: Routledge.

Terminio, N. (2009). Misurare l'inconscio? Coordinate psicoanalitiche nella ricerca in psicoterapia. Milano, Italy: Bruno Mondadori.

Thomä, H., & Kächele, H. (1989). *Psychoanalytic Practice* (Vols. 1-2). Berlin: Springer-Verlag.

Tibaldi, M. (2004). Critica archetipica. In Dizionario degli studi culturali. Roma, Italy: Meltemi editore.

Tokhi, M. O., Hossain, M. A., & Shaheed, M. H. (2003). *Parallel Computing for Real-time Signal Processing and Control*. London, UK: Springer-Verlag London. doi:10.1007/978-1-4471-0087-4

Toraldo di Francia, G. (1976). *L'indagine del mondo fisico*. Torino, Italy: Giulio Einaudi editore.

Vaccarino, G. (2006). Scienza e semantica. Milano, Italy: Edizioni Melquiades.

Vallortigara, G., & Panciera, N. (2014). Cervelli che contano. Milano, Italy: Adelphi Edizioni.

Vattimo, G., Ferraris, M., & Marconi, D. (Eds.). (1993). Enciclopedia Garzanti di Filosofia. Milano, Italy: Garzanti Editore.

Venema, Y. (2001). Temporal Logic. In The Blackwell Guide to Philosophical Logic. Oxford, UK: Basil Blackwell Publishers.

Verdiglione, A. (1977). Matematica dell'inconscio. In Feticismo, linguaggio, afasia, matematica dell'inconscio. Venezia, Italy: Marsilio Editori.

Vicario, G. B. (1997). Il tempo in psicologia. *Le Scienze, 30*(347), 43–51.

Vicario, G. B. (2005). Il tempo. Saggio di psicologia sperimentale. Bologna, Italy: Società editrice il Mulino.

Viret, J. (2012). Topological Approach of Jungian Psychology. *Acta Biotheoretica, 58*(2), 233–245. PMID:20658172

Voevodin, V. V. (1992). Mathematical Foundations of Parallel Computing. Singapore: World Scientific Publishing. doi:10.1142/1533

von Karger, B. (1995). An algebraic approach to temporal logic. In *Lecture Notes on Computer Science: Vol. 915. Proceedings of the Sixth International Joint Conference on Theory and Practice of Software Development (TAPSOFT '95)*. Berlin: Springer-Verlag. doi:10.1007/3-540-59293-8_198

von Karger, B. (2002). Temporal Algebra. In Lecture Notes in Computer Science: Vol. 2297. Algebraic and Coalgebraic Methods in the Mathematics of Program Construction. Berlin: Springer-Verlag. doi:10.1007/3-540-47797-7_9

Von Scheve, C., & Salmela, M. (Eds.). (2014). *Collective Emotions. Perspectives from Psychology, Philosophy, and Sociology*. Oxford, UK: Oxford University Press.

Von Wright, G. H. (1969). *Time, Change and Contradiction*. Cambridge, UK: Cambridge University Press.

Wang, Y. (2008). On Concept Algebra: A Denotational Mathematical Structure for Knowledge and Software Modeling. *International Journal of Cognitive Informatics and Natural Intelligence, 2*(2), 1–19. doi:10.4018/jcini.2008040101

Wang, Y. (2010). A Sociopsychological Perspective on Collective Intelligence in Metaheuristic Computing. *International Journal of Applied Metaheuristic Computing, 1*(1), 110–128. doi:10.4018/jamc.2010102606

Wang, Y., Wang, Y., Patel, S., & Patel, D. (2006). A Layered Reference Model of the Brain. *IEEE Transactions on Systems, Man and Cybernetics. Part C, Applications and Reviews, 36*(2), 124–133. doi:10.1109/TSMCC.2006.871126

Wang, Y., Zadeh, L. A., Widrow, B., Howard, N., Wood, S., Patel, S., & Zhang, D. et al. (2017). Abstract Intelligence: Embodying and Enabling Cognitive Systems by Mathematical Engineering. *International Journal of Cognitive Informatics and Natural Intelligence, 11*(1), 1–22. doi:10.4018/IJCINI.2017010101

Wang, Y., Zhang, D., & Kinsner, D. (Eds.). (2011). *Advances in Cognitive Informatics and Cognitive Computing*. Berlin: Springer-Verlag.

Watanabe, S. (1969). *Knowing and Guessing. A Quantitative Study of Inference and Information*. New York, NY: John Wiley & Sons, Inc.

Watzlawick, P., Beavin, J. H., & Jackson, D. D. (1967). Pragmatics of Human Communication. A Study of Interactional Patterns, Pathologies, and Paradoxes. New York, NY: W.W. Norton & Company.

Weinstein, A. (1996). Groupoids: Unifying Internal and External Symmetry. *Notices of the American Mathematical Society, 43*(7), 744–752.

Westphal, B. (2007). La Géocritique. Réel, fiction, espace. Paris: Les Éditions de Minuit.

White, D. R., & Jorion, P. (1996). Kinship networks and discrete structure theory: Applications and implications. *Social Networks, 18*(3), 267–314. doi:10.1016/0378-8733(95)00277-4

Whitebook, J. (1995). *Perversion and Utopia. A Study in Psychoanalysis and Critical Theory*. Cambridge, MA: The MIT Press.

Whitrow, G. J. (1988). *Time in History. Views of Time from Prehistory to the Present Day*. Oxford, UK: Oxford University Press.

Wimmer, M., & Ciompi, L. (1996). Evolutionary aspects of affective-cognitive interactions in the light of Ciompi's concept of "affect-logic". *Evolution & Cognition, 2*, 37–58.

Yang, J., Kanazawa, S., Yamaguchi, M. K., & Kuriki, I. (2016). Cortical response to categorical colour perception in infants investigated by near-infrared spectroscopy. *Proceedings of the National Academy of Sciences of the United States of America, 113*(9), 2370-2375.

Zadeh, L. A. (1965). Fuzzy Sets. *Information and Control, 8*(3), 338–353. doi:10.1016/S0019-9958(65)90241-X

Zadeh, L. A. (1968). Fuzzy Algorithms. *Information and Control, 12*(2), 94–102. doi:10.1016/S0019-9958(68)90211-8

Zadeh, L. A. (1988). Fuzzy Logic. *Computer, 21*(4), 83–93. doi:10.1109/2.53

Zapparoli, G. C. (1970). La perversione logica. I rapporti tra sessualità e pensiero nella tradizione psicoanalitica. Milano, Italy: Franco Angeli Editore.

Zeeman, E. C. (1961). The topology of the brain and the visual perception. In *Topology of 3-manifolds and related topics. Proceedings of the University of Georgia Institute.*

Zeeman, E. C. (1976a). Brain Modelling. In *Lecture Notes in Mathematics: Vol. 525. Structural Stability. The Theory of Catastrophes, and Applications in the Sciences. Proceedings of the Conference.* Berlin: Springer-Verlag.

Zeeman, E. C. (1976b). Catastrophe Theory. *Scientific American, 234*(April), 65–83. doi:10.1038/scientificamerican0476-65

Zeh, H. D. (2007). *The Physical Basis of the Direction of Time* (5th ed.). Berlin: Springer-Verlag.

Zentall, T. R. (2013). Animals represent the past and the future. *Evolutionary Psychology, 11*(3), 573–590. doi:10.1177/147470491301100307 PMID:24027784

Zepf, S., & Gerlach, A. (2012). Commentary on Kernbergs suicide prevention for psychoanalytic institutes and societies. *Journal of the American Psychoanalytic Association, 61*(4), 771–786. doi:10.1177/0003065113496634 PMID:23918822

Živaljević, R. T. (2006). *Groupoids in combinatorics – applications of a theory of local symmetries.* Preprint arXiv: math/0605508v1 [math.CO]

ENDNOTES

[1]   And this is, besides, coherent with the latest psychoanalytic researches, according to which unconscious is basically seen as a semantic-semiotic system maker (or creator) of symbols and meaning (Conrotto, 2014).

[2]   Obviously, a-temporality does not exactly coincide with synchronicity (as that involved in parallel processes), but, operatively, this latter provides the only operative means to try to realize the former. This remark is also valid in regard to the discussion of the next section about synchronous and asynchronous circuits. Anyway, we refer to the next section 6.6. for a clarifying discussion of this latter question here raised, where valid motifs why synchronous/parallel processes might simulate chief aspects of unconscious functioning, will be provided within temporal logic frameworks.

[3]   Indeed, the synchronization of neural activity in oscillatory neural networks is a general principle of information processing in the brain at both preattentional and attentional levels, this being confirmed by a model of attention based on an oscillatory neural network with a central element and models of feature binding and working memory based on multi-frequency oscillations, explained in (Borisyuk et al., 1998).

[4]   Which, in turn, depends on the notion of time considered (linear, cyclic, etc.) and its formal properties (continuity, density, etc.).

[5]   In passing, we note that groupoids are categorial structures which are widely used in theoretical informatics; see for example (Juhás, 1999). See also (Sannella & Tarlecki, 2012).

[6]   Or a "state of the things".

[7]   In this regard, see the Ph.D. thesis of Nino B. Cocchiarella, *Tense and Modal Logic. A Study in the Topology of Temporal Reference*, defended at the University of California, Los Angeles, 1965. See also (Pizzi, 1974) and, above all, (Rescher & Urquhart, 1971).

[8]   The situation is similar to that of the so-called *paraconsistent logics* (Bremer, 2005), where nevertheless time is not involved.

Chapter 7
Further Formalization Attempts of Matte Blanco's Theory, of Other Psychoanalytic Ideas, and Their Possible Applications to Informatics

ABSTRACT

We deepen the relationships between main Matte Blanco's ideas and Aristotelian logic, calling into question also phallic logic, after having premised some discussions on the possible intertwinements between logic and psychoanalysis again. Hence, further possible applications to informatics are also considered. In particular, we have outlined possible, first formalizations attempts of the processes involved in the passage from primary to secondary process according to Freudian theory, from a logical viewpoint, with the involvement of phallus logic and the usual Boolean one. Besides this, we conclude the chapter making mention to the so-called affect logic according to Luc Ciompi, with its relationships with natural sciences, as well as to other formalizations of the main psychoanalytic concepts from the topological and quasi-topological perspective, so reaching to identify possible pathways leading to fuzzy logic and other domains of application.

7.0. INTRODUCTION

In this final chapter, we give further formalizations of some main concepts of psychoanalysis and of Matte Blanco's ideas, on the basis of what has been said in the previous ones, with some possible applications to informatics. In passing, we recall that Matte Blanco main contribution was to show how extraordinarily abstract the unconscious is. He sees primary process as the outcome of the mental activities in abstraction, which are essential for the quick reactivity necessary for survival. Following (Rayner, 1998), Matte Blanco has been too an happy clinician, in particular plunging himself into a careful study of the

DOI: 10.4018/978-1-5225-4128-8.ch007

logical structures of projection and introjection and of the internal world. He remembers his seminars as a student with Melanie Klein in the 1930s, admiring, but not uncritically, her lessons, and recalling what a profound intuitive sense of the unconscious Klein possessed; but she was tied to conscious-level concepts that were inadequate to communicate about the dark regions she was in. Incidentally, the two most well-known investigators of logic and the unconscious, namely Wilfred Bion and Matte Blanco (and Lacan[1]), had links with Klein, and Bion's daughter, Parthenope Bion-Talamo, has just written a thesis comparing the ideas of the two men. Matte Blanco then moves naturally into the logical structure of projective identification, from which he goes on to propose a new way of looking at the structure of the mind.

Matte Blanco suggests that the *unrepressed* unconscious, as distinct from that which has been repressed, may be seen in terms of a *stratified bi-logic structure*, where conscious levels use an organised interplay of asymmetrical and symmetrical thought; then, with emotionality, looser symmetrisations come into play, while deeper unconscious levels manifest much higher proportions of symmetry. Afterwards, Matte Blanco makes use of the important work of his long-term friend John Bowlby, the originator of *attachment theory*, to point out, among other things, the survival importance of symmetrisations at emotional and unconscious levels. Matte Blanco, then, goes on to investigate some forms of disturbance that have hardly been thought of before, like some states of intellectual frenzy which manifest different forms of upheaval of spatial and temporal thought structures. Some might say that these were obsessive activities, but this would miss the quality of frenzy of "logical turbulence" that is being addressed. In this regard, there are, then, many other vivid and fascinating clinical examples. Now well into his stride, logical and clinical thinking come together about the notion of an object, space, dimension, outside, inside; and, lastly, Matte Blanco engages with the notion of internal world, past, present and future. This, just to remember Matte Blanco main ideas and contributions, in a flashing out.

7.1 THE POSSIBLE RELATIONSHIPS BETWEEN PSYCHOANALYSIS AND LOGIC

In order to understand better the intertwinements between psychoanalysis and logic, as established above all by Matte Blanco, it is useful to briefly discuss the central points of classical logical discipline. First of all, its basic concepts, from the psychological point of view, may be considered as specific mental operations. Among these are the notions of event, object, class, set, affirmation, negation, relation, equation, converse, and so on. For belonging to formal logic, each of these needs a precise definition. In what follows, if not otherwise specified, we mainly refer to (Rayner, 1995).

If logic is considered as a mathematical discipline, then the above concepts should be mentioned together with others of greatest precision, such as unit, quantity, enumeration (counting), addition, subtraction, zero, infinity, point, line, space, rate, rate of change, and so on. From the psychological point of view, these concepts are probably conceived by most people, but only at an intuitive level. Surely the intuitive origins of logical and mathematical concepts can often be detected at the early stages of life. For instance, it has been ascertained that a baby as young as six months can reliably detect the difference for instance between two and three objects, hence to do estimates from the rough comparison between two groups of a few elements.

This is, of course, not the same as a systematic counting, but it has rather to be considered as a precursor of it. Indeed, recent cognitive neurosciences and developmental psychology have argued in favour of a possible existence of a kind of "number sense" in the human brain[2], providing a pre-concept of number and able to establish approximate counting and comparison as early before language acquisition, while precise counting seems to be possible only with the parallel rising of the latter; cf. (Vallortigara & Panciera, 2014). There are little doubts that we all have to use many precursors and intuitions of mathematical concepts in everyday life. For instance, we are always subliminally measuring, adding, subtracting and equating as we handle things, as well as we are simple walking or driving. People can semi-automatically do this without having mathematical competences.

Another basic aspect of logic of interest for us is the process of combining logical concepts into usable conclusions. This is the general mechanism of *inference*, and it must be consistent to be commonly usable. This is often the most specialized and difficult aspect of logic and mathematics for the layman, being just the ability to perform valid inferences that distinguishes the professional logician and mathematician from the rest of us.

Coming back to Matte Blanco, there is no doubt that, though he was very competent in logic, his really original contribution does not lie here, but consists in understanding how specific logical and mathematical conceptions – such as object, set, number, equation, infinity – are intuitively used by all of us every day, above all in emotions. His insight has been in understanding human experience, not in working out complex inferences, in that he has been a psychologist rather than a logician or mathematician.

Anyway, through the ages, logicians (Hodges, 1977) have pointed out that the mind can be essentially logical. Human beings, and even other animals, have to perform at least some basic logical steps to survive. In this regard, inference, entailment and consistency, albeit quite simple and running in a short-time range, are necessary. Sometimes, human mind naturally reacts with repugnance to inconsequentialities, inconsistencies, incoherencies or incompatibilities in a sequence of ideas, but it was just Freud, for first, to point out the need to take into account as well this typical fashion of humans.

Roughly, we may say that psychoanalysis mainly deals with feelings, emotions or, in general, affects containing thoughts about inexactly generalized conceptions (*pre-conceptions*). When affects are instead made by a precise thought into *concepts* and then combined consistently with other concepts, then they become elements of thinking and liable to undergo logical inferences. Ian Mordant and Eric Rayner (Mordant, 1990; Rayner, 1995) have suggested that the term *notion* is rather useful for such inexactly generalized conceptions, i.e., pre-conceptions, which have certain thought in themselves but are intuitions and approximate; they often include too simple, even crude, impulsive value judgements. They are furthermore not fully definable, but can still be symbolized.

Logic is also addressed to identify the meanings embedded into the concepts (*semantic*). These latter are more strictly definable using words or conventional symbols and can be analysed with precision into their constituents (*analysis*). The level or realm of emotional notions or intuitions, does not coincide exactly with Freudian unconscious nor with his primary process, although they have much in common; maybe, this level should be retraced into preconscious. Likewise the realm of fully verbal, or declarative, concepts is much close to secondary process.

However, either formal logic and psychoanalysis are *analytic* disciplines. Any analytic procedure consists of separating out the elements or constituents of an entity, be it physical, formal or mental, and specifying the relationships between them. This procedure requires at least self-consciousness and intellectual reflectiveness. It occurs in psychoanalysis and equally in other forms of analysis, like mathematical, logical, linguistic, economic, political, social, chemical or physical. From this standpoint, therefore, psychoanalysis is an analytic discipline.

Thinking is always turned intentionally towards something other than itself, attributing meanings. It uses signs and symbols just to referring to meanings, such as objects, objectives, relations, forms, emotions, states, conceptions and concepts. The actual process of thinking does not involve single isolated ideas or concepts with their symbols, but rather it is a whole pattern forming a complex dynamical system, a sequence gathering together elements of knowing which will be evaluated with an aim in view. For coherent thinking to take place, the evaluation should correspond with at least some aspects of reality, this giving rise to *truthfulness*. But thought does not necessarily is always centrally aimed towards truth.

Thinking appears therefore to be a dynamic combinatorial activity in a time sequence using a group of thought elements; these latter are juxtaposed and compared. Thinking is often solitary and internal but can frequently take the usual social form of debate, dialogue or discussion. The word "argument", is then often used to mean little more than an irritable dispute, but we instead follow a long-established intellectual tradition in using such a term that refers simply to a connected series of statements intended to establish a certain position, just that to which argument refers. Afterwards, thinking truthfully necessitates of consistency, coherence as well as correspondence with at least some of reality; furthermore, its argument must not proceed between elements that contradict each other. This holds too for psychoanalytic interpretation (Codignola, 1977).

It is above all the compatibility of propositions, or of beliefs, as well as the internal coherence of their system, that most of logicians see as the main task of logic (Hodges, 1977), and, in this regard, the Aristotelian *principle of non-contradiction* is crucial, that is to say, «if a proposition, or belief, is true, then its negation is not true». This can be put alternatively as "either A or not-A, but not both". This is a fundamental basis of classical logic which, because of its disjunctive alternative "either-or" basis, it is usually called two-valued logic; Matte Blanco calls it *bivalent logic*. Human thinking, whether basically is truth-seeking or not, most often "desires" or "aims" to discover the "consequences" of something, be it a thought or an action.

At the heart of this, i.e., the discovering of certain related "consequences", there is just a purposive dedication towards the discovery of implications or entailments undergoing such "consequences". This becomes clearer when we recognize that ideas in argued thought sequences are connected of each other with terms such as: is, is not, will, will not, if-then, either-or, both-and, therefore, thus, hence, thence, because, and so, but, however, nevertheless, and many similar terms. These must stand for different operations of thought concerned with implications of one sort or another.

Importantly, most of emotional thinking of the simplest kind is then largely of the type "either A or B" (disjunction) rather than "both A and B" (conjunction), the latter being called *combinatorial*; furthermore, when an exclusive (i.e., *aut*) use of "either-or" prevails on the inclusive (i.e., *vel*) one, then splitting and polarization usually follow. So, the typical feature of emotional thinking seems to have a dualistic disjunctive nature of the type "either-or", with a certain degree of opposition.

This feature has been however noticed by several scholars who used quite different approaches. Besides many philosophers, we recall, amongst others, Melanie Klein and her paranoid-schizoid position, Piaget and his studies of the dualistic aspects of intellectual development, Ferdinand de Saussure and his binary oppositions, Jung and his polarity theory, and Lévi-Strauss' ideas on the dichotomous nature of myth and ritual.

Psychoanalysis however emphasizes that "either-or" binary polarization is also a structural feature of the unconscious, while "both-and", or combinatorial thinking, appears largely featuring the realm of verbal conscious and preconscious thought[3]. On the other hand, it should be noted that, almost paradoxically, dreams occur with an arrangement of its composing elements, which appears to the dreamer as settled by combinatorial function, although obviously they still lie in the unconscious.

Since any thinking process has an aim in that finalized, there is always a grain of anticipation or futurity in it, even when it is concerned with the distant past or with the purely imaginative. For instance, the so-called counterfactual questions – like the following one "If Eve had not eaten of the fruit of the tree of knowledge of good and evil, would mankind still have been able to have justice in its thinking?" – are often imaginative and having to do with a vague past.

From the strict point of view of logical inference, such questions are nonsense, and may only be understood if they are recognized from a metaphorical stance, so they basically symbolize deep aspects of human character and emotions. Anyway, each logical implication, in its basic conditional "if-then", contains futurity, so that it, like any other thinking process, has a sense of time at its core. This agrees with certain hypotheses on the crucial role played by time in the explication of human consciousness (Iurato et al., 2016b).

Naturally, much thinking is aimed towards deceitful ends, and very often it has to account for some aspects of reality, above all when it is finalized to search truth. It has already been recalled above that the notion of truthfulness refers only to situations where something, in one domain, represents something in another, this being *symbolization*. For truth, there must be some one-to-one correspondence, or matching, between the representation and the thing represented. Thus, if the intended matching is between an idea and some physical reality, then the idea will be testable by reference to observable external data. This is the essence of the *scientific method* whose main rules of inference are studied by *inductive logic*. If, on the other hand, we have to do with the truth within a sequence of thoughts, without any reference to external reality, then coherence, consistency or lack of contradictions in the sequence are the minimal requisites do be respected. This is the realm of *deductive logic*.

However, a suitable combination of inductive and deductive reasoning towards valid implications is essential in everyday life, even in simple and instantaneous tasks; it is certainly essential also in psychoanalysis[4]. At the same time, we should not forget the mind's capacity for untruthfulness. This is intrinsic to the nature of any pathological defence, may be passive and more or less unconscious or actively, as well as consciously intended. Furthermore, although logical reasoning is essential, it often seems not to engage with the core of the thinking about individual human selves and their emotions, which is the daily lot of analytic therapists.

Viewed in one way, many usual, typical expressions of humans are obviously false from a strict logical standpoint. Notwithstanding that, such phrases communicate some essential truths using metaphor; this and other rhetorical figures of speech, like, for example, simile, onomatopoeia, metonymy, synecdoche, etc., are the great tools for communication of emotions. This is just the realm of *rhetoric*. It is present, of course, in any poetry or drama and also in everyday therapeutic dialogue. Freud obviously was aware of this, and the first one who noticed it. Lacan then continued greatly along this way.

Thus, truth also regards affects, feelings, emotional states, character judgements, inter-subjective experiences and interpersonal relations. These may concern transient feelings, more long-lasting moods, or, longer lasting still, character traits which may go beyond emotional structures. They are the grist of psychoanalytic therapy which are definite statements and can have truth in them, so that they must have some status as *propositions*.

Yet the logicians have often neglected such forms of symbolic communication. For instance, from the strictly logical point of view, use of metaphor is often called, following Noam Chomsky, a logical "selection mistake"; cf. (Hodges, 1977). The logicians obviously recognize the importance of poetry and naturally also knows that the poet's choice of words is quite deliberate, yet they still call it a mistake. So, psychoanalytic thinking is often searching truth in emotional communication.

Among others, John Bowlby, also inspired by the Susanne Langer work on symbolization (which distinguishes between a *discursive symbolization*, mainly taking place at the social linguistic level, and a non-discursive or *presentational* one, in which the symbol has an immediate idiosyncratic sensory reference and there is an direct isomorphism between the thing symbolized and the symbol) has noted that, in animals and humans, *emotion* is an instantaneous appraisal and evaluation of the state of the external environment *simultaneously* at the internal physiological and psychological condition of the organism. Thus emotion contains, *at the same time*, data about exteroceptions, body functions (both visceral and skeletal), memories, anticipations of the future, and the state of the Self with others. To be noted here that, in human beings at least, the sense of the Self is central to any developed emotion.

7.2 FURTHER FORMALIZATIONS OF PSYCHOANALYTIC CONCEPTS AND OF MATTE BLANCO'S BI-LOGIC

The strong instinctual reduction due to *homination* (that is to say, the passage from primates to the genus *Homo*[5]), which took place around 15 millions of years ago, gave rise to the human existential problem of managing the consequent instinctual energy content which has supervened as a result of such a drive *deconstrainment*. This crucial event has taken place in concomitance with the passage from the environmental genetic adaptation to a cultural adaptation, that is to say, to that imaginative adaptation controlled by human being which is revealed to be more functional than the former because manageable, flexible and transmissible. Along this evolution, which led to *Homo sapiens* genus, a strong regression of drives occurred, which were gradually 'replaced' by the coming of the *culture* (Cuche, 2004; Iurato, 2013b,c; Spedini, 2005).

This last allows human being adapts to the environment and, conversely, to adapt this latter to the needs and projects of the former, that is to say, the culture makes possible the transformation of nature (unfortunately, at the expense of human being, seen the latest events). Human being is basically formed and shaped by culture, even in the primary needs like hunger, sleeping, sexuality, etc., which are moulded just by culture, since societies have seen to provide different responses to these physiological needs (Cuche, 2004).

But, human being is characterized, as well as by *needs*, by *desire* which is roughly meant as a sort of incoercible psychic tension which has to be necessarily, internally or externally invested. So, for the human being, it is indispensable to find *objects*[6] upon which to direct, or to invest, such an energy content. The consequent relationships established with these objects (animated or not) are generically called *object relationships*. These were explicitly introduced by post-Freudians, first of all by the Melanie Klein school, even if the notion of object relation was already present, *in nuce*, in the Freudian notion of *cathexis* of a drive (or instinct) which characterizes the inescapable human disposition to make inter-relationships with something else (which belongs to the external or own internal world), said to be the *cathexis object*, which, in turn, will be represented by the individual in various manners (Iurato, 2013b,c).

The Freudian cathexis has a *source*, an *object* and a *drive destination* (or *instinctual aim*) as fundamental constitutive elements. The first one is the (bodily) zone, or the somatic apparatus, in which the related libido excitation takes place and originates. The second one is the means by which, or with which, the drive may reach its (instinctual) aim; it is the necessary correlative of the drive destination, and is mainly determined by the personal history (above all, infantile) of the individual but constitutionally is quite undetermined since it may be either a person or a partial real or fantasmatic object. Finally, the third one is that particular and necessary activity, or that specific action, due to the push of the drive itself to obtain the given satisfaction, and that often is oriented and sustained by the *fantasmatic* or *imaginative* (symbolic) elaboration of the individual herself or himself. Hence, we sketchily have:

$$source \xrightarrow{\text{object}} drive \; destination$$

These latter notions are the generalization of the correlative ones of normal sexuality: for instance, the object may correspond to the sexual object, that is to say, the person who exerts the sexual attraction (or the fetishistic object in abnormal sexuality), while the aim corresponds to the sexual satisfaction, that is to say, it is the action due to, or raised by, drive pushes. The first (bodily) Ego formations mainly involve a correct balancing of the primary narcissism, a regulation of primary identifications (through introjection-projection mechanisms), and a beginning of a sense of reality and of a corporal image of Self (Iurato, 2013b,c).

Now, following what Freud says about the modalities of representation of dreams[7] in his main work *The Interpretation of Dreams* (of 1900), Freud says that alternative "or-or", that is to say, the logic operator "either A or B" (disjunction), is not possible in dreaming activity where instead it seems to prevail the logic operator "both A and B" (conjunction) in so far as either its possible alternatives seem to be equally present in the dream scene, as if they were equally holding both. So, Freud emphasizes that the conjunction "both A and B" is a structural feature of the unconscious, while "either A or B" (above all in its disjunctive sense) appears largely featuring the realm of verbal conscious and preconscious thought. Thus, it seems that, in the unconscious realm, there hold two kind of logic operators, a disjunction "either-or" in its non-exclusive (or inclusive) form (i.e., *vel*), and a conjunction "both-and", this latter often used to join contraries; instead, the exclusive form of disjunction "either-or" (i.e., *aut*), it seems to be a prerogative of conscious thought.

Furthermore, Freud discusses the existence of logical connections among the components of a dream, which hold simultaneously, so leaving to mean that usual logical implication of conscious thought springs out of only thanks to a *deployment* (just to use a term due to Matte Blanco) in the time. Indeed, since any conscious thinking process has an aim in that finalized, there is always a grain of anticipation or futurity in it, even when it is concerned with the distant past or with the purely imaginative. From the strict point of view of logical inference, such questions are nonsense, and may only be understood if they are recognized from a metaphorical stance, so they basically symbolize deep aspects of human character and emotions. Anyway, each logical implication, in its basic conditional "if-then", contains futurity, so that it, like any other thinking process, has a *sense of time* at its core. This highlights the basic role played by time for human consciousness.

It seems then that what is made ostensible by dream's thought, during the dreaming activity, is the (manifest) *theme* (subject-matter) of the dream thoughts, not their reciprocal *relations*, which will be explicated by the conscious interpretation of the dream in its latent content, so it seems that semantics however precedes the coming of the syntax[8]. Furthermore, as briefly mentioned above, it seems that a kind of primary chronological sequence of the thoughts of a dream, is possible as well.

Now, as discussed briefly but comprehensively in Chapter 5, the Boolean algebra $\wp$, i.e., the basic formal structure underlying Aristotelian logic, is fundamentally given by the set of all the possible sentences Ξ, equipped (after Pierce) with two basic operators, the negation $\neg$ and the conjunction $\wedge$ ("both-and") or else the disjunction $\vee$ ("either-or"), that is to say, $\wp = (\Xi, \neg, \wedge)$ or $\wp = (\Xi, \neg, \vee)$. Since formally we may freely choose between conjunction $\wedge$ or disjunction $\vee$, we have yet chosen the latter in its *aut* form, in so far as it characterizes, as has been said above, the conscious thought (also said to be *combinatorial*), while the former (often together $\vee$, but at most in its *vel* form) is a feature of unconscious thought.

Afterwards, since unconscious, according to Matte Blanco, structurally, is a not-well defined[9] aggregate of infinite sets (mainly, of thing presentations), say $\aleph$, and is characterized, as said above, by "both-and" operator (as well by "either-or" operator in its *vel* form), we may assign to it a very minimal, basic formal algebraic structure, say $\Re \doteq (\aleph, \wedge)$, in which operates primary process and where the (unconscious) logical connective $\wedge$, i.e., the "both-and" operator. This formal structure of human unconscious, however, is not complete since, to be such, we should consider at least two further operators, namely the one formalizing the *condensation* mechanism, say χ, and the other formalizing the *displacement* mechanism, say δ, so that, a minimal yet complete formal algebraic structure of unconscious is of the following type $\Re \doteq (\aleph, \wedge, \chi, \delta)$, which might give rise to another new type of algebraic structure in dependence on the algebraic properties of the operators χ and δ.

Therefore, the passage from the primary process to the secondary one may be formalized by means of a transformation Υ (of *deployment*, according to Matte Blanco) of the type:

$$\Re \doteq (\aleph, \wedge, \chi, \delta) \xrightarrow{\ \Upsilon\ } \wp \doteq (\Xi, \neg, \vee)$$

Thus, what really produces this transformation Υ, is the algebraic structure underlying Aristotelian logic, i.e., $\wp$, from the unconscious realm summarily formalized algebraically by $\Re \doteq (\aleph, \wedge, \chi, \delta)$, with $\aleph$ structured according to Matte Blanco. In $\Re \doteq (\aleph, \wedge, \chi, \delta)$, prevails the symmetry principle, while in $\wp$ prevails the asymmetry principle, with the separation of opposites taking place by means of the logic operators $\neg$ and $\vee$ in its *aut* form[10] acting on the set of all the possible sentences Ξ. Hence, Υ should formalize the bi-logic process according to Matte Blanco, as well as the crucial passage from primary process to the secondary one, with which the primary rational thought, basically formalized by $\wp$, springs out from unconscious formally structured by:

$$\Re \doteq (\aleph, \wedge, \chi, \delta)$$

A Freudian cathexis, then, as briefly recalled above, acts roughly in a manner homological to the action of the above transformation Υ: the source is relatable with the eruption of unconscious material, Υ may correspond to the (bodily or mental) modality with which free psychic energy, coming from source, transforms in bound energy of secondary process which explicates in drive destination. Anyway, what is really important about the transformation Υ, is the rising of rational thought (as discussed in the next section), basically given formally by the inseparable pair $(\Xi, \neg)$ from which, for example, language takes place[11], as well as temporal dimension, with its orientation, that arises from the consequent validity of the basic principle of non-contradiction closely related with the operator $\neg$.

Moreover, the key components of Υ, are those which allow to getting, via bi-logical modality, the (Aristotelian) logical operators $\neg$ and $\vee$ (*aut*), acting on Ξ, *from* a suitable action of the (unconscious) logical operators $\wedge$, χ (formalizing condensation) and δ (formalizing displacement) on the structural unconscious $\aleph$ and its content (coming from repression), with Ξ roughly meant as a not-well defined aggregate of infinite sets (of thing presentations) equipped with energy amounts. In any event, the transformation Υ subsumes a series of psychoanalytic notions, most of which are correlated with the fundamental passage from primary process to secondary one. However, for the sake of simplicity, in what follows, we can restrict ourselves to consider only the minimal algebraic structure of unconscious, that is to say, consider $\Re \doteq (\aleph, \wedge)$; the other two operators χ and δ, may act only with respect to $\wedge$, while their action is hindered in the conscious thought, but not in a fully manner; indeed[12], in schizophrenia (see also next section), for example, they act on the words in the same manner they act on the dream images, so their action is surely incompatible with usual Aristotelian logic, and, in place of them (i.e., χ and δ), the two logical operators $\neg$ and $\vee$ (*aut*) arise, together with non-contradiction principle. This may take place for the occurrence of certain defence mechanisms, first of all those related to negation (see Chapter 2, Section 2.8.), just by means of the function Ψ (see below).

In Chapter 4, Section 4.1.5, we have discussed on ordered groupoids, that is to say, groupoids equipped with a compatible partial order relation. In that chapter, we have also argued, following (Lawson, 2005), that any ordered groupoid is isomorphic to one constructed from a category acting, in a suitable fashion, on a certain groupoid arising from an equivalence relation. Furthermore, there, we have considered the simplest groupoids, that is, those arising from equivalence relations and said to be *combinatorial groupoids*. Then, it is possible to build ordered groupoids from combinatorial ones plus some data, namely a partial order in turn inferred from a partial pre-order relation that, quotienting, gives rise to a partial order. On its turn, such a preorder relation may be induced by a suitable category's action on the given combinatorial groupoids, so what we basically need of is the action of a given category on a combinatorial groupoid.

Now, again following what has been said in Chapter 4, Section 4.1.5., if we consider a certain category Θ as acting, via a suitable action Ψ, on the combinatorial groupoid $\aleph / \sim_s$ (which will be defined soon later), as follows:

$$\Psi : \Theta \times (\aleph / \sim_s) \to \Re_w$$

with $\Re_w$ the set of all the possible words-presentations[13] (i.e., the basic realm of consciousness), then we may obtain, according to what has been just said above, an ordered groupoids, already implemented in $\Re_w$, from which it may follow all the other usual ordered algebraic structures characterizing formally conscious activity, in first time line. The category Θ might be, for instance, the enlarged[14] class of all the possible Ego's defence mechanisms (see Chapter 2) acting, via Ψ, on the unconscious and its things-presentations, or better, on the quotient set $\aleph / \sim_s$, which is defined, more precisely, as follows[15].

In *The Interpretation of Dreams* (of 1900), Chapter VI, Section (C), Freud says that, among all the logical relations of unconscious, the one which is most favourite by the mechanism of formation of dreams, is the relation of *similarity*, say $\sim_s$, among thing presentations (belonging to $\aleph$, as an infinite set, and ruled by displacement and condensation), a relation of "as if", of "approximation", of "assonance", which will give rise to dream images. It is clearly an equivalence relation, so we may consider the quotient set $\aleph/\sim_s$. Then, the action Ψ operates as follows: to the pair $\left(\phi,[\rho]\right)\in\Theta\times(\aleph/\sim_s)$, associates the word presentation $\varphi=\Psi\left(\phi,[\rho]\right)\in\Re_w$; however, it is not excluded that more than one defence mechanism ϕ may act together on a single equivalence class of thing presentations $[\rho]$. Finally, such a word presentation $\varphi=\Psi\left(\phi,[\rho]\right)$, so obtained, is function of the thing presentation $[\rho]$, coherently with what Freud states in this regard, namely that, the conscious presentation comprehends the thing presentation plus the corresponding (just through Ψ) word presentation (Laplanche & Pontalis, 1967). Of course, there is a close correlation between Ψ and Υ, in that both try to formalize the crucial passage from primary to secondary process, with the first one related to logical aspects, the second one related to the representational (linguistic) aspects of this passage.

Now, as we have seen in Chapter 4, a pre-order relation, at least, may be obtained with a symmetry breakdown process (of inversion symmetry) acting on such an infinite combinatorial groupoids, basically for the occurrence of inequivalences among representations or configurations of a certain quotient set (like $\aleph/\sim_s$), as discussed in (Iurato et al. 2016, Sect. 5.1.), that, in the case here treated, corresponds to the clarifying insights and interpretations of psychoanalysts during analytical setting of patient telling her or his dreams and their contents, a dialectic discussion centred on the standing out of the semantic-pragmatic aspects which making just possible to point out such a distinction between (unconscious) things-representations, occurring in the manifest meaning of the dreams, in *expliciting* the related latent meaning, by psychoanalyst's work during the setting, through the right elaboration of the connected, inequivalent and distinct words-presentations. Thus, such a breaking (basically corresponding to an inversion symmetry breaking) gives rise to a pre-order relation, the fundamental prototype of any other further order relation, that is to say, the main feature of human consciousness.

7.3 THE INTERRELATIONS BETWEEN CLASSICAL LOGIC AND MATTE BLANCO'S BI-LOGIC AND SOME THEIR APPLICATIONS TO INFORMATICS

As has been already said, Ignacio Matte Blanco was a notable psychiatrist and psychoanalyst who has devoted many years of his work in studying the mathematical thought from psychoanalytical standpoint, starting from his many-years experience with schizophrenic patients. His definitive results were published in the celebrated work *The Unconscious as Infinite Sets: An Essay on Bilogic* (of 1975), which has had various editions.

In this section, whose content is drawn from (Iurato, 2013a), we mainly follow the work (Figà-Talamanca Dore, 1978) which explains the main psychoanalytic considerations, also from an epistemological viewpoint, on the logic of unconscious deduced by Matte Blanco from his already mentioned fundamental psychiatric clinic experience on schizophrenic patients. We also follow (Durst, 1988).

First, just the preface by Adriano Ossicini to (Figà-Talamanca Dore, 1978) argues on the general epistemological aspects of the psychological sciences, since the work of Matte Blanco is just directed toward these last, that is to say, he tries to establish fundamental relationships between the psychoanalysis and the exact sciences, in particular mathematics.

The work of Matte Blanco[16] is an original, interpretative afterthought of the Freudian theory through the methods of elementary logic. He starts from certain Freudian postulates which characterize the dynamical structure of the unconscious, namely *1)* displacement, *2)* condensation, *3)* absence of time,

4) substitution of the external reality with the psychic one (literal interpretation of the metaphor) and *5)* absence of mutual contradiction among the presentation of the various drives.

In particular, according to Freud[17], the usual ordinary logic rules of conscious thought are not valid for the unconscious since this operates according to another logical system. The former is ruled by a classical, assertoric (i.e., not modal) logic founded on the *material implication* and having, as fundamental laws, the *identity principle*, the *non-contradiction principle*, the *bivalent principle*, the *principle of sufficient reason* and the *principle of the excluded third* (*tertium non datur*).

Instead, according to the studies on schizophrenic thought due to Matte Blanco, the fundamental principles of the unconscious are the *generalization principle*[18] and the *symmetric principle*[19] (Figà- Talamanca Dore 1978, Ch. I, Sect. 2), through which it carries out the primary process, whereas the secondary process concerns the modus operandi of conscious thought. Subsequently, through these, Matte Blanco tries to explain the previous Freudian characteristic principles of unconscious (Figà-Talamanca Dore 1978, Ch. II). In particular, he re-examines (Figà Talamanca Dore 1978, Ch. II, Sect. 2) the classical Freudian agencies in the light of these his new principles.

According to Matte Blanco, conscious and unconscious are two different *modes of being* with respect to the psychophysics unity of the human individual, *asymmetric* and in becoming the first one, *symmetric* and static the second one: this terminology is due to the fact that the latter is regulated by the above mentioned symmetric principle, contrarily to the first one.

Following (Figà-Talamanca Dore 1978, Ch. III), the symmetry and staticity, characterizing the unconscious, do not allow any finite-dimensional space-time idea as well as any sequential logical reasoning (which relies on asymmetry, as we will see later), so that the asymmetric conscious thought seems to be the result of a sort of *symmetry breaking* of the infinite symmetric unconscious world. In passing, we recall, besides, that symmetry breaking mechanisms, according to the modern physics, are at the early basis of any fundamental physical phenomenology from the dynamical viewpoint; cf. Chapter 4.

Nevertheless, according to Matte Blanco, the conscious becoming cannot do without the being unconscious, so that it seems to be, in a certain sense, solved the secular *vexata quæstio* concerning the known *Parmenides-Heraclitean dialectic* between the logic of being and the logic of becoming (Carruccio 1971, Ch. 6, Sect. 6.2). Indeed, for Matte Blanco, the pair unconscious-conscious is inseparable[20]. The symmetric thought is unthinkable without the asymmetric one, and the limit between normality and abnormality is given by the degree of reciprocal compenetration of these two modes of being, by their ratio.

In (Figà-Talamanca Dore 1978, Ch. V), it is discussed Matte Blanco's notion of unconscious as an infinite set, resuming the distinction between *set* and *class*, as typical of formal set theory. The unconscious does not distinguish between *partial* and *total* object and, moreover, each element of any set is conceived as having only human qualities (anthropomorphization attempts). This last property is a fundamental epistemological assumption common to many theory of the history of human thought, even if Matte Blanco deduced it from psychoanalytic considerations.

In (Figà-Talamanca Dore 1978, Ch. IV), it is also discussed the notion of infinite set in mathematics, analogically compared with the symmetric mode of being of the unconscious, precisely with its property of indistinguishability between the part and the whole, in the sense that they both have the same cardinality, this just being the first notion of infinite set according to Richard Dedekind (that, inter alia, has considered the notion of infinite set as a tool to explain the world of the human thought – see (Figà-Talamanca Dore 1978, Ch. IV, pp. 47-48, footnote 3) and George Cantor. Again according to Matte Blanco, many other mathematical concepts (like that of limit process) have their origins by the attempts to asymmetrically explain the properties of the symmetric one.

In (Figà-Talamanca Dore 1978, Ch. V), it is explained some useful concepts about consciousness according to Matte Blanco: exactly, it cannot do without the asymmetric thought, in the sense that a conscious act consists in a continuous setting-up of asymmetric relations, arranged as in a net, around the *cathexis object* (that is to say, the not-well defined *thing* invested by the human desire, or better, free psychic energy). The main consciousness' activity is essentially analytic because it fundamentally subdivides every analyzed object into its constitutive components or parts (partial objects), unlike by an emotion, or an affection, which is a globally conceived symmetric thought.

Nevertheless, the symmetric and asymmetric modes are inseparable amongst them, because an entirely symmetric mode is typical of any state of loss of consciousness, whereas a complete asymmetric mode is also impossible since it would imply a total absence of either any cathexis object and any psychic energy content, which is impossible for each human being. Every normal psychic state varies within an interval (or range) including a right mixing of either these modes, but whose ratio may continuously changing yet with both modes always present. Moreover, if we consider, for instance, a mathematical argument – hence a full asymmetric thought, at least in the involved theoretical principles and at the end of his formulation – then there is always an unavoidable emotional involvement which may be described as an involvement of symmetrical type.

Therefore, albeit a certain human outcome – like a mathematical proof – may seem to be the result of a completely asymmetrical work, indeed its production is never separated from an affective component of symmetric nature. This last remark is a fundamental one for understanding the nature of a creative thought. Here, we simply observe that this fact gives a line of overall consistency to a part of the present section: indeed, a *creative thought* is just of this last type, that is to say, it is the result of a dialectical (inseparable) interaction of the two modes of being, the symmetric and the asymmetric[21]. Further, according to Matte Blanco, the consciousness may think only in a three-dimensionally way, plus eventually a fourth temporal dimension, so that the three-dimensional space seems to be the spatial dimension of consciousness and imagination. The human thought thinks mainly by three-dimensional images, also in abstraction, so confirming a suggestion due to Jacques Hadamard (Hadamard, 1945).

On the other hand, some consciousness contents are available only by means of introspection, which is an asymmetric phenomenon. According to Matte Blanco, it has a precise feature: namely, it never concerns the instant in which takes place the introspection, but it concerns the immediately previous moments (hence, the past). The human thought exists only if it is reflected on itself, or else, the most peculiar character of the human thought is just this *reflectivity*. The elusive character of the conscious thought is due to the fact that the real nature of the consciousness is *temporally* located between these two modes of being, the symmetric and the asymmetric one, so that each time we try to think a conscious content, then we *diachronically* restrict ourselves to the asymmetric mode, so completely excluding the (synchronically inevitable) symmetric components. Thus, only thinking historically, diachronically, it is possible to avoid (or minimize) the latter.

So, the shifting from symmetric to asymmetric thought of consciousness needs for a certain not empty temporal range to occur, so it is evident that *time* is a central mean for consciousness (Iurato et al., 2016b). In (Figà-Talamanca Dore 1978, Ch. VI), furthermore, it is discussed the concept of emotion which plays a fundamental role for all the psychic life, above all in the early formation of the thought. It is also describable by means of introspection. Nevertheless, it is mainly (but not completely) a symmetric phenomenon (Figà-Talamanca Dore 1978, Ch. VI, p. 68).

Finally, in (Figà-Talamanca Dore 1978, Ch. VII), it is delineated one of most important Matte Blanco' notions, to be precise that of *bi-logic*. According to Matte Blanco, the unconscious logic (or *symmetric logic*) is, as already said, mainly based on the principle of symmetry and on the principle of generalization, which regulate the so-called mode of being *symmetric*. The latter is furthermore inseparable from the mode of being *asymmetric*, regulated by the bivalent logic (as already said, the usual 'definitions' are possible only within the asymmetric thought), and vice versa, that is to say, any human psychic manifestations is the result of the interaction and/or the cooperation between these two modes of being.

And this implies that any human reasoning is the result of the combination of the rules of two main logics, that *symmetric* and the bivalent (or *asymmetric*) one, which, in turn, are interpreted as components of a unique *bi-logic*. Therefore, every human psychic phenomenon turns out to be a bi-logic process which is a mixed chain of symmetric and asymmetric sub-processes whose combination modes are, a priori, various and infinities, so giving rise to the rich variety of the human thoughts.

The emergence, at the threshold of consciousness, of a bi-logic process is related with the concept of *triad* by Matte Blanco. This last concept should be meant as a fundamental structure of the Mathematical Logic, according to which it is the entity formed by two theoretical objects related with each other by a third object called *relation*. Matte Blanco thinks that the logic-mathematical structures are the results of the application of his theory of human psyche structure based on the notion of bi-logic process. The bi-logic process has been analyzed in many therapeutic cases treated by Matte Blanco, in both normal and pathological (schizophrenic) cases. At the end, he has concluded that the normal thought takes place in a context of (logic) causality, whereas the schizophrenic one (which, as an emblematic paradigm, allows to shed a look within the unconscious realm) seems to follow an a-causal context.

Finally, in (Figà-Talamanca Dore 1978, Ch. VII, Sect. 2), it is summarized other very interesting analyses of the bi-logic structure in schizophrenic patients according to the studies conducted by Matte Blanco. For our purposes, it is simply enough to observe that the chronic schizophrenic thought continuously uses the symmetric and generalized principles in her or his reasoning. On the other hand, these latter, from a formal (or mathematical) viewpoint, imply an impossibility to establish the so-called *axiom of specification* (or of *separation*) of Formal Set Theory, according to which (Pini 1967, Ch. 1, Sect. 1), if A is a set and $p(x)$ is a statement for each x of A, then there exists a set B such that $y \in B$ if and only if $y \in A$ and $p(y)$ is true[22], in such a case, we shall write:

$$B \doteq \{y; y \in A, p(y)\}$$

The chronic schizophrenic patient, according to Matte Blanco, is unable to use such a fundamental axiom[23], hence he or she is also unable to (mentally) construct a Boolean algebra of the type $P(A)$ given by all the subsets of an arbitrary set A (to which every complete and completely distributive Boolean algebra is isomorphic, by means of certain theorems due to Alfred Tarski (Cohn 1965, Ch. V, Sect. 2) and other representation theorems provided by Marshal H. Stone). This is due to the almost total use of symmetry and generalization principles in her or his reasoning.

On the other hand, according to the just mentioned Stone's representation theorems (Atiyah & Macdonald 1969, Ch. I; Chang & Keisler 1973, Proposition 1.4.4; Pini 1967, Ch. V, Sect. 2), the two-element Boolean algebra *2* (following Halmos' notations) with support set $\{0,1\}$, is isomorphic to a Boolean algebra of the type $P(A)$ for some set A (like, for instance, the set of all maximal ideals of *2*, that is to say, its maximal spectrum). On the other hand, since *2* is the mathematical structure which formalizes the *propositional calculus*, that is to say, it is its *propositional algebra* (cf. Chapter 5, as well as (Carruccio 1971, Ch. 4) and (Pini 1967, Ch. 6)), it follows that a chronic schizophrenic patient is basically unable to construct such an algebra, that is to say, he or she is unable to perform a rigorous *syllogistic inference* (which is the general element of *2*).

This might explain, amongst other things, the great difficulties to perform a make-sense reasoning by a chronic schizophrenic patient. Furthermore, and this is a crucial point of our discussion, the two-element Boolean Algebra *2* is also the truth's value algebra of the semantics meant as the study of the various, possible interpretations of the propositional calculus (Lolli 1991, Ch. 5), whence it follows too that a chronic schizophrenic patient is unable to integrate syntax-semantics and semantics-pragmatics, as also witnessed by some recent neuropsycholinguistic researches; cf. (Iurato, 2016c) and references therein. Moreover, from an historical viewpoint, this is also coherent with the original motivations underlying George Boole's work entitled *An investigation of the laws of thought* (of 1854), in which he introduced this algebraic structure (Bara 1990, Ch. 2, Sect. 2.1.2), which were just due to the attempts to formally analyze the laws of logic considered as outcome of human thought.

Moreover, in (Bara 1995, Ch. 7, Sect. 7.3), it is confirmed that many people reason according to an incorrect inference that, in the light of what has been just said above, may be explained (following Matte Blanco) through the unavoidable presence of the symmetric thought together the asymmetric one, that is to say, by means of a bi-logic process. In (Bara 1995, Ch. 7, Sect. 7.3.1), it is discussed the structure of a syllogistic inference of the type $A \Rightarrow C$ considered as the main elementary and basic logic tool of reasoning, the primary epitome of consciousness: it is, according to the Mental Models Theory (Johnson-Laird & Bara, 1984), the result of the action of three inseparable phases, i.e., the construction, the integration and the verification.

The *construction* consists in the interpretation of the premises (relatives to A), namely, in the individual construction, for each premise, of a mental model representing the state of the things that every premises describes. The *integration* consists in the coherent integration of these various models into a unique integrated model (for instance, following Aristotle, individuating one or more so-called *intermediate terms* B between the extreme terms A and C) for the syllogistic conclusion (relatives to C). Finally, the *verification* consists in the epistemological analysis of the validity of the reached conclusion (for instance, by means of Karl R. Popper falsification method, constructing suitable counterexamples). Often, the integration phase includes the institution of possible effect-cause links between the two extreme terms. Moreover, the establishing of these last relations is mainly a creative activity, since it is not based on pre-constituted laws.

On the other hand, following (Lolli, 2005), a *conditional enunciate* is a (rational) enunciate of the type «if A then C» where A are the initial assumptions (like, for example, a single enunciate or a conjunction or a set of enunciates) considered as axioms of a certain theory, whereas C is the conclusion. Usually, in the conditional enunciates of the type $A \Rightarrow C$, A are the *hypotheses* while C is the *thesis*. Not every conditional enunciate is a theorem, since as *theorem* we mean a conditional enunciate in which C is a logical consequence of A, that is to say, if, in every interpretation of the formal language in which are formulated A and C, C is true whenever A is true, and, in such a case, we write more specifically $\vDash A \Rightarrow C$. Hence, in each theorem, the conditional enunciate $A \Rightarrow C$ means that this syllogistic inference is valid, namely it is true for every interpretation.

This leads us towards the *syntax*, independently by the *semantics* (which studies all the possible interpretations). From here, we are naturally led towards the general notion of *proof* of a theorem of the type $\vDash A \Rightarrow C$ which is the search for the chain (called *derivation*) of the formal passages each constituted by an elementary conditional enunciation through which it is overall possible to deduce C from

A. Hence, this is formally explainable as the search for a series of intermediate terms $B_1, ..., B_n$ such that the proof is formed by the chain $A \Rightarrow B_1 \Rightarrow ... \Rightarrow B_{n-1} \Rightarrow B_n \Rightarrow C$ explicable by means of the correct application of the rational logic rules.

The quest for a proof is therefore a fundamental creative process considered as a transcendental mental function in searching for the structure of being. The existence of almost one derivation of C from A for a given theorem $\vDash A \Rightarrow C$, is warranted by the known *Gödel's completeness theorem* (of 1930): this theorem has mainly a psychological function because it does not suggest any operative or methodological indication about the search or individuation of the proof strategy as well as one of its possible derivations, this confirming the nature prevalently creative of it.

On the other hand, considering, for example, an arbitrary insight process, it is then plausible to think that the long unconscious work in finding a proof (mentioned, amongst others, by Hadamard and Poincaré) is just owned to the (indivisible and homogeneous unity or) *syncretic* character of unconscious which has mainly an immediate unifying and multiple logical character[24], impossible to the asymmetric (or conscious) thought. Indeed, following what is mentioned in (Ageno 1962, Ch. 1, Sect. 10), according to Poincaré, the most insights spring out of an unexpected inner decisive inspiration often taking place in a moment in which the mind is very far from the solution to the problem under examination which has yet been, for a long time, inconclusively discussed and unconsciously incubated.

It is as if, all the elements of this searched solution, put in movement from the previous conscious study (of the problem under examination), continue to mechanically (and unconsciously) roam within a sort of 'cerebral maze' until up when, suddenly, they finally find a road along which link themselves, in a continuous chain (that is, a derivation), from the hypotheses towards the thesis. Afterwards, Hadamard says as, amongst the infinite possible choices (namely, the above road), that is to say, amongst the infinite possible (unconscious) association of ideas (which pursue the solution), just our own unconscious seems to choose the one satisfying a kind of 'beauty criterion' (with Dirac) which is ruled by a certain instinctive sense of scientific-artistic elegance. This, also in coherence with certain psychoanalytic ideas which give a precedence to primary aesthetic drive in human being, closely related with pleasure principle (Iurato, 2016a).

In turn, this sense of beauty is besides influenced by our scientific education (Ageno 1962, Ch. 1), that is to say, it is just the *method* that will become a kind of instinctive praxis, in a manner that it is impossible to explain in words. Maybe, this might be related with the continuous content exchange between explicit and implicit memories. On the other hand, following (Bara, 1990), a syllogism is nothing but an *explicitation* process of those valid and interesting conclusions *implicitly* contained into the premises. Furthermore, taking into account what has been just said by Poincaré and Hadamard, Mario Ageno (1962, Ch. 1) adds that however the (scientific) *method* cannot alone open the way to the finding of the solution to a given problem if one does not learn to discovery too new problems and to correctly formulate them.

Then, when one conducts a logic derivation of a mathematical proof, we essentially follow a bi-logic process made by symmetric steps (which have a unifying and creative character in finding the various, not a priori given, intermediate terms $B_i, i = 1, 2, ..., n$) and asymmetric steps (in applying the necessary logic tools and rules for the various partial elementary syllogistic inferences $B_i \Rightarrow B_{i+1}$ for each i); in these two inseparable types of thought and their intertwinement, it is important to consider, in relation to their occurrence, their degree of more or less *contemporaneity*. Hence, Matte Blanco bi-logic process may be considered as one of the most suitable candidate in trying to explain the primary bases of a formal creative process, whence it follows the unescapable role (or influence) played by unconscious (or symmetric) thought in finding a new mathematical proof (which is not otherwise rationally deducible – for instance, by means of generalization, analogy, extension, *reductio ad absurdum*, and so on[25]), specially as concerns the affective-emotive aspects involved in it. The unavoidable presence of symmetric thought aspects also explains why, in certain cases, the new proof of a theorem is almost never perfect in its initial form[26], but it shall reach its perfect and correct (in a certain sense, definitive) form after the subsequent correction made upon the possible initial imperfections, that is, by elimination of any symmetric thought interference.

Hadamard (1945) has then pointed out that the major part of the mathematical insights take place through images[27] and not through verbal processes. His idea is besides also confirmed by the *double codex* theory due to Wilma Bucci (Bucci 1985, 1987, 1997; Thomä & Kächele 1987-89, Vol. 1, Ch. 5, Sect. 5.4) according to which, starting from the ideas of Allan Paivio (Thomä & Kächele 1987-89, Vol. 2, Ch. 5, Sect. 5.1), there exist two equal-rank codices, that *verbal* and the *non-verbal* one. The mature thought may be placed in both these codices. In particular, the non-verbal codex is that appointed to the emotional functions and to other holistic types of thought. It works by synchronous information through parallel multiple channels (hence following a *synchronous logic*), and preside to symbolic and subsymbolic functions (Bucci, 1997).

Furthermore, in searching for a psychoanalytic psychology, Wilma Bucci (1997) points out that primary process is the modality of running of the unconscious or of the *Id* (or *Es*), mainly associated with non-verbal functions, while secondary process is the modality of conscious thought or of the *Ego*, mainly associated to verbal functions. The (non-verbal) symbolic and subsymbolic functions take place according to first modality, operating mainly through continuous parallel processes, with multiple operations occurring synchronously, and interested mainly in content rather than structure. Symbolic verbal function, instead, runs according to the second modality, via a univocal sequential channel, emitting and receiving one message at a time. All these are however intimately integrated among them to give a unitary sense of the Self (Bucci, 1997).

Thus, we would be tempted to suggest that the asymmetric thought is ruled by an *asynchronous logic*, whereas the symmetric thought is mainly ruled by a *synchronous logic*. The brain perceives and works out the reality simultaneously by means of both codices, and they are continuously in reciprocal communication through bidirectional connections and continuous referential links. The thought by images is the primary (but not the unique) and specific expression of complex emotions like desires, beliefs, expectations and other holistic sensory-motor experienced, representational and mathematical contents and others, which cannot be verbally expressed. It is evident that the Bucci's double codex theory may be closely correlated with Matte Blanco's bi-logic process and vice versa, at least from an historiographical and epistemological perspective.

Anyway, those few references and hints made here just about synchronous and asynchronous features, if suitably re-worked out and interpreted[28], might turn out to be useful from a computational standpoint, in that, as we have seen in the previous chapters, taking into account one of the main characteristics of structural unconscious, that is to say, the timelessness, then possible partial informatic simulations of its functioning, might also be performed by means of suitable coupled uses of parallel/concurrent processes as well as of synchronous/asynchronous circuits, as, for example, already discussed in the previous chapter, which here receives a further support on the basis of what has been formally argued in the present section.

7.4 THE WORK OF LUC CIOMPI ON AFFECT LOGIC AND ITS APPLICATIONS

7.4.1 Introduction: What Is Affect Logic?

We wish also mention the possible, useful and interesting links between Matte Blanco's ideas and some studies and researches in clinical and theoretical psychiatry of schizophrenia and emotional thinking, as, for instance, those made by Luc Ciompi (1991, 1994a,b, 1997, 1998, 1999, 2000, 2001, 2003, 2015) and co-workers (Ciompi & Hoffmann, 2004; Ciompi & Panksepp, 2005; Ciompi & Baatz, 2005, 2008), which are, in many respects, closely related with what has been said above. Ciompi's work has provided new psychosocial/biological models of psyche, in which the affects play a central role in organising and integrating cognition, and where human psyche is understood as a complex hierarchical structure of affective/cognitive systems of reference (or "programmes for feeling, thinking, and behaviour"), generated by repetitive concrete action. These systems store past experience in their structure, providing functional basis for further cognition and communication; affects furthermore endow these programmes with specific qualitative values (such as motivation, etc.), connect cognitive elements either *synchronically* and *diachronically* (see also Chapter 6, Section 6.5.), and contribute to their storage and mobilisation according to the context (pragmatic tasks); they participate too in differentiating cognitive systems at higher levels of abstraction. These assumptions are supported by recent neurobiological findings on the role played by limbic and hypothalamic system for the regulation of emotion, on neuronal plasticity, and on the phenomenon of state-dependent learning and memory (Ciompi, 1991).

The integrative concept of *affect logic* (or *affect-logic*) is based on a hypothesis concerning the laws of interaction between emotion and cognition. According to Ciompi and co-workers, affects are defined as global psycho-physiological states which determine the prevailing functional logic, i.e., the specific ways in which cognitive elements are selected and linked together. This besides leads, in particular, to an integrative psycho-socio-biological evolutionary model of schizophrenia, supported by clinical data, in which a specific affective-cognitive vulnerability is built up, in a first phase, through escalating interactions between unfavourable genetic-biological and psycho-social influences; in a second phase, the mental system is decompensated by psycho-social or biological stressors which induce psychosis. In a third phase, then, the great variability in long-term course is conditioned by the complex interplay of many biological and psycho-social variables. The organising functions of affects are evident in schizophrenic core phenomena such as ambivalence, incoherence, and emotional flattening (Ciompi, 1994a).

This new psycho-socio-biologically integrative concept of affect-logic, and its relevance for a comprehensive understanding and therapy of schizophrenia, has been developed by Ciompi over the past 30 years, on the basis of the literature, of clinical experience and his own research into long-term evolution, rehabilitation, effects of milieu-therapy, and nonlinear evolutionary dynamics of the illness. It postulates, basically, that fundamental affective states (comprehending emotions, feelings, moods) are continuously and inseparably linked to all cognitive functioning (or "thinking" and "logic" in a broad sense), and that affects have essential organizing and integrating effects on cognition. Schizophrenia is understood as an altered mode of affective-cognitive interaction based, possibly, on disturbed (loosened) affective-cognitive connections, and this hypothesis has led to: *i)* an integrative psycho-socio-biological model of long-term evolution of the illness; *ii)* a new understanding of psychopathological core phenomena such as ambivalence, incoherence, and emotional flattening; *iii)* an innovative therapeutic approach based on an emotion-relaxing milieu and style of care; and *iv)* the hypothesis that schizophrenia could basically be an affective (and not a cognitive[29]) disease of another kind than mania or melancholia (Ciompi, 1997).

Just in regard to the last point *iv)*, Ciompi's central hypothesis is that the critically increasing emotional tensions are capable to provoke a nonlinear phase transition from normality to psychosis, in vulnerable persons. The psychotic state should correspond, in this view, to an attempt to establish a new (and often still unstable) equilibrium which reduces the emotional tension through a global reorganization of the predominant patterns of feeling, thinking, and behaving. The hypothesis is based on this energetic understanding of emotions and on the stress-vulnerability hypothesis, being also supported by many of the notions on emotions available in this context. Moreover, Hermann Haken's theoretical concepts of *synergetics* may provide, in addition, a mathematical explanation why and how an excessive input of (here, emotional) energy in an open dynamical system (here, an habitual system of feeling, thinking, and behaviours) acts as parameter of control for the occurrence of a sudden bifurcation of its overall behaviour. They also explain how formerly marginal structural elements of the system (in this case, for example, formerly peripheral ideas of persecution which eventually become the centre of a fully structured delusional system) suddenly begin to act as a new parameter of order, or "centre of crystallisation" (in analogical terms), for a global reorganization of a critically destabilized system (Ciompi, 2015).

Affect logic is, therefore, an innovative theory on ubiquitous interactions between feeling and thinking (or emotion and cognition, affectivity and logic), which are overtly or covertly present in all human mental activities. This new framework is mainly based on the outcomes of many research findings from psychology, psychiatry, sociology, evolutionary science and neurobiology. It was firstly introduced in 1980s in Swiss and further developed since, according to the ongoing scientific progress, by Luc Ciompi and co-workers. Its main aim is to present a practically and theoretically useful synthesis of current neurobiological, psychological, psychoanalytical, socio-dynamical and evolutionary notions, besides revisited under the perspective of the general *systems theory*. Initially focused mainly on psychiatric problems, it became however clear that its basic assumptions have too a more general value. Consequently, the concept gradually developed into an interdisciplinary metatheory with implications in all the fields where affective-cognitive interactions are involved, especially in psychology, psychiatry, psychotherapy, pedagogy, advertising, politics, micro- and macro-sociological dynamics.

Following what Ciompi himself says, to briefly sum up, the five main theses of affect-logic are:

1. Emotion and cognition work together in all psychological achievements;
2. Filtering and switching effects of emotions constantly affect all cognitive functions;
3. Emotions are the decisive energies or "motors" of all thinking and behavior;
4. Critically increasing emotional tensions lead to sudden changes of the overall patterns of feeling and thinking;
5. Affective-cognitive interactions are self-similar ("fractal") on all individual and collective levels.

7.4.2 Main Definitions and Principles of Ciompi's Affect Logic

In what follows, we shall give the main definitions and the chief principles of Ciompi's affect logic, in so doing, following almost *verbatim* what Ciompi himself says personally.

The notion of *affect* – that, for most of authors, includes all kinds of emotive phenomena, while others restrict it to a particular type of subjective experience – is broadly used, says Ciompi, as an "umbrella-notion" comprehending all kinds of emotion-like phenomena, variably called emotions, feelings, or moods[30]. An *affect*, in its widest sense, is therefore "a situation-specific psycho-somatic state of variable duration, intensity, quality and degree of consciousness, characterized by specific expressive, subjective, physical and neuro-biologic features, as well as by a situation-specific pattern of energy consumption". Fundamental affects, like interest, fear, rage, joy or sadness, are atavistically rooted in all those behaviours which are relevant for survival and have been selected by evolution, such as exploration of the environment, avoidance of danger, defence against enemies, food-intake, socialisation, collaboration and bonding, sexuality, readjustment after significant losses. Their basic patterns are mostly innate, primordial, but culturally modulated[31]. Furthermore, pleasant relaxation, calmness or indifference, are also affective states in a defined sense. Hence, one is always in a certain affective state, and affective-cognitive interactions are omnipresent.

The notion of *cognition*, then, is also used in a broad sense including different specific psychic functions such as perception, attention, memory and combinatory thought. In close relation with general cybernetics and information theory (especially, to the notion of a *bit* unit, i.e., the smallest perceived difference), cognition is, again according to Ciompi, generally defined as "the capacity of distinguishing and further elaborating sensory differences (e.g., the capacity of distinguishing between black and white, warm and cold, harmless and dangerous, and so forth), and of establishing relations between these differences and differences of differences. Cognition, in this sense, too, is a basic property of living organisms which appears very early in evolution". The notion of *logic*, then, again meant in a broad sense within affect-logic, includes not only the formal (Aristotelian) logic, but also the so-called everyday logic and different types of affect-dependent logic, as we shall see later. Loosely speaking, it may be defined "as the way how cognitive elements are connected and combined in comprehensive thought, in order to form, for example, a specific theory, a world's view, a mentality or an ideology".

Ciompi says that the essential "building stones" of human psyche are integrated feeling-thinking-behaving programs, in that, simultaneously, experienced emotions, cognitions and behaviours are functionally linked and conjointly memorised, and the links among specific emotions, cognitions and behaviours are reinforced by repetition. They store past experiences which are reactivated in similar situations and function, hence, as comprehensive programs for future emotional, cognitive and motor behaviour (in short, *ECB-programs*). Also in humans, a few ECB-programs are innate (like certain fear-reactions), but most of them are acquired by experience. In this sense, integrated ECB-programs of variable degrees of complexity, are the key "building stones" of human psyche.

7.4.3 The Role of Affects and Emotions in Rational Thought and Logic From the Dynamical System Theory Viewpoint

Emotion and cognition are continually interacting in all mental activities, with specific cognitions triggering specific emotions, and specific emotions modulating and changing the related cognitive functions. *Affect logic* focuses mainly on the filtering and switching effects that basic, primordial affects, such as fear, rage, joy or sadness, continuously exert on cognition. The prevailing affective psychic state currently influences the energy, speed, form and content of thought and perception. It also modifies the focus and the hierarchy of attention, the mobilisation and storage of selected cognitions (state-dependent selective memory), and the way how affect-selected cognitions are combined together in comprehensive thought, that is in common "logic", meant in its broad sense. In doing so, cognitive elements with qualitatively similar emotional connotations (e.g., all pleasant or unpleasant aspects) are preferentially connected among them, while qualitatively dissimilar elements are preferentially disconnected (or better, repressed). In other words, specific affects have an attractor-like (or glue-like) effect on cognition processes with a qualitatively similar emotional connotation. The evolutionary function of the affects and of their selective effects on cognition is the situation-appropriated reduction of the complexity of the surrounding cognitive world, in the service of survival.

Therefore, comprehensive thought and logic, as above defined in their broad sense, are strongly dependent on the prevailing emotive state. So, Ciompi states that different types of "logic" may therefore prevail in different emotive states: there exists, for instance, a specific "logic of fear", a "logic of hate", a "logic of love", or, at the collective level, a "logic of war" or a "logic of peace". Even the apparently unemotional everyday logic is instead conditioned by underlying effects of formerly intense emotions. Everyday logic is, then, based on past experiences particularly charged emotively, which were initially related to strong conscious feelings that are, however, progressively dampened and automatized through continuous repetition and habituation[32]. In any case, the initial affects continue to exert their filtering and switching effects on everyday thought and behaviour. They condition not only all "semi-automatic" skills, like car-driving, talking, music playing, etc., but also our habitual ways of thinking. Even, all our apparently (of our own personal "mask" or) "self-evident" personality-specific, group-specific and socio-culture-specific value systems, as well as political or religious ideologies and prejudices, have been initially shaped by strong emotions such as fear, rage, pleasure or disgust, and so on. When these habitual "self-evidences" (or covers) are suddenly violated, their underlying emotional components reappear immediately.

Contrary to common beliefs, rational thought and formal logic, too, are modulated by underlying affects and emotions: logical conflicts, contradictions and paradoxes are unpleasant and, therefore, emotion-energetically spoken, dynamically uneconomic; contradiction-free solutions are instead pleasant, relaxing and dynamically economic. Seeking pleasure and avoiding displeasing tensions, plays a significant, albeit generally overlooked, role in the construction and stabilisation of formal logic and rational thought. Even here, initially, strong emotions are gradually dampened gradually the new ways of thinking become usual, routinely. They continue, however, to covertly influence rational thought and logic through the selective effects of positive feelings: pleasant solutions are systematically favoured and unpleasant solutions are avoided. Furthermore, positively "coloured" cognitive elements of scientific thought are built together, while contradictory elements are, if possible, neglected, in order to form a comprehensive scientific theory, in exactly the same way as cognitive elements with a similar emotional colour are preferentially connected, while contradictory elements are repressed, in everyday thought and logic.

The filtering and switching effects of emotions on cognition are related to another important aspect of emotions which also continues to be generally neglected, namely their energetic dimension. Different emotions are characterized by different patterns of goal-directed energy consumption with mostly stimulating and mobilizing, but, sometimes (as, for example, in freezing or depression), also inhibiting effects on thought and behaviour. Charging a mental or social system with specific emotions, is to give inputs of energy. Amount of emotional energies, as stirred up, for example, by economic, political, psychological, social or religious conflicts, are very strong pushes behind all mental or social dynamics. Besides to have qualitative features, the energetic aspects of emotions have too the advantage of being, in principle, quantifiable, which allows to explain the powerful energizing effects of emotions on individual and collective thought and behaviour in both everyday life and exceptional situations, like mass-panic, enthusiasm, rage, horror, mourning, etc.

It also leads to a deeper understanding of sudden global modifications (said to be *bifurcations* by Ciompi, but we should prefer to call them *catastrophes*) in the habitual ways of thinking and regarding both individuals or groups, until up to whole nations. To be precise, at all levels, such catastrophes occur, inevitably, when increasing emotional tensions in a mental or social system reach a critical level which cannot longer be processed by the habitual modes (or channels) of thought and behaviour. The consequence is a sudden, very often abrupt, shift of the general pattern of functioning in a new global, often opposite, regime, like in the passages from a "logic of peace" to a "logic of war", from a "logic of love" to a "logic of hate", or, as the recent research on the so-called *high expressed emotions* (HEE) has showed, from a normal to a psychotic logic and behaviour.

Similar affect-energetic mechanisms are usually at work, for example, at the sudden outbreak of violence, of wars, or of revolutions, but they also play a crucial role in other creative processes like the discovery of new solutions in art or science. In all these cases, increasing emotional tension depends on a certain critical control parameter, which determines the moment of bifurcation or catastrophe. Simultaneously, formerly marginal cognitive elements (like a formerly marginal or "crazy" idea) can suddenly turn into a new "centre of crystallisation" (said to be *order-parameter*, in analogy of critical phenomena), around which the new patterns of feeling, thinking and behaving (as a new system of value, of political, religious or scientific convictions, or a system of delusions) emerge by self-organisation. In these Ciompi's considerations, the recalls to dynamical system theory are evident, as well as the following ones about the fractal structure of affective-cognitive interactions.

Ciompi's theory of affect-logic postulates that affective-cognitive interactions are basically similar on different levels of complexity (e.g., on the individual, micro-social and macro-social level), that is, that they show a so-called *fractal structure*. Fractality is a property of a great number of natural and cultural phenomena which are intensely studied by dynamical systems theory which has many applications in numerous fields. A fractal structure is then generated by basically similar dynamical algorithms on different levels of functioning. The result is a characteristic, so-called *self-similarity* (or *scale-independence*) of structural patterns on different levels of complexity. All the above described interactions between emotion and cognition show, indeed, a basically similar structure on the individual, interpersonal, inter-group and even on the international level.

Prevailing affects such as fear or anger, for example, selectively mobilise (or inhibit) attention, memory, combinatory thought and logic in similar ways on all these levels. Intra-individual self-similarities over time furnish, for example, the basis for the projective personality tests (such as the Rorschach's ones) which explore the fact that a small fragment of mental activity may contain significant information on life-long personality traits. Psychoanalytic transference reactions, artistic style and personality formation, too, are typically self-similar on different levels of complexity. So, the notion of fractality allows a methodologically correct transfer of small-scale (e.g., individual or interpersonal) observations on large-scale (e.g., inter-group or international) processes, and-vice versa. This is very important from an epistemological viewpoint, allowing, for example, to consider a *collective affect-logic*.

Indeed, above switching and filtering effects of emotions on thought and behaviour are particularly intense at the collective level, just thanks to emotional contagion, synchronisation, imitation, conformism and other mechanisms of social reinforcement (cf. also (Contarello & Mazzara, 2002)). Collective emotions can develop enormous energies. In this regard, historically crucial macrosocial examples include the rise of the national-socialism in Germany, the Israel-Palestine conflict, the Islam-West conflict, the so-called "Arab spring", and the new Islamic state, are all spectacular yet dramatic examples of the effects of critically increasing collective emotional tensions; and further examples are provided on a daily basis. See (von Scheve & Salmela, 2014) and references therein.

The practical implications of affect-logic are then important for the techniques of communication at all levels, from everyday life and business to politics, and from the individual to the international domain.

In fact, information provided without an appropriate emotional impact will not be noticed, even if, to be remembered, however, calmness and relaxation are also highly meaningful affects in the sense of affect-logic. Successful information often depends more on the emotional "colour" of a message than on its own cognitive content. Information which meets the current emotional state of the partners of communication is preferentially noticed and accepted, while discordant information is preferentially excluded. Accordingly, therefore, skilful speakers, salesmen, politicians, mediators, negotiators, psychotherapists, performers, and others, try to adapt their verbal and non-verbal language to the emotional state of their public, respectively they try to create a shared "emotional wave-length", before delivering their message.

Then, appropriately acknowledging the omnipresent thought-modulating role of emotions changes also our understanding of rationality and of the human nature, in general, in the sense of a "homo sapiens emotionalis". On the therapeutic level, affect-logic leads to new techniques for influencing thought and behaviour through emotion-centred (rather than cognition-centred) methods of crisis intervention, of mediation, and of the treatment of mental traumatisms. A particularly interesting application of affect-logic in psychiatry is the Ciompi's therapeutic community *Soteria Berne* where patients suffering from acute schizophrenia are treated by a special Ciompi's psychotherapeutic and milieutherapeutic approach focused on the induction of a sustained emotional relaxation. Other psychiatric applications are related to general psychopathologic and psychosomatic problems, violence-prevention, crisis intervention, and body-centred psychotherapies.

In sociology, then, the concept has been successfully used for the analysis of extremist ideologies, especially national-socialism (Endert, 2006). A critique of the system-theoretical concepts of Niklas Luhmann, based on Ciompi's affect-logic and the fractality of emotion-cognition interactions, postulates basically that micro-social and macro-social dynamics can only be adequately understood by taking into account the filtering and switching effects of collective emotions on collective thought and behaviour. Other valid applications are focused on problems of pedagogy, creativity, phenomenology of consciousness, and philosophy, as well as for robotics where, as the evolutionary functions of emotions get daily increasing attention, Ciompi's theory of affect-logic has interesting and promising implications.

7.5 SOME POSSIBLE RELATIONSHIPS BETWEEN CERTAIN FORMALIZATIONS OF PSYCHOANALYSIS, TOPOLOGY AND FUZZY LOGIC

In this section, we retake some psychoanalytic considerations exposed in (Iurato et al., 2016), about Freudian topography of human psyche, hence some its possible extensions according to Lacan's theory, trying to identify the underlying topological structures according to what has been done, for instance, in (Iurato & Khrennikov, 2017). From this, some further hints in regard to possible links with *quasi-topology* (according to Michel De Glas and Jean-Pierre Desclés) and *fuzzy logic*, are put forward[33].

7.5.1 A Brief Outline of the First Freudian Topography of Human Psyche in Its Relationships With Either Quasi-Topological Structures and Fuzzy Logic

For what has been said in Chapter 4, Section 4.3., the representation association *Sachvorstellung-Wortvorstellung* (for the assumption *AC*) may be assumed, according to Freud, as characterizing consciousness, while *Triebrepräsentant*, regarding emotions-drives, is related more with the deepest and most primitive, archaic (unrepressed) meanders of the variegated unconscious realm U, where

UCC ($\subseteq U$) relies. Spatial representations (as, for example, those occurring in the dreams) are much more concentrated and structured in the *preconscious* zone, say $\Pr c$, where things-representations act. Therefore, *Triebrepräsentant* should be supposed acting on the deepest and most archaic zones of (unrepressed or structural) unconscious U, where UCC is located, and where neither usual space-time structures nor other formal structures, may exist.

Now, if we define $\mathfrak{I}_{U\Pr c} \doteq U \cap \Pr c$ as the non-void intermediate zone between unconscious U and preconscious $\Pr c$, then, little by little we go away, we depart[34] from the ancestral and dark hard core of unconscious realm U, we start to encounter preconscious zone $\Pr c$, where *Sachvorstellung* predominates, and where first spatial (like in dreams) and temporal (i.e. ordered) entities start to appear, although without a precise formal relation between them[35]. Thus, taking into account the above Freudian assumption *AC* (see Chapter 4, Sect. 4.3.) on consciousness acts based on the joint action of thing representation-word representation (see the final part of Section 7.2.) in the early dawning of consciousness, we are particularly interested first in the passage from unconscious U to preconscious $\Pr c$, in turn corresponding to the passage *Triebrepräsentant* $\rightarrow$ *Sachvorstellung*, then in the next passage from preconscious $\Pr c$ to consciousness C, on its turn corresponding to the next passage *Sachvorstellung* $\rightarrow$ *Wortvorstellung* (or, for *AC*, to *Sachvorstellung-Wortvorstellung*).

A topographic assumption[36] is truly important to be made at this point: there are not sharp and clear separation borders between the zones U, $\Pr c$ and C, whose reciprocal boundaries are quite indefinite and fluctuating, as well as they are overlapping with each other. This entails that $\mathfrak{I}_{U\Pr c} \doteq U \cap \Pr c \neq \varnothing$ which might be considered as a kind of boundary with non-zero thickness[37] (*thick boundary*) between the deepest unconscious area and the more properly preconscious zone; likewise, we might identify another similar non-empty intermediate zone $\mathfrak{I}_{\Pr c\, C} \doteq \Pr c \cap C \neq \varnothing$ between the proper preconscious zone and the conscious one C. Therefore, we have sketchily the following (first Freudian) topography $\{U, \mathfrak{I}_{U\Pr c}, \Pr c, \mathfrak{I}_{\Pr c\, C}, C\}$ with $\mathfrak{I}_{U\Pr c}$ and $\mathfrak{I}_{\Pr c\, C}$ non-void, in accordance with what Freud himself has more times stressed on the indefiniteness of the exact boundaries between the three places U, $\Pr c$ and C.

In the lands comprised among $\mathfrak{I}_{U\Pr c}$, $\Pr c$ and $\mathfrak{I}_{\Pr c\, C}$, the basic dynamical conversion from *free energy* to *bound energy*, as well as from *primary process* to *secondary process*, take place. Now, the main psychic mechanisms operating at the unconscious level, that is to say, *displacement* and *condensation* (Laplanche & Pontalis, 1967), might be suitably applied as follows. UCC is that unaccessible, deep and inscrutable zone of unconscious realm, dominated by *Triebrepräsentant*, in which the psychoanalytic setting itself does not work, is inefficient (Sasso, 2011). In $\mathfrak{I}_{U\Pr c}$, under the control of UCC, the crucial passage *Triebrepräsentant* $\rightarrow$ *Sachvorstellung* takes place, as well as displacement and condensation work there. The displacement was introduced by Freud just in relation to the clinical observation of the independence of affect from representation, studying the fashion in which energy changes and transfers along associative chains. Freud says that displacement mainly works along primary process, but it is also involved in secondary process, although acting in a restricted and limited manner and in relation to very small energy amounts.

Freud, furthermore, considers another fundamental mechanism of unconscious, that is to say, the *association*, to mean the link is being established among psychic elements making an *associative chain*. Freud reached this notion in consequence of his theory of free associations. According to him, every idea which is coming into mind (*Einfall*) apparently in an isolated fashion, in reality is always an element which refers, more or less consciously, to others, so giving rise to an associative chain which Freud calls with different names: a line (*Linie*), a thread (*Faden*), a concatenation (*Verkettung*), a string (*Zug*), and so forth. Such lines variously intersect among them, so giving rise to proper nets with nodal points (*Knotenpunkte*) through which many lines go through. Such a net will be the basis for the discourse of the subject (see Lacan), while its topology will give rise to the topographic notion of unconscious (in the first topography; cf. Chapter 2, Section 2.3.2.), precisely of the zone $\mathfrak{J}_{U\Pr c}$. Remarkably, as early Freud himself pointed out the separation or disconnection of these associative chains, which may exist also in isolation from each other (according to bifurcation processes and/or splitting processes) and in a disordered manner, thus confirming our assumption of a disconnected and non-ordered topological features of unconscious zone $\mathfrak{J}_{U\Pr c}$.

So, from what has been said so far, in the first Freudian topography as briefly described above, that is:

$$T_I \doteq \left\{ U, \mathfrak{J}_{U\Pr c}, \Pr c, \mathfrak{J}_{\Pr c\, C}, C \right\}$$

we may identify two particulars zones, $\mathfrak{J}_{U\Pr c}$ and $\mathfrak{J}_{\Pr c\, C}$, not empty, whose boundaries are yet indefinite, in accordance with what Freud himself has more times stressed on the indefiniteness of the exact boundaries between the three places U, $\Pr c$ and C. Nevertheless, just in the lands comprised among $\mathfrak{J}_{U\Pr c}$, $\Pr c$ and $\mathfrak{J}_{\Pr c\, C}$, as has been recalled above, the basic dynamical conversion from *free energy* to *bound energy*, as well as from *primary process* to *secondary process*, take place, so $\mathfrak{J}_{U\Pr c}$ and $\mathfrak{J}_{\Pr c\, C}$ play a very fundamental role in the origin and psychic development of consciousness. Just due to this indefiniteness of the boundaries of the zones $\mathfrak{J}_{U\Pr c}$ and $\mathfrak{J}_{\Pr c\, C}$, may be considered as *thick boundaries* of the domain $\Pr c$, to be precise, $\mathfrak{J}_{U\Pr c}$ as the *internal thick boundary* (or *internal border* in the quasi-topological sense of De Glas-Desclés[38]) comprised between the unconscious U and the preconscious $\Pr c$, in which operate the first censorships, and $\mathfrak{J}_{\Pr c\, C}$ as the *external thick boundary* (or *external border* in the quasi-topological sense of De Glas-Desclés) comprised between the preconscious $\Pr c$ and the consciousness C, in which operate the second censorships.

Thus, the consciousness flow springs out from psychic processes which develop roughly in the following direction[39] $U \to \mathfrak{J}_{U\Pr c} \to \Pr c \to \mathfrak{J}_{\Pr c\, C} \to C$, where the key steps are the central ones, where the transitions *Sachvorstellung* $\to$ *Wortvorstellung* take place and form the bases for the next conscious phenomena. Now, just the (non-zero) thickness of the non-empty boundary zones $\mathfrak{J}_{U\Pr c}$ and $\mathfrak{J}_{\Pr c\, C}$, seem to surround $\Pr c$, with their undefined borders (meant in the quasi-topological sense of De Glas-Desclés), to give rise a *quasi-topological space*, which is a new topological structure, introduced by De Glas and Desclés, able to formalize semantic-cognitive aspects of spatial-temporal processes, just those occurring in the preconscious and its neighbourhoods, as seen above. Indeed, such new topological schemes are able to account for those situations of confine in which there is no certainty of statement: for example, in a static situation, an object (or a place) is located relatively to a place with a certain degree of certainty (e.g., He *is near* Pisa/He *is in* Pisa/He *is out* of Pisa), while, in an evolutive spatial situation, it becomes necessary to take in account an underlying temporality as well as to have spatial uncertainty (e.g., He *arrives to* Pisa/He *enters* Pisa/He *penetrates* Pisa/He *leaves* Pisa). Classical topological representations are not sufficient for a deep semantic analysis of static and evolutive spatial situations or events (e.g., the crossing of a place, as, for example, that metaphorically involved in T_I to give rise consciousness phenomena, in which the unconscious U plays the role of internal attractor, coherently with the dynamical system standpoint discussed in (Iurato et al., 2016) in regard to the nucleus UCC), so it is necessary to extend classical topology to quasi-topological structures, the *quasi-topology* being roughly a topology of abstract sets with thick boundaries which are suitable to formally describe topology of spatial-temporal events – like crossing a space – and analyses its semantics and the related cognitive representations[40] (Desclés, 2009).

On the other hand, again the (non-zero) thickness of the non-empty boundary zones $\mathfrak{I}_{U\mathrm{Pr}c}$ and $\mathfrak{I}_{\mathrm{Pr}c\ C}$, surrounding $\mathrm{Pr}\,c$, with their undefined borders, suggest to make reference to fuzzy logic in that, just due to this last indefiniteness feature of both $\mathfrak{I}_{U\mathrm{Pr}c}$ and $\mathfrak{I}_{\mathrm{Pr}c\ C}$, in which it takes place the crucial passages *Triebrepräsentant* $\rightarrow$ *Sachvorstellung* and *Sachvorstellung* $\rightarrow$ *Wortvorstellung*, respectively, a sort of uncertainty plagues these zones in regard to *where* psychic function may be placed in a certain moment within this T_I topography of human psyche, so that the psychic domain:

$$\Delta \doteq \mathfrak{I}_{U\mathrm{Pr}c} \approx \mathrm{Pr}\,c \approx \mathfrak{I}_{\mathrm{Pr}c\ C}$$

may be suitably equipped with a structure of fuzzy set, assigning to it a so-called *membership (characteristic) function*, say f_Δ, with values in $[0,1]$, which should estimate the "degree of membership" in Δ: for example, $f_\Delta(x)$ estimates the "degree of membership" of x in Δ. So, the nearer the value of $f_\Delta(x)$ to 1, the higher the degree of membership of x in Δ. When Δ is an ordinary set, then $f_\Delta(x)$ is its characteristic function, otherwise, we speak of a *fuzzy set* (Zadeh, 1965); these have had immediate and fertile applications in informatics and computing sciences (Zadeh, 1968). From this simple remarks, we may descry[41] the possibility to implement a *fuzzy logic* (Zadeh, 1988) just in the realm of human psyche topographically described by Δ, coherently with the fact that such a logic does not provide non-contradiction principle, and, as an extension of many-values logics, is an extension too of the classical Boolean logic. So, fuzzy logic (Zadeh, 1988) is a good candidate for a possible formal framework modelling the logical functioning of Δ. This argument should then be suitably put into relation with what has been said in the previous section about the relationships between Matte Blanco's ideas and Boolean logic, on the basis of the simple correspondence rule $f_\Delta \leftrightarrow \chi_\Delta$ (the latter being the characteristic function of Δ) between fuzzy sets and ordinary Boolean sets. Finally, just in passing, we also note that the persistence of a fuzzy logic, as briefly discussed right now, is besides justified from what we have said in Chapter 6, Section 6.6., about Kripkian histories indicized by non-empty sets belonging to the hyperreal numbers system.

7.5.2 On the Topological Structure of Unconscious: Further Remarks

In this section, we make reference to some other formal aspects of unconscious, following (Iurato & Khrennikov, 2017). For other interesting applications of topology in psychoanalysis, we refer either to the first attempts made by the French school of 1960s (Balzarotti, 1972) and to the recent miscellany (Friedman & Tomšič, 2016).

7.5.2.1 On the Topology of Unconscious According to Jacques Lacan

Topological structures are considered innate, while all the other mathematical structures (algebraic, ordered, linear, and so forth), as meant, for example, in the *architecture des mathématiques* in the sense of N. Bourbaki, are considered acquired. This follows from previous studies and researches on mathematical skills and capabilities of blind mathematicians, who in particular excel in geometry with respect to the other mathematicians (Sossinsky, 2000; Zeeman, 1961). So, the study of the formal structures (especially, the topological ones) of human unconscious, seems to be particularly indicated, appreciated and useful. In (Iurato & Khrennikov, 2015), we have put forward a simple formal model of human unconscious phenomenologically based on hysteresis mechanisms, and formally laid out within p-adic analysis framework. In describing briefly this model, we have stressed the fundamental importance of temporal dimension for the origin of human consciousness, formally related with the occurrence of a primordial ordering springing out from symmetry breaking phenomena just due to the emergence of these hysteresis phenomena (Iurato et al., 2016).

These latter take place in certain zones of unconscious which are, as seen in the previous sections, not sharply identified by clear and fixed boundaries, contours or profiles, because psychoanalysis tells us that there is a kind of fluidity, undulation, evanescence in these latter which entail a certain, so to speak, topological indeterminacy subsisting from deep and primordial zones of unconscious realm to preconscious and consciousness-nearer ones. In this topographic framework, i.e., T_I , we wish further argue on other possible formal features of this model as explained in the previous sections, especially on the topological side, starting from some basic points of the well-known Jacques Lacan theory whose slogan is the celebrated (yet abused) sentence according to which "unconscious is structured like a language".

To be precise, Lacan (2014, pp. 1962-63) states that the unconscious has not to be considered as an interior put against an exterior. For Lacan, the unconscious is characterized by a confine topological structure which allows the psychic drives to lean on bodily parts with boundary. This is coherent with what we have said in (Iurato et al., 2016) above in regard to the primary relevance of boundary conditions on the diffusion of psychic energy as grounding phenomenology lying at the early bases of consciousness. The above mentioned Lacan's topology of unconscious, is moulded on that of *Möbius band* (or *strip*): indeed, the irruptions of unconscious formations into the effective discourse does not require the overcoming of any boundary, but rather they follow a continuous route like the forehand and backhand of a Möbius strip. With this emblematic topological model, Lacan has wished to describe the main interrelations between conscious and unconscious, and the related interpretation of the latter.

Indeed, although locally the Möbius band seems to have two distinct faces, it globally has instead a unique face. On the other hand, on the basis of an original rereading of classical Freudian theory, the crucial question of unconscious structure may be roughly solved, in Lacan terms, considering it as an "inscription" into a place which is *other* with respect to the conscious discourse which is however enunciated on the same versus of the former, and, since unconscious may always intervene in every point of conscious discourse, Lacan intuitively grasped the idea for which all this may be elegantly formalized by the topology of a Möbius band that, as it has a unique global face, lends itself very well to explain this crucial yet mysterious intertwinement unconscious-conscious (Chemama & Vandermersch, 1998).

7.5.2.2 On the Possible Role Played by Chirality, and All That

Roughly speaking, Möbius strip is the most elementary example of a non-trivial *fiber bundle* (see Chapter 4, Section 4.2.6.1.) whose base space is the circle and whose fiber is the real line (Choquet-Bruhat et al., 1982). Lacan has been the first psychoanalyst to have identified such basic fiber bundle structure of unconscious, and this gives credit to that possible further formal characterization of unconscious structure in terms of fibre bundles as briefly discussed in Chapter 4, Section 4.2.6.). So, we are encouraged to carry on along this line.

Möbius band is the prototype of non-orientable surfaces as every non-orientable surface contains a submanifold which is a Möbius band (Hirsch, 1976). So, we may consider the topology of the Möbius two-dimensional manifold as the most typical formal feature characterizing unconscious structure which therefore turns out to be the non-orientability. This agrees with the typical traits of unconscious according to Freud, in which any form of order cannot exist, hence any orientation.

Therefore, the rising of a primordial form of order might be correlated with the occurrence of some form of orientation, that is to say, with the passage from non-orientable structures to oriented ones.

An orientation is always related with an order because the former establishes the basic dual pair $\{-1, 1\}$ (spin down-spin up) from which to deduce the line $\mathbb{Z}$ of integers with its two-ways (or two-values) orientation. This last fact, in turn, may be equivalently related with the distinction between clockwise and anticlockwise rotations[42] (Hildebrand & Tromba, 1996; Riehl, 2010).

On the other hand, from a physical viewpoint, the occurrence of the distinction between clockwise and counterclockwise rotations may be induced, for example, by symmetry breaking of *chirality* as, for instance, induced by a *chiral anomaly*, on its turn due to a $\mathbb{Z}_2$-symmetry breaking (Bandyopadhyay 2003, Ch. 6, Sect. 6.3.2). On the other hand, chirality plays a very important role in physics, chemistry and, above all, in biology (Flügel, 2011; Riehl, 2010), where many works assume that, at a certain point in the early Earth's history, physical and/or chemical processes have triggered symmetry breaking phenomena, which occurred in an inanimate environment and allowed the initiation of life processes; therefore, a strong mirror symmetry breaking phenomenon (i.e., basically, an inversion symmetry breaking), springing out from a relatively modest asymmetry in mutual (auto)catalytic activity (in which D-enantiomers more likely catalyze other D-enantiomers than L-enantiomers, while L-enantiomers preferentially catalyze their L-brothers and sisters), is put at the early bases of the origin of life (Kafri et al., 2010).

Furthermore, fluctuations are known to promote changing in the nature of phase transitions or even destroy long-range order. It has been observed as well that fluctuations may induce symmetry breaking transitions in systems where such symmetry breaking would not have occurred in its absence. Studying autocatalytic production of chiral enantiomers from achiral reactants in reaction-diffusion systems whose mean field steady state is chiral symmetric, has shown that spatiotemporal fluctuations induce a novel chiral ordering and sharp phase transitions. This implies that an arbitrary perturbation from the chiral symmetric fixed point generated by the slightest stereo-preference, will remain as is (i.e., unamplified) and will not give rise to a global chiral symmetry breaking. In short, it has been identified a new role for fluctuations in generating a symmetry broken state in systems which are perfectly symmetric in the absence of fluctuations.

This phenomenon has been illustrated in the context of autocatalytic reaction-diffusion systems, where spatiotemporal fluctuations drive chemical systems to a chiral symmetry broken steady state (Gayathri & Rao, 2007). Indeed, just in relation to our model based on hysteresis (Iurato & Khrennikov, 2015), there are many physics studies in which chiral symmetry breaking, hence breakdown of inversion symmetry, in the charge-density wave[43] transition of certain materials (like $NbSe_3$), gives rise to drastic hysteresis effects (Hsu et al., 2013; Ong & Monceau, 1977; Van Wezel & Littlewood, 2010). Moreover, there are also important relations between chirality and hysteresis in biology (Kovacs, 1989).

Therefore, a chirality symmetry breaking, which is a phenomenon contemplated by biology, might induce just those hysteresis phenomena involved in the model exposed in (Iurato & Khrennikov, 2015), and both however inducing an ordering. Anyway, the effects of the occurrence of both chirality and hysteresis, are independent of each other as, for instance, shown by superconductivity phenomenology. Therefore, the effects entailed by both chiral and hysteresis symmetry breaking phenomena are independent of each other, so that both orders of effects are possible and equally probable to occur together. Moreover, also curvature effects may induce chirality symmetry breaking (Sloika et al., 2014). There are also interesting relations between breakdown of chiral symmetry and oscillatory chemical reactions (*chiral oscillations*) (Stich et al., 2013).

However, from an epistemological viewpoint, the proper quantitative and numerical methods of experimental physics clearly fail in probing unconscious structure, due to its basic non-directly observable nature as usually meant in natural sciences. At most, we are able to handle qualitative methods of mathematics to try to descry, even indirectly, what typical formal features human unconscious may have. From this standpoint, since topological structures are the most innate ones (Sossinsky, 2000; Zeeman, 1961), we are inclined to think that, just qualitatively, the unconscious structure of human psyche might be formally identified suitably through topological methods and its applications. Here, we have begun to outline some very basic considerations of this type as regard unconscious structure, starting from an original revisiting of Freudian thought by Jacques Lacan, the first thinker who has majorly looked at the formal aspects of psychoanalysis. Lacan tells us that unconscious has mainly a non-orientable feature, a qualitative formal trait owned by non-orientable manifolds, hence a $\mathbb{Z}_2$-symmetry.

The other higher psychic functions, from preconscious zones to consciousness, as formally characterized by other mathematical structures worked out upon the basic topological ones, seem therefore to spring out from a kind of breaking of this symmetry, so giving rise to an orientation, hence the basic dual pair $\{-1,1\}$ from which to deduce $\mathbb{Z}$ thought as an ordered algebraic system. We have called into question the breaking of chirality, which is one of the most typical phenomena occurring in biology of human evolution, trying to coherently implement it into a wider framework which also includes a previous possible model of human psyche based on hysteresis phenomena, reformulated in the formal language of *p*-adic analysis (Iurato & Khrennikov, 2015). However, just to mention a few words, besides *p*-adic analysis, a promising wider formal system might be that of *surreal numbers* system which comprises, besides *p*-adic numbers, also *hyperreal numbers* which, as we have briefly mentioned in the previous Chapter 6, may be useful to account for (time) aspects of consciousness (as regard its real numbers part) in its indissoluble links with unconscious and its unavoidable influences (as regard its hyperreal numbers part[44]). So, *surreal numbers* system[45] seems to be perhaps the most promising formal system able to globally describe the overall human psyche functioning, even if none attempt has been until now done towards this direction.

REFERENCES

Ageno, M. (1962). Le radiazioni e i loro effetti. Torino, Italy: Paolo Boringhieri Editore.

Alling, N. G. (1987). *Foundations of analysis over surreal number fields*. Amsterdam: North-Holland Publishing Company.

Arieti, S. (1974). Interpretazione della schizofrenia. Milano, Italy: Giangiacomo Feltrinelli Editore.

Arieti, S. (1976). Creatività. La sintesi magica. Roma, Italy: Il Pensiero Scientifico Editore.

Atiyah, M. F., & Macdonald, I. G. (1969). Introduction to Commutative Algebra. Reading, MA: Addison-Wesley Publishing Company, Inc.

Bajnok, B. (2013). *An Invitation to Abstract Mathematics*. New York, NY: Springer-Verlag, Inc. doi:10.1007/978-1-4614-6636-9

Balzarotti, R. (Ed.). (1972). Cahiers pour l'Analyse. Scritti scelti di analisi e teoria della scienza, a cura del Centro Ricerche 2. Torino, Italy: Editore Boringhieri.

Bandyopadhyay, P. (2003). *Geometry, Topology and Quantum Field Theory*. Dordrecht, The Netherlands: Springer Science & Business Media, B.V. doi:10.1007/978-94-017-1697-0

Bara, B. G. (1990). Scienza Cognitiva. Torino, Italy: Bollati Boringhieri editore.

Barone, F. (1965). Logica Formale e Logica Trascendentale (Vols. 1-2). Torino, Italy: Edizioni di «Filosofia».

Blumenthal, P., & Tyvaert, J.-E. (Eds.). (2003). *La cognition dans le temps. Etudes cognitives dans le champ historique des langues et des textes*. Tübingen, Germany: Max Niemeyer Verlag. doi:10.1515/9783110949490

Bria, P. (1981). Introduzione. Pensiero, mondo e problemi di fondazione. In *L'inconscio come insiemi infiniti. Saggio sulla bi-logica* (pp. xix–cxi). Torino, Italy: Giulio Einaudi editore.

Bucci, W. (1985). Dual coding: A cognitive model for psychoanalytic research. *Journal of the American Psychoanalytic Association, 33*(3), 571–607. doi:10.1177/000306518503300305 PMID:4056301

Bucci, W. (1987). *The dual code model and the interpretation of dreams*. New York, NY: Derner Institute – Adelphi University.

Bucci, W. (1997). *Psychoanalysis and Cognitive Science*. New York, NY: The Guilford Press.

CA (Collectif d'Auteurs). (1975). *La Psychanalyse*. Paris: Editions Le Livre De Poche.

Capa, R. L., Duval, C. Z., Blaison, D., & Giersch, A. (2014). Patients with schizophrenia selectively impaired in temporal order judgments. *Schizophrenia Research, 156*(1), 51–55. doi:10.1016/j.schres.2014.04.001 PMID:24768441

Carruccio, E. (1971). Mondi della Logica. Bologna, Italy: Nicola Zanichelli Editore.

Casari, E. (1972). Questioni di Filosofia della Matematica. Milano, Italy: Giangiacomo Feltrinelli Editore.

Chang, C.-C., & Keisler, H. J. (1973). Model Theory. Amsterdam: North-Holland Publishing Company, Inc.

Chemama, R., & Vandermersch, B. (Eds.). (1998). Dictionnaire de la Psychanalyse. Paris: Larousse-Bordas.

Choquet-Bruhat, Y., De Witt-Morette, C., & Dillard-Bleick, M. (1982). *Analysis, Manifolds and Physics* (Revised Edition). Amsterdam: North-Holland Publishing Company.

Ciompi, L. (1988). *The Psyche and Schizophrenia. The Bond between Affect and Logic*. Cambridge, MA: Harvard University Press.

Ciompi, L. (1991). Affects as central organising and integrating factors. A new psychosocial/biological model of the psyche. *The British Journal of Psychiatry, 159*(1), 97–105. doi:10.1192/bjp.159.1.97 PMID:1888986

Ciompi, L. (1994a). Affect logic. An integrative model of the psyche and its relations to schizophrenia. *The British Journal of Psychiatry. Supplement, 23*, 51–55. PMID:8037901

Ciompi, L. (1994b). Logica affettiva. Una ricerca sulla schizofrenia. Milano, Italy: Giangiacomo Feltrinelli Editore.

Ciompi, L. (1997). The concept of affect logic. An integrative psycho-socio-biological approach to understanding and treatment of schizophrenia. *Psychiatry, 60*(2), 158–170. doi:10.1080/00332747.1997.11024795 PMID:9257355

Ciompi, L. (1998). Is schizophrenia an affective disease? The hypothesis of affect-logic and its implications for psychopathology. In Emotions in psychopathology. Theory and research. Oxford, UK: Oxford University Press.

Ciompi, L. (1999). An affect-centred model of the psyche and its consequences for a new understanding of nonlinear psychodynamics. In Dynamics, synergetics, autonomous agents. Nonlinear system approach to cognitive psychology and cognitive science. Singapore: World Scientific Publishing.

Ciompi, L. (2000). Un modèle énergétique non linéaire de la psyché et ses applications. Confrontations psychiatriques, 33-63.

Ciompi, L. (2001). I fondamenti emozionali del pensiero. Roma, Italy: CIC-Edizioni Internazionali.

Ciompi, L. (2003). Reflections on the role of emotions in consciousness and subjectivity, from the perspective of affect logic. *Consciousness and Emotion, 4*(2), 181–196. doi:10.1075/ce.4.2.03cio

Ciompi, L. (2015). The key role of emotions in the schizophrenia puzzle. *Schizophrenia Bulletin, 41*(2), 318–322. doi:10.1093/schbul/sbu158 PMID:25481397

Ciompi, L., & Baatz, M. (2005). Do mental processes have a fractal structure? The hypothesis of affect-logic. In Fractals in Biology and Medicine (Vol. 4). Basel, Switzerland: Birkhäuser.

Ciompi, L., & Baatz, M. (2008). The energetic dimension of emotions. An evolution-based computer simulation with far-reaching implications. *Theoretical Biology, 3*(1), 42–50. doi:10.1162/biot.2008.3.1.42

Ciompi, L., & Hoffmann, H. (2004). *Soteria Berne*. An innovative milieutherapeutic approach to acute schizophrenia based on the concept of affect-logic. *World Psychiatry; Official Journal of the World Psychiatric Association (WPA), 3*, 140–146. PMID:16633478

Ciompi, L., & Panksepp, J. (2005). Energetic effects of emotions on cognitions. Complementary psychobiological and psychosocial findings. In Consciousness & Emotion. Agency, conscious choice, and selective perception. Amsterdam: John Benjamins Publishing Company. doi:10.1075/ceb.1.04cio

Codignola, E. (1977). Il vero e il falso. Saggio sulla struttura logica dell'interpretazione psicoanalitica. Torino, Italy: Editore Boringhieri.

Cohn, P. M. (1965). Universal Algebra. New York, NY: Harper & Row Publishers.

Contarello, A., & Mazzara, B. M. (2002). Le dimensioni sociali dei processi psicologici. Roma-Bari, Italy: Laterza Editori.

Conti, L., & Principe, S. (1989). Salute mentale e società. Fondamenti di psichiatria sociale. Padova, Italy: Piccin Nuova Libraria.

Cuche, D. (2004). La notion de culture dans les sciences sociales. Paris: Éditions La Découverte.

Culioli, A. (2014). L'arco e la freccia. Scritti scelti. Bologna, Italy: Società editrice il Mulino.

D'Urso, V., & Trentin, R. (1998). Introduzione alla psicologia delle emozioni. Roma-Bari, Italy: Editori Laterza.

Dalla Chiara Scabia, M. L. (1973). Istanti e individui nelle logiche temporali. *Rivista di Filosofia, 64*(2), 95–122.

Dalla Chiara Scabia, M. L. (1974). Logica. Milano, Italy: ISEDI – Istituto Editoriale Internazionale.

De Glas, M., & Desclés, J.-P. (1996). Du temps linguistique comme idéalisation d'un temps phenomenal. Intellectica – Le sémiotique/Logiques et sciences cognitives, 23(2), 159-192.

De Glas, M., & Plane, J.-L. (2005). *Une approche formelle de la typicité. Cahiers du CREA, N. 20.* Paris: Imprimerie de l'École Polytechnique.

Dehaene, S., & Brannon, E. (Eds.). (2011). *Space, Time and Number in the Brain. Searching for the Foundations of Mathematical Thought.* Amsterdam: Elsevier, Inc.

Desclés, J.-P. (2009). Relations spatiales et mouvements dans l'espace. Paper Presetned au le Séminaire GéoTAL, Rennes, France.

Devlin, K. (2006). *The Math Instinct: Why You're a Mathematical Genius (Along with Lobsters, Birds, Cats, and Dogs).* New York, NY: Thunder's Mouth Press.

Durst, M. (1988). Dialettica e bi-logica. L'epistemologia di Ignacio Matte Blanco. Milano, Italy: Marzorati Editore.

Endert, E. (2006). Über die emotionale Dimension sozialer Prozesse. Die Theorie der Affektlogik am Beispiel der Rechtsextremismus und Nationalsozialismusforschung (Theorie und Methode). Konstanz, Germany: UVK Verlagsgesellschaft mbH.

Figà-Talamanca Dore, L. (1978). La logica dell'inconscio. Roma, Italy: Edizioni Studium-Vita Nova.

Flügel, R. M. (2011). *Chirality and Life. A Short Introduction to the Early Phases of Chemical Evolution.* Berlin: Springer-Verlag.

Freud, S. (1938). Abriß der psychoanalyse. Academic Press.

Freud, S. (1957). *The Standard Edition of Complete Psychological Works of Sigmund Freud* (Vols. 1-24; J. Strachey, Trans. & Ed.). London, UK: The Hogarth Press.

Freud, S. (1979). La scissione dell'Io nel processo di difesa (1938). In Opere di Sigmund Freud, 1930-1938. L'uomo Mosè e la religione monoteistica e altri scritti (vol. 11). Torino, Italy: Editore Boringhieri.

Friedman, M., & Tomšič, S. (Eds.). (2016). Psychoanalysis: Topological Perspectives. New Conceptions of Geometry and Space in Freud and Lacan. Bielefeld, Germany: transcript Verlag. doi:10.14361/9783839434406

Galimberti, U. (2006). Dizionario di psicologia. Torino, Italy: UTET Libreria.

Gayathri, V. I., & Rao, M. (2007). Fluctuation-induced chiral symmetry breaking in autocatalytic reactiondiffusion systems. *Europhysics Letters*, *80*(2), 28001. doi:10.1209/0295-5075/80/28001

Green, A. (1993). Le travail du négatif. Paris: Les Éditions du Minuit.

Hadamard, J. (1945). The Psychology of Invention in the Mathematical Field. Princeton, NJ: Princeton University Press.

Hampe, B., & Grady, J. E. (Eds.). (2005). *From Perception to Meaning. Image Schemas in Cognitive Linguistics*. Berlin: Walter de Gruyter GmbH and Co. doi:10.1515/9783110197532

Hickmann, M., & Robert, S. (Eds.). (2006). *Space in Languages – Linguistic Systems and Cognitive Categories*. Amsterdam: John Benjamins Publishing Company. doi:10.1075/tsl.66

Hildebrand, S., & Tromba, A. (1996). *The Parsimonious Universe. Shape and Form in the Natural World*. New York, NY: Springer-Verlag, Inc. doi:10.1007/978-1-4612-2424-2

Hirsch, M. W. (1976). *Differential Topology*. New York, NY: Springer-Verlag, Inc. doi:10.1007/978-1-4684-9449-5

Hodges, W. (1977). *Logic. An Introduction to Elementary Logic*. Harmondsworth, UK: Penguin Books, Ltd.

Hsu, P.-J., Mauerer, T., Vogt, M., Yang, J. J., Seok Oh, Y., Cheong, S.-W., & Wu, W. et al. (2013). Hysteretic melting transition of a soliton lattice in a commensurate charge modulation. *Physical Review Letters*, *111*(26), 266401–266406. doi:10.1103/PhysRevLett.111.266401 PMID:24483807

Iurato, G. (2013a). Mathematical thought in the light of Matte Blanco work. *Philosophy of Mathematics Education Journal*, 27.

Iurato, G. (2013b). Σύμβολου: An attempt toward the early origins, Part 1. *Language & Psychoanalysis*, *2*(2), 77–120. doi:10.7565/landp.2013.008

Iurato, G. (2013c). Σύμβολου: An attempt toward the early origins, Part 2. *Language & Psychoanalysis*, *2*(2), 121–160. doi:10.7565/landp.2013.009

Iurato, G. (2014a). At the grounding of computational psychoanalysis: on the work of Ignacio Matte Blanco. A general history of culture overview of Matte Blanco bilogic in comparison. In *Proceedings of the 2014 IEEE 13th International Conference on Cognitive Informatics and Cognitive Computing.* Los Alamitos, CA: IEEE Computer Society Press.

Iurato, G. (2014b). The dawning of computational psychoanalysis. A proposal for some first elementary formalization attempts. *International Journal of Cognitive Informatics and Natural Intelligence, 8*(4), 50–82. doi:10.4018/ijcini.2014100104

Iurato, G. (2014c). *Alcune considerazioni critiche sul simbolismo.* Preprint No. hal-00980828 version 1. Available at HAL archives-ouvertes.

Iurato, G. (2015a). A Brief Comparison of the Unconscious as Seen by Jung and Lévi-Strauss. *Anthropology of Consciousness, 26*(1), 60–107. doi:10.1111/anoc.12032

Iurato, G. (2015b). Fetishism in Marketing. Some First Elementary Psychoanalytic Anthropology Remarks. In Business Management: A Practioners' Guide. Delhi: International Research Publication House.

Iurato, G. (2015c). A simple phylogenetic remark about certain human blood pressure values. *Journal of Biochemistry International, 2*(4), 162–165.

Iurato, G. (2016a). *A psychoanalytic enquiry on symbolic function.* Preprint No. hal-01361264 version 3. Available at HAL archives-ouvertes.

Iurato, G. (2016b). *A view of LSA/ESA in Computational Psychoanalysis.* Preprint No. hal-01353999 version 1. Available at HAL archives-ouvertes.

Iurato, G. (2016c). On Jacques Lacan Psychosis Theory and ERPs Analysis. *Journal of Biology and Nature, 5*(4), 234–240.

Iurato, G. (2016d). Some Comments on the Historical Role of *Fetishism* in Economic Anthropology. *Journal of Global Economics, Management and Business Research, 7*(1), 61–82.

Iurato, G. (2016e). *The origins of symbol. An historical-critical study of symbolic function, according to the phylo-ontogenetic perspective, as arising from the comparison of certain patterns of neuro-psychological sciences.* Paper Presented at the Satellite Event "On the edge of disciplines", Florence, Italy.

Iurato, G. (2016f). Two simple questions regarding cultural anthropology. *Journal of Global Research in Education and Social Science, 8*(1), 10–15.

Iurato, G. (2017a). An Essay in Denotational Mathematics. Rigorous Results. In Encyclopedia of Information Science and Technology (4th ed.). Hershey, PA: IGI Global.

Iurato, G. (2017b). Un raffronto critico fra la teoria platonica delle idee ed il paradosso di Kripke-Wittgenstein. In Platone nel pensiero moderno e contemporaneo (vol. 11). Villasanta (MB), Italy: Limina Mentis Edizioni.

Iurato, G. (2017c). *Rigidity of the Generalized Other, narrowness of the Otherness and demodernization, in the framework of symbolic interactionism. Ideology and Political Journal.* (in press)

Iurato, G., & Khrennikov, A. Yu. (2015). Hysteresis model of unconscious-conscious interconnection: Exploring dynamics on *m*-adic trees. *p-Adic Numbers, Ultrametric Analysis and Applications*, *7*(4), 312–321. doi:10.1134/S2070046615040068

Iurato, G., & Khrennikov, A. Yu. (2017). On the topological structure of a mathematical model of human unconscious. *p-Adic Numbers, Ultrametric Analysis and Applications*, *9*(1), 78–81. doi:10.1134/S2070046617010071

Iurato, G., Khrennikov, A. Yu., & Murtagh, F. (2016). Formal Foundations for the Origins of Human Consciousness. *p-Adic Numbers, Ultrametric Analysis and Applications*, *8*(4), 249–279. doi:10.1134/S2070046616040014

Johnson-Laird, P., & Bara, B. (1984). Syllogistic Inference. *Cognition*, *16*(1), 1–61. doi:10.1016/0010-0277(84)90035-0 PMID:6540648

Kafri, R., Markovitch, O., & Lancet, D. (2010). Spontaneous chiral symmetry breaking in early molecular networks. *Biology Direct*, *5*(38), 1–13. PMID:20507625

Kastner, R. E. (2011). The broken symmetry of time. In Quantum Retrocausation: Theory and Experiment. Melville, NY: AIP Publications. doi:10.1063/1.3663714

Khrennikov, A. Yu. (1991). *p*-Adic quantum mechanics with *p*-adic valued functions. *Journal of Mathematical Physics*, *32*(4), 932–937. doi:10.1063/1.529353

Khrennikov, A. Yu. (1998). Human subconscious as the *p*-adic dynamical system. *Journal of Theoretical Biology*, *193*(2), 179–196. doi:10.1006/jtbi.1997.0604 PMID:9714931

Khrennikov, A. Yu. (2002). *Classical and quantum mental models and Freud's theory of unconscious mind. Series in Mathematical Modelling in Physics, Enginnering and Cognitive Sciences* (Vol. 1). Växjö, Sweden: Växjö University Press.

Khrennikov, A. Yu. (2007). Toward an adequate mathematical model of mental space: Conscious/unconscious dynamics on *m*-adic trees. *Bio Systems*, *90*(3), 656–675. doi:10.1016/j.biosystems.2007.02.004 PMID:17400367

Kovacs, A. L. (1989). Degeneracy and asymmetry in Biology. In *Nonlinear Structures in Physical Systems. Pattern Formation, Chaos, and Waves. Proceedings of the 2nd Woodward Conference*. New York, NY: Springer-Verlag, Inc.

La Mantia, F. (2017). From Topology to Quasi-Topology. The Complexity of the Notional Domain. In Lecture Notes in Morphogenesis: Vol. 5. Language in Complexity. The Emerging Meaning. Springer International Publishing.

Lagache, D. (1961). *La psychanalyse et la structure de la personnalité*. Paper Presented au Colloquium International de Royaumont, Paris, France.

Lagache, D. (1965). Le modèle psychanalytique de la personnalité. In *La Folle du Logis. La psychanalyse comme science exacte* (pp. 159–183). Paris: PUF-Presses Universitaires de France.

Laplanche, J. (2000). Problematiche II. Castrazione. Simbolizzazioni. Bari-Roma, Italy: La Biblioteca.

Laplanche, J. (2001). *L'inconscio e l'Es*. Bari-Roma, Italy: La Biblioteca.

Laplanche, J. (2007). *L'après-coup*. Bari-Roma, Italy: La Biblioteca.

Laplanche, J. (2008). Sexuale. La sessualità allargata nel senso freudiano. Bari-Roma, Italy: La Biblioteca.

Laplanche, J., & Pontalis, J.-B. (1967). Vocabulaire de la psychoanalyse. Paris: Presses Universitaires de France.

Laplanche, J., & Pontalis, J.-B. (1988). Fantasma originario, fantasmi delle origini, origini del fantasma. Bologna, Italy: Società editrice il Mulino.

Lawson, M. K. (2005). Constructing ordered groupoids. *Cahiers de Topologie et Géométrie Différentielle Catégoriques*, *46*(2), 123–138.

Lévi-Strauss, C. (1975). *Razza e storia e altri studi di antropologia*. Torino, Italy: Giulio Einaudi editore.

Lévi-Strauss, C. (2008). Sull'Italia. In Claude Lévi-Strauss fotografato da Marion Kalter. Napoli, Italy: Electa Napoli.

Lévi-Strauss, C., & Eribon, D. (1988). De près et de loin. Paris: Éditions Odile Jacob.

Lis, A., Mazzeschi, C., & Zennaro, A. (2007). *La psicoanalisi. Un percorso concettuale fra tradizione e attualità (2nd ed.)*. Roma, Italy: Carocci editore.

Lis, A., Zennaro, A., Mazzeschi, C., Salcuni, S., & Parolin, L. (2003). *Breve dizionario di psicoanalisi*. Roma, Italy: Carocci editore.

Lolli, G. (1991). Introduzione alla logica formale. Bologna, Italy: Società editrice il Mulino.

Lolli, G. (2005). QED – Fenomenologia della dimostrazione. Torino, Italy: Bollati Boringhieri editore.

Matte Blanco, I. (1975). The Unconscious as Infinite Sets. An Essay in Bi-Logic. London, UK: Gerald Duckworth & Company, Ltd.

Matte Blanco, I. (1988). *Thinking, Feeling, and Being. Clinical Reflections of the Fundamental Antinomy on Human Beings and World*. London, UK: Routledge.

Maurin, K. (1997). *The Riemann Legacy. Riemann Ideas in Mathematics and Physics*. Dordrecht, The Netherlands: Kluwer Academic Publishers. doi:10.1007/978-94-015-8939-0

Mordant, I. (1990). Using attribute-memories to resolve a contradiction in the work of Matte Blanco. *The International Review of Psycho-Analysis*, *17*, 475–480.

Ong, N. P., & Monceau, P. (1977). Anomalous transport properties of a linear-chain metal $NbSe_3$. *Physical Review B: Condensed Matter and Materials Physics*, *16*(8), 3443–3455. doi:10.1103/PhysRevB.16.3443

Petrini, P., Casadei, A., & Chiricozzi, F. (Eds.). (2011). Trasgressione, violazione, perversione. Eziopatogenesi, diagnosi e terapia. Milano, Italy: FrancoAngeli.

Petrini, P., Renzi, A., Casadei, A., & Mandese, A. (2013). Dizionario di psicoanalisi. Con elementi di psichiatria, psicodinamica e psicologia dinamica. Milano, Italy: FrancoAngeli.

Pini, B. (1967). Primo Corso di Algebra. Bologna, Italy: CLUEB Editrice.

Piras, F., Piras, F., Ciullo, V., Danese, E., Caltagirone, C. & Spalletta, G. (2013). Time dysperception perspective for acquired brain injury. *Frontiers in Neurology*, *4*, 217-226.

Pizzi, C. (Ed.). (1974). La logica del tempo. Torino, Italy: Bollati Boringhieri Editore.

Poggi, S. (1977). I sistemi dell'esperienza. Bologna, Italy: Società editrice il Mulino.

Poincaré, H. J. (1958). The Value of Science. New York, NY: Dover Publications, Inc.

Pollo, M. (2016). La nostalgia dell'uroboros. Contributi a una psicologia culturale delle nuove addiction. Milano, Italy: FrancoAngeli.

Quan, P. M. (1969). *Introduction a la géométrie des variétés différentiables*. Paris: Éditions Dunod.

Radicati, L. A. (1985). Remarks on the early developments of the notion of symmetry breaking. In *Symmetries in Physics (1600-1980). Proceedings of the 1st International Meeting on the History of Scientific Ideas*. Barcelona: Servei de Publicacions, Bellaterra.

Rayner, E. (1995). *Unconscious Logic. An Introduction to Matte Blanco's Bi-Logic and its Uses*. New York, NY: Routledge.

Rayner, E. (1998). Foreword. In *The Unconscious as Infinite Sets. An Essay in Bi-Logic* (pp. xviii–xxiv). London, UK: Karnac Books, Ltd.

Redondi, P. (2007). Storie del tempo. Roma-Bari, Italy: Editori Laterza.

Reisig, W. (1988). Temporal Logic and Causality in Concurrent Systems. In R. H. Voght (Ed.), Lecture Notes in Computer Science: Vol. 335. *CONCURRENCY 1988* (pp. 121–139). Berlin: Springer-Verlag. doi:10.1007/3-540-50403-6_37

Rentz, J. (Ed.). (2002). Lecture Notes in Computer Science: Vol. 2293. Qualitative spatial reasoning with topological information. Berlin: Springer-Verlag. doi:10.1007/3-540-70736-0

Rescher, N., & Urquhart, A. (1971). Temporal Logic. Wien, Austria: Springer-Verlag GmbH. doi:10.1007/978-3-7091-7664-1

Reverberi, C., Pischedda, D., Burigo, M., & Cherubini, P. (2012). Deduction without awareness. *Acta Psychologica*, *139*(1), 244–253. doi:10.1016/j.actpsy.2011.09.011 PMID:22019058

Riehl, J. P. (2010). *Mirror-Image Asymmetry. An Introduction to the Origin and Consequences of Chirality*. Hoboken, NJ: John Wiley & Sons, Inc. doi:10.1002/9780470588888

Rose, J. R. (Ed.). (2011). *Mapping Psychic Reality. Triangulation, Communication, and Insight. Psychoanalytic Ideas*. London, UK: Karnac Books, Ltd.

Rossi, R., De Fazio, F., Gatti, U., & Rocco, G. (2008, Feb.). Perizie e consulenze psichiatriche su Diamante Stefano, Stevanin Gianfranco, Bilancia Donato, Panini Giorgio. *POL.it – The Italian On Line Psychiatric Magazine*.

Roudinesco, E. (1997). Jacques Lacan. Outline of a life, history of a system of thought. Oxford, UK: Polity Press.

Rycroft, C. (1968a). A critical dictionary of psychoanalysis. London, UK: Thomas Nelson & Sons, Ltd.

Rycroft, C. (1968b). Imagination and reality. Psychoanalytical essays 1951–1961. London, UK: The Hogarth Press, Ltd.

Sabbadini, A. (1979). Introduzione. In Il tempo in psicoanalisi. Milano, Italy: Giangiacomo Feltrinelli Editore.

Sannella, D., & Tarlecki, A. (2012). *Foundations of Algebraic Specification and Formal Software Development. Monographs in Theoretical Computer Science. An EATCS Series.* Berlin: Springer-Verlag. doi:10.1007/978-3-642-17336-3

Sasso, G. (1982). Le strutture anagrammatiche della poesia. Milano, Italy: Giangiacomo Feltrinelli Editore.

Sasso, G. (1993). La mente intralinguistica. L'instabilità del segno: anagrammi e parole dentro le parole. Genova, Italy: Marietti Editore.

Sasso, G. (1999). Struttura dell'oggetto e della rappresentazione. Roma, Italy: Casa Editrice Astrolabio-Ubaldini Editore.

Sasso, G. (2005). Psicoanalisi e Neuroscienze. Roma, Italy: Casa Editrice Astrolabio-Ubaldini Editore.

Sasso, G. (2011). La nascita della coscienza. Roma, Italy: Casa Editrice Astrolabio-Ubaldini Editore.

Scabini, E. (1973). Ideazione e psicoanalisi. Milano, Italy: Giangiacomo Feltrinelli Editore.

Schmitt, A., Hasan, A., Gruber, O., & Falkai, P. (2011). Schizophrenia as a disorder of disconnectivity. *European Archives of Psychiatry and Clinical Neuroscience, 261*(2), S150–S154. doi:10.1007/s00406-011-0242-2 PMID:21866371

Semi, A. A. (2003). La coscienza in psicoanalisi. Milano, Italy: Raffaello Cortina Editore.

Semi, A.A. (Ed.). (1989). *Trattato di Psicoanalisi* (Vols. 1-2). Milano, Italy: Raffaello Cortina Editore.

Singh, S., & Ribet, K. A. (1998). La dimostrazione dell'ultimo teorema di Fermat. *Le Scienze, 353*(70), 74–79.

Skillicorn, D. (1994). *Foundations of Parallel Programming.* Cambridge, UK: Cambridge University Press. doi:10.1017/CBO9780511526626

Sloika, M. I., Kravchuk, V. P., Sheka, D. D., & Gaididei, Y. (2014). Curvature induced chirality symmetry breaking in vortex core switching phenomena. *Applied Physics Letters, 104*(25), 252403. doi:10.1063/1.4884957

Sluzki, C. E., & Ransom, D. C. (1979). Il doppio legame: la genesi dell'approccio relazionale allo studio della famiglia. Roma, Italy: Casa Editrice Astrolabio-Ubaldini Editore.

Smirnov, V. N. (1970). *La transaction fétichique. Nouvelle Revue de Psychoanalyse, 2.*

Solms, M., & Turnbull, O. (2003). The Brain and the Inner World. An Introduction to the Neuroscience of Subjective Experience. New York, NY: Other Press, LLC.

Sossinsky, A. (2000). Nodi. Genesi di una teoria matematica. Torino, Italy: Bollati Boringhieri editore.

Souriau, J. M. (1964). *Géométrie et relativité*. Paris: Éditions Hermann.

Sparsø, J., & Furber, S. (Eds.). (2001). Principles of Asynchronous Circuit Design. A Systems Perspective. Dordrecht, The Netherlands: Springer-Science + Business Media, B.V. doi:10.1007/978-1-4757-3385-3

Spitz, R. A. (1957). No and yes. On the genesis of human communication. New York, NY: International University Press, Inc.

Stanghellini, G., Ballerini, M., Presenza, S., Mancini, M., Raballo, A., Blasi, S., & Cutting, J. (2016). Psychopathology of lived time: Abnormal time experience in persons with schizophrenia. *Schizophrenia Bulletin. The Journal of Psychoses and Related Disorders, 42*(1), 45–55.

Steedman, M. (2000). *Surface Structure and Interpretation*. Boston, MA: The MIT Press.

Stich, M., Blanco, C., & Hochberg, D. (2013). Chiral and chemical oscillations in a simple dimerization model. *Physical Chemistry Chemical Physics, 15*(1), 255–261. doi:10.1039/C2CP42620J PMID:23064600

Stirling, C. (2001). *Modal and Temporal Properties of Processes*. New York, NY: Springer-Verlag. doi:10.1007/978-1-4757-3550-5

Strocchi, F. (1981). Classification of Solutions of Non-Linear Hyperbolic Equations and Non-Linear Elliptic Problems. In Topics in Functional Analysis 1980-81. Pisa, Italy: Pubblicazioni della Scuola Normale Superiore.

Strocchi, F. (1999). Symmetry Breaking in Classical Systems and Nonlinear Functional Analysis. Pisa, Italy: Pubblicazioni della Scuola Normale Superiore.

Strocchi, F. (2000). Simmetrie e rotture di simmetrie in fisica. Corso di orientamento preuniversitario, Arezzo, Italy.

Strocchi, F. (2008). *Symmetry Breaking* (2nd ed.). Berlin: Springer-Verlag. doi:10.1007/978-3-540-73593-9

Strocchi, F. (2012). *Spontaneous Symmetry Breaking in Quantum Systems. A review for Scholarpedia*. Preprint arXiv:1201.5459v1 [physics.hist-ph]

Tabossi, P. (2009). Rappresentazione, 1. In *Psiche. Dizionario storico di psicologia, psichiatria, psicoanalisi, neuroscienze* (Vol. 2, pp. 914–919). Torino, Italy: Giulio Einaudi editore.

Tanenbaum, A. S., & Bos, H. (2015). *Modern Operating Systems* (4th ed.). Essex, UK: Pearson Education Limited.

Target, M., & Fonagy, P. (2002). The role of the father and child development. In The Importance of Fathers. A Psychoanalytic Re-evaluation. London, UK: Routledge.

Thom, R. (1972). Symmetries Gained and Lost. In: *Broken Symmetries. Proceedings of the 3rd GIFT International Seminar in Theoretical Physics organized by the Spanish-Inter-University Group in Theoretical Physics*. Saragoza, Spain: Scientific Information Service, Ltd.

Thom, R. (1980). *Stabilità strutturale e morfogenesi. Saggio di una teoria generale dei modelli*. Torino, Italy: Giulio Einaudi editore.

Thom, R. (1985). *Modelli matematici della morfogenesi*. Torino, Italy: Giulio Einaudi editore.

Thomä, H., & Kächele, H. (1989). *Psychoanalytic Practice* (Vols. 1-2). Berlin: Springer-Verlag.

Tokhi, M. O., Hossain, M. A., & Shaheed, M. H. (2003). *Parallel Computing for Real-time Signal Processing and Control*. London, UK: Springer-Verlag London. doi:10.1007/978-1-4471-0087-4

Toraldo di Francia, G. (1976). *L'indagine del mondo fisico*. Torino, Italy: Giulio Einaudi editore.

Vaccarino, G. (2006). Scienza e semantica. Milano, Italy: Edizioni Melquiades.

Vallortigara, G., & Panciera, N. (2014). Cervelli che contano. Milano, Italy: Adelphi Edizioni.

Van Wezel, J., & Littlewood, P. (2010). Chiral symmetry breaking and charge order. *Physics*, *3*, 87. doi:10.1103/Physics.3.87

Vattimo, G., Ferraris, M., & Marconi, D. (Eds.). (1993). Enciclopedia Garzanti di Filosofia. Milano, Italy: Garzanti Editore.

Venema, Y. (2001). Temporal Logic. In The Blackwell Guide to Philosophical Logic. Oxford, UK: Basil Blackwell Publishers.

Verdiglione, A. (1977). Matematica dell'inconscio. In Feticismo, linguaggio, afasia, matematica dell'inconscio. Venezia, Italy: Marsilio Editori.

Vicario, G. B. (1997). Il tempo in psicologia. *Le Scienze*, *30*(347), 43–51.

Vicario, G. B. (2005). Il tempo. Saggio di psicologia sperimentale. Bologna, Italy: Società editrice il Mulino.

Viret, J. (2012). Topological Approach of Jungian Psychology. *Acta Biotheoretica*, *58*(2), 233–245. PMID:20658172

Voevodin, V. V. (1992). Mathematical Foundations of Parallel Computing. Singapore: World Scientific Publishing. doi:10.1142/1533

von Karger, B. (1995). An algebraic approach to temporal logic. In *Lecture Notes on Computer Science: Vol. 915. Proceedings of the Sixth International Joint Conference on Theory and Practice of Software Development (TAPSOFT '95)*. Berlin: Springer-Verlag. doi:10.1007/3-540-59293-8_198

von Karger, B. (2002). Temporal Algebra. In Lecture Notes in Computer Science: Vol. 2297. Algebraic and Coalgebraic Methods in the Mathematics of Program Construction. Berlin: Springer-Verlag. doi:10.1007/3-540-47797-7_9

Von Scheve, C., & Salmela, M. (Eds.). (2014). *Collective Emotions. Perspectives from Psychology, Philosophy, and Sociology*. Oxford, UK: Oxford University Press.

Von Wright, G. H. (1969). *Time, Change and Contradiction*. Cambridge, UK: Cambridge University Press.

Wang, Y. (2008). On Concept Algebra: A Denotational Mathematical Structure for Knowledge and Software Modeling. *International Journal of Cognitive Informatics and Natural Intelligence*, *2*(2), 1–19. doi:10.4018/jcini.2008040101

Wang, Y. (2010). A Sociopsychological Perspective on Collective Intelligence in Metaheuristic Computing. *International Journal of Applied Metaheuristic Computing*, *1*(1), 110–128. doi:10.4018/jamc.2010102606

Wang, Y., Wang, Y., Patel, S., & Patel, D. (2006). A Layered Reference Model of the Brain. *IEEE Transactions on Systems, Man and Cybernetics. Part C, Applications and Reviews*, *36*(2), 124–133. doi:10.1109/TSMCC.2006.871126

Wang, Y., Zadeh, L. A., Widrow, B., Howard, N., Wood, S., Patel, S., & Zhang, D. et al. (2017). Abstract Intelligence: Embodying and Enabling Cognitive Systems by Mathematical Engineering. *International Journal of Cognitive Informatics and Natural Intelligence*, *11*(1), 1–22. doi:10.4018/IJCINI.2017010101

Wang, Y., Zhang, D., & Kinsner, D. (Eds.). (2011). *Advances in Cognitive Informatics and Cognitive Computing*. Berlin: Springer-Verlag.

Watanabe, S. (1969). *Knowing and Guessing. A Quantitative Study of Inference and Information*. New York, NY: John Wiley & Sons, Inc.

Watzlawick, P., Beavin, J. H., & Jackson, D. D. (1967). Pragmatics of Human Communication. A Study of Interactional Patterns, Pathologies, and Paradoxes. New York, NY: W.W. Norton & Company.

Weinstein, A. (1996). Groupoids: Unifying Internal and External Symmetry. *Notices of the American Mathematical Society*, *43*(7), 744–752.

Westphal, B. (2007). La Géocritique. Réel, fiction, espace. Paris: Les Éditions de Minuit.

Wetterich, C. (2005). Spontaneous Symmetry Breaking Origins for the Difference Between Time and Space. *Physical Review Letters*, *94*(1), 011692–011696. doi:10.1103/PhysRevLett.94.011602 PMID:15698063

White, D. R., & Jorion, P. (1996). Kinship networks and discrete structure theory: Applications and implications. *Social Networks*, *18*(3), 267–314. doi:10.1016/0378-8733(95)00277-4

Whitebook, J. (1995). *Perversion and Utopia. A Study in Psychoanalysis and Critical Theory*. Cambridge, MA: The MIT Press.

Whitrow, G. J. (1988). *Time in History. Views of Time from Prehistory to the Present Day*. Oxford, UK: Oxford University Press.

Wimmer, M., & Ciompi, L. (1996). Evolutionary aspects of affective-cognitive interactions in the light of Ciompi's concept of "affect-logic". *Evolution & Cognition*, *2*, 37–58.

Yang, J., Kanazawa, S., Yamaguchi, M. K., & Kuriki, I. (2016). Cortical response to categorical colour perception in infants investigated by near-infrared spectroscopy. *Proceedings of the National Academy of Sciences of the United States of America*, *113*(9), 2370-2375.

Zadeh, L. A. (1965). Fuzzy Sets. *Information and Control*, *8*(3), 338–353. doi:10.1016/S0019-9958(65)90241-X

Zadeh, L. A. (1968). Fuzzy Algorithms. *Information and Control*, *12*(2), 94–102. doi:10.1016/S0019-9958(68)90211-8

Zadeh, L. A. (1988). Fuzzy Logic. *Computer*, *21*(4), 83–93. doi:10.1109/2.53

Zapparoli, G. C. (1970). La perversione logica. I rapporti tra sessualità e pensiero nella tradizione psicoanalitica. Milano, Italy: Franco Angeli Editore.

Zeeman, E. C. (1961). The topology of the brain and the visual perception. In *Topology of 3-manifolds and related topics. Proceedings of the University of Georgia Institute*. Academic Press.

Zeeman, E. C. (1976a). Brain Modelling. In *Lecture Notes in Mathematics: Vol. 525. Structural Stability. The Theory of Catastrophes, and Applications in the Sciences. Proceedings of the Conference*. Berlin: Springer-Verlag.

Zeeman, E. C. (1976b). Catastrophe Theory. *Scientific American*, *234*(April), 65–83. doi:10.1038/scientificamerican0476-65

Zeh, H. D. (2007). *The Physical Basis of the Direction of Time* (5th ed.). Berlin: Springer-Verlag.

Zentall, T. R. (2013). Animals represent the past and the future. *Evolutionary Psychology*, *11*(3), 573–590. doi:10.1177/147470491301100307 PMID:24027784

Zepf, S., & Gerlach, A. (2012). Commentary on Kernbergs suicide prevention for psychoanalytic institutes and societies. *Journal of the American Psychoanalytic Association*, *61*(4), 771–786. doi:10.1177/0003065113496634 PMID:23918822

Živaljević, R. T. (2006). *Groupoids in combinatorics – applications of a theory of local symmetries*. Preprint arXiv: math/0605508v1 [math.CO]

ENDNOTES

[1]   In passing, we also recall the valuable work of Imre Hermann (of 1920s) on the relationships between logic and psychoanalysis; cf. (Hermann, 1989).

[2]   Regarding a wider mathematical intuition (Devlin, 2006).

[3]   Here, in discussing about "either-or" and "both-and" logic operators, we have closely followed Eric Rayner (1995). Nevertheless, just in this regard, in what follows, we prefer to make reference to the original Freudian text of *The Interpretation of Dreams* (of 1900); however, all this will be further discussed explicitly in the next section.

[4]   See also (Codignola, 1977).

[5]   See also what has been said in the Introduction (to this work).

[6]   We could consider the notion of *object* or *thing* in the wider philosophical sense. In psychoanalysis, then, a restricted sense is assumed mainly correlated to the post-Freudian notion of *object relation*. See (Laplanche & Pontalis,1967) and (Galimberti, 2006).

[7]   See Section (C), *Means of Representation in the Dream*, of Chapter VI. As recalled in the previous section, it seems yet that Eric Rayner (1995) has given a 'reverse' reading of these Freudian considerations. Here, instead, we prefer to follow directly Freud, lying close and faithful to his text.

8   This is also in agreement with the latest views on unconscious, mainly seen as a (semantic) system giving rise symbols and meanings (Conrotto, 2014).

9   Just for the nature of the unconscious realm.

10   See, above all, (Matte Blanco 1975, Part III, Ch. VIII, Sect. 6) and the clinical case there considered. In general, by tradition, formal logic has had to do with a static world, not dynamic, so that every disjunction has been often meant in its exclusive form (Pizzi 1974, N. 4, p. 259). However, we may suppose too that a bland version of the disjunction $\lor$ (*vel*) may hold in the unconscious realm, above all in proximity of the preconscious. This is supported by what is said in (Conrotto 2014, p. 34), where the author argues that, in the unconscious place, a *vel-vel* logic may hold, while an *aut-aut* logic (as well as, a "neither … nor" logic – see Chapter 5, Section 5.3. and Chapter 2, Incipit of Section 2.8.) seems rather to characterize conscious activity; on the other hand, just this disjunctive logical work is mainly due to the action of either disavowal and splitting processes (in general, the set of all psychic operations linked to negative – cf. (Green, 1993)), which roughly entails the passage from the "yes and no" to "neither … nor" (Semi 1988-89, Vol. I, Ch. 6, Sect. 6.1.6, p. 416), logical operation, this latter, which relies at the basic foundation of discriminative thought, hence consciousness. Thus, though disavowal and splitting processes are mainly unconscious, yet we should consider them (in general, the set of all psychic operators linked to negative – cf. (Green, 1993)) as primary psychic mechanisms underlying, in some way, consciousness thought. So, we might roughly say that, in going on from deep unconscious through preconscious towards consciousness, we have a basic change of the logical connectives which are, in sequence, the conjunction $\land$ (i.e., the logical copula, which is closely related, after Lacan, just with the sexual copula, which is symbolized by the phallus as main signifier – cf. (Chemama & Vandermersch 2004, p. 118)) hence the disjunction $\lor$ (*vel*), to reach disjunction $\lor$ (*aut*), according to first Freud's topography of human psyche. Anyhow, strangely enough, looking at the main logical operators acting on unconscious, it seems therefore that there is a common logical basis for either unconscious and conscious activity, in that it seems that, just in both, the "neither … nor" logical principle does hold (see Chapter 2, Incipit of Section 2.8). For all these reasons, we deem that the set of all the defence operations correlated with negation and the negative (Conrotto, 2009; Green, 1993), first of all, the disavowal, are crucial for the whole functioning of human psyche, in that they are at the early basis of the formation of the logical operators $\lor$ in both their forms *vel* and *aut*, as variously dislocated and acting on the three main zones of human psyche, according to the first Freudian topography. All this, in turn, will play a crucial role in the rising of the basic non-contradiction principle, upon which a deep critical analysis has been done by Pietro Bria (1981) in the light of Matte Blanco's work.

11   Cf. (Conrotto, 2009).

12   Here, we follow what Freud says in his work *The Unconscious* (of 1915). See also (Verdiglione 1977, p. 9).

13   We shall speak indifferently of *presentation* or *representation*, considering them as synonymous, although there is a net conceptual distinction between them, as briefly recalled in a footnote of Chapter 4, Section 4.3.1.1.

14   This because we may consider too all the other defence mechanisms introduced by other analysts, like Anna Freud, Melanie Klein, Daniel Lagache (with his working-off mechanisms), and so on (Laplanche & Pontalis, 1967).

[15] *En passant*, just in this point, we may descry useful links with the notion of unconscious according to Claude Lévi-Strauss as briefly mentioned in (Lévi-Strauss & Eribon 1988, pp. 161-163).

[16] Of such a theoretical system, herein we give only a few hints, possibly reserving us to study in-depth the thought of this Author.

[17] We recall that the above mentioned, primary unconscious logic mechanisms were deduced by Freud mainly by two main his clinical cases, precisely the so-called case of the *Rat Man* (of 1909) and that of the *Wolf Man* (of 1914-1915), thank to which Freud reached to the discovery of the neurotic-obsessive disorders (CA, 1975). Besides, from the *Rat Man* paper, Freud established some analogies between the neurosis mechanisms and the primitive mind (CA, 1975).

[18] According to this principle, the unconscious treats a single thing (individual, object, concept, etc.) as it were a member, or an element, of a class which contains other members or elements; in turn, this class is considered as a subclass of another more general class, and so forth.

[19] According to which, in the realm of unconscious, every relation is symmetric (just in the mathematical sense of this term).

[20] Nevertheless, Emanuele Severino has rightly criticized Matte Blanco to have founded an ontology from knowledge experiences and psychic sensations (Durst 1988, p. 49; Severino 2008, Ch. XVIII).

[21] This point of view has been also supported by the theses of one of the foremost scholars of schizophrenia, Silvano Arieti. In fact, on the basis of his remarkable studies on this disorder as exposed in (Arieti, 1974), he subsequently distinguished (Arieti, 1976) three main processes with which the human being thinks: a *primary* process, which is prelogic, with a paleosymbolic function, primitive, non-abstract and with individual referents; a *secondary* process which regulates the logical-formal models of the vigil thought; and, a *tertiary* process which is the result of the interaction of the first two, and culminating into the creative intuition. The first two of these three Arieti's mental processes roughly correspond to the Freudian ones. About further possible relationships between Matte Blanco's ideas and the Arieti's ones, see also (Scabini, 1973).

[22] $source \xrightarrow{\quad object \quad} drive\ destination\ true$ [respect., *false*] means that $\wp$ has [respect., does not have] the property expressed by the statement Ξ, supposing (*axiom of extensionality*), furthermore, that every element of $\neg$ has, or does not have, such a property $\wedge$, or else, that one is however able to clearly distinguish between these two basic possibilities.

[23] Mainly due, seen the previous footnote, to a wrong or mixed, confused use of the basic logical operators $\vee$ (in its *vel* and *aut* forms) and $\wp = (\Xi, \neg, \wedge)$, as described in the previous section, because of the occurrence of unconscious interferences, not elaborated enough by secondary process, which hinders a discerned use of these elementary binary logical operators.

[24] In (Iurato, 2015a), we have taken into account some similar structural aspects of the yet distinct notions of unconscious according to Claude Lévi-Strauss and Carl G. Jung. The first author considers a notion of unconscious meant as the place from which originates every form of possible thought, that is to say, it is considered as the 'place of every science', whereas the second author considers a collective unconscious that assures, amongst other, the existence of opposite pairs of *dialectic* type and not of *polar* type, inasmuch as the former reach a (Hegelian dialectic) conclusive synthesis from the initial dual elements of the opposite pair, whereas the latter keep, into a dynamical tensional state, such opposite elements without reaching any possible their synthesis (Durst, 1988; Galimberti, 2006). Thus, it would also be possible trying to explain the above syncretism character by means of the well-known *Pseudo-Scoto Law* (Carruccio, 1971) according to which,

if a proposition and its negation (like in an opposite pair) contemporaneously subsist as true, then it follows that every other possible proposition is also true, so reaching to touch clear syncretism characters.

25   In this regard, it is useful taking into account the distinction between *logical* and *mathematical processes* according to Hermann Weyl (Casari 1972, Ch. XII, Sect. 1), the second ones corresponding to the creative processes here considered. From the various, reciprocal interaction between these two basic *generative principles* of an arbitrary mathematical construction, it follows a remarkable thought's line of the modern Mathematical Philosophy.

26   See the case of the creative proof of the *last Fermat's theorem* by Andrew J. Wiles, with the collaboration of Richard Taylor, whose first form (given in the celebrated 1993 Cambridge lectures) had needed for some corrections (worked out by Wiles on the previous Cambridge version, just with the aid of his former PhD student, Richard Taylor) in order that it were correct (last 1995 proof). Nevertheless, this detracts nothing to the exceptional first creative work by Wiles and to the subsequent as much creative corrections by Wiles and Taylor. In this regard, see the interesting survey paper (Singh & Ribet, 1998) and references therein.

27   These Hadamard's suppositions seem having been recently confirmed too by some last neuroscience researches (mainly, by the neurocognitive researches on consciousness due to Stanislas Dehaene and co-workers) according to which there are fundamental and typical functional inter-correlations (*neural circuits*) between the frontal and prefrontal areas (mainly deputed to the rational and abstract thought) and the occipital-parietal ones (mainly deputed to elaboration of visual stimuli and images), considered to be at the basis of consciousness acts and of symbolic formation (Dehaene & Brannon, 2011).

28   In that these terms, above all at electronic level, are often used according to a sense not always corresponding directly to their etymological one.

29   Indeed, it is well-known that there exist many schizophrenic patients who excel in higher cognitive tasks (e.g., to solve mathematical problems).

30   See also (D'Urso & Trentin, 1998).

31   See also (Cuche, 2004).

32   In that, we refer to behaviorist trend of psychology.

33   See above all (Conrotto 2014, Ch. 1, Sect. 3, *C)*, p. 34), about a general, interesting discussion on the possible logics of either unconscious realm and conscious domain.

34   Due to life instincts (negentropy producing), against death instincts (entropy producing); cf. (Conti & Principe 1989, Part V, Ch. 3) and references therein.

35   In (Wetterich, 2005), an interesting proposal on the asymmetry between space and time is put forward. To be precise, the author argues on the radical idea according to which the difference between time and space arises as a consequence of the "dynamics" of the theory rather than being put in by hand. More precisely, he discusses a model where the "classical" or "microscopic" action does not make any difference between time and space. The time-space asymmetry is rather generated only as a property of the ground state property rather than being assumed a priori, which can be associated with spontaneous symmetry breaking. In special and general relativity time and space are treated in a unified framework. Nevertheless, a basic asymmetry between these two concepts persists, related to the signature of the metric. It is at the root of much of the complexity of physics and the universe.

[36]   To be precise, the first one, briefly recalled in Chapter 2, Section 2.3.2.

[37]   In this regard, it has to be considered too some new and interesting topological ideas in computational linguistics which have been recently introduced, among which is just that of *thick boundary* (Culioli, 2014; De Glas & Desclés, 1996; La Mantia, 2014, 2017), which we may borrow in this our discussion about the first Freudian topography. In particular, we refer to a concept similar to that of boundary (or border) of a *locological space* (an extension of the notion of ordinary topological space) in the *quasi-topological* sense of Michel De Glas and Jean-Pierre Desclés (De Glas & Desclés 1996, Sect. 3.2.; De Glas & Plane 2005, Ch. 2; Desclés, 2009).

[38]   Cf. (De Glas & Plane, 2005, Ch. 2; Desclés, 2009).

[39]   These zones may be also imaged as circular zones concentrically arranged, from the central internal nucleus $\wp = \left(\Xi, \neg, \vee \right)$ towards, gradually and radially, the most external circular annular stratum, i.e., the consciousness $\vee$. In this view, the first Freudian topography T_I is therefore suitably formalized better by the quasi-topological spaces (also said *locological spaces*) due to Michel De Glas and Jean-Pierre Desclés (see later).

[40]   See also (Blumenthal & Tyvaert, 2003; Hampe & Grady, 2005; Hickmann & Robert, 2006; Rentz, 2002; Steedman, 2000).

[41]   See also (Conrotto 2014, Ch. 1, Sect. 3, *C*), p. 34).

[42]   This may be also related with the possible occurrence of linear time from inversion symmetry breaking of cyclic time, as mentioned in Chapter 4, Section 4.3.

[43]   A periodic electronic charge modulation, often called *charge-density wave* (CDW), is roughly an ordering physical phenomenon which is accompanied by a distortion of the underlying lattice with the same periodicity, and therefore often linked with the so-called *Jahn-Teller effect* (Hsu et al., 2013).

[44]   This agrees with the fact that hyperreal numbers, in that infinitesimal means, are mentally unrecognizable, differently from real numbers.

[45]   Cf. (Alling, 1987) and (Bajnok 2013, Ch. 24).

Compilation of References

Abbagnano, N. (1998). Dizionario di Filosofia (3rd ed.). Torino, Italy: UTET Libreria.

Abbagnano, N. (1998). Dizionario di Filosofia. Terza edizione aggiornata e ampliata da Giovanni Fornero. Torino, Italy: UTET Libreria.

Abbagnano, N. (1998). *Dizionario di Filosofia. Terza edizione aggiornata e ampliata da Giovanni Fornero.* Torino, Italy: UTET Libreria.

Agazzi, E. (1976). Criteri epistemologici fondamentali delle discipline psicologiche. In *Problemi epistemologici della psicologia.* Milano, Italy: Vita e Pensiero.

Agazzi, E. (1979). Analogicità del concetto di scienza. Il problema del rigore e dell'oggettività nelle scienze umane. In *Epistemologia e scienze umane.* Milano, Italy: Editore Massimo.

Agazzi, E. (1985a). La questione del realismo scientifico. In *Scienza e filosofia. Saggi in onore di Ludovico Geymonat.* Milano, Italy: Garzanti.

Agazzi, E. (1985b). Riflessioni epistemologiche sul tema "Segno, simbolo, sintomo, comunicazione. Implicanze e convergenze fra filosofia, psichiatria e psicoanalisi". In *Segno, simbolo, sintomo, comunicazione. Implicanze e convergenze fra filosofia, psichiatria e psicoanalisi.* Genova, Italy: Edizioni Esagraph.

Agazzi, E. (2014). *Scientific Objectivity and its Contexts.* New York, NY: Springer-Verlag, Inc.; . doi:10.1007/978-3-319-04660-0

Ageno, M. (1962). Le radiazioni e i loro effetti. Torino, Italy: Paolo Boringhieri Editore.

Akhtar, S., & O'Neil, M. K. (Eds.). (2011). *On Freud's 'negation'. In The International Psychoanalytic Association – Contemporary Freud. Turning points & critical issues.* London, UK: Karnac Books, Ltd.

Albertson, M. O., & Collins, K. L. (1996). Symmetry Breaking in Graphs. *The Electronic Journal of Combinatorics, 3*(1), R18.

Albeverio, S., Kloeden, P. E., & Khrennikov, A. Yu. (1998). Human Memory as a *p*-Adic Dynamic System. *Theoretical and Mathematical Physics, 117*(3), 1414–1422. doi:10.1007/BF02557180

Alexander, F. (1948). Fundamentals of psychoanalysis. New York, NY: W.W. Norton & Company, Inc.

Alling, N. G. (1987). *Foundations of analysis over surreal number fields.* Amsterdam: North-Holland Publishing Company.

Allman, J. M. (2000). *Evolving Brains.* New York, NY: Scientific American Library. A division of HPHLP.

Ammaniti, M., & Gallese, V. (2014). La nascita dell'intersoggettività. Lo sviluppo del Sé fra psicodinamica e neurobiologia. Milano, Italy: Raffaello Cortina Editore.

Andersson, O. (1962). Studies on the Prehistory of Psychoanalysis. Stockholm, Sweden: Scandinavian University Books.

Andersson, O. (1962). Studies on the Prehistory of Psychoanalysis. Stockholm: Scandinavian University Books.

Arieti, S. (1974). Interpretazione della schizofrenia. Milano, Italy: Giangiacomo Feltrinelli Editore.

Arieti, S. (1976). Creatività. La sintesi magica. Roma, Italy: Il Pensiero Scientifico Editore.

Atiyah, M. F., & Macdonald, I. G. (1969). Introduction to Commutative Algebra. Reading, MA: Addison-Wesley Publishing Company, Inc.

Atkinson, R. L., Atkinson, R. C., Smith, E. E., Bem, D. J., & Nolen-Hoeksema, S. (Eds.). (1996). *Hilgard's Introduction to Psychology* (12th ed.). Orlando, FL: Harcourt Brace.

Atmanspacher, H. (2014a). Psychophysical correlations, synchronicity and meaning. *The Journal of Analytical Psychology, 59*(2), 181–188. doi:10.1111/1468-5922.12068 PMID:24673273

Atmanspacher, H. (2014b). Levels of unconsciousness and their formal structures. *The Journal of Analytical Psychology, 59*(3), 385–390. doi:10.1111/1468-5922.12087 PMID:24919630

Baars, B. J. (1993). How does a serial, integrated and very limited stream of consciousness emerge from a nervous system that is mostly unconscious, distributed, parallel and of enormous capacity? In *Experimental and Theoretical Studies of Consciousness, Novartis Foundation Symposium No.* 174. New York, NY: John Wiley & Sons, Ltd.

Badiou, A. (1982). Théorie du sujet. Paris: Éditions du Seuil.

Badiou, A. (1982). *Théorie du sujet.* Paris: Éditions du Seuil.

Bajnok, B. (2013). *An Invitation to Abstract Mathematics.* New York, NY: Springer-Verlag, Inc. doi:10.1007/978-1-4614-6636-9

Balsamo, M. (2009). Ripetizione, coazione a ripetere, destino. In *Psiche. Dizionario storico di psicologia, psichiatria, psicoanalisi, neuroscienze* (Vol. 2, pp. 957–962). Torino, Italy: Giulio Einaudi editore.

Balzarotti, R. (Ed.). (1972). Cahiers pour l'Analyse. Scritti scelti di analisi e teoria della scienza, a cura del Centro Ricerche 2. Torino, Italy: Editore Boringhieri.

Balzarotti, R. (Ed.). (1972). *Cahiers pour l'Analyse. Scritti scelti di analisi e teoria della scienza, a cura del Centro Ricerche 2.* Torino, Italy: Editore Boringhieri.

Bandyopadhyay, P. (2003). *Geometry, Topology and Quantum Field Theory.* Dordrecht, The Netherlands: Springer Science & Business Media, B.V. doi:10.1007/978-94-017-1697-0

Bara, B. G. (1990). Scienza Cognitiva. Torino, Italy: Bollati Boringhieri editore.

Barone, F. (1965). Logica Formale e Logica Trascendentale (2nd ed.; Vols. 1-2). Torino, Italy: Edizioni di «Filosofia».

Barratt, B. B. (2016). *Psychoanalysis and the Postmodern Impulse. Knowing and Being since Freud's Psychology.* New York, NY: Routledge.

Barthe, G., Capretta, V., & Pons, O. (2003). Setoids in type theory. *Journal of Functional Programming, 13*(2), 261–293. doi:10.1017/S0956796802004501

Bassin, F. V. (1972). *Il problema dell'inconscio. Sulle forme inconsce dell'attività nervosa superiore.* Roma, Italy: Editori Riuniti.

Bastide, R. (Ed.). (1966). Usi e significati del termine struttura nelle scienze umane e sociali. Milano, Italy: Giangiacomo Feltrinelli Editore.

Bateson, G. (1972). *Steps to an Ecology of Mind. Collected Essays in Anthropology, Psychiatry, Evolution, and Epistemology.* San Francisco, CA: Chandler Publishing Company.

Battacchi, M. W. (2006). *La conoscenza psicologia. Il metodo, l'oggetto, la ricerca.* Roma, Italy: Carocci editore.

Beals, R. L., & Hoijer, H. (1965). An Introduction to Anthropology (2nd ed.). New York, NY: The MacMillan Company.

Bell, D. (2016). *Superintelligence and World-Views.* Surrey, UK: Grosvenor House Publishing, Ltd.

Ben-Ari, M. (1993). Mathematical Logic for Computer Science. Hemel Hempstead, UK: Prentice Hall International, Ltd.

Benvenuto, S. (2005). *Perversioni. Sessualità, etica, psicoanalisi.* Torino, Italy: Bollati Boringhieri editore.

Bernardi, S., Dei, F., & Meloni, P. (Eds.). (2011). La materia del quotidiano. Per un'antropologia degli oggetti ordinari. Pisa, Italy: Pacini Editore.

Berwick, R. C., & Chomsky, N. (2016). Why Only Us. Language and Evolution. Cambridge, MA: The MIT Press. doi:10.7551/mitpress/9780262034241.001.0001

Bezoari, M., & Palombi, F. (Eds.). (2003). Epistemologia e Psicoanalisi: attualità di un confronto. Milano, Italy: Edizioni del Centro Milanese di Psicoanalisi.

Bezoari, M., & Palombi, F. (Eds.). (2003). *Epistemologia e Psicoanalisi: attualità di un confronto. Quaderni del Centro Milanese di Psicoanalisi.* Milano, Italy: Edizioni del Centro Milanese di Psicoanalisi.

Bianchi, P. (2014). La psicoanalisi e la politica delle singolarità. In L'inconscio è la politica. Milano-Udine, Italy: Mimesis Edizioni.

Bianchi, P. (2014). La psicoanalisi e la politica delle singolarità. In *L'inconscio è la politica.* Milano-Udine, Italy: Mimesis Edizioni.

Bleecker, D. (1981). *Gauge Theory and Variational Principles.* Reading, MA: Addison-Wesley Publishing Company, Inc.

Blumenthal, P., & Tyvaert, J.-E. (Eds.). (2003). *La cognition dans le temps. Etudes cognitives dans le champ historique des langues et des textes.* Tübingen, Germany: Max Niemeyer Verlag. doi:10.1515/9783110949490

Boczar, A., Teixeira da Costa Salles, A. C., Pimenta, A. C., Drawin, C. R., Eliana Rodrigues Pereira, E., Brandão Lemos Morais, M., & Beaudette Drummond, S. (2001). Psychoanalysis and Epistemology: The Interrelation Between Clinical Work, Culture and Metapsychology. *International Forum of Psychoanalysis, 10*(2), 145–150.

Bokanowski, T., & Lewkowicz, S. (Eds.). (2009). *On Freud's 'splitting of the ego in the process of defence'. In The International Psychoanalytic Association – Contemporary Freud: Turning points & critical issues.* London, UK: Karnac Books, Ltd.

Boniolo, G., & Vidali, P. (1999). Filosofia della scienza. Milano, Italy: Bruno Mondadori.

Bonnota, O., de Montalembertb, M., Kermarrecc, S., Botbold, M., Waltere, M., & Coulon, N. (2011). Are impairments of time perception in schizophrenia a neglected phenomenon? *Journal of Physiology, Paris, 105*(4-6), 164–169. doi:10.1016/j.jphysparis.2011.07.006 PMID:21803155

Borceux, F. (1989). Fasci, logica e topoi. Quaderni dell'Unione Matematica Italiana, N. 34. Bologna, Italy: Pitagora Editrice.

Borgogno, F., Luchetti, A., & Marino Coe, L. (Eds.). (2017). Il pensiero psicoanalitico italiano. Maestri, idee e tendenze dagli anni '20 ad oggi. Milano, Italy: FrancoAngeli.

Borisyuk, R., Borisyuk, G., & Kazanovich, Y. (1998). Synchronization of neural activity and information processing. *Behavioral and Brain Sciences*, *21*(6), 833. doi:10.1017/S0140525X98241768

Bottiroli, G. (2006). *Che cos'è la teoria della letteratura. Fondamenti e problemi.* Torino, Italy: Giulio Einaudi editore.

Boudon, R. (1970). *Strutturalismo e scienze umane.* Torino, Italy: Giulio Einaudi editore.

Bourguignon, A., & Manus, A. (1980). Hallucination nègative, déni de la réalité et scotomisation. *Annales Médico-Psychologiques*, *138*(2), 129–153. PMID:6992686

Brading, K., & Castellani, E. (2013). Symmetry and Symmetry Breaking. In The Stanford Encyclopedia of Philosophy. Stanford University Press.

Bremer, M. (2005). *An Introduction to Paraconsistent Logics.* Frankfurt am Main, Germany: Peter Lang Publishing.

Bria, P., & Caroppo, E. (2006). Antropologia culturale e psicopatologia. Roma, Italy: Alpes Italia.

Bria, P. (1981). Introduzione. Pensiero, mondo e problemi di fondazione. In *L'inconscio come insiemi infiniti. Saggio sulla bi-logica* (pp. xix–cxi). Torino, Italy: Giulio Einaudi editore.

Bria, P., & Caroppo, E. (2006). *Antropologia culturale e psicopatologia.* Roma, Italy: Alpes Italia.

Britton, R. (2000). Belief and Imagination. Explorations in Psychoanalysis. London, UK: Routledge.

Britton, R. (2003). Sex, Death and the Super-Ego. Experiences in Psychoanalysis. London, UK: Karnac Books, Ltd.

Britton, R., Blundell, S., & Youell, B. (2014). Il lato mancante. L'assenza del padre nel mondo interno. Milano, Italy: Mimesis edizioni.

Brown, R. (1987). From Groups to Groupoids: A Brief Survey. *Bulletin of the London Mathematical Society*, *19*(2), 113–134. doi:10.1112/blms/19.2.113

Bruhat, F. (1961). Algèbres de Lie et groupes de Lie (2nd ed.). Recife, Brazil: Instituto de Física e Matemática, Universidade do Recife.

Bruner, E. (Ed.). (2015). Human Paleoneurology. Springer International Publishing. doi:10.1007/978-3-319-08500-5

Bucci, W. (1985). Dual coding: A cognitive model for psychoanalytic research. *Journal of the American Psychoanalytic Association*, *33*(3), 571–607. doi:10.1177/000306518503300305 PMID:4056301

Bucci, W. (1987). *The dual code model and the interpretation of dreams.* New York, NY: Derner Institute – Adelphi University.

Bucci, W. (1997). *Psychoanalysis and Cognitive Science.* New York, NY: The Guilford Press.

Buneci, M. R. (2003). Topologies on the graph of the equivalence relation associated to a groupoid. *Proceedings of the International Conference on Theory and Applications of Mathematics and Informatics*, 23-32.

Buzzoni, M. (1989). Operazionismo ed ermeneutica. Saggio sullo statuto epistemologico della psicoanalisi. Milano, Italy: Franco Angeli Editore.

CA (Collectif d'Auteurs). (1975). *La Psychanalyse.* Paris: Editions Le Livre De Poche.

Cabras, A., Canarutto, D., Kolář, I., & Modugno, M. (1991). Structured Bundles. Bologna, Italy: Pitagora Editrice.

Capa, R. L., Duval, C. Z., Blaison, D., & Giersch, A. (2014). Patients with schizophrenia selectively impaired in temporal order judgments. *Schizophrenia Research*, *156*(1), 51–55. doi:10.1016/j.schres.2014.04.001 PMID:24768441

Capozza, D. (1977). Il differenziale semantico. Problemi teorici e metrici. Bologna, Italy: Casa Editrice Pàtron.

Capozzi, M., & Cellucci, C. (2014). *Breve storia della logica. Dall'Umanesimo al primo Novecento*. Morrisville, NC: Lulu Press, Inc.

Carlson, L. (1999). *Consumption and Depression in Gertrude Stein, Louis Zukofsky, and Ezra Pound*. London, UK: Palgrave-MacMillan Press, Ltd. doi:10.1057/9780230379947

Carotenuto, A. (1982). Discorso sulla metapsicologia. Torino, Italy: Bollati Boringhieri Editore.

Carotenuto, A. (1991). Trattato di psicologia della personalità e delle differenze individuali. Milano, Italy: Raffaello Cortina Editore.

Carotenuto, A. (Ed.). (1992). Dizionario Bompiani degli Psicologi Contemporanei. Milano, Italy: Bompiani.

Carotenuto, A. (Ed.). (1992). *Dizionario Bompiani degli Psicologi Contemporanei*. Milano, Italy: Bompiani.

Carruccio, E. (1971). Mondi della Logica. Bologna, Italy: Nicola Zanichelli Editore.

Carvalho, R. (2014). Synchronicity, the infinite unrepressed, dissociation and the interpersonal. *The Journal of Analytical Psychology*, *59*(3), 366–384. doi:10.1111/1468-5922.12085 PMID:24919629

Casari, E. (1972). Questioni di Filosofia della Matematica. Milano, Italy: Giangiacomo Feltrinelli Editore.

Cassinari, F. (2005). Tempo e identità. La dinamica di legittimazione nella storia e nel mito. Milano, Italy: FrancoAngeli.

Castiglioni, M., & Corradini, A. (2011). *Modelli epistemologici in psicologia. Dalla psicoanalisi al costruzionismo*. Roma, Italy: Carocci editore.

Cazeneuve, J. (1971). Sociologie du rite. Paris: PUF-Presses Universitaires de France.

Cellucci, C., & Ippoliti, E. (2016). Logica. Milano, Italy: EGEA Editore.

Cellucci, C., & Ippoliti, E. (2016). *Logica*. Milano, Italy: EGEA Editore.

Ceylan, E. M., Dönmez, A., Ünsalver, B. A., & Evrensel, A. (2016). Neural synchronization as a hypothetical explanation of the psychoanalytic unconscious. *Consciousness and Cognition*, *40*, 34–44. doi:10.1016/j.concog.2015.12.011 PMID:26744848

Chang, C.-C., & Keisler, H. J. (1973). Model Theory. Amsterdam: North-Holland Publishing Company, Inc.

Chasseguet-Smirgel, J. (1975). L'idéal du moi. Paris: Éditeur Claude Tchou.

Chasseguet-Smirgel, J. (1985). Creativity and perversion. London, UK: Free Association Books, Ltd.

Chemama, R., & Vandermersch, B. (Eds.). (1998). Dictionnaire de la Psychanalyse. Paris: Larousse-Bordas.

Cherubini, P., Giaretta, P., & Mazzocco, A. (Eds.). (2000). Ragionamento: psicologia e logica. Firenze, Italy: Giunti Gruppo Editoriale.

Chialà, S., & Curi, U. (2016). La brama dell'avere. Trento, Italy: Casa editrice Il Margine.

Chianese, D. (2009). Costruzione, Ricostruzione, Interpretazione. In *Psiche. Dizionario storico di psicologia, psichiatria, psicoanalisi, neuroscienze* (Vol. 1, pp. 280–285). Torino, Italy: Giulio Einaudi editore.

Choquet-Bruhat, Y., De Witt-Morette, C., & Dillard-Bleick, M. (1982). *Analysis, Manifolds and Physics* (Revised Edition). Amsterdam: North-Holland Publishing Company.

Ciompi, L. (1994b). Logica affettiva. Una ricerca sulla schizofrenia. Milano, Italy: Giangiacomo Feltrinelli Editore.

Ciompi, L. (1998). Is schizophrenia an affective disease? The hypothesis of affect-logic and its implications for psychopathology. In Emotions in psychopathology. Theory and research. Oxford, UK: Oxford University Press.

Ciompi, L. (1999). An affect-centred model of the psyche and its consequences for a new understanding of nonlinear psychodynamics. In Dynamics, synergetics, autonomous agents. Nonlinear system approach to cognitive psychology and cognitive science. Singapore: World Scientific Publishing.

Ciompi, L. (2000). Un modèle énergétique non linéaire de la psyché et ses applications. Confrontations psychiatriques, 33-63.

Ciompi, L. (2001). I fondamenti emozionali del pensiero. Roma, Italy: CIC-Edizioni Internazionali.

Ciompi, L., & Baatz, M. (2005). Do mental processes have a fractal structure? The hypothesis of affect-logic. In Fractals in Biology and Medicine (Vol. 4). Basel, Switzerland: Birkhäuser.

Ciompi, L., & Panksepp, J. (2005). Energetic effects of emotions on cognitions. Complementary psychobiological and psychosocial findings. In Consciousness & Emotion. Agency, conscious choice, and selective perception. Amsterdam: John Benjamins Publishing Company. doi:10.1075/ceb.1.04cio

Ciompi, L. (1988). *The Psyche and Schizophrenia. The Bond between Affect and Logic.* Cambridge, MA: Harvard University Press.

Ciompi, L. (1991). Affects as central organising and integrating factors. A new psychosocial/biological model of the psyche. *The British Journal of Psychiatry, 159*(1), 97–105. doi:10.1192/bjp.159.1.97 PMID:1888986

Ciompi, L. (1994a). Affect logic. An integrative model of the psyche and its relations to schizophrenia. *The British Journal of Psychiatry. Supplement, 23*, 51–55. PMID:8037901

Ciompi, L. (1997). The concept of affect logic. An integrative psycho-socio-biological approach to understanding and treatment of schizophrenia. *Psychiatry, 60*(2), 158–170. doi:10.1080/00332747.1997.11024795 PMID:9257355

Ciompi, L. (2003). Reflections on the role of emotions in consciousness and subjectivity, from the perspective of affect logic. *Consciousness and Emotion, 4*(2), 181–196. doi:10.1075/ce.4.2.03cio

Ciompi, L. (2015). The key role of emotions in the schizophrenia puzzle. *Schizophrenia Bulletin, 41*(2), 318–322. doi:10.1093/schbul/sbu158 PMID:25481397

Ciompi, L., & Baatz, M. (2008). The energetic dimension of emotions. An evolution-based computer simulation with far-reaching implications. *Theoretical Biology, 3*(1), 42–50. doi:10.1162/biot.2008.3.1.42

Ciompi, L., & Hoffmann, H. (2004). *Soteria Berne.* An innovative milieutherapeutic approach to acute schizophrenia based on the concept of affect-logic. *World Psychiatry; Official Journal of the World Psychiatric Association (WPA), 3*, 140–146. PMID:16633478

Codignola, E. (1977). Il vero e il falso. Saggio sulla struttura logica dell'interpretazione psicoanalitica. Torino, Italy: Editore Boringhieri.

Codignola, E. (1977). *Il vero e il falso. Saggio sulla struttura logica dell'interpretazione psicoanalitica.* Torino, Italy: Editore Boringhieri.

Cohn, P. M. (1965). Universal Algebra. New York, NY: Harper & Row Publishers.

Conrotto, F. (2000). Tra il sapere e la cura. Un itinerario freudiano. Milano, Italy: FrancoAngeli.

Conrotto, F. (2010). Per una teoria psicoanalitica della conoscenza. Milano, Italy: FrancoAngeli.

Conrotto, F. (2014). Ripensare l'inconscio. Milano, Italy: FrancoAngeli.

Conrotto, F. (2009). Negazione. In *Psiche. Dizionario storico di psicologia, psichiatria, psicoanalisi, neuroscienze* (Vol. 2, pp. 728–730). Torino, Italy: Giulio Einaudi editore.

Contardi, R. (2010). La prova del labirinto. Processo di simbolizzazione e dinamica rappresentativa in psicoanalisi. Milano, Italy: FrancoAngeli.

Contarello, A., & Mazzara, B. M. (2002). Le dimensioni sociali dei processi psicologici. Roma-Bari, Italy: Laterza Editori.

Conte, M., & Gennaro, A. (Eds.). (1989). Inconscio e processi cognitivi. Bologna, Italy: Società editrice il Mulino.

Conti, L., & Principe, S. (1989). Salute mentale e società. Fondamenti di psichiatria sociale. Padova, Italy: Piccin Nuova Libraria.

Contri, G. (1972). Nozioni fondamentali nella teoria della struttura di Jacques Lacan. In Cahiers pour l'Analyse. Scritti scelti di analisi e teoria della scienza, a cura del Centro Ricerche 2. Torino, Italy: Editore Boringhieri, pp. 244-289.

Contri, G. (1972). Nozioni fondamentali nella teoria della struttura di Jacques Lacan. In Cahiers pour l'Analyse. Scritti scelti di analisi e teoria della scienza, a cura del Centro Ricerche 2. Torino, Italy: Editore Boringhieri.

Corradi Fiumara, G. (1980). Funzione simbolica e filosofia del linguaggio. Torino, Italy: Editore Boringhieri.

Corradi Fiumara, G. (1980). *Funzione simbolica e filosofia del linguaggio* [The symbolic function: Psychoanalysis and the philosophy of language]. Torino, Italy: Editore Boringhieri.

Cotter, D. (2003). *Joyce and the Perverse Ideal*. London, UK: Routledge.

CSFG – Centro di Studi Filosofici di Gallarate. (1977). Dizionario delle idee. Firenze, Italy: G.C. Sansoni Editore.

Cuche, D. (2004). La notion de culture dans les sciences sociales. Paris: Éditions La Découverte.

Culioli, A. (2014). L'arco e la freccia. Scritti scelti. Bologna, Italy: Società editrice il Mulino.

D'Urso, V., & Trentin, R. (1998). Introduzione alla psicologia delle emozioni. Roma-Bari, Italy: Editori Laterza.

D'Urso, V., & Trentin, R. (1998). *Introduzione alla psicologia delle emozioni*. Roma-Bari, Italy: Editori Laterza.

Dalla Chiara Scabia, M. L. (1974). Logica. Milano, Italy: ISEDI – Istituto Editoriale Internazionale.

Dalla Chiara Scabia, M. L. (1973). Istanti e individui nelle logiche temporali. *Rivista di Filosofia*, *64*(2), 95–122.

Damasio, A. (1994). Descartes' Error. Emotion, Reason, and the Human Brain. New York, NY: G.P. Putnam's Sons.

Damasio, A. (1994). *Descartes' Error. Emotion, Reason, and the Human Brain*. New York, NY: G.P. Putnam's Sons.

De Glas, M., & Desclés, J.-P. (1996). Du temps linguistique comme idéalisation d'un temps phenomenal. *Intellectica – Le sémiotique/Logiques et sciences cognitives, 23*(2), 159-192.

De Glas, M., & Plane, J.-L. (2005). *Une approche formelle de la typicité. Cahiers du CREA, N. 20*. Paris: Imprimerie de l'École Polytechnique.

De Masi, F. (2016). Which is the relevant superego for clinical analytic work? In F. Borgogno, A. Luchetti, & L. M. Coe (Eds.), *Reading Italian Psychoanalysis* (pp. 279–290). Oxfordshire, UK: Routledge.

De Mijolla, A., & De Mijolla Mellor, S. (Eds.). (1996). Psychanalyse. Paris: PUF-Presses Universitaires de France.

De Mijolla, A. (Ed.). (2005). *International Dictionary of Psychoanalysis* (Vol. 1–3). Farmington Hills, MI: Thomson Gale.

De Mijolla, A., & De Mijolla Mellor, S. (Eds.). (1996). *Psychanalyse*. Paris: PUF-Presses Universitaires de France.

De Pasquali, P. (2002). Figli che uccidono. Da Doretta Graneris a Erika & Omar. Soveria Mannelli (CZ), Italy: Rubbettino Editore.

De Pasquali, P. (2002). *Figli che uccidono. Da Doretta Graneris a Erika & Omar. Soveria Mannelli (CZ)*. Italy: Rubbettino Editore.

De Waelhens, A., & Ver Eecke, W. (2001). *Phenomenology and Lacan on Schizophrenia, after the Decade of the Brain*. Leuven, Belgium: Leuven University Press.

Deacon, T. W. (1997). *The Symbolic Species. The Coevolution of Language and the Brain*. New York, NY: W.W. Norton & Company.

Dehaene, S., & Brannon, E. (Eds.). (2011). *Space, Time and Number in the Brain. Searching for the Foundations of Mathematical Thought*. Amsterdam: Elsevier, Inc.

Dei, F. (1998). La discesa agli inferi. James G. Frazer e la cultura del Novecento. Lecce, Italy: Argo Editrice.

Dei, F. (2016). Antropologia culturale (2nd ed.). Bologna, Italy: Società editrice il Mulino.

Dei, F., & Simonicca, A. (Eds.). (2008). Ragione e forme di vita. Razionalità e relativismo in antropologia (2nd ed.). Milano, Italy: FrancoAngeli.

Dei, F., & Meloni, P. (2015). *Antropologia della cultura materiale*. Roma, Italy: Carocci editore.

Deliège, R. (2006). Une historie de l'anthropologie. Écoles, auteurs, théories. Paris: Éditions du Seuil.

Deng, Y. (2013). Applied Parallel Computing. Singapore: World Scientific Publishing.

Derdzinski, A. (1992). *Geometry of the Standard Model of Elementary Particles*. Berlin: Springer-Verlag;. doi:10.1007/978-3-642-50310-8

Desclés, J.-P. (2009). Relations spatiales et mouvements dans l'espace. Communication au le Séminaire GéoTAL, Rennes, France.

Desclés, J.-P. (2009). Relations spatiales et mouvements dans l'espace. Paper Presetned au le Séminaire GéoTAL, Rennes, France.

Devlin, K. (2006). *The Math Instinct: Why You're a Mathematical Genius (Along with Lobsters, Birds, Cats, and Dogs)*. New York, NY: Thunder's Mouth Press.

Di Gregorio, L. (2003). Psicopatologia del cellulare. Dipendenza e possesso del telefonino. Milano, Italy: FrancoAngeli/LeComete.

Dijksterhuis, A., & Nordgren, L. F. (2006). A theory of unconsciouss thought. *Perspectives on Psychological Science*, *1*(2), 95–109. doi:10.1111/j.1745-6916.2006.00007.x

Dolto, F. (1984). *L'image inconsciente du corps*. Paris: Editions du Seuil.

Donati, P. (2015). L'enigma della relazione. Milano, Italy: Mimesis edizioni.

Durst, M. (1988). Dialettica e bi-logica. L'epistemologia di Ignacio Matte Blanco. Milano, Italy: Marzorati Editore.

Durst, M. (1988). *Dialettica e bi-logica. L'epistemologia di Ignacio Matte Blanco.* Milano, Italy: Marzorati Editore.

Eco, U. (1981). *Simbolo. Voce dell'Enciclopedia Einaudi* (Vol. 12). Torino, Italy: Giulio Einaudi editore.

Egidi, R. (1979). Il linguaggio delle teorie scientifiche. Esperienza ed ipotesi nell'epistemologia contemporanea. Napoli, Italy: Guida Editori.

Egidi, R. (Ed.). (1992). La svolta relativistica nell'epistemologia contemporanea. Milano, Italy: FrancoAngeli.

Ehresmann, A. C., & Vanbremeersch, J. P. (2007). *Memory Evolutive Systems. Hierarchy, Emergence, Cognition.* Amsterdam: Elsevier, B.V.

Eibl-Eibesfeldt, I. (1996). Amore e odio. Per una storia naturale dei comportamenti elementari. Milano, Italy: Edizioni Adelphi.

Eibl-Eibesfeldt, I. (1997). Le invarianti nell'evoluzione delle specie. Roma, Italy: Di Renzo Editore.

Eibl-Eibesfeldt, I. (2001). Etologia umana. Le basi biologiche e culturali del comportamento. Torino, Italy: Bollati Boringhieri editore.

Eibl-Eibesfeldt, I. (2005). Dall'animale all'uomo. Le invarianti nell'evoluzione delle specie. Roma, Italy: Di Renzo Editore.

Ekstrom, S. R. (2004). The mind beyond our immediate awareness: Freudian, Jungian, and cognitive models of the unconscious. *The Journal of Analytical Psychology*, *49*(5), 657–682. doi:10.1111/j.0021-8774.2004.00494.x

Ellis, J., Mavromatos, N. E., & Nanopoulos, D. V. (1992). The origin of space-time as W-symmetry breaking in string theory. [Part B]. *Physics Letters*, *288*(1-2), 23–30. doi:10.1016/0370-2693(92)91949-A

Endert, E. (2006). Über die emotionale Dimension sozialer Prozesse. *Die Theorie der Affektlogik am Beispiel der Rechtsextremismus und Nationalsozialismusforschung (Theorie und Methode).* Konstanz, Germany: UVK Verlagsgesellschaft mbH.

Enriques, F. (1912). Scienza e Razionalismo. Bologna, Italy: Nicola Zanichelli Editore.

Even, G., & Medina, M. (2012). *Digital Logic Design. A Rigorous Approach.* Cambridge, UK: Cambridge University Press. doi:10.1017/CBO9781139226455

Fabietti, U., & Remotti, F. (Eds.). (1998). Dizionario di Antropologia. Etnologia, Antropologia Culturale, Antropologia Sociale. Bologna, Italy: Nicola Zanichelli Editore.

Fairlamb, H. L. (1994). *Critical conditions. Postmodernity and the question of foundations.* Cambridge, UK: Cambridge University Press; . doi:10.1017/CBO9780511552762

Falzone, A. (2005). Filosofia del linguaggio e psicopatologia evoluzionistica. Soveria Mannelli (CZ), Italy: Rubbettino Editore.

Feng, E. H., & Crooks, G. E. (2008). Lenghts of time arrow. *Physical Review Letters*, *101*(9), 090602/1–4. doi:10.1103/PhysRevLett.101.090602

Fenichel, O. (1945). The psychoanalytic theory of neurosis. New York, NY: W.W. Norton & Company, Inc.

Ferretti, F. (2010). Alle origini del linguaggio umano. Il punto di vista evoluzionistico. Roma-Bari, Italy: Editori Laterza.

Ffytche, M. (2012). *The Foundation of the Unconscious. Schelling, Freud and the Birth of the Modern Psyche*. Cambridge, UK: Cambridge University Press.

Field, M. (1996). *Symmetry Breaking for Compact Lie Groups. Memoir of the AMS No. 574*. Providence, RI: American Mathematical Society Publications.

Figà-Talamanca Dore, L. (1978). La logica dell'inconscio. Roma, Italy: Edizioni Studium-Vita Nova.

Finelli, R. (2010). Perché l'inconscio non è strutturato come un linguaggio. In Compendio di Psicoanalisi e altri scritti. Roma, Italy: Newton Compton editori.

Finelli, R. (2011). Rappresentazione e linguaggio in Freud: A partire dal "Compendio di psicoanalisi". *Consecutio Temporum. Rivista di critica della postmodernità, 1*, 112-125.

Fink, K. (1993). The Bi-Logic Perception of Time. *The International Journal of Psycho-Analysis, 74*, 303–312. PMID:8491534

Flügel, R. M. (2011). *Chirality and Life. A Short Introduction to the Early Phases of Chemical Evolution*. Berlin: Springer-Verlag.

Fodor, N., & Gaynor, F. (1950). Freud: Dictionary of Psychoanalysis. New York, NY: The Philosophical Library.

Fodor, N., & Gaynor, F. (1950). *Freud: Dictionary of Psychoanalysis*. New York, NY: The Philosophical Library.

Fonagy, P., Gergely, G., Jurist, E. L., & Target, M. (2002). Affect Regulation, Mentalization, and the Development of the Self. New York, NY: Other Press.

Fonagy, P., Gergely, G., Jurist, E. L., & Target, M. (2002). *Affect Regulation, Mentalization, and the Development of the Self*. New York, NY: Other Press.

Fornari, F. (2016). Psychic birth. In F. Borgogno, A. Luchetti, & L. M. Coe (Eds.), *Reading Italian Psychoanalysis* (pp. 593–600). Oxfordshire, UK: Routledge.

Fossi, G. (1983). La psicologia dinamica: un'eredità del XX secolo. Roma, Italy: Edizioni Borla.

Fossi, G. (1984). Le teorie psicoanalitiche. Padova, Italy: Piccin Nuova Libraria.

Fossi, G. (1988). Psicoanalisi e psicoterapie dinamiche. Torino, Italy: Bollati Boringhieri editore.

Fossi, G. (2003). Una proposta evoluzionista per la psicoanalisi. Con un manuale per la pratica terapeutica e la ricerca empirica. Milano, Italy: FrancoAngeli.

Francioni, M. (1978). Psicoanalisi linguistica ed epistemologia in Jacques Lacan. Torino, Italy: Editore Boringhieri.

Francioni, M. (1982). Storia della psicoanalisi francese. Teorie e istituzioni freudiane. Torino, Italy: Editore Boringhieri.

Freni, S. (1992). Prefazione all'edizione italiana. In Capire il transfert. Milano, Italy: Raffaello Cortina Editore.

Freud, A. (1937). The Ego and the Mechanisms of Defence. London, UK: The Hogarth Press.

Freud, S. (1938). Abriß der psychoanalyse. Academic Press.

Freud, S. (1979). La scissione dell'Io nel processo di difesa (1938). In Opere di Sigmund Freud, 1930-1938. L'uomo Mosè e la religione monoteistica e altri scritti (vol. 11). Torino, Italy: Editore Boringhieri.

Freud, S. (1957). *The Standard Edition of Complete Psychological Works of Sigmund Freud* (Vol. 1-24). (J. Strachey, Trans. & Ed.). London, UK: The Hogarth Press.

Friedman, D. M. (2001). A Mind of Its Own. A Cultural History of the Penis. New York, NY: Simon & Schuster, Inc.

Friedman, M., & Tomšič, S. (Eds.). (2016). *Psychoanalysis: Topological Perspectives. New Conceptions of Geometry and Space in Freud and Lacan.* Bielefeld, Germany: Transcript Verlag; . doi:10.14361/9783839434406

Fromm, E. (1951). The Forgotten Language. An Introduction to the Understanding of Dreams, Fairy Tales, and Myths. New York, NY: Holt, Rinehart & Winston Publishing Company, Inc.

Fromm, E. (1976). To have or to be? New York, NY: Harper & Row Publishers, Inc.

Funari, E. (1988). Contestualità e specificità della psicoanalisi. In Trattato di Psicoanalisi. Volume I: Teoria e Tecnica. Milano, Italy: Raffaello Cortina Editore.

Funari, E. (1988). Contestualità e specificità della psicoanalisi. In Trattato di Psicoanalisi: Vol. 1. Teoria e Tecnica. Milano, Italy: Raffaello Cortina Editore.

Funari, E. (2007). L'irrapresentabile come origine della vita psichica. Milano, Italy: FrancoAngeli.

Funari, E. (1978). Psicoanalisi: tecnica o Weltanschauung? In *Psicoanalisi e classi sociali* (pp. 147–153). Roma, Italy: Editori Riuniti.

Fusco, A., & Tomassoni, R. (Eds.). (2013). Creatività nella psicologia letteraria, drammatica e filmica. Milano, Italy: FrancoAngeli.

Fusco, A., & Tomassoni, R. (Eds.). (2013). *Creatività nella psicologia letteraria, drammatica e filmica.* Milano, Italy: FrancoAngeli.

Gabbay, D. M., Hodkinson, I., & Reynolds, M. A. (1994). *Temporal Logic. Mathematical Foundations and Computational Aspects* (Vol. 1). Oxford, UK: Clarendon Press.

Galimberti, U. (1979). Psichiatria e fenomenologia. Milano, Italy: Giangiacomo Feltrinelli Editore.

Galimberti, U. (1983). Il corpo. Milano, Italy: Giangiacomo Feltrinelli Editore.

Galimberti, U. (2006). Dizionario di psicologia. Torino, Italy: UTET Libreria.

Galton, A. (Ed.). (1987). *Temporal Logic and its Applications.* New York, NY: Academic Press, Inc.

Gay, P. (2000). Freud. Una vita per i nostri tempi. Milano, Italy: Bompiani.

Gayathri, V. I., & Rao, M. (2007). Fluctuation-induced chiral symmetry breaking in autocatalytic reactiondiffusion systems. *Europhysics Letters*, *80*(2), 28001. doi:10.1209/0295-5075/80/28001

Gay, P. (2000). *Freud. Una vita per i nostri tempi.* Milano, Italy: Bompiani.

Giberti, F., & Rossi, R. (Eds.). (1996). Manuale di psichiatria (4th ed.). Padova, Italy: Piccin Nuova Libraria.

Giersch, A., Lalanne, L., van Assche, M., & Elliott, M.A. (2013). On disturbed time continuity in schizophrenia: an elementary impairment in visual perception? *Frontiers in Psychology*, *4*, 281-290.

Gilbert, N. D., & Miller, E. C. (2011). The graph expansion of an ordered groupoid. *Algebra Colloquium*, *18*(1), 827-842.

Gilliéron, E., & Baldassarre, M. (Ed.). (2012). Perversione e Relazione. Roma, Italy: Alpes Italia.

Giordano, M., Dello Russo, G., Pardi, F., & Patella, G. A. (1984). Tempo e inconscio. Napoli, Italy: Guida editori.

Girotto, V. (Ed.). (2013). Introduzione alla psicologia del pensiero. Bologna, Italy: Società editrice il Mulino.

Girotto, V. (Eds.). (2013). Introduzione alla psicologia del pensiero. Bologna, Italy: Società editrice il Mulino.

Givant, S., & Halmos, P. (2009). Introduction to Boolean Algebras. New York, NY: Springer Science + Business Media, LLC.

Glover, E. (1949). Psychoanalysis. London, UK: John Bale Medical Publications, Ltd.

Godement, R. (1959). Variétés Différentiables. Résumé des leçons, Textos de Matemática No. 2. Recife, Brazil: Instituto de Física e Matemática – Universidade do Recife.

Goleman, D. (1995). Emotional Intelligence. New York, NY: Bantam Books.

Golubitsky, M., & Stewart, I. (2006). Nonlinear dynamics of networks: The groupoid formalism. *Bulletin of the American Mathematical Society, 43*(3), 305–364. doi:10.1090/S0273-0979-06-01108-6

Green, A. (1993). Le travail du négatif. Paris: Les Éditions du Minuit.

Greenacre, P. (1971). Emotional growth. Psychoanalytic studies of the gifted and a great variety of other individuals. New York, NY: International Universities Press, Inc.

Grice, H. P. (1993). Logica e conversazione. Saggi su intenzione, significato e comunicazione. Bologna, Italy: Società editrice il Mulino.

Grinberg, L. (1989). La supervisione psicoanalitica. Teoria e pratica. Milano, Italy: Raffaello Cortina Editore.

Grunberger, B. (1971). *Le narcissisme. Essai de psychanalyse.* Paris: Payot.

Guay, A., & Hepburn, B. (2009). Symmetry and its Formalisms: Mathematical Aspects. *Philosophy of Science, 76*(2), 160–178. doi:10.1086/600154

Guyton, A. C. (1991). Basic Neuroscience. Anatomy & Physiology (2nd ed.). Philadelphia, PA: W.B. Saunders Company.

Hadamard, J. (1945). The Psychology of Invention in the Mathematical Field. Princeton, NJ: Princeton University Press.

Hall, C. S. (1999). *A Primer in Freudian Psychology.* New York, NY: Meridian Books.

Hampe, B., & Grady, J. E. (Eds.). (2005). *From Perception to Meaning. Image Schemas in Cognitive Linguistics.* Berlin: Walter de Gruyter GmbH and Co.; . doi:10.1515/9783110197532

Hanly, C. (2011). Studi psicoanalitici sul narcisismo. Scritti di Charles Hanly. Roma, Italy: Giovanni Fioriti Editore.

Harary, F., Norman, Z., & Cartwright, D. (Eds.). (1965). *Structural Models.* New York, NY: John Wiley and Sons, Inc.

Hartmann, H., & Loewenstein, R. M. (1962). Notes on the Superego. *The Psychoanalytic Study of the Child, 17,* 42–81.

Herlihy, M., & Shavit, H. (1999). The Topological Structure of Asynchronous Computability. *Journal of the Association for Computing Machinery, 46*(6), 858–923. doi:10.1145/331524.331529

Hermann, I. (1989). Psicoanalisi e logica. Roma, Italy: Di Renzo Editore.

Hermann, R. (1968). *Lie Groups for Physicists.* New York, NY: W.A. Benjamin, Inc.

Hickmann, M., & Robert, S. (Eds.). (2006). *Space in Languages – Linguistic Systems and Cognitive Categories.* Amsterdam: John Benjamins Publishing Company; . doi:10.1075/tsl.66

Hildebrand, S., & Tromba, A. (1996). *The Parsimonious Universe. Shape and Form in the Natural World.* New York, NY: Springer-Verlag, Inc. doi:10.1007/978-1-4612-2424-2

Hirsch, M. W. (1976). *Differential Topology*. New York, NY: Springer-Verlag, Inc. doi:10.1007/978-1-4684-9449-5

Hodges, W. (1977). *Logic. An Introduction to Elementary Logic*. Harmondsworth, UK: Penguin Books, Ltd.

Hodkinson, I., & Reynolds, M. (2007). Temporal Logic. In Handbook of Modal Logic. Amsterdam: Elsevier, B.V.

Hodkinson, I., & Reynolds, M. (2007). Temporal Logic. In Handbook of Modal Logic. Amsterdam: Elsevier.

Holloway, R. L. (1974). The Casts of Fossil Hominid Brains. *Scientific American*, *231*(1), 106–115. doi:10.1038/scientificamerican0774-106 PMID:4858755

Horkheimer, M., & Adorno, T. W. (1947). Dialektik der Aufklärung. Philosophische Fragments. Amsterdam: Querido Verlag N.V.

Hsu, P.-J., Mauerer, T., Vogt, M., Yang, J. J., Seok Oh, Y., Cheong, S.-W., & Wu, W. et al. (2013). Hysteretic melting transition of a soliton lattice in a commensurate charge modulation. *Physical Review Letters*, *111*(26), 266401–266406. doi:10.1103/PhysRevLett.111.266401 PMID:24483807

Husemoller, D. (1975). *Fibre Bundles* (2nd ed.). New York, NY: Springer-Verlag, Inc.

Imbasciati, A. (2015). Nuove teorie sul funzionamento della mente. L'istituzione psicoanalitica e gli psicoanalisti. Milano, Italy: FrancoAngeli.

Ippoliti, E. (2007). *Il vero e il plausibile*. Morrisville, NC: Lulu Press, Inc.

Iurato, G. (2013). Mathematical thought in the light of Matte Blanco work. *Philosophy of Mathematics Education Journal*, 27.

Iurato, G. (2013a). Mathematical thought in the light of Matte Blanco work. *Philosophy of Mathematics Education Journal*, 27.

Iurato, G. (2013b). Σύμβολου: An attempt toward the early origins, Part 1. Language & Psychoanalysis, 2(2), 77–120. 10.7565/landp.2013.008

Iurato, G. (2013c). Σύμβολου: An attempt toward the early origins, Part 2. Language & Psychoanalysis, 2(2), 121–160. 10.7565/landp.2013.009

Iurato, G. (2014c). *Alcune considerazioni critiche sul simbolismo*. Preprint No. hal-00980828 version 1. Available at HAL archives-ouvertes.

Iurato, G. (2015b). Fetishism in Marketing. Some First Elementary Psychoanalytic Anthropology Remarks. In Business Management: A Practioners' Guide. Delhi: International Research Publication House.

Iurato, G. (2015b). Fetishism in Marketing. Some First Elementary Psychoanalytic Anthropology Remarks. In Business Management: A Practitioners' Guide. Delhi: International Research Publication House.

Iurato, G. (2016a). *A psychoanalytic enquiry on symbolic function*. Preprint No. hal-01361264 version 3. Available at HAL archives-ouvertes.

Iurato, G. (2016b). *A view of LSA/ESA in Computational Psychoanalysis*. Preprint No. hal-01353999 version 1. Available at HAL archives-ouvertes.

Iurato, G. (2016e). *The origins of symbol. An historical-critical study of symbolic function, according to the phylo-ontogenetic perspective, as arising from the comparison of certain patterns of neuro-psychological sciences*. Paper Presented at the Satellite Event "On the edge of disciplines", Florence, Italy.

Iurato, G. (2017a). An Essay in Denotational Mathematics. Rigorous Results. In Encyclopedia of Information Science and Technology (4th ed.). Hershey, PA: IGI Global.

Iurato, G. (2017b). Un raffronto critico fra la teoria platonica delle idee ed il paradosso di Kripke-Wittgenstein. In Platone nel pensiero moderno e contemporaneo (vol. 11). Villasanta (MB), Italy: Limina Mentis Edizioni.

Iurato, G. (2014a). At the grounding of computational psychoanalysis: on the work of Ignacio Matte Blanco. A general history of culture overview of Matte Blanco bilogic in comparison. In *Proceedings of the 2014 IEEE 13th International Conference on Cognitive Informatics and Cognitive Computing*. Los Alamitos, CA: IEEE Computer Society Press.

Iurato, G. (2014b). The dawning of computational psychoanalysis. A proposal for some first elementary formalization attempts. *International Journal of Cognitive Informatics and Natural Intelligence, 8*(4), 50–82. doi:10.4018/ijcini.2014100104

Iurato, G. (2015a). A Brief Comparison of the Unconscious as Seen by Jung and Lévi-Strauss. *Anthropology of Consciousness, 26*(1), 60–107. doi:10.1111/anoc.12032

Iurato, G. (2015b). *Fetishism* in Marketing. Some First Elementary Psychoanalytic Anthropology Remarks. In *Business Management: A Practioners' Guide*. Delhi: International Research Publication House.

Iurato, G. (2015c). A simple phylogenetic remark about certain human blood pressure values. *Journal of Biochemistry International, 2*(4), 162–165.

Iurato, G. (2016c). On Jacques Lacan Psychosis Theory and ERPs Analysis. *Journal of Biology and Nature, 5*(4), 234–240.

Iurato, G. (2016d). Some Comments on the Historical Role of *Fetishism* in Economic Anthropology. *Journal of Global Economics. Management and Business Research, 7*(1), 61–82.

Iurato, G. (2016f). Two simple questions regarding cultural anthropology. *Journal of Global Research in Education and Social Science, 8*(1), 10–15.

Iurato, G. (2017a). An Essay in Denotational Mathematics. Rigorous Results. In *Encyclopedia of Information Science and Technology* (4th ed.). Hershey, PA: IGI Global.

Iurato, G. (2017c). (in press). Rigidity of the Generalized Other, narrowness of the Otherness and demodernization, in the framework of symbolic interactionism. *Ideology and Political Journal.*

Iurato, G. (2017c). *Rigidity of the Generalized Other, narrowness of the Otherness and demodernization, in the framework of symbolic interactionism. Ideology and Political Journal.* (in press)

Iurato, G., & Khrennikov, A. Yu. (2015). Hysteresis model of unconscious-conscious interconnection: Exploring dynamics on *m*-adic trees. p-Adic Numbers, Ultrametric. *Analysis and Applications, 7*(4), 312–321. doi:10.1134/S2070046615040068

Iurato, G., & Khrennikov, A. Yu. (2017). On the topological structure of a mathematical model of human unconscious. p-Adic Numbers, Ultrametric. *Analysis and Applications, 9*(1), 78–81. doi:10.1134/S2070046617010071

Iurato, G., Khrennikov, A. Yu., & Murtagh, F. (2016). Formal Foundations for the Origins of Human Consciousness. p-Adic Numbers, Ultrametric. *Analysis and Applications, 8*(4), 249–279. doi:10.1134/S2070046616040014

Jablonka, E., & Raz, G. (2009). Transgenerational Epigenetic Inheritance: Prevalence, Mechanisms, and Implications for the Study of Heredity and Evolution. *The Quarterly Review of Biology, 84*(2), 131–176. doi:10.1086/598822

Jackson, D. D. (1954). Some factors influencing the Œdipus Complex. *The Psychoanalytic Quarterly, 23*, 566–581.

Jaffé, R. (2009). Ideale dell'Io, Idealizzazione. In *Psiche. Dizionario storico di psicologia, psichiatria, psicoanalisi, neuroscienze* (Vol. 1, pp. 494–500). Torino, Italy: Giulio Einaudi editore.

Johnson-Laird, P., & Bara, B. (1984). Syllogistic Inference. *Cognition, 16*(1), 1–61. doi:10.1016/0010-0277(84)90035-0

Juhás, G. (1999). On Semantics of Petri Nets over Partial Algebra. In *SOFSEM'99: Theory and Practice of Informatics. Proceedings of the 26th Conference on Current Trends in Theory and Practice of Informatics.* Berlin: Springer-Verlag. doi:10.1007/3-540-47849-3_29

Kächele, H. (2001). Are there "Pillars of Therapeutic Wisdom" for Psychoanalytic Therapy? *European Journal of Psychoanalysis. Humanities, Philosophy. Psychothérapies, 12-13,* 151–161.

Kafri, R., Markovitch, O., & Lancet, D. (2010). Spontaneous chiral symmetry breaking in early molecular networks. *Biology Direct, 5*(38), 1–13. PMID:20507625

Kandel, E. R. (2005). Psychiatry, Psychoanalysis, and the New Biology of Mind. Washington, DC: American Psychiatric Association Publishing, Inc.

Kandel, E. R. (2005). *Psychiatry, Psychoanalysis, and the New Biology of Mind.* Washington, DC: American Psychiatric Association Publishing, Inc.

Kaplan-Solms, K., & Solms, M. (2000). Clinical Studies in Neuro-Psychoanalysis. Introduction to a Depth Neuropsychology. London, UK: Karnac Books, Ltd.

Kaplan-Solms, K., & Solms, M. (2000). *Clinical Studies in Neuro-Psychoanalysis. Introduction to a Depth Neuropsychology.* London, UK: Karnac Books, Ltd.

Kastner, R. E. (2011). The broken symmetry of time. In Quantum Retrocausation: Theory and Experiment. Melville, NY: AIP Publications. doi:10.1063/1.3663714

Kemeny, J. G. (1959). A Philosopher Looks at Science. Princeton, NJ: D. Van Nostrand Reinhold Company, Inc.

Kemeny, J. G. (1959). *A Philosopher Looks at Science.* Princeton, NJ: D. Van Nostrand Reinhold Company, Inc.

Kemeny, J. G., Snell, J. L., & Thompson, G. L. (1974). *Introduction to Finite Mathematics* (3rd ed.). Englewood Cliffs, NJ: Prentice-Hall.

Kernberg, O. (2011). Suicide prevention for psychoanalytic institutes and societies. *Journal of the American Psychoanalytic Association, 60*(4), 707–719. doi:10.1177/0003065112449861

Khan Masud, R. M. (1979). Alienation in perversions. London, UK: The Hogarth Press, Ltd.

Khan Masud, R. M. (1970). *Le fétichisme comme négation du soi. Nouvelle Revue de Psychoanalyse, 2, Numéro spécial: Objects du fétichisme. Présentation par J-B. Pontalis.* Paris: Éditions Gallimard.

Khrennikov, A. Yu. (1991). *p*-Adic quantum mechanics with *p*-adic valued functions. *Journal of Mathematical Physics, 32*(4), 932–937. doi:10.1063/1.529353

Khrennikov, A. Yu. (1998). Human subconscious as the *p*-adic dynamical system. *Journal of Theoretical Biology, 193*(2), 179–196. doi:10.1006/jtbi.1997.0604

Khrennikov, A. Yu. (2002). Classical and quantum mental models and Freud's theory of unconscious mind. In *Series in Mathematical Modelling in Physics, Enginnering and Cognitive Sciences* (Vol. 1). Växjö, Sweden: Växjö University Press.

Khrennikov, A. Yu. (2007). Toward an adequate mathematical model of mental space: Conscious/unconscious dynamics on *m*-adic trees. *Bio Systems, 90*(3), 656–675. doi:10.1016/j.biosystems.2007.02.004

Kim, W. W. (2016). History and Cultural Perspective. In Penile Augmentation. Berlin: Springer-Verlag. doi:10.1007/978-3-662-46753-4_2

Kissin, B. (1986). *Conscious and Unconscious Programs in the Brain*. New York, NY: Plenum Publishing Corporation; . doi:10.1007/978-1-4613-2187-3

Köhler, T. (2007). *Freuds Psychoanalyse. Eine Einführung* (2nd ed.). Stuttgart, Germany: W. Kohlhammer GmbH.

Kovacs, A. L. (1989). Degeneracy and asymmetry in Biology. In *Nonlinear Structures in Physical Systems. Pattern Formation, Chaos, and Waves. Proceedings of the 2nd Woodward Conference*. New York, NY: Springer-Verlag, Inc.

Kultgen, J. (1976). Lévi-Strauss on Unconscious Social Structures. *The Southwestern Journal of Philosophy*, *7*(1), 153–159. doi:10.5840/swjphil19767118

Kuper, J. (Ed.). (1988). *A Lexicon of Psychology, Psychiatry and Psychoanalysis*. London, UK: Routledge.

La Forgia, M. (1992). Sincronicità. In Trattato di Psicologia Analitica (vol. 2). Torino, Italy: UTET.

La Forgia, M. (1992). Sincronicità. In Trattato di Psicologia Analitica (Vols. 1-2). Torino, Italy: UTET.

La Mantia, F. (2017). From Topology to Quasi-Topology. The Complexity of the Notional Domain. In Lecture Notes in Morphogenesis: Vol. 5. Language in Complexity. The Emerging Meaning. Springer International Publishing.

La Mantia, F. (2017). From Topology to Quasi-Topology. The Complexity of the Notional Domain. In Lecture Notes in Morphogenesis: Vol. 5. Language in Complexity: The Emerging Meaning. Springer International Publishing.

Lacan, J. (2014). *The Seminar of Jacques Lacan. Book X: The Anxiety (J. A. Miller* (A. R. Price Trans. & Ed.). Malden, MA: Polity Press.

Lacan, J. (2014). *The Seminar of Jacques Lacan. Book X: The Anxiety* (J. A. Miller, Ed.; A. R. Price, Trans.). Malden, MA: Polity Press.

Lacas, M.-L. (2007). La démarche originale de Gisela Pankow. Gisela Pankows original thought processes. LÉvolution Psychiatrique, 72(1), 15–24. 10.1016/j.evopsy.2006.11.001

Làdavas, E., & Berti, A. (2014). Neuropsicologia (3rd ed.). Bologna, Italy: Società editrice il Mulino.

Lagache, D. (1961). *La psychanalyse et la structure de la personnalité*. Paper Presented au Colloquium International de Royaumont, Paris, France.

Lagache, D. (1961). La psychanalyse et la structure de la personnalité. In *La psycanalyse. Recherche et enseignement Freudiens de la Société Française de Psychanalyse, N. 6: Perspectives structurales*. Paris: Presses Universitaires de France-PUF.

Lagache, D. (1965). Le modèle psychanalytique de la personnalité. In *La Folle du Logis. La psychanalyse comme science exacte* (pp. 159–183). Paris: PUF-Presses Universitaires de France.

Lakatos, I. (1978). Philosophical Papers (Vols. 1-2). Cambridge, UK: Cambridge University Press.

Lakatos, I. (1978). *Philosophical Papers*. Cambridge, UK: Cambridge University Press.

Lambert, K., & Brittain, G. G., Jr. (1979). An Introduction to the Philosophy of Science. Reseda, CA: Ridgeview Publishing Company.

Lambert, K., & Brittain, G. G. Jr. (1979). *An Introduction to the Philosophy of Science*. Reseda, CA: Ridgeview Publishing Company.

Lample-De-Groot, J. (1962). Ego ideal and Superego. *The Psychoanalytic Study of the Child*, *17*, 94–106.

Langs, R. (1990). Guida alla psicoterapia. Un'introduzione all'approccio comunicativo. Torino, Italy: Bollati Boringhieri editore.

Laplanche, J. (2000). Problematiche II. Castrazione. Simbolizzazioni. Bari-Roma, Italy: La Biblioteca.

Laplanche, J. (2008). Sexuale. La sessualità allargata nel senso freudiano. Bari-Roma, Italy: La Biblioteca.

Laplanche, J., & Pontalis, J.-B. (1967). Vocabulaire de la psychoanalyse. Paris: Presses Universitaires de France.

Laplanche, J., & Pontalis, J.-B. (1988). Fantasma originario, fantasmi delle origini, origini del fantasma. Bologna, Italy: Società editrice il Mulino.

Laplanche, J. (2001). *L'inconscio e l'Es*. Bari-Roma, Italy: La Biblioteca.

Laplanche, J. (2007). *L'après-coup. Bari-Roma, Italy: La Biblioteca*. Preprint available at www.math.berkeley.edu

Laplanche, J., & Pontalis, J.-B. (1967). *Vocabulaire de la psychoanalyse*. Paris: Presses Universitaires de France.

Lauro-Grotto, R. (2014a). Formal Approaches in the Age of Mirror Neurons. Hints from Psychoanalytic Theories and Practice. In *Proceedings of the 2014 IEEE 13th International Conference on Cognitive Informatics and Cognitive Computing*. Los Alamitos, CA: IEEE Computer Society Press.

Lauro-Grotto, R. (2014b). Paradigmi metapsicologici. Con tre scritti inediti di Freud. Pisa, Italy: ETS-Editrice tecnico-scientifica.

Lauro-Grotto, R. (2008). The unconscious as an ultrametric set. *The American Imago, 64*(4), 52–62. doi:10.1353/aim.2008.0009

Lawson, M. K. (2005). Constructing ordered groupoids. *Cahiers de Topologie et Géométrie Différentielle Catégoriques, 46*(2), 123–138.

Lenz Dunker, I. (2008). Psychology and Psychoanalysis in Brazil. From Cultural Syncretism to the Collapse of Liberal Individualism. *Theory & Psychology, 18*(2), 223–236. doi:10.1177/0959354307087883

Lerner, D. (Ed.). (1961). Quality and Quantity. New York, NY: The Free Press of Glencoe.

Lerner, D. (Ed.). (1961). *Quality and Quantity*. New York, NY: The Free Press of Glencoe.

Lévi-Strauss, C. (2008). Sull'Italia. In Claude Lévi-Strauss fotografato da Marion Kalter. Napoli, Italy: Electa Napoli.

Lévi-Strauss, C., & Eribon, D. (1988). De près et de loin. Paris: Éditions Odile Jacob.

Lévi-Strauss, C. (1975). *Razza e storia e altri studi di antropologia*. Torino, Italy: Giulio Einaudi editore.

Lévi-Strauss, C., & Eribon, D. (1988). *Da vicino e da lontano. Discutendo con Claude Lévi-Strauss*. Milano, Italy: Rizzoli.

Levitz, K., & Levitz, H. (1979). *Logic and Boolean Algebra*. Woodbury, NY: Barron's Educational Series, Inc.

Lewin, R. (1996). Communicating with the schizophrenic superego. *The Journal of the American Academy of Psychoanalysis, 24*(4), 709–736.

Lewis, C. I. (1912). Implication and the Algebra of Logic. *Mind, 21*(84), 522–531. doi:10.1093/mind/XXI.84.522

Lis, A., Mazzeschi, C., & Zennaro, A. (2007). *La psicoanalisi. Un percorso concettuale fra tradizione e attualità* (2nd ed.). Roma, Italy: Carocci editore.

Lis, A., Zennaro, A., Mazzeschi, C., Salcuni, S., & Parolin, L. (2003). *Breve dizionario di psicoanalisi*. Roma, Italy: Carocci editore.

Loewald, H. W. (1988). Sublimation. Inquires into Theoretical Psychoanalysis. New Haven, CT: Yale University Press.

Loewald, H. W. (1989). Papers on Psychoanalysis. New Haven, CT: Yale University Press.

Loewald, H. W. (1962). The Superego and the Ego-Ideal. II. Superego and Time. *The International Journal of Psycho-Analysis*, *43*, 264–268.

Lolli, G. (1991). Introduzione alla logica formale. Bologna, Italy: Società editrice il Mulino.

Lolli, G. (2000). Un logico esamina i modelli mentali. In Ragionamento: psicologia e logica. Firenze, Italy: Giunti Gruppo Editoriale.

Lolli, G. (2005). *QED – Fenomenologia della dimostrazione*. Torino, Italy: Bollati Boringhieri editore.

Longhin, L. (1992). Alle origini del pensiero psicoanalitico. Roma, Italy: Edizioni Borla.

Longhin, L. (2016). La mente emotiva. Conoscerla e curarla. Milano, Italy: FrancoAngeli.

Longhin, L., & Mancia, M. (1998). Temi e problemi in psicoanalisi. Torino, Italy: Bollati Boringhieri editore.

Luborsky, L., & Crits-Christoph, P. (1992). Capire il transfert. Milano, Italy: Raffaello Cortina Editore.

Luborsky, L., & Crits-Christoph, P. (1992). *Capire il transfert*. Milano, Italy: Raffaello Cortina Editore.

Lusetti, V. (2008). Psicopatologia antropologica. Roma, Italy: EUR-Edizioni Universitarie Romane.

Macola, E. (Ed.). (2014). Sublimazione e perversione. Attualità Lacaniana. Rivista della Scuola Lacaniana di Psicoanalisi, 18, 7-108.

Maffei, L. (2014). Elogio della lentezza. Bologna, Italy: Società editrice il Mulino.

Maffei, L. (2016). Elogio della ribellione. Bologna, Italy: Società editrice il Mulino.

Main, R. (2014). The cultural significance of synchronicity for Jung and Pauli. *The Journal of Analytical Psychology*, *59*(2), 174–180. doi:10.1111/1468-5922.12067 PMID:24673272

Mancia, M. (Ed.). (1990). Super-Io e Ideale dell'Io. Roma, Italy: Casa Editrice Astrolabio-Ubaldini Editore.

Mancia, M. (Ed.). (1990). *Super-Io e Ideale dell'Io*. Roma, Italy: Casa Editrice Astrolabio-Ubaldini Editore.

Mancia, M. (Ed.). (2006). *Psychoanalysis and Neuroscience*. Milan, Italy: Springer-Verlag Italia; . doi:10.1007/88-470-0550-7

Manzi, G. (2013). Il grande racconto dell'evoluzione umana. Bologna, Italy: Società editrice il Mulino.

Marchi, D. (2016). Il mistero di Homo naledi. Chi era e come viveva il nostro lontano cugino africano: storia di una scoperta rivoluzionaria. Milano, Italy: Mondadori Libri.

Marchi, D. (2016). *Il mistero di Homo naledi. Chi era e come viveva il nostro lontano cugino africano: storia di una scoperta rivoluzionaria*. Milano, Italy: Mondadori Libri.

Marcuse, H. (1964). One-Dimensional Man. Studies in the Ideology of Advanced Industrial Society. Boston, MA: Beacon Press, Inc.

Marcuse, H. (1964). *One-Dimensional Man. Studies in the Ideology of Advanced Industrial Society.* Boston, MA: Beacon Press, Inc.

Matte Blanco, I. (1975). The Unconscious as Infinite Sets. An Essay in Bi-Logic. London, UK: Gerald Duckworth & Company, Ltd.

Matte Blanco, I. (1975). *The Unconscious as Infinite Sets. An Essay in Bi-Logic.* London, UK: Gerald Duckworth & Company, Ltd.

Matte Blanco, I. (1988). *Thinking, Feeling, and Being. Clinical Reflections of the Fundamental Antinomy on Human Beings and World.* London, UK: Routledge.

Matthews, G. C. (1998). Neurobiology. Molecules, Cells, and Systems. Oxford, UK: Blackwell Science, Ltd.

Matthews, P. T. (1974). *Introduction to Quantum Mechanics.* Maidenhead, UK: McGraw-Hill Publishing Company Limited.

Maurin, K. (1997). *The Riemann Legacy. Riemann Ideas in Mathematics and Physics.* Dordrecht, The Netherlands: Kluwer Academic Publishers. doi:10.1007/978-94-015-8939-0

McCulloch, W. S. (1965). *Embodiments of Mind.* Cambridge, MA: The MIT Press.

Mellino, M. (2005). La critica postcoloniale. Decolonizzazione, capitalismo e cosmopolitismo nei postcolonial studies. Roma, Italy: Meltemi editore.

Mendes, E.P.R. (1995). Vicissitudes da clínica psicanalítica contemporânea. *Reverso, Belo Horizonte, 40.*

Miller, P. H. (1983). *Theories of Developmental Psychology.* New York, NY: W.H. Freeman & Co.

Milrod, D. (2002). The superego. Its formation, structure, and functioning. *The Psychoanalytic Study of the Child, 57,* 131–148.

Minsky, M. (1975). A Framework for the Representation Knowledge. In The Psychology of Computer Vision. New York, NY: McGraw-Hill Book Company.

Mitchell, S. A., & Black, M. J. (1995). *Freud and beyond. A History of Modern Psychoanalysic Thought.* New York, NY: Basic Books. A Division of Harper Collins Publishers.

Moore, B. E., & Fine, B. D. (Eds.). (1990). Psychoanalytic Terms and Concepts. New York, NY: The American Psychoanalytic Association.

Moore, D. S. (2015). *The Developing Genome. An Introduction to Behavioural Epigenetics.* New York, NY: Oxford University Press.

Moravia, S. (2004). Ragione strutturale e universi di senso. Saggio su Lévi-Strauss. Firenze, Italy: Casa Editrice Le Lettere.

Moravia, S. (2004). Ragione strutturale e universi di senso. Saggio sul pensiero di Claude Lévi-Strauss. Firenze, Italy: Casa Editrice Le Lettere.

Mordant, I. (1990). Using attribute-memories to resolve a contradiction in the work of Matte Blanco. *The International Review of Psycho-Analysis, 17,* 475–480.

Morgan, J., & Tian, G. (2007). *Ricci Flow and the Poincaré Conjecture. Clay Mathematics Monographs, Volume No. 3.* Providence, RI: American Mathematical Society Publications.

Murtagh, F. (2014b). Mathematical representations of Matte Blancos bi-logic, based on metric space and ultrametric or hierarchical topology: Towards practical application. Language and Psychoanalysis, 3(2), 40–63. 10.7565/landp.2014.008

Murtagh, F. (2012a). Ultrametric model of mind, I [Review]. p-Adic Numbers, Ultrametric. *Analysis and Applications, 4*(3), 193–206. doi:10.1134/S2070046612030041

Murtagh, F. (2012b). Ultrametric model of mind, II. Application to text content analysis. p-Adic Numbers, Ultrametric. *Analysis and Applications, 4*(3), 207–221. doi:10.1134/S2070046612030053

Murtagh, F. (2013). The new science of complex systems through ultrametric analysis. Application to search and discovery, to narrative and to thinking. p-Adic Numbers, Ultrametric. *Analysis and Applications, 5*(4), 326–337. doi:10.1134/S2070046613040067

Murtagh, F. (2014a). Pattern recognition of subconscious underpinnings of cognition using ultrametric topological mapping of thinking and memory. *International Journal of Cognitive Informatics and Natural Intelligence, 8*(4), 1–16. doi:10.4018/ijcini.2014100101

Murtagh, F. (2014c). Pattern Recognition in Mental Processes: Determining Vestiges of the Subconscious through Ultrametric Component Analysis. In *Proceedings of the 2014 IEEE 13th International Conference on Cognitive Informatics and Cognitive Computing.* Los Alamitos, CA: IEEE Computer Society Press; . doi:10.1109/ICCI-CC.2014.6921455

Murtagh, F. (2017). *Data Science Foundations. Geometry and Topology of Complex Hierarchic Systems and Big Data Analytics.* Boca Raton, FL: Chapman & Hall/CRC Press.

Murtagh, F., & Iurato, G. (2016). Human Behaviour, Benign or Malevalent: Understanding the Human Psyche, Performing Therapy, based on Affective Mentalization and Matte-Blancos Bi-Logic. *Annals of Translational Medicine, 4*(24), 486–496. doi:10.21037/atm.2016.12.37

Murtagh, F., & Iurato, G. (2017). (in press). Visualization of Jacques Lacan's Registers of the Psychoanalytic Field, and Discovery of Metaphor and of Metonymy. Analytical Case Study of Edgar Allan Poe's "The Purloined Letter". *Language and Psychoanalysis.*

Murtagh, F., & Iurato, G. (2017). Visualization of Jacques Lacan's Registers of the Psychoanalytic Field, and Discovery of Metaphor and of Metonymy. Analytical Case Study of Edgar Allan Poe's "The Purloined Letter". *Language and Psychoanalysis.* (in press)

My thanks go to the Director of IGI Global Publisher, Jan Travers, as well as to my Assistant Development Editor, Jordan Tepper, for what they have done to make possible this new publication.

Nagel, T. (1993). Summary. In *Experimental and Theoretical Studies of Consciousness. Novartis Foundation Symposium No.* 174. New York, NY: John Wiley & Sons, Ltd.

Nannini, S. (2007). Naturalismo cognitivo. Per una teoria materialistica della mente. Macerata, Italy: Edizioni Quodlibet.

Nannini, S. (2011). L'anima e il corpo. Un'introduzione storica alla filosofia della mente. Roma-Bari, Italy: Laterza Editori.

Nannini, S. (2007). *Naturalismo cognitivo. Per una teoria materialistica della mente.* Macerata, Italy: Edizioni Quodlibet.

Nannini, S. (2011). *L'anima e il corpo. Un'introduzione storica alla filosofia della mente.* Roma-Bari, Italy: Laterza Editori.

Nannini, S. (2015). Time and Consciousness in Cognitive Naturalism. *Rivista Internazionale di Filosofia e Psicologia, 6*(3), 458–473.

Napolitano, F. (2009). Rappresentazione, 2. In *Psiche. Dizionario storico di psicologia, psichiatria, psicoanalisi, neuroscienze* (Vol. 2, pp. 919–923). Torino, IT: Giulio Einaudi editore.

Neubauer, K. (2004). Semantica storica. In Dizionario degli studi culturali. Roma, Italy: Meltemi editore.

Neuman, Y. (2016). Computational Personality Analysis. Introduction, Practical Applications and Novel Directions. Springer International Publishing.

Neuman, Y. (2014). *Introduction to Computational Cultural Psychology*. Cambridge, UK: Cambridge University Press.

Neuman, Y. (2016). *Computational Personality Analysis. Introduction, Practical Applications and Novel Directions*. Springer International Publishing.

Nicasi, S. (1981). Meccanismi di difesa. Studio su Freud. Milano, Italy: il Saggiatore.

Nunberg, H. (1932). Allgemeine Neurosenlehre auf psychoanalytischer Grundlage. Berlin: Verlag Hans Hüber.

Nunberg, H. (1932). *Allgemeine Neurosenlehre auf psychoanalytischer Grundlage* [Principles of psychoanalysis: Their application to the neuroses]. Berlin: Verlag Hans Hüber.

Øhrstrøm, P., & Hasle, P. F. V. (Eds.). (1995). *Temporal Logic. From Ancient Ideas to Artificial Intelligence. Studies in Linguistics and Philosophy, Volume No. 57*. Dordrecht, The Netherlands: Kluwer Academic Publishers.

Oliverio, A. (1982). Biologia e comportamento. Bologna, Italy: Nicola Zanichelli Editore.

Oliverio, A. (1984). Storia naturale della mente. Torino, Italy: Editore Boringhieri.

Oliverio, A. (2008). Geografia della mente. Territori cerebrali e comportamenti umani. Milano, Italy: Raffaello Cortina Editore.

Oliverio, A. (2009). La vita nascosta del cervello. Firenze, Italy: Giunti Editore.

Oliverio, A. (2011). Prima lezione di neuroscienze. Roma-Bari, Italy: Editori Laterza.

Oliverio, A. (2016). Il cervello e linconscio. Psicobiettivo, 36(3), 251–259. 10.3280/PSOB2016-003015

Oliverio, A. (2017). Il cervello che impara. Neuropedagogia dall'infanzia alla vecchiaia. Firenze, Italy: Giunti Editore.

Ong, N. P., & Monceau, P. (1977). Anomalous transport properties of a linear-chain metal $NbSe_3$. *Physical Review B: Condensed Matter and Materials Physics, 16*(8), 3443–3455. doi:10.1103/PhysRevB.16.3443

Palombi, F. (2002). Il legame instabile. Attualità del dibattito psicoanalisi-scienza. Milano, Italy: FrancoAngeli.

Pankow, G. (1977). L'uomo e la sua psicosi. Milano, Italy: Giangiacomo Feltrinelli Editore.

Pankow, G. (1979). Struttura familiare e psicosi. Milano, Italy: Giangiacomo Feltrinelli Editore.

Panksepp, J., & Biven, L. (2012). The Archeology of Mind. Neuroevolutionary Origins of Human Emotion. New York, NY: W.W. Norton & Company.

Panksepp, J., & Biven, L. (2012). *The Archeology of Mind. Neuroevolutionary Origins of Human Emotion*. New York, NY: W.W. Norton & Company.

Papagno, C. (2010). Neuropsicologia della memoria. Bologna, Italy: Società editrice il Mulino.

Parsons, T. (1970). *Social Structure and Personality*. New York, NY: The Free Press. A Division of The Macmillan Company.

Percacci, R. (1986). Geometry of Nonlinear Field Theories. Singapore: World Scientific Publishing. doi:10.1142/0251

Peterburs, J., Nitsch, A. M., Miltner, W. H. R., & Straube, T. (2013). Impaired representation of time in schizophrenia is linked to positive symptoms and cognitive demand. *PLoS ONE, 8*(6), e67615/1–7. doi:10.1371/journal.pone.0067615 PMID:23826328

Petersen, W. P., & Arbenz, P. (2004). *Introduction to Parallel Computing*. New York, NY: Oxford University Press, Inc.

Petit, C., & Prévost, G. (1971). Genetica ed evoluzione. Milano, Italy: Arnoldo Mondadori Editore.

Petocz, A. (2004). *Freud, psychoanalysis and symbolism*. Cambridge, UK: Cambridge University Press.

Petrilli, S., & Ponzio, A. (2005). *Semiotics Unbounded. Interpretive Routes Through the Open Network of Signs*. Toronto: The University of Toronto Press; . doi:10.3138/9781442657113

Petrini, P., Casadei, A., & Chiricozzi, F. (Eds.). (2011). Trasgressione, violazione, perversione. Eziopatogenesi, diagnosi e terapia. Milano, Italy: FrancoAngeli.

Petrini, P., Renzi, A., Casadei, A., & Mandese, A. (2013). Dizionario di psicoanalisi. Con elementi di psichiatria, psicodinamica e psicologia dinamica. Milano, Italy: FrancoAngeli.

Petrini, P., Casadei, A., & Chiricozzi, F. (Eds.). (2011). *Trasgressione, violazione, perversione. Eziopatogenesi, diagnosi e terapia*. Milano, Italy: FrancoAngeli.

Petrini, P., Renzi, A., Casadei, A., & Mandese, A. (2013). *Dizionario di psicoanalisi. Con elementi di psichiatria, psicodinamica e psicologia dinamica*. Milano, Italy: FrancoAngeli.

Piattelli Palmarini, M. (1987). Scienza come cultura. Protagonisti, luoghi e idee delle scienze contemporanee. Milano, Italy: Arnoldo Mondadori Editore.

Piattelli Palmarini, M. (1987). *Scienza come cultura. Protagonisti, luoghi e idee delle scienze contemporanee*. Milano, Italy: Arnoldo Mondadori Editore.

Pierce, B. C. (2002). *Types and Programming Languages*. Cambridge, MA: The MIT Press.

Pieri, P. F. (2005). *Dizionario junghiano (Edizione ridotta)*. Torino, Italy: Bollati Boringhieri editore.

Pini, B. (1967). Primo Corso di Algebra. Bologna, Italy: CLUEB Editrice.

Piras, F., Piras, F., Ciullo, V., Danese, E., Caltagirone, C. & Spalletta, G. (2013). Time dysperception perspective for acquired brain injury. *Frontiers in Neurology, 4*, 217-226.

Piscicelli, U. (1994). Sessuologia. Teoremi psicosomatici e relazionali. Padova, Italy: Piccin Nuova Libraria.

Pizzi, C. (Ed.). (1974). La logica del tempo. Torino, Italy: Bollati Boringhieri Editore.

Poggi, S. (1977). I sistemi dell'esperienza. Bologna, Italy: Società editrice il Mulino.

Poincaré, H. J. (1958). The Value of Science. New York, NY: Dover Publications, Inc.

Pollo, M. (2016). La nostalgia dell'uroboros. Contributi a una psicologia culturale delle nuove addiction. Milano, Italy: FrancoAngeli.

Pollo, M. (2016). *La nostalgia dell'uroboros. Contributi a una psicologia culturale delle nuove addiction*. Milano, Italy: FrancoAngeli.

Possenti, V. (Ed.). (1979). Epistemologia e scienze umane. Milano, Italy: Editore Massimo.

Preziosi, P. (1992). Fondamenti di neuropsicofarmacologia. Padova, Italy: Piccin Nuova Libraria.

Putnam, H. (1975). Filosofia della logica. Nominalismo e realismo nella logica contemporanea. Milano, Italy: ISEDI – Istituto Editoriale Internazionale.

Putnam, H. (1956). Mathematics and the Existence of Abstract Entities. *Philosophical Studies*, 7(6), 81–88. doi:10.1007/BF02221758

Putnam, H. (1975). *Filosofia della logica. Nominalismo e realismo nella logica contemporanea*. Milano, Italy: ISEDI – Istituto Editoriale Internazionale.

Quan, P. M. (1969). *Introduction a la géométrie des variétés différentiables*. Paris: Éditions Dunod.

Radicati, L. A. (1985). Remarks on the early developments of the notion of symmetry breaking. In *Symmetries in Physics (1600-1980). Proceedings of the 1st International Meeting on the History of Scientific Ideas*. Barcelona: Servei de Publicacions, Bellaterra.

Rayner, E. (1995). *Unconscious Logic. An Introduction to Matte Blanco's Bi-Logic and its Uses*. New York, NY: Routledge.

Rayner, E. (1998). Foreword. In *The Unconscious as Infinite Sets. An Essay in Bi-Logic* (pp. xviii–xxiv). London, UK: Karnac Books, Ltd.

Recalcati, M. (2003). Introduzione alla psicoanalisi contemporanea. Milano, Italy: Bruno Mondadori Editore.

Recalcati, M. (2007a). Elogio dell'inconscio. Dodici argomenti in difesa della psicoanalisi. Milano, Italy: Bruno Mondadori.

Recalcati, M. (2007b). Lo psicoanalista e la città. L'inconscio e il discorso del capitalista. Roma, Italy: manifestolibri.

Recalcati, M. (2010). L'uomo senza inconscio. Figure della nuova clinica psicoanalitica. Milano, Italy: Raffaello Cortina Editore.

Recalcati, M. (2016). *Jacques Lacan* (vols. 1-2). Milano, Italy: Raffaello Cortina Editore.

Recalcati, M. (2016). *Jacques Lacan* (Vols. 1-2). Milano, Italy: Raffaello Cortina Editore.

Redondi, P. (2007). Storie del tempo. Roma-Bari, Italy: Editori Laterza.

Reich, A. (1954). Early identifications as archaic elements in the Superego. *Journal of the American Psychoanalytic Association*, 2(2), 218–238. doi:10.1177/000306515400200203

Reisig, W. (1988). Temporal Logic and Causality in Concurrent Systems. In R. H. Voght (Ed.), Lecture Notes in Computer Science: Vol. 335. *CONCURRENCY 1988* (pp. 121–139). Berlin: Springer-Verlag. doi:10.1007/3-540-50403-6_37

Rentz, J. (Ed.). (2002). Lecture Notes in Computer Science: Vol. 2293. Qualitative spatial reasoning with topological information. Berlin: Springer-Verlag. doi:10.1007/3-540-70736-0

Rescher, N., & Urquhart, A. (1971). Temporal Logic. Wien, Austria: Springer-Verlag GmbH. doi:10.1007/978-3-7091-7664-1

Reverberi, C., Pischedda, D., Burigo, M., & Cherubini, P. (2012). Deduction without awareness. *Acta Psychologica*, 139(1), 244–253. doi:10.1016/j.actpsy.2011.09.011

Riehl, J. P. (2010). *Mirror-Image Asymmetry. An Introduction to the Origin and Consequences of Chirality*. Hoboken, NJ: John Wiley & Sons, Inc. doi:10.1002/9780470588888

Riolo, F. (2009). Trasformazione. In *Psiche. Dizionario storico di psicologia, psichiatria, psicoanalisi, neuroscienze* (Vol. 2, pp. 1112–1116). Torino, Italy: Giulio Einaudi editore.

Rose, J. R. (Ed.). (2011). *Mapping Psychic Reality. Triangulation, Communication, and Insight. Psychoanalytic Ideas.* London, UK: Karnac Books, Ltd.

Rosenzweig, M. R., Bennett, E. L., & Diamond, M. C. (1972). On the Role of Environmental Stimulation on Brain Plasticity. *Scientific American, 226*(2), 22–29. doi:10.1038/scientificamerican0272-22 PMID:5062027

Rossi, R., De Fazio, F., Gatti, U., & Rocco, G. (2008, Feb.). Perizie e consulenze psichiatriche su Diamante Stefano, Stevanin Gianfranco, Bilancia Donato, Panini Giorgio. *POL.it – The Italian On Line Psychiatric Magazine.*

Roudinesco, E. (1997). Jacques Lacan. Outline of a life, history of a system of thought. Oxford, UK: Polity Press.

Roudinesco, E. (2008). Da vicino e da lontano. Claude Lévi-Strauss e la psicoanalisi. In Lévi-Strauss Fuori di sé. Macerata, Italy: Quodlibet.

Roudinesco, E. (2008). *Da vicino e da lontano.* Claude Lévi-Strauss e la psicoanalisi. In *Lévi-Strauss Fuori di sé.* Macerata, Italy: Quodlibet.

Russo, J. A. (2007). Psychoanalysis in Brazil – Institutionalization and Dissemination among the Lay Public. *Estudios Interdisciplinarios de America Latina y el Caribe, 18*(1), 63–80.

Rycroft, C. (1968a). A critical dictionary of psychoanalysis. London, UK: Thomas Nelson & Sons, Ltd.

Rycroft, C. (1968b). Imagination and reality. Psychoanalytical essays 1951–1961. London, UK: The Hogarth Press, Ltd.

Sabbadini, A. (1979). Introduzione. In Il tempo in psicoanalisi. Milano, Italy: Giangiacomo Feltrinelli Editore.

Sabbadini, A. (1979). Introduzione. In *Il tempo in psicoanalisi.* Milano, Italy: Giangiacomo Feltrinelli Editore.

Sanchez-Cardenas, M. (2011). Matte Blancos thought and epistemological pluralism in psychoanalysis. *The International Journal of Psycho-Analysis, 92*(4), 811–831. doi:10.1111/j.1745-8315.2011.00381.x

Sanchez-Cardenas, M. (2016). Clinical applications of Matte Blancos thinking. *The International Journal of Psycho-Analysis, 97*(6), 1547–1573. doi:10.1111/1745-8315.12515

Sandler, J. J. (Ed.). (1981). La ricerca in psicoanalisi (vols. 1-2). Torino, Italy: Bollati Boringhieri editore.

Sandler, J. J. (Ed.). (1981). La ricerca in psicoanalisi (Vols. 1-2). Torino, Italy: Bollati Boringhieri editore.

Sandler, J., Holder, A., & Meers, D. (1963). The Ego Ideal and the Ideal Self. *The Psychoanalytic Study of the Child, 18*, 139–158.

Sannella, D., & Tarlecki, A. (2012). *Foundations of Algebraic Specification and Formal Software Development. Monographs in Theoretical Computer Science. An EATCS Series.* Berlin: Springer-Verlag; . doi:10.1007/978-3-642-17336-3

Sasso, G. (1982). Le strutture anagrammatiche della poesia. Milano, Italy: Giangiacomo Feltrinelli Editore.

Sasso, G. (1993). La mente intralinguistica. L'instabilità del segno: anagrammi e parole dentro le parole. Genova, Italy: Marietti Editore.

Sasso, G. (1999). Struttura dell'oggetto e della rappresentazione. Roma, Italy: Casa Editrice Astrolabio-Ubaldini Editore.

Sasso, G. (2005). Psicoanalisi e Neuroscienze. Roma, Italy: Casa Editrice Astrolabio-Ubaldini Editore.

Sasso, G. (2011). La nascita della coscienza. Roma, Italy: Casa Editrice Astrolabio-Ubaldini Editore.

Sasso, G. (1982). *Le strutture anagrammatiche della poesia.* Milano, Italy: Giangiacomo Feltrinelli Editore.

Sasso, G. (1993). *La mente intralinguistica. L'instabilità del segno: anagrammi e parole dentro le parole.* Genova, Italy: Marietti Editore.

Sasso, G. (1999). *Struttura dell'oggetto e della rappresentazione.* Roma, Italy: Casa Editrice Astrolabio-Ubaldini Editore.

Sasso, G. (2005). *Psicoanalisi e Neuroscienze* [The development of consciousness]. Roma, Italy: Casa Editrice Astrolabio-Ubaldini Editore.

Sasso, G. (2011). *La nascita della coscienza.* Roma, Italy: Casa Editrice Astrolabio-Ubaldini Editore.

Scabini, E. (1973). Ideazione e psicoanalisi. Milano, Italy: Giangiacomo Feltrinelli Editore.

Scabini, E. (1973). *Ideazione e psicoanalisi.* Milano, Italy: Giangiacomo Feltrinelli Editore.

Schmitt, A., Hasan, A., Gruber, O., & Falkai, P. (2011). Schizophrenia as a disorder of disconnectivity. *European Archives of Psychiatry and Clinical Neuroscience, 261*(2), S150–S154. doi:10.1007/s00406-011-0242-2 PMID:21866371

Segalen, M. (1998). Rites et rituels contemporains. Paris: Les Éditions Nathan.

Segalen, M. (1998). *Rites et rituels contemporains.* Paris: Les Éditions Nathan.

Semi, A. A. (2003). La coscienza in psicoanalisi. Milano, Italy: Raffaello Cortina Editore.

Semi, A.A. (Ed.). (1989). *Trattato di Psicoanalisi* (Vols. 1-2). Milano, Italy: Raffaello Cortina Editore.

Severino, E. (2008). La strada. La follia e la gioia. Milano, Italy: BUR Saggi.

Silvestri, D. (2013). Linguistica implicita e linguistica esplicita. In Simposio Lévi-Strauss. Uno sguardo dall'oggi. Milano, Italy: il Saggiatore.

Singh, S., & Ribet, K. A. (1998). La dimostrazione dell'ultimo teorema di Fermat. *Le Scienze, 353*(70), 74–79.

Siri, G. (Ed.). (1976). Problemi epistemologici della psicologia. Milano, Italy: Vita e Pensiero.

Siri, G. (Ed.). (1976). *Problemi epistemologici della psicologia.* Milano, Italy: Vita e Pensiero.

Skelton, R. (1984). Understanding Matte Blanco. *The International Journal of Psycho-Analysis, 65,* 453–460.

Skelton, R. (1990). Generalizations from Freud to Matte Blanco. *The International Review of Psycho-Analysis, 17,* 471–474.

Skillicorn, D. (1994). *Foundations of Parallel Programming.* Cambridge, UK: Cambridge University Press. doi:10.1017/CBO9780511526626

Sloika, M. I., Kravchuk, V. P., Sheka, D. D., & Gaididei, Y. (2014). Curvature induced chirality symmetry breaking in vortex core switching phenomena. *Applied Physics Letters, 104*(25), 252403. doi:10.1063/1.4884957

Sluzki, C. E., & Ransom, D. C. (1979). Il doppio legame: la genesi dell'approccio relazionale allo studio della famiglia. Roma, Italy: Casa Editrice Astrolabio-Ubaldini Editore.

Sluzki, C. E., & Ransom, D. C. (1979). *Il doppio legame: la genesi dell'approccio relazionale allo studio della famiglia.* Roma, Italy: Casa Editrice Astrolabio-Ubaldini Editore.

Smirnov, V. N. (1970). *La transaction fétichique.* Nouvelle Revue de Psychoanalyse, 2.

Solms, M., & Turnbull, O. (2003). The Brain and the Inner World. An Introduction to the Neuroscience of Subjective Experience. New York, NY: Other Press, LLC.

Solomon, P., & Patch, V. D. (1974). Handbook of Psychiatry. Los Altos, CA: Lange Medical Publications.

Somenzi, V. (1998). Prefazione. In Categorie, tempo e linguaggio. Quaderni di Methodologia, N. 5. Roma, Italy: Società Stampa Sportiva.

Somenzi, V. (1998). Prefazione. In *Categorie, tempo e linguaggio. Quaderni di Methodologia, N. 5*. Roma, Italy: Società Stampa Sportiva.

Sossinsky, A. (2000). Nodi. Genesi di una teoria matematica. Torino, Italy: Bollati Boringhieri editore.

Souriau, J. M. (1964). *Géométrie et relativité*. Paris: Éditions Hermann.

Sparsø, J., & Furber, S. (Eds.). (2001). Principles of Asynchronous Circuit Design. A Systems Perspective. Dordrecht, The Netherlands: Springer-Science + Business Media, B.V. doi:10.1007/978-1-4757-3385-3

Spedini, G. (2005). Antropologia evoluzionistica (2nd ed.). Padova, Italy: Piccin Nuova Libraria.

Spitz, R. A. (1957). No and yes. On the genesis of human communication. New York, NY: International University Press, Inc.

Stanghellini, G., Ballerini, M., Presenza, S., Mancini, M., Raballo, A., Blasi, S., & Cutting, J. (2016). Psychopathology of lived time: Abnormal time experience in persons with schizophrenia. *Schizophrenia Bulletin. The Journal of Psychoses and Related Disorders, 42*(1), 45–55.

Steedman, M. (2000). *Surface Structure and Interpretation*. Boston, MA: The MIT Press.

Stich, M., Blanco, C., & Hochberg, D. (2013). Chiral and chemical oscillations in a simple dimerization model. *Physical Chemistry Chemical Physics, 15*(1), 255–261. doi:10.1039/C2CP42620J PMID:23064600

Stirling, C. (2001). *Modal and Temporal Properties of Processes*. New York, NY: Springer-Verlag. doi:10.1007/978-1-4757-3550-5

Strocchi, F. (1981). Classification of Solutions of Non-Linear Hyperbolic Equations and Non-Linear Elliptic Problems. In Topics in Functional Analysis 1980-81. Pisa, Italy: Pubblicazioni della Scuola Normale Superiore.

Strocchi, F. (1999). Symmetry Breaking in Classical Systems and Nonlinear Functional Analysis. Pisa, Italy: Pubblicazioni della Scuola Normale Superiore.

Strocchi, F. (2000). Simmetrie e rotture di simmetrie in fisica. Corso di orientamento preuniversitario, Arezzo, Italy.

Strocchi, F. (2000). Simmetrie e rotture di simmetrie in fisica. Corso di orientamento preuniversitario, Cortona, Italy.

Strocchi, F. (2012). *Spontaneous Symmetry Breaking in Quantum Systems. A review for Scholarpedia*. Preprint arXiv:1201.5459v1

Strocchi, F. (2012). *Spontaneous Symmetry Breaking in Quantum Systems. A review for Scholarpedia*. Preprint arXiv:1201.5459v1 [physics.hist-ph]

Strocchi, F. (2008). *Symmetry Breaking* (2nd ed.). Berlin: Springer-Verlag. doi:10.1007/978-3-540-73593-9

Tabossi, P. (2009). Rappresentazione, 1. In *Psiche. Dizionario storico di psicologia, psichiatria, psicoanalisi, neuroscienze* (Vol. 2, pp. 914–919). Torino, Italy: Giulio Einaudi editore.

Tallis, R. (2002). Hidden Minds. A History of the Unconscious. New York, NY: Arcade Publishing, Inc.

Tanenbaum, A. S., & Bos, H. (2015). *Modern Operating Systems* (4th ed.). Essex, UK: Pearson Education Limited.

Target, M., & Fonagy, P. (2002). The role of the father and child development. In The Importance of Fathers. A Psychoanalytic Re-evaluation. London, UK: Routledge.

Target, M., & Fonagy, P. (2002). The role of the father and child development. In The Importance of Fathers. A Psychoanalytic Re-Evaluation. London, UK: Routledge.

Target, M., & Fonagy, P. (2002). The role of the father and child development. In *The Importance of Fathers. A Psychoanalytic Re-evaluation*. London, UK: Routledge.

Tartabini, A., & Giusti, F. (2006). Origine ed evoluzione del linguaggio. Scimpanzé, ominidi e uomini moderni. Napoli, Italy: Liguori Editore.

Tartabini, A., & Giusti, F. (2006). Origine ed evoluzione del linguaggio. Scimpanzé, Ominidi e uomini moderni. Napoli, Italy: Liguori Editore.

Terminio, N. (2009). Misurare l'inconscio? Coordinate psicoanalitiche nella ricerca in psicoterapia. Milano, IT: Bruno Mondadori.

Terminio, N. (2009). Misurare l'inconscio? Coordinate psicoanalitiche nella ricerca in psicoterapia. Milano, Italy: Bruno Mondadori.

Thom, R. (1972). Symmetries Gained and Lost. In *Broken Symmetries. Proceedings of the 3rd GIFT International Seminar in Theoretical Physics organized by the Spanish-Inter-University Group in Theoretical Physics*. Saragoza, Spain: Scientific Information Service, Ltd.

Thom, R. (1972). Symmetries Gained and Lost. In: *Broken Symmetries. Proceedings of the 3rd GIFT International Seminar in Theoretical Physics organized by the Spanish-Inter-University Group in Theoretical Physics*. Saragoza, Spain: Scientific Information Service, Ltd.

Thomä, H., & Kächele, H. (1989). *Psychoanalytic Practice* (vols. 1-2). Berlin: Springer-Verlag.

Thomä, H., & Kächele, H. (1989). *Psychoanalytic Practice* (Vols. 1-2). Berlin: Springer-Verlag.

Thomä, H., & Kächele, H. (1989). *Psychoanalytic Practice* (Vol. 1-2). Berlin: Springer-Verlag.

Thom, R. (1980). *Stabilità strutturale e morfogenesi. Saggio di una teoria generale dei modelli*. Torino, Italy: Giulio Einaudi editore.

Thom, R. (1985). *Modelli matematici della morfogenesi*. Torino, Italy: Giulio Einaudi editore.

Tibaldi, M. (2004). Critica archetipica. In Dizionario degli studi culturali. Roma, Italy: Meltemi editore, pp. 115-121.

Tibaldi, M. (2004). Critica archetipica. In Dizionario degli studi culturali. Roma, Italy: Meltemi editore.

Tokhi, M. O., Hossain, M. A., & Shaheed, M. H. (2003). *Parallel Computing for Real-time Signal Processing and Control*. London, UK: Springer-Verlag London. doi:10.1007/978-1-4471-0087-4

Toraldo di Francia, G. (1976). *L'indagine del mondo fisico*. Torino, Italy: Giulio Einaudi editore.

Uznadze, D. N., Prangisvili, A. S., Bassin, F. V., & Razran, G. (1972). *L'inconscio nella psicologia sovietica*. Roma, Italy: Editori Riuniti.

Vaccarino, G. (2006). Scienza e semantica. Milano, Italy: Edizioni Melquiades.

Vallortigara, G., & Panciera, N. (2014). Cervelli che contano. Milano, Italy: Adelphi Edizioni.

Van Lommel, P. (2016). Coscienza oltre la vita. La scienza delle esperienze di premorte. Torino, Italy: Edizioni Amrita.

Van Wezel, J., & Littlewood, P. (2010). Chiral symmetry breaking and charge order. *Physics*, *3*, 87. doi:10.1103/Physics.3.87

Vattimo, G., Ferraris, M., & Marconi, D. (Eds.). (1993). Enciclopedia Garzanti di Filosofia. Milano, Italy: Garzanti Editore.

Vattimo, G., Ferraris, M., & Marconi, D. (Eds.). (1993). *Enciclopedia Garzanti di Filosofia*. Milano, Italy: Garzanti Editore.

Vegetti Finzi, S. (1990). Storia della psicoanalisi. Autori, opere, teorie (1895-1990). Milano, Italy: Arnoldo Mondadori Editore.

Vegetti Finzi, S. (Ed.). (1976). Il bambino nella psicoanalisi. Testi di S. Freud, Jung, Reich, Klein, A. Freud, Spitz, Winnicott, Musatti, Fornari, Erikson, Laing, Lacan, Mannoni. Bologna, Italy: Nicola Zanichelli Editore.

Venema, Y. (2001). Temporal Logic. In The Blackwell Guide to Philosophical Logic. Oxford, UK: Basil Blackwell Publishers.

Verdiglione, A. (1977). Matematica dell'inconscio. In Feticismo, linguaggio, afasia, matematica dell'inconscio. Fa parte di VEL – Collana-rivista di psicoanalisi diretta da Armando Verdiglione. Venezia, Italy: Marsilio Editori.

Verdiglione, A. (1977). Matematica dell'inconscio. In Feticismo, linguaggio, afasia, matematica dell'inconscio. Venezia, Italy: Marsilio Editori.

Verdiglione, A. (1977). Matematica dell'inconscio. In *Feticismo, linguaggio, afasia, matematica dell'inconscio*. Venezia, Italy: Marsilio Editori.

Vicario, G. B. (2005). Il tempo. Saggio di psicologia sperimentale. Bologna, Italy: Società editrice il Mulino.

Vicario, G. B. (1997). Il tempo in psicologia. *Le Scienze*, *30*(347), 43–51.

Viret, J. (2012). Topological Approach of Jungian Psychology. *Acta Biotheoretica*, *58*(2), 233–245.

Voevodin, V. V. (1992). Mathematical Foundations of Parallel Computing. Singapore: World Scientific Publishing. doi:10.1142/1533

von Karger, B. (1995). An algebraic approach to temporal logic. In *Lecture Notes in Computer Science: Vol. 915. Proceedings of the Sixth International Joint Conference on Theory and Practice of Software Development (TAPSOFT '95)*. Berlin: Springer-Verlag. doi:10.1007/3-540-59293-8_198

von Karger, B. (2002). Temporal Algebra. In Lecture Notes in Computer Science: Vol. 2297. Algebraic and Coalgebraic Methods in the Mathematics of Program Construction. Berlin: Springer-Verlag. doi:10.1007/3-540-47797-7_9

Von Scheve, C., & Salmela, M. (Eds.). (2014). *Collective Emotions. Perspectives from Psychology, Philosophy, and Sociology*. Oxford, UK: Oxford University Press.

Von Wright, G. H. (1969). *Time, Change and Contradiction*. Cambridge, UK: Cambridge University Press.

Wang, Y. (2008). On Concept Algebra: A Denotational Mathematical Structure for Knowledge and Software Modeling. *International Journal of Cognitive Informatics and Natural Intelligence*, *2*(2), 1–19. doi:10.4018/jcini.2008040101

Wang, Y. (2010). A Sociopsychological Perspective on Collective Intelligence in Metaheuristic Computing. *International Journal of Applied Metaheuristic Computing*, *1*(1), 110–128. doi:10.4018/jamc.2010102606

Wang, Y., Wang, Y., Patel, S., & Patel, D. (2006). A Layered Reference Model of the Brain. *IEEE Transactions on Systems, Man and Cybernetics. Part C, Applications and Reviews*, *36*(2), 124–133. doi:10.1109/TSMCC.2006.871126

Wang, Y., Zadeh, L. A., Widrow, B., Howard, N., Wood, S., Patel, S., & Zhang, D. et al. (2017). Abstract Intelligence: Embodying and Enabling Cognitive Systems by Mathematical Engineering. *International Journal of Cognitive Informatics and Natural Intelligence, 11*(1), 1–22. doi:10.4018/IJCINI.2017010101

Wang, Y., Zhang, D., & Kinsner, D. (Eds.). (2011). *Advances in Cognitive Informatics and Cognitive Computing*. Berlin: Springer-Verlag.

Watanabe, S. (1969). *Knowing and Guessing. A Quantitative Study of Inference and Information*. New York, NY: John Wiley & Sons, Inc.

Watzlawick, P., Beavin, J. H., & Jackson, D. D. (1967). Pragmatics of Human Communication. A Study of Interactional Patterns, Pathologies, and Paradoxes. New York, NY: W.W. Norton & Company.

Watzlawick, P., Beavin, J. H., & Jackson, D. D. (1967). *Pragmatics of Human Communication. A Study of Interactional Patterns, Pathologies, and Paradoxes*. New York, NY: W.W. Norton & Company.

Weinstein, A. (1996). Groupoids: Unifying Internal and External Symmetry. *Notices of the American Mathematical Society, 43*(7), 744–752.

Westphal, B. (2007). La Géocritique. Réel, fiction, espace. Paris: Les Éditions de Minuit.

Westphal, B. (2007). *La Géocritique. Réel, fiction, espace*. Paris: Les Éditions de Minuit.

Wetterich, C. (2005). Spontaneous Symmetry Breaking Origins for the Difference Between Time and Space. *Physical Review Letters, 94*(1), 011692–011696. doi:10.1103/PhysRevLett.94.011602 PMID:15698063

Whitebook, J. (1995). *Perversion and Utopia. A Study in Psychoanalysis and Critical Theory*. Cambridge, MA: The MIT Press.

White, D. R., & Jorion, P. (1996). Kinship networks and discrete structure theory: Applications and implications. *Social Networks, 18*(3), 267–314. doi:10.1016/0378-8733(95)00277-4

Whitrow, G. J. (1988). *Time in History. Views of Time from Prehistory to the Present Day*. Oxford, UK: Oxford University Press.

Wimmer, M., & Ciompi, L. (1996). Evolutionary aspects of affective-cognitive interactions in the light of Ciompi's concept of "affect-logic". *Evolution & Cognition, 2*, 37–58.

Yang, J., Kanazawa, S., Yamaguchi, M. K., & Kuriki, I. (2016). Cortical response to categorical colour perception in infants investigated by near-infrared spectroscopy. *Proceedings of the National Academy of Sciences of the United States of America, 113*(9), 2370–2375.

Zadeh, L. A. (1965). Fuzzy Sets. *Information and Control, 8*(3), 338–353. doi:10.1016/S0019-9958(65)90241-X

Zadeh, L. A. (1968). Fuzzy Algorithms. *Information and Control, 12*(2), 94–102. doi:10.1016/S0019-9958(68)90211-8

Zadeh, L. A. (1988). Fuzzy Logic. *Computer, 21*(4), 83–93. doi:10.1109/2.53

Zanforlin, M. (1971). Prefazione. In Evoluzione e modificazione del comportamento. Torino, Italy: Editore Boringhieri.

Zapparoli, G. C. (1970). La perversione logica. I rapporti tra sessualità e pensiero nella tradizione psicoanalitica. Milano, Italy: Franco Angeli Editore.

Zapparoli, G. C. (1970). *La perversione logica. I rapporti tra sessualità e pensiero nella tradizione psicoanalitica*. Milano, Italy: Franco Angeli Editore.

Zeeman, E. C. (1961). The topology of the brain and the visual perception. In *Topology of 3-manifolds and related topics. Proceedings of the University of Georgia Institute*. Academic Press.

Zeeman, E. C. (1976a). Brain Modelling. In *Lecture Notes in Mathematics: Vol. 525. Structural Stability. The Theory of Catastrophes, and Applications in the Sciences. Proceedings of the Conference*. Berlin: Springer-Verlag.

Zeeman, E. C. (1976b). Catastrophe Theory. *Scientific American, 234*(April), 65–83. doi:10.1038/scientificamerican0476-65

Zeh, H. D. (2007). *The Physical Basis of the Direction of Time* (5th ed.). Berlin: Springer-Verlag.

Zentall, T. R. (2013). Animals represent the past and the future. *Evolutionary Psychology, 11*(3), 573–590. doi:10.1177/147470491301100307 PMID:24027784

Zepf, S., & Gerlach, A. (2012). Commentary on Kernbergs suicide prevention for psychoanalytic institutes and societies. *Journal of the American Psychoanalytic Association, 61*(4), 771–786. doi:10.1177/0003065113496634

Živaljević, R. T. (2006). *Groupoids in combinatorics – applications of a theory of local symmetries*. Preprint arXiv: math/0605508v1 [math.CO]

About the Author

Giuseppe Iurato, with a BA in Mathematics from University of Pisa, Italy, a MA in Mathematics from University of Catania, Italy, and a PhD in Applied Physics (with curriculum in: History and Education of Science) from University of Palermo, Italy, is an external research collaborator of the *International Center for Mathematical Modeling* of the Faculty of Technology of the Linneaus University, Vaxio, Sweden, and has been past member of the Editorial Review Board of the *International Journal of Software Science and Computational Intelligence* (IJSSCI), published by IGI Global Publisher, Hershey (PA), USA. His main research interests regard the interrelations between humanities with natural and exact sciences.

Index

M

Matte Blanco, Ignacio 2-3, 7, 11, 17, 20, 24, 29, 31, 33, 38, 88, 92, 96-97, 99, 101, 108-109, 114-119, 121-130, 132-141, 144, 146-153, 165, 180, 183-184, 188-189, 191, 193, 198, 200, 206, 214-216, 218-219, 222, 227, 231, 235, 240, 243, 247, 249-250, 255-258, 260-262, 264-271, 279, 285-287, 289-290, 296-297

Modal Logic 92, 183, 207, 209, 215, 232-233, 243, 254

N

Negative 38, 42-43, 57-59, 66-68, 70, 106, 108-109, 130, 150, 212, 296

P

P-Adic Numbers 25, 29, 93, 97, 137, 167, 185, 189, 217, 244, 282, 288

Parallel Computing 20, 103, 179, 190, 195-196, 219-222, 227-228, 240, 248, 251-252, 293

Phallic Logic 1, 11, 17, 38, 59, 136, 222, 255

Psychiatry 26, 36, 84, 94, 101, 117, 175, 185-186, 193, 245, 250, 255, 271-272, 276, 284, 291

Psychoanalysis 1-3, 5, 7-33, 35-46, 49-55, 59-60, 62, 67, 76, 83-85, 87, 89-92, 94-100, 104, 112, 114, 116-119, 126, 136-137, 140-141, 152, 154, 160, 163, 165-167, 172, 174-177, 179-182, 184-190, 192, 197-198, 206, 211, 213-216, 219, 228, 235-248, 250, 253, 255-259, 264, 276, 279-280, 282-283, 286-287, 291, 294-295

S

Sequential Computing 222, 227

Structuralisms 1

Structural Unconscious 17, 114, 127-128, 137, 139, 147, 222, 227, 230-231, 235, 263, 270

Surreal Numbers 282

Symbolism 31, 38, 60, 65, 99, 107-108, 126, 190, 209, 248

Symmetry 36, 63, 104, 114, 119-122, 124-126, 128, 130-131, 136, 139-148, 150-153, 161, 164, 166-167, 171-172, 174, 176, 180, 182, 185, 191, 194-196, 198-199, 202-203, 213, 217, 224, 236, 245, 253, 256, 262, 264-265, 267, 280-282, 286, 288, 290-294, 298-299

Symmetry Breaking 36, 136, 142-145, 147-148, 150-152, 161, 164, 166-167, 171-172, 174, 176, 180, 185, 191, 194-196, 198-199, 202-203, 213, 224, 236, 264-265, 280-282, 286, 288, 290-294, 298-299

Synchronicity 96, 231, 234-236, 238, 247, 254

T

Temporal Logic 90, 92, 98, 103, 181-183, 190, 192, 195-196, 198, 209, 215, 218-221, 227-228, 232-235, 242-243, 248-249, 252, 254, 290, 293

Time 2-3, 7, 12, 20, 28, 30, 35, 43-46, 48, 53, 57, 59-60, 62-63, 65-66, 69, 72, 74, 77, 81, 83, 85, 88-89, 91, 96, 98-99, 102-104, 107, 111-112, 114-118, 120, 122-125, 128, 130-134, 136-137, 141, 147, 150-151, 153, 158, 161, 165-167, 171-174, 176, 179-180, 182, 185, 187, 190-191, 194, 196-197, 200-202, 205, 208-209, 212, 215, 217, 221, 223-224, 226-230, 232-235, 237, 240-242, 245, 248-249, 251-255, 258-261, 263-264, 266, 269-270, 275, 282, 285, 288, 290, 292-295, 298-299

Topology 26, 29-30, 63, 97, 158-159, 162-163, 175, 183, 189, 197, 234, 243, 245, 253-255, 276, 278-281, 283, 286, 288, 295

U

Unconscious 2, 7, 9-11, 13, 16-17, 21, 24-27, 29, 31-32, 34, 36, 38-53, 55, 58-60, 63, 65-67, 70-72, 74, 76-77, 80-84, 86, 88-89, 92-96, 99-100, 102, 105-106, 112, 114, 118-122, 124-125, 127-135, 137, 139-141, 144-145, 147, 152-153, 156-160, 165-173, 175, 184-188, 191, 194, 199-200, 202-206, 216-219, 222-236, 238, 240, 243-245, 247, 249, 254-259, 261-267, 269-270, 276-279, 281-282, 287-290, 296-298

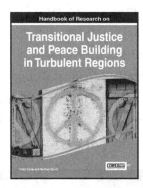
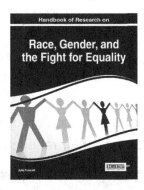

Stay Current on the Latest Emerging Research Developments

Become an IGI Global Reviewer for Authored Book Projects

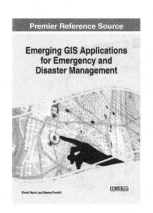

Premier Reference Source

Emerging GIS Applications for Emergency and Disaster Management

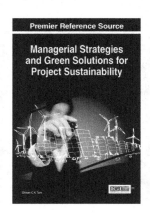

Premier Reference Source

Managerial Strategies and Green Solutions for Project Sustainability

Premier Reference Source

Comparative Approaches to Using R and Python for Statistical Data Analysis

Premier Reference Source

Solutions for High-Touch Communications in a High-Tech World

The overall success of an authored book project is dependent on quality and timely reviews.

In this competitive age of scholarly publishing, constructive and timely feedback significantly decreases the turnaround time of manuscripts from submission to acceptance, allowing the publication and discovery of progressive research at a much more expeditious rate. Several IGI Global authored book projects are currently seeking highly qualified experts in the field to fill vacancies on their respective editorial review boards:

Applications may be sent to:
development@igi-global.com

Applicants must have a doctorate (or an equivalent degree) as well as publishing and reviewing experience. Reviewers are asked to write reviews in a timely, collegial, and constructive manner. All reviewers will begin their role on an ad-hoc basis for a period of one year, and upon successful completion of this term can be considered for full editorial review board status, with the potential for a subsequent promotion to Associate Editor.

If you have a colleague that may be interested in this opportunity, we encourage you to share this information with them.

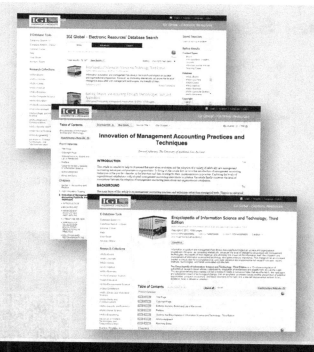

Information Resources Management Association

Advancing the Concepts & Practices of Information Resources Management in Modern Organizations

Become an IRMA Member

Members of the **Information Resources Management Association (IRMA)** understand the importance of community within their field of study. The Information Resources Management Association is an ideal venue through which professionals, students, and academicians can convene and share the latest industry innovations and scholarly research that is changing the field of information science and technology. Become a member today and enjoy the benefits of membership as well as the opportunity to collaborate and network with fellow experts in the field.

IRMA Membership Benefits:

- **One FREE Journal Subscription**
- **30% Off Additional Journal Subscriptions**
- **20% Off Book Purchases**
- Updates on the latest events and research on Information Resources Management through the IRMA-L listserv.
- Updates on new open access and downloadable content added to Research IRM.
- A copy of the Information Technology Management Newsletter twice a year.
- A certificate of membership.

IRMA Membership $195

Scan code or visit **irma-international.org** and begin by selecting your free journal subscription.

Membership is good for one full year.